RV Camping in

STATE PARKS

ROUNDABOUT
PUBLICATIONS

Published by:

Roundabout Publications
P.O. Box 569
LaCygne, KS 66040

Phone: 800-455-2207
Internet: www.RoundaboutPublications.com

Library of Congress Control Number: 2021938203

ISBN-10: 1-885464-79-7
ISBN-13: 978-1-885464-79-8

In memory of David J. Davin

About the Author

This edition of RV Camping in State Parks is dedicated to the memory of David (D.J.) Davin. When D.J. first came to us with the idea of publishing a book about state parks, we knew it would be a big undertaking but he was interested in tackling the job. He wanted to create a book for other RVers to use as they travelled across America.

The first edition of RV Camping in State Parks was released in 2004. For the next 13 years, D.J. provided us with updates to the state park information. Overall, six editions of his book was published. He passed away in late 2017 at the age of 83.

D.J. Davin was a retired sales and marketing executive. He and his wife, Kay, were married for more than 60 years. They enjoyed the RV lifestyle and made several cross-country junkets, travelled extensively in the West and have stayed in many of the parks listed in this book. They also have been volunteer campground hosts with Oregon State Parks.

Thanks D.J.

Contents

Introduction

About this Book

Millions of people enjoy camping in state parks every year. This guide is designed to help you find them. Although there are several thousand state parks in America, not all are included here. In this book, we focus on those parks that can accommodate and have camping sites for recreational vehicles.

The book is organized by state; Hawaii is not included. Each chapter displays a state map marked with park locations. The maps are intended to provide you with a visual of where parks are located within the state.

On the page following the map is contact information for the agency that manages the parks and recreation areas within the state. Information includes a mailing address, phone number, reservation phone number, and website.

A *Park Locator* chart follows the contact information and lists each park alphabetically. The chart also includes the Map Grid ID for cross referencing to the map. This list is helpful if you are already familiar with a park's name.

Next is each park's name and description and is generally organized as follows:

Contact and Location Information

- Address and phone number
- General location and directions
- GPS coordinates

Park Features

- Activities (hike, bike, golf, swim, fish, etc.)
- Amenities (visitor center, marina, store, etc.)
- Unique attractions (historical, scenic, etc.)

Camping Details

- Open season
- Cost per night
- Number of sites
- Types of hookups
- Facilities (restrooms, showers, RV dump, etc.)

A Note About the Cost to Camp

We have provided a general range for the per night cost to camp. Several factors can increase or decrease the amount you ultimately pay.

- Type of hookup(s)
- Site location (prime, waterfront, etc)
- Weekend, holiday, off-season
- Resident vs. non-resident of a state
- Daily park entrance fee
- Miscellaneous fees for some amenities

A new trend is also emerging with online reservations. The closer a park is to being fully reserved, the higher the camp site price becomes (supply & demand).

With the increased popularity of camping in general, and state parks specifically, some states are now requiring reservations to camp. Also, some may even require advance notice to just enter the park.

The best practice is to plan ahead and reserve your site as soon as you are able.

Alabama

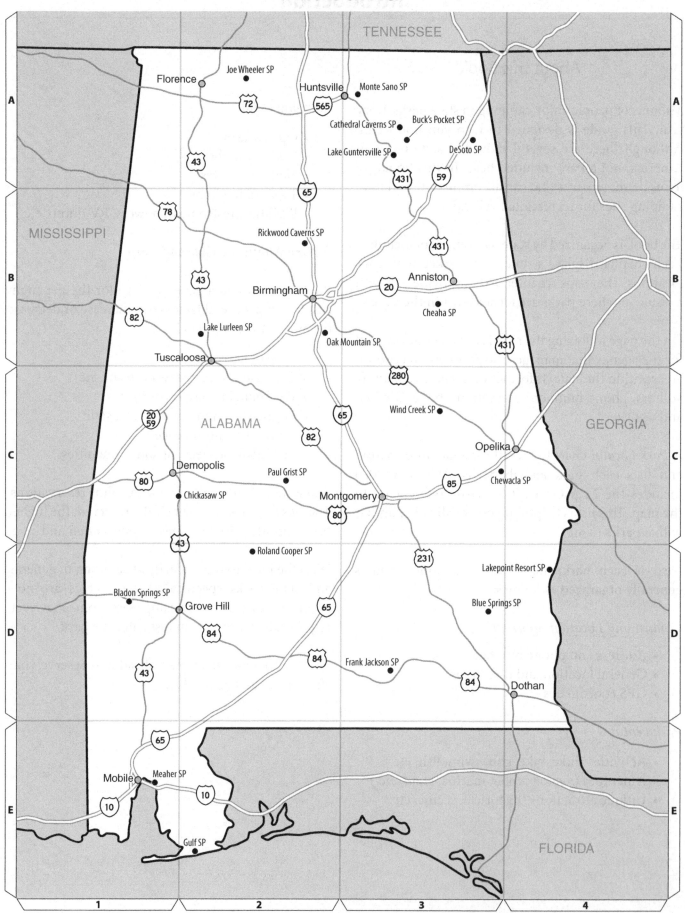

Alabama

Alabama State Parks Division
64 N Union St, Room 538
Montgomery, AL 36130

Phone: (800) 252-7275
Internet: www.alapark.com
Reservations: Online or call park. Also (800) 252-7275

Alabama Park Locator

Alabama Parks

Bladon Springs State Park

3921 Bladon Rd, Bladon Springs, AL 36919. Phone: (205) 459-3459. Located 12 miles W of Coffeeville via US 84 and CR 31. GPS: 31.735024, -88.199430. Wildlife viewing. Bird watching. Open all year. Operated by Choctaw County. Reservations: (205) 574-9613. $30 or less. 10 full hookup sites.

Blue Springs State Park

2595 State Hwy 10, Clio, AL 36017. Phone: (334) 397-4875. Located 6 miles E of Clio on AL 10 about 15 miles W of US 431. GPS: 31.663520, -85.507625. Lake in park. Spring-fed swimming pool, fishing, boating (rentals). Hiking, biking trails. Bird watching. Open all year. $30 or less. 47 sites, 7 full hookup, 40 with water and electric. Restrooms; showers.

Buck's Pocket State Park

393 County Road 174, Grove Oak, AL 35975. Phone: (256) 659-6288. Located on Lake Guntersville, 2 miles N of Grove Oak. Northbound travelers use exit 205 off I-59 to CR 20 to AL 227. Southbound travelers use exit 218 off I-59 to AL 35 to Rainsville, S on AL 75 to AL 227, follow signs to park. GPS: 34.475074, -86.055202. Fishing, boating. Hiking, ORV trails. Scenic overlook. Open all year. $30 or less. 23 sites, 13 full hookup, 10 with water and electric. Restrooms; showers. Laundry facilities. Dump station.

Cathedral Caverns State Park

637 Cave Rd, Woodville, AL 35769. Phone: (256) 728-8193. Located 7 miles SE of Woodville via Cathedral Caverns Hwy. GPS: 34.571340, -86.224250. Hiking trails. Welcome center. Cave tours (fee charged). Gemstone mining. Open all year. $20 or less. 11 sites with water and electric. Restrooms; showers.

Cheaha State Park

19644 Hwy 281, Delta, AL 36258. Phone: (256) 488-5111. Located in Talladega National Forest, 12 miles S of I-20 off AL 281 near Anniston. GPS: 33.470542, -85.821373. Lake in park. Swimming, fishing, boating (pedal boat rentals). Hiking, biking trails. Camp store. Restaurant. Waterfalls. Two museums. Open all year. $30 or less. 73 full hookup sites. Restrooms; showers.

Chewacla State Park

124 Shell Toomer Pkwy, Auburn, AL 36830. Phone: (334) 887-5621. Located on Chewacla Lake, 4 miles S of Auburn off I-85 at exit 51. GPS: 32.554348, -85.481389. Lake in park. Swimming, fishing, boating (no boat ramp, rentals). Hiking, biking trails. Open all year. $41 or more. 36 full hookup sites. Restrooms; showers. Dump station.

Chickasaw State Park

26955 US Hwy 43, Gallion, AL 36742. Phone: (334) 295-8230. Located on US 43 about 4 miles N of Linden. GPS: 32.361907, -87.779629. Wading pool. Wildlife viewing. Bird watching. Open all year. $20 or less. 3 sites with water and electric. Some primitive sites. Restrooms; no showers.

DeSoto State Park

7104 DeSoto Pkwy NE, Fort Payne, AL 35967. Phone: (256) 845-5380. Located 8 miles NE of Fort Payne near I-59 & US 11. GPS: 34.501386, -85.618836. Swimming pool, fishing, boating. Hiking, biking, equestrian trails. Eight waterfalls. Zipline. Camp store. Nature center. Restaurant. Museum. Open all year. $40 or less. 94 full hookup sites. Restrooms; showers. Laundry facilities.

Frank Jackson State Park

100 Jerry Adams Dr, Opp, AL 36467. Phone: (334) 493-6988. Located on Lake Jackson in the town of Opp on US 331. GPS: 31.296831, -86.274548. Lake in park. Swimming beach, fishing, boating. Walking trails. Wildlife viewing. Open all year. $40 or less. 32 full hookup sites with cable TV service. Restrooms; showers.

Gulf State Park

20115 State Hwy 135, Gulf Shores, AL 36542. Phone: (251) 948-7275. Located in the city of Gulf Shores on the Gulf of Mexico. GPS: 30.259754, -87.649072. Two miles of white sand beaches. Lake in park. Swimming pool, fishing, boating/paddling (rentals). Hiking, biking trails. Camp store. Nature center. Restaurant. Open all year. $41 or more. 496 full hookup sites. Restrooms; showers. Laundry facilities.

Joe Wheeler State Park

4401 McLean Dr, Rogersville, AL 35652. Phone: (256) 247-1184. Located on Wheeler Lake, 1.5 miles W of Rogersville on US 72. GPS: 34.805426, -87.318078. Lake in park. Swimming beach, fishing, boating (rentals). Hiking, biking trails. Golf course. Disc golf. Camp store. Marina. Restaurant. Open all year. $30 or less. 116 sites, 110 full hookup. Restrooms; showers.

Lake Guntersville State Park

1155 Lodge Dr, Guntersville, AL 35976. Phone: (256) 571-5455. Located 6 miles NE of Guntersville off Hwy 227. GPS: 34.382483, -86.198413. Swimming beach, fishing, boating (rentals). Hiking, biking, equestrian (rentals) trails. Golf course. Camp store. Nature center. Marina, Restaurant. Zipline. Open all year. $30 or less. 321 sites with water and electric, some with sewer hookups. Restrooms; showers. Laundry facilities.

Lake Lurleen State Park

13226 Lake Lurleen Rd, Coker, AL 35452. Phone: (205) 339-1558. Located on Lake Lurleen, 12 miles NW of Tuscaloosa via US 82 and CR 21. GPS: 33.297366, -87.676677. Swimming beach, fishing, boating (rentals). Hiking, biking trails. Golf course. Camp store. Nature center. Open all year. $30 or less. 91 sites, 35 full hookup, 56 with water and electric. Restrooms; showers. Dump station.

Lakepoint State Park

104 Lakepoint Dr, Eufaula, AL 36027. Phone: (334) 687-8011. Located 7 miles N of Eufaula on US 431 near Georgia state line. GPS: 31.987526, -85.114125. Swimming pool, fishing, boating (rentals). Hiking, nature trails. Wildlife viewing. Camp store. Marina. Restaurants. Open all year. $30 or less. 192 sites with water and electric (some with sewer). Some pull-through, some on the lake. Restrooms; showers. Laundry facilities. Dump station.

Meaher State Park

5200 Battleship Pkwy E, Spanish Fort, AL 36577. Phone: (251) 626-5529. Located on US 90 (Old Spanish Trail) N of I-10 exit 30. GPS: 30.668914, -87.935292. Fishing, boating. Hiking trails. Bird watching. Open all year. $40 or less. 61 full hookup sites. Restrooms; showers. Laundry facilities.

Monte Sano State Park

5105 Nolen Ave, Huntsville, AL 35801. Phone: (256) 534-3757. Located in the city of Huntsville, 8 miles SE of city center off US 431. GPS: 34.744333, -86.518861. Hiking, biking trails. Disc golf. Camp store. Museum, planetarium.

Open all year. $30 or less. 74 sites, 15 full hookup (some pull-thrus), 59 with water and electric. Restrooms; showers. Laundry facilities. Dump station.

Oak Mountain State Park

200 Terrace Dr, Pelham, AL 35124. Phone: (205) 620-2520. Located E of I-65 exit 246 along AL 119 (15 miles S of Birmingham). GPS: 33.360825, -86.709117. Two lakes in park. Swimming beach and aquapark, fishing, boating (rentals, no gas motors). Hiking, biking, equestrian (rentals), nature trails. Golf course, driving range, grill. Archery range. Camp store. Wildlife center. Oak Mountain Interpretive Center. Marina, Restaurant. Open all year. $40 or less. 84 sites, 57 full hookup, 27 with water and electric. Restrooms; showers. Laundry facilities. Dump station.

Paul Grist State Park

1546 Grist Rd, Selma, AL 36701. Phone: (334) 872-5846. Located 15 miles N of Selma via CR 37. GPS: 32.602183, -86.990620. Lake in park. Swimming (lake), fishing, boating (rentals). Hiking, equestrian trails. Bird watching. Open all year. $30 or less. 11 full hookup sites. Restrooms; showers.

Rickwood Caverns State Park

370 Rickwood Park Rd, Warrior, AL 35180. Phone: (205) 647-9692. Located 4 miles W of I-65 exit 284. GPS: 33.876241, -86.864525. Swimming pool . Hiking trails. Cave tours (fee charged). Gemstone mining. Gift shop. Open all year. $30 or less. 13 sites with water and electric. Restrooms; showers.

Roland Cooper State Park

285 Deer Run Dr, Camden, AL 35726. Phone: (334) 682-4838. Located on Dannelly Reservoir, 6 miles NE of Camden on AL 41 (about 37 miles SW of Selma). GPS: 32.052837, -87.248119. Lake in park. Fishing, boating. Bird watching. Camp store. Open all year. $30 or less. Park managed by Recreational Resource Management. For reservations call (334) 682-4838 or online at: www.camprrm.com. 47 full hookup sites. Restrooms; showers. Dump station.

Wind Creek State Park

4325 State Hwy 128, Alexander City, AL 35010. Phone: (256) 329-0845. Located on Lake Martin, 7 miles SE of Alexander City off AL 63 and AL 128. GPS: 32.859122, -85.935899. Lake in park. Swimming beach, fishing, boating (rentals). Hiking, equestrian trails. Guided trail rides on horse back. Bird watching. Miniature golf. Archery range. Camp store. Marina, Outdoor restaurant. Zipline. Open all year. $40 or less. 586 sites (157 waterfront), 268 full hookup, 318 with water and electric. Restrooms; showers. Laundry facilities. Equestrian area, 16 sites.

Alaska

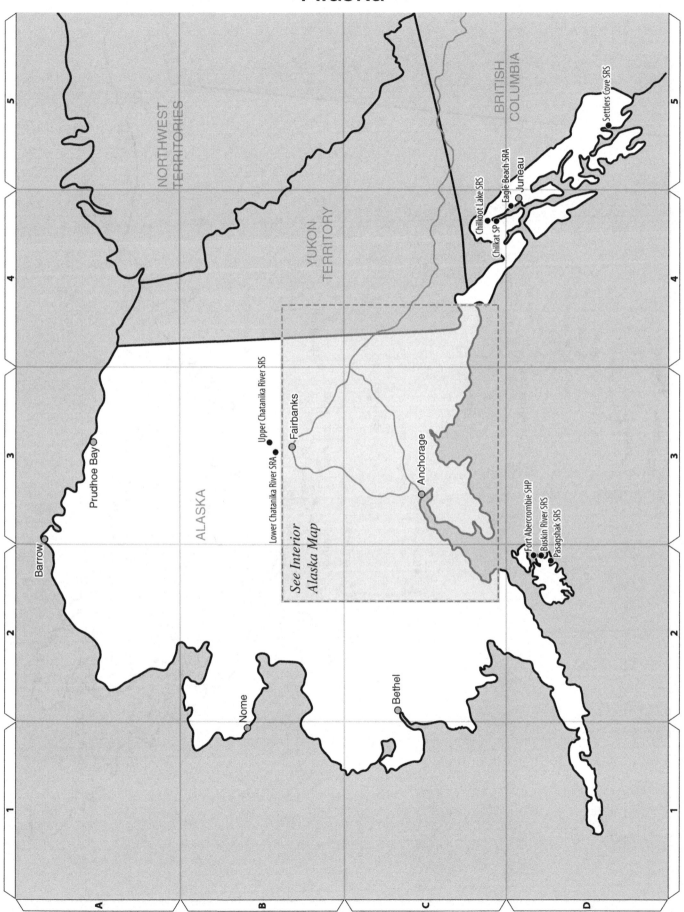

Interior Alaska

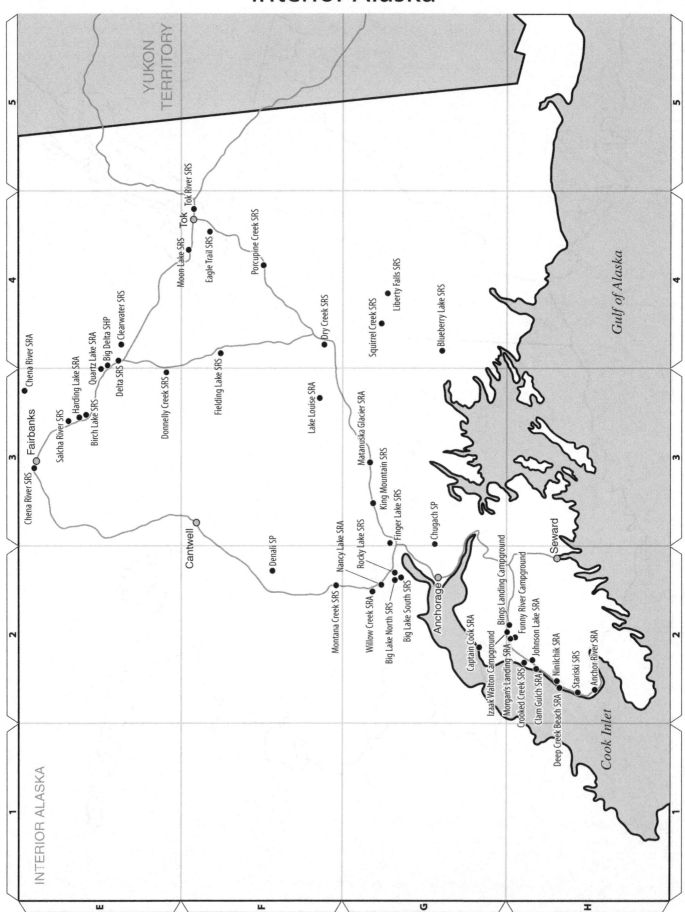

YUKON TERRITORY

Gulf of Alaska

INTERIOR ALASKA

Tok River SRS

Tok

Moon Lake SRS

Eagle Trail SRS

Porcupine Creek SRS

Liberty Falls SRS

Blueberry Lake SRS

Dry Creek SRS

Squirrel Creek SRS

Chena River SRA

Quartz Lake SRA

Big Delta SHP

Clearwater SRS

Harding Lake SRA

Delta SRS

Salcha River SRS

Birch Lake SRS

Donnelly Creek SRS

Fielding Lake SRS

Lake Louise SRA

Fairbanks

Chena River SRS

Matanuska Glacier SRA

King Mountain SRS

Cantwell

Denali SP

Nancy Lake SRA

Rocky Lake SRS

Finger Lake SRS

Chugach SP

Seward

Montana Creek SRS

Willow Creek SRA

Big Lake North SRS

Big Lake South SRS

Anchorage

Captain Cook SRA

Bings Landing Campground

Funny River Campground

Johnson Lake SRA

Izaak Walton Campground

Morgan's Landing SRA

Ninilchik SRA

Crooked Creek SRS

Clam Gulch SRA

Stariski SRS

Anchor River SRA

Deep Creek Beach SRA

Cook Inlet

Alaska

Division of Parks & Outdoor Recreation
550 W 7th Ave, Ste 1380
Anchorage, AK 99501

Phone: (907) 269-8700
Internet: www.alaskastateparks.org
Reservations: Online or call park.

Alaska Park Locator

Alaska Parks

Anchor River State Recreation Area

157 Sterling Hwy, Homer, AK 99603. Located 15 miles NW of Homer along the Sterling Hwy. GPS: 59.770971, -151.836652. Fishing, boating. Hiking. Wildlife viewing. Five campgrounds. Open May-Sep. No reservations accepted. $20 or less. 186 sites, no hookups. Drinking water. Restrooms; no showers.

Big Delta State Historic Park

274 Richardson Hwy, Delta Junction, AK 99737. Located 8 miles N of Delta Junction on AK 2 (Richardson Hwy). GPS: 64.153935, -145.841555. Walking tours. Museum, historic buildings. Cafe, gift shop. Open May-Sep. No reservations accepted. $20 or less. 25 sites, no hookups. Drinking water. Dump station. Restrooms; no showers.

Big Lake North State Recreation Site

16905 W Northshore Dr, Big Lake, AK 99652. Phone: (907) 240-9797. Located 13 miles W of Wasilla. GPS: 61.545599, -149.854577. Swimming beach, fishing, boating. Wildlife viewing. Camp store. Open all year. Operated by Great Holiday Campgrounds, phone (907) 240-9797, online reservations http://greatholidaycampgrounds. com. $20-25 per night, per vehicle. 60 sites, no hookups. Drinking water. 40-foot limit. Restrooms; no showers.

Big Lake South State Recreation Site

4678 S Big Lake Rd, Big Lake, AK 99652. Phone: (907) 240-9797. Located 15 miles W of Wasilla via AK 3 and Big Lake Rd. GPS: 61.532829, -149.831810. Swimming beach, fishing, boating. Wildlife viewing. Open May-Sep. Operated by Great Holiday Campgrounds, phone (907) 240-9797, online reservations http://greatholidaycampgrounds.com. $20 per night. 20 sites, no hookups. Drinking water. 40-foot limit. Restrooms; no showers.

Bings Landing Campground

80 Sterling Hwy, Sterling, AK 99672. Phone: (907) 262-5581. Located 3 miles SE of Sterling. GPS: 60.516708, -150.700943. Fishing, boating. Hiking trails. Wildlife viewing. Bird watching. No reservations accepted. $20 or less. 36 sites, no hookups. Drinking water. Restrooms; no showers.

Birch Lake State Recreation Site

305.5 Richardson Hwy, Salcha, AK 99714. Follow Richardson Hwy to park sign, park is at the end of the road. GPS: 64.315238, -

146.643848. Swimming beach, fishing, boating. Wildlife viewing. Bird watching. Open all year. No reservations accepted. $20 or less. 19 sites, no hookups. Drinking water. Restrooms; no showers.

Blueberry Lake State Recreation Site

23 Richardson Hwy, Valdez, AK 99686. Located about 25 miles E of Valdez via Richardson Hwy. GPS: 61.125103, -145.679911. Fishing. Hiking trails. Wildlife viewing. Berry picking. Open May-Sep. No reservations accepted. $20 or less. 25 sites, no hookups. Restrooms; no showers.

Buskin River State Recreation Site

4.5 W Rezanof Dr, Kodiak, AK 99637. From downtown go W on Center St to Rezanof Dr. GPS: 57.756647, -152.500089. Fishing. Hiking, biking trails. Wildlife viewing. Bird watching. Beach combing. Berry picking. No reservations accepted. $20 or less. 15 sites, no hookups. Drinking water. 40-foot limit. Restrooms; no showers.

Captain Cook State Recreation Area

39 Kenai Spur Hwy, Nikiski, AK 99635. Phone: (907) 522-8368. Located about 25 miles N of Kenai on the North Kenai Road to milepost 36. GPS: 60.807023, -151.012804. Lake in park. Fishing, boating. Hiking, biking trails. Wildlife viewing. Bird watching. Beach combing. Berry picking. No reservations accepted. $20 or less. 53 sites, no hookups. Drinking water. Restrooms; no showers.

Chena River State Recreation Area

Chena Hot Springs Rd, Fairbanks, AK 99709. 254,000 acre park accessed along Chena Hot Springs Rd between miles 26 and 51. Three camping areas.

Red Squirrel Campground: Mile 43 Chena Hot Springs Rd, off Steese Hwy. GPS: 64.934602, -146.286203. Fishing, boating. Hiking, ATV trails. Wildlife viewing. $20 or less. 5 sites, no hookups. Drinking water. Restrooms; no showers.

Rosehip Campground: Mile 27 Chena Hot Springs Rd, off Steese Hwy. GPS: 64.877104, -146.764966. Fishing, boating. Hiking ATV trails. Wildlife viewing. $20 or less. 37 sites, no hookups. Drinking water. Restrooms; no showers.

Granite Tors Campground: Mile 39 Chena Hot Springs Rd, off Steese Hwy. GPS: 64.903334, -146.362437. Fishing, boating. Hiking, ATV trails. Wildlife viewing. $20 or less. 24 sites, no hookups. Drinking water. Restrooms; no showers.

Chena River State Recreation Site

3530 Geraghty Ave, Fairbanks, AK 99709. Located in Fairbanks near the intersection of Airport Way and University Ave. GPS: 64.839082, -147.808230. Fishing, boating. Hiking, biking, walking trails. Bird watching. Open May-Sep. $18-28 per night. 60 sites, 11 with water and electric, 5 electric only. Drinking water. 55-foot limit. Restrooms; no showers. Dump station.

Chilkat State Park

7 Mud Bay Rd, Haines, AK 99827. Located 7 miles S of Haines along Mud Bay Rd. GPS: 59.139147, -135.369410. Lake in park. Fishing, boating. Hiking trails. Wildlife viewing. Information center. No reservations accepted. $20 or less. 35 sites, no hookups. 35-foot limit. Restrooms; no showers.

Chilkoot Lake State Recreation Site

10 Lutak Rd, Haines, AK 99827. Located 9 miles N of Haines via Lutak Rd. GPS: 59.335882, -135.561718. Fishing, boating. Wildlife viewing. No reservations accepted. $20 or less. 32 sites, no hookups. Drinking water. 35-foot limit. Restrooms; no showers.

Chugach State Park

Eagle River, AK 99577. A 495,000 acre park located E of Anchorage accessible via Glenn Hwy and Seward Hwy. Three camping areas.

Bird Creek Campground: 101.2 Seward Hwy, Chugach, AK 99540. Located about 20 miles SE of Anchorage, just E of Bird Creek Bridge. GPS: 60.972148, -149.460050. Lake in park. Fishing, boating. Hiking, biking, ATV trails. Wildlife viewing. Open all year. No reservations accepted. $20 or less. 28 sites, no hookups. Drinking water. 35-foot limit. Restrooms; no showers. 20 overflow sites.

Eagle River Campground: 12.6 Glenn Highway, Eagle River, AK 99577. Located 12 miles N of Anchorage, 1 mile S of the town of Eagle River. GPS: 61.306360, -149.571788. Fishing. Hiking trails. Wildlife viewing. Open May-Sep. $20 or less. 57 sites, no hookups. Drinking water. Restrooms; no showers. Dump station. Overflow area with 10 sites.

Eklutna Campground: 26.5 Glenn Highway, Eklutna, AK 99567. Located off Glenn Hwy at the Eklutna Turn-off. Follow Eklutna Lake road to the end. GPS: 61.409417, -149.145631. Lake in park. Fishing, boating. Hiking, biking, equestrian, ATV trails. Wildlife viewing. Open all year. No reservations accepted. $20 or less. 50 sites, no hookups. Drinking water. Restrooms; no showers. Overflow area with 15 sites.

Clam Gulch State Recreation Area

117 Sterling Highway, Soldotna, AK 99669. Located about 20 miles S of Soldotna via AK 1. GPS: 60.238518, -151.39611. Fishing, boating. Hiking, biking trails. Wildlife viewing. Scenic views. Open May-Sep. No reservations accepted. $20 or less. 120 sites, no hookups. Drinking water. 35-foot limit. Restrooms; no showers.

Clearwater State Recreation Site

1415 Alaska Hwy, Delta Junction, AK 99737. Located E of Delta Junction about 11 miles N of the Alaska Hwy at Clearwater Rd. GPS: 64.053476, -145.432544. Fishing, boating. Walking trails. Wildlife viewing. Bird watching. Open May-Sep. No reservations accepted. $20 or less. 17 sites, no hookups. Drinking water. Restrooms; no showers.

Crooked Creek State Recreation Site

Coho Loop Rd, Soldotna, AK 99669. Located about 18 miles SW of Soldotna . Go N on Cohoe Loop Rd off Sterling Hwy. GPS: 60.321475, -151.286568. Fishing. Hiking trails. Wildlife viewing. No reservations accepted. $20 or less. 79 sites, no hookups. Drinking water. 35-foot limit. Restrooms; no showers.

Deep Creek Beach State Recreation Area

136 Sterling Hwy, Homer, AK 99603. Located about 35 miles N of Homer along the Sterling Hwy. GPS: 60.031453, -151.702147. Fishing, boating. ATV riding. Wildlife viewing. Scenic overlook. No reservations accepted. $20 or less. 100 sites, no hookups. Drinking water. 35-foot limit. Restrooms; no showers.

Delta State Recreation Site

267 Richardson Hwy, Delta Junction, AK 99737. Located just N of Delta Junction on AK 2. GPS: 64.053165, -145.734635. Directly across the highway from the recreation site is the Delta River. No reservations accepted. $20 or less. 25 sites, no hookup. Drinking water. Restrooms; no showers.

Denali State Park

Trapper Creek, AK 99683. Phone: (907) 745-3975. Located about 140 miles N of Anchorage along the George Parks Hwy from mile 137.2 to mile 162.7. Five camping areas.

Byers Lake Campground: 147 Parks Hwy. GPS: 62.745116, -150.120431. Lake in park. Fishing, boating (rentals, no gas motors). Hiking trails. Wildlife viewing. Visitor center nearby. Open May-Sep. No reservations accepted. $20 or less. 73 sites, no hookups. Drinking water. 35-foot limit. Restrooms; no showers. Dump station.

Denali View North Campground: 162.7 Parks Hwy. GPS: 62.886220, -149.786221. Hiking trails. Wildlife viewing. Scenic viewpoint. Open May-Sep. No reservations accepted. $20 or less. 20 sites, no hookups. Drinking water. Restrooms; no showers.

Denali View South Campground: 134.8 Parks Hwy. GPS: 62.592979, -150.239149. Hiking trails. Wildlife viewing. Scenic viewpoint. Open May-Sep. No reservations accepted. $20 or less. 9 sites, no hookups. Drinking water. Restrooms; no showers.

K'esugi Ken Campground: 135.4 Parks Hwy. GPS: 62.592060, -150.229052. Interpretive center and trail. Walking/biking trails. Wildlife viewing. Open May-Sep. $40 or less. 32 sites with electric hookups. Drinking water. 75-foot limit. Restrooms; no showers.

Lower Troublesome Creek Campground: 137.2 Parks Hwy. GPS: 62.625775, -150.227574. Fishing. Hiking trails. Wildlife viewing. Open May-Sep. No reservations accepted. $20 or less. 20 sites, no hookups. Drinking water. Restrooms; no showers.

Donnelly Creek State Recreation Site

238 Richardson Hwy, Delta Junction, AK 99737. Located 32 miles S of Delta Junction at milepost 238 on Richardson Hwy. GPS: 63.674033, -145.883520. Fishing. Wildlife viewing. No reservations accepted. $20 or less. 12 sites, no hookups. Drinking water. Restrooms; no showers.

Dry Creek State Recreation Site

117 Richardson Hwy, Glennallen, AK 99588. Located 4 miles N of Glennallen on Richardson Hwy. GPS: 62.152754, -145.471711. Fishing. Hiking trails. Wildlife viewing. Open May-Sep. No reservations accepted. $20 or less. 50 sites, no hookups. Restrooms; no showers.

Eagle Beach State Recreation Area

26 Glacier Hwy, Juneau, AK 99801. Located about 27 miles N of Juneau. GPS: 58.527791, -134.816564. Fishing, boating. Hiking, biking, walking, trails. Wildlife viewing. Bird watching. Beach combing. No reservations accepted. $20 or less. 26 sites, no hookups. Drinking water. 35-foot limit. Restrooms; no showers.

Eagle Trail State Recreation Site

109 Tok Cutoff, Tok, AK 99780. Located 16 miles S of Tok at mile 109.5 of the Tok Cut-Off Hwy. GPS: 63.161847, -143.195835. Hiking, nature trails. Wildlife viewing. No reservations accepted. $20 or less. 35 sites, no hookups. Drinking water. Restrooms; no showers.

Fielding Lake State Recreation Site

200 Richardson Hwy, Delta Junction, AK 99737. Located about 65 miles S of Delta Junction at mile 200.5 on Richardson Hwy. GPS: 63.192948, -145.647810. Fishing, boating. Hiking trails. Wildlife viewing. No reservations accepted. $20 or less. 17 sites, no hookups. Drinking water. Restrooms; no showers.

Finger Lake State Recreation Site

7278 E Bogard Rd, Wasilla AK 99654. Phone: (907) 745-8950. Located about 7 miles NE of Wasilla. GPS: 61.609859, -149.264433. Swimming beach, fishing, boating. Wildlife viewing. Open May-Sep. $30 or less. 24 sites, no hookups. Drinking water. 35-foot limit. Restrooms; no showers.

Fort Abercrombie State Historic Park

1400 Abercrombe Dr, Kodiak AK 99615. Located about 4 miles N of Kodiak. GPS: 57.834535, -152.357360. Lake in park. Swimming (lake), fishing. Hiking, biking, interpretive trails. Scenic view, beach access. In 1970 Ft. Abercrombie was listed on the National Register of Historic Places and in 1985, the park was designated a National Historic Landmark. Open May-Sep. No reservations accepted. $20 or less. 5 sites, no hookups. Drinking water. 20-foot limit. Restrooms; no showers.

Funny River State Recreation

12 Funny River Rd, Soldotna AK 99669. Located 12 miles E of Soldotna at the confluence of the Funny and Kenai Rivers. GPS: 60.492381, -150.862996. Fishing. Wildlife viewing. Bird watching. No reservations accepted. $20 or less. 10 sites, no hookups. Drinking water. 40-foot limit. Restrooms; no showers.

Harding Lake State Recreation Area

321 Richardson Hwy, Fairbanks, AK 99714. Located about 42 miles S or Fairbanks on Salcha Dr. GPS: 64.437630, -146.875920. Fishing, boating. Hiking, nature trails. Wildlife viewing. No reservations accepted. $20 or less. 78 sites, no hookups. Drinking water. Restrooms; no showers. Dump station.

Izaak Walton Campground

81 Sterling Hwy, Sterling, AK 99672. In Sterling just E of the Moose River bridge. GPS: 60.535735, -150.751117. Fishing, boating. Wildlife viewing. No reservations accepted. $20 or less. 31 sites, no hookups. Drinking water. 32-foot limit. Restrooms; no showers.

Johnson Lake State Recreation Area

110 Sterling Hwy, Kasilof, AK 99610. Located about 15 miles S of Soldotna on Johnson Lake Loop Rd. GPS: 60.296630, -151.265864. Fishing, boating. Walking trails. Wildlife viewing. Scenic views. Open May-Sep. No reservations accepted. $20 or less. 51 sites, no hookups. Drinking water. 35-foot limit. Restrooms; no showers.

King Mountain State Recreation Site

33915 N Glenn Hwy, Chickaloon, AK 99674. Located about 29 miles NE of Palmer via Glenn Hwy eastbound to milepost 78.6. GPS: 61.775789, 148.494529. Fishing. Hiking trails. ATV trails nearby. Wildlife viewing. Open Mar-Sep. Operated by Great Holiday Campgrounds, phone (907) 240-9797, online reservations http://greatholidaycampgrounds.com. $25 per night. 22 sites, no hookups. Drinking water. 40-foot limit. Restrooms; no showers.

Lake Louise State Recreation Area

17 Lake Louise Rd, Glennallen, AK 99588. Located about 43 miles west and north of Glennallen. Mile 158 Glenn Highway to Lake Louise Rd. GPS: 62.281643, -146.542805. Fishing, boating. Hiking, biking trails. Wildlife viewing. Bird watching. Berry picking. Northern Lights viewing. Open all year. No reservations accepted. $20 or less. 67 sites, no hookups. Drinking water. Restrooms; no showers.

Liberty Falls State Recreation Site

23 Edgerton Hwy, Chitina, AK 99566. Located about 57 miles S of Glennallen via AK 4 and AK 10. GPS: 61.621642, -144.546834. Hiking trails. Wildlife viewing. Scenic viewpoint, waterfall. Open May-Sep. No reservations accepted. $20 or less. 10 sites, no hookups. Drinking water. Restrooms; no showers.

Lower Chatanika River State Recreation Area

11 Elliott Hwy, Fairbanks, AK 99712. 400-acre park located about 20 miles N of Fairbanks at mile 10.5 of the Elliot Hwy. Two camping areas.

Olnes Pond Campground: Located one mile W of the Elliott Hwy about 21 miles N of Fairbanks. GPS: 65.077018, -147.744719. Lake in park. Fishing, boating. Hiking ATV trails. Wildlife viewing. Berry picking. Open all year. No reservations accepted. $20 or less. 15 sites, no hookups. Drinking water. Restrooms; no showers.

Whitefish Campground: Located about 21 miles N of Fairbanks just off Elliot Hwy. GPS: 65.084896, -147.727981. Fishing, boating. Hiking, ATV trails. Wildlife viewing. Berry picking. Open May-Sep. No reservations accepted. $20 or less. 25 sites, no hookups. Drinking water. Restrooms; no showers.

Matanuska Glacier State Recreation Area

101 Glenn Hwy, Palmer, AK 99645. Phone: (907) 745-5151. Located about 52 miles E of Palmer at milepost 101 of the Glenn Hwy. GPS: 61.800556, -147.814875. River rafting. Hiking, nature trails. Glacier trekking. Wildlife viewing. Glacier viewing platforms. Scenic byway adjacent to park. Open until closed by winter snow. $20 or less. 12 sites, no hookups. Drinking water. Restrooms; no showers.

Morgan's Landing State Recreation Area

83 Sterling Hwy, Sterling, AK 99672. Located 5 miles S of Sterling Hwy via Scout Lake Loop Rd and Lou Morgan Rd. GPS: 60.501002, -150.864437. Fishing, boating. Hiking trails. Wildlife viewing. No reservations accepted. $20 or less. 51 sites, no hookups. Drinking water. 35-foot limit. Restrooms; no showers.

Montana Creek State Recreation Site

96 Parks Hwy, Trapper Creek, AK 99688. Phone: (907) 733-5267. Located about 54 miles N of Wasilla via Glenn Hwy to George Parks Hwy N to milepost 96.6, park entrance on the left. GPS: 62.103447, -150.059371. Fishing. Hiking, biking, walking trails. Wildlife viewing. Camp store. Open all year. For reservations call (907) 733-5267, online at www.montanacreekcampground.com. $30 or less. 36 sites, no hookups.Drinking water. Restrooms; no showers.

Moon Lake State Recreation Site

1332 Alaska Hwy, Tok, AK 99780. Phone: (907) 505-0319. Located 15 miles NW of Tok at milepost 1332 on Alaska Hwy. GPS: 63.375691, -143.544630. Swimming beach, fishing, boating. Wildlife viewing. No reservations accepted. $20 or less. 15 sites, no hookups. Drinking water. Restrooms; no showers.

Nancy Lake State Recreation Area

67 Parks Hwy, Willow, AK 99688. 22,685 acre park located about 25 miles W of Wasilla. Two camping areas. To enter the Nancy Lake Recreation Area, turn W onto Nancy Lake Pkwy at Mile 67.3 of the Parks Hwy. From there, the Nancy Lake Pkwy travels 6.5 miles SW to South Rolly Lake campground. Fishing, boating. Hiking trails. Wildlife viewing. Bird watching.

Nancy Lake State Recreation Site: Located along Parks Hwy about 3 miles S of Willow. GPS: 61.701891, -150.005427. No reservations accepted. $20 or less. 30 sites, no hookups. Drinking water. Restrooms; no showers.

South Rolly Lake Campground: Located near the end of Nancy Lake Pkwy, which is about 2.5 miles S of Willow. GPS: 61.667070, -150.141259. No reservations accepted. $30 or less. 98 sites, no hookups. Drinking water. Restrooms; no showers.

Ninilchik State Recreation Area

135 Sterling Hwy, Homer, AK 99603. Located 40 miles south of Soldotna. Located at milepost 135 of the Sterling Hwy. Fishing. Hiking trails. Wildlife viewing. Bird watching. Three camping areas.

Ninilchik River Campground: Located at milepost 134.4 of the Sterling Hwy. GPS: 60.052815, -151.651898. No reservations accepted. $20 or less. 39 sites, no hookups. 35-foot limit. Restrooms; no showers.

Ninilchick River Scenic Overlook: Located at milepost 135 of the Sterling Hwy. GPS: 60.048663, -151.653864. No reservations accepted. $20 or less. 9 sites, no hookups. 35-foot limit. Restrooms; no showers.

Ninilchik View Campground: Located at milepost 135.7 of the Sterling Hwy. GPS: 60.46160, -151.670854. No reservations accepted. $20 or less. 14 sites, no hookups.

Pasagshak State Recreation Site

20 Pasagshak River Rd, Kodiak, AK 99615. Located about 39 miles S of Kodiak. GPS: 57.458364, -152.449745. Fishing, kayaking. Wildlife viewing. Beach combing. No reservations accepted. $20 or less. 6 sites, no hookups. 40-foot limit. Drinking water. Restrooms; no showers.

Porcupine Creek State Recreation Site

64 Tok Cut-off Highway, Tok, AK 99780. Phone: (907) 822-3973. Located about 62 miles S of Tok on the Tok cut-off near the Nebesna Rd Intersection. GPS: 62.726604, -143.868401. Fishing. Hiking trails. Wildlife viewing. Area operated by Hart D. Ranch. For information call (907) 822-3973. $20 or less. 12 sites, no hookups, Drinking water. Restrooms; no showers.

Quartz Lake State Recreation Area

277 Richardson Hwy, Delta Junction, AK 99737. 556-acre park located about 12 miles N of Delta Junction. Swimming, fishing, boating. Hiking, ATV trails. Wildlife viewing. Two camping areas.

Lost Lake Trail Campground: Located about 13 miles N of Delta Junction on Quartz Lake Rd. GPS: 64.197790, -145.837875. No reservations accepted. $20 or less. 12 sites, no hookups. Drinking water. Restrooms; no showers.

Quartz Lake Campground: Located about 14 miles N of Delta Junction on Quartz Lake Rd. GPS: 64.197570, -145.828520. No reservations accepted. $20 or less. 103 sites, no hookups. Drinking water. Restrooms; no showers.

Rocky Lake State Recreation Site

14806 W Rocky St, Big Lake, AK 99652. Phone: (907) 240-9797. Located about 14 miles W of Wasilla via AK 3 and Big Lake Rd. GPS: 61.557792, -149.822342. Fishing, boating. Jet powered watercraft not allowed on lake. Wildlife viewing. Open Mar-Sep. Operated by Great Holiday Campgrounds, phone (907) 240-9797, online reservations http://greatholidaycampgrounds.com.

$20-25 per night. 10 sites, no hookups. Drinking water. 30-foot limit. Restrooms; no showers.

Salcha River State Recreation Site

323 Richardson Hwy, Fairbanks, AK 99703. Located about 40 miles SE of Fairbanks at milepost 323.3 on Richardson Hwy. GPS: 64.469466, -146.928421. Fishing, boating. Wildlife viewing. Bird watching. No reservations accepted. $20 or less. 6 sites, no hookups. Drinking water. Restrooms; no showers.

Settlers Cove State Recreation Site

18 N Tongass Hwy, Ketchikan, AK 99903. Located about 18 miles NW of Ketchikan. GPS: 55.509973, -131.727574. Lake in park. Fishing, boating (canoe/kayak). Hiking trails. Wildlife viewing. Waterfall viewing deck. Open all year. No reservations accepted. $20 or less. 13 sites, no hookups. Drinking water. 35-foot limit. Restrooms; no showers.

Squirrel Creek State Recreation Site

79 Richardson Hwy, Copper Center, AK 99573. Phone: (907) 822-5932. Located about 35 miles S of Glennallen. GPS: 61.667054, -145.177288. Lake in park. Fishing. Wildlife viewing. No reservations accepted. $20 or less. 25 sites, no hookups. Drinking water. Restrooms; no showers.

Stariski State Recreation Site

152 Sterling Hwy, Anchor Point, AK 99556. Located about 20 miles N of Homer at milepost 152. GPS: 59.841550, -151.811518. Scenic viewpoint. Wildlife viewing. Open May-Sep. No reservations accepted. $20 or less. 13 sites, no hookups. Drinking water. 35-foot limit. Restrooms; no showers. Dump station.

Tok River State Recreation Site

1309 Alaska Hwy, Tok, AK 99780. Phone: (907) 505-0319. Located about 4.5 miles E of Tok at milepost 1309 on Alaska Hwy. GPS: 63.325164, -142.831428. Fishing, boating. Hiking, walking trails. Wildlife viewing. No reservations accepted. $20 or less. 27 sites, no hookups. Drinking water. 60-foot limit. Restrooms; no showers.

Upper Chatanika River State Recreation Site

39 Steese Hwy, Fairbanks, AK 99712. Located about 47 miles NE of Fairbanks at milepost 39 on Steese Hwy. GPS: 65.232263, -146.883472. Fishing, boating. Wildlife viewing. No reservations accepted. $20 or less. 24 sites, no hookups. Drinking water. Restrooms; no showers.

Willow Creek State Recreation Area

70 Parks Hwy, Willow, AK 99688. Located about 5 miles NW of Willow via AK 3 and Willow Creek Pkwy. GPS: 61.773140, -150.162341. Fishing, boating. River rafting. Hiking trails. Wildlife viewing. Bird watching. Open May-Sep. No reservations accepted. $20 or less. 140 sites, no hookups. Drinking water. Restrooms; no showers.

Arizona

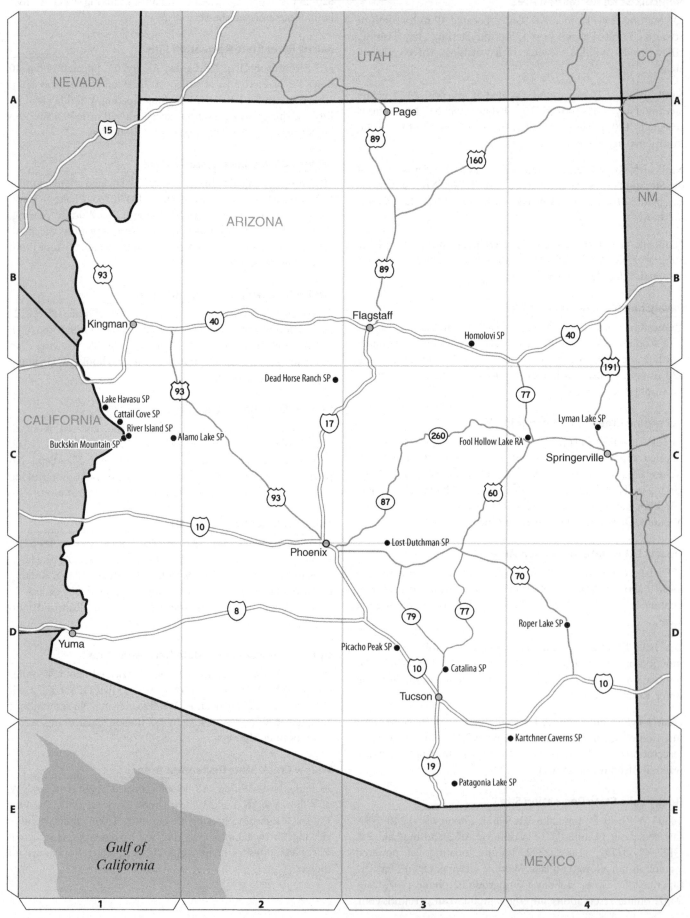

Arizona

Arizona State Parks
23751 N 23rd Ave Ste 190
Phoenix, AZ 85085

Phone: (877) 697-2757.
Internet: www.azstateparks.com
Reservations: Online or (877) 697-2757

Arizona Park Locator

Arizona Parks

Alamo Lake State Park

Alamo Rd, Wenden, AZ 85357. Phone: (928) 669-2088. Remote location in western Arizona about 37 miles N of US 60 from Wenden via county roads. GPS: 34.235330, -113.555393. Swimming, fishing, boating. Hiking, biking trails. Wildlife viewing. Visitor center, park store. Open all year. $15-25 per night. 185 sites, 19 full hookup, 80 with water and electric. Restrooms; showers. Dump station.

Buckskin Mountain State Park

5476 N US 95, Parker, AZ 85344. Phone: (928) 667-3231. Located about 12 miles NE of Parker on AZ 95. GPS: 34.255633, -114.162425. Lake in park. Swimming, fishing, boating. Hiking trails. Wildlife viewing. Scenic viewpoint. Visitor center, gift shop. Open all year. $35-40 per night. 68 sites, 15 full hookup, 53 with water and electric. Restrooms; showers. Dump station.

Catalina State Park

11570 N Oracle Rd, Tucson, AZ 85740. Phone: (520) 628-5798. Located about 9 miles N of Tucson on AZ 77 at mile marker 81. GPS: 32.423978, -110.925584. Hiking, biking, equestrian, nature trails. Wildlife viewing. Bird watching. Visitor center, park store. Open all year. 120 sites with water and electric. Restrooms; showers. Dump station. Equestrian camp, 16 corrals.

Cattail Cove State Park

Lake Havasu City, AZ 86405. Phone: (928) 855-1223. Located in western Arizona 15 miles S of Lake Havasu City on AZ 95, on Colorado River (north of Buckskin Mountain SP). GPS: 34.353826, -114.166975. Lake in park. Swimming beach, fishing, boating. Hiking trails. Bird watching. Visitor center, park store. Open all year. Reservations recommended, especially in winter months. $30-35 per night. 61 sites with water and electric. Restrooms; showers. Dump station.

Dead Horse Ranch State Park

675 Dead Horse Ranch Rd, Cottonwood, AZ 86326. Phone: (928) 634-5283. Located in northern Arizona, 39 miles W of Sedona on AZ 89A. GPS: 34.753752, -112.021135. Lake in park. Fishing. Hiking, biking, equestrian trails. Wildlife viewing. Bird watching. Visitor center, park store. Equestrian concessionaire offers guided trail rides. Open all year. $30-35 per night. 110 sites with water and electric. 65-foot limit. Restrooms; showers. Dump station.

Fool Hollow Lake Recreation Area

1500 N Fools Hollow Lake Rd, Show Low, AZ 85901. Phone: (989) 537-3680. Located in northeastern Arizona, 2 miles N of US 60 near Show Low. Fishing, swimming; boat ramp. GPS: 34.273711, -110.065921. Swimming (lake), fishing, boating (rentals). Hiking, biking (rentals) trails. Wildlife viewing. Visitor center, park store. Open all year. $25-35 per night. 92 sites with water and electric (some with sewer). 40-foot limit. Restrooms; showers. Dump station.

Homolovi State Park

Winslow, AZ 86047. Phone: (928) 289-4106. Located in north-central Arizona, 12 miles NE of I-40 exit 257 on AZ 87. GPS: 35.031445, -110.646756. Hiking, nature trails. Wildlife viewing. Visitor center, park store, gift shop. Museum. Observatory. Open all year. $18-30 per night. 53 sites, 44 with water and electric (some pull-thrus). 83-foot limit (pull-thru sites). Restrooms; showers. Dump station.

Kartchner Caverns State Park

2890 S Hwy 90, Benson, AZ 85602. Phone: (520) 586-4100. Cave tour reservations: (520) 586-2283. Located in southeastern Arizona, 9 miles S of I-10 exit 302 via AZ 90. GPS: 31.836143, -110.348006. Hiking, walking trails. Wildlife viewing. Bird watching. Discovery center, cafe, gift shop. Museum. Big tourist attraction park; reservations strongly recommended for cave tours (limited walk-up tickets available daily). Open all year. Reservations strongly recommended, especially in winter months when both caverns are open. $30-35 per night. 62 sites with water and electric. 60-foot limit. Restrooms; showers. Dump station.

Lake Havasu State Park

699 London Bridge Rd, Lake Havasu City, AZ 86403. Phone: (928) 855-2784. Located in western Arizona, 6 miles S of Lake Havasu City on AZ 95. GPS: 34.493191, -114.358994. Swimming beaches, fishing, boating (rentals). Nature, walking trails. Bird watching. Visitor center, park store, gift shop. Interpretive Garden.

London Bridge, two miles from park. Open all year. Reservations recommended, especially in winter months. $35-40 per night. 47 sites with water and electric. Restrooms; showers. Dump station.

Lost Dutchman State Park

6109 N Apache Trail, Apache Junction, AZ 85219. Phone: (480) 982-4485. Located 5 miles N of Apache Junction on AZ 88, off US 60 (Superstition Hwy). GPS: 33.454942, -111.484120. Hiking, biking, nature trails. Wildlife viewing. Visitor center, park store, gift shop. Open all year. $25-35 per night. 134 sites, 68 with water and electric. Restrooms; showers. Dump station.

Lyman Lake State Park

St. Johns, AZ 85936. Phone: (928) 337-4441. Located in eastern Arizona, 11 miles S of St. Johns via US 191. GPS: 34.360915, -109.376315. Swimming (lake), fishing, boating. Hiking trails. Wildlife viewing. Bird watching. Visitor center, park store, gift shop. Open all year. $20-33 per night. 56 sites, 13 full hookup, 25 with water and electric. Restrooms; showers. Dump station.

Patagonia Lake State Park

400 Patagonia Lake Rd, Patagonia, AZ 85624. Phone: (520) 287-6965. Remote location in southern Arizona near Nogales off AZ 82, 35 miles S of I-10 exit 281. GPS: 31.494546, -110.854459. Swimming beach, fishing, boating (rentals). Hiking trail (1/2 mile). Hiking and equestrian trails nearby. Wildlife viewing. Bird watching. Visitor center, park store. Marina. Pontoon Boat Tours. Open all year. $25-30 per night. 105 sites with water and electric; some pull-through sites. Restrooms; showers. Dump station.

Picacho Peak State Park

Eloy, AZ 85131. Phone: (520) 466-3183. Located northwest of Tucson at I-10 exit 219. GPS: 32.651413, -111.418071. Hiking, nature, walking trails. Wildlife viewing. Bird watching. Visitor center, park store, gift shop. Open all year. $25-30 per night. 85 sites with electric only; some pull-through sites. Drinking water. Restrooms; showers. Dump station.

River Island State Park

5200 N Hwy 95; Parker, AZ 85344. Phone (928) 667-3386. Located 12 miles NW of Parker off AZ 95. GPS: 34.254009, -114.137820. Swimming beach, fishing, boating. 1/2-mile hiking trail, others nearby. Bird watching. Visitor center, park store. Open all year. $30 per night. 29 sites with water and electric; 19 pull-throughs. 65-foot limit. Restrooms; showers. Dump station. Eight beachfront campsites on the grass overlooking Colorado River with 20-amp service and water. These sites are for small campers up to 24 feet.

Roper Lake State Park

101 East Roper Lake Rd, Safford, AZ 85546. Phone: (928) 428-6760. Located in southeast Arizona about 28 miles N of I-10 exit 352 via US 191. GPS: 32.753497, -109.706152. Swimming beach, fishing, boating. Hiking, nature trails. Bird watching. Visitor center, park store, gift shop. Open all year. $20-30 per night. 50 sites, 45 with water and electric, 5 no hookups. 45-foot limit. Restrooms; showers. Dump station.

Arkansas

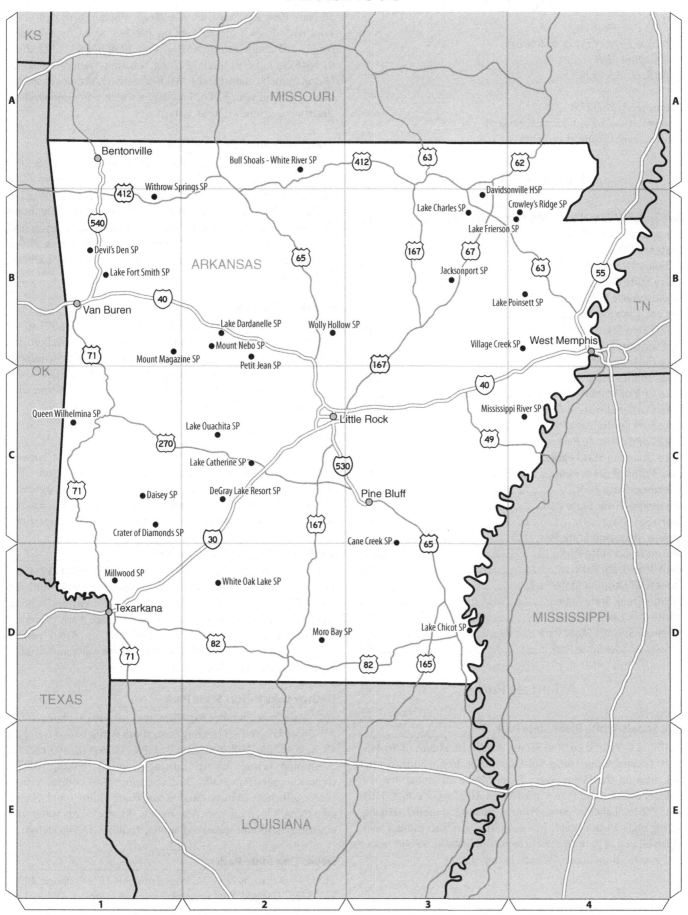

Arkansas

Arkansas Dept. of Parks & Tourism
One Capitol Mall
Little Rock, AR 72201

Phone: (888) 287-2757
Internet: www.ArkansasStateParks.com
Reservations: Online or call park.

Arkansas Park Locator

Arkansas Parks

Bull Shoals-White River State Park

153 Dam Overlook Ln, Bull Shoals, AR 72619. Phone: (870) 445-3629. Located about 9 miles S of AR/MO state line in north-central Arkansas on the White River. From Mountain Home, travel 6 miles N on AR 5 and then 8 miles W on AR 178. GPS: 36.351101, -92.588626. Lake in park. Fishing, boating (rentals). Hiking, biking trails. Visitor center, gift shop. Marina. Observation tower. Open all year. $40 or less. 93 sites, 63 full hookup, 30 with water and electric. Restrooms; showers. Dump station.

Cane Creek State Park

50 State Park Rd, Star City, AR 71667. Phone: (870) 628-4714. Located 5 miles E of Star City on AR 293. Star City is located on US 425 about 24 miles SE of Pine Bluff. GPS: 33.912320, -91.764659. Lake in park. Fishing, boating (rentals). Hiking, biking (rentals), nature trails. Wildlife viewing. Visitor center, gift shop. Open all year. $30 or less. 29 sites with water and electric. Restrooms; showers. Dump station.

Crater of Diamonds State Park

209 State Park Rd, Murfreesboro, AR 71958. Phone: (870) 285-3113. Located on AR 301 about 2 miles SE of Murfreesboro. GPS: 34.041215, -93.676198. Swimming pool, water park. Walking trails. Wildlife observation blind. Cafe. Visitor center. Diamond Discovery Center. Digging for diamonds search area, if you find a diamond, it is yours to keep. Open all year. $40 or less. 47 full hookup sites (all 50 amp). Restrooms; showers. Laundry facilities. Dump station.

Crowley's Ridge State Park

2092 Hwy 168 N, Paragould, AR 72450. Phone: (870) 573-6751. Located in northeastern Arkansas 17 miles N of Jonesboro via AR 141. GPS: 36.044455, -90.666217. Lakes in park. Swimming beach, fishing, boating (rentals). Hiking, walking trails. Bird watching. Visitor center. Open all year. $30 or less. 18 sites with water and electric. Restrooms; showers. Dump station.

Daisy State Park

103 East Park, Kirby, AR 71950. Phone: (870) 398-4487. Located 1/4 mile S of Daisy off US 70 near AR 27 on Lake Greeson. GPS: 34.233586, -93.740758. Lake in park. Fishing, boating (rentals). Nature, ATV trails. Visitor center. Open all year. $30 or less. 82 sites with water and electric. Restrooms; showers. Dump station.

Davidsonville Historic State Park

8047 Hwy 166 S, Pocahontas, AR 72455. Phone: (870) 892-4708. Located about 11 miles SW of Pocahontas via US 62 and AR 166. GPS: 36.158644, -91.056768. Lake in park. Fishing, boating (rentals). Hiking, walking trails. Visitor center. Park preserves the site of historic Davidsonville, established in 1815. Open all year. $40 or less. 19 sites, 12 full hookup, 7 with water and electric. Restrooms; showers. Dump station.

DeGray Lake Resort State Park

2027 State Park Entrance Rd, Bismarck, AR 71929. Phone: (501) 865-5850. Located on DeGray Lake about 6 miles N of I-30 Exit 78 near Caddo Valley via AR 7. GPS: 34.254116, -93.132784. Swimming beach, fishing, boating (rentals). Hiking, biking (rentals), equestrian trails. Bird watching. Golf course. Visitor center, gift shop. Marina. Guided horseback riding tours. Scenic lake tours. Open all year. $40 or less. 81 sites with water and electric. Restrooms; showers. Laundry facilities. Dump station.

Devils Den State Park

11333 W Arkansas Hwy 74, West Fork, AR 72774. Phone: (479) 761-3325. Located S of Fayetteville about 16 miles SW of I-49

Exit 53 via AR 170. Note: Large RVs should not use AR 74 from I-49 Exit 45 due to steep and winding roads. GPS: 35.780176, -94.250295. Lake in park. Swimming pool, fishing, boating (rentals). Hiking, biking, equestrian trails. Visitor center. Park store, gift shop, cafe. Open all year. $40 or less. 61 sites, 44 full hookup, 4 with water and electric, 13 with either water or electric only. Restrooms; showers. Laundry facilities. And 42 sites with water and electric hookups in the horse camp. Dump station.

Jacksonport State Park

205 Avenue St, Newport, AR 72112. Phone: (870) 523-2143. Located on White River in Jacksonport on AR 69, 3 miles N of Newport. GPS: 35.629145, -91.313058. River in park. Swimming beach, fishing, boating. Walking trails. Visitor center, store, gift shop. Museum. Open all year. $30 or less. 20 sites with water and electric (all 50 amp). Restrooms; showers. Dump station.

Lake Catherine State Park

1200 Catherine Park Rd, Hot Springs, AR 71913. Phone: (501) 844-4176. Located on Lake Catherine, SE of Hot Springs on AR 171 near Malvern. From I-30 exit 97, go 12 miles N on AR 171. GPS: 34.437689, -92.919815. Swimming beach, fishing, boating (rentals). Hiking, equestrian, nature trails. Visitor center, store, gift shop. Marina. Guided horseback rides. Open all year. $40 or less. 68 sites with water and electric. Restrooms; showers. Dump station.

Lake Charles State Park

3705 Hwy 25, Powhatan, AR 72458. Phone: (870) 878-6595. Located on Lake Charles in northeastern Arkansas near Hoxie. From Hoxie, 8 miles NW on US 63 then 6 miles S on AR 25. GPS: 36.065453, -91.152967. Swimming beach, fishing, boating (rentals). Hiking, nature, walking trails. 3-D archery range. Visitor center, store, gift shop. Nature center. Open all year. $40 or less. 60 sites with water and electric (some with sewer). Restrooms; showers. Dump station.

Lake Chicot State Park

2542 Hwy 257, Lake Village, AR 71653. Phone: (870) 265-5480. Located on Lake Chicot on AR 144, 8 miles NE of Lake Village. Exit US 65 at AR 144, E 9 miles to park. GPS: 33.371710, -91.195753. Swimming pool, fishing, boating (rentals). Hiking, biking (rentals) trails. Bird watching. Park store. Visitor center. Marina. Open all year. $40 or less. 122 sites with water and electric (some with sewer). Restrooms; showers. Laundry facilities. Dump station.

Lake Dardanelle State Park

2428 Marina Rd, Russellville, AR 72802. Phone: (479) 967-5516. Located on Lake Dardanelle near Russellville in north-central Arkansas. Two camping areas.

Dardanelle Campground: Located about 4 miles W of Dardanelle via AR 22. GPS: 35.253085, -93.212506. Swimming beach, fishing, boating. Wildlife viewing. Bird watching. Marina. Open all year. $30 or less. 18 sites with water and electric. Restrooms; showers. Dump station.

Russellville Campground: Located about 6 miles W of town center via US 64 and Marina Rd. GPS: 35.284820, -93.201724. Swimming beach, fishing, boating (rentals). Walking trails. Wildlife viewing. Bird watching. Visitor center. Marina. Party barge or kayak tours. Open all year. $30 or less. 57 sites, 30 full hookup, 27 with water and electric. Restrooms; showers. Dump station.

Lake Fort Smith State Park

15458 Shepard Springs Rd, Mountainburg, AR 72946. Phone: (479) 369-2469. Located on Lake Fort Smith about 8 miles N of Mountainburg. GPS: 35.696374, -94.119167. Swimming pool, fishing, boating (rentals). Hiking, biking, nature trails. Wildlife viewing. Visitor center, gift shop. Marina. Open all year. $40 or less. 30 sites, 20 full hookup, 10 with water and electric. Restrooms; showers.

Lake Frierson State Park

7904 Hwy 141, Jonesboro, AR 72401. Phone: (870) 932-2615. Located on Lake Frierson about 10 miles N of Jonesboro on AR 141. GPS: 35.972251, -90.716114. Fishing, boating (rentals). Hiking, nature trails. Wildlife viewing. Visitor center, gift shop. Open all year. $30 or less. 4 sites with water and electric. Restrooms; no showers. A bathhouse and dump station are at nearby Crowley's Ridge State Park.

Lake Ouachita State Park

5451 Mountain Pine Rd, Mountain Pine, AR 71956. Phone: (501) 767-9366. Located about 16 miles N of Hot Springs via AR 227. GPS: 34.618565, -93.176717. Swimming beach, fishing, scuba diving, boating (rentals). Hiking trail. Wildlife viewing. Visitor center, store, gift shop. Marina. Open all year. $40 or less. 58 full hookup sites. Restrooms; showers. Dump station.

Lake Poinsett State Park

5752 State Park Ln, Harrisburg, AR 72432. Phone: (870) 578-2064. Located in northeastern Arkansas about 3 miles SE of Harrisburg via AR 163. GPS: 35.532814, -90.687128. Fishing, boating (rentals). Hiking trail. Visitor center. Marina. Kayak tours available. Open all year. $30 or less. 26 sites with water and electric. Restrooms; showers. Dump station.

Millwood State Park

1564 Hwy 32 E, Ashdown, AR 71822. Phone: (870) 898-2800. Located about 27 miles N of Texarkana via US 71 and AR 32. GPS: 33.677428, -93.987523. Lake in park. Fishing, boating (rentals). Hiking, biking, nature, walking trails. Bird watching. Visitor center. Marina, store, gifts. Open all year. $40 or less. 42 sites, 27 full hookup, 15 with water and electric. Restrooms; showers. Dump station.

Mississippi River State Park

2955 Hwy 44, Marianna AR, 72360. Phone: (870) 295-4040. Located in southeast Arkansas about 10 miles SE of Marianna via AR 44. GPS: 34.710140, -90.699041. Lake in park. Swimming beaches, fishing, boating. Hiking, nature trails. Wildlife viewing.

Bird watching. Visitor center. Open all year. $40 or less. 14 full hookup sites (all 50 amp). Restrooms; showers. Dump station.

Moro Bay State Park

6071 Hwy 600, Jersey, AR 71651. Phone: (870) 463-8555. Located in southern Arkansas about 24 miles NE of El Dorado via US 63. GPS: 33.300764, -92.345276. Fishing, boating (rentals). Nature trails. Wildlife viewing. Visitor center, store, gift shop. Marina. Open all year. $40 or less. 23 full hookup sites. Restrooms; showers. Dump station.

Mount Magazine State Park

16878 Hwy 309 S, Paris, AR 72855. Phone: (479) 963-8502. Located about 17 miles S of Paris via AR 309. GPS: 35.171736, -93.644559. Hiking, biking (rentals), equestrian, ATV trails. Wildlife viewing. Scenic overlooks. Visitor center, gift shop. Wildflower and butterfly garden. Restaurant. Rock climbing. Hang gliding launch areas. Open all year. $40 or less. 18 full hookup sites. Restrooms; showers. Dump station.

Mount Nebo State Park

16728 W State Hwy 155, Dardanelle, AR 72834. Phone: (479) 229-3655. Located seven miles W of Dardenelle via AR 155. Note: Highway 155 is a winding road; trailers longer than 24 feet are not recommended. GPS: 35.218901, -93.252248. Swimming pool. Hiking, biking (rentals) trails. Wildlife viewing. Visitor center, store, gifts. Open all year. $30 or less. 24 sites with water and electric. Restrooms; showers. Dump station at nearby Lake Dardanelle State Park.

Petit Jean State Park

1285 Petit Jean Mountain Rd, Morrilton, AR 72110. Phone: (501) 727-5441. Located about 16 miles W of Morrilton via AR 9 and AR 154. GPS: 35.126883, -92.912457. Lake in park. Swimming pools, fishing, boating (rentals). Hiking, biking, walking trails. Scenic viewpoints. Visitor center, gift shop. Lodge, restaurant. Scenic drive. Open all year. $40 or less. 125 sites, 35 full hookup, 90 with water and electric. Restrooms; showers. Dump station.

Queen Wilhelmina State Park

3877 Hwy 88 W, Mena, AR 71953. Phone: (479) 394-2863. Located about 12 miles NW of Mena via AR 88. GPS: 34.685438, -94.373384. Hiking trails. Wildlife viewing. Scenic overlook. Miniature golf. Miniature railroad. Lodge, restaurant, gifts. Scenic drive. Open all year. $30 or less. 35 sites with water and electric. Restrooms; showers. Dump station.

Village Creek State Park

201 County Road 754, Wynne, AR 72396. Phone: (870) 238-9406. Located in northeast Arkansas about 7 miles SE of Wynne via AR 284. GPS: 35.161722, -90.717587. Lakes in park. Swimming beaches, fishing, boating (rentals). Hiking, biking, equestrian, nature trails. Golf course, driving range, clubhouse. Visitor center, store, gift shop. Museum. Open all year. $40 or less. 96 sites, 23 full hookup, 73 with water and electric. Restrooms; showers.

Dump station. Equestrian campground with water and electric hookups.

White Oak Lake State Park

563 Highway 387, Bluff City, AR 71722. Phone: (870) 685-2748. Located in a state forest about 21 miles SE of Prescott via AR 24. GPS: 33.688621, -93.117140. Fishing, boating (rentals). Hiking, biking (rentals), nature trails. Wildlife viewing. Bird watching. Visitor center, store, gifts. Marina. Open all year. $30 or less. 41 sites with water and electric. Restrooms; showers. Dump station.

Withrow Springs State Park

33424 Spur 23, Huntsville, AR 72740. Phone: (479) 559-2593. Located in the Ozark Mountains on AR 23 about 6 miles N of Huntsville. GPS: 36.163237, -93.721935. Swimming pool, fishing, boating/floating (rentals). Hiking trails. Visitor center. Open all year. $40 or less. 30 full hookup sites. Restrooms; showers. Dump station.

Woolly Hollow State Park

82 Woolly Hollow Rd, Greenbrier, AR 72058. Phone: (501) 679-2098. Located in central Arkansas about 8 miles NE of Greenbrier via AR 285. GPS: 35.288007, -92.288050. Lake in park. Swimming beach, fishing, boating (rentals). Hiking, biking, walking trails. Park office, snack bar, gifts. Open all year. $40 or less. 30 full hookup sites. Restrooms; showers. Dump station.

California

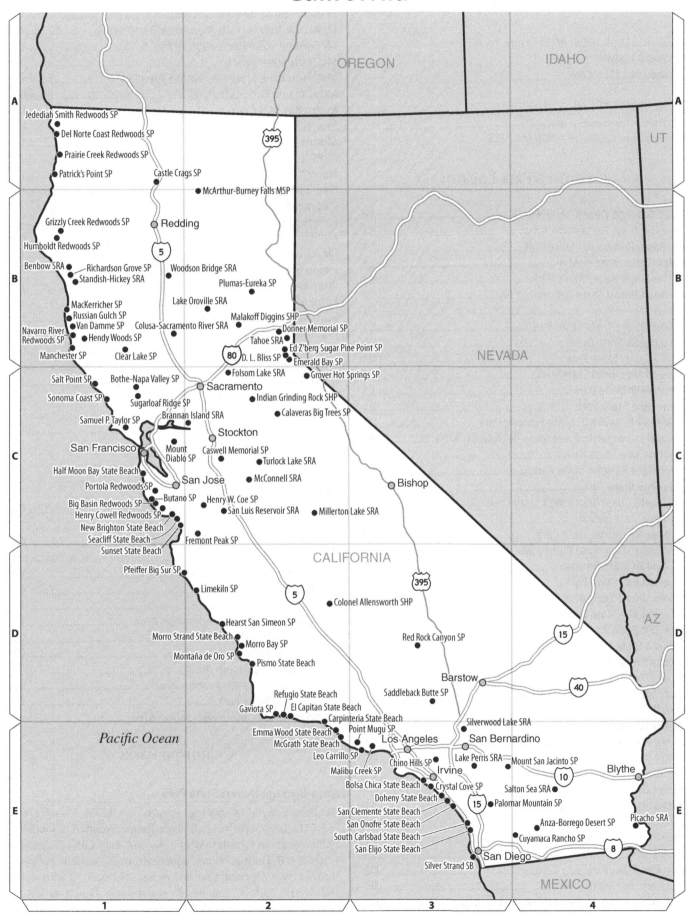

California

California Department of Parks and Recreation
PO Box 942896
Sacramento, CA 94296

Phone: (800) 777-0369
Internet: www.parks.ca.gov
Reservations: Online or (800) 444-7275

California Park Locator

California Parks

Anza-Borrego Desert State Park

200 Palm Canyon Dr, Borrego Springs, CA 92004. Phone: (760) 767-5311. Largest park in California. Remote location in southern California about 65 miles SW of Indio on CA 78. GPS: 33.268643, -116.405470. Hiking, biking, equestrian trails. Wildlife viewing. Visitor center. Open all year. $40 or less. 145 sites, 52 with water and electric. 35-foot limit. Restrooms; showers. Dump station.

Benbow State Recreation Area

1600 Hwy 101, Garberville, CA 95542. Phone: (707) 923-3238 or (707) 247-3318 (winter). Located in northern California about 4 miles S of Garberville via US 101 and Benbow Dr. Note: Large vehicles and RVs should enter the park from South Benbow Drive because there is a one-lane road coming from the north that is difficult for RVs to navigate. GPS: 40.058627, -123.784428. Swimming beach, fishing, boating. Hiking trails. Open all year. $40 or less. 75 sites, 2 with water and electric. Drinking water. 30-foot limit. Restrooms; showers. Dump station.

Big Basin Redwoods State Park

21600 Big Basin Way, Boulder Creek, CA 95006. Phone: (831) 338-8860. Located in central California about 25 miles N of Santa Cruz on CA 236. GPS: 37.172402, -122.221943. Swimming. Hiking, biking, equestrian, walking trails. Wildlife viewing. Scenic viewpoint. Camp store. Visitor center. Nature museum. Waterfalls. Food service. Five campgrounds open seasonally. $40 or less. 82 sites, no hookups. Drinking water. Length limit: motorhome 27-foot, trailer 24-foot. Restrooms; showers. Dump station.

Bolsa Chica State Beach

17851 Pacific Coast Hwy, Huntington Beach, CA 92649. Phone: (714) 377-5691. Located in southern California in Huntington Beach. GPS: 33.695691, -118.048193. Swimming, fishing, surfing. Hiking, biking, walking trails. Wildlife viewing. Bird watching. Visitor center. Food service. Open all year. $41 or more. 50 sites with water and electric. 40-foot limit. Restrooms; showers. Dump station.

Bothe-Napa Valley State Park

3801 Saint Helena Hwy, Calistoga, CA 94515. Phone: (707) 942-4575. Located in northern California about 5 miles N of Saint Helena on CA 128. GPS: 38.552633, -122.522845. Swimming pool. Hiking, biking, nature trails. Wildlife viewing. Visitor center. Museum. Managed by Napa County. Open all year. $40 or less. 30 sites, no hookups. Drinking water. Length limit: motorhome 31-foot, trailer 24-foot. Restrooms; showers.

Brannan Island State Recreation Area

Folsom, CA 95630. Phone: (916) 777-6671. Located in central California about 3 miles NE of Rio Vista on CA 160. GPS: 38.110468, -121.696997. Swimming beach, fishing, boating, surfing. Hiking, biking trails. Wildlife viewing. Scenic viewpoint. Visitor center. Open all year. $40 or less. 114 sites, 12 with water and electric. Drinking water. 36-foot limit. Restrooms; showers. Dump station.

Butano State Park

Pescadero, CA 94060. Phone: (650) 879-2040. Located in central California about 30 miles N of Santa Cruz via CA 1. GPS: 37.210231, -122.329390. Hiking, biking, equestrian trails. Guided nature walks. Wildlife viewing. Visitor center. Open Apr-Nov. $40 or less. 21 sites, no hookups. Drinking water. 24-foot limit. Restrooms; no showers.

Calaveras Big Trees State Park

1170 East Highway 4, Arnold, CA 95223. Phone: (209) 795-2334. Located about 24 miles NE of Angels Camp in central California on CA 4. GPS: 38.277366, -120.309738. Swimming beach, fishing. Hiking, biking, nature trails. Wildlife viewing. Visitor center, bookstore, museum. Open seasonally. $40 or less. 52 sites, no hookups. Drinking water. 30-foot limit. Restrooms; showers. Dump station.

Carpinteria State Beach

5361 6th Street, Carpinteria, CA 93013. Phone: (805) 684-2811. Located about 12 miles SE of Santa Barbara via US 101. GPS: 34.392542, -119.521290. Swimming, fishing, scuba diving, surfing. Hiking trails. Scenic viewpoint. Visitor center. Open seasonally. $41 or more. 105 sites, 80 full hookup, 25 with water and electric. 35-foot limit. Restrooms; showers. Dump station.

Castle Crags State Park

20022 Castle Creek Rd, Castella, CA 96017. Phone: (530) 235-2684. Located in northern CA off I-5 Exit 774 about 6 miles SW of Dunsmuir. GPS: 41.148352, -122.321487. Fishing. Hiking trails. Wildlife viewing. Scenic viewpoint. Pedestrian suspension bridge over the river. Open all year. $30 or less. 19 sites, no hookups. Drinking water. Length limit: motorhome 27-foot, trailer 21-foot. Restrooms; showers.

Caswell Memorial State Park

28000 S Austin Rd, Ripon, CA 95366. Phone: (209) 599-3810. Located in central California about 6 miles SW of Ripon via Doak Blvd. GPS: 37.700420, -121.182669. Swimming beaches, fishing, boating. Hiking, biking, nature trails. Wildlife viewing. Bird watching. Open all year. $30 or less. 24 sites, no hookups. Drinking water. Length limit: motorhome 24-foot, trailer 21-foot. Restrooms; showers.

Chino Hills State Park

4721 Sapphire Rd, Chino Hills, CA 91709. Phone: (951) 780-6222. Located about 13 miles NW of Corona via CA 91 and CA 71. GPS: 33.944337, -117.703641. Hiking, biking, equestrian trails. Wildlife viewing. Scenic viewpoint. Visitor center. Museum. Open all year. 20 sites, no hookups. Drinking water. 28-foot limit. Restrooms; showers.

Clear Lake State Park

5300 Soda Bay Rd, Kelseyville, CA 95451. Phone: (707) 279-2267. Located in northern California, N of Kelseyville off CA 29/175. GPS: 39.010655, -122.813995. Swimming beach, fishing, boating (rentals). Scuba diving/Snorkeling. Hiking, biking, trails. Wildlife viewing. Camp store. Visitor center. Museum. Open seasonally. $40 or less. 146 sites, no hookups. Drinking water. 35-foot limit. Restrooms; showers. Dump station.

Colonel Allensworth State Historic Park

4011 Grant Dr, Earlimart, CA 93219. Phone: (661) 849-3433. Located in south-central California about 45 miles NW of Bakersfield off CA 43. GPS: 35.866477, -119.391729. Hiking, biking trails. Wildlife viewing. Visitor center. Museum. Historic buildings. Open all year. $20 or less. 15 sites, no hookups. Drinking water. Length limit: motorhome 35-foot, trailer 27-foot. Restrooms; showers. Dump station.

Colusa-Sacramento River State Recreation Area

Levee St, Colusa, CA 95932. Phone: (530) 329-9198. Located in north-central California in the City of Colusa. GPS: 39.217945, -122.014802. Fishing, boating. Hiking, equestrian trails. Wildlife viewing. Bird watching. Managed by the City of Colusa. Open all year. $41 or more. 12 sites, 6 with electric hookups. Drinking water. Length limit: motorhome 27-foot, trailer 24-foot. Restrooms; showers. Dump station.

Crystal Cove State Park

8471 N Coast Hwy, Laguna Beach, CA 92651 Phone: (949) 494-3539. Located about 3 miles N of Laguna Beach via CA 1. GPS: 33.564451, -117.822271. Swimming beach, fishing, boating, surfing. Scuba diving/Snorkeling. Hiking, biking, equestrian, walking trails. Wildlife viewing. Scenic viewpoints. Visitor center. Open all year. $41 or more. 27 sites with water and electric. 35-foot limit. Restrooms; showers. Dump station.

Cuyamaca Rancho State Park

13652 Highway 79, Julian, CA 92036. Phone: (760) 765-3020. Located in southern California about 11 miles S of Julian on CA 79. GPS: 32.928570, -116.560108. Lake in park. Hiking, biking, equestrian trails. Wildlife viewing. Visitor center. Museum. Two campgrounds open all year. $30 or less. 166 sites, no hookups. Drinking water. 30-foot limit. Restrooms; showers. Dump station.

D. L. Bliss State Park

Tahoma, CA 96142. Phone: (530) 525-7277. Located about 17 miles S of Tahoe City on CA 89. GPS: 38.978018, -120.102853. Lake in park. Swimming beach, fishing, boating, scuba diving/snorkeling. Hiking, nature trails. Wildlife viewing. Scenic viewpoints. Visitor center. Museum. Open seasonally. $40 or less. 150 sites, no hookups. Dump station. Length limit: motorhome 18-foot, trailer 15-foot. Restrooms; showers.

Del Norte Coast Redwoods State Park

Highway 101, Crescent City, CA 95531. Phone: (707) 465-7335. Located in northern California about 7 miles S of Crescent City via US 101. GPS: 41.699714, -124.120609. Fishing, surfing, scuba diving/snorkeling. Hiking, biking, equestrian trails. Wildlife viewing. Bird watching. Open May-Sep. $40 or less. 142 sites, no hookups. Drinking water. Length limit: motorhome 28-foot, trailer 24-foot. Restrooms; showers. Dump station.

Doheny State Beach

25300 Dana Point Harbor Dr, Dana Point, CA 92629. Phone: (949) 496-6171. Located on the coast between San Diego and Long Beach off CA 1, 1 mile W of I-5, exit 79. GPS: 33.463868, -117.687334. Swimming, fishing, surfing. Hiking, biking trails. Wildlife viewing. Visitor center. Food service. Open all year.

$40 or less. 118 sites, no hookups. Drinking water. 35-foot limit. Restrooms; showers. Dump station.

Donner Memorial State Park

12593 Donner Pass Rd, Truckee, CA 96161. Phone: (530) 582-7892. Located about 3 miles W of Truckee via Donner Pass Rd off I-80 exit 184. GPS: 39.324089, -120.233367. Lake in park. Swimming beach, fishing, boating (rentals), surfing. Hiking trails. Wildlife viewing. Visitor center. Museum. The Pioneer Monument honors those who risked their lives to reach California during the 1840s. Open May-Oct. $40 or less. 152 sites, no hookups. Drinking water. Length limit: motorhome 28-foot, trailer 24-foot. Restrooms; showers.

Ed Z'berg Sugar Pine Point State Park

Highway 89, Tahoma, CA 96142. Phone: (530) 525-7982. Located about 24 miles S of Truckee via CA 89. GPS: 39.058387, -120.120613. Lake in park. Swimming beach, fishing, boating, scuba diving/snorkeling. Hiking, biking trails. Wildlife viewing. Visitor center. Nature center. Museum. Ehrman Mansion. Open all year. $40 or less. 120 sites, no hookups. Drinking water. Length limit: motorhome 32-foot, trailer 26-foot. Restrooms; showers. Dump station.

El Capitan State Beach

US Hwy 101, Goleta, CA 93117. Phone: (805) 968-1033. Located in southern California about 17 miles W of Santa Barbara on US 101. GPS: 34.460101, -120.023617. Swimming, fishing, boating, scuba diving/snorkeling, surfing. Hiking, biking, nature trails. Camp store. Open all year. $41 or more. 132 sites, no hookups. Drinking water. 42-foot limit. Restrooms; showers.

Emerald Bay State Park

Highway 89, Tahoma, CA 96142. Phone: (530) 541-3030. Located about 20 miles S of Tahoe City via CA 89. GPS: 38.951652, -120.085793. Lake in park. Swimming beach, fishing, boating (rentals), scuba diving/snorkeling. Hiking, nature trails. Scenic viewpoint. Visitor center. Museum. Designated a National Natural Landmark. Note: no vehicle access to the lakeshore of Emerald Bay or Vikingsholm. Visitors walk to the lake from the Vikingsholm Parking Lot (1 mile walk) or via the Rubicon Trail. Open seasonally. $40 or less. 97 sites, no hookups. Drinking water. Length limit: motorhome 18-foot, trailer 15-foot. Restrooms; showers.

Emma Wood State Beach

Pacific Coast Hwy, Ventura, CA 93001. Phone: (805) 968-1033. Located about 3 miles NW of Ventura via US 101 and CA 1. GPS: 34.295310, -119.341193. Swimming, fishing, surfing. Biking trails. Open all year. $40 or less. 90 sites, no hookups. No water. 45-foot limit. No restrooms or showers.

Folsom Lake State Recreation Area

7755 Folsom-Auburn Rd, Folsom, CA 95630. Phone: (916) 988-0205. Located about 25 miles NE of Sacramento. Two camping areas.

Beals Point Campground: Located just N of Folsom Dam about 3 miles N of the City of Folsom. GPS: 38.719241, -121.175456. Swimming beach, fishing, boating (rentals). Hiking, biking (rentals), equestrian trails. Scenic viewpoint. Visitor center. Marina, store. Open all year. $40 or less. 69 sites, 20 full hookups, 49 no hookups. Drinking water. 31-foot limit. Restrooms; showers. Dump station.

Peninsula Campground: Located about 20 miles S of Auburn via CA 49 and Rattlesnake Bar Rd. GPS: 38.766454, -121.108980. No swimming, fishing, boating (rentals). Hiking, biking (rentals), equestrian trails. Scenic viewpoint. Visitor center. Marina, store. Open Apr-Sep. $40 or less. 96 sites, no hookups. Drinking water. Length limit: motorhome 24-foot, trailer 18-foot. Restrooms; showers. Dump station.

Fremont Peak State Park

San Juan Canyon Road, San Juan Bautista, CA 95045. Phone: (831) 623-4526. Located about 10 miles S of San Juan Bautista via San Juan Canyon Rd; road is narrow in places. GPS: 36.761520, -121.496547. Hiking, biking trails. Wildlife viewing. Bird watching. Scenic viewpoint. Astronomical observatory. Open Mar-Nov. $30 or less. 8 sites, no hookups. Drinking water. 25-foot limit. Restrooms; no showers.

Gaviota State Park

17620 Gaviota Beach Rd, Gaviota, CA 93117. Phone: (805) 968-1033. Located about 33 miles W of Santa Barbara via US 101. GPS: 34.473404, -120.229472. Swimming beach, fishing, boating. Hiking, equestrian trails. Scenic viewpoint. Camp store. Open seasonally. $40 or less. 39 sites, no hookups. Drinking water. Length limit: motorhome 28-foot, trailer 25-foot. Restrooms; showers.

Grizzly Creek Redwoods State Park

16949 Hwy 36, Carlotta, CA 95528. Phone: (707) 777-3683. Located about 22 miles E of Fortuna via US 101 and CA 36. GPS: 40.486976, -123.904957. Swimming beach, fishing, boating. Hiking, walking trails. Visitor center. Open seasonally. $40 or less. 26 sites, no hookups. Drinking water. 24-foot limit. Restrooms; showers.

Grover Hot Springs State Park

3415 Hot Springs Rd, Markleeville, CA 96120. Phone: (530) 694-2248. Located about 4 miles W of Markleeville via Hot Springs Rd. GPS: 38.695563, -119.836945. Hot springs pool (both hot and cool water pools), fishing. Hiking, biking trails. Wildlife viewing. May-Oct. $30 or less. 76 sites, no hookups. Drinking water. Length limit: motorhome 27-foot, trailer 24-foot. Restrooms; showers.

Half Moon Bay State Beach

95 Kelly Ave, Half Moon Bay, CA 94019. Phone: (650) 726-8819. Located off CA 1 about 1 mile W of town center. GPS: 37.467342, -122.444784. Swimming, fishing, boating, surfing. Hiking, biking, equestrian trails. Wildlife viewing. Scenic viewpoint. Visitor center. Open all year. $41 or more. 52 sites, 34 with electric. Drinking water. 40-foot limit. Restrooms; showers. Dump station.

Hearst San Simeon State Park

750 Hearst Castle Road, San Simeon, CA 93452. Phone (805) 927-2010. Located about 5 miles S of San Simeon and the Hearst Castle Visitor Center along CA 1. GPS: 35.599110, -121.124672. Swimming beach, fishing, boating, surfing, scuba diving/snorkeling. Hiking, nature trails. Wildlife viewing. Scenic viewpoint. Open all year. $40 or less. 183 sites, no hookups. Drinking water. 35-foot limit. Restrooms; showers. Dump station.

Hendy Woods State Park

18599 Philo-Greenwood Rd, Philo, CA 95466. Phone: (707) 895-3141. Located about 33 miles SE of Mendocino via CA 1 and CA 128. GPS: 39.077634, -123.480276. Swimming beach, fishing, boating. Hiking trails. Wildlife viewing. Camp store. Visitor center. Open all year. $41 or more. 82 sites, no hookups. Drinking water. 35-foot limit. Restrooms; showers. Dump station.

Henry Cowell Redwoods State Park

2591 Graham Hill Rd, Scotts Valley, CA 95060. Phone: (831) 438-2396. Located about 4 miles N of Santa Cruz via CA 1 and Graham Hill Rd. GPS: 37.029911, -122.040167. Swimming (river), fishing. Hiking, biking, equestrian trails. Wildlife viewing. Bird watching. Scenic viewpoint. Visitor center. Museum. Roaring Camp Railroad, a tourist railroad is next to the park. Open Mar-Nov. $40 or less. 107 sites, no hookups. Drinking water. Length limit: motorhome 35-foot, trailer 31-foot. Restrooms; showers.

Henry W. Coe State Park

9000 E Dunne Ave, Morgan Hill, CA 95037. Phone: (408) 779-2728. Located about 14 miles NE of Morgan Hill off US 101. Access road is narrow and winding; not recommended for large RVs. GPS: 37.186647, -121.546906. Swimming (at least 5 mile hike to reach swimming areas), fishing, boating. Hiking, biking, equestrian trails. Wildlife viewing. Scenic viewpoint. Camp store. Visitor center. Museum. Open seasonally. $20 or less. 10 sites, no hookups. Drinking water. Length limit: motorhome 22-foot, trailer 20-foot. Restrooms (vault toilets); no showers.

Humboldt Redwoods State Park

Weott, CA 95571. Phone: (707) 946-2409. The park's visitor center is located along CA 254 about 47 miles S of Eureka. Swimming, fishing, boating. Hiking, biking, equestrian trails. Visitor center. 32-mile Avenue of the Giants auto tour. Three camping areas.

Albee Creek Campground: Located about 5 miles W of US 101 Exit 663 via Bull Creek Flats Rd and Mattole Rd. GPS: 40.353101, -124.008061. Open May-Oct. $40 or less. 40 sites, no hookups. Drinking water nearby. 24-foot limit. Restrooms; showers.

Burlington Campground: Located 1.5 miles S of Weott via CA 254/Avenue of the Giants. GPS: 40.308607, -123.909091. Open all year. $40 or less. 57 sites, no hookups. Drinking water nearby. 24-foot limit. Restrooms; showers.

Hidden Springs Campground: Located 1 mile N of Myers Flat via CA 254/Avenue of the Giants. GPS: 40.275217, -123.864097. Open May-Sep. $40 or less. 154 sites, no hookups. Drinking water nearby. 24-foot limit. Restrooms; showers.

Indian Grinding Rock State Historic Park

14881 Pine Grove-Volcano Rd, Pine Grove, CA 95665. Phone: (209) 296-7488. Located in central California about 8 miles E of Jackson via CA 88. GPS: 38.421863, -120.643231. Hiking, nature trails. Wildlife viewing. Visitor center. Museum. Open all year. $30 or less. 22 sites, no hookups. Drinking water. 27-foot limit. Restrooms; showers.

Jedediah Smith Redwoods State Park

1440 Highway 199, Crescent City, CA 95531. Phone: (707) 464-6101. Located 9 miles NE of Crescent City via US 101 and US 199. GPS: 41.798202, -124.084317. Swimming beach, fishing, boating. Hiking, biking, equestrian trails. Visitor center. Open all year. $40 or less. 87 sites, no hookups. Drinking water. Length limit: motorhome 25-foot, trailer 21-foot. Restrooms; showers. Dump station.

Lake Oroville State Recreation Area

400 Glen Dr, Oroville, CA 95966. Phone: (530) 538-2219. Located about 7 miles E of Oroville via CA 162. GPS: 39.520807, -121.440318. Swimming beach, fishing, boating (rentals), surfing, scuba diving/snorkeling. Hiking, biking, equestrian trails. Scenic viewpoint. Visitor center, store. Marina, store. Museum. Two campgrounds open all year. $40 or less. 278 sites, no hookups. Drinking water. Length limit: motorhome 40-foot, trailer 31-foot. Restrooms; showers. Dump station.

Lake Perris State Recreation Area

17801 Lake Perris Dr, Perris, CA 92571. Phone: (951) 940-5600. Located in southern California about 18 miles SE of Riverside between I-215 and CA 60. GPS: 33.871700, -117.178135. Swimming beach, fishing, boating (rentals), surfing, scuba diving/snorkeling. Hiking, biking, equestrian trails. Bird watching. Camp store. Visitor center. Museum. Open all year. $41 or more. 431 sites, 264 with water and electric. Drinking water. 31-foot limit. Restrooms; showers. Dump station.

Leo Carrillo State Park

35000 W Pacific Coast Hwy, Malibu, CA 90265. Phone: (310) 457-8143. Located about 28 miles NW of Santa Monica via CA 1. GPS: 34.046580, -118.933726. Swimming beach, fishing, boating, surfing, scuba diving/snorkeling. Hiking, nature trails. Wildlife viewing. Scenic viewpoint. Camp store. Visitor center. Open all year. $41 or more. 135 sites, no hookups. Drinking water. 31-foot limit. Restrooms; showers. Dump station.

Limekiln State Park

63025 Highway 1, Big Sur, CA 93920. Phone: (831) 434-1996. Located on CA coast S of Monterey, 28 miles S of Big Sur via CA 1. GPS: 36.010006, -121.518257. Swimming beach, fishing. Hiking trails. Wildlife viewing. Scenic viewpoint. Waterfall. Open all year. $40 or less. 12 sites, no hookups. Drinking water. Length limit: motorhome 24-foot, trailer 15-foot. Restrooms; showers.

MacKerricher State Park

24100 MacKerricher Park Rd, Fort Bragg, CA 95437. Phone: (707) 937-5804. Located about 3 miles N of Fort Bragg via CA 1. GPS: 39.489302, -123.789520. The park extends approximately nine miles along the coast. Small lake in park. Fishing, boating, surfing, scuba diving/snorkeling. Hiking, biking, equestrian trails. Wildlife viewing. Visitor center. Open all year. $41 or more. 104 sites, no hookups. Drinking water. 35-foot limit. Restrooms; showers. Dump station.

Malakoff Diggins State Historic Park

23579 N Bloomfield Rd, Nevada City, CA 95959. Phone: (530) 265-2740. Located about 26 miles NE of Nevada City via CA 49 and Tyler Foote Rd. GPS: 39.376789, -120.898182. Lake in park. Swimming, fishing, boating. Hiking, equestrian trails. Scenic viewpoint. Visitor center. Museum. Park preserves the history of North Bloomfield and hydraulic mining. Open May-Sep. $40 or less. 30 sites, no hookups. Drinking water. Length limit: motorhome 24-foot, trailer 18-foot. Restrooms; no showers.

Malibu Creek State Park

1925 Las Virgenes Rd, Calabasas, CA 91302. Phone: (818) 880-0367. Located 7 miles SE of Agoura Hills via US 101 and Las Virgenes Rd. GPS: 34.100334, -118.712709. Swimming, fishing. Hiking, biking, equestrian trails. Wildlife viewing. Visitor center. Open all year. $41 or more. 63 sites, no hookups. Drinking water. 30-foot limit. Restrooms; showers. Dump station.

Manchester State Park

44500 Kinney Rd, Mendocino, CA 95459. Phone: (707) 937-5804. Located about 1.5 miles NW of Manchester via CA 1 and Kinney Rd. GPS: 38.980911, -123.698853. Fishing, boating, surfing, scuba diving/snorkeling. Hiking trails. Wildlife viewing. Open May-Sep. $40 or less. 40 sites, no hookups. Drinking water. Length limit: motorhome 30-foot, trailer 22-foot. Restrooms; no showers. Dump station.

McArthur-Burney Falls Memorial State Park

24898 Highway 89, Burney, CA 96013. Phone: (530) 335-2777. Located about 11 miles N of Burney via CA 299 and CA 89. GPS: 41.011804, -121.650583. Lake in park. Swimming beach, fishing, boating (rentals), surfing, scuba diving/snorkeling. Hiking, equestrian trails. Wildlife viewing. Scenic viewpoint. Camp store. Visitor center. Open all year. $40 or less. 104 sites, no hookups. 32-foot limit. Restrooms; showers. Dump station.

McConnell State Recreation Area

8800 McConnell Rd, Ballico, CA 95303. Phone: (209) 394-7755. Located about 5 miles E of Delhi via El Capitan Way and Pepper St. GPS: 37.416790, -120.713415. Swimming beach, fishing, boating. Hiking trails. Open all year. $30 or less. 13 sites, no hookups. Drinking water. Length limit: motorhome 30-foot, trailer 24-foot. Restrooms; showers.

McGrath State Beach

2211 Harbor Blvd, Oxnard, CA 93035. Phone: (805) 968-1033. Located about 5 miles S of Ventura via Harbor Blvd. GPS: 34.228642, -119.256899. Swimming, fishing, surfing. Wildlife viewing. Open all year. $41 or more. 173 sites, no hookups. Drinking water. Length limit: motorhome 34-foot, trailer 30-foot. Restrooms; showers. Dump station.

Millerton Lake State Recreation Area

47597 Road 145, Friant, CA 93626. Phone: (559) 822-2332. Located about 27 miles N of Fresno via CA 41 and CA 145. GPS: 37.018720, -119.693199. Swimming beach, fishing, boating (rentals), surfing, scuba diving/snorkeling. Hiking, biking, equestrian, nature trails. Bird watching. Scenic viewpoint. Marina, store. Open all year. $40 or less. 147 sites, 28 with electric hookups (some with sewer). Drinking water. 36-foot limit. Restrooms; showers. Dump station.

Montaña de Oro State Park

3550 Pecho Valley Rd, Los Osos, CA 93402. Phone: (805) 772-7434. Located about 4 miles S of Los Oso via Pecho Valley Rd. GPS: 35.274021, -120.884815. Beach area, swimming, surfing, scuba diving/snorkeling. Hiking, biking, equestrian trails. Scenic viewpoint. Visitor center. Open all year. $30 or less. 50 sites, no hookups. Drinking water. 27-foot limit. Restrooms; no showers. Equestrian camp.

Morro Bay State Park

1 State Park Rd, Morro Bay, CA 93442. Phone: (805) 772-7434. Located 1.5 miles S of Morro Bay via Main St. GPS: 35.346737, -120.840940. Fishing, boating (rentals), surfing, scuba diving/snorkeling. Hiking, biking trails. Bird watching. Scenic viewpoint. Golf course. Marina, cafe. Museum. Open all year. $40 or less. 134 sites, 30 with water and electric. Drinking water. 35-foot limit. Restrooms; showers. Dump station.

Morro Strand State Beach

Yerba Buena and Highway 1, Morro Bay, CA 93452. Phone: (805) 772-8812. Located in southern California about 2 miles S of Cayucos via CA 1. GPS: 35.402257, 120.867935. Swimming, fishing, surfing. Bird watching. Scenic viewpoint. Open all year. $40 or less. 82 sites, 25 full hookup, 57 with no hookups. Drinking water. 40-foot limit for full hookup sites, 24-foot all other sites. Restrooms; outdoor showers. Campers may use the showers at nearby Morro Bay State Park.

Mount Diablo State Park

96 Mitchell Canyon Rd, Clayton, CA 94517. Phone: (925) 837-2525. Located in central California, SE of Walnut Creek, about 7 miles E of Danville (I-680 exit 39). GPS: 37.842798, -121.920331. Hiking, biking, equestrian trails. Wildlife viewing. Scenic viewpoint. Visitor center. Museum. Open all year. $30 or less. 53 sites, no hookups. Drinking water. 20-foot limit. Restrooms; showers.

Mount San Jacinto State Park

25905 Highway 243, Idyllwild, CA 92549. Phone: (951) 659-2607. Located in southern California about 23 miles E of Hemet. Hiking, equestrian, nature trails. Wildlife viewing. Scenic viewpoints. Visitor center. Museum. Two camping areas.

Idyllwild Campground: Located in Idyllwild along CA 243. GPS: 33.747705, -116.714927. Open all year. $40 or less. 13 sites, 3 full hookup, 1 with water and electric, 4 electric only. Drinking water. 24-foot limit. Restrooms; showers.

Stone Creek Campground: Located 6 miles N of Idyllwild via CA 243. GPS: 33.784351, -116.749132. Open May-Oct. $40 or less. 14 sites, 6 with electric hookups. Drinking water. 24-foot limit. Restrooms; no showers.

Navarro River Redwoods State Park

Highway 128, Albion, CA 95410. Phone: (707) 937-5804. Located in northern California about 10 miles S of Mendocino. Swimming beach, fishing, boating. Hiking trails. Wildlife viewing. Scenic viewpoint. Two camping areas.

Navarro Beach Campground: Located about 10 miles S of Mendocino along CA 1. GPS: 39.191810, -123.758266. Open all year. No reservations accepted. $40 or less. 10 sites, no hookups. No water. Length limit: motorhome 30-foot, trailer 24-foot. Restrooms (chemical toilets); no showers.

Paul M. Dimmick Campground: Located about 18 miles SE of Mendocino via CA 1 and CA 128. GPS: 39.157140, -123.635125. Open all year. $40 or less. 26 sites, no hookups. Drinking water. Length limit: motorhome 30-foot, trailer 24-foot. Restrooms (vault toilets); no showers.

New Brighton State Beach

1500 Park Ave, Capitola, CA 95010. Phone: (831) 464-6329. Located about 6 miles E of Santa Cruz via CA 1. GPS: 36.981438, -121.934849. Swimming, fishing, surfing. Hiking trails. Beach combing. Scenic viewpoint. Visitor center, store. Open all year. $40 or less. 111 sites, 11 with electric hookups. Drinking water. 36-foot limit. Restrooms; showers. Dump station.

Palomar Mountain State Park

19952 State Park Rd, Palomar, CA 92060. Phone: (760) 742-3462. Located about 28 miles northwest of Santa Ysabel via CA 79 and CR S7. GPS: 33.342145, 116.901505. Lake in park. Fishing. Hiking trails. Scenic viewpoints. Visitor center. Open all year. $30 or less. 31 sites, no hookups. Drinking water nearby. Length limit: motorhome 27-foot, trailer 24-foot. Restrooms; no showers.

Patrick's Point State Park

4150 Patrick's Point Dr, Trinidad, CA 95570. Phone: (707) 677-3570. Located about 29 miles N of Eureka via US 101. GPS: 41.134735, -124.155134. Beach area, swimming not recommended. Fishing, surfing, scuba diving/snorkeling. Hiking, nature, walking trails. Scenic viewpoint. Visitor center. Open all year. $40 or less. 109 sites, no hookups. Drinking water. 31-foot limit. Restrooms; showers. Dump station.

Pfeiffer Big Sur State Park

47225 Highway 1, Big Sur, CA 93920. Phone: (831) 667-2315. Located in central California about 26 miles S of Carmel on CA 1. GPS: 36.251079, -121.783479. There is no beach or ocean access in this park. Swimming (river), fishing. Hiking, nature trails. Wildlife viewing. Camp store. Open all year. $40 or less. 189 sites, no hookups. Length limit: motorhome 32-foot, trailer 27-foot. Restrooms; showers. Dump station.

Picacho State Recreation Area

Picacho Road, Winterhaven, CA 92283. Phone: (760) 996-2963. Remote location in southeast California on Colorado River about 24 miles N of Winterhaven. Note: Picacho Rd from Winterhaven is paved for the first 6 miles. The last 18 miles is a dirt road. If using a mapping device make sure you are routed via Picacho Rd from Winterhaven. The secondary route into the park from Ogilby Rd through Indian Pass is a 4X4 only route. GPS: 33.022339, -114.616981. Swimming beach, fishing, boating. Hiking trails. Wildlife viewing. Bird watching. Scenic viewpoint. Open all year. No reservations accepted. $20 or less. 54 sites, no hookups. Drinking water. Length limit: motorhome 35-foot, trailer 30-foot. Restrooms; showers. Dump station.

Pismo State Beach

Oceano, CA 93445. Phone: (805) 473-7220. Located in southern California S of the City of Pismo Beach along CA 1. Fishing, surfing, scuba diving/snorkeling. Hiking trails. Wildlife viewing. Bird watching. Visitor center. Two camping areas.

North Beach Campground: Located about 1 mile S of town center via CA 1. GPS: 35.132625, -120.635662. Open all year. $40 or less. 103 sites, no hookups. Length limit: motorhome 36-foot, trailer 31-foot. Restrooms; showers. Dump station.

Oceano Campground: Located on Pier Ave about 3 miles S of town center via CA 1. GPS: 35.106945, -120.627735. Open all year. $40 or less. 80 sites, 40 with electric hookups. Length limit: motorhome 36-foot, trailer 31-foot. Restrooms; showers.

Plumas-Eureka State Park

310 Johnsville Rd, Blairsden, CA 96103. Phone: (530) 836-2380. Located in central California about 7 miles W of Blairsden via Graeagle Johnsville Rd off CA 89. GPS: 39.742317, -120.707402. Small lake in park. Fishing, boating. Hiking, trails. Camp store. Visitor center. Mining museum and historic area. Open May-Sep. $40 or less. 43 sites, no hookups. Drinking water. Length limit: motorhome 28-foot, trailer 24-foot. Restrooms; showers. Dump station.

Point Mugu State Park

9000 W Pacific Coast Hwy, Malibu, CA 90265. Phone: (805) 488-1827. Located in southern California about 15 miles S of Oxnard via CA 1. GPS: 34.070840, -119.012510. Five miles of ocean shoreline. Beach area, swimming, fishing, boating, surfing, scuba diving/snorkeling. Hiking, biking, equestrian trails. Wildlife viewing. Visitor center. Open all year. $40 or less. 126 sites, no hookups. Drinking water. 31-foot limit. Restrooms; showers. Dump station.

Portola Redwoods State Park

9000 Portola State Park Road, La Honda, CA 94020. Phone: (650) 948-9098. Located 9 miles SE of La Honda via Alpine Rd and Portola State Park Rd. GPS: 37.252942, -122.217104. Swimming (creeks). Hiking trails. Wildlife viewing. Visitor center. Museum. Open Apr-Oct. $40 or less. 55 sites, no hookups. Drinking water. Length limit: motorhome 24-foot, trailer 21-foot. Restrooms; showers.

Prairie Creek Redwoods State Park

127011 Newton B Drury Pkwy, Orick, CA 95555. Phone: (707) 465-7335. Located in northern California about 50 miles N of Eureka via US 101. Fishing, surfing. Hiking, biking, nature, walking trails. Bird watching. Visitor center. Three scenic drives. Two camping areas.

Elk Prairie Campground: 6 miles N of Orick via US 101 and Newton B Drury Scenic Pkwy. GPS: 41.359159, -124.028657. Open all year. $40 or less. 75 sites, no hookups. Drinking water. Length limit: motorhome 27-foot, trailer 24-foot. Restrooms; showers.

Gold Bluffs Beach Campground: 8 miles N of Orick via US 101 and Davison Rd. For cabover camper or tent-only; no trailers of any kind are allowed on Davison Rd. GPS: 41.383633, -124.068496. Open all year. No reservations accepted. $40 or less. 26 sites, no hookups. Drinking water. Restrooms; showers.

Red Rock Canyon State Park

37749 Abbott Dr, Cantil, CA 93519. Phone: (661) 839-6553. Located about 26 miles N of Mojave via CA 14. GPS: 35.365228, -117.982860. Hiking, equestrian, OHV trails. Wildlife viewing. Visitor center. Open all year. No reservations accepted. $30 or less. 50 sites, no hookup. Drinking water. 30-foot limit. Restrooms (pit toilets); no showers.

Refugio State Beach

10 Refugio Beach Rd, Goleta, CA 93117. Phone: (805) 968-1033. Located in southern California about 24 miles W of Santa Barbara via US 101. GPS: 34.464590, -120.069446. Swimming, fishing, boating, surfing, scuba dive. Hiking, biking trails. Camp store. Open all year. $41 or more. 66 sites, no hookups. Length limit: motorhome 30-foot, trailer 27-foot. Restrooms; showers.

Richardson Grove State Park

1600 US Hwy 101, Garberville, CA 95442. Phone: (707) 247-3318. Located in northern California about 7 miles S of Garberville via US 101. GPS: 40.022706, -123.793836. Swimming (river), fishing, boating. Hiking, nature trails. Wildlife viewing. Scenic viewpoint. Visitor center. Open all year. $40 or less. 167 sites, no hookups. Drinking water. Length limit: motorhome 30-foot, trailer 24-foot. Restrooms; showers.

Russian Gulch State Park

Hwy 1, Mendocino, CA 95460. Phone: (707) 937-5804. Located in northern California about 2 miles N of Mendocino on CA 1. GPS: 39.330770, -123.801155. Beach area, swimming, fishing, boating, surfing, scuba diving/snorkeling. Hiking, biking, equestrian trails. Wildlife viewing. Scenic viewpoint. Open all year. $41 or more.

30 sites, no hookups. Drinking water. 24-foot limit. Restrooms; showers.

Saddleback Butte State Park

43230 172nd St, East Lancaster, CA 93534. Phone: (661) 946-6092. Located in southern California about 20 miles E of Lancaster via Ave J off CA 14 exit 43. GPS: 34.676366, -117.825236. Hiking, biking, equestrian trails. Wildlife viewing. Scenic viewpoint. Visitor center. Open all year. No reservations accepted. $20 or less. 37 sites, no hookups. Drinking water. 30-foot limit. Restrooms; no showers. Dump station.

Salt Point State Park

25050 Coast Highway 1, Jenner, CA 95450. Phone: (707) 847-3221. Located in northern California, 18 miles N of Jenner on CA 1. GPS: 38.569588, -123.322037. Beach area, fishing, boating, surfing, scuba diving/snorkeling. Hiking trails. Visitor center. Open all year. $40 or less. 109 sites, no hookups. Drinking water. Length limit: motorhome 31-foot, trailer 27-foot. Restrooms; no showers.

Salton Sea State Recreation Area

100-225 State Park Road, North Shore, CA 92254. Phone: (760) 393-3052. Located in southern California about 24 miles SE of Indio via CA 111. Swimming beach, fishing, boating (rentals), surfing. Hiking, nature trails. Wildlife viewing. Bird watching. Camp store. Visitor center. Marina. Museum. Three camping areas.

Headquarters Campground: Located about 24 miles SE of Indio via CA 111. GPS: 33.504202, -115.914166. Open all year. $30 or less. 15 full hookup sites. 35-foot limit. Restrooms; showers. Dump station.

Mecca Beach Campground: Located about 25 miles SE of Indio via CA 111. GPS: 33.492045, -115.901217. Open all year. $30 or less. 109 sites, some with full hookups. Drinking water. 35-foot limit. Restrooms; showers.

New Camp Campground: Located about 24 miles SE of Indio via CA 111. GPS: 33.501610, -115.912527. Open all year. $20 or less. 26 sites, 4 with electric hookups. Drinking water. 35-foot limit. Restrooms; showers. Dump station.

Samuel P. Taylor State Park

8889 Sir Francis Drake Blvd, Lagunitas, CA 94938. Phone: (415) 488-9897. Located 13 miles W of San Rafael via Sir Francis Drake Blvd. GPS: 38.019325, -122.729930. Hiking, biking, equestrian, nature trails. Wildlife viewing. Open all year. $40 or less. 60 sites, no hookups. Drinking water. Length limit: motorhome 31-foot, trailer 27-foot. Restrooms; showers.

San Clemente State Beach

225 W Calafia Ave, San Clemente, CA 92672. Phone: (949) 492-3156. Located in San Clemente near I-5 Exit 73. GPS: 33.406461, -117.600141. Swimming, fishing, surfing, scuba diving/snorkeling. Hiking, biking trails. Wildlife viewing. Visitor center. Open all year. $41 or more. 72 sites with full hookups. 30-foot limit. Restrooms; showers. Dump station.

San Elijo State Beach

2050 S Coast Hwy 101, Cardiff, CA 92007. Phone: (760) 753-5091. Located about 2 miles west and south from I-5 Exit 42 in Encinitas. GPS: 33.021487, -117.284318. Swimming, fishing, surfing, scuba diving/snorkeling. Biking trails. Scenic viewpoints. Camp store. Visitor center. Open all year. $40 or less. 171 sites, 28 with water and electric hookups. Drinking water. Dump station. 24-foot limit for sites with hookups, 35-foot limit all other sites. Restrooms; showers. Laundry facilities.

San Luis Reservoir State Recreation Area

31426 Gonzaga Rd, Gustine, CA 95322. Phone: (209) 826-1197. Located in central California about 12 miles W of Los Banos. Three lakes in park. Swimming beach, fishing, boating, surfing. Hiking, equestrian, OHV trails. Wildlife viewing. Scenic viewpoint. Visitor center. Four camping areas.

Basalt Campground: Located about 14 miles W of Los Banos via CA 152. GPS: 37.032334, -121.066343. Open all year. $30 or less. 79 sites, no hookups. Drinking water. 30-foot limit. Restrooms; showers. Dump station.

Los Banos Creek Campground: Located on Los Banos Creek Reservoir about 11 miles SW of the City of Los Banos via Pioneer Rd and Canyon Rd. GPS: 36.986532, -120.939661. Most sites cannot accommodate trailers or motor homes because of limited turn around space. Open all year. No reservations accepted. $30 or less. 14 sites, no hookups. Drinking water. 30-foot limit. Restrooms (chemical toilets); no showers.

Medeiros Campground: Located 10 miles W of Los Banos via CA 152. GPS: 37.065130, -121.023967. Open all year. No reservations accepted. $30 or less. Scattered sites along the southern shore of O'Neill Forebay; no hookups. Drinking water. 30-foot limit. Restrooms (chemical toilets); no showers.

San Luis Creek Campground: Located about 16 miles W of Los Banos via CA 152. GPS: 37.106309, -121.066120. Open all year. $40 or less. 53 sites with water and electric hookups. 30-foot limit. Restrooms (chemical toilets); no showers. Dump station.

San Onofre State Beach

San Clemente, CA 92672. Phone: (949) 492-4872. Located in southern California, S of San Clemente. Swimming, fishing, boating, surfing, scuba diving/snorkeling. Hiking, biking, nature trails. Wildlife viewing. Bird watching. Two camping areas.

San Mateo Campground: Located about 3.5 miles SE of San Clemente via I-5 and Cristianitos Rd. GPS: 33.408221, -117.584803. Open all year. $40 or less. 157 sites, 67 with water and electric hookups. 25-foot limit. Restrooms; showers. Dump station.

San Onofre Bluffs Campground: Located about 7 miles S of San Clemente via I-5 and Old Highway 101. GPS: 33.354433, -117.529597. Open all year. $40 or less. 175 sites, no hookups. 25-foot limit. Restrooms (chemical toilets); cold outdoor showers. Dump station.

Seacliff State Beach

201 State Park Dr, Aptos, CA 95003. Phone: (831) 685-6500. Located about 8 miles E of Santa Cruz via CA 1. GPS: 36.972706, -121.912775. Swimming, fishing, surfing. Hiking, biking trails. Visitor center. Open all year. $41 or more. 64 sites, 26 with full hookups. Drinking water. Length limit: motorhome 40-foot, trailer 36-foot. Restrooms; showers.

Silver Strand State Beach

5000 Highway 75, Coronado, CA 92118. Phone: (619) 435-5184. Located about 6 miles S of Coronado via CA 75. GPS: 32.634854, -117.142102. Swimming, fishing, surfing, scuba diving/snorkeling. Hiking, biking trails. Wildlife viewing. Open all year. $41 or more. 122 sites, no hookups. Drinking water. 40-foot limit. Restrooms; cold showers in beach area. Dump station.

Silverwood Lake State Recreation Area

14651 Cedar Circle, Hesperia, CA 92345. Phone: (760) 389-2281. Located about 30 miles N of San Bernardino via I-15 and CA 138. GPS: 34.283932, -117.352792. Lake in park. Swimming beaches, fishing, boating (rentals), surfing. Hiking, biking, equestrian, nature trails. Wildlife viewing. Bird watching. Camp store. Visitor center. Marina. Open all year. $41 or more. 136 sites, 40 with sewer hookups. Drinking water. 31-foot limit. Restrooms; showers. Dump station.

Sonoma Coast State Park

3095 Highway 1, Bodega Bay, CA 94923. Phone: (707) 875-3483. Located in northern California along the Pacific Coast Highway between Jenner and Bodega Bay. Beach area, swimming, fishing, boating, surfing, scuba diving/snorkeling. Hiking, equestrian trails. Bird watching. Scenic viewpoint. Visitor center. Marina. Two camping areas.

Bodega Dunes Campground: Located one mile N of Bodega Bay via CA 1. GPS: 38.341923, -123.056618. Open all year. $40 or less. 99 sites, no hookups. 31-foot limit. Restrooms; showers. Dump station.

Wright's Beach Campground: Located about 6 miles N of Bodega Bay via CA 1. GPS: 38.400196, -123.093563. Open all year. $40 or less. 27 sites, no hookups. 31-foot limit. Restrooms; no showers. No dump station.

South Carlsbad State Beach

7201 Carlsbad Blvd, Carlsbad, CA 92008. Phone: (760) 438-3143. Located in southern California about 5 miles S of Carlsbad via Carlsbad Blvd or from I-5 exit 43 (Poinsettia Ln). GPS: 33.101308, -117.318662. Swimming, fishing, surfing. Biking trails. Scenic viewpoints. Camp store. Visitor center. Open all year. $40 or less. 223 sites, 14 with full hookups. Drinking water. 35-foot limit. Restrooms; showers. Laundry facilities. Dump station.

Standish-Hickey State Recreation Area

69350 Highway 101, Leggett, CA 95455. Phone: (707) 925-6482. Located about 2 miles N of Leggett via US 101. GPS: 39.878033, -123.726561. Swimming beach, fishing, boating. Hiking, nature trails. Open all year. $40 or less. 161 sites, no hookups. Length limit: motorhome 27-foot, trailer 24-foot. Restrooms; showers.

Sugarloaf Ridge State Park

2605 Adobe Canyon Rd, Kenwood, CA 95452. Phone: (707) 833-5712. Located in central California about 4 miles NE of Kenwood via CA 12 and Adobe Canyon Rd. GPS: 38.437716, -122.516267. Hiking, biking, equestrian trails. Wildlife viewing. Scenic viewpoint. Visitor center. Museum. Open all year. $40 or less. 49 sites, no hookups. Drinking water. Length limit: motorhome 27-foot, trailer 24-foot. Restrooms; no showers.

Sunset State Beach

201 Sunset Beach Rd, Watsonville, CA 95076. Phone: (831) 763-7062. Located about 6 miles W of Watsonville via Beach St and San Andreas Rd. GPS: 36.896972, -121.837505. Swimming, fishing, surfing. Hiking trails. Scenic viewpoint. Open all year. $40 or less. 90 sites, no hookups. Drinking water. 31-foot limit. Restrooms; showers.

Tahoe State Recreation Area

Highway 28, Tahoe City, CA 96145. Phone: (530) 583-3074. Located about 15 miles S of Truckee via CA 89 and CA 28. GPS: 39.175306, -120.135496. Lake in park. Swimming beach, fishing, surfing. Biking trails. Marina nearby. Open May-Sep. $40 or less. 27 sites, no hookups. Drinking water. Length limit: motorhome 21-foot, trailer 15-foot. Restrooms; showers.

Turlock Lake State Recreation Area

22600 Lake Road, LaGrange, CA 95329. Phone: (209) 874-2056. Located about 25 miles E of Modesto via CA 132. GPS: 37.629331, -120.579342. Lake in park. Swimming beach, fishing, boating, surfing. Wildlife viewing. Scenic viewpoints. Open all year. $40 or less. 66 sites, no hookups. Length limit: motorhome 27-foot, trailer 24-foot. Restrooms; showers.

Van Damme State Park

Mendocino, CA 95460. Phone: (707) 937-5804. Located about 3 miles S of Mendocino via CA 1. GPS: 39.274468, -123.790118. Fishing, boating (kayak rentals and tours), surfing, scuba diving/ snorkeling. Hiking, biking, walking trails. Bird watching. Scenic viewpoint. Visitor center. Open all year. $41 or more. 74 sites, no hookups. Drinking water nearby. 35-foot limit. Restrooms; showers. Dump station.

Woodson Bridge State Recreation Area

25340 South Ave, Corning, CA 96021. Phone: (530) 839-2112. Located in northern California, 6 miles E of I-5 Exit 630 in Corning. GPS: 39.912052, -122.087687. Fishing. Hiking, equestrian trails. Wildlife viewing. Bird watching. A boat launch ramp is located across the road in the county park. Open all year. $40 or less. 37 sites, no hookups. Drinking water nearby. 31-foot limit. Restrooms; showers.

Colorado

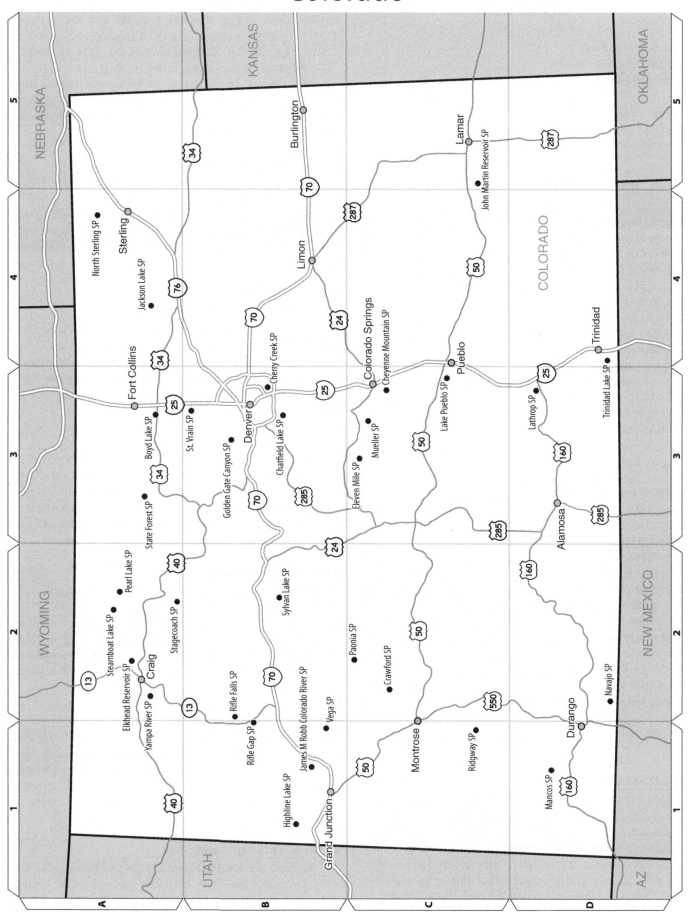

Colorado

Colorado State Parks
1313 Sherman St, 6th Floor
Denver, CO 80203

Phone: (303) 297-1192
Internet: cpw.state.co.us
Reservations: Required, all parks. Online or (800) 244-5613

Colorado Park Locator

Colorado Parks

Boyd Lake State Park

3720 N CR 11-C, Loveland, CO 80538. Phone: (970) 669-1739. Located in Loveland on the western shore of Boyd Lake about 4 miles NE of town center. GPS: 40.430822, -105.042792. Swimming beach, fishing, boating (rentals). Hiking, biking, trails. Visitor center. Marina, store. Open all year. $36 per night. 148 pull-thru sites with 50-amp electric. Drinking water. 40-foot limit. Restrooms; showers. Laundry facilities. Dump station.

Chatfield Lake State Park

11500 N Roxborough Park Rd, Littleton, CO 80125. Phone: (303) 791-7275. Located 12 miles S of Littleton town center via US 85, Titan Rd, and Roxborough Park Rd. GPS: 39.536487, -105.059134. Swimming beach, fishing, boating (rentals). Hiking, biking, equestrian (rentals) trails. Wildlife viewing. Marina, store. Four camping areas open all year. $36-41 per night. 197 sites, 146 full hookup, 51 with electric only. Drinking water. Restrooms; showers. Laundry facilities. Dump station.

Cherry Creek State Park

4201 S Parker Rd, Aurora, CO 80014. Phone: (303) 690-1166. Located 3 miles S of I-225 Exit 4 via CO 83 and Lehigh Ave. GPS: 39.649303, -104.841239. Lake in park. Swimming beach, fishing, boating. Hiking, biking, equestrian (rentals) trails. Bird watching. Marina. Model Airplane Field. Outdoor shooting range. Open all year. $41 per night. 101 full hookup sites. Restrooms; showers. Laundry facilities. Dump station.

Cheyenne Mountain State Park

410 JL Ranch Heights, Colorado Springs, CO 80926. Phone: (719) 576-2016. Located 8 miles S of Colorado Springs via CO 115. GPS: 38.737972, -104.828932. Hiking, biking, equestrian trails. Archery range. Visitor center, gift shop. Four camping loops open all year. $41 per night. 51 full hookup sites. Restrooms; showers. Laundry facilities.

Crawford State Park

40468 Highway 92, Crawford, CO 81415. Phone: (970) 921-5721. Located about 32 miles E of Delta via CO 92. GPS: 38.672286, -107.598069. Lake in park. Swimming beach, fishing, boating. Hiking, biking trails. Visitor center, gift shop. Two campgrounds open all year. $32-35 per night. 61 sites, 16 full hookup, 45 with water and electric. Restrooms; showers. Dump station.

Eleven Mile State Park

4229 CR 92, Lake George, CO 80827. Phone: (719) 748-3401. Remote location about 38 miles W of Colorado Springs via US 24 and CR 92. GPS: 38.950507, -105.530845. Lake in park. Fishing, boating (rentals). Hiking, biking, nature trails. Bird watching. Visitor center, gift shop. Marina. Nine campgrounds open all year. $28-36 per night. 324 sites, 51 with electric hookups. Restrooms; showers. Dump station.

Elkhead Reservoir State Park

135 County Road 28, Craig, CO 81625. Phone: (970) 276-2061. Located 10 miles NE of Craig via US 40, CR 29 and CR 28. GPS: 40.562887, -107.389297. Swimming beach, fishing, boating. Hiking trails. Wildlife viewing. Open all year. $22-30 per night. 46 sites, 30 with electric hookups. No water. Restrooms; no showers.

Golden Gate Canyon State Park

92 Crawford Gulch Rd, Golden, CO 80403. Phone: (303) 582-3707. Located 14 miles NW of Golden via Golden Gate Canyon Rd. GPS: 39.875548, -105.449671. Fishing. Hiking, biking,

equestrian trails. Wildlife viewing. Visitor center. Open all year. $36 per night. 59 sites with electric hookups. Restrooms; showers. Laundry facilities. Dump station.

Highline Lake State Park

1800 11.8 Road, Loma, CO 81524. Phone: (970) 858-7208. Located 6 miles N of Loma via CO 139 and Q Rd. GPS: 39.269813, -108.837158. Two lakes in park. Swimming beach, fishing, boating. Hiking, biking, walking trails. Wildlife viewing. Bird watching. Visitor center, store, gifts. Open all year. $14-28 per night. 33 sites, no hookups. Drinking water. Restrooms; showers. Laundry facilities. Dump station.

Jackson Lake State Park

26363 CR 3, Orchard, CO 80649. Phone: (970) 645-2551. Located about 9 miles NW of Weldona via CO 144. GPS: 40.380604, -104.091216. Swimming, fishing, boating. Nature, walking, OHV trails. Wildlife viewing. Bird watching. Visitor center. Marina. Six camping loops; 3 open all year, 3 open Apr-Sep. $28-36 per night. 229 sites, 140 with electric hookups. Restrooms; showers. Laundry facilities. Dump station.

James M. Robb Colorado River State Park

361-32 Rd, Clifton, CO 81520 (Park office). The park consists of five separate units between Fruita and Island Acres. Swimming (only at Island Acres), fishing, boating. Hiking, biking trails. OHV riding nearby. Bird watching. Two camping areas.

Island Acres: 1055 Interstate 70, Palisade, CO 81526. Phone: (970) 464-0548. Located off I-70 Exit 47 about 5 miles E of Palisades. GPS: 39.168842, -108.300082. Open all year. $36-41 per night. 72 sites, 38 full hookup, 34 with electric. Restrooms; showers. Laundry facilities. Dump station.

Fruita: 595 Hwy 340, Fruita, CO 81521. Phone: (970) 858-9188. Located one-half mile S of I-70 Exit 19 in Fruita. GPS: 39.149004, -108.741558. Open all year. $36-41 per night. 44 sites, 22 full hookup, 22 with electric. Restrooms; showers. Laundry facilities. Dump station.

John Martin Reservoir State Park

30703 County Road 24, Hasty, CO 81044. Phone: (719) 829-1801. Located about 2 miles S of US 50 in Hasty. GPS: 38.083874, -102.952811. Swimming beach, fishing, boating. Hiking, biking, equestrian trails. Bird watching. Two camping areas open all year. $17-28 per night. 213 sites, 109 with electric hookups. Restrooms; showers. Laundry facilities. Dump station.

Lake Pueblo State Park

640 Pueblo Reservoir Rd, Pueblo, CO 81005. Phone: (719) 561-9320. Located about 8 miles W of Pueblo via CO 96. GPS: 38.254160, -104.731999. Swimming beach, fishing, boating (rentals). Biking trails. Visitor center. Marinas. Three camping areas open all year. $24-36 per night. 393 sites, 272 with electric hookups. Restrooms; showers. Dump station.

Lathrop State Park

70 County Road 502, Walsenburg, CO 81089. Phone: (719) 738-2376. Located 3.5 miles W of Walsenburg via US 160. GPS: 37.602645, -104.832922. Two lakes in park. Swimming beach, fishing, boating. Hiking, biking, equestrian, walking trails. Bird watching. Golf course. Archery range. Camp store. Visitor center. Two camping areas open all year. $28-36 per night. 103 sites, 82 with electric hookups. Restrooms; showers. Dump station.

Mancos State Park

42545 County Road N, Mancos, CO 81328. Phone: (970) 533-7065. Located about 5 miles N of Mancos via CR 42. GPS: 37.399942, -108-269523. Lake in park. No swimming in lake, fishing, boating (rentals). Hiking, biking, equestrian trails. Wildlife viewing. Bird watching. Two campgrounds, Main and West. West campground closed in winter, Main open all year. $18-22 per night. 32 sites, no hookups. Drinking water (Main campground only). Vault toilets; no showers. Dump station.

Mueller State Park

21045 Highway 67, Divide, CO 80814. Phone: (719) 687-2366. Located 4 miles S of Divide via CO 67. GPS: 38.885419, -105.160288. Hiking, biking, equestrian trails. Wildlife viewing. Bird watching. Visitor center, store. Open all year. $28-36 per night. 112 sites, 99 with electric hookups. 45-foot limit. Restrooms; showers. Laundry facilities. Dump station. Two equestrian camp sites.

Navajo State Park

1526 County Road 982, Arboles, CO 81121. Phone: (970) 883-2208. Located about 36 miles SW of Pagosa Springs via US 160 and CO 151. GPS: 37.008974, -107.407722. Lake in park. No swimming allowed, fishing, boating (rentals). Hiking, biking, equestrian trails. Wildlife viewing. Visitor center. Marina. Sailing tours and sailing lessons are available. Three camping areas, two open all year. $24-41 per night. 118 sites, 39 full hookup, 41 with electric. 55-foot limit. Restrooms; showers. Laundry facilities. Dump station.

North Sterling State Park

24005 County Road 330, Sterling, CO 80751. Phone: (970) 522-3657. Located about 15 miles N of Sterling via CR 39 and CR 37. GPS: 40.789471, -103.264904. Lake in park. Swimming beach, fishing, boating (rentals). Hiking, biking, equestrian trails. Bird watching. Archery range. Visitor center. Marina, store. Three campgrounds. Elk campground is open all year. Inlet Grove and Chimney View campgrounds are open May-Sep. $28-36 per night. 141 sites, 97 with electric hookups. Restrooms; showers. Laundry facilities. Dump station.

Paonia State Park

Crawford, CO 81415. Phone: (970) 921-5721. Located 18 miles N of Paonia via CO 133. GPS: 38.987660, -107.348412. Lake in park. Fishing, boating. Notes: Fishing in reservoir from mid-June to mid-August. Fly fishing for trout on streams below dam is more productive. Boating allowed from mid-June until mid-August, or until the water level drops enough to close the boat ramp. At that point, only carry on boats are allowed. Two campgrounds open all year. $18 per night. 13 sites, no hookups. No water. Vault toilets; no showers. No trails in park.

Pearl Lake State Park

Clark, CO 80428. Phone: (970) 879-3922. Located 26 miles N of Steamboat Springs via CR 129 and CR 209. GPS: 40.787310, -106.892508. Fishing, boating. Hiking trails. Wildlife viewing. Open seasonally. $24 per night. 38 sites, no hookups. Drinking water. Restrooms; no showers. Campers may use shower, laundry and dump station facilities at nearby Steamboat Lake State Park.

Ridgway State Park

28555 Highway 550, Ridgway, CO 81432. Phone: (970) 626-5822. Located 29 miles S of Montrose via US 550. GPS: 38.212833, -107.733293. Lake in park. Swimming beach, fishing, boating (rentals). Hiking, biking trails. Wildlife viewing. Bird watching. Scenic viewpoint. Visitor center, gift shop. Marina, store. Open all year. $26-32 per night. 280 sites (less in winter), 81 full hookup, 187 with water and electric. Restrooms; showers. Laundry facilities. Dump station.

Rifle Falls State Park

5775 Hwy 325, Rifle, CO 81650. Phone: (970) 625-1607. Located about 13 miles N of I-70 Exit 90 in Rifle via CO 13 and CO 325. GPS: 39.674099, -107.700059. Fishing. Hiking trails. Scenic viewpoint. Triple waterfall. Open all year. $30-36 per night. 13 sites with electric hookups. Drinking water. Restrooms; no showers.

Rifle Gap State Park

5275 Highway 325, Rifle, CO 81650. Phone: (970) 625-1607. Located about 9 miles N of I-70 Exit 90 in Rifle via CO 13 and CO 325. GPS: 39.634694, -107.735419. Lake in park. Swimming, fishing, boating. Wildlife viewing. Visitor center, gift shop. Five areas spread out along the northern shore of the reservoir, open all year. $20-38 per night. 89 sites, 36 full hookup, 23 with electric. Restrooms; showers. Dump station.

Saint Vrain State Park

3785 Weld County Road 24 1/2, Firestone, CO 80504. Phone: (303) 678-9402. Located near Longmont just W of I-25 Exit 240. GPS: 40.167942, -104.991374. Seven ponds in park. No swimming allowed, fishing, boating. Hiking, biking, walking trails. Bird watching. All camping areas are at the east end of the park. Open all year. $36-41 per night. 87 sites, 45 full hookup, 42 with electric. Restrooms; showers. Dump station.

Stagecoach State Park

25500 County Road 14, Oak Creek, CO 80467. Phone: (970) 736-2436. Located about 16 miles S of Steamboat Springs via US 40, CO 131, and CR 14. GPS: 40.288328, -106.861573. Lake in park. Swimming beach, fishing, boating (rentals). Hiking, biking, equestrian trails. Bird watching. Marina. Open all year. $28-36

per night. 92 sites, 65 with electric hookups. Restrooms; showers. Dump station.

State Forest State Park

56750 Hwy 14, Walden, CO 80480. Phone: (970) 723-8366. Located about 23 miles SE of Walden via CO 14. GPS: 40.511692, -106.010135. Lake in park. Fishing, boating. Hiking, biking, equestrian, nature, OHV trails. Bird watching. Scenic viewpoint. Visitor center, gift shop. Five camping areas open all year. $28-36 per night. 187 sites, 32 with electric hookups. Drinking water. Restrooms (vault toilets); no showers.Dump station. Two equestrian camping areas.

Steamboat Lake State Park

61105 County Road 129, Clark, CO 80428. Phone: (970) 879-3922. Located about 8 miles N of Clark via CR 129. GPS: 40.808614, -106.952430. Lake in park. Swimming beach, fishing, boating (rentals). Hiking, biking, equestrian (guided rides available) trails. Bird watching. Visitor center, gift shop. Marina, store. Open all year. $16-32 per night. 188 sites, 73 with electric hookups. Restrooms; showers. Laundry facilities. Dump station.

Sylvan Lake State Park

10200 Brush Creek Rd, Eagle, CO 81631. Phone: (970) 328-2021. Located about 16 miles S of I-70 Exit 147 near Eagle via Brush Creek Rd. GPS: 39.481200, -106.734649. Fishing, boating (rentals). Hiking, biking, equestrian, walking trails. OHV trails in national forest accessed from park. Bird watching. Visitor center. Marina. Two camping areas open all year. $14-28 per night. 46 sites, no hookups. Drinking water. Restrooms; showers. Dump station.

Trinidad Lake State Park

32610 Hwy 12, Trinidad, CO 81082. Phone: (719) 846-6951. Located about 5 miles W of Trinidad via CO 12. GPS: 37.145433, -104.570323. Fishing, boating. Hiking, biking, equestrian trails. Archery range. Visitor center, store. Two camping areas open all year. $28-41 per day. 73 sites, 63 with electric hookups. Restrooms; showers. Laundry facilities. Dump station. Full hookups are available at seven sites during the summer.

Vega State Park

15247 N 6/10 Rd, Collbran, CO 81624. Phone: (970) 487-3407. Located about 11 miles E of Collbran via Hwy 330. GPS: 39.215935, -107.814213. Lake in park. Swimming, fishing, boating. Hiking, biking, equestrian trails. OHV trails in national forest accessed from park. Bird watching. Visitor center, gift shop. Four camping areas open all year (limited in winter). $30 per night. 99 sites, 33 with water and electric. Restrooms; showers. Dump station.

Yampa River State Park

6185 W US Hwy 40, Hayden, CO 81639. Phone: (970) 276-2061. Located 14 miles E of Craig via US 40. GPS: 40.490919, -107.312394. Fishing, boating. Nature trail. Wildlife viewing. Bird watching. Visitor center. Open all year. $32 per night. 35 sites with electric hookups. Restrooms; showers. Laundry facilities. Dump station.

Connecticut

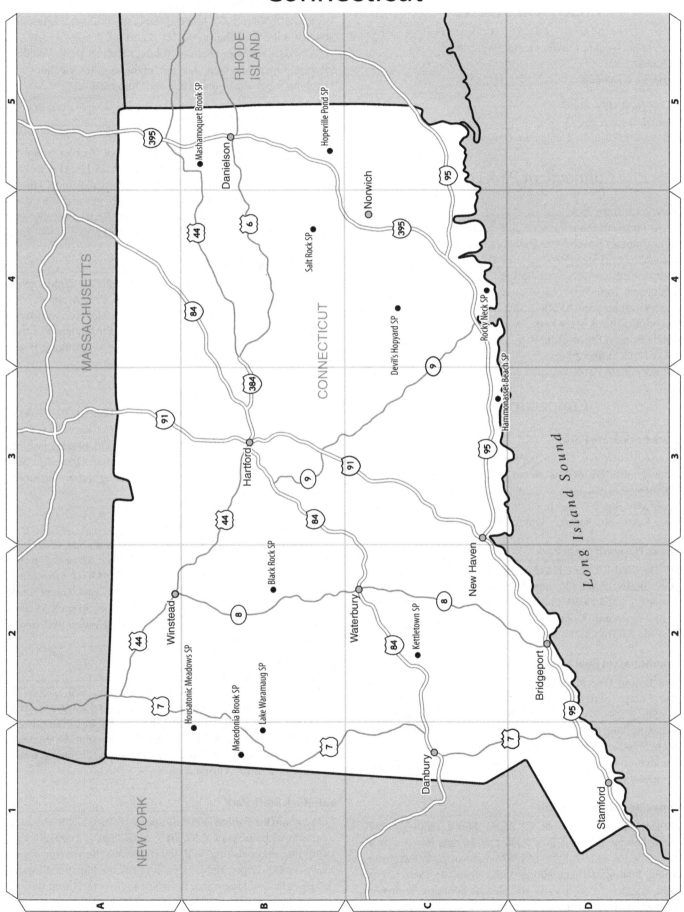

Connecticut

Dept. of Energy and Environmental Protection
79 Elm St
Hartford, CT 06106

Phone: (860) 424-3200
Internet: www.ct.gov
Reservations: Required, all parks. Online or (877) 668-2267

Connecticut Park Locator

Connecticut Parks

Black Rock State Park

Route 6, Watertown, CT 06795. Phone: (860) 283-8088. Located about 4 miles NE of Watertown via US 6. GPS: 41.654155, -73.098669. Lake in park. Swimming beach, fishing. Hiking trails. Open May-Sep. $27 per night. 78 sites, no hookups. Drinking water. Restrooms; showers. Dump station.

Devil's Hopyard State Park

366 Hopyard Rd, East Haddam, CT 06423. Phone: (860) 526-2336. Located off CT 434 about 11 miles SE of East Haddam. GPS: 41.484066, -72.340630. Fishing. Hiking, biking. Bird watching. Scenic viewpoint. Open Apr-Oct. $24 per night. 21 sites, no hookups. Restrooms; no showers.

Hammonasset Beach State Park

1288 Boston Post Rd, Madison, CT 06443. Phone: (203) 245-1817. Located about 1.5 miles S of I-95 Exit 62 near Madison via CT 450. GPS: 41.270409, -72.557770. Swimming, fishing, boating. Biking, walking trails. Bird watching. Camp store. Nature center. Open May-Sep. $30-45 per night. 558 sites, water and electric available at some sites. Drinking water. Restrooms; showers. Dump station.

Hopeville Pond State Park

929 Hopeville Rd, Griswold, CT 06351. Phone: (860) 376-2920. Located about 1.5 miles E of I-395 Exit 24 near Jewett City via CT 201. GPS: 41.607011, -71.919876. Lake in park. Swimming, fishing, boating. Hiking, biking trails. Open May-Sep. $27 per night. 80 sites, 11 with water and electric hookups. Restrooms; showers. Dump station.

Housatonic Meadows State Park

US Route 7, Sharon, CT 06069. Phone: (860) 672-6772. Located about 9 miles E of Sharon via CT 4 and US 7. GPS: 41.838272, -73.379851. Fishing, boating, tubing. Hiking trails. Wildlife viewing. Open May-Sep. $27 per night. 61 sites, no hookups. Drinking water. Restrooms; showers. Dump station.

Kettletown State Park

1400 Georges Hill Rd, Southbury, CT 06488. Phone: (203) 264-5678 or (203) 264-5169. Located about 3 miles S of I-84 exit 14 near Southbury via Georges Hill Rd. GPS: 41.430119, -73.202580. Lake in park. No swimming allowed, fishing. Hiking trails. Wildlife viewing. Open May-Sep. $27 per night. 61 sites, no hookups. Drinking water. 28-foot limit. Restrooms; showers. Dump station.

Lake Waramaug State Park

30 Lake Waramaug Rd, New Preston, CT 06777. Phone: (860) 868-0220. Located about 5 miles NW of Preston via CT 45 and North Shore Rd. GPS: 41.707898, -73.383766. Swimming, fishing, boating (rentals). Wildlife viewing. Bird watching. Open May-Sep. $27 per night. 76 sites, no hookups. Drinking water. Restrooms; showers. Dump station.

Macedonia Brook State Park

159 Macedonia Brook Rd, Kent, CT 06757. Phone: (860) 927-3238 or (860) 927-4100. Located about 4 miles N of Kent via CT 341 and Macedonia Brook Rd. GPS: 41.766387, -73.494869. Fishing. Hiking trails. Wildlife viewing. Bird watching. Open Apr-Sep. $24 per night. 51 sites, no hookups. Drinking water. Restrooms (vault toilets); no showers.

Mashamoquet Brook State Park

147 Wolf Den Dr, Pomfret Center, CT 06259. Phone: (860) 928-6121. Located about 6 miles W of I-395 Exit 41 near Dayville via CT 101 and US 44. GPS: 41.861148, -71.983053. Swimming, fishing. Hiking, nature trails. Wildlife viewing. Two campgrounds open Apr-Sep. $24 per night (plus $15 for hookup site). 53 sites, 1 with water and electric hookups. Drinking water. Restrooms; showers. Dump station.

Rocky Neck State Park

244 W Main St, Niantic, CT 06357. Phone: (860) 739-5471. Located about one mile S of I-95 exit 72 near East Lyme. GPS: 41.315894, 72.241310. Swimming, fishing. Hiking, biking trails. Bird watching. Scenic viewpoint. Food concession. Open May-Sep. $30 per night. 160 sites, no hookups. Drinking water. Restrooms; showers. Dump station.

Salt Rock State Park

173 Scotland Rd, Baltic, CT 06330. Phone: (860) 822-0884. Located 2 miles N of Baltic via CT 97. GPS: 41.642888, -72.092130. Two swimming pools, fishing. Walking trails. Wildlife viewing. Open May-Sep. $45-52 per night. 71 sites, 14 full hookup, 9 with water and electric. Drinking water. Restrooms; showers. Dump station.

Delaware

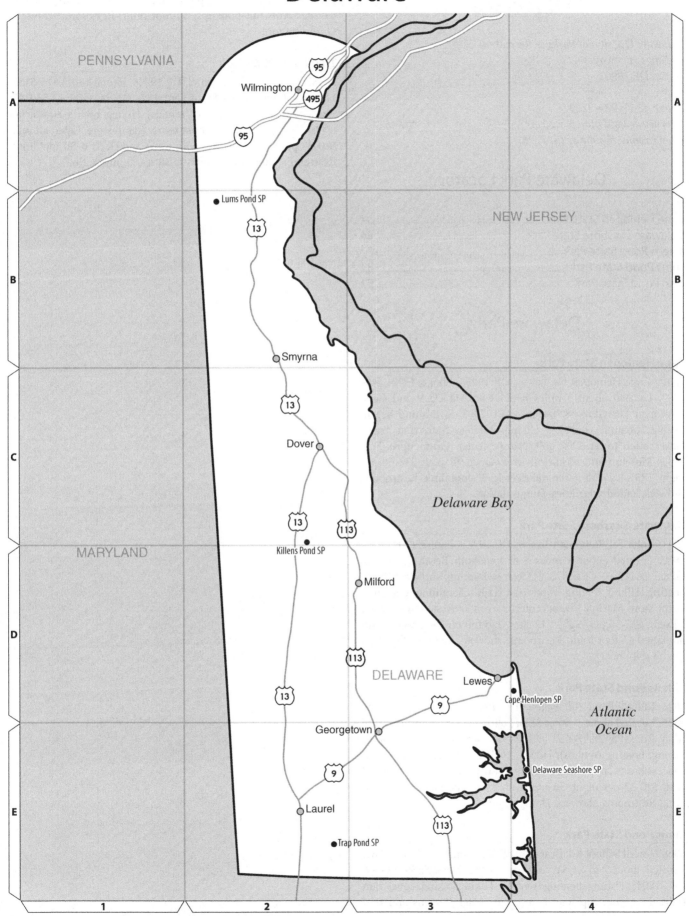

Delaware

Delaware Division of Parks & Recreation
89 Kings Highway
Dover, DE 19901

Phone: (302) 739-9220
Internet: www.destateparks.com
Reservations: Online or (877) 987-2757

Delaware Park Locator

Delaware Parks

Cape Henlopen State Park

15099 Cape Henlopen Dr, Lewes, DE 19958. Phone: (302) 645-8983. Located about 3 miles E of Lewes via US 9 and Cape Henlopen Dr. GPS: 38.780466, -75.102307. Swimming beach, fishing, boating (rentals). Hiking, biking, equestrian trails. Observation tower. Disc golf. Nature center. Camp store. Fort Miles Museum and Historical Area. Open all year. $32-60 per night. 120 sites with water and electric. 35-foot limit. Restrooms; showers. Laundry facilities. Dump station.

Delaware Seashore State Park

39415 Inlet Rd, Rehoboth Beach, DE 19971. Phone: (302) 227-2800. Located about 8 miles S of Rehoboth Beach via DE 1. GPS: 38.611209, -75.064735. Ocean swimming, surfing, fishing, boating. Hiking, biking, equestrian trails. Clamming, crabbing. Camp store. Marina. Visitor center. Two on-site restaurants. Open all year. $25-55 per night. 312 sites, 226 full hookup, 86 with no hookups. 45-foot limit. Restrooms; showers. Laundry facilities. Dump station.

Killens Pond State Park

5025 Killens Pond Rd, Felton, DE 19943. Phone: (302) 284-4526. Located about 5 miles SE of Felton via US 13 and Paradise Alley Rd. GPS: 38.976627, -75.534917. Swimming (waterpark), fishing, boating (rentals). Hiking, biking trails. Disc golf. Food concessions. Camp store. Nature center. Waterpark. Open all year. $20-37 per night. 56 sites with water and electric. 40-foot limit. Restrooms; showers. Dump station.

Lums Pond State Park

1068 Howell School Rd, Bear, DE 19701. Phone: (302) 368-6989. Located about 7 miles SW of Bear via DE 71. GPS: 39.550040, -75.718043. Fishing, boating (rentals). Hiking, biking, equestrian trails. Disc golf. Zip line. Equestrian center (lessons and trail rides). Nature center. Camp store. Open all year. $25-45 per night. 64 sites with full hookups. 50-foot limit. Restrooms; showers. Dump station.

Trap Pond State Park

33587 Baldcypress Ln, Laurel, DE 19956. Phone: (302) 875-5153. Located about 6 miles SE of Laurel via DE 24. GPS: 38.530397, -75.475247. Fishing, boating (rentals). Hiking, biking, equestrian trails. Disc golf. Pontoon boat tours. Camp store. Open all year. $20-37 per night. 124 sites with water and electric. 50-foot limit. Restrooms; showers. Laundry facilities. Dump station.

Florida

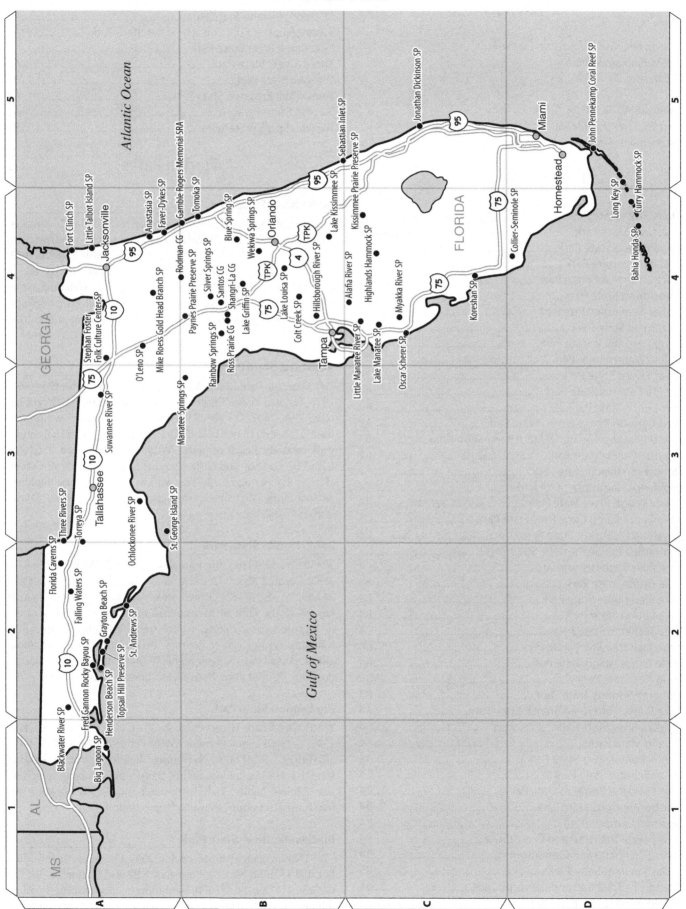

Florida

Florida Division of Recreation & Parks
3900 Commonwealth Blvd.
Tallahassee, FL 32399

Phone: (850) 245-2157
Internet: www.FloridaStateParks.org
Reservations: Online or (800) 326-3521

Florida Park Locator

Florida Parks

Alafia River State Park

14326 S CR 39, Lithia, FL 33547. Phone: (813) 672-5320. Located about 20 miles NE of I-75 Exit 240 (240A for southbound travelers) near Ruskin via FL 674 and CR 39. GPS: 27.780117, -82.144023. Numerous small lakes in park. Fishing, boating. Hiking, biking (rentals), equestrian trails. Wildlife viewing. Bird watching. Open all year. $22 per night. 30 sites with water and electric hookups. 55-foot limit. Restrooms; showers. Dump station. Equestrian camp, 12 sites.

Anastasia State Park

300 Anastasia Park Rd, St. Augustine, FL 32080. Phone: (904) 461-2033. Located about 3 miles S of Saint Augustine via Hwy A1A. GPS: 29.877302, -81.280253. Four miles of beach, swimming, fishing, boating (rentals), surfing. Hiking, biking (rentals), nature, walking trails. Beach combing. Wildlife viewing. Bird watching. Island Beach Shop and Grill. Coquina Quarry historic site. Open all year. $28 per night. 139 sites with water and electric hookups. 38-foot limit. Restrooms; showers. Laundry facilities. Dump station.

Bahia Honda State Park

36850 Overseas Hwy, Big Pine Key, FL 33043. Phone: (305) 872-2353. Located about 15 miles W of Marathon via US 1. GPS: 24.659799, -81.274324. Beach area, swimming, fishing, boating (access to the Gulf of Mexico and the Atlantic Ocean), scuba diving/snorkeling. Biking, nature trails. Wildlife viewing. Bird watching. Visitor center. Marina. Park concession; store, food, gifts. Open all year. $36 per night. 48 sites with water and electric hookups. 50-foot limit. Restrooms; showers. Dump station.

Big Lagoon State Park

12301 Gulf Beach Hwy, Pensacola, FL 32507. Phone: (850) 492-1595. Located about 15 miles SW of Pensacola via FL 292. GPS: 30.314559, -87.411126. Swimming beaches, fishing, boating (rentals). Hiking, biking, nature trails. Bird watching. Open all year. $20 per night. 75 sites with water and electric hookups. 40-foot limit. Restrooms; showers. Dump station.

Blackwater River State Park

7720 Deaton Bridge Rd, Milton, FL 32564. Phone: (850) 983-5363. Located 15 miles NE of Milton via US 90 and Deaton Bridge Rd. GPS: 30.711729, -86.878370. Swimming beaches, fishing, boating, tubing (rentals). Hiking, biking, nature trails. Bird watching.

Open all year. $20 per night. 30 sites with full hookups. 50-foot limit. Restrooms; showers. Dump station.

Blue Spring State Park

2100 W French Ave, Orange City, FL 32763. Phone: (386) 775-3663. Located in Orange City about 2 miles W of town via French Ave. GPS: 28.951470, -81.333592. Swimming, fishing, boating, tubing (rentals), scuba diving/snorkeling. Hiking, nature trails. Bird watching. Boat tours. Park concession; store, food, gifts, rentals. Thursby House historic site. Open all year. $24 per night. 51 sites with water and electric hookups. 40-foot limit. Restrooms; showers. Dump station.

Collier-Seminole State Park

20200 E Tamiami Trail, Naples, FL 34114. Phone: (239) 394-3397. Located about 17 miles SE of Naples via US 41. GPS: 25.991654, -81.591702. Fishing, boating. Hiking, biking, nature trails. Wildlife viewing. Bird watching. Guided canoe trips. The Bay City Walking Dredge, designated a National Historic Mechanical Engineering Landmark, is on display inside the park. Open all year. $22 per night. 105 sites with water and electric hookups. 50-foot limit. Restrooms; showers. Laundry facilities. Dump station.

Colt Creek State Park

16000 SR-471, Lakeland, FL 33809. Phone: (863) 815-6761. Located about 21 miles N of Lakeland via US 98 and FL 471. GPS: 28.302329, -82.053523. Lakes in park. Fishing, boating (no gas motors). Hiking, biking, equestrian, nature, trails. Wildlife viewing. Bird watching. Open all year. $24 per night. 27 sites with water and electric hookups. 70-foot limit. Restrooms; showers. Dump station. Equestrian campground with 10 primitive sites.

Curry Hammock State Park

56200 Overseas Hwy, Marathon, FL 33050. Phone: (305) 289-2690. Located on US 1 about 5 miles E of Marathon. GPS: 24.741572, -80.981899. 1,200-foot beach area, swimming, fishing, boating (rentals), snorkeling. Biking, nature trails. Bird watching. Open all year. $36 per night. 28 sites with water and electric hookups. 70-foot limit. Restrooms; showers. Dump station.

Falling Waters State Park

1130 State Park Rd, Chipley, FL 32428. Phone: (850) 638-6130. Located about 2 miles SE of I-10 Exit 120 near Chipley via FL 77 and CR 77A. GPS: 30.730813, -85.528863. Lake in park. Swimming beach, fishing. Nature trails. Bird watching. Florida's highest waterfall. Historic sites include remnants of the first oil well ever drilled in Florida and parts of a grist mill. Open all year. $18 per night. 24 sites with water and electric hookups. 40-foot limit. Restrooms; showers. Dump station.

Faver-Dykes State Park

1000 Faver-Dykes Rd, St. Augustine, FL 32086. Phone: (904) 794-0997. Located about 2 miles E of I-95 Exit 298 near St. Augustine. GPS: 29.667375, -81.268642. Fishing, boating (canoe rentals). Hiking, nature trails. Bird watching. Open all year. $18 per night. 30 sites with water and electric hookups. 35-foot limit. Restrooms; showers. Dump station.

Florida Caverns State Park

3345 Caverns Rd, Marianna, FL 32446. Phone: (850) 482-1228. Located 3 miles N of Marianna on FL 166. GPS: 30.808601, -85.213212. Swimming , fishing, boating (canoe rentals). Hiking, biking, equestrian trails. Visitor center, self-guided museum. Park concession; food, cave tour tickets, gifts. Open all year. $20 per night. 30 sites with full hookups. 32-foot limit. Restrooms; showers. Dump station. Equestrian camp, 6 sites, 3 with water and electric hookups. 40-foot limit.

Fort Clinch State Park

2601 Atlantic Ave, Fernandina Beach, FL 32034. Phone: (904) 277-7274. Located about 2 miles E of Fernandina Beach via Atlantic Ave. GPS: 30.670127, -81.434649. Swimming in the Atlantic Ocean, fishing (free fishing clinics), surfing. Beach combing. Hiking, biking trails. Bird watching. Visitor center, store, gifts. Museum. One of the most well-preserved 19th-century forts in the country. Open all year. $26 per night. 63 sites with water and electric hookups. 40-foot limit. Restrooms; showers. Laundry facilities. Dump station.

Fred Gannon Rocky Bayou State Park

4281 SR-20, Niceville, FL 32578. Phone: (850) 833-9144. Located about 4 miles SE of Niceville via FL 20. GPS: 30.497029, -86.431863. Fishing, boating. Hiking, biking (park roads), nature trails. A former WWII gunnery and bombing practice range. Open all year. $16 per night. 42 sites with water and electric hookups. 50-foot limit. Restrooms; showers. Laundry facilities.

Gamble Rogers Memorial State Recreation Area

3100 S Oceanshore Blvd, Flagler Beach, FL 32136. Phone: (386) 517-2086. Located about 3 miles S of Flagler Beach via A1A Hwy. GPS: 29.437939, -81.108948. Half-mile stretch of beach, swimming, fishing, boating, surfing. Hiking, biking (park roads), walking trails. Wildlife viewing. Bird watching. Open all year. $28 per night. 68 sites with water and electric hookups. 47-foot limit. Restrooms; showers. Laundry facilities. Dump station.

Grayton Beach State Park

357 Main Park Rd, Santa Rosa, FL 32459. Phone: (850) 267-8300. Located about 8 miles SE of Santa Rosa Beach via US 98 and CR 283. GPS: 30.331550, -86.157079. Beach area and lake in park. Swimming, fishing, boating. Hiking, biking, nature trails. Wildlife viewing. Bird watching. Open all year. $30 per night. 59 sites with water and electric hookups (some with sewer). 40-foot limit. Restrooms; showers.

Henderson Beach State Park

17000 Emerald Coast Pkwy, Destin, FL 32541. Phone: (850) 837-7550. Located about 3 miles E of Destin via US 98. GPS: 30.385225, -86.446814. More than a mile of sandy beach. Swimming, fishing. Nature trail. Bird watching. Open all year. $30 per night. 60 sites with water and electric hookups. 60-foot limit. Restrooms; showers. Laundry facilities. Dump station.

Highlands Hammock State Park

5931 Hammock Rd, Sebring, FL 33872. Phone: (863) 386-6094. Located about 7 miles W of Sebring via US 98 and CR 634. GPS: 27.470992, -81.530639. Hiking, biking (rentals), equestrian, nature trails. Bird watching. Museum. Tram tours provide a close-up look at alligators, birds, deer and other wildlife. Open all year. $22 per night. 116 sites with water and electric hookups. 50-foot limit. Restrooms; showers. Laundry facilities. Dump station.

Hillsborough River State Park

15402 US-301 N, Thonotosassa, FL 33592. Phone: (813) 987-6771. Located about 7 miles N of Thonotosassa via US 301. GPS: 28.140443, -82.227273. Swimming pool (poolside cafe and store), fishing, boating (canoe/kayak rentals). Hiking, biking, equestrian, nature trails. Interpretative Center for Fort Foster Historic State Park, tours available. Open all year. $24 per night. 112 sites with water and electric hookups. 50-foot limit. Restrooms; showers. Laundry facilities. Dump station.

John Pennekamp Coral Reef State Park

Mile 102.5 Overseas Highway, Key Largo, FL 33037. Phone: (305) 676-3777. Located along US-1 north of Key Largo. GPS: 25.125896, -80.407133. Swimming beaches, fishing, boating (rentals), scuba diving/snorkeling. Hiking trails. Wildlife viewing. Visitor center, 30,000 gallon saltwater aquarium. Marina, dive shop, scuba diving tours. Park concession, restaurant, boat tours. Open all year. $36 per night. 47 sites with water and electric hookups. 57-foot limit. Restrooms; showers. Laundry facilities. Dump station.

Jonathan Dickinson State Park

16450 SE Federal Hwy, Hobe Sound, FL 33455. Phone: (772) 546-2771. Located about 5 miles S of Hobe Sound via US 1. GPS: 27.003406, -80.101370. Swimming beach, fishing, boating (rentals). Hiking, biking, equestrian, nature trails. Wildlife viewing. Bird watching. Visitor center. Pontoon boat tours. Guided horseback rides. Park concession; food and beverage garden, rentals. Open all year. $26 per night. 142 sites, 90 full hookup, 52 with water and electric. 40-foot limit. Restrooms; showers. Laundry facilities. Dump station. Equestrian camp, 5 sites.

Kissimmee Prairie Preserve State Park

33104 NW 192nd Ave, Okeechobee, FL 34972. Phone: (863) 462-5360. Located 27 miles NW of Okeechobee via US 98 and CR 700A. GPS: 27.539221, -81.022676. Hiking, biking (rentals), equestrian, nature trails. Wildlife viewing. Bird watching. Visitor center. Ranger-led prairie buggy tours. Open all year. $16 per night. 35 sites with water and electric hookups. 65-foot limit. Restrooms; showers. Laundry facilities. Dump station. Equestrian sites with electric and water hookups.

Koreshan State Park

3800 Corkscrew Rd, Estero, FL 33928. Phone: (239) 992-0311. Located 2 miles W of I-75 Exit 123 near Estero via Corkscrew Rd. GPS: 26.432395, -81.814945. Fishing, boating (canoe/kayak rentals). Hiking, nature trails. Wildlife viewing. Self-guided or ranger led tours of the 19th century religious settlement. Eleven

buildings on the National Register of Historic Places. Open all year. $26 per night. 60 sites with water and electric hookups. 40-foot limit. Restrooms; showers. Laundry facilities. Dump station.

Lake Griffin State Park

3089 US-441/27, Fruitland Park, FL 34731. Phone: (352) 360-6760. Located in Fruitland Park along US 441 at Berckman St. GPS: 28.857461, -81.902255. No swimming, fishing, boating (canoe/kayak rentals). Nature trail. Pontoon boat tours. Open all year. $18 per night. 40 sites, 7 full hookup, 33 with water and electric. 40-foot limit. Restrooms; showers. Laundry facilities. Dump station.

Lake Kissimmee State Park

14248 Camp Mack Rd, Lake Wales, FL 33898. Phone: (863) 696-1112. Located about 17 miles NE of Lake Wales via FL 60, Boy Scout Camp Rd, and Camp Mack Rd. GPS: 27.969178, -81.380187. Fishing, boating (rentals). Hiking, biking (rentals), equestrian trails. Bird watching. Observation tower. Marina. Park concession; store, snacks. Open all year. $20 per night. 60 sites with water and electric hookups. 55-foot limit. Restrooms; showers. Laundry facilities. Dump station. Primitive equestrian camping.

Lake Louisa State Park

7305 US Hwy 27, Clermont, FL 34714. Phone: (352) 394-3969. Located about 9 miles S of Clermont via US 27. GPS: 28.45556, -81.723368. Swimming, fishing, boating (no boat ramp-hand carry only, canoe/kayak rentals). Hiking, biking (rentals), equestrian, nature trails. Wildlife viewing. Bird watching. Open all year. $24 per night. 60 sites with water and electric hookups. 50-foot limit. Restrooms; showers. Dump station. Equestrian area and 5 primitive campsites.

Lake Manatee State Park

20007 State Road 64 E, Bradenton, FL 34212. Phone: (941) 741-3028. Located 15 miles E of Bradenton via FL 64. GPS: 27.477040, -82.347248. Swimming, fishing, boating (rentals). Hiking, biking (rentals) trails. Bird watching. Open all year. $22 per night. 60 sites with water and electric hookups. 65-foot limit. Restrooms; showers. Dump station.

Little Manatee River State Park

215 Lightfoot Rd, Wimauma, FL 33598. Phone: (813) 671-5005. Located about 7 miles SW of Wimauma via FL 674 and US 301. GPS: 27.663157, -82.373699. Fishing, boating (canoe rentals). Hiking, biking, equestrian, nature trails. Wildlife viewing. Bird watching. Open all year. $22 per night. 30 sites with water and electric hookups. 68-foot limit. Restrooms; showers. Laundry facilities. Dump station. Equestrian camp with 4 sites.

Little Talbot Island State Park

12157 Heckscher Dr, Jacksonville, FL 32226. Phone: (904) 251-2320. Located about 20 miles E of I-95 Exit 358A in Jacksonville via FL 105. GPS: 30.458239, -81.418400. Over five miles of beaches, swimming, fishing, boating (canoe/kayak rentals), surfing.

Hiking, biking, nature trails. Wildlife viewing. Bird watching. Visitor center. Open all year. $24 per night. 36 sites with water and electric hookups. 30-foot limit. Restrooms; showers. Laundry facilities. Dump station.

Long Key State Park

67400 Overseas Hwy, Long Key, FL 33001. Phone: (305) 664-4815. Located along US 1 at mile marker 67.5 in Florida Keys, between Key Largo and Marathon. GPS: 24.815570, -80.823299. Swimming, fishing, boating (kayak rentals), snorkeling. Hiking, biking, nature trails. Bird watching. Open all year. $36 per night. 60 sites with water and electric hookups. 36-foot limit. Restrooms; showers. Dump station.

Manatee Springs State Park

11650 NW 115th St, Chiefland, FL 32626. Phone: (352) 493-6072. Located about 8 miles W of Chiefland via FL 320. GPS: 29.496144, -82.966263. Swimming, fishing, boating (canoe/kayak rentals), scuba diving/snorkeling. Hiking, biking, walking trails. Wildlife viewing. Park concession; gear rentals, pontoon boat tours. Open all year. $20 per night. 66 sites with water and electric hookups. 40-foot limit. Restrooms; showers. Dump station.

Mike Roess Gold Head Branch State Park

6239 State Road 21, Keystone Heights, FL 32656. Phone: (352) 473-4701. Located 6 miles NE of Keystone Heights via FL 21. GPS: 29.847568, -81.961556. Lake in park. Swimming, fishing, boating (canoe rentals). Hiking, biking (park roads), equestrian, nature trails. Wildlife viewing. Bird watching. Open all year. $20 per night. 73 sites, 64 with water and electric hookups. 45-foot limit. Restrooms; showers. Laundry facilities. Dump station.

Myakka River State Park

13208 State Road 72, Sarasota, FL 34241. Phone: (941) 361-6511. Located 9 miles E of I-75 Exit 205 in Sarasota via FL 72. GPS: 27.240230, -82.315547. Fishing, boating (canoe/kayak rentals). Hiking, biking (rentals), equestrian, nature trails. Wildlife viewing. Bird watching. Visitor center. Boat tours. Park concessions; cafe, gift shops. Open all year. $26 per night. 90 sites with water and electric hookups. 35-foot limit. Restrooms; showers. Laundry facilities. Dump station.

O'Leno State Park

410 SE O'Leno Park Rd, High Springs, FL 32643. Phone: (386) 454-1853. Located in north-central FL, W of I-75, 7 miles N of High Springs via US 41. GPS: 29.919502, -82.603589. Swimming (river), fishing, boating (canoe rentals). Hiking, biking (rentals), nature, walking trails. Bird watching. Nature center. Museum. Open all year. $18 per night. 61 sites with water and electric hookups. 50-foot limit. Restrooms; showers. Dump station.

Ochlockonee River State Park

429 State Park Rd, Sopchoppy, FL 32358. Phone: (850) 962-2771. Located about 37 miles SW of Tallahassee via US 319. GPS: 29.998956, -84.484914. Swimming, fishing, boating (rentals), tubing. Hiking, biking trails. Wildlife viewing. Bird watching.

Open all year. $18 per night. 30 sites with water and electric hookups. 40-foot limit. Restrooms; showers. Dump station.

Oscar Scherer State Park

1843 S Tamiami Trail, Osprey, FL 34229. Phone: (941) 483-5956. Located along US 41, 13 miles S of Sarasota. GPS: 27.170311, -82.475716. Lake in park. Swimming beach, fishing, boating (canoe/kayak rentals), snorkeling. Hiking, biking trails. Wildlife viewing. Bird watching. Nature center. Open all year. $26 per night. 104 sites with water and electric hookups. 36-foot limit. Restrooms; showers. Laundry facilities. Dump station.

Paynes Prairie Preserve State Park

100 Savannah Blvd, Micanopy, FL 32667. Phone: (352) 466-3397. Located 10 miles S of Gainesville via US 441. GPS: 29.519860, -82.295149. Lake in park. Fishing, boating. Hiking, biking, equestrian, walking trails. Bird watching. Observation tower. Visitor center. Open all year. $18 per night. 50 sites with water and electric hookups. 58-foot limit. Restrooms; showers. Dump station.

Rainbow Springs State Park

19158 SW 81st Place Rd, Dunnellon, FL 34432. Phone: (352) 465-8555. Located 3 miles N of Dunnellon on US 41. Campground entrance is 2 miles N of CR 484 at SW 180th Ave. GPS: 29.086750, -82.417198. Swimming, fishing, boating (canoe/kayak rentals), tubing, snorkeling. Nature trails. Bird watching. Camp store. Visitor center. Gardens and waterfalls. Park concession; sandwiches and snacks. Open all year. $30 per night. 60 sites with full hookups. 103-foot limit. Restrooms; showers. Laundry facilities. Dump station.

Rodman Campground

108 Rodman Dam Rd, Palatka, FL 32177. Phone: (386) 326-2846. Located about 15 miles SW of Palatka via FL 19. GPS: 29.520905, -81.796041. Lake in park. Fishing, boating. Hiking, biking, equestrian trails. Wildlife viewing. Bird watching. Open all year. $22 per night. 38 sites with water and electric hookups. 40-foot limit. Restrooms; showers. Dump station.

Ross Prairie Trailhead and Campground

10660 SW Hwy 200, Dunnellon, FL 34431. Phone: (352) 732-2606. Located along FL 200 about 15 miles SW of Ocala. GPS: 29.039041, -82.296809. Hiking, biking, equestrian trails. Wildlife viewing. Bird watching. Open all year. $22 per night. 14 pull-thru sites with water and electric hookups. Restrooms; showers. Dump station. Equestrian camp with 14 sites.

Santos Trailhead and Campground

3080 SE 80th St, Ocala, FL 34470. Phone: (352) 369-2693. Located five miles SE of Ocala via US 27. GPS: 29.106198, -82.093718. Hiking, biking, equestrian, walking trails. Wildlife viewing. Open all year. $22 per night. 23 sites with water and electric hookups. 55-foot limit. Restrooms; showers. Dump station.

Sebastian Inlet State Park

9700 S Highway A1A, Melbourne Beach, FL 32951. Phone: (321) 984-4852. Located along Highway A1A, 15 miles S of Melbourne Beach. GPS: 27.856022, -80.446509. Over three miles of Atlantic beach. Swimming, fishing, boating (canoe/kayak rentals), surfing, scuba diving/snorkeling. Hiking, biking, nature trails. Wildlife viewing. Bird watching. Visitor center. Marina. Restaurant, gift shop. Two museums. Open all year. $28 per night. 51 sites with water and electric hookups. 40-foot limit. Restrooms; showers. Laundry facilities. Dump station.

Shangri-La Trailhead and Campground

12788 SW 69th Ct, Ocala, FL 34476. Phone: (352) 347-1163. Located five miles W of I-75 Exit 341 near Ocala via CR 484. GPS 29.037401, -82.234987. Hiking, biking, equestrian trails. Wildlife viewing. Bird watching. Open all year. $18 per night. 24 pull-thru sites, no hookups. Drinking water. 50-foot limit. Restrooms; showers. Dump station.

Silver Springs State Park

1425 NE 58th Ave, Ocala, FL 34470. Phone: (352) 236-7148. Located 6 miles E of Ocala via Silver Springs Blvd and NE 7th St. GPS: 29.201052, -82.050785. Fishing, boating (canoe/kayak rentals). Hiking, biking, equestrian trails. Wildlife viewing. Bird watching. Museum and Environmental Center. Glass bottom boat tours. Park concessions; cafe and sweets shop. Pioneer Village, replica of a 19th century pioneer settlement. Open all year. $24 per night. 59 sites with water and electric hookups. 50-foot limit. Restrooms; showers. Laundry facilities. Dump station.

St. Andrews State Park

4607 State Park Ln, Panama City Beach, FL 32408. Phone: (850) 708-6100. Located about 5 miles SE of Panama City Beach via Thomas Dr. GPS: 30.135122, -85.742362. Gulf of Mexico on one side and St. Andrews Bay on the other. Swimming, fishing, boating (canoe/kayak rentals), surfing, scuba diving/snorkeling. Hiking, biking (park roads) trails. Wildlife viewing. Bird watching. Shuttle boat tours. Park concession; store, gifts, gear rental. Open all year. $28 per night. 60 sites with water and electric hookups. 45-foot limit. Restrooms; showers. Laundry facilities. Dump station.

St. George Island State Park

1900 E Gulf Beach Dr, St. George Island, FL 32328. Phone: (850) 927-2111. Located about 14 miles SE of Eastpoint via FL 300. GPS: 29.721143, -84.745566. Nine miles of beaches along the Gulf coast, swimming, fishing, boating. Hiking, biking, nature trails. Wildlife viewing. Bird watching. Open all year. $24 per night. 60 sites with water and electric hookups. 43-foot limit. Restrooms; showers. Dump station.

Stephan Foster Folk Culture Center State Park

11016 Lillian Saunders Dr, White Springs, FL 32096. Phone: (386) 397-4331. Located on Suwannee River in White Springs, just W of town center. GPS: 30.335805, -82.770010. Fishing, boating. Hiking, biking, equestrian, nature trails. Visitor center. Museum and Carillon Tower. Craft Square with demonstrating artists.

Open all year. $20 per night. 45 sites with water and electric hookups. 100-foot limit. Restrooms; showers. Dump station.

Suwannee River State Park

3631 201st Path, Live Oak, FL 32060. Phone: (386) 362-2746. Located about 13 miles NW of Live Oak via US 90. GPS: 30.383170, -83.167417. Fishing, boating. Hiking, biking trails. Bird watching. Open all year. $22 per night. 30 sites with full hookups. 45-foot limit. Restrooms; showers. Laundry facilities. Dump station.

Three Rivers State Park

7908 Three Rivers Park Rd, Sneads, FL 32460. Phone: (850) 482-9006. Located on FL 271, 2 miles N of Sneads. GPS: 30.739029, -84.935888. Lake in park. Fishing, boating (canoe rentals). Hiking, biking, nature trails. Bird watching. Open all year. $16 per night. 30 sites with water and electric hookups. 50-foot limit. Restrooms; showers. Dump station.

Tomoka State Park

2099 N Beach St, Ormond Beach, FL 32174. Phone: (386) 676-4050. Located 4 miles N of Ormond Beach via North Beach St. GPS: 29.339792, -81.083339. Fishing, boating (canoe rentals). Hiking, biking, nature trails. Wildlife viewing. Park concession; store, snacks, gifts. Open all year. $24 per night. 100 sites with water and electric hookups. 34-foot limit. Restrooms; showers. Laundry facilities. Dump station.

Topsail Hill Preserve State Park

7525 W County Hwy 30A, Santa Rosa Beach, FL 32459. Phone: (850) 267-8330. Located in Santa Rosa Beach off US 98 at CR 30A. GPS: 30.371280, -86.273918. Three miles of sand beaches. Lakes in park. Swimming (pool and Gulf of Mexico), fishing, boating (rentals). Hiking, biking (rentals) trails. Wildlife viewing. Bird watching. Camp store. Visitor center. Cafe. Open all year. $42 per night. 156 full hookup sites. 45-foot limit. Restrooms; showers. Laundry facilities.

Torreya State Park

2576 NW Torreya Park Rd, Bristol, FL 32321. Phone: (850) 643-2674. Located 12 miles N of Bristol via FL 12 and Torreya Park Rd. GPS: 30.558743, -84.949687.

Fishing, boating (small vessels). Hiking trails. Bird watching. Museum. Gregory House tours, an 1840s plantation home. Open all year. $16 per night. 30 sites with water and electric hookups. 30-foot limit. Restrooms; showers.

Wekiwa Springs State Park

1800 Wekiwa Cir, Apopka, FL 32712. Phone: (407) 553-4383. Located W of I-4 Exit 94 near Wekiwa Springs via FL 434 and Wekiwa Springs Rd. GPS: 28.710920, -81.462699. Lake in park. Swimming, fishing, boating (canoe/kayak rentals), snorkeling. Hiking, biking, equestrian trails. Bird watching. Nature center. Park concession; food, snacks, gifts and gear. Open all year. $24 per night. 60 sites with water and electric hookups (some with sewer). 50-foot limit. Restrooms; showers. Dump station.

Georgia

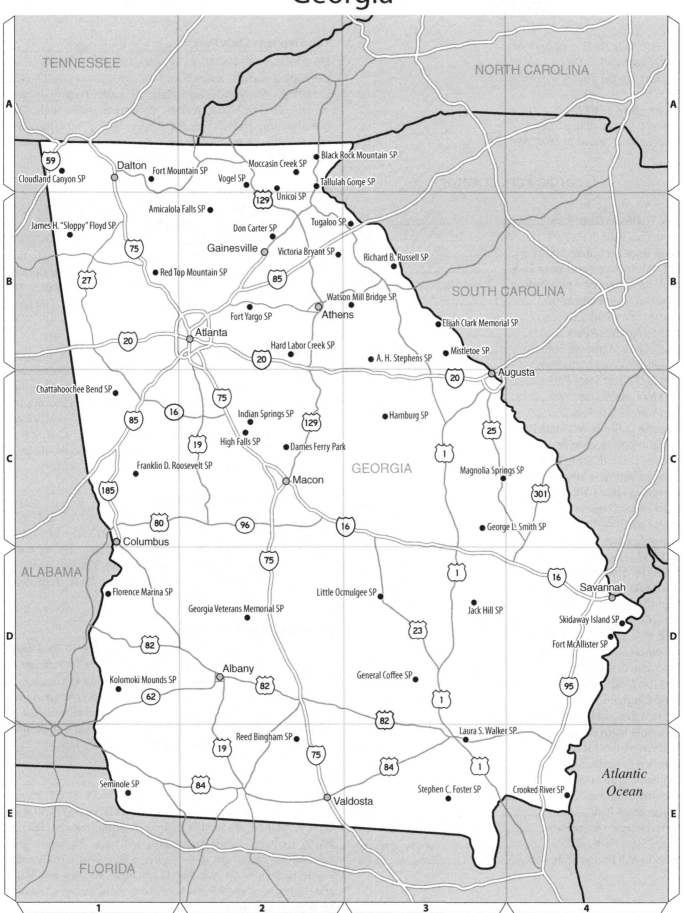

TENNESSEE

NORTH CAROLINA

59
Dalton
Fort Mountain SP
Moccasin Creek SP
Black Rock Mountain SP
Cloudland Canyon SP
Vogel SP
Tallulah Gorge SP
129
Unicoi SP
Amicalola Falls SP
James H. "Sloppy" Floyd SP
Don Carter SP
Tugaloo SP
75
Gainesville
Victoria Bryant SP
Richard B. Russell SP
SOUTH CAROLINA
27
Red Top Mountain SP
85
Watson Mill Bridge SP
Fort Yargo SP
Athens
Elijah Clark Memorial SP
20
Atlanta
Hard Labor Creek SP
Mistletoe SP
20
A. H. Stephens SP
Augusta
20
Chattahoochee Bend SP
75
Indian Springs SP
Hamburg SP
85
16
129
25
19
High Falls SP
Dames Ferry Park
1
GEORGIA
Franklin D. Roosevelt SP
Macon
Magnolia Springs SP
185
301
80
96
16
George L. Smith SP
Columbus
ALABAMA
75
1
16
Savannah
Florence Marina SP
Little Ocmulgee SP
Skidaway Island SP
Georgia Veterans Memorial SP
Jack Hill SP
Fort McAllister SP
82
23
Albany
82
Kolomoki Mounds SP
General Coffee SP
1
95
62
1
82
Reed Bingham SP
Laura S. Walker SP
19
75
Seminole SP
84
75
84
1
Stephen C. Foster SP
Crooked River SP
Atlantic Ocean
Valdosta

FLORIDA

Georgia

Georgia State Parks & Historic Sites
2600 Highway 155 SW
Stockbridge, GA 30281

Phone: (800) 864-7275
Internet: www.gastateparks.org
Reservations: Online or (800) 864-7275

Georgia Park Locator

Georgia Parks

A.H. Stephens State Park

456 Alexander St NW, Crawfordville, GA 30631. Phone: (706) 456-2602. Located 3 miles N of I-20 Exit 148 via GA 22. GPS: 33.560252, -82.897291. Three lakes in park. Fishing, boating (rentals). Hiking, biking (rentals), equestrian, nature trails. Civil War Museum. Open all year. $30-32 per night. 25 sites with water and electric hookups. 50-foot limit. Restrooms; showers. Laundry facilities. Dump station. Equestrian camping area, 29 sites.

Amicalola Falls State Park

418 Amicalola Falls State Park Rd, Dawsonville, GA 30534. Phone: (706) 344-1500. Located 15 miles NW of Dawsonville via GA 343 and GA 52. The road to access the campground is at a 25% grade. GPS: 34.557850, -84.249949. Fishing. Hiking, walking trails. Bird watching. Scenic viewpoint. 3-D Archery range. Visitor center. Lodge, restaurant. Zip lines. Guided hikes. Open all year. $44 per night. 24 sites with water and electric hookups. 90-foot limit. Restrooms; showers. Laundry facilities. Dump station.

Black Rock Mountain State Park

3085 Black Rock Mtn Pkwy, Mountain City, GA 30562. Phone: (706) 746-2141. Located about 2 miles W of US 23 in Mountain City; steep grade. GPS: 34.904745, -83.412524. Small lake in park. Fishing, boating. Hiking, walking trails. Scenic viewpoint. Visitor center, gift shop. Open all year. $34-38 per night. 44 sites with water and electric hookups. 50-foot limit. Restrooms; showers. Laundry facilities. Dump station.

Chattahoochee Bend State Park

425 Bobwhite Way; Newnan, GA 30263. Phone: (770) 254-7271. Located 16 miles NW of Newnan. GPS: 33.422391, -84.982152. Fishing, boating (canoe/kayak rentals). Hiking, biking trails. Wildlife viewing. Gift shop. Open all year. $28 per night. 37 sites with water and electric hookups. 40-foot limit. Restrooms; showers. Laundry facilities. Dump station.

Cloudland Canyon State Park

122 Cloudland Canyon Park Rd, Rising Fawn, GA 30738. Phone: (706) 657-4050. Located 6 miles E of I-59 Exit 11 in Trenton via GA 136. GPS: 34.817118, -85.488386. Fishing (pond). Hiking, biking (rentals), equestrian trails. Wildlife viewing. Scenic viewpoint. Disc golf. Camp store, gift shop. Waterfalls. Open all year. $32-38 per night. 72 sites with water and electric hookups. 50-foot limit. Restrooms; showers. Laundry facilities. Dump station.

Crooked River State Park

6222 Charlie Smith Senior Hwy, St. Mary's GA 31558. Phone: (912) 882-5256. Located 7 miles N of Saint Mary's via GA 40 Spur. GPS: 30.843644, -81.558045. Fishing, boating (rentals). Hiking, biking (rentals), nature trails. Bird watching. Miniature golf. Information center, gift shop. Nature center. Boat tours, guided kayak trips. Open all year. $34-42 per night. 63 sites with water and electric hookups. 85-foot limit. Restrooms; showers. Laundry facilities. Dump station.

Dames Ferry Park

9546 Highway 87, Juliette GA 31046. Phone: (478) 994-7945. Located 12 miles E of I-75 Exit 185 in Forsyth via GA 18 and US 23. GPS: 33.044173, -83.757720. Lake in park. Fishing, boating. Bird watching. Open all year. $35-38 per night. 30 sites with electric hookups. 50-foot limit. Restrooms; showers. Dump station.

Don Carter State Park

5000 North Browning Bridge Rd, Gainesville, GA 30506. Phone: (678) 450-7726. Located 12 miles N of Gainesville via US 129 and GA 284. GPS: 34.388259, -83.746719. Lake in park. Swimming beach, fishing, boating (rentals). Hiking, biking, equestrian, nature trails. Wildlife viewing. Visitor center, gift shop. Guided horseback rides. Open all year. $32-35 per night. 44 sites with water and electric hookups (some with sewer). 90-foot limit. Restrooms; showers. Dump station.

Elijah Clark Memorial State Park

2959 McCormick Hwy, Lincolnton, GA 30817. Phone: (706) 359-3458. Located 7 miles NE of Lincolnton via US 378. GPS: 33.853630, -82.403509. Lake in park. Swimming beach, fishing, boating (canoe rentals). Hiking trails. Wildlife viewing. Miniature golf. Log Cabin Museum. Open all year. $32-38 per night. 172 sites with water and electric hookups. 50-foot limit. Restrooms; showers. Dump station.

Florence Marina State Park

218 Florence Rd, Omaha, GA 31821. Phone: (229) 838-6870. Located 16 miles W of Lumpkin via GA 39C. GPS: 32.086906, -85.041572. Lake in park. Fishing, boating (rentals). Nature trail. Bird watching. Miniature golf. Interpretive center. Marina. Trading Post. Museum. Open all year. $32-34 per night. 41 full hookup sites. 120-foot limit. Restrooms; showers. Laundry facilities. Dump station.

Fort McAllister State Park

3894 Fort McAllister Rd, Richmond Hill, GA 31324. Phone: (912) 727-2339. Located 10 miles E of I-95 Exit 90 in Richmond Hill via GA 144. GPS: 31.889554, -81.199426. Fishing, boating (canoe/kayak rentals). Hiking, biking (rentals), nature trails. Bird watching. Lookout Tower. Earthwork Fort, tours. Civil War museum, gift shop. Open all year. $33-42 per night. 67 sites with water and electric hookups (some with sewer). 50-foot limit. Restrooms; showers. Laundry facilities. Dump station.

Fort Mountain State Park

181 Fort Mountain Park Rd, Chatsworth, GA 30705. Phone: (706) 422-1932. Located 8 miles E of Chatsworth via GA 52. GPS: 34.760422, -84.707053. Lake in park. Swimming beach, fishing, boating (rentals). Hiking, biking, equestrian trails. Miniature golf. Stone fire tower. Open all year. $34-38 per night. 70 sites with water and electric hookups. 50-foot limit. Restrooms; showers. Dump station.

Fort Yargo State Park

210 S Broad St, Winder, GA 30680. Phone: (770) 867-3489. Located 1 mile S of Winder via GA 81. GPS: 33.984325, -83.733061. Lake in park. Swimming beach, fishing, boating (rentals). Hiking, biking (rentals) trails. Disc golf. Miniature golf. Nature center, gift shop. A 1792 log fort. Open all year. $34-36 per night. 46 sites with water and electric hookups (some with sewer). 50-foot limit. Restrooms; showers. Dump station.

Franklin D. Roosevelt State Park

2970 Highway 190, Pine Mountain, GA 31822. Phone: (706) 663-4858. Located 11 miles E of I-185 Exit 34 via GA 18 and GA 354. GPS: 32.838455, -84.815664. Lake in park. Swimming pool, fishing, boating (rentals). Hiking, equestrian trails. Bird watching. Visitor center, gift shop. Trading Post. Guided horseback rides. Open all year. $30 per night. 115 sites with water and electric hookups. 85-foot limit. Restrooms; showers. Laundry facilities. Dump station.

General Coffee State Park

46 John Coffee Rd, Nicholls, GA 31554. Phone: (912) 384-7082. Located 6 miles E of Douglas via GA 32. GPS: 31.508853, -82.755276. Lake in park. Fishing, boating (rentals). Hiking, biking (rentals), equestrian trails. Bird watching. Heritage Farm with log cabins, tobacco barn, cane mill and other exhibits. Gift shop. Open all year. $30-32 per night. 50 sites with water and electric hookups (some with sewer). 50-foot limit. Restrooms; showers. Laundry facilities. Dump station. Four equestrian sites available.

George L. Smith State Park

371 George L Smith State Park Rd, Twin City, GA 30471. Phone: (478) 763-2759. Located about 4 miles SE of Twin City via US 80 and state park road. GPS: 32.550828, -82.125903. Lake in park. Fishing, boating (canoe/kayak rentals). Hiking, biking trails. Bird watching. Parrish Mill and Pond, a combination gristmill, saw mill, covered bridge and dam built in 1880. Open all year. $33-36 per night. 24 sites with water and electric hookups. 40-foot limit. Restrooms; showers. Laundry facilities. Dump station.

Georgia Veterans Memorial State Park

2459 US Hwy 280 W, Cordele, GA 31015. Phone: (800) 459-1230. Located 9 miles W of I-75 Exit 101 in Cordele via US 280. GPS: 31.951431, -83.904922. Lake in park. Swimming beach, fishing, boating (rentals). Hiking, biking, nature trails. Archery & Air Gun Range. Marina, grill. Restaurant and lakeside bar. Military Museum. Lake Blackshear Resort & Golf Club and Georgia Veterans Memorial Golf Course. SAM Shortline Excursion Train. Open all year. $60-65 per night. 82 sites with water and electric hookups. 50-foot limit. Restrooms; showers. Laundry facilities. Dump station.

Hamburg State Park

6071 Hamburg State Park Rd, Mitchell, GA 30820. Phone: (478) 552-2393. Located 17 miles N of Sandersville via GA 15 and GA 248. GPS: 33.205542, -82.790658. Lake in park. Fishing, boating (rentals). Hiking trails. Wildlife viewing. Museum. Restored 1921 water-powered gristmill. Trading Post. Open all year. $28-32 per night. 32 sites with water and electric hookups. 40-foot limit. Restrooms; showers. Laundry facilities. Dump station.

Hard Labor Creek State Park

5 Hard Labor Creek Rd, Rutledge, GA 30663. Phone: (706) 557-3001. Located in north-central GA, 3 miles N of Rutledge via Fairplay St or via Old Mill Rd off US 278. GPS: 33.664150, -83.605763. Two lakes in park. Swimming beach, fishing, boating (rentals). Hiking, biking, equestrian trails. Bird watching. Golf course, pro shop. Miniature golf. Open all year. $35-59 per night. 51 sites with water and electric hookups (some with sewer). 45-foot limit. Restrooms; showers. Laundry facilities. Dump station. Equestrian camp with 11 sites.

High Falls State Park

76 High Falls Park Dr, Jackson, GA 30233. Phone: (478) 993-3053. Located 35 miles N of Macon and 1.5 miles E of I-75 Exit 198 via High Falls Rd. GPS: 33.179285, -84.017775. Lake in park. Swimming pool, fishing, boating (rentals). Hiking trails. Miniature golf. Visitor center. Open all year. $35-38 per night. 106 sites with water and electric hookups (some with sewer). 50-foot limit. Restrooms; showers. Dump station.

Indian Springs State Park

678 Lake Clark Rd, Flovilla, GA 30216. Phone: (770) 504-2277. Located about 6 miles SE of Jackson via US 23 and GA 42. GPS: 33.247518, -83.921241. Lake in park. Fishing, boating (rentals). Hiking, biking, nature trails. Miniature golf. Nature center. Museum. Open all year. $32 per night. 62 sites with water and electric hookups. 60-foot limit. Restrooms; showers. Laundry facilities. Dump station.

Jack Hill State Park

162 Park Ln, Reidsville, GA 30453. Phone: (912) 557-7744. Located in Reidsville off US 280, south of I-16 Exit 98. GPS: 32.082565, -82.122825. Small lake in park. Fishing, boating (rentals). Nature trail. Golf course, pro shop. Miniature golf. Gift shop. Open all year. $30-35 per night. 29 sites with water and electric hookups (some with sewer). 60-foot limit. Restrooms; showers. Laundry facilities. Dump station.

James H. "Sloppy" Floyd State Park

2800 Sloppy Floyd Lake Rd, Summerville, GA 30747. Phone: (706) 857-0826. Located 4 miles S of Summerville via US 27. GPS: 34.439832, -85.337582. Two lakes in park. Fishing, boating (rentals). Hiking, walking trails. Bird watching. Open all year. $31-33 per night. 24 sites with water and electric hookups (some with sewer). 50-foot limit. Restrooms; showers. Laundry facilities. Dump station.

Kolomoki Mounds State Park

205 Indian Mounds Rd, Blakely, GA 39823. Phone: (229) 724-2150. Located 8 miles N of Blakely via Main St and First Kolomoki Rd; follow signs. GPS: 31.470641, -84.933056. Two lakes in park. Swimming beach, fishing, boating (rentals). Hiking trails.

Miniature golf. Eight Indian Mounds. Museum, built around an excavated mound. Open all year. $26-30 per night. 25 sites with water and electric hookups. 79-foot limit. Restrooms; showers. Dump station.

Laura S. Walker State Park

5653 Laura Walker Rd, Waycross, GA 31503. Phone: (912) 287-4900. Located 10 miles SE of Waycross via US 82 and GA 177. GPS: 31.143427, -82.214114. Lake in park. Swimming beach, fishing, boating (rentals). Hiking, biking (rentals), nature trails. Wildlife viewing. Bird watching. Golf course, club house, pro shop. Visitor center. Open all year. $32-36 per night. 44 sites with water and electric hookups (some with sewer). 40-foot limit. Restrooms; showers. Laundry facilities. Dump station.

Little Ocmulgee State Park

80 Live Oak Trail, Helena, GA, 31037. Phone: (877) 591-5572. Located 2 miles N of McRae via US 319. GPS: 32.091285, -82.890164. Lake in park. Swimming pool and beach, fishing, boating (rentals). Hiking trails. Wildlife viewing. Golf course, club house, pro shop. Miniature golf. Visitor center, trading post. Lodge, restaurant. Open all year. $35-50 per night. 54 sites with water and electric hookups (some with sewer). 40-foot limit. Restrooms; showers. Laundry facilities. Dump station.

Magnolia Springs State Park

1053 Magnolia Springs Dr, Millen, GA 30442. Phone: (478) 982-1660. Located 5 miles N of Millen via US 25. GPS: 32.873375, -81.961783. Small lake in park. Fishing, boating (rentals). Hiking, biking (rentals), walking trails. Wildlife viewing. Visitor center. History center. Museum. Natural Spring with boardwalk. Open all year. $33-36 per night. 26 sites with water and electric hookups. 40-foot limit. Restrooms; showers. Laundry facilities. Dump station.

Mistletoe State Park

3725 Mistletoe Rd, Appling, GA 30802. Phone: (706) 541-0321. Located 11 miles N of I-20 Exit 175 near Thomson via GA 150 and Mistletoe Rd. GPS: 33.642992, -82.385035. Lake in park. Swimming beach, fishing, boating (rentals). Hiking, biking, nature trails. Bird watching. Open all year. $32-35 per night. 93 sites with water and electric hookups (some with sewer). 50-foot limit. Restrooms; showers. Laundry facilities. Dump station.

Moccasin Creek State Park

3655 State Hwy 197, Clarkesville, GA 30523. Phone: (706) 947-3194. Located 21 miles N of Clarkesville via GA 197. GPS: 34.844843, -83.588956. Lake in park. Fishing, boating (rentals). Hiking, biking trails. Wildlife observation tower. Trading Post. Open all year. $34-36 per night. 53 sites with water and electric hookups. 40-foot limit. Restrooms; showers. Laundry facilities. Dump station.

Red Top Mountain State Park

50 Lodge Rd SE, Acworth, GA 30102. Phone: (770) 975-0055. Located 2 miles E of I-75 Exit 285 near Cartersville via Red

Top Mountain Rd. GPS: 34.147718, -84.707131. Lake in park. Swimming beach, fishing, boating (rentals), skiing. Hiking, biking, walking trails. Visitor center. Marina. Open all year. $25-40 per night. 93 sites, 69 with water and electric, 24 no hookups. 40-foot limit. Restrooms; showers. Dump station.

Reed Bingham State Park

542 Reed Bingham Rd, Adel, GA 31620. Phone: (229) 896-3551. Located 6 miles W of I-75 Exit 39 in Adel via GA 37. GPS: 31.161286, 83.538465. Lake in park. Swimming beach, fishing, boating (rentals), skiing. Hiking, biking (rentals), nature trails. Wildlife viewing. Bird watching. Miniature golf. Guided Boat Tours. Open all year. $30-38 per night. 46 sites with water and electric hookups (some with sewer). 50-foot limit. Restrooms; showers. Laundry facilities. Dump station.

Richard B. Russell State Park

2650 Russell State Park Dr, Elberton, GA 30635. Phone: (706) 213-2045. Located 9 miles NE of Elberton via GA 77 and Ruckersville Rd. GPS: 34.179906, -82.764640. Lake in park. Swimming beach, fishing, boating (rentals). Hiking, biking (rentals), nature trails. Golf course. Disc golf. Information center. Open all year. $33-35 per night. 27 sites with water and electric hookups. 35-foot limit. Restrooms; showers. Laundry facilities. Dump station.

Seminole State Park

7870 State Park Rd, Donalsonville, GA 39845. Phone: (229) 861-3137. Located in SW corner of Georgia, 16 miles S of Donalsonville via GA 39; on Lake Seminole. GPS: 30.805205, -84.879546. Lake in park. Swimming beach, fishing, boating (rentals), skiing, tubing. Hiking, nature trails. Wildlife viewing. Bird watching. Miniature golf. Open all year. $32-38 per night. 50 sites with water and electric hookups. 40-foot limit. Restrooms; showers. Laundry facilities. Dump station.

Skidaway Island State Park

52 Diamond Causeway, Savannah, GA 31411. Phone: (912) 598-2300. Located about 15 miles S of Savannah via Truman Pkwy and GA 204. GPS: 31.947115, -81.052721. Hiking, biking (rentals) trails. Wildlife viewing. Interpretive center. Open all year. $45-53 per night. 87 sites with water and electric hookups (some with sewer). 70-foot limit. Restrooms; showers. Laundry facilities. Dump station.

Stephen C. Foster State Park

17515 Highway 177, Fargo, GA 31631. Phone: (912) 637-5274. Located 18 miles NE of Fargo via GA 177. GPS: 30.823474, -82.364320. Located within the Okefenokee National Wildlife Refuge. Fishing, boating (rentals). Hiking, biking trails. Wildlife viewing. Bird watching. Visitor center. Guided boat tours of the swamp. Guided hikes. Open all year. $35-37 per night. 66 sites with water and electric hookups. 50-foot limit. Restrooms; showers. Laundry facilities. Dump station.

Tallulah Gorge State Park

338 Jane Hurt Yarn Dr, Tallulah Falls, GA 30573. Phone: (706) 754-7981. Located about 20 miles NE of Cornelia via US 23. GPS: 34.742831, -83.396412. The gorge is two miles long and nearly 1,000 feet deep. Swimming beach, fishing, boating. Hiking, biking, walking trails. Scenic viewpoint. Archery range. Interpretive center. Gift shop. Five waterfalls. Suspension bridge. Open all year. $34-37 per night. 50 sites with water and electric hookups. 50-foot limit (many 25-foot). Restrooms; showers. Dump station.

Tugaloo State Park

1763 Tugaloo State Park Rd, Lavonia, GA 30553. Phone: (706) 356-4362. Located 7.5 miles N of Lavonia via GA 328 and Tugaloo State Park Rd. GPS: 34.495416, -83.066620. Lake in park. Swimming beach, fishing, boating (rentals), skiing, sailing. Hiking trails. Miniature golf. Visitor center. Open all year. $35-38 per night. 105 sites with water and electric hookups. 50-foot limit. Restrooms; showers. Laundry facilities. Dump station.

Unicoi State Park

1788 Highway 356, Helen, GA 30545. Phone: (800) 573-9659. Located 2 miles NE of Helen via GA 356. GPS: 34.723975, -83.721905. Lake in park. Swimming beach, fishing, boating. Hiking, biking trails. Archery & Air Gun Range. Visitor center. Lodge and restaurant. Zip lines. Open all year. $55-70 per night. 51 sites with water and electric hookups (some with sewer). 40-foot limit. Restrooms; showers. Dump station.

Victoria Bryant State Park

1105 Bryant Park Rd, Royston, GA 30662. Phone: (706) 245-6270. Located 4 miles W of Royston via US 29 and GA 327. GPS: 34.298849, -83.158576. Swimming pool, fishing (two ponds). Hiking, biking (rentals), nature trails. Wildlife viewing. Golf course, club house, pro shop. Archery range. Visitor center, gift shop. Open all year. $30-32 per night. 27 sites with water and electric hookups. 50-foot limit. Restrooms; showers. Laundry facilities. Dump station.

Vogel State Park

405 Vogel State Park Rd, Blairsville, GA 30512. Phone: (706) 745-2628. Located 10 miles S of Blairsville via US 19. GPS: 34.765801, -83.923982. Lake in park. Swimming beach, fishing, boating (rentals). Hiking, biking (rentals), nature trails. Miniature golf. Visitor center. Museum. General store. Open all year. $34-38 per night. 90 sites with water and electric hookups. 40-foot limit. Restrooms; showers. Laundry facilities. Dump station.

Watson Mill Bridge State Park

650 Watson Mill Rd, Comer, GA 30629. Phone: (706) 783-5349. Located 3 miles S of Comer off GA 22; on South Fork River. GPS: 34.023420, -83.071932. Fishing, boating (rentals). Hiking, biking, equestrian trails. Longest covered bridge in the state. Open all year. $30-32 per night. 21 sites with water and electric hookups. 50-foot limit. Restrooms; showers. Laundry facilities. Dump station. Equestrian camp, 11 sites with electric hookups.

Idaho

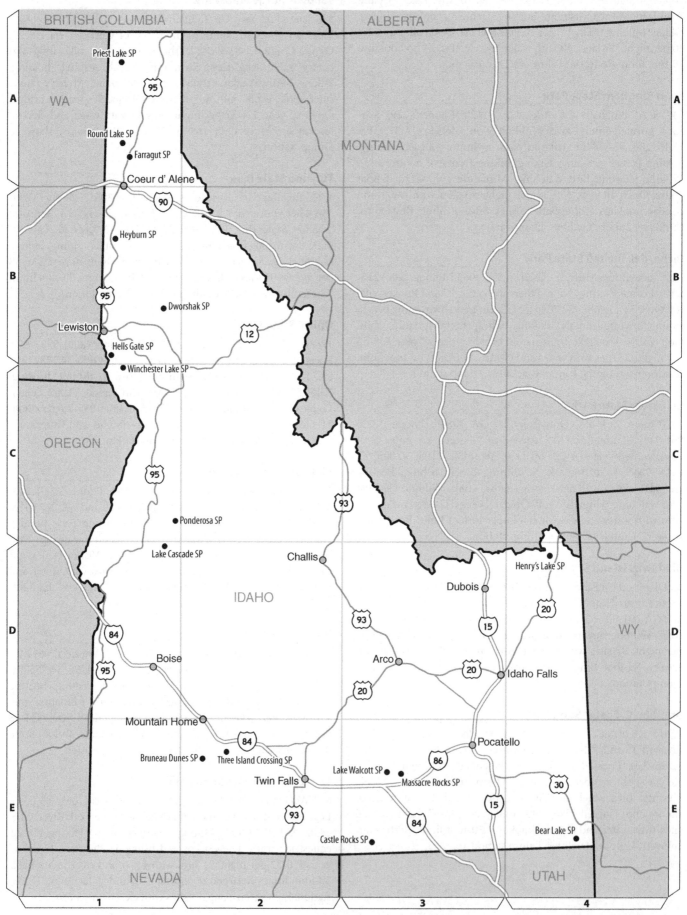

Idaho

Idaho Dept. of Parks & Recreation
5657 Warm Springs Ave
Boise, ID 83716

Phone: (208) 334-4199
Internet: https://parksandrecreation.idaho.gov
Reservations: Online or (888) 922-6743

Idaho Park Locator

Idaho Parks

Bear Lake State Park

3rd N 10th E, St. Charles, ID 83272. Phone: (208) 945-2325. Located 21 miles S of Montpieler via US 30, Dingle Rd, Merkley Lake Rd, and Eastshore Rd. GPS: 42.029213, -111.258199. Half of Bear Lake is located in Idaho, the other half in Utah. Swimming, fishing, boating, sailing. Biking trails. Bird watching. Visitor center. Scenic drive. Open all year. $28-31 per night. 47 sites with electric hookups. Drinking water. 60-foot limit. Restrooms (vault toilets); no showers. Dump station.

Bruneau Dunes State Park

27608 Sand Dunes Rd, Bruneau, ID 83647. Phone: (208) 366-7919. Located 16 miles south and west of I-84 Exit 112 in Hammett via ID 78. GPS: 42.912079, -115.715050. Lake in park. Fishing, boating. Hiking, biking, equestrian trails. Bird watching. Visitor center. Museum. Tallest single-structured sand dune in North America. Observatory. Open all year. $14-29 per night. 117 sites, 82 with water and electric, 35 no hookups. 65-foot limit. Restrooms; showers. Dump station. Equestrian area, 19 sites.

Castle Rocks State Park

748 East 2800 South, Almo, ID 83312. Phone: (208) 824-5901. Located 2 miles S of Almo via Elba-Almo Rd and Smoky Mountain Dr. GPS: 42.076952, -113.651694. Fishing. Hiking, biking, equestrian trails. Bird watching. Disc golf. Visitor center. Museum. Rock climbing. Scenic drive. Open all year. $35 per night. 37 sites with electric hookups. 60-foot limit. Restrooms; showers. Dump station. Equestrian area, 6 sites.

Dworshak State Park

9934 Freeman Creek, Lenore, ID 83541. Phone: (208) 476-5994. Located about 25 miles E of Kendrick via Southwick Rd and Freeman Creek Rd. The last two miles of access road to the park is steep and narrow. GPS: 46.573360, -116.278847. Lake in park. Swimming, fishing, boating (rentals), sailing. Hiking trails. Bird watching. Disc golf. Marina. Open all year. $14-29 per night. 104 sites, 45 with water and electric hookups, 12 with electric only. 50-foot limit. Restrooms; showers. Dump station.

Farragut State Park

13550 E Hwy 54, Athol, ID 83801. Phone: (208) 683-2425. Located along ID 54 about 5 miles E of Athol. GPS: 47.951534, -116.603432. Lake in park. Swimming beach, fishing, boating, sailing. Hiking, biking, equestrian trails. Bird watching. Disc golf. Visitor center. Museum. Tree To Tree Adventure Park (zip lines, swings). Open all year. $24-35 per night. 265 sites, 48 full hookup, 156 with water and electric, 61 no hookups. 60-foot limit. Restrooms; showers. Dump station.

Hells Gate State Park

5100 Hells Gate Rd, Lewiston, ID 83501. Phone: (208) 799-5015. Located 4 miles S of Lewiston on Snake River Ave. GPS: 46.370425, -117.053556. Lake in park. Swimming, fishing, boating, sailing. Hiking, biking, equestrian, walking trails. Bird watching. Disc golf. Visitor center. Marina, store. Jet boat rides. Lewis and Clark Discovery Center. Open all year. $23-35 per night. 86 sites, 10 full hookup, 49 with water and electric. 60-foot limit. Restrooms; showers. Dump station.

Henrys Lake State Park

3917 E 5100 N, Island Park, ID 83429. Phone: (208) 558-7532. Located along US 20 near mile post 401, 40 miles N of Ashton. GPS: 44.618176, -111.368607. Swimming, fishing, boating, sailing. Hiking, biking, nature trails. Bird watching. Open May-Oct. $30-35 per night. 83 sites, 8 full hookup, 58 with water and electric, 17 sites electric only. 40-foot limit. Restrooms; showers. Dump station.

Heyburn State Park

57 Chatcolet Rd, Plummer, ID 83851. Phone: (208) 686-1308. Located 6 miles E of Plummer via ID 5. GPS: 47.353771, -116.772079. Lakes in park. Swimming, fishing, boating (rentals), sailing. Hiking, biking, equestrian trails. Bird watching. Park store. Visitor center. Marina. Open May-Sep. $28-32 per night. 56 sites, 15 full hookup, 41 with water and electric. 55-foot limit. Restrooms; showers. Dump station. Equestrian sites available.

Lake Cascade State Park

100 Kellys Parkway, Cascade, ID 83611. Phone: (208) 382-6544. Visitor center is located south end of Cascade along ID 5. GPS: 44.507512, -116.030883. Swimming, fishing, boating (kayak rentals), sailing. Hiking, biking, equestrian trails. Bird watching. Visitor center. Multiple camping areas open all year. The sites are located along 86 miles of shoreline. $23-32 per night. 247 sites, 83 with electric (some with water and sewer), 164 no hookups. 40-foot limit. Restrooms; showers. Dump station.

Lake Walcott State Park

959 E Minidoka Dam Rd, Rupert, ID 83350. Phone: (208) 436-1258. Located 16 miles NE of I-84 Exit 211 near Heyburn via ID 24 and Minidoka Dam Rd. GPS: 42.675129, -113.483374. Swimming, fishing, boating, sailing. Hiking, biking, walking trails. Wildlife viewing. Bird watching. Disc golf. Visitor center. Open all year. $14-31 per night. 40 sites, 22 with water and electric hookups. 60-foot limit. Restrooms; showers. Dump station.

Massacre Rocks State Park

3592 N Park Ln, American Falls, ID 83211. Phone: (208) 548-2672. Located 11 miles SW of American Falls just off I-86 Exit 28. GPS: 42.670451, -112.995343. Fishing, boating. Hiking, biking, walking trails. Wildlife viewing. Bird watching. Disc golf. Visitor center. Museum. Rock climbing. Open all year. $14-29 per night. 42 sites with water and electric hookups. 55-foot limit. Restrooms; showers. Dump station.

Ponderosa State Park

1920 N Davis Ave, McCall, ID 83638. Phone: (208) 634-2164. Located 2 miles NE of McCall. GPS: 44.925097, -116.088925. Lake in park. Swimming, fishing, boating (rentals), sailing. Hiking, biking, walking trails. Bird watching. Visitor center. Open May-Sep. $14-32 per night. 162 sites, 50 full hookup, 112 with water and electric. 35-foot limit. Restrooms; showers. Dump station.

Priest Lake State Park

314 Indian Creek Park Rd, Coolin, ID 83821. Phone: (208) 443-2200. Located 40 miles N of Priest River via ID 57 and East Shore Rd. GPS: 48.618898, -116.828167. Lake in park. Swimming, fishing, boating (rentals), sailing. Hiking, biking trails. Wildlife viewing. Bird watching. Disc golf. Park store. Visitor center. Open all year. $30-37 per night. 151 sites, some with water and electric (some with sewer). 50-foot limit. Restrooms; showers. Dump station.

Round Lake State Park

1880 Dufort Rd, Sagle, ID 83860. Phone: (208) 263-3489. Located 5 miles S of Sagle via US 95 and Dufort Rd. GPS: 48.167030, -116.636920. Swimming, fishing, boating (rentals), sailing. Hiking, biking trails. Wildlife viewing. Bird watching. Visitor center. Open all year. $24-33 per night. 51 sites, 16 with water and electric. 35-foot limit motorhome; 24-foot trailer limit. Restrooms; showers. Dump station.

Three Island Crossing State Park

1083 S Three Island Park Dr, Glenns Ferry, ID 83623. Phone: (208) 366-2394. Located 2 miles S of I-84 Exit 121 in Glenns Ferry. GPS: 42.944713, -115.318009. Fishing. Hiking, biking, walking trails. Bird watching. Disc golf. Visitor center. Oregon Trail river crossing site; with Oregon Trail history and education center. Original wagon ruts and Conestoga replicas. Scenic drive. Open all year. $26-31 per night. 82 sites with water and electric hookups. 60-foot limit. Restrooms; showers. Dump station.

Winchester Lake State Park

1786 Forest Rd, Winchester, ID 83555. Phone: (208) 924-7563. Located 35 miles SE of Lewiston on US 95, W of Winchester on Winchester Lake. GPS: 46.235917, -116.627852. Swimming, fishing, boating (rentals). Hiking, biking trails. Wildlife viewing. Bird watching. Visitor center. Scenic drive. Open all year. $14-31 per night. 68 sites, 46 with water and electric hookups. 70-foot limit. Restrooms; showers. Dump station.

Illinois

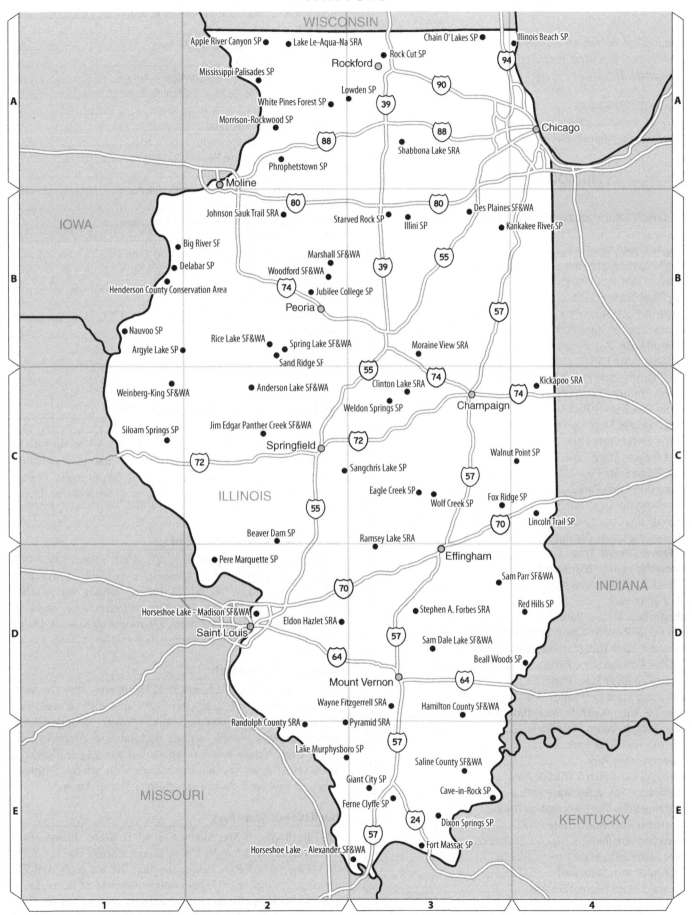

WISCONSIN

Apple River Canyon SP ● ● Lake Le-Aqua-Na SRA ● Chain O' Lakes SP ● Illinois Beach SP

Rock Cut SP

94

Mississippi Palisades SP ● Rockford

90

Lowden SP

A ● White Pines Forest SP ● 39 A

Morrison-Rockwood SP ●

88 88

● Chicago

Shabbona Lake SRA ●

● Phrophetstown SP

● Moline

80 80 ● Des Plaines SF&WA

Johnson Sauk Trail SRA ● Starved Rock SP ● ● Illini SP ● Kankakee River SP

IOWA Big River SF ● 55

B Delabar SP ● Marshall SF&WA ● 39 B

Henderson County Conservation Area ● Woodford SF&WA ● 57

74 ● Jubilee College SP

Peoria

● Nauvoo SP Rice Lake SF&WA ● ● Spring Lake SF&WA Moraine View SRA ●

Argyle Lake SP ● Sand Ridge SF ● Kickapoo SRA ●

Weinberg-King SF&WA ● ● Anderson Lake SF&WA 55 Clinton Lake SRA ● 74 74

Weldon Springs SP ● Champaign

Jim Edgar Panther Creek SF&WA ● Walnut Point SP ●

C Siloam Springs SP ● Springfield 72 57 C

72 Sangchris Lake SP ● Fox Ridge SP ●

Eagle Creek SP ● 57 Lincoln Trail SP ●

ILLINOIS Wolf Creek SP ● 70

55 Beaver Dam SP ● Ramsey Lake SRA ●

● Pere Marquette SP Effingham

Sam Parr SF&WA ●

70 INDIANA

Horseshoe Lake - Madison SF&WA ● Stephen A. Forbes SRA ● Red Hills SP ●

Eldon Hazlet SRA ●

D Saint Louis 57 Sam Dale Lake SF&WA ● D

64 Beall Woods SP ●

Mount Vernon 64

Wayne Fitzgerrell SRA ● Hamilton County SF&WA ●

Randolph County SRA ● ● Pyramid SRA 57

Lake Murphysboro SP ● Saline County SF&WA ●

Giant City SP ● Cave-in-Rock SP ●

E Ferne Clyffe SP ● 24 E

57 Dixon Springs SP ● KENTUCKY

MISSOURI

Horseshoe Lake - Alexander SF&WA ● 57 ● Fort Massac SP

1 2 3 4

Illinois

Illinois Dept. of Natural Resources
One Natural Resources Way
Springfield, IL 62702

Phone: (217) 782-6302
Internet: www.dnr.illinois.gov
Reservations: www.exploremoreil.com, no phone reservations.

Illinois Park Locator

Illinois Parks

Anderson Lake State Fish & Wildlife Area

647 N State Highway 100, Astoria, IL 61501. Phone: (309) 759-4484. Located 11 miles N of Browning via IL 100. GPS: 40.196556, -90.203292. Fishing, boating. Wildlife viewing. Bird watching. Open all year. Reservations not accepted. $8 per night. 30 sites, no hookups. Drinking water. Restrooms; no showers. Dump station.

Apple River Canyon State Park

8763 E Canyon Rd, Apple River, IL 61001. Phone: (815) 745-3302. Located 6 miles SE of Apple River via North Canyon Park Rd. GPS: 42.450349, -90.051613. Fishing. Hiking, nature trails. Wildlife viewing. Bird watching. Open all year. $8 per night. 49 sites, no hookups. Drinking water. Restrooms; no showers. Dump station.

Argyle Lake State Park

640 Argyle Park Rd, Colchester, IL 62326. Phone: (309) 776-3422. Located 2 miles N of Colchester via Coal St. GPS: 40.448536, -90.805466. Fishing, boating, scuba diving. Hiking, biking, equestrian trails. Wildlife viewing. Bird watching. Archery range. Camp store. Nature center. Open all year. $18-25 per night. 128 sites, 110 with electric hookups (some with sewer). Drinking water. 42-foot limit. Restrooms; showers. Dump station.

Beall Woods State Park

9285 Beall Woods Ave, Mount Carmel, IL 62863. Phone: (618) 298-2442. Located 9 miles SW of Mount Carmel via IL 1. GPS: 38.347966, -87.835859. Fishing, boating. Hiking trails. Wildlife viewing. Open all year. No reservations accepted. $8 per night. 16 sites, no hookups. Restrooms; no showers. Dump station.

Beaver Dam State Park

14548 Beaver Dam Ln, Plainview, IL 62685. Phone: (217) 854-8020. Located 7 miles SW of Carlinville via Alton Rd and Shipman Rd. GPS: 39.209685, -89.975424. Lake in park. Fishing, boating (rentals). Hiking trails. Wildlife viewing. Bird watching. Observation deck. Archery range. Restaurant. Open all year. $20-25 per night. 84 sites with electric hookups. Drinking water. 45-foot limit. Restrooms; showers. Dump station.

Big River State Forest

1337 Township Rd 2850N, Keithsburg, IL 61443. Phone: (309) 374-2496. Located on Mississippi River about 4 miles S of Keithsburg. GPS: 41.051626, -90.934838. Fishing, boating. Hiking, equestrian trails. Wildlife viewing. Bird watching. Scenic drive. Open all year. $8 per night. 65 sites, no hookups. Drinking water. Restrooms; no showers. Dump station. Equestrian camp.

Cave-in-Rock State Park

1 New State Park Rd, Cave-in-Rock, IL 62919. Phone: (618) 289-4325. Located on the Ohio River about 49 miles E of I-24 Exit 16 near Vienna via IL 146. GPS: 37.468493, -88.159882. Fishing, boating. Hiking trails. Marina, store, gifts. Restaurant (at lodge). Open all year. No reservations accepted. $20 per night. 34 sites with electric hookups. Drinking water. 60-foot limit. Restrooms; showers. Dump station.

Chain O' Lakes State Park

8916 Wilmot Rd, Spring Grove, IL 60081. Phone: (847) 587-5512. Located 7 miles E of Richmond via IL 173 and Wilmot Rd. GPS: 42.457401, -88.205469. Fishing, boating (rentals). Hiking, biking, equestrian (rentals) trails. Wildlife viewing. Bird watching. Park concession; food, snacks, gear. Open all year. $12-25 per night. 238 sites, 151 with electric hookups. Drinking water. 40-foot limit. Restrooms; showers. Dump station.

Clinton Lake State Recreation Area

7251 Ranger Rd, DeWitt, IL 61735. Phone: (217) 935-8722. Located 12 miles E of Clinton via IL 54. GPS: 40.163329, -88.787991. Swimming beach, fishing, boating, skiing. Hiking, biking, equestrian trails. Wildlife viewing. Archery range. Park concession; grill, camp supplies. Open all year. $10-25 per night. 308 sites, 17 full hookup, 277 with electric. Drinking water. 40-foot limit. Restrooms; showers. Dump station.

Delabar State Park

RR 2 Box 27, Oquawka, IL 61469. Phone: (309) 374-2496. Located on Mississippi River about 1.5 miles N of Oquawka via Third St. GPS: 40.957829, -90.940803. Fishing, boating. Hiking trails. Wildlife viewing. Marina (nearby). Open all year. $18 per night. 54 sites with electric hookups. Drinking water. Restrooms; no showers. Dump station.

Des Plaines State Fish & Wildlife Area

24621 N River Rd, Wilmington, IL 60481. Phone: (815) 423-5326. Located about 2 miles W of I-55 Exit 241 near Wilmington. GPS: 41.372144, -88.207081. Lake in park. Fishing, boating, skiing. Equestrian trail. Wildlife viewing. Archery range. Open Apr-Oct. No reservations accepted. $8 per night. 24 sites, no hookups. Drinking water. Dump station.

Dixon Springs State Park

982 State Highway 146, Golconda, IL 62938. Phone: (618) 949-3394. Located 10 miles W of Golconda via IL 146. GPS: 37.380384, -88.665902. Swimming pool, fishing, boating. Hiking, nature trails. Wildlife viewing. Bird watching. Park concession; snacks, beverages. Open all year. $18 per night. 38 sites with electric hookups. Drinking water. 42-foot limit. Restrooms; showers. Dump station.

Eagle Creek State Park

2641 Eagle Creek Rd, Findlay, IL 62534. Phone: (217) 756-8260. Located 4 miles SE of Findlay via Division St and county roads. GPS: 39.501577, -88.713097. Lake in park. Fishing, boating, skiing. Hiking, equestrian, nature trails. Wildlife viewing. Golf course. Marinas. Open all year. $20 per night. 103 sites with electric hookups. Drinking water. 60-foot limit. Restrooms; showers. Dump station.

Eldon Hazlet State Recreation Area

20100 Hazlet Park Rd, Carlyle, IL 62231. Phone: (618) 594-3015. Located 7 miles NE of Carlyle via IL 127. GPS: 38.654648, -89.330255. Lake in park. Swimming pool, fishing, boating, skiing. Hiking, biking trails. Wildlife viewing. Bird watching. Scenic viewpoint. Archery range. Camp store. Open all year. $20 per night. 327 sites with electric hookups. Drinking water. 40-foot limit. Restrooms; showers. Dump station.

Ferne Clyffe State Park

90 Office Dr, Goreville, IL 62939. Phone: (618) 995-2411. Located 2 miles S of Goreville via IL 37. GPS: 37.532564, -88.966416. Lake in park. Fishing. Hiking, equestrian, nature trails. Wildlife viewing. Bird watching. Rock climbing. Open Apr-Dec. $20 per night. 59 sites with electric hookups. Drinking water. 60-foot limit. Restrooms; showers. Dump station. Equestrian camp, 25 sites.

Fort Massac State Park

1308 E 5th St, Metropolis, IL 62960. Phone: (618) 524-4712. Located along US-45 east end of town. GPS: 37.147408, -88.713143. Lake in park. Fishing, boating, skiing. Hiking, biking trails. Disc golf. Visitor center and historic site. Museum, replica 1802 fort. Open all year. $20 per night. 50 sites with electric hookups. Drinking water. 68-foot limit. Restrooms; showers. Dump station.

Fox Ridge State Park

18175 State Park Rd, Charleston, IL 61920. Phone: (217) 345-6416. Located 8 miles S of Charleston via IL 130. GPS: 39.402774, -88.134849. Fishing, boating. Hiking, biking, equestrian trails. Wildlife viewing. Bird watching. Scenic viewpoint. Nature center. Open all year. $20 per night. 42 sites with electric hookups. Drinking water. 40-foot limit. Restrooms; showers. Dump station.

Giant City State Park

235 Giant City Rd, Makanda, IL 62958. Phone: (618) 457-4836. Located 12 miles S of Carbondale via Giant City Rd. GPS: 37.606630, -89.167279. Fishing (ponds). Hiking, equestrian, nature trails. Wildlife viewing. Lookout tower. Archery range. Visitor center. Lodge, restaurant, gifts. Rock climbing. Open all year. $20 per night. 85 sites with electric hookups. Drinking water. 40-foot limit. Restrooms; showers. Dump station.

Hamilton County State Fish & Wildlife Area

10279 Sunrise Point Rd, McLeansboro, IL 62859. Phone: (618) 773-4340. Located 8 miles E of McLeansboro via IL 14. GPS: 38.064666, -88.404695. Lake in park. Fishing, boating. Hiking, equestrian trails. Wildlife viewing. Bird watching. Nature center. Park concession; food, drinks. Open all year. $10-20 per night. 59 sites, 51 with electric hookups. Drinking water. 45-foot limit. Restrooms; showers. Dump station.

Henderson County Conservation Area

RR 1 Box 118, Keithsburg, IL 61437. Phone: (309) 374-2496. Located SW of Gladstone via Elm St and Gladstone Lake Rd. GPS: 40.857579, -90.975470. Lake in park. Fishing, boating. Wildlife viewing. Open all year. No reservations accepted. $8 per night. 25 sites, no hookups. Restrooms (vault toilets); no showers. Dump station.

Horseshoe Lake - Alexander State Fish & Wildlife Area

21204 Promised Land Rd, Miller City, IL 62962. Phone: (618) 776-5689. Located 14 miles NW of I-57 Exit 1 near Cairo via IL 3 and Promised Land Rd. GPS: 37.137010, -89.346309. Fishing, boating. Wildlife viewing. Open all year. No reservations accepted. $10-20 per night. 88 sites, 78 with electric, 10 no hookups. Drinking water. Restrooms; showers. Dump station.

Horseshoe Lake - Madison State Fish & Wildlife Area

3321 Highway 111, Granite City, IL 62040. Phone: (618) 931-0270. Located 3 miles N of I-70 Exit 6 near Fairmont City via IL 111. GPS: 38.699602, -90.066100. Fishing, boating. Hiking trails. Wildlife viewing. Open May-Sep. No reservations accepted. $8 per night. 26 sites, no hookups. Drinking water. Restrooms; no showers. Dump station.

Illini State Park

2660 E 2350th Rd, Marseilles, IL 61341. Phone: (815) 795-2448. Located on the south shore of the Illinois River in Marseilles. GPS: 41.318643, -88.710980. Fishing, boatingHiking, biking trails. Wildlife viewing. Bird watching. Park concession; food, drinks. Open all year. $10-20 per night. 100 sites, 45 sites with electric hookups. Drinking water. 40-foot limit. Restrooms; showers. Dump station.

Illinois Beach State Park

Zion, IL 60099. Phone: (847) 662-4811. Located in Zion near the junction of N Sheridan Rd and W Wadsworth Rd. GPS: 42.430157, -87.810132. Lake in park. Swimming beach, fishing, boating, scuba diving. Hiking, biking trails. Wildlife viewing.

Scenic viewpoint. Marina. Lodge, restaurant, gifts. Open Apr-Sep. $25 per night. 241 sites with electric hookups. Drinking water. 60-foot limit. Restrooms; showers. Dump station.

Jim Edgar Panther Creek State Fish & Wildlife Area

10149 County Hwy 11, Chandlerville, IL 62627. Phone: (217) 452-7741. Located 7 miles SE of Chandlerville via CR 2 and CR 11. GPS: 39.988923, -90.070571. Lake in park. Fishing, boating. Hiking, biking, equestrian trails. Wildlife viewing. Bird watching. Archery range. Open all year. $20-25 per night. 84 sites, 19 full hookup, 65 electric only. Drinking water. 60-foot limit. Restrooms; showers. Dump station.

Johnson-Sauk Trail State Recreation Area

28616 Sauk Trail Road, Kewanee, IL 61443. Phone: (309) 853-2425. Located 7 miles N of Kewanee via IL 78. GPS: 41.329330, -89.890880. Lake in park. Fishing, boating (rentals). Hiking, biking trails. Wildlife viewing. Bird watching. Archery range. Marina. Park concession; cafe, camp store. Open all year. $20 per night. 70 sites with electric hookups. Drinking water. 40-foot limit. Restrooms; showers. Dump station.

Jubilee College State Park

13921 W Route 150, Brimfield, IL 61517. Phone: (309) 446-3758. Located 5 miles W of Brimfield via US 150. GPS: 40.821386, -89.807213. Fishing (limited). Hiking, biking, equestrian trails. Wildlife viewing. Bird watching. Open Apr-Oct. $10-20 per night. 147 sites, 107 with electric, 40 no hookups. Drinking water. 40-foot limit. Restrooms; showers. Dump station. Equestrian camp area.

Kankakee River State Park

5314 W Route 102, Bourbonnais, IL 60914. Phone: (815) 933-1383. Located on IL 102 about 6 miles NW of Kankakee, on Kankakee River. GPS: 41.203532, -87.979471. Fishing, boating. Hiking, biking, equestrian trails. Wildlife viewing. Bird watching. Archery range. Nature center. Museum. Guided trail rides, pony rides, carriage rides, riding lessons. Two camping areas open Mar-Oct. $8-25 per night. 200 sites, 150 with electric, 50 no hookups. Drinking water. 45-foot limit. Restrooms; showers. Dump station.

Kickapoo State Recreation Area

10906 Kickapoo Park Rd, Oakwood, IL 61858. Phone: (217) 442-4915. Located 4 miles NE of Oakwood via Oakwood Rd and Glenburn Creek Rd. GPS: 40.137179, -87.739461. Twenty two deep-water ponds. Fishing, boating (rentals), scuba diving. Hiking, biking (rentals), equestrian, nature trails. Wildlife viewing. Bird watching. Archery range. Park concession; restaurant, camp supplies. Open all year. $8-20 per night. 184 sites, 101 with electric hookups. Drinking water. 50-foot limit. Restrooms; showers. Dump station.

Lake Le-Aqua-Na State Recreation Area

8542 N Lake Rd, Lena, IL 61048. Phone: (815) 369-4282. Located 3 miles N of Lena via North Lake Rd. GPS: 42.420916, -89.824019.

Lake in park. Swimming beach, fishing, boating. Hiking, biking, equestrian trails. Wildlife viewing. Open all year. $10-20 per night. 149 sites, 136 sites with electric, 13 no hookups. Drinking water. 40-foot limit. Restrooms; showers. Dump station.

Lake Murphysboro State Park

52 Cinder Hill Dr, Murphysboro, IL 62966. Phone: (618) 684-2867. Located 3 miles W of Murphysboro via IL 149. GPS: 37.777674, -89.388496. Fishing, boating. Hiking trails. Wildlife viewing. Scenic viewpoint. Archery range. Open all year. $10-20 per night. 63 sites, 44 sites with electric, 19 no hookups. Drinking water. 40-foot limit. Restrooms; showers. Dump station.

Lincoln Trail State Park

16985 E 1350th Rd, Marshall, IL 62441. Phone: (217) 826-2222. Located 4 miles S of Marshall via IL 1. GPS: 39.346621, -87.703568. Lake in park. Fishing, boating (rentals). Hiking trails. Wildlife viewing. Restaurant. Park concession; food, drinks, camp supplies. Two campgrounds open all year. $8-20 per night. 199 sites, 164 with electric hookups. Drinking water. 40-foot limit. Restrooms; showers. Dump station.

Lowden State Park

1411 N River Rd, Oregon, IL 61061. Phone: (815) 732-6828. Located 2 miles N of Oregon via Norther River Rd from IL 64. GPS: 42.035246, -89.325061. Fishing, boating. Hiking trails. Wildlife viewing. Open all year. $10-20 per night. 118sites, 80 with electric, 38 no hookups. 40-foot limit. Restrooms; showers. Dump station.

Marshall State Fish & Wildlife Area

236 State Route 26, Lacon, IL 61540. Phone: (309) 246-8351. Located 5 miles S of Lacon via IL 26. GPS: 40.954315, -89.428678. Fishing, boating. Hiking trails. Wildlife viewing. Bird watching. Open all year. $18 per night. 22 sites with electric hookups. Drinking water. 42-foot limit. Restrooms; no showers. Dump station.

Mississippi Palisades State Park

16327A State Route 84, Savanna, IL 61074. Phone: (815) 273-2731. Located about 4 miles N of Savanna via IL 84. GPS: 42.144260, -90.168744. Fishing, boating. Hiking trails. Wildlife viewing. Scenic viewpoint. Rock climbing. Open all year. $20 per night. 241 sites with electric hookups. Drinking water. 40-foot limit. Restrooms; showers. Dump station.

Moraine View State Recreation Area

27374 Moraine View Park Rd, LeRoy, IL 61752. Phone: (309) 724-8032. Located 7 miles N of I-74 Exit 149 in LeRoy via CR 2600. GPS: 40.413563, -88.737325. Lake in park. Swimming beach, fishing, boating (rentals). Hiking, equestrian trails. Wildlife viewing. Bird watching. Scenic viewpoint. Archery range. Camp store. Restaurant. Open all year. $10-20 per night. 239 sites, 137 with electric, 102 no hookups. Drinking water. 40-foot limit. Restrooms; showers. Dump station. Equestrian campground.

Morrison-Rockwood State Park

18750 Lake Rd, Morrison, IL 61270. Phone: (815) 772-4708. Located 2 miles N of Morrison via Crosby Rd. GPS: 41.840684, -89.968946. Lake in park. Fishing, boating (rentals). Hiking, equestrian trails. Wildlife viewing. Bird watching. Archery range. Marina. Park concession; restaurant, camp supplies. Open all year. $20 per night. 92 sites with electric hookups. Drinking water. 40-foot limit. Restrooms; showers. Dump station.

Nauvoo State Park

980 S Bluff St, Nauvoo, IL 62354. Phone: (217) 453-2512. Located in Nauvoo about 12 miles N of Hamilton via IL 96. GPS: 40.544139, -91.385609. Lake in park. Fishing, boating. Hiking trails. Bird watching. Museum. Open all year. $20 per night. 105 sites with electric hookups. Drinking water. 40-foot limit. Restrooms; showers. Dump station.

Pere Marquette State Park

13112 Visitor Center Ln, Grafton, IL 62037. Phone: (618) 786-3323. Located 6 miles W of Grafton via IL 100. GPS: 38.968364, -90.535507. Swimming, fishing, boating. Hiking, biking, equestrian trails. Bird watching. Scenic viewpoint. Visitor center. Lodge, restaurant, gifts. Museum. Rock climbing. Riding stables, trail rides. Free guided hikes. Open all year. $20 per night. 80 sites with electric hookups. Drinking water. 40-foot limit. Restrooms; showers. Dump station.

Prophetstown State Park

Riverside Drive & Park Ave, Prophetstown, IL 61277. Phone: (815) 537-2926. Located NE of town center. GPS: 41.672517, -89.931770. Fishing, boating. Hiking trails. Wildlife viewing. Open May-Oct. $20 per night. 86 sites with electric hookups. Drinking water. 40-foot limit. Restrooms; showers. Dump station.

Pyramid State Recreation Area

1562 Pyramid Park Rd, Pinckneyville, IL 62274. Phone: (618) 357-2574. Located 8 miles S of Pinckneyville via IL 127 and Pyatt-Cutler Rd. GPS: 38.004123, -89.416466. Lake in park. Fishing, boating. Hiking, biking, equestrian trails. Wildlife viewing. Archery range. Open all year. No reservations accepted. $8 per night. 28 sites, no hookups. Drinking water. Restrooms; no showers. Dump station.

Ramsey Lake State Recreation Area

Ramsey Lake Rd, Ramsey, IL 62080. Phone: (618) 423-2215. Located 2 miles NW of Ramsey via county roads off US 51. GPS: 39.159780, -89.128038. Fishing, boating (rentals). Hiking, biking, equestrian trails. Wildlife viewing. Bird watching. Scenic viewpoint. Park concession; food, camp supplies. Open all year. $10-20 per night. 135 sites, 90 with electric, 45 no hookups. Drinking water. 40-foot limit. Restrooms; showers. Dump station.

Randolph County State Recreation Area

4301 S Lake Dr, Chester, IL 62233. Phone: (618) 826-2706. Located 5 miles N of Chester via Palestine Rd. GPS: 37.972022,

-89.807728. Lake in park. Fishing, boating. Hiking, equestrian trails. Wildlife viewing. Bird watching. Open all year. $10-18 per night. 146 sites, 51 with electric, 95 no hookups. Drinking water. 42-foot limit. Restrooms; showers. Dump station. Equestrian area, 8 stalls and 4 primitive camp sites.

Red Hills State Park

3571 Ranger Ln, Sumner, IL 62466. Phone: (618) 936-2469. Located along US 50 between Olney and Lawrenceville. GPS: 38.730753, -87.833575. Lake in park. Fishing, boating. Hiking, biking, equestrian trails. Bird watching. Restaurant. Open all year. $20 per night. 103 sites with electric hookups. Drinking water. 40-foot limit. Restrooms; showers. Dump station.

Rice Lake State Fish & Wildlife Area

19721 N US-24, Canton, IL 61520. Phone: (309) 647-9184. Located 12 miles SE of Canton via IL 9 and US 24. GPS: 40.476608, -89.950328. Fishing, boating. Hiking trails. Wildlife viewing. Bird watching. Open all year. No reservations accepted. $20 per night. 32 sites with electric hookups. Drinking water. Restrooms; showers. Dump station.

Rock Cut State Park

7318 Harlem Rd, Loves Park, IL 61111. Phone: (815) 885-3311. Located 1 mile W of I-39/90 Exit 8 near Caledonia via IL 173. GPS: 42.359140, -88.975802. Two lakes in park. Swimming beach, fishing, boating (rentals). Hiking, biking (rentals), equestrian trails. Wildlife viewing. Bird watching. Park concessions; cafe, camp supplies, gifts. Open all year. $20-25 per night. 270 sites with electric hookups. Drinking water. 40-foot limit. Restrooms; showers. Dump station.

Saline County State Fish & Wildlife Area

85 Glen O. Jones Rd, Equality, IL 62934. Phone: (618) 276-4405. Located 5 miles SW of Equality via Shawnee Forest Rd. GPS: 37.691447, -88.377425. Lake in park. Fishing, boating (rentals). Hiking, equestrian trails. Wildlife viewing. Bird watching. Open all year. No reservations accepted. $8 per night. 25 sites, no hookups. Drinking water. Restrooms; no showers. Dump station.

Sam Dale Lake State Fish & Wildlife Area

620 County Road 1910N, Johnsonville, IL 62850. Phone: (618) 835-2292. Located 3 miles NW of Johnsonville via county roads. GPS: 38.536187, -88.565621. Lake in park. Fishing, boating (rentals). Hiking, equestrian trails. Wildlife viewing. Park concessions; restaurant, camp supplies. Open all year. $18 per night. 68 sites with electric hookups. Drinking water. 60-foot limit. Restrooms; showers. Dump station.

Sam Parr State Fish & Wildlife Area

13225 E State Hwy 23, Newton, IL 63448. Phone: (618) 783-2661. Located 3 miles NE of Newton via IL 33. GPS: 39.011103, -88.126956. Lake in park. Fishing, boating. Hiking, biking, equestrian trails. Wildlife viewing. Bird watching. Scenic viewpoint. Open all year. $18 per night. 30 sites with electric hookups. Drinking water. 42-foot limit. Restrooms; no showers. Dump station.

Sand Ridge State Forest

25799E County Road 2300N, Forest City, IL 61532. Phone: (309) 597-2212. Located 20 miles NE of Havana via US 136 and county roads. GPS: 40.390946, -89.866338. Hiking, biking, equestrian trails. Wildlife viewing. Bird watching. Scenic viewpoint. Archery range. Open all year. $8 per night. 27 sites, no hookups. Drinking water. 40-foot limit. Restrooms (vault toilets); no showers. Dump station.

Sangchris Lake State Park

9898 Cascade Rd, Rochester, IL 62563. Phone: (217) 498-9208. Located 9 miles SE of Rochester via Cardinal Hill Rd and CR 9 S. GPS: 39.656117, -89.487473. Fishing, boating. Hiking, equestrian trails. Bird watching. Archery range. Two campgrounds open all year. $10-20 per night. 185 sites, 135 with electric, 50 no hookups. Drinking water. 40-foot limit. Restrooms; showers. Dump station.

Shabbona Lake State Recreation Area

4201 Shabbona Grove Rd, Shabbona, IL 60550. Phone: (815) 824-2106. Located 8 miles E of I-39 Exit 87 via US 30 and Preserve Rd. GPS: 41.757231, -88.869830. Fishing, boating (rentals). Hiking, biking trails. Wildlife viewing. Archery range. Camp store. Marina. Park concessions; restaurant, gear, gifts. Open all year. $25 per night. 150 sites with electric hookups. Drinking water. 40-foot limit. Restrooms; showers. Dump station.

Siloam Springs State Park

938 E 3003rd Lane, Clayton, IL 62324. Phone: (217) 894-6205. Located 13 miles S of Clayton at US 24 via county roads. GPS: 39.893630, -90.930688. Lake in park. Fishing, boating (rentals), scuba diving. Hiking, biking, equestrian trails. Wildlife viewing. Bird watching. Archery range. Park concession; food, snacks, drinks, supplies. Open all year. $10-20 per night. 104 sites, 86 with electric, 18 no hookups. Drinking water. 40-foot limit. Restrooms; showers. Dump station.

Spring Lake State Fish & Wildlife Area

7982 S Park Rd, Manito, IL 61546. Phone: (309) 968-7135. Located in northwestern IL about 25 miles SW of Peoria, on the E side of the Illinois River, off IL 29. GPS: 40.467866, -89.841772. Fishing, boating (rentals). Hiking trails. Wildlife viewing. Bird watching. Archery range. Open all year. No reservations accepted. $8 per night. 60 sites, no hookups. Drinking water. Restrooms; no showers. Dump station.

Starved Rock State Park

2678 N Illinois Route 178, Utica, IL 61373. Phone: (815) 667-4726. Located 7 miles E of I-39 Exit 54 near Oglesby via Walnut St and IL 71. GPS: 41.302874, -88.979290. Fishing, boating (rentals). Hiking trails. Wildlife viewing. Bird watching. Visitor center. Lodge, restaurant. Park concessions; food, drinks, gifts, camp supplies. Open all year. $25 per night. 129 sites with electric hookups. Drinking water. 40-foot limit. Restrooms; showers. Dump station.

Stephen A. Forbes State Recreation Area

6924 Omega Rd, Kinmundy, IL 62854. Phone: (618) 547-3381. Located about 7 miles SE of Kinmundy via county roads. GPS: 38.736178, -88.773079. Lake in park. Swimming beach, fishing, boating (rentals), skiing. Hiking, biking, equestrian trails. Wildlife viewing. Bird watching. Scenic viewpoint. Marina. Park concessions; restaurant, store, gifts. Open all year. $20 per night. 115 sites with electric hookups. Drinking water. 40-foot limit. Restrooms; showers. Dump station. Equestrian camp, 21 sites with electric hookups.

Walnut Point State Park

2331 E County Road 370 N, Oakland, IL 61943. Phone: (217) 346-3336. Located 4 miles N of Oakland via CR 2400 E. GPS: 39.697073, -88.038516. Lake in park. Fishing, boating (rentals). Hiking, biking trails. Wildlife viewing. Bird watching. Scenic viewpoint. Restaurant. Open all year. $10-20 per night. 40 sites, 34 with electric hookups. Drinking water. 40-foot limit. Restrooms; showers. Dump station.

Wayne Fitzgerrell State Recreation Area

11094 Ranger Rd, Whittington, IL 62897. Phone: (618) 629-2320. Located about 2 miles W I-57 Exit 77 near Whittington via IL 154. GPS: 38.109140, -88.930148. Lake in park. Swimming, fishing, boating, skiing. Hiking, biking, equestrian trails. Wildlife viewing. Bird watching. Scenic viewpoint. Open all year. $20 per night. 243 sites with electric hookups. Drinking water. 40-foot limit. Restrooms; showers. Dump station.

Weinberg-King State Fish & Wildlife Area

State Highway 101, Augusta, IL 62311. Phone: (217) 392-2345. Located 3 miles E of Augusta via IL 101. GPS: 40.226550, -90.894749. Fishing. Hiking, equestrian trails. Wildlife viewing. Bird watching. Archery range. Open all year. $18 per night. 29 sites with electric hookups. Drinking water. 40-foot limit. Restrooms; no showers. Dump station. Equestrian camp, 19 sites with electric hookups.

Weldon Springs State Park

4734 Weldon Springs Rd, Clinton, IL 61727. Phone: (217) 935-2644. Located 3 miles SE of Clinton via IL 10 and Magill St. GPS: 40.121913, -88.931427. Lake in park. Fishing, boating (rentals). Hiking, biking, nature trails. Wildlife viewing. Open all year. $20 per night. 75 sites with electric hookups. Drinking water. 40-foot limit. Restrooms; showers. Dump station.

White Pines Forest State Park

6712 West Pines Rd, Mount Morris, IL 61054. Phone: (815) 946-3717. Located about 8 miles S of Mount Morris via IL 64, Ridge Rd and Pines Rd. GPS: 41.988915, -89.464899. Fishing. Hiking, nature trails. Bird watching. Restaurant. Open all year. $10-20 per night. 103 sites, 3 with electric hookups. Drinking water. 40-foot limit. Restrooms; showers. Dump station.

Wolf Creek State Park

1837 N Wolf Creek Rd, Windsor, IL 61957. Phone: (217) 459-2831. Located on Lake Shelbyville, 9 miles NW of Windsor via IL 32 and county roads. GPS: 39.478909, -88.688145. Lake in park. Swimming beach, fishing, boating (rentals), skiing. Hiking, equestrian trails. Wildlife viewing. Marina. Open all year. $20 per night. 304 sites with electric hookups. Drinking water. 60-foot limit. Restrooms; showers. Dump station.

Woodford State Fish & Wildlife Area

Low Point, IL 61545. Phone: (309) 822-8861. Located about 14 miles N of Peoria via IL 26. GPS: 40.879227, -89.456460. Due to periodic flooding of the Illinois River, it is advisable to call ahead and check on conditions before you visit. Fishing, boating. Hiking, biking trails. Bird watching. Open Apr-Sep. No reservations accepted. $8 per night. 40 sites, no hookups. Drinking water. Pit toilets; no showers. Dump station.

Indiana

Indiana

Indiana Dept. of Natural Resources
402 West Washington St, Room W160A
Indianapolis, IN 46204

Phone: (317) 232-4200
Internet: www.in.gov/dnr/parklake
Reservations: www.camp.in.gov or (866) 622-6746

Indiana Park Locator

Indiana Parks

Brookville Lake (Mounds SRA & Quakertown SRA)

14108 IN 101, Brookville, IN 47012. Phone: (765) 647-2657. Mounds SRA is located 7 miles N of Brookville via IN 101. Quakertown SRA is 16 miles N of Brookville via IN 101 and Dunlapsville Rd. GPS: 39.503087, -84.949379. Swimming beach, fishing, boating (rentals), skiing. Hiking, equestrian trails. Wildlife viewing. Bird watching. Archery and shooting range. Camp store. Marinas. Two recreation areas open all year. $23-40 per night. 450 sites, 65 full hookup, 388 with electric. Drinking water. Restrooms; showers. Dump station.

Brown County State Park

1405 State Route 46W, Nashville, IN 47448. Phone: (812) 988-6406. Located 2 miles S of Nashville via IN 46. Campers must enter via West Gate. GPS: 39.176663, -86.270164. Swimming pool, fishing. Hiking, biking, equestrian trails. Scenic viewpoint, 90' fire tower. Camp store. Nature center. Lodge, restaurant, water park. Open all year. $12-30 per night. 429 sites, 401 with electric, 28 no hookups. Drinking water. Restrooms; showers. Dump station.

Cagles Mill Lake (Lieber State Recreation Area)

1317 W Lieber Rd, Cloverdale, IN 46120. Phone: (765) 795-4576. Located 3 miles S of I-70 Exit 37 near Cloverdale via IN 243. GPS: 39.486961, -86.875160. Swimming pool, fishing, boating (rentals), skiing. Hiking trails. Nature center. Aquatic Center. Open all year. $16-30 per night. 216 sites, 120 with electric, 96 no hookups. Drinking water. Restrooms; showers. Dump station.

Cecil M. Harden Lake (Raccoon SRA)

1588 S Raccoon Pkwy, Rockville, IN 47872. Phone: (765) 344-1412. Located 9 miles E of Rockville via US 36. GPS: 39.758352, -87.073968. Swimming beach, fishing, boating (rentals), skiing. Hiking trails. Wildlife viewing areas. Archery range. Camp store. Marina. Historic Mansfield 1880's Roller Mill, tours. Open all year. $16-30 per night. 312 sites, 240 with electric, 72 no hookups. Drinking water. Restrooms; no showers. Dump station.

Chain O'Lakes State Park

2355 E 75 S, Albion, IN 46701. Phone: (260) 636-2654. Located about 5 miles SE of Albion via IN 9. GPS: 41.341313, -85.401470. Swimming beach, fishing, boating (rentals). Hiking trails. Wildlife viewing. Camp store. Nature center. Historic one-room Stanley Schoolhouse. Open all year. $12-30 per night. 413 sites, 331 with electric, 82 no hookups. Drinking water. Restrooms; showers. Dump station.

Charlestown State Park

12500 Highway 62, Charlestown, IN 47111. Phone: (812) 256-5600. Located 5 miles SE of Charlestown via IN 3, IN 62, and Jersey Ave. GPS: 38.429807, -85.635518. Fishing. Hiking trails. Bird watching. Open all year. $23-40 per night. 192 sites, 60 full hookup, 132 with electric. Drinking water. Restrooms; showers. Dump station.

Clifty Falls State Park

2221 Clifty Dr, Madison, IN 47250. Phone: (812) 273-8885. Located 2 miles W of Madison via IN 56. GPS: 38.759138, -85.421002. Swimming pool. Hiking trails. Bird watching. Nature center. Restaurant. Open all year. $16-30 per night. 169 sites, 106 with electric, 63 no hookups. Drinking water. Restrooms; no showers. Laundry facilities. Dump station.

Hardy Lake State Park

5620 N Hardy Lake Rd, Scottsburg, IN 47170. Phone: (812) 794-3800. Located about 8 miles E of I-65 Exit 34 near Austin via IN 256 and county roads. GPS: 38.776625, -85.705579. Swimming beach, fishing, boating, skiing. Hiking trails. Bird watching. Archery range. Open all year. $12-30 per night. 164 sites, 149 with electric, 15 no hookups. Drinking water. Restrooms; showers. Dump station.

Harmonie State Park

3451 Harmonie State Park Rd, New Harmony, IN 47631. Phone: (812) 682-4821. Located about 29 miles NW of Evansville via IN 66. GPS: 38.090076, -87.944613. Swimming pool, fishing, boating. Hiking, biking, equestrian, nature trails. Wildlife viewing. Nature center. Open all year. $23-30 per night. 200 sites with electric hookups. Drinking water. Restrooms; no showers. Dump station.

Indiana Dunes State Park

1600 N 25 E, Chesterton, IN 46304. Phone: (219) 926-1952. Located 2.5 miles N of I-94 Exit 26B via IN 49. GPS: 41.657763, -87.063869. Lake in park. Swimming beach, fishing. Hiking trails. Bird watching. Camp store. Nature center. Open all year. $23-30 per night. 140 sites with electric hookups. Drinking water. Restrooms; showers. Dump station.

Lincoln State Park

Indiana Highway 162, Lincoln City, IN 47552. Phone: (812) 937-4710. Located about 7 miles S of I-64 Exit 57A near Dale via US 231 and IN 162. GPS: 38.111223, -86.998084. Two lakes in park. Swimming beach, fishing, boating (rentals). Hiking, nature trails. Wildlife viewing. Camp store. Nature center. Historic Colonel Jones Home, tours. Abraham Lincoln Bicentennial Plaza. Open all year. $12-30 per night. 269 sites, 150 with electric, 119 no hookups. Drinking water. Restrooms; showers. Dump station.

McCormick's Creek State Park

250 McCormick's Creek Park Rd, Spencer, IN 47460. Phone: (812) 829-2235. Located 2 miles E of Spencer along IN 46. GPS: 39.284205, -86.726268. Swimming pool. Hiking, equestrian, nature trails. Camp store. Nature center. Scenic waterfalls. Open all year. $12-30 per night. 221 sites, 189 with electric, 32 no hookups. Drinking water. Restrooms; showers. Dump station.

Mississinewa Lake State Park

4673 S 625 E, Peru, IN 46970. Phone: (765) 473-6528. Located about 9 miles SE of Peru via IN 19. GPS: 40.697898, -85.954580. Swimming beach, fishing, boating, skiing. Hiking, biking trails. Bird watching. Disc golf. Radio-Control flying field. Open all year. $16-40 per night. 431 sites, 39 full hookup, 335 with electric, 57 no hookups. Drinking water. Restrooms; showers. Dump station.

Monroe Lake State Park

4850 S State Road 446, Bloomington, IN 47401. Phone: (812) 837-9546. Located about 9 miles SE of Bloomington via IN 446.

GPS: 39.092760, -86.423346. Swimming beaches, fishing, boating (rentals), skiing. Hiking trails. Camp store. Nature center. Marina. Open all year. $16-30 per night. 320 sites, 226 with electric, 94 no hookups. Drinking water. Restrooms; showers. Dump station.

Mounds State Park

4306 Mounds Rd, Anderson, IN 46017. Phone: (765) 642-6627. Located 4 miles E of Anderson via IN 232 or 4 miles W of I-69 Exit 234. GPS: 40.095961, -85.619112. Swimming pool, fishing (river). Hiking trails. Camp store. Nature center. Park features 10 unique earthworks built by prehistoric Indians. Open all year. $23-30 per night. 75 sites with electric hookups. Drinking water. Restrooms; no showers.

O'Bannon Woods State Park

7234 Old Forest Rd SW, Corydon, IN 47112. Phone: (812) 738-8232. Located 11 miles SW of I-64 Exit 105 near Corydon via IN 62 and IN 462. GPS: 38.199314, -86.265934. Swimming pool, fishing, boating. Hiking, biking, equestrian trails. Nature center. Restored, working haypress barn and a pioneer farmstead. Wyandotte Caves, tours. Aquatic center. Open all year. $16-30 per night. 328 sites, 281 with electric, 47 no hookups. Drinking water. Restrooms; showers. Dump station.

Ouabache State Park

4930 E State Road 201, Bluffton, IN 46714. Phone: (260) 824-0926. Located 3 miles SE of Bluffton via IN 124 and IN 201. GPS: 40.725123, -85.122455. Lake in park. Swimming beach, fishing, boating. Hiking, biking trails. Wildlife viewing. Scenic viewpoint, 100-foot tower. Nature center. A 20-acre American bison exhibit. Open all year. $23-30 per night. 122 sites with electric hookups. Drinking water. Restrooms; showers. Dump station.

Patoka Lake

3084 N Dillard Rd, Birdseye, IN 47513. Phone: (812) 685-2464. Located 9 miles NE of Birdseye via IN 145 and IN 164. GPS: 38.384477, -86.647129. Swimming beach, fishing, boating (rentals), skiing. Hiking, biking trails. Bird watching. Disc golf. Archery range. Camp store. Nature center. Marinas. Open all year. $12-30 per night. 500 sites, 455 with electric, 45 no hookups. Drinking water. Restrooms; showers. Dump station.

Pokagon State Park

450 Lane 100 Lake James, Angola, IN 46703. Phone: (260) 833-2012. Located 6 miles W of Fremont and 1.5 miles W of I-69 Exit 354 via IN 727. GPS: 41.707663, -85.022641. Lakes in park. Swimming beach, fishing, boating (rentals). Hiking, biking, equestrian trails. Camp store. Nature center. Guided horseback rides. Open all year. $16-30 per night. 273 sites, 200 with electric, 73 no hookups. Drinking water. Restrooms; showers. Dump station.

Potato Creek State Park

25601 State Road 4, North Liberty, IN 46554. Phone: (574) 656-8186. Located 16 miles SW of South Bend via US 31 and IN 4. GPS: 41.534999, -86.362026. Lake in park. Swimming beach, fishing, boating (rentals). Hiking, biking (rentals), equestrian trails. Wildlife viewing area. Camp store. Nature center. Open all year. $23-30 per night. 287 sites with electric hookups. Drinking water. Restrooms; showers. Dump station. 70 equestrian sites with electric.

Prophetstown State Park

5545 Swisher Rd, West Lafayette, IN 47906. Phone: (765) 567-4919. Located 2 miles south and east of I-65 Exit 178 near Battle Ground via River Rd, Burnetts Rd, and N 9th St. GPS: 40.497379, -86.842477. Swimming pool (aquatic center). Hiking, biking trails. Scenic viewpoint. Farm at Prophetstown, 1920s farm. Open all year. $23-40 per night. 110 sites, 55 full hookup, 55 with electric. Drinking water. Restrooms; showers. Dump station.

Salamonie Lake State Park

9214 Lost Bridge West, Andrews, IN 46702. Phone: (260) 468-2125. Located 6 miles SE of Largo, off US 24. GPS: 40.766440, -85.627374. Lake in park. Swimming beach, fishing, boating, skiing. Hiking, biking, equestrian trails. Bird watching. Nature center. Open all year. $12-30 per night. 283 sites, 245 with electric, 38 no hookups. Drinking water. Restrooms; showers. Dump station. Equestrian camp, 50 sites.

Shades State Park

7751 S 890 W, Waveland, IN 47989. Phone: (765) 435-2810. Located 17 miles SW of Crawfordsville via IN 47 and IN 234. GPS: 39.929583, -87.072544. Fishing, boating. Hiking trails. Camp store. Pine Hills Nature Preserve. Open all year. $16-19 per night. 105 sites, no hookups. Drinking water. Restrooms; showers. Dump station.

Shakamak State Park

6265 W State Road 48, Jasonville, IN 47438. Phone: (812) 665-2158. Located 2 miles NW of Jasonville via IN 48. GPS: 39.176294, -87.234444. Three lakes in park. Swimming pool (aquatic center), fishing, boating (rentals). Hiking trails. Camp store. Nature center. Open all year. $16-40 per night. 164 sites, 8 full hookup, 114 with electric, 42 no hookups. Drinking water. Restrooms; showers. Dump station.

Spring Mill State Park

3333 State Road 60 E, Mitchell, IN 47446. Phone: (812) 849-3534. Located about 3 miles E of Mitchell via IN 60. GPS: 38.723378, -86.416949. Lake in park. Swimming pool, fishing, boating (rentals). Hiking, biking (rentals) trails. Camp store. Nature center. Restaurant. Twin Caves Boat Tours. Restored Pioneer Village, founded in 1814, contains 20 historic buildings. Open all year. $12-30 per night. 223 sites, 187 with electric, 36 no hookups. Drinking water. Restrooms; no showers. Dump station.

Summit Lake State Park

5993 N Messick Rd, New Castle, IN 47362. Phone: (765) 766-5873. Located about 5.5 miles E of Mount Summit via US 36 and Messick Rd. GPS: 40.020651, -85.303112. Swimming beach, fishing, boating (rentals). Hiking, nature trails. Wildlife viewing.

Bird watching. Camp store. Open all year. $23-30 per night. 120 sites with electric hookups. Drinking water. Restrooms; showers. Dump station.

Tippecanoe River State Park

4200 N US-35, Winamac, IN 46996. Phone: (574) 946-3213. Located 4.5 miles N of Winamac via US 35. GPS: 41.117313, -86.602535. Fishing, boating. Hiking, equestrian trails. Wildlife viewing. Scenic viewpoint, 90-foot fire tower. Nature center. Open all year. $23-30 per night. 112 sites with electric hookups. Drinking water. Restrooms; showers. Dump station. Equestrian camp, 56 sites no hookups.

Turkey Run State Park

8121 E Park Rd, Marshall, IN 47859. Phone: (765) 597-2635. Located 25 miles SW of Crawfordsville via IN 47. GPS: 39.878787, -87.213761. Swimming pool, fishing. Hiking trails. Wildlife viewing. Camp store. Nature center. Restaurant. Colonel Richard Lieber Cabin. Open all year. $23-30 per night. 213 sites with electric hookups. Drinking water. Restrooms; no showers. Dump station.

Versailles State Park

1387 US-50, Versailles, IN 47042. Phone: (812) 689-6424. Located 1 mile E of Versailles along US 50. GPS: 39.061474, -85.234095. Lake in park. Swimming pool, fishing, boating (rentals). Hiking, biking, equestrian trails. Wildlife viewing. Scenic viewpoint. Camp store. Open all year. $23-30 per night. 226 sites with electric hookups. Drinking water. Restrooms; showers. Dump station. Equestrian camp, 9 sites with electric hookups.

Whitewater Memorial State Park

1418 S State Road 101, Liberty, IN 47353. Phone: (765) 458-5565. Located 2 miles S of Liberty via IN 101. GPS: 39.612116, -84.942382. Lake in park. Swimming beach, fishing, boating (rentals). Hiking, equestrian trails. Bird watching. Camp store. Marinas. Hayrides, guided trail rides. Open all year. $16-30 per night. 281 sites, 236 with electric, 45 no hookups. Drinking water. Restrooms; showers. Dump station. Equestrian camp, 37 sites (some with electric hookups).

Iowa

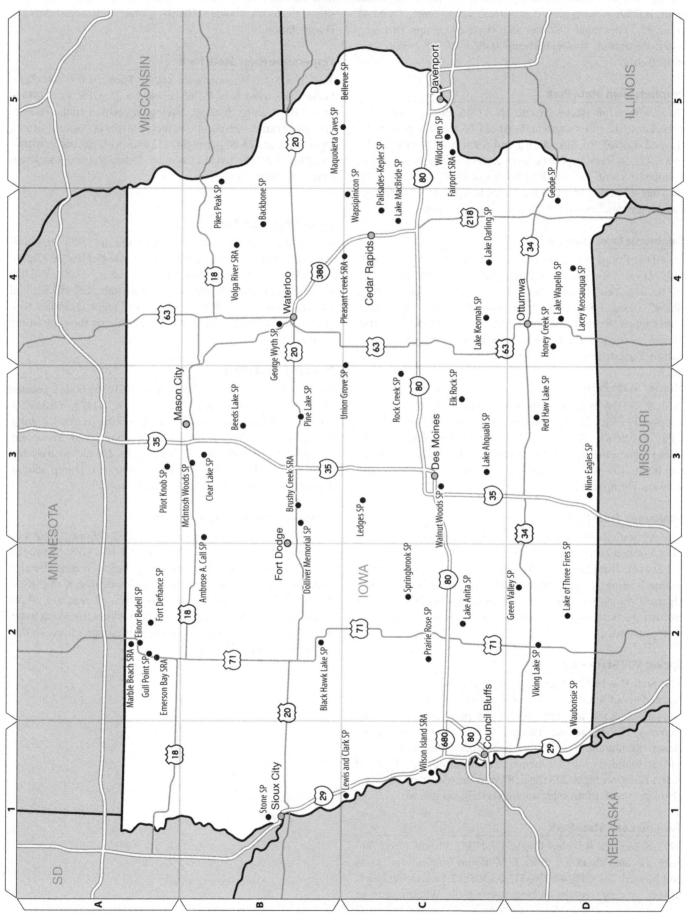

Iowa

State Parks Bureau
Iowa Department of Natural Resources
Wallace State Office Building
502 E 9th St, 4th Floor
Des Moines, IA 50319

Information: (515) 725-8200
Internet: iowadnr.gov
Reservations: Online or (877) 427-2757

Iowa Park Locator

Iowa Parks

Ambrose A. Call State Park

2007 Call Park Dr, Algona, IA 50511. Phone: (641) 581-4835. Located 1.5 miles SW of Algona via Orton Rd. GPS: 43.054777, -94.241943. Hiking trails. Disc golf. Open Apr-Oct. Reservations not accepted. $10-16 per night. 16 sites, 13 with electric hookups. Vault toilets; no showers.

Backbone State Park

1347 129th St, Dundee. IA 52038. Phone: (536) 924-2527. Located 2.5 miles N of Dundee via 140th St. GPS: 42.601026, -91.532585. Swimming beach, fishing, boating (rentals). Hiking, biking trails. Bird watching. Museum. Rock climbing. Two campgrounds open all year. $14-20 per night. 108 sites, 49 with electric, 59 no hookups. Drinking water. 60-foot limit. Restrooms; showers. Dump station.

Beeds Lake State Park

1422 165th St, Hampton, IA 50441. Phone: (641) 456-2047. Located 4 miles NW of Hampton via IA 3 and IA 134. GPS: 42.767199, -93.236592. Swimming beach, fishing, boating. Hiking, biking trails. Bird watching. Open all year. $16 per night. 91 sites with electric hookups. Drinking water. 65-foot limit. Restrooms; showers. Dump station.

Bellevue State Park

24668 Hwy 52 Bellevue, IA 52031. Phone: (563) 872-4019. Located 3 miles S of Bellevue via US 52. GPS: 42.222808, -90.396738. Hiking, walking trails. Wildlife viewing. Scenic viewpoint. Nature center. Butterfly garden. Open all year. $12-18 per night. 36 sites, 31 with electric hookups, 5 no hookups. Drinking water. 55-foot limit. Restrooms; showers. Dump station.

Black Hawk Lake State Park

228 S Blossom, Lake View, IA 51450. Phone: (712) 657-8712. Located in west-central IA in Lake View on Black Hawk Lake, near US 71 & IA 175. GPS: 42.292111, -95.018468. Swimming beach, fishing, boating. Hiking, biking trails. Disc golf. Open all year. $12-21 per night. 126 sites, 87 with electric (some with water), 39 no hookups. Drinking water. 90-foot limit. Restrooms; showers. Dump station.

Brushy Creek State Recreation Area

2802 Brushy Creek Road, Lehigh, IA 50557. Phone: (515) 543-8298. Located 17 miles SE of Fort Dodge via US 20 and county roads. GPS: 42.391021, -93.989177. Lake in park. Swimming beach, fishing, boating. Hiking, biking trails. Bird watching. Shooting range. Open all year. $20-26 per night. 37 sites, 8 full hookup, 29 with electric. Drinking water. 70-foot limit. Restrooms; showers. Dump station. Equestrian camp, 112 sites.

Clear Lake State Park

6490 South Shore Dr, Clear Lake, IA 50428. Phone: (641) 357-4212. Located 4 miles SW of I-35 Exit 194 in Clear Lake via US 18 and N 8th St. GPS: 43.111016, -93.388992. Swimming beach, fishing, boating (rentals), skiing. Hiking, biking trails. Wildlife viewing. Open all year. $14-26 per night. 175 sites, 6 full hookup, 161 with electric, 8 no hookups. Drinking water. 109-foot limit. Restrooms; showers. Dump station.

Dolliver Memorial State Park

2757 Dolliver Park Ave, Lehigh, IA 50557. Phone: (515) 359-2539. Located 4 miles NW of Lehigh via 290th St and Dolliver Park Ave. GPS: 42.391367, -94.079335. Fishing, boating. Hiking trails. Wildlife viewing. Historic sites, Native American mounds. Open all year. $16 per night. 19 sites with electric hookups. Drinking water. 65-foot limit. Restrooms; showers. Dump station.

Elinor Bedell State Park

1619 260th Ave, Spirit Lake, IA 51360. Phone: (712) 337-3211. Located 2.5 miles SE of Spirit Lake via US 71 and 250th Ave. GPS: 43.411930, -95.067689. Fishing, boating. Hiking, biking, walking trails. Open all year. $26 per night. 8 full hookup sites. Drinking water. 70-foot limit. Restrooms; showers. Dump station.

Elk Rock State Park

811 146th Ave, Knoxville, IA 50138. Phone: (641) 842-6008. Located 7 miles N of Knoxville via SR-14. GPS: 41.399021, -93.086529. Lake in park. Fishing, boating. Hiking, biking, equestrian trails. Bird watching. Open all year. $12-18 per night. 31 sites, 22 with electric, 9 no hookups. Drinking water. 70-foot limit. Restrooms; showers. Dump station. Equestrian area with 49 sites.

Emerson Bay State Recreation Area

3100 Emerson St, Okoboji, IA 51351. Phone: (712) 337-3211. Located about 4 miles NW of Milford via IA 86 and Okoboji Ave. GPS: 43.355695, -95.175329. Lake in park. Fishing, boating. Wildlife viewing. Bird watching. Open all year. $20-26 per night. 82 sites, 24 full hookup, 58 with electric. Drinking water. 70-foot limit. Restrooms; showers. Dump station.

Fairport State Recreation Area

1884 Wildcat Den Rd, Muscatine, IA 52761. Phone: (563) 263-4337. Located 7 miles E of Muscatine via IA 22. GPS: 41.432855, -90.924070. Fishing, boating. Bird watching. Open all year. $18 per night. 42 sites with electric hookups. Drinking water. 50-foot limit. Restrooms; showers. Dump station.

Fort Defiance State Park

3642 174th St, Estherville, IA 51334. Phone: (712) 337-3211. Located 2.5 miles W of Estherville via Central Ave and 170th St. GPS: 43.392032, -94.869417. Hiking, biking, equestrian trails. Wildlife viewing. Bird watching. Scenic viewpoint. Open all year. No reservations accepted. $16 per night. 8 sites with electric hookups. Vault toilets; no showers.

Geode State Park

3333 Racine Ave, Danville, IA 52623. Phone: (319) 392-4601. Located 6 miles SW of Danville via Danville Rd and CR 79. GPS: 40.825132, -91.380373. Lake in park. Swimming beach, fishing, boating. Hiking, biking (park roads) trails. Wildlife viewing. Open all year. $12-24 per night. 91 sites, 31 full hookup, 36 with electric, 24 no hookups. Drinking water. Restrooms; showers. Dump station.

George Wyth State Park

3659 Wyth Rd, Waterloo, IA 50703. Phone: (319) 232-5505. Located between Waterloo and Cedar Falls off US 218 at Airport Blvd. GPS: 42.532219, -92.402593. Four lakes in park. Swimming beach, fishing, boating. Hiking, biking, walking trails. Bird watching. Open all year. $12-18 per night. 66 sites, 47 with electric, 19 no hookups. Drinking water. 60-foot limit. Restrooms; showers. Dump station.

Green Valley State Park

1480 130th St, Creston, IA 50801. Phone: (641) 782-5131. Located 5 miles N of Creston via Green Valley Rd. GPS: 41.114424, -94.382950. Lake in park. Swimming beach, fishing, boating. Hiking, biking trails. Open all year. $14-26 per night. 97 sites, 19 full hookup, 61 with electric, 17 no hookups. Drinking water. 97-foot limit. Restrooms; showers. Dump station.

Gull Point State Park

1500 Harpen St, Milford, IA 51351. Phone: (712) 337-3211. Located 5 miles N of Milford via US 71 and IA 86. GPS: 43.371233, -95.168864. Lake in park. Fishing, boating, skiing. Hiking, biking, nature trails. Bird watching. Open all year. $10-16 per night. 104 sites, 52 with electric, 52 no hookups. Drinking water. 45-foot limit. Restrooms; showers. Dump station.

Honey Creek State Park

12194 Honey Creek Rd, Moravia, IA 52571. Phone: (641) 724-3739. Located 12 miles SW of Maravia via CR J18. GPS: 40.860429, -92.934108. Lake in park. Swimming beach, fishing, boating (rentals). Hiking, biking (rentals) trails. Scenic viewpoint. Golf course. Resort, restaurant. Indoor water park. Open all year. $16-22 per night. 149 sites, 28 full hookup, 75 with electric. Drinking water. 90-foot limit. Restrooms; showers. Dump station.

Lacey Keosauqua State Park

22895 Lacey Trail, Keosauqua, IA 52565. Phone: (319) 293-3502. Located 2 miles SW of town via IA 1 and Park Rd. GPS: 40.709745, -91.979050. Lake in park. Swimming beach, fishing, boating (electric motors only). Hiking, biking trails. Bird watching. Open all year. $12-24 per night. 64 sites, 13 full hookup, 38 with electric (10 with water), 13 no hookups. Drinking water. 104-foot limit. Restrooms; showers. Dump station.

Lake Ahquabi State Park

16510 118th Ave, Indianola, IA 50125. Phone: (515) 961-7101. Located 6 miles SW of Indianola via US 65. GPS 41.295810, -93.591522. Swimming beach, fishing, boating (rentals). Hiking, biking trails. Wildlife viewing. Park concession; snacks, drinks. Open all year. $14-20 per night. 113 sites, 84 with electric, 29 no hookups. Drinking water. 60-foot limit. Restrooms; showers. Dump station.

Lake Anita State Park

55111 750th St, Anita, IA 50020. Phone: (712) 762-3564. Located less than one mile S of Anita via Michigan Ave. GPS: 41.432612, -94.761930. Swimming beach, fishing, boating. Hiking, biking, walking trails. Wildlife viewing. Bird watching. Open all year. $14-26 per night. 161 sites, 40 full hookup, 52 with electric, 69 no hookups. Drinking water. 70-foot limit. Restrooms; showers. Dump station.

Lake Darling State Park

111 Lake Darling Rd, Brighton, IA 52540. Phone: (319) 694-2323. Located 4 miles W of Brighton via IA 1. GPS: 41.176922, -91.887299. Swimming beach, fishing, boating (rentals). Hiking, biking trails. Bird watching. Open all year. $14-26 per night. 80 sites, 15 full hookup, 50 with electric, 15 no hookups. Drinking water. 120-foot limit. Restrooms; showers. Dump station.

Lake Keomah State Park

2720 Keomah Ln, Oskaloosa, IA 52577. Phone: (641) 673-6975. Located 7 miles E of Oskaloosa via IA 92. GPS: 41.286387, -92.543017. Swimming beach, fishing, boating (electric motors only). Hiking, biking trails. Bird watching. Open all year. $10-16 per night. 65 sites, 41 with electric, 24 no hookups. Drinking water. 39-foot limit. Restrooms; showers. Dump station.

Lake MacBride State Park

3225 Hwy 382 NE Solon, IA 52333. Phone: (319) 624-2200. Located 5 miles west of Solon via Hwy 382. GPS: 41.798897, -91.572979. Swimming beach, fishing, boating (rentals). Hiking, biking, nature trails. Bird watching. Two campgrounds open all year. Northern unit: $20-26 per night. 43 sites, 11 full hookup, 32 with electric. Drinking water. 65-foot limit. Restrooms; showers. Dump station. Southern unit: $12 per night. 56 sites, no hookups. Drinking water. 30-foot limit. Restrooms; no showers.

Lake of Three Fires State Park

2303 Lake Rd, Bedford, IA 50833. Phone: (712) 523-2700. Located 4 miles N of Bedford via Lake Rd. GPS: 40.712816, -94.683411. Swimming beach, fishing, boating. Hiking, biking, equestrian trails. Bird watching. Open all year. $12-18 per night. 123 sites, 38 with electric hookups. Drinking water. 65-foot limit. Restrooms; showers. Dump station. Equestrian camp.

Lake Wapello State Park

15248 Campground Rd, Drakesville, IA 52552. Phone: (641) 722-3371. Located 6 miles NW of Drakesville via 180th St and Eagle Blvd. GPS: 40.824868, -92.570498. Swimming beach, fishing, boating. Hiking, biking, nature trails. Bird watching. Open all year. $12-24 per night. 72 sites, 15 full hookup, 34 with electric, 23 no hookups. Drinking water. Restrooms; showers. Dump station.

Ledges State Park

1515 P Ave, Madrid, IA 50156. Phone: (515) 432-1852. Located 7 miles S of Boone via US 30 and Quill Ave. GPS: 41.993822, -93.874864. Fishing, boating. Hiking, nature trails. Wildlife viewing. Scenic canyon drive. Open all year. $14-26 per night. 82 sites, 16 full hookup, 53 with electric, 13 no hookups. Drinking water. 83-foot limit. Restrooms; showers. Dump station.

Lewis and Clark State Park

21914 Park Loop, Onawa, IA 51040. Phone: (712) 423-2829. Located 3 miles east and north of I-29 Exit 112 near Onawa via IA 175 and Park Loop. GPS: 42.046653, -96.162535. Lake in park. Swimming beach, fishing, boating. Hiking, nature trails. Wildlife viewing. Visitor center, full-sized reproduction of Lewis and Clark's keelboat. Open all year. $20-26 per night. 106 sites, 13 full hookup, 93 with electric. Drinking water. 90-foot limit. Restrooms; showers. Dump station.

Maquoketa Caves State Park

9688 Caves Road, Maquoketa, IA 52060. Phone: (563) 652-5833. Located 6.5 miles NW of US 61 in Maquoketa via IA 428. GPS: 42.119857, -90.777015. Hiking trails. Wildlife viewing. Scenic viewpoint. Interpretive center. Park has about 13 caves. Some can be explored by walking, others are for serious spelunkers. Open all year. $20 per night. 24 sites with electric hookups. Drinking water. 68-foot limit. Restrooms; showers. Dump station.

Marble Beach State Recreation Area

12320 240th Ave, Spirit Lake, IA 51360. Phone: (712) 337-3211. Located about 4 miles N of Spirit Lake via Peoria Ave and 240th Ave. GPS: 43.469301, -95.124873. Lake in park. Swimming beach, fishing, boating, skiing. Hiking, biking trails. Bird watching. Open all year. $14-26 per night. 221 sites, 64 full hookup, 38 with electric (some with water), 119 no hookups. Drinking water. 80-foot limit. Restrooms; showers. Dump station.

McIntosh Woods State Park

1200 E Lake St, Ventura, IA 50482. Phone: (641) 829-3847. Located 6 miles W of I-35 Exit 194 in Clear Lake via US 18. GPS: 43.125677, -93.458776. Lake in park. Swimming beach, fishing, boating. Hiking, biking, walking trails. Wildlife viewing blind. Bird watching. Open all year. $12-18 per night. 49 sites, 45 with electric hookups. Drinking water. 65-foot limit. Restrooms; showers. Dump station.

Nine Eagles State Park

23678 Dale Miller Rd, Davis City, IA 50065. Phone: (641) 442-2855. Located 6 miles SE of Davis City via Dale Miller Rd. GPS: 40.591772, -93.753428. Lake in park. Swimming beach, fishing, boating. Hiking, biking, equestrian . Bird watching. Open all year. $10-16 per night. 55 sites, 28 with electric, 27 no hookups. Drinking water. 76-foot limit. Restrooms; showers. Dump station. Equestrian area, 7 primitive sites.

Palisades-Kepler State Park

700 Kepler Dr, Mount Vernon, IA 52314. Phone: (319) 895-6039. Located 4 miles W of Mount Vernon via US 30. GPS: 41.909190, -91.508481. Fishing (river), boating. Hiking trails. Wildlife viewing. Rock climbing. Open all year. $14-20 per night. 44 sites, 31 with electric, 13 no hookups. Drinking water. 81-foot limit. Restrooms; showers. Dump station.

Pikes Peak State Park

32264 Pikes Peak Rd, McGregor, IA 52157. Phone: (563) 873-2341. Located 2.5 miles S of McGregor via Great River Rd. GPS: 42.994838, -91.166051. Hiking, biking, walking trails. Wildlife viewing. Scenic viewpoint. Scenic drive. Effigy Mounds National Monument seven miles north of the park. Open all year. $14-20 per night. 67 sites, 50 with electric, 17 no hookups. Drinking water. 64-foot limit. Restrooms; showers. Dump station.

Pilot Knob State Park

2148 340th St, Forest City, IA 50436. Phone: (641) 581-4835. Located 5 miles E of Forest City via IA 9 and IA 332. GPS: 43.254095, -93.559707. Lake in park. Fishing. Hiking, biking, equestrian trails. Wildlife viewing. Observation tower. Open all year. $10-16 per night. 60 sites, 48 with electric, 12 no hookups. Drinking water. Restrooms; showers. Dump station.

Pine Lake State Park

22620 County Hwy S56, Eldora, IA 50627. Phone: (641) 858-5832. Located 2.5 miles NE of Eldora via IA 175 and CR S56. GPS: 42.376830, -93.068264. Swimming beach, fishing (lake and river), boating (electric motors only). Hiking, biking, walking trails. Wildlife viewing. Open all year. $12-18 per night. 118 sites, 94 with electric, 24 no hookups. Drinking water. 100-foot limit. Restrooms; showers. Dump station.

Pleasant Creek State Recreation Area

4530 McClintock Rd, Palo, IA 52324. Phone: (319) 436-7716. Located 15 miles NW of Cedar Rapids and 3.5 miles N of Palo via Palo marsh Rd. GPS: 42.129169, -91.820388. Lake in park. Swimming beach, fishing, boating, scuba diving. Hiking, biking, equestrian trails. Wildlife viewing. Open all year. $14-20 per night. 67 sites, 54 with electric, 13 no hookups. Drinking water. 95-foot limit. Restrooms; showers. Dump station.

Prairie Rose State Park

680 Road M47, Harlan, IA 51537. Phone: (712) 773-2701. Located 10 miles SE of Harlan via IA 44 and Road M47. GPS: 41.600289, -95.212224. Lake in park. Swimming beach, fishing, boating. Hiking, biking, nature trails. Wildlife viewing. Open all year. $14-26 per night. 97 sites, 8 full hookup, 69 with electric, 20 no hookups. Drinking water. 65-foot limit. Restrooms; showers. Dump station.

Red Haw Lake State Park

24550 US 34, Chariton, IA 50049. Phone: (641) 774-5632. Located 2 miles E of Chariton via US 34. GPS: 41.003709, -93.278311. Lake in park. Swimming beach, fishing, boating. Hiking, nature trails. Bird watching. Open all year. $16 per night. 62 sites with electric hookups. Drinking water. 55-foot limit. Restrooms; showers. Dump station.

Rock Creek State Park

5627 Rock Creek East, Kellogg, IA 50135. Phone: (641) 236-3722. Located about 9 miles north and east of I-80 Exit 173 near Kellogg via IA 224 and Hwy F27. GPS: 41.756743, -92.837382. Lake in park. Swimming beach, fishing, boating (rentals). Hiking, biking, equestrian trails. Park concession store. Open all year. $14-20 per night. 193 sites, 98 with electric, 95 no hookups. Drinking water. 50-foot limit. Restrooms; showers. Dump station.

Springbrook State Park

2437 160th Rd, Guthrie Center, IA 50115. Phone: (641) 747-3591. Located 9 miles N of Guthrie Center via IA 25 and 160th Rd. GPS: 41.771105, -94.466980. Lake in park. Swimming beach, fishing, boating (no gas motors). Hiking, biking, nature trails. Wildlife viewing. Open all year. $12-18 per night. 119 sites, 81 with electric, 38 no hookups. Drinking water. Restrooms; showers. Dump station.

Stone State Park

5001 Talbot Rd, Sioux City, IA 51103. Phone: (712) 255-4698. Located 7 miles NW of Sioux City via I-29 and SR-12. GPS: 42.559338, -96.466991. Small 2-acre lake and Big Sioux River in park. Fishing, boating. Hiking, biking, equestrian, nature trails. Wildlife viewing. Nature center. Scenic drive. Open all year. $12-18 per night. 29 sites, 10 with electric, 19 no hookups. Drinking water. 42-foot limit. Restrooms; showers.

Union Grove State Park

1215 220th St, Gladbrook, IA 50635. Phone: (641) 473-2556. Located about 5 miles S of Gladbrook via Hwy T47. GPS: 42.123647, -92.725017. Lake in park. Swimming beach, fishing, boating. Hiking trails. Bird watching. Waterfall. Open all year. $12-24 per night. 25 sites, 9 full hookup, 2 with electric, 14 no hookups. Drinking water. 40-foot limit. Restrooms; showers. Dump station.

Viking Lake State Park

2780 Viking Lake Rd, Stanton, IA 51573. Phone: (712) 829-2235. Located 4 miles E of Stanton via US 34 and 230 St. GPS: 40.971668, -95.043823. Swimming beach, fishing, boating. Hiking, biking, nature trails. Wildlife viewing. Open all year. $14-26 per night. 141 sites, 22 full hookup, 94 with electric, 25 no hookups. Drinking water. 80-foot limit. Restrooms; showers. Dump station.

Volga River State Recreation Area

10225 Ivy Rd, Fayette, IA 52142. Phone: (563) 425-4161. Located in about 7 miles NE of Fayette via IA 150 and Ivy Rd. GPS: 42.893937, -91.765771. Lake in park. fishing, boating. Hiking, biking, equestrian trails. Bird watching. Open all year. $18-24 per night. 50 sites, 33 full hookup, 7 with electric, 10 no hookups. Drinking water. 90-foot limit. Restrooms; showers. Dump station. Equestrian area, 34 sites with electric hookups.

Walnut Woods State Park

3155 SE Walnut Woods Dr, West Des Moines, IA 50265. Phone: (515) 285-4502. Located 4 miles east and north of I-35 Exit 68 via IA 5. GPS: 41.542044, -93.741103. Fishing (river), boating. Hiking trails. Bird blind observation station. Open all year. $20-26 per night. 22 sites, 9 full hookup, 13 with electric. Drinking water. 71-foot limit. Restrooms; no showers. Dump station.

Wapsipinicon State Park

21301 CR E34, Anamosa, IA 52205. Phone: (319) 462-2761. Located on Wapsipinicon River about 15 miles NE of Marion via US 151. GPS: 42.095942, -91.288652. Fishing (river), boating. Hiking, biking trails. Wildlife viewing. Golf course. Park is listed on the National Register of Historic Places. Open all year. $10-16 per night. 20 sites, 13 with electric, 7 no hookups. Drinking water. 60-foot limit. Restrooms; showers.

Waubonsie State Park

2585 Waubonsie Park Rd, Hamburg, IA 51640. Phone: (712) 382-2786. Located near Hamburg about 6 miles E of I-29 Exit 10 via IA 2. GPS: 40.674496, -95.688467. Lake in park. Fishing, boating (electric motors only). Hiking, biking, equestrian trails. Wildlife viewing. Scenic drive. Open all year. $12-18 per night. 42 sites, 25 with electric, 17 no hookups. Drinking water. 100-foot limit. Restrooms; showers. Dump station. Equestrian campground, 36 non-electric sites.

Wildcat Den State Park

1884 Wildcat Den Road, Muscatine, IA 52761. Phone: (563) 263-4337. Located 10 miles E of Muscatine via IA 22. GPS: 41.468911, -90.886367. Fishing, boating. Hiking trails. Pine Creek Grist Mill, built in 1848, listed on the National Register of Historic Places. Open all year. Not suitable for large RVs. $9 per night. 20 sites, no hookups. Drinking water. 37-foot limit. Vault toilets. No showers.

Wilson Island State Recreation Area

32801 Campground Ln, Missouri Valley, IA 51555. Phone: (712) 642-2069. Located near Loveland about 6 miles W of I-29 Exit 72 via Desoto Ave. GPS: 41.489144, -96.009643. Fishing (river), boating. Hiking, biking trails. Wildlife viewing. Bird watching. Open Apr-Oct. $14-20 per night. 41 sites, 33 with electric, 8 no hookups. Drinking water. Restrooms; showers. Dump station.

Kansas

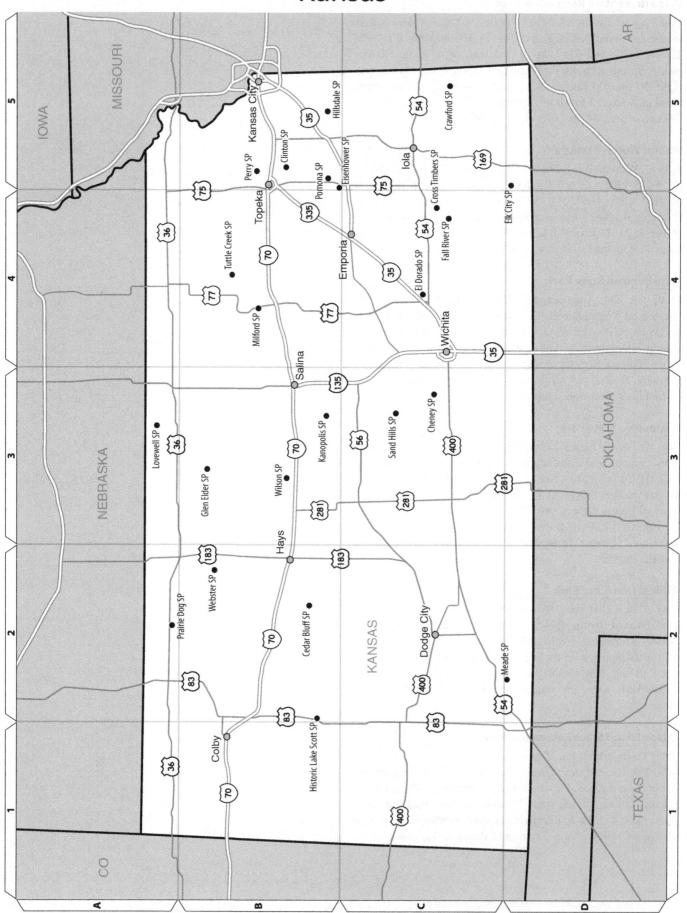

Kansas

Kansas Dept. of Wildlife & Parks
512 SE 25th Ave
Pratt, KS 67124

Phone: (620) 672-5911
Internet: www.ksoutdoors.com
Reservations: Online or call park.

Kansas Park Locator

Kansas Parks

Cedar Bluff State Park

32001 147 Hwy, Ellis, KS 67637. Phone: (785) 726-3212. Located near Ellis about 13 miles S of I-70 Exit 135 via KS 147. GPS: 38.811132, -99.732220. Lake in park. Swimming beach, fishing, boating, skiing. Hiking, biking, nature trails. Wildlife viewing. Scenic viewpoint. Open all year. $10-24 per night. 449 sites, 23 full hookup, 126 with water and electric, 300 no hookups. Drinking water. 100-foot limit. Restrooms; showers. Dump station.

Cheney State Park

16000 NE 50th St, Cheney, KS 67025. Phone: (316) 542-3664. Located about 32 miles W of Wichita via US 400 and KS 251. GPS: 37.720731, -97.834068. Lake in park. Swimming beach, fishing, boating, skiing. Hiking, biking, nature trails. Bird watching. Park store. Two Marinas. Open all year. $10-24 per night. 691 sites, 10 full hookup, 229 with water and electric, 452 no hookups. Drinking water. 87-foot limit. Restrooms; showers. Dump station.

Clinton State Park

798 N 1415 Rd, Lawrence, KS 66049. Phone: (785) 842-8562. Located near Lawrence about 5 miles S of I-70/Kansas Turpike Exit 197 via KS 10. GPS: 38.941939, -95.354297. Lake in park. Swimming beach, fishing, boating (rentals), skiing. Hiking, biking trails. Wildlife viewing. Archery range. Park store. Nature center. Marina. Restaurant. Mountain bike skills course. Open all year. $10-24 per night. 379 sites, 61 full hookup, 145 with water and electric, 173 no hookups. Drinking water. 80-foot limit. Restrooms; showers. Laundry facilities. Dump station.

Crawford State Park

1 Lake Rd, Farlington, KS 66734. Phone: (620) 362-3671. Located 18 miles SW of Fort Scott via US 69 and KS 7. GPS: 37.644673, -94.815603. Lake in park. Swimming beach, fishing, boating, skiing. Hiking, biking trails. Bird watching. Marina, restaurant. Six campgrounds open all year. $10-23 per night. 99 sites, 45 with water and electric, 26 electric only, 28 no hookups. Drinking water. Restrooms; showers. Laundry facilities. Dump station.

Cross Timbers State Park

144 Hwy 105, Toronto, KS 66777. Phone: (620) 637-2213. Located S of Toronto off KS 105. GPS: 37.779780, -95.943096. Lake in park. Swimming beach, fishing, boating (rentals). Hiking, biking trails. Wildlife viewing. Information center. Open all year. $10-24 per night. 242 sites, 15 full hookup, 37 with water and electric, 10 electric only, 180 no hookups. Drinking water. 85-foot limit. Restrooms; showers. Dump station.

Eisenhower State Park

29810 S Fairlawn Rd, Osage City, KS 66523. Phone: (785) 528-4102. Located near Melvern about 12 miles N of I-35 Exit 155 via US 75 and KS 278. GPS: 38.528499, -95.745566. Lake in park. Swimming beach, fishing, boating (rentals), skiing. Hiking, biking, equestrian trails. Disc golf. Archery range. Park store. Nature center. Open all year. $10-24 per night. 261 sites, 37 full hookup, 81 with water and electric, 68 electric only, 75 no hookups. Drinking water. 100-foot limit. Restrooms; showers. Laundry facilities. Dump station. Equestrian area, 15 sites with water and electric hookups.

El Dorado State Park

618 NE Bluestem Rd, El Dorado, KS 67042. Phone: (316) 321-7180. Located near El Dorado off I-35 Exit 76 via US 77. GPS: 37.833640, -96.784778. Lake in park. Swimming beaches, fishing, boating (rentals), skiing. Hiking, biking, equestrian, nature, walking trails. Scenic viewpoint. Archery range. Park store. Information center. Marina. Arboretum. Four campgrounds open all year. $10-24 per night. 1,196 sites, 164 full hookup, 307 with water and electric, 125 electric only, 600 no hookups. Drinking water. 100-foot limit. Restrooms; showers. Laundry facilities. Dump station. Equestrian camping area, 29 primitive sites.

Elk City State Park

4825 Squaw Creek Rd, Independence, KS 67301. Phone: (620) 331-6295. Located 5 miles NW of Independence via US 160 and county roads. GPS: 37.259463, -95.768544. Lake in park. Swimming beach, fishing, boating, skiing, windsurfing. Hiking, biking, nature trails. Bird watching. Archery range. Open all year. $10-24 per night. 128 sites, 11 full hookup, 75 with water and electric, 42 no hookups. Drinking water. 110-foot limit. Restrooms; showers. Laundry facilities. Dump station.

Fall River State Park

2381 Casner Creek Rd, Fall River, KS 67047. Phone: (620) 637-2213. Located on Fall River Lake about 18 miles NW of Fredonia via US 400 & Z50 Rd. GPS: 37.652842, -96.097210. Lake in park. Swimming beach, fishing, boating. Hiking trails. Wildlife viewing. Bird watching. Open all year. $10-23 per night. 138 sites, 45 with water and electric, 93 no hookups. Drinking water. 70-foot limit. Restrooms; showers. Dump station.

Glen Elder State Park

2131 180 Rd, Glen Elder, KS 67446. Phone: (785) 545-3345. Located along US 24 just W of Glen Elder. GPS: 39.513934, -98.339139. Lake in park. Swimming beach, fishing, boating (rentals), skiing, parasailing. Hiking, biking trails. Bird watching. Scenic viewpoint. Marina. Waconda Heritage Village, a living museum. Open all year. $10-23 per night. 360 sites, 120 with water and electric, 240 no hookups. Drinking water. 80-foot limit. Restrooms; showers. Dump station.

Hillsdale State Park

26001 W 255th St, Paola, KS 66071. Phone: (913) 594-3600. Located near Ottawa about 18 miles E of I-35 Exit 187 via KS 68. GPS: 38.645662, -94.917953. Lake in park. Swimming beach, fishing, boating (rentals), skiing. Hiking, biking, equestrian, walking trails. Wildlife viewing. Marina. Open all year. $10-24 per night. 319 sites, 60 full hookup, 181 with water and electric, 78 no hookups. Drinking water. 84-foot limit. Restrooms; showers. Laundry facilities. Dump station.

Historic Lake Scott State Park

101 W Scott Lake Dr, Scott City, KS 67871. Phone: (620) 872-2061. Located 13 miles N of Scott City via KS 95. GPS: 38.665593, -100.919379. Lake in park. Swimming beach, fishing, boating. Hiking, biking, equestrian, nature trails. Wildlife viewing. Scenic drive. Historic sites, building. More than 26 archeological sites in and adjacent to the park. Open all year. $10-24 per night. 155 sites, 5 full hookup, 50 with water and electric, 100 no hookups. Drinking water. Restrooms; showers. Dump station.

Kanopolis State Park

200 Horsethief Rd, Marquette, KS 67464. Phone: (785) 546-2565. Located about 13 miles NW of Marquette via KS 4 and KS 141. GPS: 38.644935, -97.987442. Lake in park. Swimming beach, fishing, boating, skiing. Hiking, biking, equestrian (rentals), nature trails. Bird watching. Park store. Marina. Scenic drive. Open all year. $10-24 per night. 333 sites, 16 full hookup, 54 with water

and electric, 63 electric only, 200 no hookups. Drinking water. 90-foot limit. Restrooms; showers. Dump station. Equestrian camp. 40 sites, 13 with water and electric, 17 electric only, 10 no hookups.

Lovewell State Park

2446 250 Rd, Webber, KS 66970. Phone: (785) 753-4971. Located about 18 miles NE of Mankato via US 36 and KS 14. GPS: 39.906367, -98.043019. Lake in park. Swimming beach, fishing, boating (rentals), skiing. Hiking trails. Wildlife viewing. Disc golf. Archery range. Park store. Marina, grill. Open all year. $10-24 per night. 460 sites, 28 full hookup, 93 with water and electric, 33 electric only, 306 no hookups. Drinking water. 50-foot limit. Restrooms; showers. Dump station.

Meade State Park

13051 V Rd, Meade, KS 67864. Phone: (620) 873-2572. Located in southwestern Kansas about 13 miles SW of town via KS 23. GPS: 37.170796, -100.434413. Lake in park. Swimming beach, fishing, boating. Hiking, biking, nature trails. Wildlife viewing. Park store. Visitor center. Open all year. $10-23 per night. 96 sites, 42 with water and electric, 54 no hookups. Drinking water. 100-foot limit. Restrooms; showers. Dump station.

Milford State Park

3612 State Park Rd, Milford, KS 66514. Phone: (785) 238-3014. Located near Junction City about 9 miles N of I-70 Exit 295 via US 77 and KS 57. GPS: 39.103499, -96.894710. Lake in park. Swimming beach, fishing, boating, skiing. Hiking, biking, equestrian trails. Wildlife viewing. Bird watching. Park store. Nature center. Marina. Open all year. $10-24 per night. 245 sites, 53 full hookup, 90 with water and electric, 102 no hookups. Drinking water. 75-foot limit. Restrooms; showers. Laundry facilities. Dump station.

Perry State Park

5441 W Lake Rd, Ozawkie, KS 66070. Phone: (785) 246-3449. Located about 12 miles NE of Topeka via US 24 and KS 237. GPS: 39.144249, -95.488795. Lake in park. Swimming beach, fishing, boating. Hiking, biking, equestrian, nature trails. Bird watching. Open all year. $10-23 per night. 318 sites, 118 with water and electric, 200 no hookups. Drinking water. 100-foot limit. Restrooms; showers. Dump station. Equestrian camp, 16 sites with water and electric hookups.

Pomona State Park

22900 S Highway 368, Vassar, KS 66543. Phone: (785) 828-4933. Located 30 miles S of Topeka on the south shore of Pomona Reservoir, about 1 mile N of K-268 on K-368. GPS: 38.652156, -95.600852. Lake in park. Swimming beach, fishing, boating, skiing. Hiking, biking trails. Wildlife viewing. Park store. Marina. Restaurant. Open all year. $10-24 per night. 292 sites, 45 full hookup, 97 with water and electric, 150 no hookups. Drinking water. 70-foot limit. Restrooms; showers. Laundry facilities. Dump station.

Prairie Dog State Park

13037 State Highway 261, Norton, KS 67654. Phone: (785) 877-2953. Located on Sebelius Reservoir, 5 miles W of Norton via US 36 and KS 261. GPS: 39.812640, -99.963968. Lake in park. Swimming beach, fishing, boating, skiing, parasailing. Hiking, biking, nature trails. Scenic viewpoint. Archery range. Marina. Restaurant. Open all year. $10-24 per night. 164 sites, 10 full hookup, 67 with water and electric, 12 electric only, 75 no hookups. Drinking water. 110-foot limit. Restrooms; showers. Laundry facilities. Dump station.

Sand Hills State Park

4207 E 56th Ave, Hutchinson, KS 67502. Phone: (316) 542-3664. Located 6 miles NE of Hutchinson via KS 61 and 56th Ave. GPS: 38.115578, -97.856965. Lake in park. Fishing. Hiking, biking, equestrian trails. Wildlife viewing. Bird watching. Open all year. $10-24 per night. 64 sites, 44 full hookup, 20 with water and electric. Drinking water. Restrooms; showers. Dump station.

Tuttle Creek State Park

5800 A River Pond Rd, Manhattan, KS 66502. Phone: (785) 539-7941. Located near Manhattan about 16 miles N of I-70 Exit 313 via KS 177 and US 24. GPS: 39.257390, -96.579887. Lake in park. Swimming beach, fishing, boating (rentals), skiing, scuba diving. Hiking, biking, equestrian, nature trails. Wildlife viewing. Disc golf. Archery range. Shooting Range. Park store. Marina. Open all year. $10-24 per night. 719 sites, 13 full hookup, 167 with water and electric, 39 electric only, 500 no hookups. Drinking water. 100-foot limit. Restrooms; showers. Laundry facilities. Dump station.

Webster State Park

1140 Ten Rd, Stockton, KS 67669. Phone: (785) 425-6775. Located 10 miles W of Stockton via US 24. GPS: 39.417107, -99.435796. Lake in park. Fishing, boating, skiing. Hiking, biking trails. Bird watching. Scenic viewpoint. Park store. Open all year. $10-23 per night. 253 sites, 87 with water and electric, 66 electric only, 100 no hookups. Drinking water. 102-foot limit. Restrooms; showers. Dump station.

Wilson State Park

#3 State Park Rd, Sylvan Grove, KS 67481. Phone: (785) 658-2465. Located on Wilson Lake about 5 miles N of I-70 Exit 206 via KS 232. GPS: 38.911809, -98.501249. Lake in park. Swimming beach, fishing, boating (rentals). Hiking, biking, walking trails. Marina. Scenic drive. Open all year. $10-24 per night. 239 sites, 4 full hookup, 105 with water and electric, 30 electric only, 100 no hookups. Drinking water. Restrooms; showers. Laundry facilities. Dump station.

Kentucky

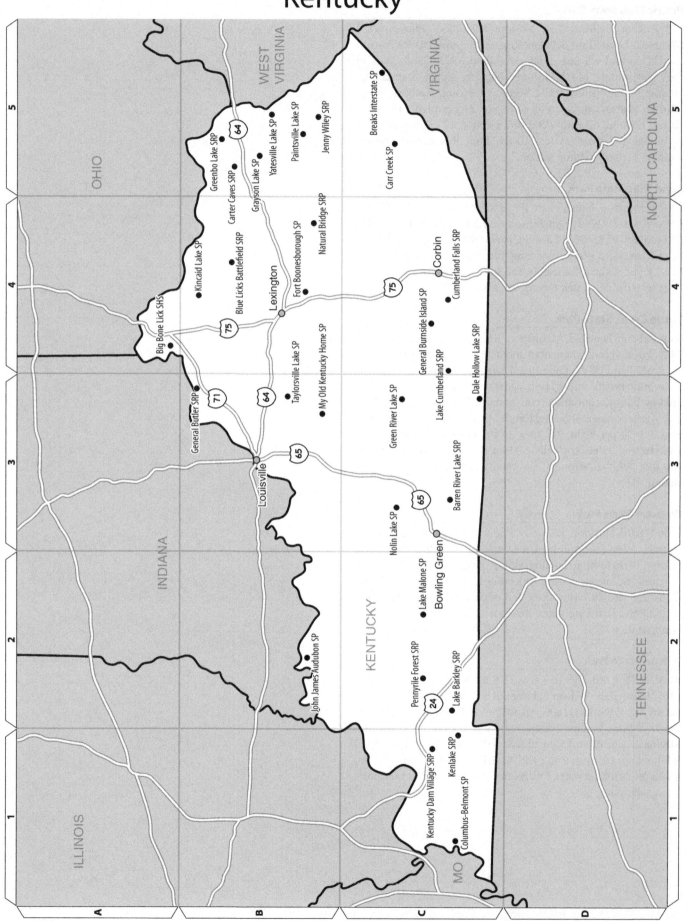

OHIO

WEST VIRGINIA

VIRGINIA

NORTH CAROLINA

INDIANA

ILLINOIS

KENTUCKY

TENNESSEE

MO

Breaks Interstate SP

Greenbo Lake SRP

Paintsville Lake SP

Jenny Wiley SRP

Yatesville Lake SP

Carter Caves SRP

Grayson Lake SP

Carr Creek SP

Kincaid Lake SP

Blue Licks Battlefield SRP

Natural Bridge SRP

Fort Boonesborough SP

Lexington

Cumberland Falls SRP

Corbin

Big Bone Lick SHS

Cumberland Falls SRP

General Burnside Island SP

Taylorsville Lake SP

My Old Kentucky Home SP

Dale Hollow Lake SRP

General Butler SRP

Louisville

Green River Lake SP

Lake Cumberland SRP

Barren River Lake SRP

Nolin Lake SP

Bowling Green

Lake Malone SP

John James Audubon SP

Pennyrile Forest SRP

Lake Barkley SRP

Kenlake SRP

Kentucky Dam Village SRP

Columbus-Belmont SP

Kentucky

Kentucky State Parks
2 Hudson Hollow Rd, Unit 1
Frankfort, KY 40601

Phone: (502) 564-2172
Internet: parks.ky.gov
Reservations: Online or call park.

Kentucky Park Locator

Kentucky Parks

Barren River Lake State Resort Park

1149 State Park Rd, Lucas, KY 42156. Phone: (270) 646-2151. Located about 11 miles NE of Scottsville via US 31E. GPS: 36.854359, -86.056422. Swimming beach, fishing, boating (rentals). Hiking, biking trails. Bird watching. Golf course, pro shop. Park store, gift shop. Information center. Marina. Lodge, restaurant, bar. Open Apr-Oct. $20-35 per night. 99 sites with water and electric hookups (some with sewer). 103-foot limit. Restrooms; showers. Laundry facilities. Dump station.

Big Bone Lick State Historic Site

3380 Beaver Rd, Union, KY 41091. Phone: (859) 384-3522. Located about 9 miles SW of Union via US 42 and KY 338. GPS: 38.883795, -84.747273. Swimming pool. Hiking, walking trails. Bird watching. Miniature golf. Camp store. Visitor center. Museum. Bison herd. Open Mar-Nov. $25-30 per night. 62 sites with water and electric hookups. 47-foot limit. Restrooms; showers. Laundry facilities. Dump station.

Blue Licks Battlefield State Resort Park

10299 Maysville Rd, Carlisle, KY 40311. Phone: (859) 289-5507. Located 10 miles N of Carlisle via Hwy 1455 and US 68. GPS: 38.429246, -83.992059. Swimming pool, fishing, boating. Hiking, biking trails. Bird watching. Miniature golf. Nature center. Lodge, restaurant. Museum. Gift shop. Historic site. Open Mar-Nov. $20-28 per night. 51 sites with water and electric hookups. 54-foot limit. Restrooms; showers. Dump station.

Breaks Interstate State Park

627 Commission Circle, Breaks, VA 24607. Phone: (276) 865-4413. Located on Kentucky/Virginia state line about 8 miles SE of Elkhorn City, Kentucky, via KY 80. GPS: 37.295325, -82.297812. Lake in park. Swimming pool, water park, fishing, boating (rentals), rafting. Hiking, biking, equestrian trails. Scenic viewpoint. Golf course. Camp store. Visitor center. Open Mar-Nov. $20-35 per night, 138 sites with water and electric hookups. 62-foot limit. Restrooms; showers. Laundry facilities. Dump station.

Carr Creek State Park

2086 Smithboro Rd, Sassafras, KY 41759. Phone: (606) 642-4050. Located 3 miles E of Sassafras via KY 15. GPS: 37.229492, -83.004165. Lake in park. Swimming beach, fishing, boating (rentals). Biking trails. Wildlife viewing. Marina. Open Apr-Nov. $22-25 per night. 39 sites with water and electric hookups. 60-foot limit. Restrooms; showers. Laundry facilities. Dump station.

Carter Caves State Resort Park

344 Caveland Dr, Olive Hill, KY 41164. Phone: (606) 286-4411. Located near Olive Hill about 4 miles N of I-64 Exit 161 via US 60 and KY 182. GPS: 38.375498, -83.130709. Lake in park. Swimming pool, fishing, boating. Hiking, biking, equestrian trails. Wildlife viewing. Bird watching. Miniature golf. Archery range. Rock climbing. Welcome center, gift shop. Restaurant. Cave tours. Open all year. $20-33 per night. 90 sites, 19 full hookup, 71 with water and electric. 64-foot limit. Restrooms; showers. Laundry facilities. Dump station. Equestrian area, 8 sites with full hookups. $35-38 per night.

Columbus-Belmont State Park

350 Park Rd, Columbus, KY 42032. Phone: (270) 677-2327. Located near the Mississippi River about 10 miles SW of Bardwell via KY 123. GPS: 36.762040, -89.107310. Fishing (river), boating. Hiking trails. Bird watching. Scenic viewpoint. Miniature golf. Information Center. Museum. Snack bar. Gift shop. Scenic drive. Open all year. $22-34 per night. 38 sites, 10 full hookup, 28 with water and electric. 53-foot limit. Restrooms; showers. Laundry facilities. Dump station.

Cumberland Falls State Resort Park

7351 Highway 90, Corbin, KY 40701. Phone: (606) 528-4121. Located near Corbin about 15 miles SW of I-75 Exit 25 via Cumberland Falls Rd. GPS: 36.838271, -84.343320. Swimming pool, fishing (river), boating. Hiking trails. Bird watching. Observation deck. Camp store. Information center. Lodge, restaurant. Waterfalls. 1937 Fire tower. Gift shop. Gem mining. Guided horseback trail rides. Open Mar-Nov. $27-33 per night. 50 sites with water and electric hookups. 30-foot limit. Restrooms; showers. Laundry facilities. Dump station.

Dale Hollow Lake State Resort Park

5970 State Park Rd, Burkesville, KY 42717. Resort: (270) 433-7431. Located about 13 miles SE of Burkesville via KY90, SR-449, and SR-1206. GPS: 36.653453, -85.291843. Swimming pool, fishing, boating. Hiking, biking (rentals), equestrian trails. Bird watching. Scenic viewpoint. Golf course, pro shop. Miniature golf. Camp store. Information center. Marina, store. Restaurant, bar. Cindy Cave, guided tours. Open Mar-Nov. $25-40 per night. 120 sites, 40 full hookup, 80 with water and electric. 41-foot limit. Restrooms; showers. Laundry facilities. Dump station. Equestrian area with 24 sites. $30-40 per night.

Fort Boonesborough State Park

4375 Boonesboro Rd, Richmond, KY 40475. Phone: (859) 527-3131. Located near Richmond about 5 miles E of I-75 Exit 95 via KY 627. GPS: 37.898037, -84.268102. Swimming pool, fishing, boating. Hiking, biking trails. Miniature golf. Camp store. Museum. Fort reconstructed as a working fort complete with cabins, blockhouses and furnishings, period craft demonstrations. Gift shop, handmade pioneer items. Open all year. $31-38 per night. 156 sites, 18 full hookup, 148 with water and electric. 60-foot limit. Restrooms; showers. Laundry facilities. Dump station.

General Burnside Island State Park

8801 S Hwy 27, Burnside, KY 42519. Phone: (606) 561-4104. Located just S of Burnside via US 27. GPS: 36.980568, -84.601421. Lake in park. Fishing, boating (rentals), skiing. Wildlife viewing. Bird watching. Golf course. Marina. Open Mar-Nov. $24-27 per night. 94 sites with water and electric hookups. 60-foot limit. Restrooms; showers. Laundry facilities. Dump station.

General Butler State Resort Park

1608 Hwy 227, Carrollton, KY 41008. Phone: (502) 732-4384. Located about 2 miles S of Carrollton via KY 227. GPS: 38.669219, -85.151150. Lake in park. Swimming pool, fishing, boating (rentals). Hiking, biking, walking trails. Bird watching. Scenic viewpoint. Miniature golf. Lodge, gift shop, restaurant, lounge. Butler-Turpin historic home built in 1859, tours. Open all year. $32-43 per night. 111 sites, 9 full hookup, 102 with water and electric. 60-foot limit. Restrooms; showers. Laundry facilities. Dump station.

Grayson Lake State Park

314 Grayson Lake State Park Rd, Olive Hill, KY 41164. Phone: (606) 474-9727. Located 10 miles S of Grayson via KY 7. GPS: 38.201220, -83.028683. Fishing, boating (rentals). Hiking, biking trails. Wildlife viewing. Scenic viewpoint. Golf course, pro shop. Information center. Open Mar-Nov. $25-28 per night. 71 sites with water and electric hookups. 69-foot limit. Restrooms; showers. Laundry facilities. Dump station.

Green River Lake State Park

179 Park Office Rd, Campbellsville, KY 42718. Phone: (270) 465-8255. Located about 8 miles S of Campbellsville via KY 55 and KY 1061. GPS: 37.273345, -85.316738. Swimming beach, fishing, boating (rentals), skiing. Hiking, biking (rentals) trails. Bird watching. Miniature golf. Camp store. Information center. Gift shop. Marina, restaurant. Open Mar-Dec. $26-34 per night. 167 sites with water and electric hookups. 51-foot limit. Restrooms; showers. Laundry facilities. Dump station.

Greenbo Lake State Resort Park

965 Lodge Rd, Greenup, KY 41144. Phone: (606) 473-7324. Located about 11 miles S of Greenup via KY 1 and KY 1711. GPS: 38.484077, -82.889885. Swimming pool (no lake swimming), fishing, boating (rentals). Hiking, biking (rentals), equestrian trails. Bird watching. Miniature golf. Camp store. Marina. Lodge, gift shop, restaurant. Open all year. $18-41 per night. 79 sites, 42 full hookup, 37 with water and electric. 100-foot limit. Restrooms; showers. Laundry facilities. Dump station.

Jenny Wiley State Resort Park

75 Theatre Ct, Prestonsburg, KY 41653. Phone: (606) 889-1790. Located 3 miles N of Prestonsburg via KY 3 and KY 321. GPS: 37.715739, -82.740729. Lake in park. Swimming beach, fishing, boating (rentals), skiing, scuba diving. Hiking, biking trails. Scenic viewpoint. Camp store. Nature center. Gift shop. Marina. Lodge, restaurant, bar. Elk viewing tour. Open Mar-Nov. $23-35 per night. 121 sites, 61 full hookups, 60 with water and electric hookups. 95-foot limit. Restrooms; showers. Laundry facilities. Dump station.

John James Audubon State Park

3100 US Hwy 41 N, Henderson, KY 42419. Phone: (270) 826-2247. Located along US 41 in Henderson, N end of town. GPS: 37.881254, -87.563561. Lake in park. Swimming beach, fishing, boating (rentals). Hiking, biking, nature, walking trails. Wildlife viewing. Bird watching. Scenic viewpoint. Golf course, pro shop. Nature center. Museum, gift shop. Open Mar-Nov. $26-34 per night. 69 sites with water and electric hookups. 63-foot limit. Restrooms; showers. Dump station.

Kenlake State Resort Park

542 Kenlake Rd, Hardin, KY 42048. Phone: (270) 474-2211. Located 9 miles E of Hardin via KY 402 and US 68. GPS: 36.771874, -88.138147. Lake in park. Swimming beach, fishing, boating (rentals), skiing. Hiking, biking (rentals) trails. Bird watching. Information center. Marina, restaurant. Lodge, gift shop, restaurant. Botanical Garden. Open Mar-Nov. $19-28 per night. 90 sites with water and electric hookups. 39-foot limit. Restrooms; showers. Laundry facilities. Dump station.

Kentucky Dam Village State Resort Park

113 Administration Dr, Calvert City, KY 42044. Phone: (270) 362-4271. Located about 5 miles E of Calvert City via KY 282. GPS: 37.012577, -88.282007. Lake in park. Swimming beach, fishing, boating (rentals). Hiking, biking, walking trails. Golf course, pro shop. Camp store. Marina. Lodge, restaurant, lounge. Open Mar-Nov. $22-27 per night. 221 sites with water and electric hookups. 57-foot limit. Restrooms; showers. Laundry facilities. Dump station.

Kincaid Lake State Park

565 Kincaid Park Rd, Falmouth, KY 41040. Phone: (859) 654-3531. Located 4 miles N of Falmouth via KY 159. GPS: 38.723696, -84.281488. Swimming pool, fishing, boating (rentals). Hiking trails. Wildlife viewing. Golf course, pro shop. Miniature golf. Camp store, gift shop. Marina. Open Apr-Nov. $22-28 per night. 84 sites with water and electric hookups. 67-foot limit. Restrooms; showers. Laundry facilities. Dump station.

Lake Barkley State Resort Park

3500 State Park Rd, Cadiz, KY 42211. Phone: (270) 924-1131. Located 8 miles SW of Cadiz via US 68 and KY 1489. GPS: 36.854945, -87.914755. Swimming pool (lodge guest) beach, fishing, boating (rentals), skiing. Hiking, biking (rentals) trails. Bird watching. Golf course, pro shop. Trap shooting. Marina, store, grill. Lodge, restaurant, bar. Open Mar-Nov. $17-24 per night. 79 sites with water and electric hookups. 65-foot limit. Restrooms; showers. Laundry facilities. Dump station.

Lake Cumberland State Resort Park

5465 State Park Rd, Jamestown, KY 42629. Phone: (270) 343-3111. Located 13 miles S of Jamestown via US 127 and State Park Rd. GPS: 36.919981, -85.043983. Swimming pool, fishing, boating (rentals), skiing. Hiking trails. Wildlife viewing. Scenic viewpoint. Disc golf. Miniature golf. Nature center, store, gifts. Marina. Lodge, restaurant, bar. Open Mar-Dec. $20-26 per night. 124 sites with water and electric hookups. 41-foot limit. Restrooms; showers. Laundry facilities. Dump station.

Lake Malone State Park

331 State Route Rd 8001, Dunmore, KY 42339. Phone: (270) 657-2111. Located about 4 miles W of Dunmore via KY 973. GPS: 37.075299, -87.040405. Swimming beach, fishing, boating. Hiking trails. Wildlife viewing. Scenic viewpoint. Marina, store. Open Mar-Nov. $22-25 per night. 25 sites with water and electric hookups. 70-foot limit. Restrooms; showers. Laundry facilities. Dump station.

My Old Kentucky Home State Park

501 E Stephen Foster Ave, Bardstown, KY 40004. Phone: (502) 348-3502. Located 1.5 miles SE of Bardstown via US 150 and Parkview Ave. GPS: 37.798272, -85.457526. Bird watching. Golf course, pro shop. Visitor center. Historic Mansion, tours. Open Mar-Nov. $24-33 per night. 39 sites, 5 full hookup, 34 with water and electric. 55-foot limit. Restrooms; showers. Dump station.

Natural Bridge State Resort Park

2135 Natural Bridge Rd, Slade, KY 40376. Phone: (606) 663-2214. Located 3 miles S of Slade via KY11. GPS: 37.766568, -83.674674. Lake in park. Swimming pool, fishing, boating (rentals). Hiking trails. Wildlife viewing. Scenic viewpoint. Miniature golf. Nature center. Lodge, gift shop, restaurant, bar. Sky Lift ride. Two camping areas open Mar-Nov. $26-34 per night. 87 sites, 51 with water and electric hookups, 6 electric only, 30 water only. 57-foot limit. Restrooms; showers. Laundry facilities. Dump station.

Nolin Lake State Park

2998 Brian Creek Rd, Mammoth Cave, KY 42259. Phone: (270) 286-4240. Located about 25 miles W of Munfordville via KY 88 and KY 1827. GPS: 37.296080, -86.212841. Swimming beach, fishing, boating, skiing. Hiking, biking trails. Camp store. Nature center. Scenic drive. Open all year. $22-24 per night. 32 sites with water and electric hookups. 90-foot limit. Restrooms; showers. Laundry facilities. Dump station.

Paintsville Lake State Park

1551 KY 2275, Staffordsville, KY 41256. Phone: (606) 297-8486. Located 5 miles W of Paintsville via KY 40 and KY 2275. GPS: 37.842930, -82.878659. Swimming beach, fishing, boating (rentals), skiing. Hiking, biking, equestrian, walking trails. Wildlife viewing. Marina. Open all year. $30-32 per night. 32 full hookup sites. 48-foot limit. Restrooms; showers. Laundry facilities.

Pennyrile Forest State Resort Park

20781 Pennyrile Lodge Rd, Dawson Springs, KY 42408. Phone: (270) 797-3421. Located 8 miles S of Dawson Springs via KY 109 and KY 398. GPS: 37.072398, -87.656183. Lake in park. Swimming beach, fishing, boating (rentals). Hiking, biking, equestrian trails. Bird watching. Golf course, pro shop. Miniature golf. Camp store. Lodge, gift shop, restaurant. Scenic drive. Open all year. $20-25 per night. 68 sites with water and electric hookups. 60-foot limit. Restrooms; showers. Laundry facilities. Dump station. Equestrian area, 8 sites with full hookups. $35-40 per night.

Taylorsville Lake State Park

1320 Park Rd, Taylorsville, KY 40046. Phone: (502) 477-8713. Located about 9 miles E of Taylorsville via KY 44 and KY 248. GPS: 38.028936, -85.255707. Swimming beach, fishing, boating (rentals), skiing. Hiking, biking (rentals), equestrian trails. Information center. Marina, store, deli. Open Apr-Dec. $26-29 per night. 45 sites with water and electric hookups. 67-foot limit. Restrooms; showers. Laundry facilities. Dump station. Equestrian area, 10 sites with water and electric hookups. $28-32 per night.

Yatesville Lake State Park

2667 Pleasant Ridge Rd, Louisa, KY 41230. Phone: (606) 673-1492. Located about 9 miles SW of Louisa via KY 32 and KY 3215. GPS: 38.096683, -82.682451. Swimming beach, fishing, boating (rentals), skiing. Hiking, biking, equestrian trails. Bird watching. Golf course, pro shop. Miniature golf. Marina, store. Open Mar-Nov. $24-26 per night. 27 sites with water and electric hookups. 35-foot limit. Restrooms; showers. Laundry facilities. Dump station.

Louisiana

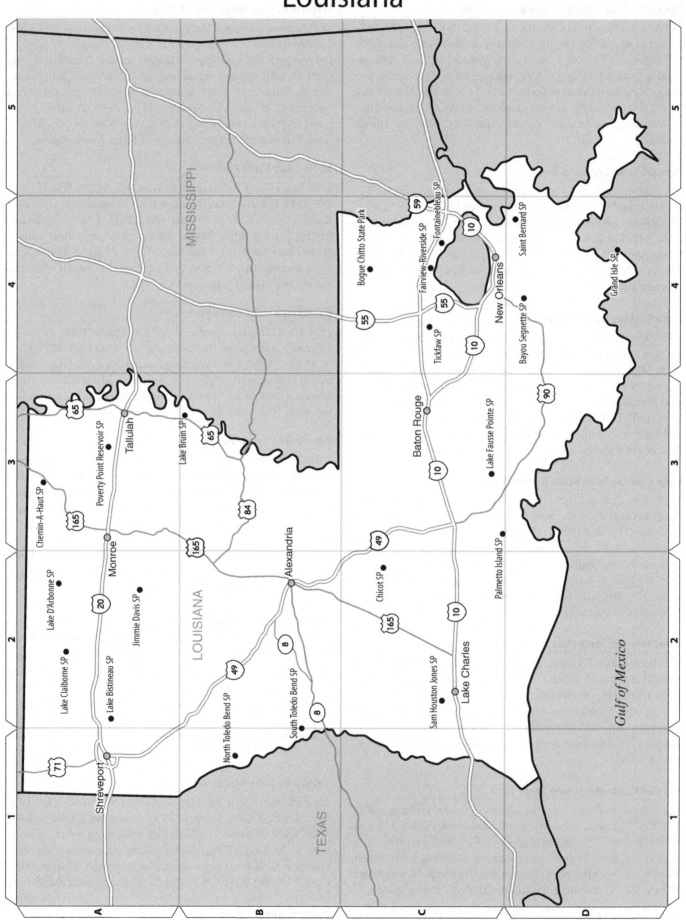

Louisiana

Louisiana Office of State Parks
PO Box 44426
Baton Rouge, LA 70804

Phone: (225) 342-8111 or (888) 677-1400
Internet: www.crt.state.la.us/louisiana-state-parks
Reservations: Online or call park.

Louisiana Park Locator

Louisiana Parks

Bayou Segnette State Park

7777 Westbank Expressway, Westwego, LA 70094. Phone: (504) 736-7140. Located in southwestern Westwego along the Westbank Expressway (Business US 90). GPS: 29.887746, -90.162501. Swimming pool, fishing, boating. Hiking, nature trails. Wildlife viewing. Bird watching. Open all year. $25-33 per night. 99 sites with water and electric hookups. 50-foot limit. Restrooms; showers. Laundry facilities. Dump station.

Bogue Chitto State Park

17049 State Park Blvd, Franklinton, LA 70438. Phone: (985) 839-5707. Located about 8 miles S of Franklinton via LA 25. GPS: 30.767527, -90.157307. Lake in park. Swimming beach, tubing, fishing, boating (rentals). Hiking, biking, equestrian (rentals), walking trails. Wildlife viewing. Bird watching. Disc golf. Visitor center. Open all year. $25-33 per night. 81 sites, 49 full hookup, 32 with water and electric. 88-foot limit. Restrooms; showers. Dump station.

Chemin-A-Haut State Park

14656 State Park Rd, Bastrop, LA 71220. Phone: (318) 283-0812. Located about 10 miles N of Bastrop via US 425. GPS: 32.910473, -91.849458. Lake in park. Swimming pool, fishing, boating (rentals). Hiking, biking, equestrian, walking trails. Bird watching. Visitor center. Open all year. $25-33 per night. 26 sites with full hookups. 60-foot limit. Restrooms; showers. Dump station.

Chicot State Park

3469 Chicot Park Rd, Ville Platte, LA 70586. Phone: (337) 363-2403. Located 8 miles N of Ville Platte via LA 3042. GPS: 30.790071, -92.284510. Lake in park. Swimming pool, fishing, boating (rentals). Hiking, biking, walking trails. Wildlife viewing. Visitor center. Louisiana State Arboretum. Open all year. $25-33 per night. 198 sites with water and electric hookups. 75-foot limit. Restrooms; showers. Laundry facilities. Dump station.

Fairview Riverside State Park

119 Fairview Dr, Madisonville, LA 70447. Phone: (985) 845-3318. Located 1 mile E of Madisonville via LA 22. GPS: 30.408865, -90.140217. Lake in park. Fishing, boating. Hiking, nature, walking trails. Bird watching. Otis House Museum, originally built in the 1880s, tours. Boat tours. Open all year. $20-33 per night. 81 sites with water and electric hookups. 58-foot limit. Restrooms; showers. Laundry facilities. Dump station.

Fontainebleau State Park

67883 Highway 1089, Mandeville, LA 70448. Phone: (985) 624-4443. Located 3 miles SE of Mandeville via US 190. GPS: 30.345091, -90.022743. Lake in park. Swimming beach, fishing, boating. Hiking, biking, nature, walking trails. Bird watching. Visitor center. Open all year. $18-33 per night. 167 sites, 8 full hookup, 122 with water and electric, 37 no hookups. 135-foot limit. Restrooms; showers. Laundry facilities. Dump station.

Grand Isle State Park

Admiral Craik Dr, Grand Isle, LA 70358. Phone: (985) 787-2559. Located 2 miles E of town along LA 1. GPS: 29.257915, -89.956429. On Gulf of Mexico. Swimming beach, fishing, boating. Hiking, walking trails. Bird watching. Observation tower. Visitor center. Open all year. $25-33 per night. 49 sites with water and electric hookups. 80-foot limit. Restrooms; showers. Dump station.

Jimmie Davis State Park

1209 State Park Rd, Chatham, LA 71226. Phone: (318) 249-2595. Located 7 miles SW of Chatham via LA 4 and Lakeshore Dr. GPS: 32.258377, -92.518344. Lake in park. Swimming beach, fishing, boating, skiing. Hiking, biking, walking trails. Bird watching. Open all year. $20-33 per night. 73 sites with water and electric hookups. 74-foot limit. Restrooms; showers. Laundry facilities. Dump station.

Lake Bistineau State Park

103 State Park Rd, Doyline, LA 71023. Phone: (318) 745-3503. Located 7 miles S of Doyline via LA 163. GPS: 32.441195, -93.387222. Swimming beach, fishing, boating (rentals). Hiking,

biking, equestrian, walking trails. Bird watching. Disc golf. Visitor center. Open all year. $20-33 per night. 61 sites with water and electric hookups. 62-foot limit. Restrooms. Dump station.

Lake Bruin State Park

201 State Park Rd, Saint Joseph, LA 71366. Phone: (318) 766-3530. Located 4 miles NE of Saint Joseph via LA 605 and LA 604. GPS: 31.961802, -91.200110. Swimming beach, fishing, boating (rentals). Hiking, biking, walking trails. Bird watching. Open all year. $20-33 per night. 48 sites with water and electric hookups. 69-foot limit. Restrooms; showers. Laundry facilities. Dump station.

Lake Claiborne State Park

225 State Park Rd, Homer, LA 71040. Phone: (318) 927-2976. Located 11 miles SE of Homer via LA 146. GPS: 32.724939, -92.922940. Swimming beach, fishing, boating (rentals), skiing. Hiking, biking, nature trails. Bird watching. Scenic viewpoint. Disc golf. Open all year. $20-33 per night. 87 sites with water and electric hookups. 80-foot limit. Restrooms; showers. Laundry facilities. Dump station.

Lake D'Arbonne State Park

3628 Evergreen Rd, Farmerville, LA 71241. Phone: (318) 368-2086. Located 6 miles W of Farmerville via LA 2. GPS: 32.783074, -92.490888. Swimming pool, fishing, boating (rentals), skiing. Hiking, biking trails. Wildlife viewing. Scenic viewpoint. Disc golf. Visitor center. Open all year. $20-33 per night. 58 sites with water and electric hookups. 63-foot limit. Restrooms; showers. Laundry facilities. Dump station.

Lake Fausse Pointe State Park

5400 Levee Rd, Saint Martinville, LA 70582. Phone: (337) 229-4764. Located about 20 miles E of Saint Martinville via LA 96, LA 679 and Bayou Benoit Levee Rd. GPS: 30.062050, -91.608290. Water playground. Fishing, boating (rentals). Hiking, biking, nature trails. Wildlife viewing. Visitor center. Open all year. $20-33 per night. 46 sites, 14 full hookup, 32 with water and electric. 80-foot limit. Restrooms; showers. Laundry facilities. Dump station.

North Toledo Bend State Park

2907 North Toledo Park Rd, Zwolle, LA 71486. Phone: (318) 645-4715. Located about 9 miles SW of Zwolle via LA 482 and LA 3229. GPS: 31.563834, -93.735691. Lake in park. Swimming pool, fishing, boating (rentals). Hiking, biking trails. Wildlife viewing. Scenic viewpoint. Open all year. $20-33 per night. 63 sites with water and electric hookups. 45-foot limit. Restrooms; showers. Laundry facilities. Dump station.

Palmetto Island State Park

19501 Pleasant Rd, Abbeville, LA 70510. Phone: (337) 893-3930. Located 10 miles S of Abbeville via LA 82 and LA 690. GPS: 29.869532, -92.150435. Lake in park. Water playground. Fishing, boating (rentals). Hiking, biking, walking trails. Wildlife viewing. Visitor center. Open all year. $20-33 per night. 96 sites, 20 full hookup, 76 with water and electric. 80-foot limit. Restrooms; showers. Dump station.

Poverty Point Reservoir State Park

1500 Poverty Point Pkwy, Delhi, LA 71232. Phone: (318) 878-7536. Located about 2 miles N of Delhi via LA 17. GPS: 32.483134, -91.493590. Lake in park. Water playground. Swimming beach, fishing, boating (rentals). Hiking, biking, nature trails. Wildlife viewing. Marina, store. Open all year. $20-33 per night. 54 sites, 45 full hookup, 9 with water and electric. 140-foot limit. Restrooms; showers. Laundry facilities. Dump station.

Saint Bernard State Park

501 Saint Bernard Pkwy, Braithwaite, LA 70040. Phone: (504) 682-2101. Located 17 miles SE of New Orleans via LA 46 and LA 39. GPS: 29.864275, -89.900523. Water playground, swimming pool, fishing, boating. Hiking, biking, nature trails. Bird watching. Open all year. $20-28 per night. 51 sites with water and electric hookups. 63-foot limit. Restrooms; showers. Laundry facilities. Dump station.

Sam Houston Jones State Park

107 Sutherland Rd, Lake Charles, LA 70611. Phone: (337) 855-2665. Located near Lake Charles about 6 miles N of I-10 Exit 27 via LA 378. GPS: 30.299904, -93.256185. Fishing, boating (rentals). Hiking, biking, nature trails. Wildlife viewing. Bird watching. Disc golf. Visitor center. Open all year. $20-33 per night. 58 sites, 38 with water and electric, 20 no hookups. 75-foot limit. Restrooms; showers. Dump station.

South Toledo Bend State Park

120 Bald Eagle Rd, Anacoco, LA 71403. Phone: (337) 286-9075. Located about 16 miles W of Anacoco via LA 111, LA 392 and LA 191. GPS: 31.215607, -93.575157. Lake in park. Swimming beach, fishing, boating. Hiking, biking, nature, ATV trails. Wildlife viewing. Bird watching. Observation deck. Visitor center. Open all year. $20-33 per night. 55 sites with water and electric hookups. 90-foot limit. Restrooms; showers. Dump station.

Tickfaw State Park

27225 Patterson Rd, Springfield, LA 70462. Phone: (225) 294-5020. Located 7 miles SW of Springfield via LA 1037. GPS: 30.381525, -90.631260. Water playground. Fishing, boating (canoe rentals). Hiking, biking, walking trails. Wildlife viewing. Scenic viewpoint. Nature center, gift shop, 800-gallon aquarium. Open all year. $18-28 per night. 50 sites, 30 with water and electric hookups, 20 water only. 78-foot limit. Restrooms; showers. Laundry facilities. Dump station.

Maine

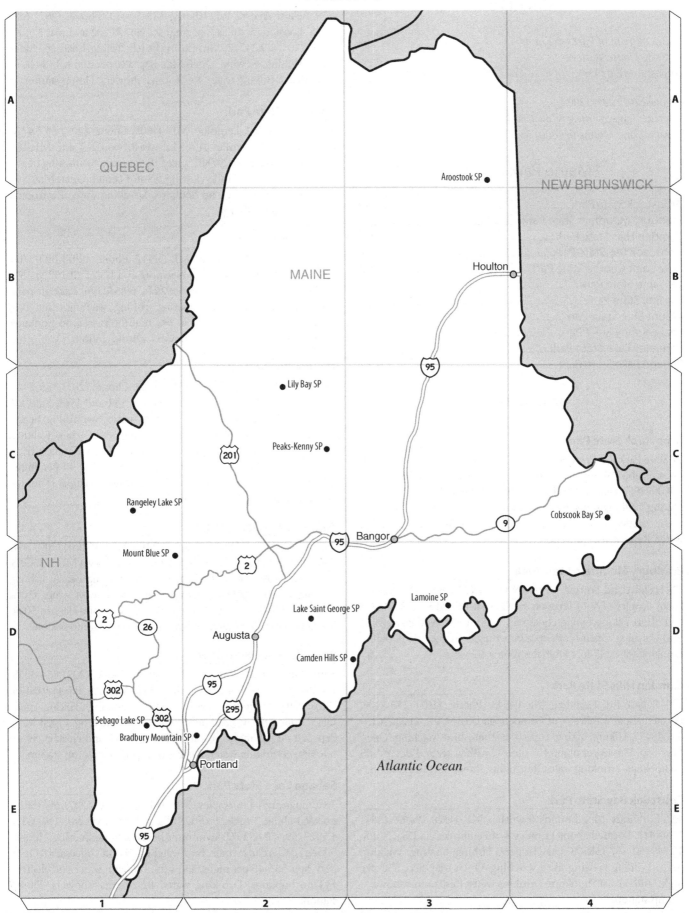

QUEBEC

NEW BRUNSWICK

Aroostook SP ●

MAINE

Houlton ○

95

Lily Bay SP ●

Peaks-Kenny SP ●

201

Rangeley Lake SP ●

Cobscook Bay SP ●

9

NH

Mount Blue SP ●

2

95 Bangor ○

2

Lamoine SP ●

26

Lake Saint George SP ●

Augusta ○

95

Camden Hills SP ●

302

295

Sebago Lake SP ●

302

Bradbury Mountain SP ●

Portland ○

Atlantic Ocean

95

Maine

Maine Bureau of Parks & Lands
22 State House Station
Augusta, ME 04333

Phone: (207) 287-3200
Internet: www.maine.gov/dacf/parks
Reservations: Online or (800) 332-1501

Maine Park Locator

Maine Parks

Aroostook State Park

87 State Park Rd, Presque Isle, ME 04769. Phone: (207) 768-8341. Located about 6 miles S of Presque Isle via US 1. GPS: 46.615469, -68.008197. Lake in park. Swimming beach, fishing, boating. Hiking, walking trails. Bird watching. Open May-Sep. $25-35 per night. 35 sites, 5 with water and electric, 25 no hookups. Drinking water. Restrooms; showers.

Bradbury Mountain State Park

528 Hallowell Rd, Pownal, ME 04069. Phone: (207) 688-4712. Located about 6 miles NW of Freeport via Pownal Rd. GPS: 43.899164, -70.179120. Hiking, biking, equestrian, nature trails. Wildlife viewing. Bird watching. Open May-Sep. $25 per night. 31 sites, no hookups. Drinking water. 35-foot limit. Restrooms; showers.

Camden Hills State Park

280 Belfast Rd, Camden, ME 04843. Phone: (207) 236-3109. Located about 2 miles N of Camden via US 1. GPS: 44.230361, -69.048435. Hiking, biking, equestrian trails. Bird watching. Open May-Sep. $35-45 per night. 107 sites, 42 with water and electric, 65 no hookups. Drinking water. Restrooms; showers. Dump station.

Cobscook Bay State Park

40 S Edmunds Rd, Edmunds Township, ME 04628. Phone: (207) 726-4412. Located about 11 miles S of Pembroke via US 1. GPS: 44.849750, -67.158508. Lake in park. Fishing, boating. Walking trails. Wildlife viewing. Bird watching. Open May-Sep. $30 per night. 106 sites, no hookups. Drinking water. Restrooms; showers. Dump station.

Lake Saint George State Park

278 Belfast-Agusta Rd, Liberty, ME 04949. Phone: (207) 589-4255. Located 27 miles E of Augusta via US 202 and ME 3. GPS: 44.397707, -69.347179. Swimming beach, fishing, boating. Hiking trails. Wildlife viewing. Open May-Sep. $30 per night. 38 sites, no hookups. Drinking water. Restrooms; showers. Dump station.

Lamoine State Park

23 State Park Rd, Lamoine, ME 04605. Phone: (207) 667-4778. Located about 10 miles SE of Ellsworth via US 1 and ME 184. GPS: 44.454646, -68.297887. Oceanfront park. Swimming beach, fishing, boating. Wildlife viewing. Visitor center. Open May-Sep. $30 per night. 61 sites, no hookups. Drinking water. Restrooms; showers. Dump station.

Lily Bay State Park

13 Myrle's Way, Greenville, ME 04441. Phone: (207) 695-2700. Located about 60 miles N of Newport and I-95 Exit 157 via ME 7, SR-23, and SR-6. GPS: 45.569201, -69.542396. Lake in park. Swimming beach, fishing, boating. Hiking, walking trails. Bird watching. Open May-Sep. $30 per night. 65 sites, no hookups. Drinking water. Restrooms; showers. Dump station.

Mount Blue State Park

187 Webb Beach Rd, Weld, ME 04285. Phone: (207) 585-2347. Located 12 miles N of Dixfield via ME 142 and West Side Rd. GPS: 44.681791, -70.449246. Lake in park. Swimming beach, fishing, boating (rentals). Hiking, biking, equestrian, walking, ATV trails. Bird watching. Nature center. Guided canoe trips, walks, and nature programs. Open May-Sep. $30-40 per night. 136 sites, 12 with water and electric, 124 no hookups. Drinking water. Restrooms; showers. Dump station.

Peaks-Kenny State Park

401 State Park Rd, Dover-Foxcroft, ME 04426. Phone: (207) 564-2003. Located about 6 miles N of Dover-Foxcroft via ME 153. GPS: 45.258808, -69.278852. Lake in park. Swimming beach, fishing, boating (canoe rentals). Hiking trails. Wildlife viewing. Open May-Sep. $30-40 per night. 56 sites, 6 with water and electric, 50 no hookups. Drinking water. Restrooms; showers. Dump station.

Rangeley Lake State Park

South Shore Drive, Rangeley, ME 04970. Phone: (207) 864-3858. Located 35 miles N of US 2 at Mexico via ME 17. GPS: 44.918175, -70.699594. Swimming beach, fishing, boating. Hiking trails. OHV trails nearby. Wildlife viewing. Bird watching. Open May-Sep. $30-40 per night. 50 sites, 11 with water and electric, 39 no hookups. Drinking water. Restrooms; showers. Dump station.

Sebago Lake State Park

3 Campground Ln, Naples, ME 04055. Phone: (207) 693-6613. Located about 3 miles S of US 302 at Naples via ME 114. GPS: 43.929759, -70.583671. Swimming beach, fishing, boating. Hiking, biking (park roads) trails. Bird watching. Food concession. Open May-Sep. $35-45 per night. 250 sites, 106 with water and electric, 144 no hookups. Drinking water. Restrooms; showers. Dump station.

Maryland

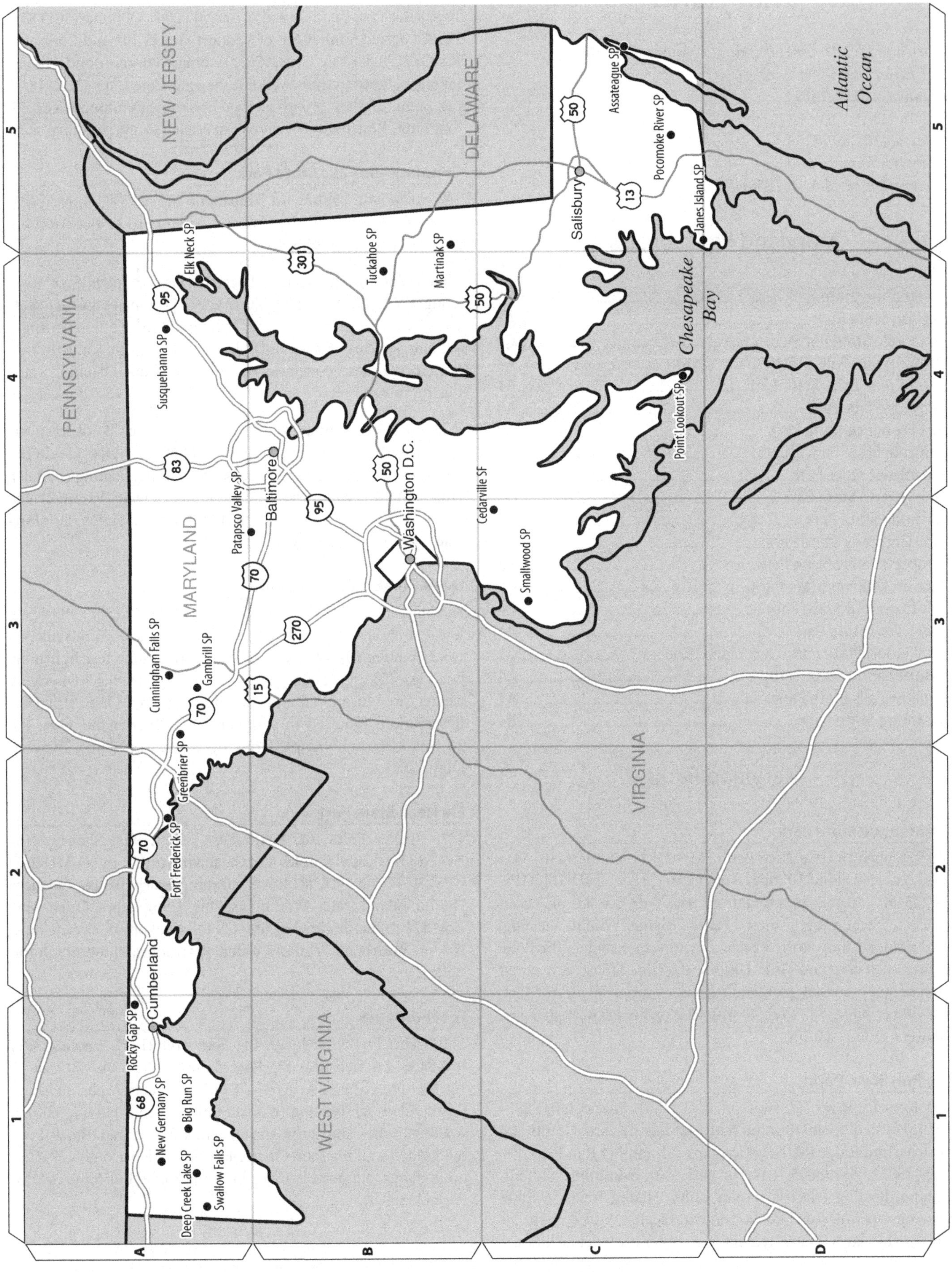

NEW JERSEY
DELAWARE
PENNSYLVANIA
MARYLAND
WEST VIRGINIA
VIRGINIA
Atlantic Ocean
Chesapeake Bay
Assateague SP
Pocomoke River SP
Janes Island SP
Salisbury
Martinak SP
Tuckahoe SP
Elk Neck SP
Susquehanna SP
Point Lookout SP
Cedarville SF
Smallwood SP
Washington D.C.
Baltimore
Patapsco Valley SP
Cunningham Falls SP
Gambrill SP
Greenbrier SP
Fort Frederick SP
Cumberland
Rocky Gap SP
New Germany SP
Big Run SP
Deep Creek Lake SP
Swallow Falls SP
50
13
301
95
83
70
270
15
68
1
2
3
4
5
A
B
C
D

Maryland

Maryland Department of Natural Resources
580 Taylor Ave
Annapolis, MD 21401

Phone: (410) 260-8367
Internet: dnr.maryland.gov
Reservations: Online or (888) 432-2267

Maryland Park Locator

Maryland Parks

Assateague State Park

6915 Stephen Decatur Hwy, Berlin, MD 21811. Phone: (410) 641-2918. Located about 10 miles S of Ocean City, via MD 611. GPS: 38.235490, -75.138630. Oceanfront park with 2 miles of ocean beaches. Swimming, fishing, boating. Biking. Wildlife viewing, wild ponies. Camp store. Visitor center. Nature center. The Pony Express Giftshop and Grill. Historic Rackliffe House, a restored 18th-century coastal plantation house, tours. Open Apr-Oct. $27-39 per night. 342 sites, 40 with electric hookups. Restrooms; showers. Dump station.

Big Run State Park

10368 Savage River Rd, Swanton, MD 21561. Phone: (301) 895-5453. Located about 13 miles S of I-68 Exit 22 near Grantsville via Chestnut Ridge Rd, New Germany Rd, and Big Run Rd. GPS: 39.544502, -79.138803. Lake in park. No swimming allowed. Fishing, boating (electric motors only). Hiking trails. Wildlife viewing. Open all year. No reservations accepted. $10 per night. 29 sites, no hookups. Water hydrant. Two waterless toilet facilities.

Cedarville State Forest

10201 Bee Oak Road, Brandywine MD 20613. Phone: (301) 888-1410. Located 6 miles NE of Waldorf via US 301 and Cedarville Rd. GPS: 38.646955, -76.829927. Fishing, four-acre pond. Hiking, biking, equestrian trails. Wildlife viewing. Open Apr-Oct. $18-25 per night. 27 sites, 9 with electric hookups. Drinking water. 65-foot limit. Restrooms; showers. Equestrian camp, primitive sites.

Cunningham Falls State Park

14039 Catoctin Hollow Rd, Thurmont, MD 21788. Phone: (301) 271-7574. Located in the Catoctin Mountains of north-central Maryland. Two camping areas.

Manor Area Campground: Located about 3 miles S of town along US 15. GPS: 39.589552, -77.433851. Open Apr-Oct. $21-28 per night. Fishing, boating. Hiking, biking, equestrian trails. Wildlife viewing. Scales and Tales Aviary. Historic Catoctin Iron Furnace. 21 sites, 10 with electric, 11 no hookups. Drinking water. Restrooms; showers.

William Houck Campground: Located 3 miles W of town via MD 77. GPS: 39.622740, -77.468601. Open Apr-Oct. $21-28 per night. Lake in park. Swimming beach, fishing, boating (rentals). Hiking, biking, equestrian trails. Wildlife viewing. Visitor center. Snack bar. 106 sites, 33 with electric, 73 no hookups. Drinking water. Restrooms; showers.

Deep Creek Lake State Park

898 State Park Rd, Swanton, MD 21561. Phone: (301) 387-5563. Located about 20 miles S of I-68 Exit 14A near Grantsville via US 219. GPS: 39.512334, -79.297973. Swimming beach, fishing, boating. Hiking, biking trails. Wildlife viewing. Discovery Center, an educational and interpretive center. Open Apr-Dec. Reservations required in summer. $21-28 per night. 112 sites, 26 with electric hookups. Drinking water. Restrooms; showers. Dump station.

Elk Neck State Park

4395 Turkey Point Rd, North East, MD 21901. Phone: (410) 287-5333. Located 9 miles S of the town North East via MD 272. GPS: 39.479760, -75.981497. Swimming beach, fishing, boating. Hiking, biking trails. Wildlife viewing. Camp store. Open Apr-Nov. $21-28 per night. 250 sites, 28 full hookup, 19 electric only, 203 no hookups. Drinking water. Restrooms; showers. Dump station.

Fort Frederick

11100 Fort Frederick Road, Big Pool MD 21711. Phone: (301) 842-2155. Located near Big Pool about 1 mile S of I-70 Exit 12 via MD 56. GPS: 39.617960, -78.002502. Lake in park. Fishing (lake and river), boating (electric motors only). Hiking, biking, walking trails. Camp store. Visitor center. Museum. Historic Fort, self guided walking tour. Open May-Nov. $15 per night. 29 sites, no hookups. No potable water in campground but some nearby. Portable toilets.

Gambrill State Park

8602 Gambrill Park Rd, Frederick, MD 21702. Phone: (301) 271-7574. Located about 6 miles NW of Frederick via US 40. GPS: 39.455678, -77.494151. Fishing (small pond). Hiking, biking, equestrian trails. Wildlife viewing. Scenic viewpoint. Nature center. Open Apr-Oct. $19-25 per night. 19 sites, 6 with electric, 13 no hookups. Drinking water. Restrooms; showers. Dump station.

Greenbrier State Park

c/o South Mountain Recreation Area, 21843 National Pike, Boonsboro, MD 21713. Phone: (301) 791-4767. Located 10 miles SE of Hagerstown via US 40. GPS: 39.541533, -77.608634. Lake in park. Swimming beach, fishing, boating (rentals). Hiking, biking trails. Wildlife viewing. Camp store. Visitor center. Open Apr-Oct. $21-28 per night. 165 sites, 40 with electric, 125 no hookups. Drinking water. Restrooms; showers. Dump station.

Janes Island State Park

26280 Alfred Lawson Dr, Crisfield, MD 21817. Phone: (410) 968-1565. Located 2.4 miles N of Crisfield via Richardson Ave and Jacksonville Rd. GPS: 38.009143, -75.844816. Lake in park. Swimming beach, fishing, boating (rentals). Hiking, biking trails. Bird watching. Camp store. Visitor center. Open Apr-Nov. $21-28 per night. 104 sites, 49 with electric, 55 no hookups. Drinking water. Restrooms; showers. Dump station.

Martinak State Park

137 Deep Shore Rd, Denton, MD 21629. Phone: (410) 820-1668. Located 2 miles S of Denton via MD 404. GPS: 38.866093, -75.836371. Fishing, boating (rentals). Hiking, biking Wildlife viewing. Visitor center. Open Mar-Nov. $19-25 per night. 63 sites, 30 with electric, 33 no hookups. Drinking water. Restrooms; showers. Dump station.

New Germany State Park

349 Headquarters Ln, Grantsville, MD 21536. Phone: (301) 895-5453. Located near Grantsville about 5 miles S of I-68 Exit 22 via Chestnut Ridge Rd and New Germany Rd. GPS: 39.630623, -79.128794. Lake in park. Swimming beach, fishing, boating (rentals). Hiking, biking, walking trails. Wildlife viewing. Visitor center, gift shop, snack bar. Nature center. Open Apr-Nov. $19-28 per night. 48 sites, 2 with electric, 46 no hookups. Drinking water. Restrooms; showers. Dump station.

Patapsco Valley State Park

8020 Baltimore National Pike, Ellicott City, MD 21043. Phone: (410) 461-5005. The park extends along 32 miles of the Patapsco River in central Maryland. The campground is on US 40 about 13 miles W of downtown Baltimore. Note: RVs over 11 feet 1 inch in height must use the eastbound US 40 entrance. GPS: 39.295015, -76.786012. Fishing (river), boating. Hiking, biking, equestrian trails. Wildlife viewing. Scenic viewpoint. Visitor center. Open Apr-Oct. $18-22 per night. 73 sites, 30 with electric, 43 no hookups. Drinking water. Restrooms; showers. Dump station.

Pocomoke River State Park

3461 Worcester Hwy, Snow Hill, MD 21863. Phone: (410) 632-2566. The park is situated on the Pocomoke River, SW of Snow Hill. Two camping areas.

Milburn Landing: 3036 Nassawango Rd, Pocomoke City, MD 21851. Located 8 miles SW of Snow Hill via MD 12 and Nassawango Rd. GPS: 38.128375, -75.491887. Fishing, boating. Hiking, biking trails. Bird watching. Open Apr-Dec. $18-25 per night. 32 sites, 26 with electric, 6 no hookups. Drinking water. Restrooms; showers. Dump station.

Shad Landing: 3461 Worcester Hwy, Snow Hill, MD 21863. Located 4 miles SW of Snow Hill via US 113. GPS: 38.132064, -75.437474. Swimming pool, fishing, boating (rentals). Hiking, biking trails. Bird watching. Visitor center. Nature center. Marina, store, gifts, deli. Open all year. $21-28 per night. 175 sites, 60 with electric, 115 no hookups. Drinking water. Restrooms; showers. Laundry facilities (at marina). Dump station.

Point Lookout State Park

11175 Point Lookout Rd, Scotland, MD 20687. Phone: (301) 872-5688. Located about 11 miles S of Saint Mary's City via MD 5. GPS: 38.063261, -76.333994. Lake in park. Swimming beach, fishing, boating (rentals). Hiking, biking trails. Scenic viewpoint. Camp store. Visitor center. Nature center. Marina. Civil War Museum. Open Apr-Nov. $21-39 per night. 143 sites, 26 full hookup, 33 with electric, 84 no hookups. Drinking water. Restrooms; showers. Dump station.

Rocky Gap State Park

17600 Campers Hill Dr, Flintstone, MD 21530. Phone: (301) 722-1488. Located 7 miles NE of Cumberland at I-68 Exit 50. GPS: 39.715016, -78.638945. Lake in park. Swimming beach, fishing, boating (rentals). Hiking, biking trails. Camp store. Visitor center, cafe. Rocky Gap Casino Resort (casino, hotel, comedy club, restaurants, golf course, spa, pool), located in park. Open May-Dec. $21-28 per night. 278 sites, 30 with electric, 248 no hookups. Drinking water. Restrooms; showers. Dump station.

Smallwood State Park

2750 Sweden Point Rd, Marbury, MD 20658. Phone: (301) 743-7613. Located 2 miles SW of Marbury via MD 224. GPS: 38.555731, -77.174833. Fishing, boating. Hiking, nature trails. Bird watching. Discovery Center, features live animal displays. Marina, store. Retreat House historic area, a restored 18th century tidewater plantation and a 19th century tobacco barn. Open Apr-Nov. $28 per night. 15 sites with electric hookups. Drinking water. Restrooms; showers. Dump station.

Susquehanna State Park

4122 Wilkinson Road, Havre de Grace MD 21078. Phone: (410) 557-7994. Located near Havre de Grace about 5 miles NW of I-95 Exit 89 via MD 155, MD 161, and Rock Run Rd. GPS: 39.610787, -76.163585. Fishing (river), boating. Hiking, biking, equestrian trails. Steppingstone Farm Museum. Rrestored Rock Run Historic Area with working gristmill, Carter-Archer Mansion, Jersey Toll

House and the remains of the Susquehanna & Tidewater Canal. Open May-Nov. $21-28 per night. 69 sites, 6 with electric, 63 no hookups. Drinking water. Restrooms; showers. Dump station.

Swallow Falls State Park

2470 Maple Glade Road, Oakland MD 21550. Phone: (301) 387-6938. Located 8 miles N of Oakland via Herrington Manor Rd. GPS: 39.494114, -79.420195. Fishing (river). Hiking, biking trails. Scenic viewpoint. Camp store. Visitor center. Scenic 53-foot waterfall. Open Apr-Dec. $21-33 per night. 65 sites, 3 full hookup, 3 water and electric, 59 no hookups. Drinking water. 36-foot limit (many are 20-feet or less). Restrooms; showers. Dump station.

Tuckahoe State Park

13070 Crouse Mill Rd, Queen Anne, MD 21657. Phone: (410) 820-1688. Located 5 miles N of Queen Anne via Eveland Rd. GPS: 38.977622, -75.929475. Lake in park. Fishing, boating (rentals). Hiking, biking, equestrian trails. Wildlife viewing. Disc golf. Visitor center. Arboretum. Scales & Tales Programs (see wildlife up close). Open Mar-Nov. $21-28 per night. 54 sites, 33 with electric, 21 no hookups. Drinking water. Restrooms; showers. Dump station.

Massachusetts

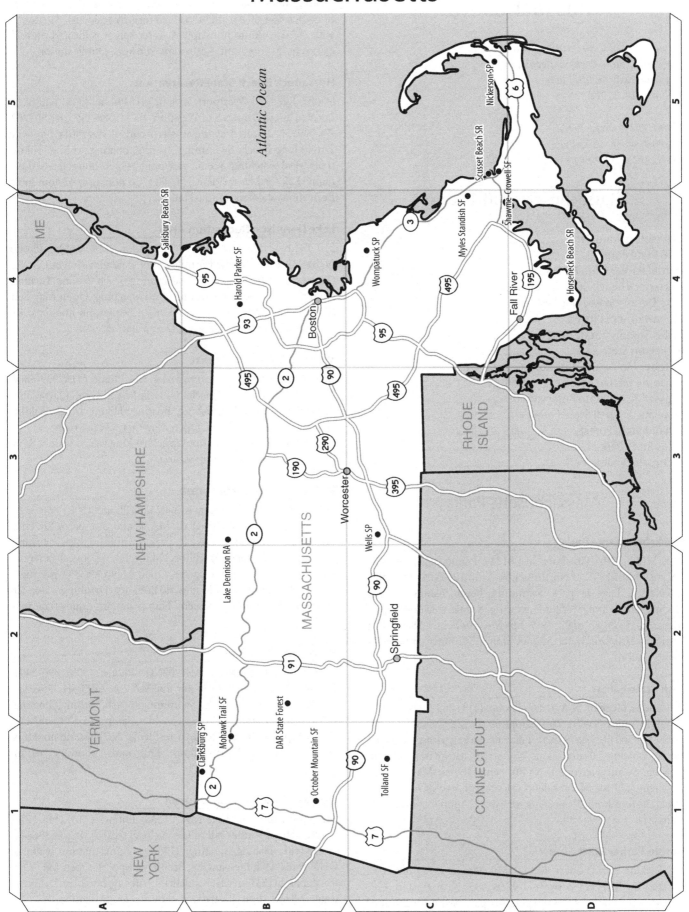

Massachusetts

Department of Conservation & Recreation
Division of State Parks & Recreation
251 Causeway St, 9th Floor
Boston, MA 02114

Phone: (617) 626-1250
Internet: www.mass.gov
Reservations: Online or (877) 422-6762

Massachusetts Park Locator

Massachusetts Parks

Clarksburg State Park

1199 Middle Rd, Clarksburg, MA 01247. Phone: (413) 664-8345. Located 4 miles NE of North Adams via MA 8. GPS: 42.733897, -73.076181. Lake in park. Swimming beach, fishing, boating. Hiking, nature trails. Wildlife viewing. Scenic viewpoint. Open May-Sep. $54 per night ($17 for MA resident). 18 sites, no hookups. Drinking water. 35-foot limit. Restrooms; showers. No dump station.

DAR State Forest

78 Cape St, Goshen, MA 01032. Phone: (413) 268-7098. Located about 14 miles NW of Northampton via MA 9 and MA 112. GPS: 42.456643, -72.791320. Lake in park. Swimming beach, fishing, boating. Hiking, biking, equestrian, nature trails. Wildlife viewing. Scenic viewpoint. Nature center. Open May-Oct. $54 per night ($17 for MA resident). 31 sites, no hookups. Drinking water. 30-foot limit. Restrooms; showers. Dump station (at HQ complex).

Harold Parker State Forest

133 Jenkins Rd, Andover, MA. 01810. Phone: (978) 686-3391. Located on MA 114 between I-95 & 495, N of Boston. GPS: 42.610477, -71.090454. Several ponds in park. Swimming, fishing, boating (non-motorized). Hiking, biking, equestrian trails. Open May-Oct. $54-60 per night ($17-23 for MA resident). 31 sites, 11 with electric, 20 no hookups. A water spigot is located on each campsite. 40-foot limit. Restrooms; showers. Dump station.

Horseneck Beach State Reservation

5 John Reed Rd, Westport, MA 02791. Phone: (508) 636-8817. Located about 6 miles S of Westport via MA 88. GPS: 41.501762, -71.039955. Located at the western end of Buzzard's Bay with 2-mile long beach. Swimming, fishing, boating, sailing. Hiking trails. Bird watching. Scenic viewpoint. Open May-Oct. $70 per night ($22 for MA resident). 96 sites, no hookups. 42-foot limit. Restrooms; showers. Dump station.

Lake Dennison Recreation Area

219 Baldwinville State Rd, Winchendon, MA 01436. Phone: (978) 939-8962. Located 3 miles N of Baldwinville via US 202. GPS: 42.647748, -72.081597. Swimming beach, fishing, boating. Hiking, biking, equestrian trails. Bird watching. Open May-Sep. $54 per night ($17 for MA resident). 139 sites, no hookups. 40-foot limit. Restrooms; showers. Dump station.

Mohawk Trail State Forest

Cold River Road, Charlemont, MA 01339. Phone: (413) 339-5504. Located 4 miles W of Charlemont via MA 2. GPS: 42.638236, -72.936096. Swimming, fishing, boating. Hiking trails. Wildlife viewing. Scenic viewpoint. Open May-Oct. $54 per night ($17 for MA resident). 43 sites, no hookups. Drinking water. 30-foot limit. Restrooms; showers. Dump station.

Myles Standish State Forest

194 Cranberry Rd, Carver, MA 02330. Phone: (508) 866-2526. Located 7 miles SE of Carver via MA 58 and Cranberry Rd. GPS: 41.839086, -70.691437. Lake in park. Swimming beach, fishing, boating (non-motorized), sailing. Hiking, biking, equestrian trails. Wildlife viewing. Visitor center. Open May-Oct. $54 per night ($17 for MA resident). 304 sites, no hookups. Drinking water. 30-foot limit. Restrooms; showers. Dump station. Equestrian area, 32 sites.

Nickerson State Park

3488 Main St, Brewster, MA 02631. Phone: (508) 896-3491. Located 3 miles E of Brewster via MA 6A. GPS: 41.775295, -70.030715. Lake in park. Swimming beach, fishing, boating. Hiking, biking trails. Wildlife viewing. Camp store. Open May-Oct. $70 per night ($22 for MA resident). 325 sites, no hookups. Drinking water. 35-foot limit. Restrooms; showers. Dump station.

October Mountain State Forest

317 Woodland Rd, Lee, MA 01238. Phone: (413) 243-1778. Located about 3 miles NE of Lee via local roads. GPS: 42.336241, -73.233781. Fishing, boating. Hiking, biking, nature, walking, OHV trails. Wildlife viewing. Scenic viewpoint. Open May-Oct. $54 per night ($17 for MA resident). 47 sites, no hookups. Drinking water. 34-foot limit. Restrooms; showers. Dump station.

Salisbury Beach State Reservation

State Reservation Road, Salisbury, MA 01952. Phone: (978) 462-4481. Located about 3 miles E of Salisbury via MA 1A. GPS: 42.832516, -70.818302. Nearly 4 miles of coastline. Swimming beach, fishing, boating. Nature, walking trails. Bird watching. Scenic viewpoint. Open Apr-Nov. $70-80 per night ($22-32 for MA resident). 484 sites, 324 with electric, 160 no hookups. Drinking water. 40-foot limit. Restrooms; showers. Dump station.

Scusset Beach State Reservation

20 Scusset Beach Rd, Sagamore, MA 02562. Phone: (508) 888-0859. Located on Cape Cod Bay near Sagamore about 2 miles E of US 6/MA 3 Exit 1A via Scusset Beach Rd. GPS: 41.777798, -70.504850. Salisbury Beach overlooks the point at which the Merrimack River feeds the Atlantic Ocean. Swimming beach, fishing, boating. Biking, equestrian, walking trails. Scenic viewpoint. Open all year. $70-80 per night ($22-32 for MA resident). 98 sites with electric hookups. Drinking water. 40-foot limit. Restrooms; showers. Dump station.

Shawme-Crowell State Forest

42 Main St, Sandwich, MA 02563. Phone: (508) 888-0351. Located 2 miles N of US 6 Exit 2 near Sandwich via MA 130. GPS: 41.762690, -70.518179. On the western end of Cape Cod. Hiking, equestrian trails. Wildlife viewing. Nature center. Open Apr-Oct. $54 per night ($17 for MA resident). 285 sites, no hookups. Drinking water. 30-foot limit. Restrooms; showers. Dump station.

Tolland State Forest

410 Tolland Rd, East Otis, MA 01029. Phone: (413) 269-6002. Located 7 miles S of Otis via MA 8. GPS: 42.144844, -73.049512. Lake in park. Swimming beach, fishing, boating, sailing. Hiking, biking trails. Wildlife viewing. Open May-Oct. $54 per night ($17 for MA resident). 93 sites, no hookups. Drinking water. 35-foot limit. Restrooms; showers. No dump station.

Wells State Park

159 Walker Pond Rd, Sturbridge, MA 01566. Phone: (508) 347-9257. Located about 5 miles N of Sturbridge via US 20 and MA 49. GPS: 42.146558, -72.060610. Lake in park. Swimming beach, fishing, boating. Hiking, biking, equestrian trails. Wildlife viewing. Scenic viewpoint. Nature center. Open May-Oct. Reservations required in summer. $54 per night ($17 for MA resident). 55 sites, no hookups. Drinking water. 30-foot limit. Restrooms; showers. No dump station.

Wompatuck State Park

204 Union St, Hingham, MA 02043. Phone: (617) 895-8245. Located about 4 miles SE of Hingham via MA 228 and Union St. GPS: 42.202853, -70.846964. Lake in park. No swimming allowed. Fishing, boating. Hiking, biking, equestrian, walking trails. Wildlife viewing. Visitor center. Open May-Oct. $54-60 per night ($17-23 for MA resident). 260 sites, 125 with electric, 135 no hookups. Drinking water. 40-foot limit. Restrooms; showers. Dump station.

Michigan

Michigan

Michigan Dept. of Natural Resources
Parks and Recreation
PO Box 30257
Lansing, MI 48909

Phone: (517) 284-7275
Internet: www.michigan.gov/dnr
Reservations: Online or (800) 447-2757

Michigan Park Locator

Michigan Parks

Albert E. Sleeper State Park

6573 State Park Rd, Caseville, MI 48725. Phone: (989) 856-4411. Located 5 miles NE of Caseville via MI 25. GPS: 43.979550, -83.210318. Lake in park. Swimming beach, fishing, boating (rentals). Hiking, biking, nature trails. Open Apr-Oct. $20-32 per night. 226 sites with electric hookups. Drinking water. Restrooms; showers. Dump station.

Algonac State Park

8732 River Rd, Marine City, MI 48039. Phone: (810) 765-5605. Located about 6 miles S of Marine City via MI 29. GPS: 42.651338, -82.516901. Half-mile of St. Clair River frontage. Fishing, boating. Hiking, walking trails. Wildlife viewing. Archery range and trap shooting. Two campgrounds open Mar-Nov. $20-32 per night. 296 sites with electric hookups. Drinking water. Restrooms; showers. Dump station.

Aloha State Park

4347 Third St, Cheboygan, MI 49721. Phone: (231) 625-2522. Located 10 miles S of Cheboygan via MI 27 and MI 33. GPS: 45.525155, -84.465498. Lake in park. Swimming beach, fishing, boating. Hiking, biking (rentals) trails. Open Apr-Oct. $22-34 per night. 285 sites with electric hookups. Drinking water. Restrooms; showers. Dump station.

Baraga State Park

1300 US-41 S, Baraga, MI 49908. Phone: (906) 353-6558. Located 1/2 mile S of Baraga via US 41. GPS: 46.760701, -88.500332. Lake in park. Fishing, boating. Hiking, nature, OHV trails. Wildlife viewing. Open May-Nov. $22-34 per night. 95 sites, 14 full hookup, 81 with electric. Drinking water. Restrooms; showers. Dump station.

Bay City State Park

3582 State Park Dr, Bay City, MI 48706. Phone: (989) 684-3020. Located about 5 miles E of I-75 Exit 168 near Bay City. GPS: 43.667293, -83.907612. Lake in park. Swimming beach, fishing. Hiking, biking, nature trails. Wildlife viewing. Scenic viewpoint. Visitor center. Open Apr-Oct. $20-29 per night. 193 sites with electric hookups. Drinking water. Restrooms; showers. Dump station.

Bewabic State Park

720 Idlewild Rd, Crystal Falls, MI 49920. Phone: (906) 875-3324. Located 4 miles W of Crystal Falls via US 2. GPS: 46.094355, -88.425386. Lake in park. Swimming beach, fishing, boating (rentals). Hiking, OHV trails. Wildlife viewing. Open May-Oct. $17-24 per night. 122 sites, 119 with electric, 3 no hookups. Drinking water. Restrooms; showers. Dump station.

Brighton Recreation Area

6360 Chilson Rd, Howell, MI 48843. Phone: (810) 229-6566. Located W of Detroit, 6 miles W of Brighton via W Main St/ Brighton Rd to Chilson Rd. GPS: 42.506310, -83.858860. Lakes in park. Swimming beach, fishing, boating (rentals). Hiking, biking, equestrian trails. Bird watching. Disc golf. Open all year. $17-25 per night. 194 sites, 144 with electric, 50 no hookups. Drinking water. Restrooms; showers. Dump station. Equestrian area with 19 primitive sites.

Brimley State Park

9200 W 6 Mile Road, Brimley, MI 49715. Phone: (906) 248-3422. Located 1 miles NE of Brimley via MI 221 and 6 Mile Rd. GPS: 46.412876, -84.556158. Lake in park. Swimming beach, fishing, boating. Wildlife viewing. Scenic viewpoint. Open May-Oct. $20-29 per night. 237 sites with electric hookups. Drinking water. Restrooms; showers. Dump station.

Burt Lake State Park

6635 State Park Dr, Indian River, MI 49749. Phone: (231) 238-9392. Located just W of I-75 Exit 310 near Indian River. GPS: 45.401439, -84.619582. Swimming beach, fishing, boating. Hiking trails. Wildlife viewing. Scenic viewpoint. Camp store. Open May-Nov. $22-34 per night. 306 sites with electric hookups. Drinking water. Restrooms; showers. Dump station.

Charles Mears State Park

400 W Lowell St, Pentwater, MI 49449. Phone: (231) 869-2051. Located just W of Pentwater town center via Lowell St. GPS: 43.782514, -86.439084. Lake in park. Swimming beach, fishing. Hiking trails. Park store. Open Apr-Oct. $33 per night. 175 sites with electric hookups. Drinking water. Restrooms; showers. Dump station.

Cheboygan State Park

4490 Beach Rd, Cheboygan, MI 49721. Phone: (231) 627-2811. Located about 4 miles E of Cheboygan via US 23. GPS: 45.658202, -84.417584. Lake in park. Swimming beach, fishing, boating (kayak rentals). Hiking, biking trails. Wildlife viewing. Open May-Oct. $20-25 per night. 76 sites with electric hookups. Drinking water. Restrooms; showers. Dump station.

Clear Lake State Park

20500 M-33 North, Atlanta, MI 49709. Phone: (989) 785-4388. Located 9 miles N of Atlanta via MI 33. GPS: 45.132254, -84.184132. Swimming beach, fishing, boating (rentals). Hiking, biking, OHV trails. Disc golf. Open all year. $20-29 per night. 178 sites with electric hookups. Drinking water. Restrooms; showers. Dump station.

Fayette Historic State Park

4785 11 Rd, Garden, MI 49835. Phone: (906) 644-2603. Located about 8 miles SW of Garden via MI 183. GPS: 45.712412, -86.667676. Lake in park. Swimming beach, fishing, boating (rentals), scuba diving. Hiking, biking trails. Scenic viewpoint. Visitor center. Historic townsite, tours. Open May-Dec. $20-29 per night. 61 sites with electric hookups. Drinking water. Restrooms; showers. Dump station.

Fisherman's Island State Park

Bell's Bay Rd, Charlevoix, MI 49720. Phone: (231) 547-6641. Located 4 miles W of Charlevoix via US 31 and Bells Bay Rd. GPS: 45.307999, -85.310385. Lake in park. Swimming beach, fishing, boating. Hiking trails. Bird watching. Open May-Sep. $17 per night. 81 sites, no hookups. Hand-pumped water. Vault toilets. No dump station.

Fort Custer Recreation Area

5163 Fort Custer Dr, Augusta, MI 49012. Phone: (269) 731-4200. Located just E of Augusta via MI 96/Dickman Rd. GPS: 42.320169, -85.349423. Three lakes in park. Swimming beach, fishing, boating (rentals). Hiking, biking, equestrian trails. Park store. Open all year. $20-29 per night. 219 sites with electric hookups. Drinking water. Restrooms; showers. Dump station. Equestrian area, 7 primitive sites.

Fort Wilkins Historic State Park

15223 US Hwy 41, Copper Harbor, MI 49918. Phone: (906) 289-4215. Located 1 miles E of Copper Harbor via US 41. GPS: 47.467677, -87.862027. Lake in park. Fishing, boating. Hiking, biking, nature trails. Scenic viewpoint. Park store. Open May-Oct. $20-29 per night. 159 sites with electric hookups. Drinking water. Restrooms; showers. Laundry facilities. Dump station.

Grand Haven State Park

1001 Harbor Ave, Grand Haven, MI 49417. Phone: (616) 847-1309. Located 1 mile W of Grand Haven via Harbor Dr. GPS: 43.056187, -86.246024. Lake in park. Swimming beach, fishing, boating. Hiking trails. Scenic viewpoint. Park store. Open May-Oct. $21-37 per night. 174 sites, most with electric hookups. Drinking water. Restrooms; showers. Dump station.

Harrisville State Park

248 State Park Rd, Harrisville, MI 48740. Phone: (989) 724-5126. Located about 1 mile S of Harrisville via US 23. GPS: 44.647361, -83.297771. Lake in park. Swimming beach, fishing, boating. Hiking, biking (rentals) trails. Bird watching. Open Apr-Oct. $28-32 per night. 195 sites with electric hookups. Drinking water. Restrooms; showers. Dump station.

Hartwick Pines State Park

3612 State Park Dr, Grayling, MI 49738. Phone: (989) 348-7068. Located 7 miles N of Grayling and 2 miles E of I-75 Exit 259. GPS: 44.738891, -84.686859. Four small lakes and river in park. Fishing, boating (rentals). Hiking, biking trails. Park store. Visitor center. Hartwick Pines Logging Museum, live demonstrations. Open Apr-Oct. $22-38 per night. 100 sites, 36 full hookup, 64 with electric. Drinking water. Restrooms; showers. Dump station.

Highland Recreation Area

5200 Highland Rd, White Lake, MI 48383. Phone: (248) 889-3750. Located 3 miles W of White Lake via MI 59. GPS: 42.636026, -83.544569. Lake in park. Swimming beach, fishing, boating. Hiking, biking, equestrian trails. Visitor center. Open Apr-Sep. $20 per night. 25 sites, no hookups. Access to water and two vault toilets near campground entrance. No dump station.

Holland State Park

2215 Ottawa Beach Rd, Holland, MI 49424. Phone: (616) 399-9390. Located 6 miles W of Holland via Ottawa Beach Rd. GPS: 42.779180, -86.198985. Lake in park. Swimming beach, fishing, boating (rentals). Hiking trails. Park store. Open Apr-Oct. $33-45 per night. 309 sites, 31 full hookup, 278 with electric. Drinking water. Restrooms; showers. Dump station.

Holly Recreation Area

8100 Grange Hall Rd, Holly, MI 48442. Phone: (248) 634-8811. Located 2 miles E of I-75 Exit 101 near Holly. GPS: 42.819799, -83.526441. Lake in park. Swimming beach, fishing, boating (rentals). Hiking, biking trails. Disc golf. Radio control flying field. Open Mar-Nov. $20-29 per night. 159 sites, 144 with electric, 15 no hookups. Drinking water. Restrooms; showers. Dump station.

Indian Lake State Park

8970 W County Road 442, Manistique, MI 49854. Phone: (906) 341-2355. Located 5 miles W of Manistique via CR 442. GPS: 45.943611, -86.331806. Swimming beach, fishing, boating (rentals). Hiking, walking trails. Wildlife viewing. Two camping areas open Apr-Oct. $20-29 per night. 217 sites, 145 with electric, 72 no hookups. Drinking water. Restrooms; showers. Dump station.

Interlochen State Park

4167 Highway M-137, Interlochen, MI 49643. Phone: (231) 276-9511. Located just S of town via MI 137. GPS: 44.628601, -85.765011. Lakes in park. Swimming beach, fishing, boating. Wildlife viewing. Park store. Two campgrounds open Apr-Oct. $17-29 per night. 444 sites, 392 with electric, 52 no hookups. Drinking water. Restrooms; showers. Dump station.

Ionia State Recreation Area

2880 W David Hwy, Ionia, MI 48846. Phone: (616) 527-3750. Located 7 miles SW of Ionia via MI 66 and David Hwy. GPS: 42.941472, -85.119616. Lake in park. Swimming beach, fishing, boating . Hiking, biking, equestrian trails. Bird watching. Disc golf. Open Apr-Nov. $20-22 per night. 100 sites with electric hookups. Drinking water. Restrooms; showers. Dump station. Equestrian area, 46 primitive sites.

J.W. Wells State Park

N7670 Highway M-35, Cedar River, MI 49887. Phone: (906) 863-9747. Located 1 miles S of Cedar River via MI 35. GPS: 45.388803, -87.368095. Lake in park. Swimming beach, fishing, boating. Hiking trails. Open Apr-Oct. $20-26 per night. 150 sites with electric hookups. Drinking water. Restrooms; showers. Dump station.

Keith J. Charters Traverse City State Park

1132 US 31 N, Traverse City, MI 49686. Phone: (231) 922-5270. Located about 4 miles E of Traverse City via US 31. GPS: 44.747844, -85.553874. Lake in park. Swimming beach, fishing, boating. Hiking, biking trails. Bird watching. Open Apr-Nov. $33-37 per night. 348 sites with electric hookups. Drinking water. Restrooms; showers. Dump station.

Lake Gogebic State Park

N 9995 Highway M-64, Marenisco, MI 49947. Phone: (906) 842-3341. Located 11 miles E of Marenisco via MI 64. GPS: 46.456893, -89.569436. Swimming beach, fishing, boating. Hiking trail. Wildlife viewing. Open Apr-Oct. $17-28 per night. 127 sites, 105 with electric (some with sewer), 22 no hookups. Drinking water. Restrooms; showers. Dump station.

Lake Hudson Recreation Area

5505 Morey Hwy, Clayton, MI 49235. Phone: (517) 445-2265. Located about 2 miles S of Clayton via MI 156. GPS: 41.824794, -84.259628. Lake in park. Swimming beach, fishing, boating. Hiking trails. Designated dark sky preserve. Open Apr-Nov. $20 per night. 50 sites with electric hookups. Hand-pump water. Vault toilets. No dump station.

Lakeport State Park

7605 Lakeshore Rd, Lakeport, MI 48059. Phone: (810) 327-6224. Located just N of town along MI 25. GPS: 43.124285, -82.497268. Lake in park. Swimming beach, fishing. Wildlife viewing. Camp store. Open Apr-Oct. $30-34 per night. 250 sites with electric hookups. Drinking water. Restrooms; showers. Dump station.

Leelanau State Park

15310 N Lighthouse Point Rd, Northport, MI 49670. Phone: (231) 386-5422. Located in northwestern MI at end of MI 201 on Lake Michigan, N of Traverse City. GPS: 45.209892, -85.547538. Lake in park. Swimming beach. Hiking trails. Wildlife viewing. Scenic viewpoint. Park store. Grand Traverse Lighthouse, self-guided tours. Open Apr-Nov. $17 per night. 52 sites, no hookups. Drinking water. Vault toilets. No dump station.

Ludington State Park

8800 W Highway M-116, Ludington, MI 49431. Phone: (231) 843-2423. Located about 7 miles N of Ludington via MI 116. GPS: 44.032419, -86.504701. Lake in park. Swimming beach, fishing (lake and river), boating (rentals). Hiking, biking (rentals) trails. Scenic viewpoint. Park store. Big Sable Point Lighthouse, tours. Open all year. $17-37 per night. 344 sites with electric hookups. Drinking water. Restrooms; showers. Dump station.

McLain State Park

18350 Highway M-203, Hancock, MI 49930. Phone: (906) 482-0278. Located 10 miles N of Hancock via MI 203. GPS: 47.237030, -88.608896. Lake in park. Fishing. Hiking trails. Wildlife viewing. Park store. Keweenaw Waterway Lighthouse. Open May-Oct. $22-30 per night. 98 sites with electric hookups. Drinking water. Restrooms; showers. Dump station.

Metamora-Hadley Recreation Area

3871 Herd Rd, Metamora, MI 48455. Phone: (810) 797-4439. Located 7 miles SW of I-69 Exit 155 near Lapper via MI 24 and Pratt Rd. GPS: 42.945037, -83.357034. Lake in park. Swimming beach, fishing, boating (rentals). Hiking, biking (rentals) trails. Camp store. Open Apr-Nov. $20-25 per night. 214 sites with electric hookups. Drinking water. Restrooms; showers. Dump station.

Muskallonge Lake State Park

29881 CR 407, Newberry, MI 49868. Phone: (906) 658-3338. Located 28 miles N of Newberry via MI 123 and CR 407. GPS: 46.676760, -85.627676. Swimming beach, fishing, boating. Hiking, OHV trails. Wildlife viewing. Open Apr-Oct. $20-29 per night. 159 sites with electric hookups. Drinking water. Restrooms; showers. Dump station.

Muskegon State Park

3560 Memorial Dr, North Muskegon, MI 49445. Phone: (231) 744-3480. Located 6 miles W of North Muskegon via Ruddiman Dr and Memorial Dr. GPS: 43.262053, -86.355941. Lake in park. Swimming beach, fishing, boating. Hiking trails. Wildlife viewing. Open May-Oct. $25-37 per night. 244 sites with electric hookups. Drinking water. Restrooms; showers. Dump station.

Newaygo State Park

2793 Beech St, Newaygo, MI 49337. Phone: (231) 856-4452. Located 16 miles NE of Newaygo via MI 37 and E 40th St. GPS: 43.501778, -85.582856. Lake in park. Swimming beach, fishing, boating (rentals). Hiking trails. Wildlife viewing. Disc golf. Open May-Oct. $17 per night. 99 sites, no hookups. Drinking water. Vault toilets. Dump station.

North Higgins Lake State Park

11747 N Higgins Lake Dr, Roscommon, MI 48653. Phone: (989) 821-6125. Located about 5 miles W of I-75 Exit 244 near Roscommon. GPS: 44.514745, -84.759404. Swimming beach, fishing, boating (rentals). Hiking, biking trails. Open all year. $22-34 per night. 174 sites with electric hookups. Drinking water. Restrooms; showers. Dump station.

Onaway State Park

3622 N Highway M-211, Onaway, MI 49765. Phone: (989) 733-8279. Located 5 miles N of Onaway via Hwy M-211. GPS: 45.432307, -84.229043. Lake in park. Swimming beach, fishing, boating (rentals). Wildlife viewing. Open Apr-Nov. $20-22 per night. 82 sites with electric hookups. Drinking water. Restrooms; showers. Dump station.

Orchard Beach State Park

2064 N Lakeshore Rd, Manistee, MI 49660. Phone: (231) 723-7422. Located about 3 miles N of Manistee via US 31 and MI 110. GPS: 44.283739, -86.313604. Lake in park. Swimming beach. Hiking trails. Bird watching. Open May-Oct. $22-42 per night. 166 sites, 16 full hookup, 150 with electric. Drinking water. Restrooms; showers. Dump station.

Otsego Lake State Park

7136 Old 27 S, Gaylord, MI 49735. Phone: (989) 732-5485. Located 7 miles S of Gaylord via Old Hwy 27. GPS: 44.928725, -84.689765. Swimming beach, fishing, boating (rentals). Hiking, biking, walking trails. Bird watching. Park store. Open Apr-Oct. $22-30 per night. 155 sites with electric hookups. Drinking water. Restrooms; showers. Dump station.

P.H. Hoeft State Park

5001 US 23 N, Rogers City, MI 49779. Phone: (989) 734-2543. Located 5 miles W of Rogers City via US 23. GPS: 45.468323, -83.885046. Lake in park. Swimming beach. Hiking, biking, walking trails. Bird watching. Open Apr-Nov. $20-33 per night. 126 sites with electric hookups (some with sewer). Drinking water. Restrooms; showers. Dump station.

P.J. Hoffmaster State Park

6585 Lake Harbor Rd, Muskegon, MI 49441. Phone: (231) 798-3711. Located 12 miles S of Muskegon town center via US 31. GPS: 43.136790, -86.268575. Three miles of sandy shoreline along Lake Michigan. Swimming. Hiking trails. Wildlife viewing. Scenic viewpoint. Visitor center. Open Apr-Oct. $25-37 per night. 297 sites with electric hookups. Drinking water. Restrooms; showers. Dump station.

Petoskey State Park

2475 Highway M-119, Petoskey, MI 49770. Phone: (231) 347-2311. Located 4 miles NE of Petoskey via US 31 and MI 119. GPS: 45.406623, -84.908577. Lake in park. Swimming beach, fishing, boating (rentals). Hiking, biking (rentals) trails. Scenic viewpoint. Park store. Open May-Oct. $33-37 per night. 180 sites with electric hookups. Drinking water. Restrooms; showers. Dump station.

Pinckney Recreation Area

8555 Silver Hill Rd, Pinckney, MI 48169. Phone: (734) 426-4913. Located about 10 miles SW of Pinckney via Patterson Lake Rd; follow signs. Campground address is 21237 Kaiser Rd, Gregory MI 48137. GPS: 42.424077, -84.041345. Lake in park. Swimming beach, fishing, boating (rentals). Hiking, biking, equestrian trails.

Wildlife viewing. Open Apr-Nov. $17-32 per night. 186 sites, 161 with electric, 25 no hookups. Drinking water. Restrooms; showers. Dump station.

Pontiac Lake Recreation Area

7800 Gale Rd, Waterford, MI 48327. Phone: (248) 666-1020. Located about 6 miles W of Waterford Township via Andersonville Rd and White Lake Rd. GPS: 42.686237, -83.472739. Swimming beach, fishing, boating (rentals). Hiking, biking, equestrian trails. Radio control flying field. Shooting range with a rifle/pistol, hand trap, archery and knife range. Open Apr-Oct. $30 or less. 176 sites with electric hookups. Drinking water. Restrooms; showers. Dump station. Equestrian area, 25 sites.

Porcupine Mountains Wilderness State Park

33303 Headquarters Rd, Ontonagon, MI 49953. Phone: (906) 885-5275. Located 16 miles W of Ontonagon via MI 64. GPS: 46.821816, -89.639086. Lake in park. Swimming beach, fishing, boating (rentals). Hiking, biking (rentals) trails. Scenic viewpoint. Disc golf. Park store. Visitor center. Open May-Oct. $20-28 per night. 100 sites with electric hookups. Drinking water. Restrooms; showers. Dump station.

Port Crescent State Park

1775 Port Austin Rd, Port Austin, MI 48467. Phone: (989) 738-8663. Located 4 miles SW of Port Austin via MI 25. GPS: 44.006892, -83.051637. Lake in park. Swimming beach, fishing. Hiking trails. Wildlife viewing. Scenic viewpoint. Open Apr-Oct. $33 per night. 142 sites with electric hookups. Drinking water. Restrooms; showers. Dump station.

Proud Lake Recreation Area

3500 N Wixom Rd, Commerce Township, MI 48382. Phone: (248) 685-2433. Located 5 miles N of I-96 Exit 159 near Wixom via Wixom Rd. GPS: 42.562090, -83.526304. Fishing, boating (rentals). Hiking, biking, equestrian trails. Park store. Cafe. Open Apr-Nov. $25-29 per night. 130 sites with electric hookups. Drinking water. Restrooms; showers. Dump station.

Rifle River Recreation Area

2550 E Rose City Rd, Lupton, MI 48635. Phone: (989) 473-2258. Located just S of Lupton. GPS: 44.414819, -84.025042. Lakes in park. Swimming beach, fishing, boating. Hiking, biking trails. Scenic viewpoint. Multiple camping areas open all year. $13-28 per night. 174 sites, 75 with electric, 99 no hookups. Drinking water. Restrooms; showers. Dump station.

Seven Lakes State Park

14390 Fish Lake Rd, Holly, MI 48442. Phone: (248) 634-7271. Located about 3 miles NW of Holly. GPS: 42.816948, -83.648249. Swimming beach, fishing, boating (rentals). Hiking, biking trails. Park store. Open May-Nov. $25 per night. 70 sites with electric hookups. Drinking water. Restrooms; showers. Dump station.

Silver Lake State Park

9679 W State Park Rd, Mears, MI 49436. Phone: (231) 873-3083. Located about 5 miles W of Mears via Fox Rd and Hazel Rd. GPS:

43.663029, -86.493609. Swimming beach, fishing, boating. Hiking trails. ORV Scramble Area. Open Mar-Oct. $25-33 per night. 200 sites with electric hookups. Drinking water. Restrooms; showers. Dump station.

Sleepy Hollow State Park

7835 E Price Rd, Laingsburg, MI 48848. Phone: (517) 651-6217. Located 5 miles NW of Laingsburg via Meridian Rd and Price Rd. GPS: 42.941875, -84.401342. Lake in park. Swimming beach, fishing, boating (rentals). Hiking, biking, equestrian trails. Disc golf. Park store. Open Apr-Oct. $25 per night. 181 sites with electric hookups. Drinking water. Restrooms; showers. Dump station.

South Higgins Lake State Park

106 State Park Dr, Roscommon, MI 48653. Phone: (989) 821-6374. Located about 7 miles W of I-75 Exit 239 near Roscommon via Robinson Lake Rd and Higgins Lake Dr. GPS: 44.424088, -84.679607. Swimming beach, fishing, boating (rentals). Hiking, biking trails. Park store. Open Apr-Nov. $25-45 per night. 400 sites, 39 full hookup, 361 with electric. Drinking water. Restrooms; showers. Dump station.

Sterling State Park

2800 State Park Rd, Monroe, MI 48162. Phone: (734) 289-2715. Located 1.5 miles E of I-75 Exit 15 near Monroe. GPS: 41.921008, -83.340919. Lake in park. Swimming beach, fishing, boating (rentals). Hiking, biking trails. Bird watching. Open Apr-Oct. $28-40 per night. 256 sites, 80 full hookup, 176 with electric. Drinking water. Restrooms; showers. Dump station.

Straits State Park

720 Church St, Saint Ignace, MI 49781. Phone: (906) 643-8620. Located less than a mile E of I-75 Exit 344/344A via Church St. GPS: 45.855103, -84.719463. Lake in park. Boating (paddling, carry-in). Nature trail. Wildlife viewing. Scenic viewpoint. Open Apr-Nov. $20-34 per night. 270 sites, 255 with electric, 15 no hookups. Drinking water. Restrooms; showers. Dump station.

Tahquamenon Falls State Park

41382 W Highway M-173, Paradise, MI 49768. Phone: (906) 492-3415. Located 10 miles W of Paradise via MI 123. GPS: 46.610681, -85.206264. Lake in park. Swimming beach, fishing, boating (rentals). Hiking trails. Scenic viewpoint. Park store, cafe. Three camping areas open all year. $17-32 per night. 296 sites, 260 with electric, 36 no hookups. Drinking water. Restrooms; showers. Dump station.

Tawas Point State Park

686 Tawas Beach Rd, East Tawas, MI 48730. Phone: (989) 362-5041. Located 3 miles SE of East Tawas via Tawas Beach Rd. GPS: 44.258772, -83.442419. Two miles of sandy shoreline along Lake Huron. Swimming, fishing, boating. Hiking, biking trails. Tawas Point Lighthouse, guided tours. Food and drink concessions. Open Apr-Nov. $33 per night. 193 sites with electric hookups. Drinking water. Restrooms; showers. Dump station.

Twin Lakes State Park

6204 E Poyhonen Rd, Toivola, MI 49965. Phone: (906) 288-3321. Located 9 miles S of Toivola via MI 26. GPS: 46.890906, -88.857681. Swimming beach, fishing, boating. Hiking, nature trails. Wildlife viewing. Open May-Oct. $20-29 per night. 62 sites with electric hookups. Drinking water. Restrooms; showers. Dump station.

Van Buren State Park

23960 Ruggles Rd, South Haven, MI 49090. Phone: (269) 637-2788. Located 5 miles S of South Haven via Blue Star Hwy. GPS: 42.333643, -86.304843. Lake in park. Swimming beach. Hiking, biking trails. Open Apr-Oct. $28-32 per night. 220 sites with electric hookups. Drinking water. Restrooms; showers. Dump station.

Van Riper State Park

851 County Road AKE, Champion, MI 49814. Phone: (906) 339-4461. Located 1 mile NW of Champion off US 41. GPS: 46.520851, -87.984841. Lake in park. Swimming beach, fishing, boating (kayak rentals). Hiking, biking trails. Wildlife viewing. Open May-Oct. $17-29 per night. 187 sites, 147 with electric, 40 no hookups. Drinking water. Restrooms; showers. Dump station.

Walter J. Hayes State Park

1220 Wamplers Lake Rd, Onsted, MI 49265. Phone: (517) 467-7401. Located off US 12 about 7 miles NE of Onsted. GPS: 42.067941, -84.136386. Lake in park. Swimming beach, fishing, boating (rentals). Hiking trails. Bird watching. Open Apr-Oct. $28-32 per night. 185 sites with electric hookups (10 with water). Drinking water. Restrooms; showers. Dump station.

Warren Dunes State Park

12032 Red Arrow Hwy, Sawyer, MI 49125. Phone: (269) 426-4013. Located 2 miles S of I-94 Exit 16 near Sawyer. GPS: 41.909389, -86.587519. Lake in park. Swimming beach. Hiking trails. Wildlife viewing. Park store. Open Apr-Oct. $25-45 per night. 219 sites with electric hookups (some full hookup sites). Drinking water. Restrooms; showers. Dump station.

Waterloo Recreation Area

16345 McClure Rd, Chelsea, MI 48118. Phone: (734) 475-8307. Located in southeastern Michigan, NW of Ann Arbor. Lakes in park. Swimming beach, fishing, boating (rentals). Hiking, biking, equestrian (rentals) trails. Disc golf. Park store. Visitor center. Four camping areas.

Equestrian Campground: Located 4 miles N of I-94 Exit 153 via Clear Lake Rd, Harvey Rd, and Loveland Rd. GPS: 42.335754, -84.131319. Open all year. $17 per night. 25 sites, no hookups. Solar well pump for water. Vault toilets. Showers available at the Sugarloaf Lake Campground.

Green Lake Campground: Located north of Chelsea about 5.5 miles north of I-94 Exit 159 via MI 52. GPS: 42.361668, -84.062524. Open Apr-Nov. $17 per night. 25 sites, no hookups. Vault toilets.

Portage Lake Campground: Located 3 miles N of I-94 Exit 147 via Race Rd and Seymour Rd. GPS: 42.328817, -84.241119. Open all year. $20-32 per night. 136 sites with electric hookups. Drinking water. Restrooms; showers. Dump station.

Sugarloaf Lake Campground: Located 4 miles N of I-94 Exit 153 via Clear Lake Rd, Harvey Rd, and Loveland Rd. GPS: 42.340708, -84.122280. Open May-Oct. $28-32 per night. 164 sites with electric hookups. Drinking water. Restrooms; showers. Dump station.

Wilderness State Park

903 Wilderness Park Dr, Carp Lake, MI 49718. Phone: (231) 436-5381. Located 12 miles NW of Carp Lake via Cecil Bay Rd and Wilderness Park Dr. GPS: 45.745865, -84.900022. Has 26 miles of sandy shoreline along Lake Michigan. Swimming, fishing, boating. Hiking, biking trails. Open Apr-Nov. $25-45 per night. 438 sites, 18 full hookup, 420 with electric hookups. Drinking water. Restrooms; showers. Dump station.

William Mitchell State Park

6093 E Highway M-115, Cadillac, MI 49601. Phone: (231) 775-7911. Located along Hwy M 115 about 4 miles W of town center. GPS: 44.238291, -85.454609. Lake in park. Swimming beach, fishing, boating (rentals). Hiking, nature trails. Wildlife viewing. Scenic viewpoint. Visitor center. Open all year. $33-37 per night. 221 sites with electric hookups. Drinking water. Restrooms; showers. Dump station.

Wilson State Park

910 N First St, Harrison, MI 48625. Phone: (989) 539-3021. Located about 1 mile N of Harrison via First St. GPS: 44.028892, -84.805294. Lake in park. Swimming beach, fishing, boating (rentals). Open May-Nov. $22 per night. 158 sites with electric hookups. Drinking water. Restrooms; showers. Dump station.

Yankee Springs Recreation Area

2104 S Briggs Rd, Middleville, MI 49333. Phone: (269) 795-9081. Located 10 miles S of Middleville via MI 37 and MI 179. GPS: 42.619910, -85.513168. Lake in park. Swimming beach, fishing, boating. Hiking, biking, equestrian trails. Wildlife viewing. Park store. Three camping areas open Apr-Nov. $17-28 per night. 278 sites, 200 with electric, 78 no hookups. Drinking water. Restrooms; showers. Dump station. Equestrian area, 25 primitive sites.

Young State Park

2280 Boyne City Rd, Boyne City, MI 49712. Phone: (231) 582-7523. Located two miles NW of Boyne City. GPS: 45.236030, -85.057417. Lake in park. Swimming beach, fishing, boating (rentals). Hiking, biking trails. Disc golf. Park store. Three camping areas open May-Oct. $33-37 per night. 240 sites with electric hookups. Drinking water. Restrooms; showers. Dump station.

Minnesota

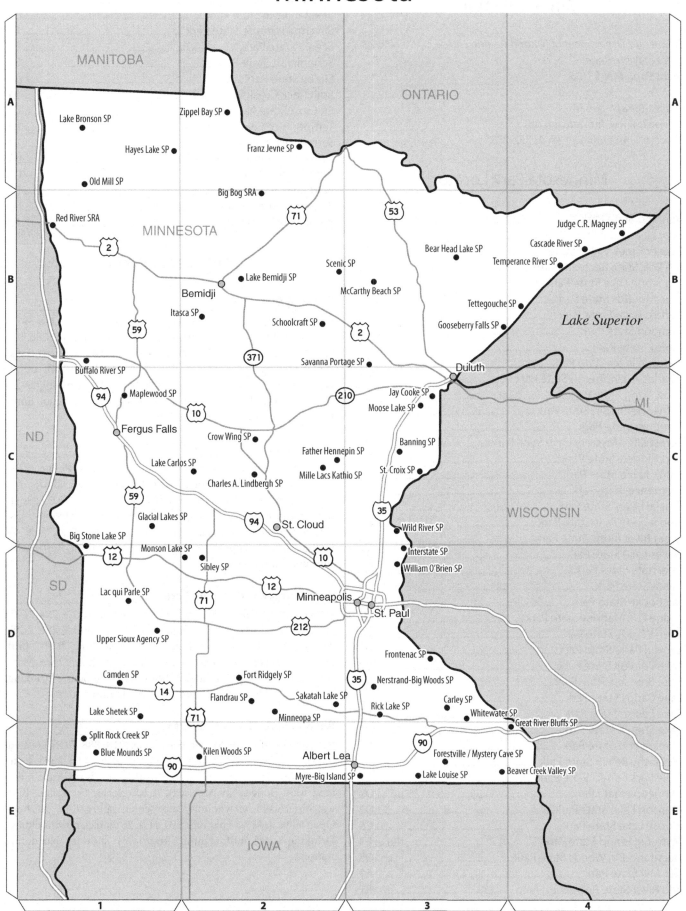

Minnesota

Minnesota Department of Natural Resources
500 Lafayette Road
Saint Paul, MN 55155

Phone: (888) 646-6367
Internet: www.dnr.state.mn.us
Reservations: Online or (866) 857-2757

Minnesota Park Locator

Minnesota Parks

Banning State Park

PO Box 643, Sandstone, MN 55072. Phone: (320) 216-3910. Located just E of I-35 Exit 195 near Sandstone. GPS: 46.179639, -92.848781. Fishing (river), boating. Hiking, biking, walking trails. Bird watching. Scenic viewpoint. Rock climbing. Park office, gift shop. Scenic waterfall. Open Apr-Nov. $24-34 per night. 33 sites, 11 with electric hookups. Drinking water. 50-foot limit. Restrooms; showers. Dump station.

Bear Head Lake State Park

9301 Bear Head Lake State Park Rd, Ely, MN 55731. Phone: (218) 235-2520. Located on Bear Head Lake on CR 128 off US 169, about 11 miles E of Tower. GPS: 47.794430, -92.078722. Lake in park. Swimming beach, fishing, boating (rentals). Hiking trails. Wildlife viewing. Open all year. $25-35 per night. 73 sites, 45 with electric hookups. Drinking water. 60-foot limit. Restrooms; showers. Dump station.

Beaver Creek Valley State Park

15954 CR 1, Caledonia, MN 55921. Phone: (507) 724-2107. Located 5 miles W of Caledonia via MN 76 and CR 1. GPS: 43.644494, -91.578861. Fishing. Hiking, walking trails. Bird watching. Scenic viewpoint. Park office, gift shop. Open May-Nov. $20-30 per night. 42 sites, 16 with electric hookups. Drinking water. 55-foot limit. Restrooms; showers. Dump station.

Big Bog State Recreation Area

PO Box 428, Waskish, MN 56685. Phone: (218) 888-7310. Located on MN 72 just N of Waskish. GPS: 48.170820, -94.512593. Lake in park. Swimming beach, fishing, boating. Bog boardwalk, mile-long walk (longest in America), is wheelchair accessible. Bird watching. Scenic viewpoint. Visitor center, nature store, gift shop. Open all year. $23-33 per night. 31 sites, 26 with electric hookups. Drinking water. 60-foot limit. Restrooms; showers. No dump station.

Big Stone Lake State Park

35889 Meadowbrook State Park Rd, Ortonville, MN 56278. Phone: (320) 839-3663. Located 8 miles NW of Ortonville via MN 7. GPS: 45.391531, -96.530370. Swimming beach, fishing, boating (rentals). Hiking trails. Visitor center. Open Apr-Oct. $23-33 per night. 37 sites, 10 with electric hookups. Drinking water. 48-foot limit. Restrooms; showers. Dump station.

Blue Mounds State Park

1410 161st Street, Luverne, MN 56156. Phone: (507) 283-6050. Located 3 miles N of Luvern on Blue Mounds Lake; (I-90, exit 12) off US 75 on CR 20. GPS: 43.716592, -96.190670. Fishing (creek). Hiking, biking, nature trails. Wildlife viewing (bison herd). Rock climbing. Visitor center. Nature store, gift shop. Historic Manfred House. Open all year. $24-34 per night. 73 sites, 40 with electric hookups. Drinking water. 50-foot limit. Restrooms; showers. Dump station.

Buffalo River State Park

565 155th St S, Glyndon, MN 56547. Phone: (218) 498-2124. Located 5 miles E of Glyndon via US 10. GPS: 46.870840, -96.474675. Swimming beach, fishing. Hiking, nature trails. Scenic viewpoint. Park office, gift shop. Open all year. $24-34 per night. 44 sites, 35 with electric hookups. Drinking water. 60-foot limit. Restrooms; showers. Dump station.

Camden State Park

1897 Camden Park Rd, Lynd, MN 56157. Phone: (507) 872-7031. Located about 3 miles SW of Lynd via MN 23. GPS: 44.355850, -95.919829. Lake in park. Swimming beach, fishing, boating (rentals). Hiking, biking, equestrian, nature trails. Scenic viewpoint. Park office, nature store, gift shop. Open Apr-Oct. $24-34 per night. 80 sites, 47 with electric hookups. Drinking water. 60-foot limit. Restrooms; showers. Dump station. Equestrian camp, 12 sites.

Carley State Park

c/o Whitewater State Park, 19041 Hwy 74, Altura, MN 55910. Phone: (507) 312-2300. Located 4 miles S of Plainview via CR 4. GPS: 44.110013, -92.169941. Fishing (river). Hiking trails. Wildlife viewing. Scenic viewpoint. Open May-Sep. $20 per night. 20 sites, no hookups. Drinking water. 30-foot limit. Vault toilets. No showers. No dump station.

Cascade River State Park

3481 W Highway 61, Lutsen, MN 55612. Phone: (218) 387-6000. Located on Lake Superior between Lutsen and Grand Marais on MN 61 at mile post 101. GPS: 47.711038, -90.510674. Lake in park. Fishing, boating, skiing. Hiking trails. Scenic viewpoint. Waterfalls. Open all year. $23-33 per night. 40 sites, 21 with electric hookups. Drinking water. 35-foot limit. Restrooms; showers. Dump station.

Charles A. Lindbergh State Park

1615 Lindbergh Dr S, Little Falls, MN 56345. Phone: (320) 616-2525. Located on Mississippi River, 1 mile SW of Little Falls off US 10. GPS: 45.958909, -94.388254. Fishing (river), boating (canoe rentals). Hiking trails. Scenic viewpoint. Visitor center. Nature store, gift shop. Museum and childhood home of famous aviator Charles A. Lindbergh are adjacent to the park. Open Apr-Sep. $20-30 per night. 38 sites, 15 with electric hookups. Drinking water. 50-foot limit. Restrooms; showers. Dump station.

Crow Wing State Park

3124 State Park Rd, Brainerd, MN 56401. Phone: (218) 825-3075. Located about 10 miles SW of Brainerd via MN 371. GPS: 46.272837, -94.332248. Fishing (river), boating (rentals). Hiking, biking, walking trails. Wildlife viewing. Scenic viewpoint. Park office, gift shop. Open Apr-Sep. $23-33 per night. 59 sites, 12 with electric hookups. Drinking water. 45-foot limit. Restrooms; showers. Dump station.

Father Hennepin State Park

41294 Father Hennepin Park Rd, Isle, MN 56342. Phone: (320) 676-8763. Located 1 mile W of Isle via MN 27. GPS: 46.143686, -93.482865. Lake in park. Swimming beach, fishing, boating. Hiking, walking trails. Scenic viewpoint. Park office, gift shop. Two campgrounds open May-Oct. $23-33 per night. 103 sites, 51 with electric hookups. Drinking water. 60-foot limit. Restrooms; showers. Dump station.

Flandrau State Park

1300 Summit Ave, New Ulm, MN 56073. Phone: (507) 233-1260. Located about 2 miles S of town center near Summit Ave and 10th St. GPS: 44.293653, -94.465498. Swimming in a sand-bottom swimming pond, fishing (river), boating (carry-in). Hiking trails. Wildlife viewing. Scenic viewpoint. Park office, gift shop. Three campgrounds open all year. $24-34 per night. 84 sites, 34 with electric hookups. Drinking water. 66-foot limit. Restrooms; showers. Dump station.

Forestville / Mystery Cave State Park

21071 CR 118, Preston, MN 55965. Phone: (507) 352-5111. Located 17 miles W of Preston via MN 16, CR 5, and CR 118. GPS: 43.633748, -92.226026. Fishing (streams). Hiking, equestrian trails. Visitor center, nature store, gift shop. Cave tours. Historic Forestville tours, a restored 1800s village. Open Apr-Nov. $25-35 per night. 73 sites, 23 with electric hookups. Drinking water. 50-foot limit. Restrooms; showers. Dump station. Equestrian camp, 55 sites (23 with electric).

Fort Ridgely State Park

72158 County Road 30, Fairfax, MN 55332. Phone: (507) 426-7840. Located 6 miles S of Fairfax via MN 4. GPS: 44.447964, -94.726739. Hiking, biking, equestrian trails. Scenic viewpoint. Visitor center. Historic Fort Ridgely and museum. Open Apr-Oct. $23-33 per night. 33 sites, 15 with electric hookups. Drinking water. 60-foot limit. Restrooms; showers. Dump station. Equestrian camp, 14 sites (13 with electric).

Franz Jevne State Park

State Highway 11, Birchdale, MN 56629. Phone: (218) 647-8592. Located about 3 miles NE of Birchdale via MN 11 and CR 85. GPS: 48.641502, -94.058249. Fishing (river). Hiking, walking trails. Wildlife viewing. Open Apr-Oct. No reservations accepted. $20-30 per night. 18 sites, 2 with electric hookups. Drinking water. 30-foot limit. Vault toilets. No showers. No Dump station.

Frontenac State Park

29223 County 28 Blvd, Frontenac, MN 55026. Phone: (651) 345-3401. Located about a mile N of town via Galia Ave. GPS: 44.523740, -92.342310. Lake in park. Fishing. Hiking, biking, nature trails. Wildlife viewing. Bird watching. Scenic viewpoint. Park office, nature store, gift shop. Open all year. $24-34 per night. 58 sites, 19 with electric hookups. Drinking water. 53-foot limit. Restrooms; showers. Dump station.

Glacial Lakes State Park

25022 County Road 41, Starbuck, MN 56381. Phone: (320) 239-2860. Located 5 miles S of Starbuck via MN 29 and CR 41. GPS: 45.541315, -95.531483. Swimming beach, fishing, boating (rentals). Hiking, biking, equestrian, nature trails. Scenic viewpoint. Park office, gift shop. Open Apr-Oct. $23-33 per night. 37 sites, 14 with electric hookups. Drinking water. 45-foot limit. Restrooms; showers. Dump station. Equestrian area, 8 sites.

Gooseberry Falls State Park

3206 Highway 61 East, Two Harbors, MN 55616. Phone: (218) 595-7100. Located 13 miles NE of Two Harbors via MN 61. GPS: 47.138370, -91.467325. Lake in park. Hiking, biking, walking trails. Wildlife viewing. Visitor center, gift shop. Scenic waterfalls. Open all year. $25 per night. 69 sites, no hookups. Drinking water. 40-foot limit. Restrooms; showers. Dump station.

Great River Bluffs State Park

43605 Kipp Dr, Winona, MN 55987. Phone: (507) 312-2650. Located 20 miles SE of Winona via US 14/61 and CR 3.Can also be reached from I-90 Exit 266 by following CR 3 north 1 mile to park entrance. GPS: 43.939568, -91.408464. Hiking, nature trails. Bird watching. Scenic viewpoint. Park office, gift shop. Open all year. $23 per night. 31 sites, no hookups. Drinking water. 60-foot limit. Restrooms; showers. No Dump station.

Hayes Lake State Park

48990 County Road 4, Roseau, MN 56751. Phone: (218) 425-7504. Located about 24 miles SE of Roseau via MN 89 and CR 4. GPS: 48.637782, -95.545501. Swimming beach, fishing, boating (canoe/kayak rentals). Hiking, biking, equestrian trails. Bog boardwalk. Wildlife viewing. Scenic viewpoint. Open May-Oct. $23-33 per night. 35 sites, 18 with electric hookups. Drinking water. 40-foot limit. Restrooms; showers. Dump station.

Interstate State Park

307 Milltown Rd, Taylors Falls, MN 55084. Phone: (651) 539-4500. Located about a mile southwest of Taylors Falls via US 8. GPS: 45.394817, -92.667749. Fishing (river), boating (rentals). Hiking trails. Scenic viewpoint. Rock climbing. Visitor center, gift shop. Open Apr-Oct. $24-34 per night. 37 sites, 22 with electric hookups. Drinking water. 45-foot limit. Restrooms; showers. Dump station.

Itasca State Park

36750 Main Park Dr, Park Rapids, MN 56470. Phone: (218) 669-7251. Minnesota's oldest state park. Located 22 miles N of Park Rapids via US 71. GPS: 47.193872, -95.165594. Lakes in park. Swimming beach, fishing, boating (rentals). Hiking, biking (rentals), walking trails. Bird watching. Scenic viewpoint. Visitor center, gift shop. Restaurant. Itasca State Park itself is designated as a National Register Historic District. There are many historic sites within the park. Two campgrounds open all year. $25-35 per night. 223 sites, 160 with electric hookups. Drinking water. 60-foot limit. Restrooms; showers. Dump station.

Jay Cooke State Park

780 Highway 210, Carlton, MN 55718. Phone: (218) 673-7000. Located 3 miles E of Carlton via MN 210. GPS: 46.655239, -92.372735. Lake in park. Hiking, biking, equestrian, walking trails. Wildlife viewing. Scenic viewpoint. Visitor center, nature store, gift shop. Swinging suspension bridge. Pioneer cemetery. Open all year. $25-35 per night. 79 sites, 21 with electric hookups. Drinking water. 60-foot limit. Restrooms; showers. Dump station.

Judge C.R. Magney State Park

4051 E Highway 61, Grand Marais, MN 55604. Phone: (218) 387-6300. Located 14 miles NE of Grand Marais via MN 61. GPS: 47.817480, -90.053646. Lake in park. Fishing. Hiking, nature trails. Wildlife viewing. Restaurant (across the highway from park). Scenic waterfalls. Open May-Oct. $20 per night. 27 sites, no hookups. Drinking water. 45-foot limit. Restrooms; showers. No dump station.

Kilen Woods State Park

50200 860th St, Lakefield, MN 56150. Phone: (507) 832-6034. Located 9 miles NE of Lakefield via MN 86 and CR 24. GPS: 43.731083, -95.068081. Fishing, boating. Hiking trails. Bird watching. Scenic viewpoint. Open May-Oct. $20-30 per night. 33sites, 11 with electric hookups. Drinking water. 50-foot limit. Restrooms; showers.

Lac qui Parle State Park

14047 20th St NW, Watson, MN 56295. Phone: (320) 734-4450. Located about 6 miles NW of Watson via US 59, CR 13 and CR 32. GPS: 45.044322, -95.879049. Lake in park. Swimming beach, fishing, boating. Hiking, equestrian trails. Wildlife viewing area. Bird watching. Scenic viewpoint. Visitor center, nature store. Park is listed on the National Register of Historic Places. A number of WPA-built historic facilities can be found within the park. Two campgrounds open May-Oct. $23-41 per night. 67 sites, 9 full hookup, 58 with electric. Drinking water. 60-foot limit. Restrooms; showers. Dump station.

Lake Bemidji State Park

3401 State Park Road, Bemidji, MN 56601. Phone: (218) 308-2300. Located about 7 miles N of town via US 71 and CR 20. GPS: 47.535299, -94.826825. Swimming beach, fishing, boating (rentals). Hiking, biking (rentals), walking trails. Bird watching. Scenic viewpoint. Visitor center, nature store, gift shop. Marina. Open all year. $24-34 per night. 95 sites, 43 with electric hookups. Drinking water. 50-foot limit. Restrooms; showers. Dump station.

Lake Bronson State Park

3793 230th St, Lake Bronson, MN 56734. Phone: (218) 754-2200. Located 2 miles E of town via CR 28. GPS: 48.724318, -96.625621. Swimming beach, fishing, boating (rentals). Hiking, biking, equestrian, nature, walking trails. Wildlife viewing. Observation tower. Visitor center. Three campgrounds open all year. $23-33 per night. 152 sites, 67 with electric hookups. Drinking water. 50-foot limit. Restrooms; showers. Dump station.

Lake Carlos State Park

2601 County Road 38 NE, Carlos, MN 56319. Phone: (320) 852-7200. Located about 4 miles NW of Carlos via MN 29 and MN 38. GPS: 46.000672, -95.334923. Swimming beach, fishing, boating (rentals). Hiking, equestrian, nature trails. Wildlife viewing area. Bird watching. Scenic viewpoint. Park office, nature store, gift shop. Visitor center. Two campgrounds open all year. $25-35 per night. 121 sites, 81 with electric hookups. Drinking water. 50-foot limit. Restrooms; showers. Dump station. Equestrian camp, 7 primitive sites.

Lake Louise State Park

c/o Forestville/Mystery Cave State Park, 21071 County Road 118, Preston, MN 55965. Phone: (507) 352-5111. Located 2 miles N of LeRoy via 770th Ave. GPS: 43.535957, -92.512947. Swimming beach, fishing, boating. Hiking, biking, equestrian trails. Open May-Sep. $20-30 per night. 20 sites, 11 with electric hookups. Drinking water. 45-foot limit. Restrooms; showers. Dump station. Equestrian camp, 6 primitive sites.

Lake Shetek State Park

163 State Park Rd, Currie, MN 56123. Phone: (507) 763-3256. Located 3 miles NW of Currie via CR 38 and State Park Rd. GPS: 44.101428, -95.690731. Swimming beach, fishing, boating (rentals). Hiking, biking, walking trails. Scenic viewpoint. Park office, gift shop. Visitor center. Open all year. $23-41 per night. 66 sites, 32 full hookup, 32 with electric hookups. Drinking water. 70-foot limit. Restrooms; showers. Dump station.

Maplewood State Park

39721 Park Entrance Rd, Pelican Rapids, MN 56572. Phone: (218) 863-8383. Located 7 miles E of Pelican Rapids via MN 108. GPS: 46.538645, -95.953152. Lakes in park. Swimming beach, fishing, boating (rentals). Hiking, biking, equestrian trails. Wildlife viewing. Bird watching. Scenic viewpoint. Park office, gift shop. Open all year. $24-34 per night. 71 sites, 32 with electric hookups. Drinking water. 50-foot limit. Restrooms; showers. Dump station. Equestrian campground, 24 sites with no hookups.

McCarthy Beach State Park

7622 McCarthy Beach Road, Side Lake, MN 55781. Phone: (218) 274-7200. Located one mile W of town via McCarthy Beach Rd. GPS: 47.670678, -93.031034. Lakes in park. Swimming beach, fishing, boating (rentals). Hiking, biking, equestrian trails. Bird watching. Park office, nature store, gift shop. Two campgrounds open Apr-Nov. $20-33 per night. 86 sites, 21 with electric hookups. Drinking water. 40-foot limit. Restrooms; showers. Dump station. The Side Lake Campground has narrow roads with sharp turns and may not be suitable for some large RVs.

Mille Lacs Kathio State Park

15066 Kathio State Park Rd, Onamia, MN 56359. Phone: (320) 532-3523. Located 8 miles NW of Onamia via US 169. GPS: 46.135441, -93.725191. Lakes in park. Swimming beach, fishing, boating (rentals). Hiking, equestrian, nature trails. Bird watching. Observation tower. Park office, nature store, gift shop. Visitor center. Two campgrounds open all year. $23-35 per night. 70 sites, 22 with electric hookups. Drinking water. 60-foot limit. Restrooms; showers. Dump station. Equestrian camp, 10 sites. Restrooms but no showers or hookups.

Minneopa State Park

54497 Gadwall Rd, Mankato, MN 56001. Phone: (507) 386-3910. Located about 6 miles W of Mankato via US 169 and MN 68. Bison range in park. GPS: 44.157284, -94.090487. Fishing. Hiking, biking, walking trails. Wildlife viewing (bison herd). Bird watching. Scenic viewpoint. Visitor center. Scenic waterfalls. Seppmann Mill, a wind driven grist mill. Open all year. $24-34 per night. 61 sites, 6 with electric hookups. Drinking water. 60-foot limit. Restrooms; showers. Dump station.

Monson Lake State Park

1690 15th St NE, Sunburg, MN 56289. Phone: (320) 366-3797 or (320) 354-2055. Located 5 miles SW of Sunburg via CR 7 and CR 18. GPS: 45.318400, -95.275939. Fishing, boating. Hiking trail. Bird watching. Open all year. $20-30 per night. 20 sites, 6 with electric hookups. Drinking water. 70-foot limit. Restrooms; showers. No dump station.

Moose Lake State Park

4252 County Road 137, Moose Lake, MN 55767. Phone: (218) 460-7001. Located 1/4 mile E of I-35 Exit 214 near Moose Lake. GPS: 46.436279, -92.735776. Swimming beach, fishing, boating (rentals). Hiking, walking trails. Wildlife viewing. Open Apr-Nov. $23-33 per night. 33 sites, 20 with electric hookups. Drinking water. 60-foot limit. Restrooms; showers. No dump station.

Myre-Big Island State Park

19499 780th Ave, Albert Lea, MN 56007. Phone: (507) 668-7060. Located 2 miles east and south of I-35 Exit 11 in Albert Lea via CR 38. GPS: 43.637314, -93.308951. Lake in park. Swimming beach, fishing, boating (rentals). Hiking, biking, nature, walking trails. Bird watching. Park office, nature store, gift shop. Two campgrounds open all year. $24-34 per night. 93 sites, 32 with electric hookups. Drinking water. 60-foot limit. Restrooms; showers. Dump station.

Nerstrand-Big Woods State Park

9700 170th St E, Nerstrand, MN 55053. Phone: (507) 384-6140. Located 2 miles W of town via MN 246 and CR 40. GPS: 44.342041, -93.105380. Hiking, nature trails. Wildlife viewing. Park office, nature store. Visitor center. Scenic waterfalls. Open all year. $24-34 per night. 51 sites, 27 with electric hookups. Drinking water. 60-foot limit. Restrooms; showers. Dump station.

Old Mill State Park

33489 240th Ave NW, Argyle, MN 56713. Phone: (218) 754-2200. Located 14 miles E of Argyle via CR 4. GPS: 48.361429, -96.565606. Swimming beach. Hiking, equestrian, nature trails. Wildlife viewing. Scenic viewpoint. Log cabin and a steam-powered flour mill. Swinging bridge. Open May-Oct. $20-30 per night. 26 sites, 10 with electric hookups. Drinking water. 67-foot limit. Restrooms; showers. No dump station.

Red River State Recreation Area

515 2nd St NW, East Grand Forks, MN 56721. Phone: (218) 773-4950. Located on the Red River in East Grand Forks, off US 2. GPS: 47.929514, -97.029294. Fishing, boating. Hiking, biking, walking trails. Bird watching. Several restaurants within close walking distance. Open May-Sep. $23-41 per night. 109 sites, 98 full hookup, 3 electric only. Drinking water. 60-foot limit. Restrooms; showers. No dump station.

Rice Lake State Park

8485 Rose St, Owatonna, MN 55060. Phone: (507) 414-6191. Located about 8 miles E of Owatonna via CR 19. GPS: 44.092857, -93.063882. Fishing (limited), boating (canoe rentals). Note: Rice Lake is very shallow, canoe and kayaks are best for boating. Hiking, walking trails. Bird watching. Scenic viewpoint. Park office, gift shop. Open all year. $23-33 per night. 40 sites, 18 with electric hookups. Drinking water. 55-foot limit. Restrooms; showers. No dump station.

Sakatah Lake State Park

50499 Sakatah Lake State Park Rd, Waterville, MN 56096. Phone: (507) 698-7851. Located 2 miles E of Waterville via MN 60. GPS: 44.218995, -93.531924. Fishing, boating (rentals). Hiking, biking, walking trails. Park office, nature store, gift shop. Open all year. $23-33 per night. 62 sites, 14 with electric hookups. Drinking water. 55-foot limit. Restrooms; showers. Dump station.

Savanna Portage State Park

55626 Lake Place, McGregor, MN 55760. Phone: (218) 419-1500. Located 18 miles NE of McGregor via MN 65 and Lake Ave. GPS: 46.818531, -93.176465. Continental Divide runs through park. Lake in park. Swimming beach, fishing, boating (rentals). Hiking, biking, nature trails. Scenic viewpoint. Open all year. $23-33 per

night. 61 sites, 18 with electric hookups. Drinking water. 55-foot limit. Restrooms; showers. Dump station.

Scenic State Park

56956 Scenic Highway 7, Bigfork, MN 56628. Phone: (218) 743-3362. Located 7 miles SE of Bigfork via Scenic Hwy 7. GPS: 47.703111, -93.566943. Lake in park. Swimming beach, fishing, boating (rentals). Hiking, nature trails. Scenic viewpoint. Park office, nature store, gift shop. Two campgrounds open all year. $23-33 per night. 93 sites, 23 with electric hookups. Drinking water. 50-foot limit. Restrooms; showers. Dump station.

Schoolcraft State Park

9042 Schoolcraft Ln NE, Deer River, MN 56636. Phone: (218) 328-8982. Located about 17 miles W of Grand Rapids via US 2, MN 6, CR 28, and CR 74. GPS: 47.223108, -93.804960. Fishing (river), boating. Hiking, nature trails. Open May-Sep. $20 or less. 28 sites, no hookups. Drinking water. 40-foot limit. Vault toilets. No showers. No dump station.

Sibley State Park

800 Sibley Park Rd NE, New London, MN 56273. Phone: (320) 354-2055. Located 5 miles W of New London via MN 9 and CR 148. GPS: 45.313613, -95.032733. Lake in park. Swimming beach, fishing, boating (rentals). Hiking, biking, equestrian, nature, walking trails. Wildlife viewing area. Bird watching. Scenic viewpoint. Beach store, rentals. Park office, nature store, gift shop. Visitor center. Two campgrounds open all year. $25-35 per night. 132 sites, 87 with electric hookups. Drinking water. 70-foot limit. Restrooms; showers. Dump station. Equestrian campground, 9 sites. Vault toilets, water available.

Split Rock Creek State Park

336 50th Ave, Jasper, MN 56144. Phone: (507) 348-7908. Located 5 miles NE of Jasper via MN 23 and CR 20. GPS: 43.895936, -96.366134. Lake in park. Swimming beach, fishing. boating (rentals). Hiking, equestrian, walking trails. Wildlife viewing. Bird watching. Park office, nature store, gifts. Open May-Oct. $23-33 per night. 34 sites, 21 with electric hookups. Drinking water. 52-foot limit. Restrooms; showers. Dump station.

St. Croix State Park

30065 St. Croix Park Rd, Hinckley, MN 55037. Phone: (320) 384-6591. Located 15 miles E of I-35 Exit 183 in Hinckley via MN 48. GPS: 46.011957, -92.617761. Lake in park. Swimming beach, fishing, boating (rentals). Hiking, biking, equestrian, walking trails. Wildlife viewing. Bird watching. Observation tower. Visitor center, nature store, gifts. Park is listed as a National Historic Landmark. Three campgrounds open all year. $25-35 per night. 211 sites, 71 with electric hookups. Drinking water. 60-foot limit. Restrooms; showers. Dump station. Equestrian camp, 40 sites (19 with electric).

Temperance River State Park

State Highway 61, Schroeder, MN 55613. Phone: (218) 663-3100. Located in northeastern Minnesota on MN 61 just N of

Schroeder. GPS: 47.556593, -90.871299. Fishing (river), boating. Hiking, nature trails. Scenic viewpoint. Rock climbing. Park office, nature store, gifts. Scenic waterfalls. Open all year. $24-34 per night. 52 sites, 18 with electric hookups. Drinking water. 60-foot limit. Restrooms; showers. No dump station.

Tettegouche State Park

5702 State Highway 61, Silver Bay, MN 55614. Phone: (218) 353-8800. Located along MN 61 about 4 miles NE of Silver Bay. GPS: 47.339839, -91.196258. Lake in park. Fishing, boating (rentals). Hiking, biking, ATV trails. Bird watching. Scenic viewpoint. Rock climbing. Visitor center, gift shop. Scenic waterfalls. Open all year. $25-35 per night. 28 sites, 22 with electric hookups. Drinking water. 60-foot limit. Restrooms; showers. No dump station.

Upper Sioux Agency State Park

5908 Highway 67, Granite Falls, MN 56241. Phone: (320) 564-4777. Located about 8 miles SE of Granite Falls via MN 67. GPS: 44.737098, -95.460340. Fishing (river). Hiking, equestrian trails. Bird watching. Scenic viewpoint. Visitor center, nature store, gifts. Open May-Oct. $22-32 per night. 34 sites, 14 with electric hookups. Drinking water. 60-foot limit. Restrooms; showers. No dmp station. Equestrian camp, 45 sites (7 with electric hookups).

Whitewater State Park

19041 Highway 74, Altura, MN 55910. Phone: (507) 312-2300. Located 7 miles W of Altura via Center St and MN 74. GPS: 44.063006, -92.043413. Swimming beach, fishing (river). Hiking, nature trails. Scenic viewpoint. Visitor center. Nature store, gifts. Open all year. $25-35 per night. 110 sites, 85 with electric hookups. Drinking water. 50-foot limit. Restrooms; showers. Dump station.

Wild River State Park

39797 Park Trail, Center City, MN 55012. Phone: (651) 583-2125. Located 14 miles E of I-35 Exit 147 in North Branch via MN 95 and St Croix Trail. GPS: 45.523150, -92.749232. Fishing, boating. Hiking, biking, equestrian, walking trails. Wildlife viewing area. Scenic viewpoint. Park office, nature store, gifts. Visitor center. Open all year. $25-35 per night. 94 sites, 34 with electric hookups. Drinking water. 60-foot limit. Restrooms; showers. Dump station. Equestrian camp, 20 sites (18 with electric hookups).

William O'Brien State Park

16821 O'Brien Trail North, Marine on St. Croix, MN 55047. Phone: (651) 539-4980. Located about 2 miles N of town via MN 95. GPS: 45.224953, -92.765411. Swimming beach, fishing (river), boating (rentals). Hiking, biking, walking trails. Bird watching. Park office, gift shop. Visitor center. Two campgrounds open all year. $25-35 per night. 114 sites, 71 with electric hookups. Drinking water. 60-foot limit. Restrooms; showers. Dump station.

Zippel Bay State Park

3684 54th Ave NW, Williams, MN 56686. Phone: (218) 783-6252. Located 12.5 miles NW of Williams via CR 2 and CR 8. GPS: 48.847760, -94.850004. Lake in park. Swimming beach, fishing, boating (canoe rentals). Hiking, equestrian trails. Bird watching. Visitor center, nature store, gifts. Marina. Open Apr-Oct. $23 per night. 57 sites, no hookups. Drinking water. 60-foot limit. Restrooms; showers. Dump station.

Mississippi

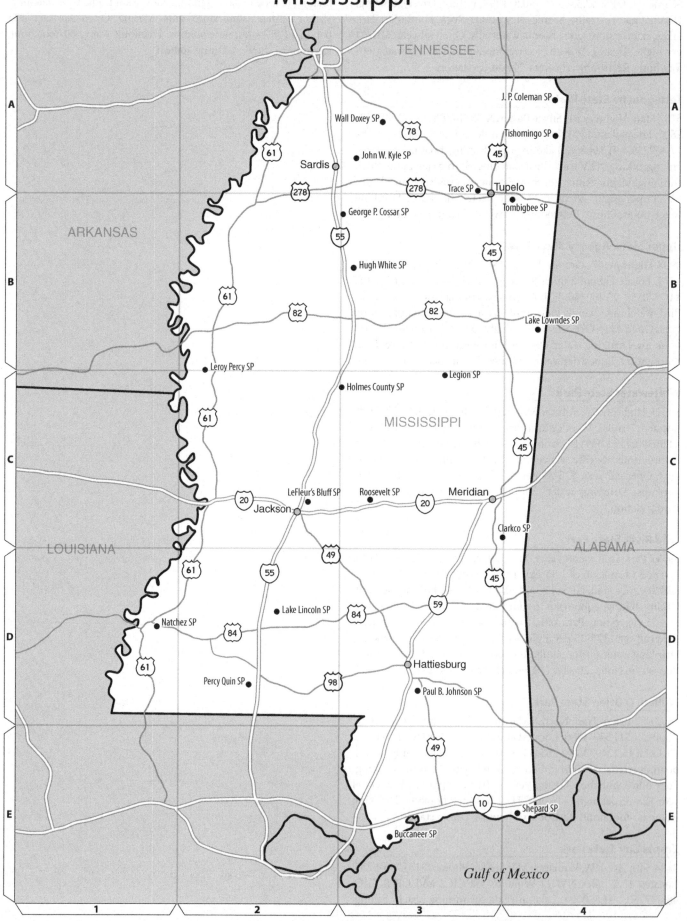

Mississippi

Mississippi Dept. of Wildlife, Fisheries and Parks
1505 Eastover Dr
Jackson, MS 39211

Phone: (601) 432-2400
Internet: www.mdwfp.com
Reservations: Online or call park.

Mississippi Park Locator

Mississippi Parks

Buccaneer State Park

1150 South Beach Blvd, Waveland, MS 39576. Phone: (228) 467-3822. Located 2 miles off US 90 on Beach Blvd in Waveland. GPS: 30.260652, -89.405342. On the Gulf of Mexico. Water park. Swimming pool, fishing (ocean). Hiking, biking, nature trails. Bird watching. Disc golf. Camp store. Activity center. Restaurant. Open all year. $28-45 per night. 276 sites, 206 full hookup, 70 with water and electric. Drinking water. 63-foot limit. Restrooms; showers. Laundry facilities. Dump station.

Clarkco State Park

386 Clarko Rd, Quitman, MS 39355. Phone: (601) 776-6651. Located 20 miles S of Meridian via US 45. GPS: 32.104199, -88.703425. Lake in park. Splash pad, swimming (lake), fishing, boating, skiing. Hiking, biking, nature trails. Observation tower. Disc golf. Open all year. $22-28 per night. 43 full hookup sites. 40-foot limit. Restrooms; showers. Laundry facilities. Dump station.

George P. Cossar State Park

165 County Road 170, Oakland, MS 38948. Phone: (622) 623-7356. Located 5 miles E of I-55 exit 227 near Oakland via MS 32. GPS: 34.124623, -89.882241. Lake in park. Fishing, boating, skiing. Hiking, biking, nature trails. Bird watching. Disc golf. Miniature golf. Visitor center. Two campgrounds open all year. $22-28 per night. 111 sites, 76 full hookup, 35 with water and electric. Drinking water. 40-foot limit. Restrooms; showers. Laundry facilities. Dump station.

Holmes County State Park

5369 State Park Rd, Durant, MS 39063. Phone: (662) 653-3351. Located 1 mile E of I-55 Exit 150 near Durant via MS 424. GPS: 33.027504, -89.918614. Open all year. No reservations accepted. $22 per night. Lake in park. Fishing, boating. Wildlife viewing. 28 sites with water and electric hookups. Restrooms; showers. Laundry facilities. Dump station.

Hugh White State Park

3170 State Park Rd, Grenada, MS 38902. Phone: (662) 226-4934. Located 5 miles E of Grenada via MS 8 and MS 333. GPS: 33.811703, -89.772765. Lake in park. Swimming beach, fishing, boating, skiing. Hiking trails. Golf course, pro shop. Disc golf. Visitor center. Open all year. $22 per night. 163 sites with water and electric hookups. 40-foot limit. Restrooms; showers. Laundry facilities. Dump station.

J. P. Coleman State Park

613 County Road 321, Iuka, MS 38852. Phone: (662) 423-6515. Located about 14 miles N of Iuka via MS 25 and CR 321. GPS: 34.930780, -88.168389. Lake in park. Swimming pool, fishing, boating, sailing, skiing. Biking. Miniature golf. Lodge, visitor center, park office. Marina. Open all year. $24-28 per night. 69 full hookup sites. 42-foot limit. Restrooms; showers. Laundry facilities. Dump station.

John W. Kyle State Park

4235 State Park Rd, Sardis, MS 38666. Phone: (662) 487-1345. Located about 8 miles E of Sardis and I-55 Exit 252 via MS 315. GPS: 34.411204, -89.805536. Lake in park. Swimming pool, fishing, boating, skiing. Biking. Golf course, pro shop. Visitor center. Open all year. $22-28 per night. 200 sites, 46 full hookup, 154 with water and electric. 40-foot limit. Restrooms; showers. Laundry facilities. Dump station.

Lake Lincoln State Park

2573 Sunset Rd NE, Wesson, MS 39191. Phone: (601) 643-9044. Located about 5 miles E of Wesson via Timberlane Rd and Sunset Rd. GPS: 31.674175, -90.341566. Swimming beach, fishing, boating, skiing. Hiking, nature trails. Disc golf. Open all year. $22-28 per night. 71 sites, 22 full hookup, 49 with water and electric hookups. 80-foot limit. Restrooms; showers. Laundry facilities. Dump station.

Lake Lowndes State Park

3319 Lake Lowndes Rd, Columbus, MS 39702. Phone: (662) 328-2110. Located 10 miles SE of Columbus via MS 69. GPS: 33.439624, -88.304885. Fishing, boating, skiing. Hiking, biking, equestrian trails. Bird watching. Disc golf. Visitor center. Open all year. $22-28 per night. 50 full hookup sites. 40-foot limit. Restrooms; showers. Laundry facilities. Dump station.

LeFleur's Bluff State Park

3315 Lakeland Terrace, Jackson, MS 39216. Phone: (601) 987-3923. Just E of I-55 Exit 98 in Jackson. GPS: 32.331336, -90.150367. Lake in park. Fishing, boating. Nature trails. Golf course, pro shop, driving range. Disc golf. Open all year. $22 per night. 28 sites with water and electric hookups. Restrooms; showers. Dump station.

Legion State Park

635 Legion State Park Rd, Louisville, MS 39339. Phone: (662) 773-8323. Located 2 miles NE of Louisville via N Columbus Ave. GPS: 33.146164, -89.039959. Lake in park. Fishing, boating. Nature trail. Wildlife viewing. Archery range. Open all year. $24 per night. 15 full hookup sites. 40-foot limit. Restrooms; showers.

Leroy Percy State Park

1400 Highway 12 W, Hollandale, MS 38748. Phone: (662) 827-5436. Located 5 miles W of Hollandale via MS 12. Mississippi's oldest state park. GPS: 33.160960, -90.936132. Lake in park. Fishing, boating. Nature trail. Wildlife viewing. Disc golf. Open all year. $24 per night. 16 full hookup sites. 40-foot limit. Restrooms; showers. Laundry facilities. Dump station.

Natchez State Park

230-B Wickliff Rd, Natchez, MS 39120. Phone: (601) 442-2658. Located 10 miles NE of Natchez via US 61 at Stanton. GPS: 31.612410, -91.237383. Lake in park. Fishing, boating. Nature trail. Wildlife viewing. Disc golf. Two campgrounds open all year. $22-24 per night. 50 sites, 6 full hookup, 44 with water and electric. 47-foot limit. Restrooms; showers. Laundry facilities. Dump station.

Paul B. Johnson State Park

319 Geiger Lake Rd, Hattiesburg, MS 39401. Phone: (601) 582-7721. Located 15 miles S of Hattiesburg via US 49. GPS: 31.141894, -89.248039. Lake in park. Splash pad. Swimming beach, fishing, boating, skiing. Hiking, biking, nature trails. Disc golf. Visitor center. Open all year. $24-28 per night. 125 full hookup sites. 75-foot limit. Restrooms; showers. Laundry facilities. Dump station.

Percy Quin State Park

2036 Percy Quin Dr, McComb, MS 39648. Phone: (601) 684-3938. Located 6 miles S of McComb off I-55 Exit 13. GPS: 31.191911, -90.497185. Lake in park. Swimming pool and beach, fishing, boating, skiing. Hiking, biking, nature trails. Bird watching. Golf course, pro shop. Camp store. Visitor center. Marina. Open all year. $24-28 per night. 100 full hookup sites. 40-foot limit. Restrooms; showers. Laundry facilities. Dump station.

Roosevelt State Park

2149 Highway 13 S, Morton, MS 39117. Phone: (601) 732-6316. Located just N of I-20 Exit 77 near Morton. GPS: 32.318253, -89.674017. Lake in park. Swimming pool, water slide, fishing, boating, skiing. Hiking, biking, nature trails. Wildlife viewing. Bird watching. Scenic viewpoint. Disc golf. Visitor center. Open all year. $22-28 per night. 109 sites, 82 full hookup, 27 with water and electric. 40-foot limit. Restrooms; showers. Laundry facilities. Dump station.

Shepard State Park

1034 Graveline Rd, Gautier, MS 39553. Phone: (228) 497-2244. Located 3 miles W of Pascagoula on Gulf of Mexico, off US 90 at Gautier. Operated by City of Gautier. GPS: 30.373046, -88.626476. Fishing, boating. Hiking, biking trails. Wildlife viewing. Disc golf. Archery range. Visitor center. Open all year. $24 per night. 28 sites with water and electric hookups. Restrooms; showers. Dump station.

Tishomingo State Park

105 County Road 90, Tishomingo, MS 38873. Phone: (662) 438-6914. Located off the Natchez Trace at mile marker 304. GPS: 34.618983, -88.198183. Lake in park. Swimming pool, fishing, boating (canoe rentals). Hiking trails. Bird watching. Disc golf. Rock climbing. Scenic Natchez Trace Parkway runs through park. Open all year. $22 per night. 62 sites with water and electric hookups. 40-foot limit. Restrooms; showers. Laundry facilities. Dump station.

Tombigbee State Park

254 Cabin Dr, Tupelo, MS 38804. Phone: (662) 842-7669. Located 6 miles SE of Tupelo via MS 6 and State Park Rd. GPS: 34.230653, -88.626183. Lake in park. Fishing, boating. Hiking, biking, nature trails. Disc golf. Visitor center. Open all year. $22-24 per night. 20 sites, 18 full hookup, 2 with water and electric. 40-foot limit. Restrooms; showers. Laundry facilities. Dump station.

Trace State Park

2139 Faulkner Rd, Belden, MS 38826. Phone: (662) 489-2958. Located 17 miles W of Tupelo via US 45 and US 278. GPS: 34.260145, -88.886535. Lake in park. Fishing. Hiking, biking, equestrian, ORV trails. Bird watching. Disc golf. Pontotoc Country Club's 18-hole golf course is next to park. Open all year. $24-28 per night. 76 full hookup sites. 40-foot limit. Restrooms; showers. Laundry facilities. Dump station.

Wall Doxey State Park

3946 Highway 7 S, Holly Springs, MS 38635. Phone: (662) 252-4231. Located 7 miles S of Holly Springs via MS 7. GPS: 34.664733, -89.460737. Lake in park. Fishing, boating. Hiking, biking trail. Disc golf. Visitor center. Open all year. $22 per night. 64 sites with water and electric hookups. 40-foot limit. Restrooms; showers. Laundry facilities. Dump station.

Missouri

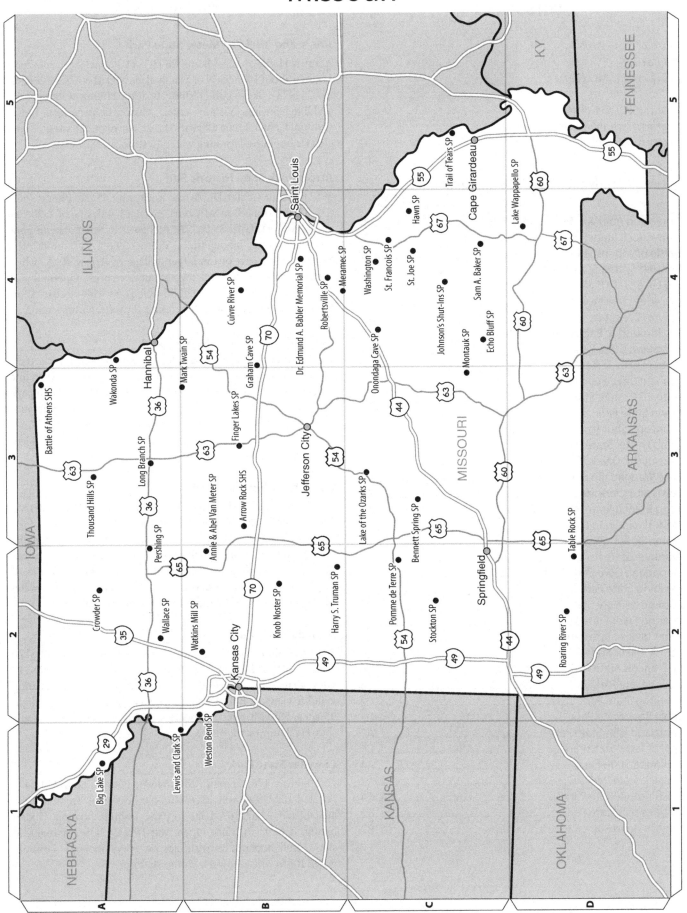

Missouri

Missouri State Parks
PO Box 176
Jefferson City, MO 65102

Phone: (800) 334-6946
Internet: www.mostateparks.com
Reservations: Online or (877) 422-6766

Missouri Park Locator

Missouri Parks

Annie and Abel Van Meter State Park

32146 N Highway 122, Miami, MO 65344. Phone: (660) 886-7537. Located about 14 miles N of Marshall via MO 41. GPS: 39.258362, -93.262423. Lake in park. Fishing, boating. Hiking, walking trails. Wildlife viewing. Visitor center. Missouri's American Indian Cultural Center. Open all year. $12-25 per night. 21 sites, 12 with electric hookups. Drinking water. Restrooms; showers.

Arrow Rock State Historic Site

39521 Visitor Center Dr, Arrow Rock, MO 65320. Phone: (660) 837-3330. Located on Missouri River, 13 miles N of 1-70 Exit 98 via MO 41. GPS: 39.063223, -92.946381. Small lake in park. Fishing. Hiking, biking trails. Visitor center. Restaurant. This historic site is part of the larger Village of Arrow Rock, which features quaint stores and several antique shops. Open all year. $13-30 per night. 47 sites, 1 full hookup, 34 with electric, 12 no hookups. Drinking water. Restrooms; showers. Dump station.

Battle of Athens State Historic Site

12378 Athens State Park Rd, Revere, MO 63465. Phone: (660) 877-3871. Located on Hwy CC, off MO 81, near Iowa state line, on Des Moines River. GPS: 40.588333, -91.710806. Lake in park. Fishing (river), boating. Hiking trails. Site includes interpretation and tours of the battlefield as well as a number of historic buildings. Open all year. $13-25 per night. 29 sites, 15 with electric, 14 no hookups. Restrooms; showers.

Bennett Spring State Park

26250 Hwy 64A, Lebanon, MO 65536. Phone: (417) 532-4338. Located on MO 64, 12 miles NW of Lebanon (I-44 exit 129). GPS: 37.725412, -92.856351. Swimming pool, fishing, boating (rentals). Hiking, biking, trails. Park store. Nature center. Restaurant. Five campgrounds open all year. $13-30 per night. 186 sites, 48 full hookup, 123 with electric, 15 no hookups. Drinking water. Restrooms; showers. Laundry facilities. Dump station.

Big Lake State Park

204 Lake Shore Dr, Craig, MO 64437. Phone: (660) 442-3770. Located SW of Mound City near Kansas state line on MO 111. GPS: 40.086216, -95.342919. Swimming pool, fishing, boating. Wildlife viewing. Bird watching. Open all year. $13-25 per night. 75 sites, 58 with electric hookups. Drinking water. Restrooms; showers. Dump station.

Crowder State Park

76 Highway 128, Trenton, MO 64683. Phone: (660) 359-6473. Located off US 65, on MO 146, 4 miles W of Trenton. GPS: 40.090847, -93.672167. Lake in park. Fishing, boating. Hiking, biking, equestrian trails. Open Mar-Nov. $13-30 per night. 39 sites, 5 full hookup, 29 with electric, 5 no hookups. Drinking water. Restrooms; showers. Dump station.

Cuivre River State Park

678 State Route 147, Troy, MO 63379. Phone: (636) 528-7247. Located about 6 miles NE of Troy via MO 47 and MO 147. GPS: 39.031025, -90.910386. Lake in park. Swimming beach, fishing, boating. Hiking, biking, equestrian trails. Wildlife viewing. Scenic viewpoint. Visitor center. Open all year. $13-30 per night. 92 sites, 31 full hookup, 19 with electric, 42 no hookups. Drinking water. Restrooms; showers. Laundry facilities. Dump station. Equestrian camp, 13 sites (8 with electric hookups).

Dr. Edmund A. Babler Memorial State Park

800 Guy Park Dr, Wildwood, MO 63005. Phone: (636) 458-3813. Located 20 miles W of St. Louis off MO 109, between US 40 and MO 100. GPS: 38.617409, -90.689792. Hiking, biking, equestrian trails. Scenic viewpoint. Visitor center, gifts. Open all year. $13-25 per night. 72 sites, 47 with electric, 25 no hookups. Drinking water. Restrooms; showers. Dump station.

Echo Bluff State Park

34489 Echo Bluff Dr, Eminence, MO 65466. Phone: (844) 322-3246. Located in SE Missouri, 11 miles N of Eminence on MO 19, on Sinking Creek. GPS: 37.313617, -91.401554. Swimming, fishing, boating. Hiking, biking trails. Park store. Lodge, restaurant. Open all year. $13-37 per night. 60 sites, 41 full hookup, 19 with water and electric. Restrooms; showers. Dump station.

Finger Lakes State Park

1505 E Peabody Rd, Columbia, MO 65202. Phone: (573) 443-5315. Located 10 miles N of Columbia (1-70 exit 123) off US 63. GPS: 39.101656, -92.318114. Swimming beach, fishing, boating. Hiking, biking, ORV trails. Open all year. $13-25 per night. 35 sites, 16 with electric, 19 no hookups. Drinking water. Restrooms; showers. Dump station.

Graham Cave State Park

217 Hwy TT, Danville, MO 63361. Phone: (573) 564-3476. Located on Loutre River, 2 miles W of Danville (I-70 exit 170) on Hwy TT. GPS: 38.909448, -91.572438. Lake in park. Fishing, boating. Hiking, biking trails. Visitor center. Cave tours. Open all year. $12-23 per night. 52 sites, 18 with electric hookups. Drinking water. Restrooms; showers. Laundry facilities. Dump station.

Harry S. Truman State Park

28761 State Park Rd, Warsaw, MO 65355. Phone: (660) 438-7711. Located off MO 7 on Hwy UU, on Lake of the Ozarks (Truman Lake), W of US 65 at Warsaw. GPS: 38.271670, -93.446802. Lake in park. Swimming beach, fishing, boating (rentals). Hiking trails. Park store. Marina. Six campgrounds; one is open all year. $10-27 per night. 182 sites, 117 with electric hookups. Drinking water. Restrooms; showers. Laundry facilities. Dump station.

Hawn State Park

12096 Park Dr, Sainte Genevieve, MO 63670. Phone: (573) 883-3603. Located 14 miles SW of I-55 exit 150 via MO 32 and MO 144. GPS: 37.830961, -90.228342. Hiking, walking trails. Wildlife viewing. Bird watching. Scenic viewpoint. Open all year. $13-

25 per night. 49 sites, 25 with electric hookups. Drinking water. Restrooms; showers. Laundry facilities.

Johnson's Shut-Ins State Park

148 Taum Sauk Tr, Middlebrook, MO 63656. Phone: (573) 546-2450. Located in remote section of southeast MO near Mark Twain National Forest, on Hwy N, SW of Park Hills and US 67. GPS: 37.550042, -90.846612. Swimming, fishing . Hiking, biking (rentals), equestrian trails. Camp store. Park store. Visitor center. Open all year. $13-30 per night. 68 sites, 19 full hookup, 21 with electric, 28 no hookups. Drinking water. Restrooms; showers. Laundry facilities. Dump station.

Knob Noster State Park

873 SE 10 Road, Knob Noster, MO 65336. Phone: (660) 563-2463. Located on MO 23, outside Knob Noster, off US 50. GPS: 38.751401, -93.581529. Two small lakes in park. Fishing, boating (canoe). Hiking, biking, equestrian trails. Wildlife viewing. Visitor center. Open all year. $13-23 per night. 68 sites, 41 with electric hookups. Drinking water. Restrooms; showers. Laundry facilities. Dump station.

Lake of the Ozarks State Park

403 Highway 134, Kaiser, MO 65047. Phone: (573) 348-2694. Located on Lake of the Ozarks near Osage Beach (US 54) via MO 42 and MO 134. GPS: 38.123746, -92.561918. Swimming beaches, fishing, boating (rentals). Hiking, biking, equestrian trails. Rock climbing. Park store. Camp store. Visitor center. Marinas. Cave tours. Open all year. $13-25 per night. 182 sites, 124 with electric hookups. Drinking water. Restrooms; showers. Laundry facilities. Dump station.

Lake Wappapello State Park

8005 State Highway 172, Williamsville, MO 63967. Phone: (573) 297-3232. Located 16 miles N of Popular Bluff off US 67. GPS: 36.939742, -90.334158. Swimming beach, fishing, boating (rentals). Hiking, biking, equestrian trails. Bird watching. Park store. Two campgrounds; one is open all year. $14-22 per night. 72 sites, 68 with electric hookups. Drinking water. Restrooms; showers. Laundry facilities. Dump station.

Lewis and Clark State Park

801 Lake Crest Blvd, Rushville, MO 64484. Phone: (816) 579-5564. Located on MO 138, on the Missouri River, 20 miles SW of St. Joseph. GPS: 39.538785, -95.053450. Lake in park. Fishing, boating. Hiking, biking trail. Bird watching. Open all year. $13-25 per night. 69 sites, 62 with electric hookups. Drinking water. Restrooms; showers. Laundry facilities. Dump station.

Long Branch State Park

28615 Visitor Center Rd, Macon, MO 63552. Phone: (660) 773-5229. Located on Long Branch Lake, 2 miles W of the US 63/US 36 junction, outside Macon. GPS: 39.771968, -92.526462. Lake in park. Swimming beach, fishing, boating (rentals). Hiking, biking trails. Park store. Marina. Open all year. $13-28 per night. 74 sites,

56 with electric hookups. Drinking water. Restrooms; showers. Dump station.

Mark Twain State Park

37352 Shrine Rd, Florida, MO 65283. Phone: (573) 565-3440. Located on MO 107, NE of Moberly, N of MO 154 on Mark Twain Lake. GPS: 39.466270, -91.799227. Lake in park. Swimming beach, fishing, boating. Hiking, biking trails. Wildlife viewing. Scenic viewpoint. The Mark Twain Birthplace State Historic Site is located adjacent to the park. Three campgrounds open all year. $12-25 per night. 93 sites, 71 with electric hookups. Drinking water. Restrooms; showers. Laundry facilities. Dump station.

Meramec State Park

115 Meramec Park Dr, Sullivan, MO 63080. Phone: (573) 468-6072. Located on Meramec River, 3 miles E of Sullivan (1-44 exit 225) on MO 185. GPS: 38.206660, -91.102187. Swimming, fishing (river), boating, rafting (rentals). Hiking trails. Park store. Visitor center. Restaurant. Fisher Cave, tours. Open all year. $13-30 per night. 209 sites, 20 full hookup, 14 with water and electric, 124 electric only, 51 no hookups. Drinking water. Restrooms; showers. Laundry facilities. Dump station.

Montauk State Park

345 County Road 6670, Salem, MO 65560. Phone: (573) 548-2201. Located 22 miles SW of Salem via MO 32 and MO 119. GPS: 37.453863, -91.677978. Fishing (river). Hiking, biking trails. Lodge, store, restaurant, snack bar, soda fountain. Montauk Mill, a gristmill built in 1896. Much of the original machinery used to grind the grain is still intact. Open all year. $13-25 per night. 146 sites, 116 with electric hookups. Drinking water. Restrooms; showers. Laundry facilities. Dump station.

Onondaga Cave State Park

7556 Highway H, Leasburg, MO 65535. Phone: (573) 245-6576. Located 5 miles SE of Leasburg via Hwy H. GPS: 38.064368, -91.230356. Lake in park. Fishing. Hiking, biking trails. Wildlife viewing. Park store. Visitor center. A National Natural Landmark, cave tours. Open all year. $13-27 per night. 64 sites, 45 with water and electric hookups. Drinking water. Restrooms; showers. Laundry facilities. Dump station.

Pershing State Park

29277 MO 130, Laclede, MO 64651. Phone: (660) 963-2299. Located 4 miles SW of Laclede via US 36 and MO 130. GPS: 39.758654, -93.213009. Four small lakes in park. Fishing, boating (no launch ramps). Hiking, walking trails. Bird watching. Observation tower. Open all year. $13-23 per night. 38 sites, 26 with electric hookups. Drinking water. Restrooms; showers. Laundry facilities. Dump station.

Pomme de Terre State Park

23451 Park Entrance Road, Pittsburg, MO 65724. Phone: (417) 852-4291. Located 5 miles S of Hermitage via MO 254 and MO 64. GPS: 37.883065, -93.303468. Lake in park. Swimming beaches, fishing, boating (rentals). Hiking, biking (rentals) trails. Two park stores. Marina, grill, store. Two camping areas open all year. $10-27 per night. 236 sites, 20 with electric and water hookups, 181 electric only, 35 no hookups. Drinking water. Restrooms; showers. Laundry facilities. Dump station.

Roaring River State Park

12716 Farm Road 2239, Cassville, MO 65625. Phone: (417) 847-2539. Located 7 miles S of Cassville via MO 112. GPS: 36.578733, -93.830335. Swimming pool, fishing (river). Hiking trails. Park store. Nature center. Restaurant. Three campgrounds, one open all year. $14-26 per night. 168 sites, 1 full hookup, 126 with electric, 41 no hookups. Drinking water. Restrooms; showers. Laundry facilities. Dump station.

Robertsville State Park

900 State Park Dr, Robertsville, MO 63072. Phone: (636) 257-3788. Located just W of Robertsville along Hwy O. GPS: 38.419878, -90.817936. Fishing (river), boating. Hiking trails. Wildlife viewing. Bird watching. Open all year. $12-25 per night. 25 sites, 14 with electric hookups. Drinking water. Restrooms; showers. Laundry facilities. Dump station.

Sam A. Baker State Park

5580 State Highway 143, Patterson, MO 63956. Phone: (573) 856-4411. Located on St. Francois River, 4 miles N of Patterson on MO 143, W of US 67. GPS: 37.257062, -90.505428. Swimming, wading, tubing, fishing, boating (rentals). Hiking, biking, equestrian trails. Park store. Visitor center/nature center. Restaurant. Two RV campgrounds, one open all year. $13-25 per night. 175 sites, 131 with electric hookups. Drinking water. Restrooms; showers. Laundry facilities. Dump station. Equestrian camp open Mar-Nov. 21 sites, 10 with electric hookups.

St. Francois State Park

8920 US Hwy 67 N, Bonne Terre, MO 63628. Phone: (573) 358-2173. Located 6 miles N of Bonne Terre via US 67. GPS: 37.956071, -90.534457. River swimming allowed, no designated area. Fishing, boating (motorized boats not recommended). Hiking, equestrian trails. Wildlife viewing. Rock climbing. Open all year. $13-23 per night. 109 sites, 63 with electric hookups. Drinking water. Restrooms; showers. Laundry facilities. Dump station.

St. Joe State Park

2800 Pimville Rd, Park Hills, MO 63601. Phone: (573) 431-1069. Located 5 miles S of Park Hills via MO 32 and Pimville Rd. GPS: 37.803502, -90.506819. Lakes in park. Swimming beaches, fishing, boating (canoe/kayak rentals), scuba diving. Hiking, biking, equestrian trails. Shooting range. Park store. Radio controlled flying field. Two campgrounds open all year. $13-25 per night. 73 sites, 40 with electric hookups. Drinking water. Restrooms; showers. Laundry facilities. Dump station.

Stockton State Park

19100 Highway 215, Dadeville, MO 65635. Phone: (417) 276-4259. Located on Stockton Lake about 10 miles S of Stockton via

MO 39 and MO 215. GPS: 37.605249, -93.738509. Lake in park. Swimming beach, fishing, boating (rentals). Hiking, biking trails. Park store. Marina, grill. Two campgrounds open all year. $13-25 per night. 70 sites, 53 with electric hookups. Drinking water. Restrooms; showers. Laundry facilities. Dump station.

Table Rock State Park

5272 State Highway 165, Branson, MO 65616. Phone: (417) 334-4704. Located about 10 miles SW of Branson via US 65 and MO 165. GPS: 36.583375, -93.309750. Lake in park. Swimming, fishing, boating (rentals). Hiking, biking (rentals), walking trails. Marina, store, grill. Boat tours. Two campgrounds open all year. $13-30 per night. 157 sites, 41 full hookup, 73 with electric, 43 no hookups. Drinking water. Restrooms; showers. Laundry facilities. Dump station.

Thousand Hills State Park

29431 State Highway 157, Kirksville, MO 63501. Phone: (660) 665-6995. Located on Forest Lake, 5 miles W of Kirksville via MO 6 and MO 157. GPS: 40.195998, -92.646889. Lake in park. Swimming beach, fishing, boating (rentals). Hiking, biking trails. Bird watching. Marina, store. Restaurant. Two campgrounds open all year. $13-25 per night. 53 sites, 38 with electric hookups. Drinking water. Restrooms; showers. Dump station.

Trail of Tears State Park

429 Moccasin Springs, Jackson, MO 63755. Phone: (573) 290-5268. Located 11 miles N of Cape Girardeau via MO 177. GPS: 37.438409, -89.480431. Lake in park. Swimming beach, fishing (river & lake), boating. Hiking, equestrian, nature trails. Scenic viewpoint. Visitor center. Two campgrounds, one open all year. $13-28 per night. 52 sites, 7 full hookup, 10 with electric, 35 no hookups. Drinking water. Restrooms; showers. Laundry facilities. Dump station.

Wakonda State Park

32836 State Park Rd, LaGrange, MO 63448. Phone: (573) 655-2280. Located 3 miles S of LaGrange via US 61. GPS: 40.007165, -91.523128. Six lakes in park. Swimming beach, fishing, boating (rentals). Hiking, biking, walking trails. Bird watching. Two campgrounds open all year. $13-30 per night. 81 sites, 9 full hookup, 65 with electric, 7 no hookups. Drinking water. Restrooms; showers. Laundry facilities. Dump station.

Wallace State Park

10621 NE Highway 121, Cameron, MO 64429. Phone: (816) 632-3745. Located 2 miles E of I-35 Exit 48 near Cameron via US 69 and MO 121. GPS: 39.660448, -94.213286. Small lake in park. Fishing, boating (small boats, no boat ramp). Hiking trails. Four camping areas, two open all year. $13-25 per night. 81 sites, 42 with electric hookups. Drinking water. Restrooms; showers. Laundry facilities. Dump station.

Washington State Park

13041 State Highway 104, DeSoto, MO 63020. Phone: (636) 586-5768. Located 11 miles SW of DeSoto via MO 21 and MO 104. GPS: 38.085306, -90.694609. Swimming pool, fishing (river), boating (rentals). Hiking trails. Wildlife viewing. Scenic viewpoint. Park store. Interpretive center. Concession stand. Open all year. $10-23 per night. 49 sites, 23 with electric hookups. Drinking water. Restrooms; showers. Laundry facilities. Dump station.

Watkins Mill State Park

26600 Park Road N, Lawson, MO 64062. Phone: (816) 580-3387. Located 7 miles E of I-35 Exit 26 in Kearney via MO 92. GPS: 39.389670, -94.265010. Lake in park. Swimming beach, fishing, boating. Hiking, biking, equestrian trails. Visitor center. Adjacent to park is Watkins Woolen Mill State Historic Site. A National Historic Landmark and National Engineering Landmark. Guided tours available. Open all year. $13-25 per night. 91 sites, 74 with electric hookups. Drinking water. Restrooms; showers. Laundry facilities. Dump station.

Weston Bend State Park

16600 Highway 45 N, Weston, MO 64098. Phone: (816) 640-5443. Located 3 miles S of Weston via MO 45. GPS: 39.392288, -94.866317. Hiking, biking, walking trails. Scenic overlook. Learn about the area's history of tobacco production and trade by reading the interpretive display at the tobacco barn. Open all year. $13-25 per night. 34 sites with electric hookups. Drinking water. Restrooms; showers. Laundry facilities. Dump station.

Montana

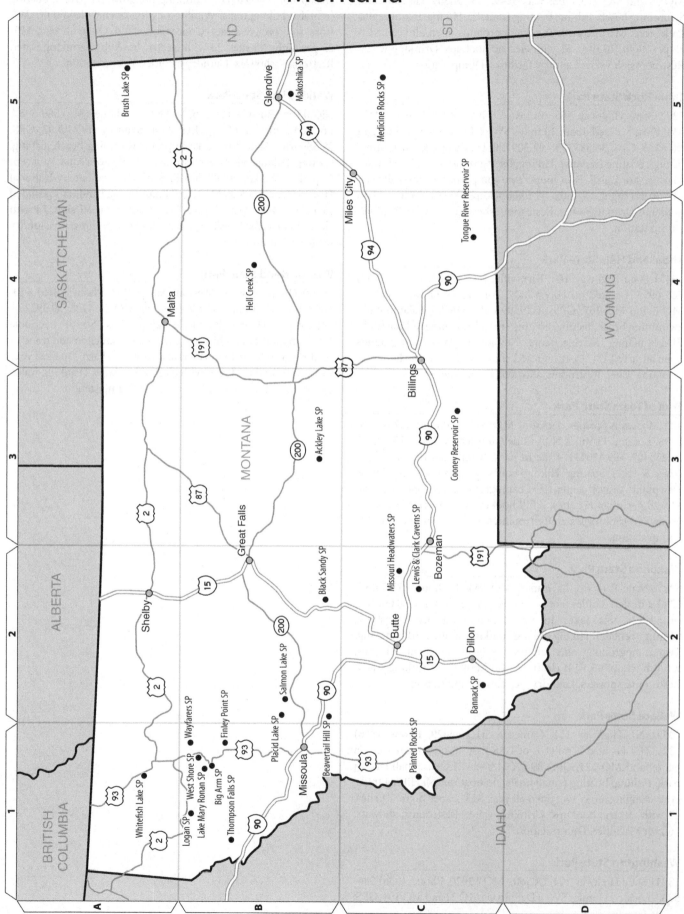

Montana

Montana Fish, Wildlife & Parks
1420 E 6th Ave
Helena, MT 59620

Phone: (406) 444-3750
Internet: www.stateparks.mt.gov
Reservations: Online or call park.

Montana Park Locator

Montana Parks

Ackley Lake State Park

989 Ackley Lake Rd, Hobson, MT 59452. Phone: (406) 727-1212. Located 6 miles SW of Hobson via MT 400. GPS: 46.95795, -109.94090. Swimming fishing, boating, skiing. Wildlife viewing. Bird watching. Open all year. No reservations accepted. $14-28 per night. 26 sites, no hookups. No water.

Bannack State Park

721 Bannack Rd, Dillon, MT 59725. Phone: (406) 834-3413. Located 25 miles W of Dillon via MT 278. Near Bannack ghost town. GPS: 45.160684, -112.994215. Fishing. Hiking, biking, equestrian, walking trails. Wildlife viewing. Bird watching. Visitor center. Store, gift shop. Best preserved ghost town in Montana. Park is a National Historic Landmark and the site of Montana's first major gold discovery on July 28, 1862. Tours available. Open all year. $14-28 per night. 24 sites, no hookups. Drinking water. 45-foot limit. Restrooms; no showers.

Beavertail Hill State Park

29895 Bonita Station Rd, Clinton, MT 59825. Phone: (406) 677-6804. Located S of I-90 Exit 130, 26 miles E of Missoula. GPS: 46.72047, -113.57628. Fishing (river), boating. Hiking, nature trails. Wildlife viewing. Bird watching. Open May-Oct. $14-28 per night. 24 sites with electric hookups. Drinking water. 70-foot limit. Restrooms; no showers.

Big Arm State Park

28031 Big Arm State Park Rd, Big Arm, MT 59910. Phone: (406) 849-5256. Located on US 93, west side of Flathead Lake, 14 miles N of Polson. GPS: 47.80534, -114.31339. Lake in park. Swimming beach, fishing, boating, skiing, scuba diving. Hiking, biking, nature trails. Bird watching. Visitor center. Open Apr-Oct. $14-28 per night. 40 sites, no hookups. Drinking water. 40-foot limit. Restrooms; showers.

Black Sandy State Park

6563 Hauser Dam Rd, Helena, MT 59602. Phone: (406) 458-3221 or (406) 495-3270. Located 8 miles NE of I-15 Exit 200 via Lincoln Rd and Hauser Dam Rd. GPS: 46.744689, -111.886811. Lake in park. Swimming, fishing, boating, skiing. Hiking, biking trails. Wildlife viewing. Open all year. $14-28 per night. 35 sites, 29 with electric hookups. Drinking water. 35-foot limit. Restrooms; no showers. Dump station.

Brush Lake State Park

Mailing address: PO Box 134, Medicine Lake, MT 59247. Phone: (406) 377-6256. Remote location in northeastern MT, near North Dakota state line. Located 25 miles NE of Medicine Lake via MT 16 and E Reserve Hwy. GPS: 48.605039, -104.102700. Swimming beach, no fishing (due to the mineral make-up of lake, there are no fish), boating, skiing, scuba diving. Hiking, walking trails. Wildlife viewing. Open May-Nov. $14-28 per night. 12 sites with electric hookups. Drinking water. 40-foot limit. Restrooms; no showers.

Cooney Reservoir State Park

86 Lake Shore Rd, Roberts, MT 59070. Phone: (406) 445-2326. Located 7 miles N of Roberts via Cooney Rd. GPS: 45.441544, -109.205353. Swimming, fishing, boating, skiing. Hiking, biking trails. Bird watching. Open all year. $14-28 per night. 72 sites, 21 with electric hookups. Drinking water. 80-foot limit. Restrooms; showers.

Finley Point State Park

31453 Finley Point Rd, Finley Point, MT 59860. Phone: (406) 887-2715. Located 12 miles NE of Polson via US 93 and MT 35. GPS: 47.755307, -114.082062. Lake in park. Swimming beach, fishing, boating, skiing. Hiking trails. Wildlife viewing. Marina. Open Apr-Oct. $14-28 per night. 18 sites with electric hookups. Drinking water. 50-foot limit. Restrooms; no showers.

Hell Creek State Park

2456 Hell Creek Rd, Jordan, MT 59337. Phone: (406) 557-2362. Remote location on Fort Peck Lake, 25 miles N of Jordan via MT 543 and Hell Creek Rd. GPS: 47.614816, -106.886941. Lake in park. Swimming beach, fishing, boating, skiing. Hiking trails. Wildlife viewing. Marina. Open all year. $14-28 per night. 71 sites, 44 with electric hookups. Drinking water. 75-foot limit. Restrooms; showers. Dump station.

Lake Mary Ronan State Park

50623 Lake Mary Ronan Rd, Dayton, MT 59860. Phone: (406) 849-5082 or (406) 755-2706. Located 7 miles NW of Dayton. GPS: 47.927971, -114.381670. Swimming beach, fishing, boating. Hiking trail. Wildlife viewing. Open all year. $14-28 per night. 25 sites with electric hookups. Drinking water. 40-foot limit. Restrooms; no showers.

Lewis & Clark Caverns State Park

25 Lewis & Clark Caverns Rd, Whitehall, MT 59759. Phone: (406) 287-3541. Located about 15 miles E of Whitehall via I-90 and MT 2. GPS: 45.822875, -111.851547. Fishing (river), boating. Hiking, biking trails. Bird watching. Scenic viewpoint. Visitor center, gift shop, food concession. Guided cave tours. Open all year. $14-28 per night. 39 sites, 18 with electric hookups. Drinking water. 71-foot limit. Restrooms; showers. Dump station.

Logan State Park

77518 US Hwy 2, Libby, MT 59923. Phone: (406) 293-7190 or (406) 751-4590. Located 45 miles SE of Libby via US 2. GPS: 48.033133, -115.066141. Lake in park. Swimming, fishing, boating, skiing. Hiking trails. Wildlife viewing. Open May-Sep. $14-28 per night. 37 sites, 33 with electric hookups. Drinking water. 45-foot limit. Restrooms; showers. Dump station.

Makoshika State Park

1301 Snyder Ave, Glendive, MT 59330. Phone: (406) 377-6256. Located just SE of Glendive via Snyder St. GPS: 47.076431, -104.695620. Hiking, biking, equestrian trails. Wildlife viewing. Scenic viewpoint. Disc golf. Visitor center, gift shop. Museum. Park houses many fossil remains of such dinosaurs as Tyrannosaurus rex and Triceratops. Open all year. $12-28 per night. 15 sites, no hookups. Drinking water. 60-foot limit. Restrooms; no showers.

Medicine Rocks State Park

1141 Highway 7, Ekalaka, MT 59324. Phone: (406) 377-6256. Located about 12 miles NE of Ekalaka via MT 7. GPS: 46.045501, -104.458166. Hiking, biking trails. Wildlife viewing. Bird watching. Scenic viewpoint. Listed on the National Register of Historic Places. Open all year. $12-28 per night. No reservations accepted. 12 sites, no hookups. Drinking water. 50-foot limit. Vault toilets; no showers.

Missouri Headwaters State Park

1585 Trident Rd, Three Forks, MT 59752. Phone: (406) 285-3610. Located 4 miles NE of I-90 Exit 278 near Three Forks via Frontage Rd and Trident Rd. GPS: 45.920344, -111.499680. Swimming, fishing, river floating, boating. Hiking, biking, equestrian trails. Wildlife viewing. Bird watching. Here the Jefferson, Madison, and Gallatin rivers merge to form the 2,300 mile Missouri River. A National Historic Landmark. Open all year. $14-28 per night. 17 sites, no hookups. Drinking water. 47-foot limit. Restrooms; no showers.

Painted Rocks State Park

8809 W Fork Rd, Darby, MT 59829. Phone: (406) 273-4253 (Travelers' Rest State Park). Located about 30 miles S of Darby via MT 473. GPS: 45.681287, -114.300938. Lake in park. Swimming, fishing, boating. Hiking trails. Wildlife viewing. Bird watching. Open all year. No reservations accepted. $14-28 per night. 25 sites, no hookups. 35-foot limit. Vault toilets. No water, showers or dump station.

Placid Lake State Park

5001 N Placid Lake Rd, Seeley Lake, MT 59868. Phone: (406) 677-6804. Located 8 miles S of Seeley Lake via MT 83 and Placid Creek Rd. GPS: 47.119340, -113.503231. Lake in park. Swimming beach, fishing, boating, skiing. Hiking, biking, walking trails. Wildlife viewing. Open May-Nov. $14-28 per night. 40 sites, 17 with electric hookups. Drinking water. 41-foot limit. Restrooms; showers.

Salmon Lake State Park

2329 Highway 83 N, Seeley Lake, MT 59868. Phone: (406) 677-3731. Located 8 miles SE of Seeley Lake via MT 83. GPS: 47.094447, -113.397909. Lake in park. Swimming beach, fishing, boating, skiing. Hiking, biking trails. Bird watching. Open May-Sep. $14-28 per night. 23 sites, 16 with electric hookups. Drinking water. 45-foot limit. Restrooms; showers.

Thompson Falls State Park

2220 Blue Slide Rd, Thompson Falls, MT 59873 (406) 827-3110. Located on Clark Fork River, 3 miles N of Thompson Falls via MT 200 and Blue Slide Rd. GPS: 47.616358, -115.386551. Lake in park. Swimming, fishing, boating. Hiking, nature, walking trails. Wildlife viewing. Bird watching. Open May-Sep. $14-28 per night. 18 sites, no hookups. 35-foot limit. Vault toilets. No showers or dump station.

Tongue River Reservoir State Park

290 Campers Point, Decker, MT 59025. Phone: (406) 757-2298. Located 27 miles N of Sheridan, Wyoming and 7 miles N of Decker via MT 314. GPS: 45.095659, -106.814022. Lake in park (12 mile long reservoir). Swimming beach, fishing, boating (rentals), skiing. Hiking trails. Wildlife viewing. Bird watching. Marina, store. Six campgrounds. Open May-Sep. $14-28 per night. 156 sites, 81 with electric hookups. Drinking water. 80-foot limit. Vault toilets. No showers. Dump station.

Wayfarers State Park

8600 Highway 35, Bigfork, MT 59911. Phone: (406) 837-4196. Located just S of Bigfork along MT 35. GPS: 48.054791, -114.075473. Lake in park. Swimming, fishing, boating, skiing.

Hiking, nature trails. Wildlife viewing. Scenic viewpoint. Open Apr-Oct. $14-28 per night. 29 sites, 1 accessible site with electric, 28 no hookups. Drinking water. 40-foot limit. Restrooms; showers. Dump station.

West Shore State Park

17768 Highway 93, Lakeside, MT 59922. Phone: (406) 844-3044. Located 5 miles S of Lakeside via US 93. GPS: 47.950137, -114.191044. Lake in park. Swimming, fishing, boating (rentals), skiing. Hiking, biking trails. Wildlife viewing. Scenic viewpoint. Open Apr-Sep. $18-28 per night. 26 sites, 12 with electric hookups. Drinking water. 45-foot limit. Vault toilets. No showers or dump station.

Whitefish Lake State Park

1615 W Lakeshore, Whitefish, MT 59937. Phone: (406) 862-3991. Located about 3 miles NW of Whitefish via US 93 and State Park Rd. GPS: 48.422749, -114.369106. Swimming beach, fishing, boating (rentals), skiing. Hiking, biking trails. Wildlife viewing. Open Apr-Oct. $18-28 per night. 25 sites, 1 accessible site with electric, 24 no hookups. Drinking water. 45-foot limit. Restrooms; showers.

Nebraska

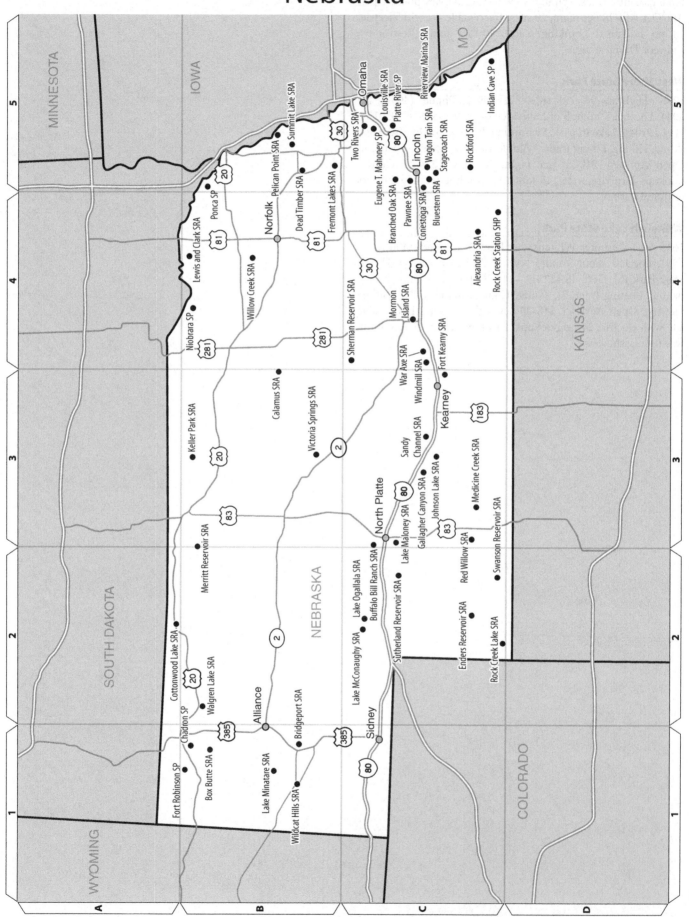

Nebraska

Nebraska Game & Parks Commission
2200 N 33rd St
Lincoln, NE 68503

Phone: (402) 471-0641
Internet: outdoornebraska.gov
Reservations: Online or (402) 471-1414

Nebraska Park Locator

Nebraska Parks

Alexandria State Recreation Area

57426 710th Road, Fairbury, NE 68352. Phone: (402) 729-5777. Located 4 miles E of Alexandria via NE 85G. GPS: 40.234209, -97.329969. Lakes in park. Swimming beach, fishing, boating (no ramps). Hiking, biking trails. Wildlife viewing. Park store. Open all year. No reservations accepted. $15-30 per night. 53 sites, 45 with electric hookups. Drinking water. Restrooms; no showers. Dump station.

Bluestem State Recreation Area

Sprague, NE 68503. Phone: (402)796-2362. Located 8 miles E of Crete via Sprague Rd. GPS: 40.633168, -96.799195. Lake in park. Swimming beach, fishing, boating. Wildlife viewing. Archery range. Open all year. No reservations accepted. $15 per night. 19 sites, no hookups. Drinking water. Vault toilets. Dump station. Dispersed camping also available.

Box Butte State Recreation Area

Crawford, NE 69339. Phone: (308) 665-2903. Located 10 miles N of Hemingford via Rd 70. GPS: 42.465584, -103.084011. Lake in park. Swimming beach, fishing, boating. Bird watching. Open all year. No reservations accepted. $15-30 per night. 14 sites with electric hookups. Drinking water. Vault toilets. Dispersed camping also available.

Branched Oak State Recreation Area

12000 W Branched Oak Rd, Raymond, NE 68428. Phone: (402) 783-3400. Located 16 miles NW of Lincoln via US 34 and NE 79. GPS: 40.973382, -96.891340. Lake in park. Swimming beaches, fishing, boating (rentals). Hiking, biking, equestrian trails. Wildlife viewing. Scenic viewpoint. Disc golf. Archery and shooting range. Marina, store, grill. Four camping areas open all year. $15-35 per night. 295 sites, 12 full hookup, 283 with electric. Drinking water. 65-foot limit. Restrooms; showers. Dump station. Equestrian area, 15 sites with electric hookups.

Bridgeport State Recreation Area

Bridgeport, NE 69336. Phone: (308) 436-3777. Located just NW of Bridgeport. GPS: 41.677360, -103.115127. Lake in park. Swimming beach, fishing, boating. Wildlife viewing. Open all year. No reservations accepted. $15 per night. 72 sites, no hookups. Drinking water. Vault toilets. Dump station.

Buffalo Bill Ranch State Recreation Area

2921 Scouts Rest Ranch Rd, North Platte, NE 69101. Phone: (308) 535-8035. Located one mile N of US 30 in North Platte via Buffalo Bill Ave. GPS: 41.162769, -100.791466. Lake in park. Fishing, boating (rentals). Hiking trails. Wildlife viewing. Archery range. Guided horseback rides. Float trips. Next to park is the Buffalo Bill Ranch State Historical Park. Open all year. No reservations accepted. $15-30 per night. 23 sites with electric hookups. Drinking water. Vault toilets.

Calamus State Recreation Area

42285 York Point Rd, Burwell, NE 68823. Phone: (308) 346-5666. Located 8 miles NW of Burwell via NE 96. GPS: 41.850072, -99.213205. Lake in park. Swimming beach, fishing, boating (rentals). Hiking trails. Bird watching. Scenic viewpoint. Fish hatchery, self-guided tours. Food and gear concessions. Three camping areas open all year. $15-30 per night. 132 sites with electric hookups. Drinking water. 50-foot limit. Restrooms; showers. Dump station.

Chadron State Park

15951 Hwy 385, Chadron, NE 69337. Phone: (308) 432-6167. Located 9 miles S of Chadron via US 385. GPS: 42.708575, -103.006869. Lake in park. Swimming pool, fishing, boating (rentals). Hiking, biking, equestrian trails. Scenic viewpoint. Archery range. Park store, gift shop. Guided horseback rides. Open all year. $15-30 per night. 70 sites with electric hookups. Drinking water. 65-foot limit. Restrooms; showers. Laundry facilities. Dump station.

Conestoga State Recreation Area

3800 NW 105th St, Denton, NE 68524. Phone: (402) 796-2362. Located 2 miles N of Denton via NE 55A. GPS: 40.771587, -96.853480. Lake in park. Swimming beach, fishing, boating. Hiking, biking trails. Wildlife viewing. Disc golf. Archery and shooting range. Open all year. No reservations accepted. $15-30 per night. 33 sites, 25 with electric hookups. Drinking water. Vault toilets. Dump station. Dispersed camping also available.

Cottonwood Lake State Recreation Area

Merriman, NE 69218. Phone: (308) 684-3428. Located 1 mile E of Merriman via US 20. GPS: 42.921356, -101.679705. Lake in park. Fishing, boating. Wildlife viewing. Bird watching. Open all year. No reservations accepted. $10-15 per night. 30 sites, no hookups. Drinking water. Vault toilets.

Dead Timber State Recreation Area

227 County Road & 12 Blvd, Scribner, NE 68057. Phone: (402) 727-2922. Located 7 miles NW of Scribner via US 275. GPS: 41.720079, -96.684658. Lake in park. Fishing, boating (no motors). Hiking trails. Wildlife viewing. Open all year. $25 per night. 17 sites with electric hookups. Drinking water. Vault toilets.

Enders Reservoir State Recreation Area

73122 338th Ave, Enders, NE 69027. Phone: (308) 394-5118. Located along US 6 just SE of Enders. GPS: 40.435832, -101.521284. Swimming beach, fishing, boating. Wildlife viewing. Open all year. No reservations accepted. $15-30 per night. 32 sites with electric hookups. Drinking water. Restrooms; showers. Dump station.

Eugene T. Mahoney State Park

28500 West Park Hwy, Ashland, NE 68003. Phone: (402) 944-2523. Located just N of I-80 Exit 426 near Ashland. GPS: 41.017302, -96.316862. Lake in park. Aquatic center, swimming pool, fishing, boating (paddleboat rentals). Hiking, biking, equestrian, walking trails. Observation tower. Golf driving range. Disc golf. Miniature golf. Venture Climb (indoor 42-foot climbing wall). Activity center. Marina, store, food, snacks. Lodge, restaurant. Go Ape, a high-ropes adventure course through the forest canopy, features suspended obstacles and zip lines. Guided horseback rides. Two campgrounds open all year. $25-35 per night. 148 sites, 7 full hookup, 141 with electric. Drinking water. 55-foot limit. Restrooms; showers. Laundry facilities. Dump station.

Fort Kearny State Recreation Area

1020 V Road, Kearney, NE 68847. Phone: (308) 865-5305. Located 5 miles S of I-80 Exit 279 near Kearney via NE 10 and NE 50A. GPS: 40.655277, -98.989434. Lakes in park. Swimming beach, fishing, boating (no ramps). Hiking, biking, nature trails. Bird watching. Disc golf. Interpretive center. Guided horseback rides. Two campgrounds open all year. $15-30 per night. 120 sites with electric hookups. Drinking water. 54-foot limit. Restrooms; showers. Dump station.

Fort Robinson State Park

3200 Highway 20, Crawford, NE 69339. Phone: (308) 665-2900. Located 4 miles W of Crawford via US 20. GPS: 42.665551, -103.466604. Lake in park. Indoor swimming pool, fishing, boating (rentals). Hiking, biking (rentals), equestrian trails. Wildlife viewing (buffalo and longhorn herds). Golf course. Visitor center. Restaurant. Museums. Guided horseback rides. Jeep and horse-drawn tours. Stagecoach rides. Operated as a fort from the early days of the Old West until after World War II. Many original buildings survive and others have been reconstructed. Two campgrounds open all year. $15-35 per night. 130 sites, 32 full hookup, 70 with electric, 28 no hookups. Drinking water. 70-foot limit. Restrooms; showers. Laundry facilities. Dump station. Equestrian camp, 24 sites with electric hookups.

Fremont Lakes State Recreation Area

4349 W State Lakes Rd, Fremont, NE 68025. Phone: (402) 727-2922. Located along US 30 about 4 miles W of Fremont. GPS: 41.451459, -96.568085. Swimming beach, fishing, boating, skiing. Hiking trails. Bird watching. Disc golf. Convenience store, grill. Four campgrounds open all year. $15-30 per night. 168 sites with electric hookups. Drinking water. 70-foot limit (some 100' plus). Restrooms; showers. Dump station.

Gallagher Canyon State Recreation Area

1 East Park Dr 25A, Elwood, NE 68937. Phone: (308) 785-2685. Located 11 miles S of I-80 Exit 222 near Cozad via NE 21. GPS: 40.735430, -99.977954. Canal connects with the Plum Creek Reservoir and Johnson Lake. Fishing, boating. Wildlife viewing. Open all year. No reservations accepted. $10 per night. 24 sites, no hookups. No water. Vault toilets.

Indian Cave State Park

65296 720 Rd, Shubert, NE 68437. Phone: (402) 883-2575. Located about 8 miles E of Shubert via NE 67 and NE 64E. GPS: 40.265114, -95.579736. Fishing (river), boating. Hiking, biking, equestrian trails. Wildlife viewing. Scenic viewpoint. Archery range. Guided horseback rides. Restored schoolhouse and general store from the old river town of St. Deroin. Open all year. $15-30 per night. 134 sites with electric hookups. Drinking water. 65-foot limit. Restrooms; showers. Laundry facilities. Dump station.

Johnson Lake State Recreation Area

1 East Park Dr 25A, Elwood NE 68937. Phone: (308) 785-2685. Located 8 miles S of I-80 Exit 237 near Lexington via US 283. GPS: 40.684654, -99.829176. Swimming beach, fishing, boating. Hiking, biking trails. Bird watching. Marina. Two campgrounds open all year. $15-30 per night. 112 sites with electric hookups. Drinking water. 42-foot limit. Restrooms; showers. Dump station.

Keller Park State Recreation Area

Ainsworth, NE 68714. Phone: (402) 684-2921. Located 14 miles NE of Ainsworth via US 20 and US 183. GPS: 42.669851, -99.765249. Five small lakes in park. Fishing, boating (electric motor and non-powered boats). Hiking trails. Wildlife viewing. Bird watching. Open all year. No reservations accepted. $10-25 per night. 50 sites, 25 with electric hookups. Drinking water. Vault toilets. Dump station.

Lake Maloney State Recreation Area

301 E State Farm Rd, North Platte, NE 69101. Phone: (308) 535-8025. Located 6 miles S of I-80 Exit 177 near North Platte via US 83. GPS: 41.048993, -100.801883. Swimming beaches, fishing, boating. Wildlife viewing. Open all year. No reservations accepted. $10-30 per night. 256 sites, 56 with electric hookups. Drinking water. Restrooms; showers. Dump station.

Lake McConaughy State Recreation Area

1475 Highway 61 N, Ogallala, NE 69153. Phone: (308) 284-8800. Located 9 miles N of I-80 Exit 126 near Ogallala via NE 61. GPS: 41.206574, -101.670245. Nebraska's largest reservoir. Swimming beaches, fishing, boating (rentals), skiing, scuba diving. Hiking trails. Bird watching. Archery range. Visitor center, gift shop. Marina. Lodges, restaurants. Five campgrounds open all year. Reservations required. $10-40 per night. 347 sites, 92 full hookup, 119 with electric, 136 no hookups. Drinking water. 60-foot limit. Restrooms; showers. Dump station.

Lake Minatare State Recreation Area

Stonegate Road, Minatare, NE 69356. Phone: (308) 783-2911. Located 10 miles N of Minatare via Stonegate Rd. GPS: 41.944896, -103.519379. Swimming beach, fishing, boating (kayak rentals), skiing. Bird watching. Lighthouse/observation tower. Three camping areas open all year. $15-30 per night. 101 sites with electric hookups. Drinking water. 61-foot limit. Restrooms; showers. Laundry facilities. Dump station.

Lake Ogallala State Recreation Area

1475 Highway 61 N, Ogallala, NE 69153. Phone: (308) 284-8800. Located 13 miles N of I-80 Exit 126 near Ogallala via NE 61. GPS: 41.234920, -101.67254. Swimming beach, fishing, boating. Hiking, biking trail. Bird watching. Two campgrounds open all year. Reservations required. $15-30 per night. 285 sites, 82 with electric, 203 no hookups. Drinking water. 45-foot limit. Restrooms; showers. Dump station, nearby.

Lewis and Clark State Recreation Area

54731 897 Road, Crofton, NE 68730. Phone: (402) 388-4169. Located 12 miles NE of Crofton via NE 121. GPS: 42.833408, -97.577482. Lake in park. Swimming beach, fishing, boating, skiing, scuba diving. Hiking, biking, equestrian trails. Bird viewing blind. Disc golf. Marina, store. Open all year. $15-35 per night. 192 sites, 4 full hookup, 188 with electric. Drinking water. 50-foot limit. Restrooms; showers. Dump station.

Louisville State Recreation Area

15810 Highway 50, Louisville, NE 68037. Phone: (402) 234-6855. Located just NW of town along NE 50. GPS: 41.003893, -96.164970. Lakes in park. Swimming beach, floating playground, fishing, boating (rentals). Hiking, biking (rentals) trails. Bird watching. Scenic viewpoint. Park store. Three camping areas open all year. $15-30 per night. 236 sites, 223 with electric, 13 no hookups. Drinking water. 70-foot limit. Restrooms; showers. Dump station.

Medicine Creek State Recreation Area

40611 Road 728, Cambridge, NE 69022. Phone: (308) 697-4667. Located 11 miles N of Cambridge via US 34 and NE 73A. GPS: 40.386190, -100.219041. Lake in park. Swimming beach, fishing, boating. Wildlife viewing. Disc golf. Archery range. Open all year. $10-30 per night. 106 sites, 72 with electric, 34 no hookups. Drinking water. 40-foot limit. Restrooms; showers. Dump station. Several primitive camp areas around the lake.

Merritt Reservoir State Recreation Area

Highway 97, Valentine, NE 69201. Phone: (402) 376-3320. Located 27 miles SW of Valentine via NE 97. GPS: 42.625741, -100.860450. Fishing, boating. Wildlife viewing. Bird watching. Park concession; gear, food, boat rentals. Resort, restaurant, store (just outside park area). Four campgrounds open all year. $15-30 per night. 89 sites with electric hookups. Drinking water. 60-foot limit. Restrooms; showers. Dump station.

Mormon Island State Recreation Area

7425 S US Hwy 281, Doniphan, NE 68832. Phone: (308) 385-6211. Located just N of I-80 Exit 312 near Doniphan along US 281. GPS: 40.823652, -98.377738. Lake in park. Swimming beaches, fishing, boating. Bird watching. Two campgrounds open all year. $15-30 per night. 71 sites, 34 with electric hookups. Drinking water. 55-foot limit. Restrooms; showers. Dump station.

Niobrara State Park

89261 522 Ave, Niobrara, NE 68760. Phone: (402) 857-3373. Located 2 miles W of Niobrara via NE 12. GPS: 42.751439, -98.065950. Lake in park. Swimming pool, fishing, boating. Hiking, biking, equestrian trails. Wildlife viewing. Interpretive center. Buffalo cookouts with entertainment. Guided horseback rides. Open all year. $15-30 per night. 76 sites with electric hookups. Drinking water. 65-foot limit. Restrooms; showers. Laundry facilities. Dump station.

Pawnee State Recreation Area

3900 NW 105th St, Lincoln, NE 68524. Phone: (402) 796-2362. Located 14 miles NW of Lincoln via US 34. GPS: 40.858833, -96.872709. Lake in park. Swimming beaches, fishing, boating, skiing. Hiking, biking, equestrian trails. Wildlife viewing. Disc golf. Archery and shooting ranges. Park store. Open all year. $15-30 per night. 102 sites, 68 with electric hookups. Drinking water. 53-foot limit. Restrooms; showers. Dump station. An additional 97 primitive sites are available.

Pelican Point State Recreation Area

Country Road KL, Tekamah, NE 68061. Phone: (402) 468-5611. Located 9 miles NE of Tekamah via CR GH and CR 45. GPS: 41.834768, -96.112866. Fishing (river), boating. Wildlife viewing. Open all year. No reservations accepted. $15 per night. 6 sites, no hookups. No water. Vault toilets.

Platte River State Park

14421 346th St, Louisville, NE 68037. Phone: (402) 234-2217. GPS: 40.986778, -96.216537. Located SW of Omaha, between South Bend and Louisville, via 346th St off NE 66. Lake in park. Splash park, swimming pool, fishing, boating (rentals). Hiking, biking trails. Two observation towers. Archery and shooting range. Marina. Lodge, restaurant. Guided horseback rides. Open all year. $30-35 per night. 48 full hookup sites. 55-foot limit. Restrooms; showers.

Ponca State Park

88090 Spur 26 E, Ponca, NE 68770. Phone: (402) 755-2284. Located 2 miles N of Ponca via NE 26E Spur. GPS: 42.593451, -96.710994. Aquatic center, swimming pool, fishing (river), boating. Hiking, biking trails. Wildlife viewing. Bird watching. Scenic viewpoint. Golf course, clubhouse. Archery and shooting range. Education center. Guided horseback rides. Guided bird tours. Open all year. $15-30 per night. 92 sites with electric hookups. Drinking water. 60-foot limit. Restrooms; showers. Dump station.

Red Willow State Recreation Area

72718 Trail 2, McCook, NE 69001. Phone: (308) 345-5899. Located 13 miles N of McCook via US 83. GPS: 40.366105, -100.658478. Lake in park. Swimming beach, fishing, boating. Hiking, biking trails. Bird watching. Scenic viewpoint. Archery range. Marina. Open all year. No reservations accepted. $15-30 per night. 48 sites with electric hookups. Drinking water. Restrooms; showers. Dump station.

Riverview Marina State Recreation Area

Nebraska City, NE 68410. Phone: (402) 873-7222. Located adjacent to the Missouri River in Nebraska City on 4th St. GPS: 40.692082, -95.850621. Fishing (river), boating. Open all year. No reservations accepted. $15-25 per night. 24 sites with electric hookups. Drinking water. Restrooms; no showers.

Rock Creek Lake State Recreation Area

73122 338th Ave, Enders, NE 69027. Phone: (308) 394-5118. Located 4 miles NW of Parks. GPS: 40.086206, -101.762971. Swimming, fishing, boating. Wildlife viewing. Open all year. No reservations accepted. $15 per night. 43 sites, no hookups. Drinking water. Vault toilets.

Rock Creek Station State Historical Park

57426 710th Rd, Fairbury, NE 68352. Phone: (402) 729-5777. Located 8 miles E of Fairbury via NE 15 and 711th Rd. GPS: 40.117186, -97.063735. Hiking, biking, equestrian, walking trails. Deep ruts, carved by the many wagons that traveled the Oregon and California trails remain plainly visible at this park. Includes reconstructed historic buildings, living history demonstrations and a visitor center. Open all year. $15-25 per night. 25 sites with electric hookups. Drinking water. 58-foot limit. Restrooms; showers. Dump station. Equestrian camp area, 20 sites.

Rockford State Recreation Area

Beatrice, NE 68503. Phone: (402) 729-5777. Located 11 miles SE of Beatrice via US 136 and Rockford Lake Recreation Rd. GPS: 40.226478, -96.576886. Lake in park. Swimming beach, fishing, boating. Hiking trail. Open all year. No reservations accepted. $15-30 per night. 72 sites, 30 with electric hookups. Drinking water. Vault toilets.

Sandy Channel State Recreation Area

1020 V Rd, Kearney, NE 68847. Phone: (308) 865-5305. Located 2 miles S of I-80 Exit 257 near Elm Creek via US 183. GPS: 40.668360, -99.380321. Six small lakes in park. Fishing, floating, boating (electric motor only). Hiking trails. Bird watching. Open all year. No reservations accepted. $15 per night. 30 sites, no hookups. Drinking water. Vault toilets.

Sherman Reservoir State Recreation Area

79025 Sherman Dam Rd, Loup City, NE 68853. Phone: (308) 745-0230. Located 4 miles E of Loup City via 790th Rd. GPS: 41.286172, -98.899797. Fishing, boating. Hiking, nature, walking trails. Wildlife viewing. Marina. Open all year. No reservations accepted. $15 per night. 360 sites, no hookups. Drinking water. Restrooms; showers. Dump station.

Stagecoach State Recreation Area

Panama Road, Hickman, NE 68372. Phone: (402) 796-2362. Located 2 miles SW of Hickman via 68th St and Panama Rd. GPS: 40.597633, -96.647712. Lake in park. Fishing, boating. Bird watching. Open all year. No reservations accepted. $15-30 per night. 72 sites, 22 with electric hookups. Drinking water. Vault toilets.

Summit Lake State Recreation Area

2787 County Road G, Tekamah, NE 68061. Phone: (402) 374-1727. Located 5 miles W of Tekamah via NE 32 and CR G. GPS: 41.761867, -96.300319. Swimming beach, fishing, boating. Hiking, biking trails. Archery range. Open all year. No reservations accepted. $15-30 per night. 43 sites, 30 with electric hookups. Drinking water. Vault toilets. Shower house. Dump station.

Sutherland Reservoir State Recreation Area

301 E State Farm Rd, North Platte, NE 69101. Phone: (308) 535-8025. Located 4 miles S of I-80 Exit 158 near Sutherland via NE 25. GPS: 41.091423, -101.160075. Swimming beach, fishing, boating. Bird watching. Open all year. No reservations accepted. $10-15 per night. 85 sites, no hookups. Drinking water. Vault toilets.

Swanson Reservoir State Recreation Area

36166 Road 44B, Trenton, NE 69044. Phone: (308) 334-5493. Located 5 miles W of Trenton via NE 25 and NE 44B. GPS: 40.146762, -101.073191. Swimming beach, fishing, boating. Marina, store. Two campgrounds open all year. No reservations accepted. $15-30 per night. 64 sites with electric hookups. Drinking water. Restrooms; showers. Dump station.

Two Rivers State Recreation Area

27702 F St, Waterloo, NE 68069. Phone: (402) 359-5165. Located 8 miles SW of Waterloo via US 275 and NE 92. GPS: 41.219216, -96.349810. Lake in park. Swimming beach, fishing (lake and river), boating. Hiking, biking, equestrian trails. Wildlife viewing. Concession stand; snacks, food. Six camping areas open all year. $15-30 per night. 207 sites, 143 with electric hookups (12 with water). Drinking water. 60-foot limit. Restrooms; showers. Dump station. Equestrian camp area.

Victoria Springs State Recreation Area

43400 Highway 21A Spur, Anselmo, NE 68813. Phone: (308) 749-2235. Located 6 miles E of Anselmo via NE 21A Spur. GPS: 41.611244, -99.748332. Lake in park. Fishing, boating (electric motors only, paddleboat rentals). Nature, walking trails. Wildlife viewing. Historic buildings. Open all year. $15-30 per night. 27 sites, 21 with electric hookups. Drinking water. 50-foot limit. Restrooms; showers. Dump station.

Wagon Train State Recreation Area

Hickman, NE 68503. Phone: (402) 796-2362. Located 4 miles E of Hickman via NE 55P. GPS: 40.625459, -96.576680. Lake in park. Swimming beach, fishing, boating. Hiking, biking trail (one mile). Open all year. No reservations accepted. $15-30 per night. 28 sites with electric hookups. Drinking water. Restrooms. Dump station.

Walgren Lake State Recreation Area

15951 Highway 385, Chadron, NE 69337. Phone: (308) 432-6167. Located 7 miles SE of Hay Springs via US 20 and Walgren Lake Rd. GPS: 42.635892, -102.631362. Fishing, boating. Bird watching. Open all year. No reservations accepted. $10 per night. 40 sites, no hookups. Drinking water. Vault toilets.

War Axe State Recreation Area

Highway 10D, Shelton, NE 68840. Phone: (308) 468-5700. Located just N of I-80 Exit 291 near Shelton. GPS: 40.724932, -98.740602. Lake in park. Fishing, boating (electric motors only). Open all year. No reservations accepted. $10 per night. 8 sites, no hookups. Drinking water. Restrooms; no showers.

Wildcat Hills State Recreation Area

210615 Highway 71, Gering, NE 69341. Phone: (308) 436-3777. Located 12 miles S of Scottsbluff via NE 71. GPS: 41.706697, -103.677395. Hiking, biking, equestrian trails. Wildlife viewing. Bird watching. Scenic viewpoint. Shooting complex and archery range. Nature center, gift shop. Open all year. No reservations accepted. $15 per night. 12 sites, no hookups. Drinking water. Vault toilets.

Willow Creek State Recreation Area

54376 852 Road, Pierce, NE 68767. Phone: (402) 329-4053. Located 5 miles SW of Pierce via 549th Ave. GPS: 42.171076, -97.562713. Lake in park. Swimming beach, fishing, boating, skiing. Hiking, biking, equestrian trails. Archery range. Open all year. $15-30 per night. 165 sites with electric hookups. Drinking water. 65-foot limit. Restrooms; showers. Equestrian camp, 10 sites with electric hookups.

Windmill State Recreation Area

2625 Lowell Rd, Gibbon, NE 68840. Phone: (308) 468-5700. Located N of I-80 Exit 285 near Gibbon. GPS: 40.706906, -98.844494. Lakes in park. Swimming beach, fishing, boating (electric motors only, no ramps). Hiking, biking, nature trails. Open all year. $15-30 per night. 69 sites with electric hookups. Drinking water. Restrooms; showers. Dump station.

Nevada

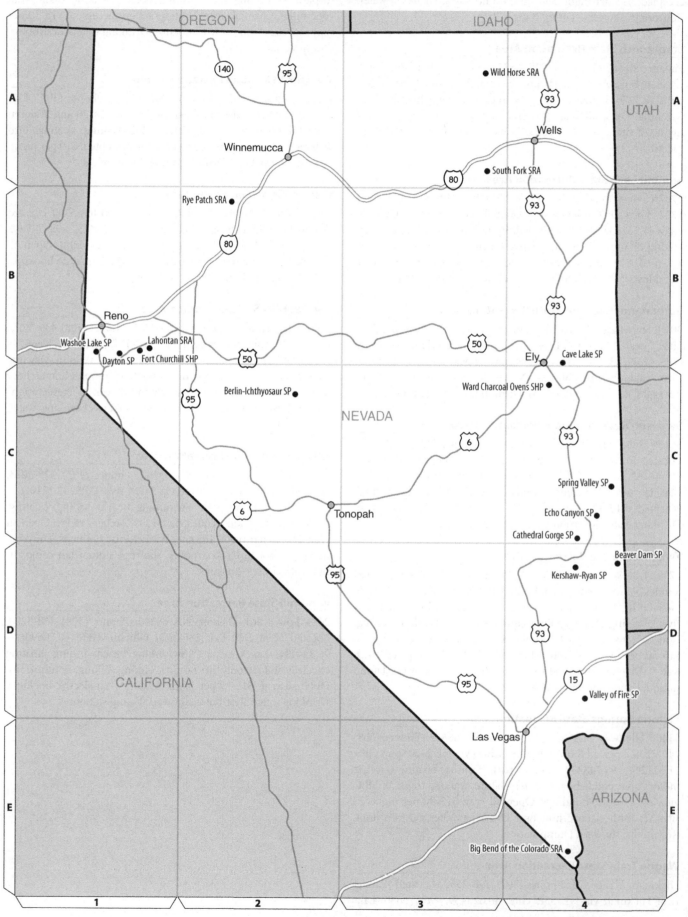

Nevada

Nevada Division of State Parks
901 S Stewart St, Ste 5005
Carson City, NV 89701

Phone: (775) 684-2770
Internet: www.parks.nv.gov
Reservations: Call park.

Nevada Park Locator

Nevada Parks

Beaver Dam State Park

Beaver Dam Road, Caliente NV 89008. Phone: (775) 728-8101. Located 33 miles E of Caliente via US 93 and Beaver Dam Rd. GPS: 37.518132, -114.082996. Fishing. Hiking, biking, equestrian trails. Wildlife viewing. Bird watching. Two campgrounds open all year. $20 per night. 34 sites, no hookups. Drinking water. 28-foot limit. Vault toilets.

Berlin-Ichthyosaur State Park

HC 61 Box 61200, Austin, NV 89310. Phone: (775) 964-2440. Located 20 miles E of Gabbs via NV 361 and NV 844. GPS: 38.882342, -117.610228. Hiking, biking, equestrian trails. Bird watching. Park contains a town built in the 1890s that is preserved in a state of arrested decay, self guided tours. Fossil House and Diana Mine tours. Open all year. $20 per night. 14 sites, no hookups. Drinking water. 25-foot limit. Restrooms nearby. Dump station.

Big Bend of the Colorado State Recreation Area

4220 S Needles Hwy, Laughlin, NV 89029. Phone: (702) 298-1859. Located about 7 miles S of Laughlin via Needles Hwy. GPS: 35.118516, -114.643521. Swimming beach, fishing (river), boating. Hiking, biking trails. Bird watching. Scenic viewpoint. Open all year. No reservations accepted. $35 per night. 24 full hookup sites. 60-foot limit. Restrooms; showers. Dump station.

Cathedral Gorge State Park

111 Cathedral Gorge State Park Road, Panaca, NV 89042. Phone: (775) 728-8101. Located 2 miles NW of Panaca via NV 319 and US 93. GPS: 37.803511, -114.407050. Hiking, biking, equestrian walking trails. Bird watching. Visitor center, gift shop. Open all year. $30 per night. 22 sites with electric hookups. Drinking water. 40-foot limit. Restrooms; showers. Dump station.

Cave Lake State Park

US 93, Success Summit, Ely, NV 89315. Phone: (775) 728-8100. Located 13 miles SE of Ely via US 50 and NV 486. GPS: 39.191241, -114.693830. Lake in park. Swimming, fishing, boating. Hiking, biking, equestrian trails. Bird watching. Two campgrounds. Lake View campground is open all year but may close in extremely cold conditions. Elk Flat is open May-Oct. No reservations accepted. $20 per night. 38 sites, no hookups. Drinking water. Restrooms; showers. Dump station.

Dayton State Park

825 US Hwy 50 East, Dayton NV 89403. Phone: (775) 687-5678. Located 1 mile N of Dayton via US 50. GPS: 39.249394, -119.588008. Fishing (river). Hiking, biking trails. Bird watching. Park features the remains of the Rock Point Mill built in 1861. Open all year. $20 per night. 10 sites, no hookups. Drinking water. 34-foot limit. Restrooms; no showers. Dump station.

Echo Canyon State Park

HC 74 Box 295, Pioche, NV 89043. Phone: (775) 962-5103. Located 12 miles E of Pioche via NV 322 and Echo Dam Rd. GPS: 37.910755, -114.269394. Lake in park. Swimming, fishing, boating. Hiking, biking, equestrian trails. Bird watching. Two campgrounds open all year. $30 per night. 53 sites, 20 full hookup, 33 no hookups. Drinking water. Restrooms; showers. Dump station.

Fort Churchill State Historic Park

10000 US Hwy 95A, Silver Springs, NV 89429. Phone: (775) 577-2345. Located 9 miles S of Silver Springs via US 95-ALT. GPS: 39.294924, -119.267342. Fishing (river), boating. Hiking, biking, equestrian trails. Bird watching. Visitor center. Fort Churchill was built in 1861 to provide protection for early settlers and guard Pony Express mail runs. Today the ruins are preserved in a state of arrested decay. Open all year. No reservations accepted. $20 per night. 20 sites, no hookups. Drinking water. Restrooms; no showers. Dump station.

Kershaw-Ryan State Park

Caliente, NV 89008. Phone: (775) 726-3564. Located about 3 miles S of Caliente via US 93 and NV 317. GPS: 37.586348, -114.533323. Hiking, biking trails. Wildlife viewing. Open all year. $30 per night. 16 sites with water and electric hookups. 30-foot limit. Restrooms; showers. Dump station.

Lahontan State Recreation Area

16799 Lahontan Dam Road, Fallon NV 89406. Phone: (775) 577-2226. Located 5 miles SE of Silver Springs via US 95-ALT and Fir Ave. GPS: 39.378979, -119.201192. Lake in park. Fishing, boating, skiing. Hiking, equestrian trails. Wildlife viewing. Bird watching. Open all year. $20 per night. 26 sites, no hookups. Drinking water. 65-foot limit. Restrooms; showers. Dump station.

Rye Patch State Recreation Area

2505 Rye Patch Reservoir Rd, Lovelock, NV 89419. Phone: (775) 442-0135. Located 25 miles NE of Lovelock via I-80. GPS: 40.469626, -118.306569. Lake in park. Swimming beach, fishing, boating, skiing. Hiking, biking, equestrian, nature, OHV trails. Two campgrounds open all year. $20 per night. 47 sites, no hookups. Drinking water. Restrooms; showers. Dump station.

South Fork State Recreation Area

353 Lower South Fork #8, Spring Creek, NV 89815. Phone: (775) 744-4346. Located 18 miles SW of Spring Creek via NV 227 and NV 228. GPS: 40.656331, -115.752329. Lake in park. Swimming, fishing, boating. Hiking, biking, equestrian trails. Wildlife viewing. Open all year. No reservations accepted. $20 per night. 25 sites, no hookups. Drinking water. 30-foot limit. Restrooms; showers. Dump station.

Spring Valley State Park

Pioche, NV 89043. Phone: (775) 962-5102. Located 18 miles NE of Pioche via NV 322. GPS: 38.023364, -114.202522. Lake in park. Swimming, fishing, boating. Hiking trail. Bird watching. Tour historic ranches built in the late 1800s. Two campgrounds open all year. Snow may make winter access difficult. $20 per night. 44 sites, no hookups. Drinking water. 35-foot limit. Restrooms; showers.

Valley of Fire State Park

29450 Valley of Fire Rd, Overton, NV 89040. Phone: (702) 397-2088. Located 16 miles E of I-15 Exit 75 near Moapa. GPS: 36.422272, -114.549234. Hiking, biking trails. Bird watching. Visitor center, gift shop. Park contains ancient, petrified trees and petroglyphs dating back more than 2,000 years. Two campgrounds open all year. No reservations accepted. $25-35 per night. 72 sites, 22 with water and electric hookups. Drinking water. 50-foot limit. Restrooms; showers. Dump station.

Ward Charcoal Ovens State Historical Park

Ely, NV 89315. Phone: (775) 289-1693. Located 16 miles S of Ely via US 50 and Cave Valley Rd. GPS: 39.040352, -114.854881. Fishing. Hiking, biking, equestrian, OHV trails. Wildlife viewing. Park features six beehive shaped charcoal ovens that were used from 1876 through 1879 to help process rich silver ore, open for touring. Open all year. $20 per night. 16 sites, no hookups. Drinking water. 35-foot limit. Vault toilets.

Washoe Lake State Park

4855 Eastlake Blvd, Carson City, NV 98704. Phone: (775) 687-4319. Located 3 miles NE of I-580 Exit 10 near Carson City via Eastlake Blvd. GPS: 39.241613, -119.763412. Fishing, boating. Hiking, biking, equestrian trails. Bird watching. Scenic viewpoint. Visitor center. Open all year. $20-30 per night. 49 sites, 24 with water and electric hookups. Drinking water. 45-foot limit. Restrooms; showers. Dump station. Equestrian camp area.

Wild Horse State Recreation Area

Elko, NV 89801. Phone: (775) 385-5939. Located 66 miles N of I-80 Exit 301 in Elko via NV 225. GPS: 41.670879, -115.799186. Lake in park. Swimming beach, fishing, boating. Hiking, biking, equestrian, OHV trails. Wildlife viewing. Visitor center. Open all year. $20 per night. 34 sites, no hookups. Drinking water. 45-foot limit. Restrooms; showers. Dump station.

New Hampshire

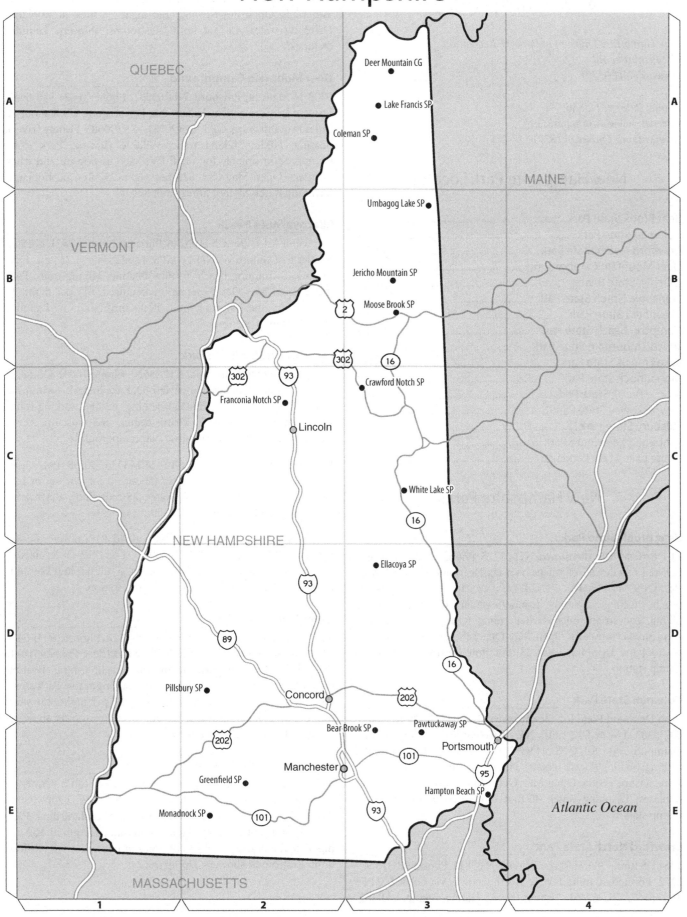

QUEBEC

Deer Mountain CG

Lake Francis SP

Coleman SP

MAINE

Umbagog Lake SP

VERMONT

Jericho Mountain SP

Moose Brook SP

Crawford Notch SP

Franconia Notch SP

Lincoln

White Lake SP

NEW HAMPSHIRE

Ellacoya SP

Pillsbury SP

Concord

Bear Brook SP

Pawtuckaway SP

Portsmouth

Manchester

Greenfield SP

Hampton Beach SP

Monadnock SP

Atlantic Ocean

MASSACHUSETTS

New Hampshire

New Hampshire Division of Parks & Recreation
172 Pembroke Rd
Concord, NH 03301

Phone: (603) 271-3556
Internet: www.nhstateparks.org
Reservations: Online or (877) 647-2757

New Hampshire Park Locator

New Hampshire Parks

Bear Brook State Park

61 Deerfield Rd, Allenstown, NH 03275. Phone: (603) 485-9869. Located 6 miles SE of Allenstown via Deerfield Rd and Lower Rd. GPS: 43.115649, -71.328144. Lake in park. Swimming beach, fishing, boating (canoe/rowboat rentals). Hiking, biking, equestrian trails. Archery range. Camp store. Antique snowmobile museum. Open May-Oct. $25 per night. 95 sites, no hookups. Drinking water. 38-foot limit. Restrooms; showers. Dump station.

Coleman State Park

1166 Diamond Pond Rd, Stewartstown, NH 03597. Phone: (603) 237-5382. Located 12 miles NE of Colebrook via NH 26 and Diamond Pond Rd. GPS: 44.943755, -71.328494. Lake in park. Fishing, boating (kayak rentals). Hiking, biking, ATV trails. Park store. Visitor center. Open May-Oct. $25 per night. 24 sites, no hookups. Drinking water. 40-foot limit. Restrooms; showers. Dump station.

Crawford Notch State Park

1464 US Route 302; Harts Location, NH 03812. Phone: (603) 374-2272. Located 20 miles NW of North Conway via US 302. GPS: 44.155167, -71.363461. Fishing (river). Hiking, biking, walking trails. Wildlife viewing. Park store. Visitor center, gift shop. Waterfalls. Open Jun-Nov. $25 per night. 36 sites, no hookups. Drinking water. 40-foot limit. Restrooms; showers. Laundry facilities.

Deer Mountain Campground

5309 N Main St, Pittsburg, NH 03592. Phone: (603) 538-6965. Located in Connecticut Lakes State Forest along US 3 about 18 miles N of Pittsburg. GPS: 45.190961, -71.190585. Fishing (river), boating. Hiking, biking trails. Wildlife viewing. Park store. Campground suitable for small RVs such as pop-up and truck campers. Open May-Oct. $23 per night. 25 sites, no hookups. Drinking water. 25-foot limit. Vault toilets.

Ellacoya State Beach

266 Scenic Rd, Gilford, NH 03246. Phone: (603) 293-7821. Located 5 miles E of Gilford via NH 11. GPS: 43.572834, -71.354452. Lake in park. Swimming beach, fishing, boating. Hiking trails. Park store. Open May-Oct. Reservations required. $47 per night. 38 full hookup sites. 50-foot limit. Restrooms; showers. Laundry facilities. Dump station.

Franconia Notch State Park

260 Tramway Dr, Franconia, NH 03580. Phone: (603) 823-8800. Located 9 miles S of Franconia via I-93. Lake in park. Swimming beach, fishing, boating (rentals). Hiking, biking, walking trails. Rock climbing. Park store. Visitor center. Ski museum. Aerial tramway (at Cannon Mountain). Two campgrounds.

Lafayette Place campground. GPS: 44.143330, -71.683194. Open May-Oct. $25 per night. 70 sites (about 50 for pop-up or tent only), no hookups. Drinking water. 28-foot limit. Restrooms; showers. Laundry facilities.

Canon Mountain RV Park (self-contained RV's only). Located west of I-93 Exit 34C. GPS: 44.143602, -71.684717. Open all year. Reservations required. $25-40 per night. 7 full hookup sites. 40-foot limit. Restrooms; no showers. Dump station.

Greenfield State Park

52 Campground Rd, Greenfield, NH 03047. Phone: (603) 547-3497. Located 1 mile W of Greenfield via NH 136. GPS: 42.951071, -71.888075. Lake in park. Swimming beach, fishing, boating (canoe/kayak rentals). Hiking, biking, walking trails. Park store. Open May-Oct. Reservations required. $25 per night. 251 sites, no hookups. Drinking water. 38-foot limit. Restrooms; showers. Laundry facilities. Dump station.

Hampton Beach State Park

160 Ocean Blvd, Hampton, NH 03842. Phone: (603) 926-8990. Located 4 miles SE of Hampton via NH 101. GPS: 42.899080, -70.815127. Atlantic ocean-front. Swimming beach, fishing. Park store. Visitor center. Open all year. Reservations required. $50 per night. 28 full hookup sites (no pop-ups or tents allowed). 40-foot limit. Restrooms; showers. Dump station.

Jericho Mountain State Park

298 Jericho Lake Rd, Berlin, NH 03570. Phone: (603) 752-4758. Located in northern NH, 4 miles W of Berlin off NH 110. GPS: 44.498955, -71.245804. Lake in park. Swimming beach, fishing, boating. Hiking, biking, equestrian, walking, OHV trails. Bird watching. Scenic viewpoint. Park store. Visitor center. Open all year. $25 per night. 9 sites, no hookups. Drinking water. 40-foot limit. Restrooms; showers. Laundry facilities.

Lake Francis State Park

439 River Rd, Pittsburg, NH 03592. Phone: (603) 538-6965. Located 8 miles E of Pittsburg via US 3. GPS: 45.060102, -71.303433. Swimming beach, fishing, boating (canoe/kayak rentals). Hiking, biking, walking, OHV trails. Park store. Visitor center. Open May-Oct. $25-35 per night. 17 sites, 9 with water and electric hookups. Drinking water. 40-foot limit. Restrooms; showers. Dump station.

Monadnock State Park

116 Poole Rd, Jaffrey, NH 03452. Phone: (603) 532-8862. Located 5 miles NW of Jaffrey via NH 124 and Dublin Rd. GPS: 42.861581, -72.060895. Lake in park. Hiking trails. Park store. Park designated a National Natural Landmark. Open all year. $25 per night. 34 sites (suitable for pop-up trailers), 4 with electric hookups. Drinking water. 30-foot limit. Restrooms; showers.

Moose Brook State Park

30 Jimtown Rd, Gorham, NH 03581. Phone: (603) 466-3860. Located 3 miles W of Gorham via US 2. GPS: 44.400921, -71.230111. Swimming beach, fishing. Hiking, biking trails. Park store. Open May-Oct. $25 per night. 30 sites, no hookups. Drinking water. 40-foot limit. Restrooms; showers.

Pawtuckaway State Park

40 Pawtuckaway Rd, Nottingham, NH 03290. Phone: (603) 895-3031. Located 4 miles N of Raymond via NH 156 and Mountain Rd. GPS: 43.077305, -71.171532. Lake in park. Swimming beach, fishing, boating (canoe/kayak rentals). Hiking, biking, equestrian trails. Wildlife viewing. Scenic viewpoint. Park store. Open May-Oct. $25-30 per night. 120 sites, no hookups. Drinking water. 38-foot limit. Restrooms; showers.

Pillsbury State Park

100 Pillsbury State Park Rd, Washington, NH 03280. Phone: (603) 863-2860. Located 4 miles N of Washington via NH 31. GPS: 43.232798, -72.120590. Lake in park. Fishing, boating (canoe/kayak rentals). Hiking, biking trails. Wildlife viewing. Open May-Oct. $23 per night. 18 sites, no hookups. Drinking water. 38-foot limit. Vault toilets.

Umbagog Lake State Park

235 E Route 26, Cambridge, NH 03579. Phone: (603) 482-7795. Located 8 miles SE of Errol via NH 26. GPS: 44.702796, -71.050392. Swimming beach, fishing, boating (canoe/kayak rentals). Wildlife viewing. Park store. Open May-Oct. $35 per night. 27 sites with water and electric hookups. 40-foot limit. Restrooms; showers. Dump station.

White Lake State Park

94 State Park Rd, Tamworth, NH 03886. Phone: (603) 323-7350. Located 15 miles S of Conway via NH 16. GPS: 43.836006, -71.208570. Swimming beach, fishing, boating (rentals). Biking, walking trails. Park store. Open May-Oct. $25-30 per night. 90 sites, no hookups. Drinking water. 38-foot limit. Restrooms; showers. Dump station.

New Jersey

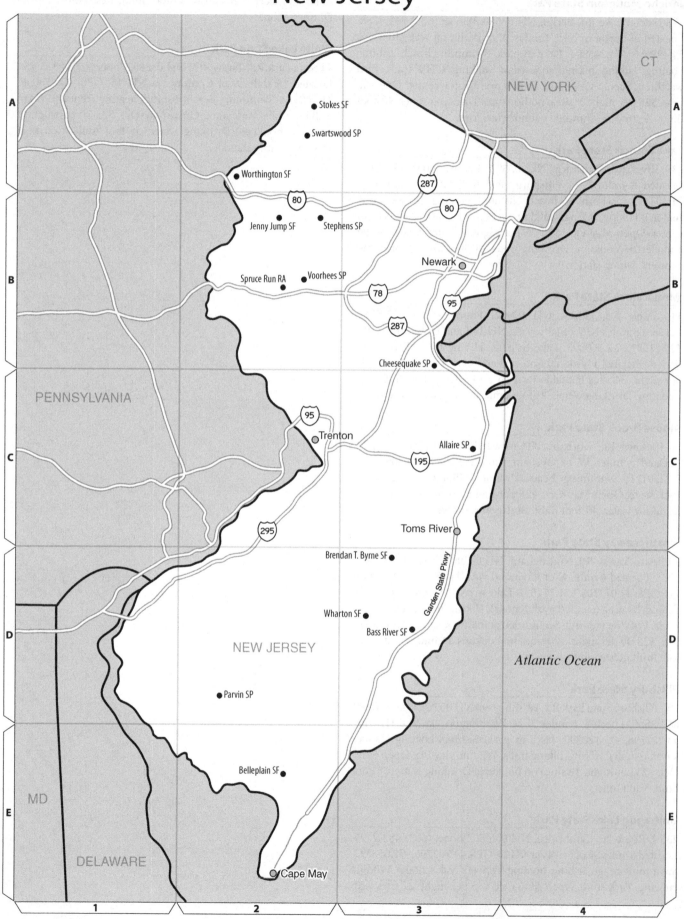

- Stokes SF
- Swartswood SP
- Worthington SF
- Jenny Jump SF
- Stephens SP
- Newark
- Spruce Run RA
- Voorhees SP
- Cheesequake SP
- Trenton
- Allaire SP
- Toms River
- Brendan T. Byrne SF
- Wharton SF
- Bass River SF
- Parvin SP
- Belleplain SF
- Cape May

NEW YORK
CT
PENNSYLVANIA
NEW JERSEY
Atlantic Ocean
MD
DELAWARE

New Jersey

New Jersey Dept. of Environmental Protection
State Park Service
PO Box 420
Trenton, NJ 08625

Phone: (609) 984-0370
Internet: www.nj.gov/dep/parksandforests
Reservations: www.camping.nj.gov or call park.

New Jersey Park Locator

New Jersey Parks

Allaire State Park

4265 Atlantic Ave, Farmingdale, NJ 07727. Phone: (732) 938-2371. Located .5 mile north and east of I-195 Exit 31B near Farmingdale. GPS: 40.165477, -74.146735. Lake in park. Fishing, boating. Hiking, biking, equestrian, nature trails. Bird watching. Visitor center, museum. Nature center. Historic Allaire Village. Pine Creek Railroad. Open all year. $25 per night. 45 sites, no hookups. Drinking water. Restrooms; showers. Laundry facilities. Dump station.

Bass River State Forest

762 Stage Rd, Tuckerton, NJ 08087. Phone: (609) 296-1114. Located 5 miles W of Tuckerton via Stage Rd. GPS: 39.621202, -74.423615. Lake in park. Swimming beach, fishing, boating (rentals). Hiking, biking, equestrian, nature, walking trails. Wildlife viewing. Interpretive center. Food concession. Two camping areas open all year. $25 per night. 176 sites, no hookups. Drinking water. Restrooms; showers. Laundry facilities. Dump station.

Belleplain State Forest

1 Henkinsifkin Rd, Woodbine, NJ 08270. Phone: (609) 861-2404. Located 2 miles W of Woodbine via Webster St. GPS: 39.248752, -74.841394. Lake in park. Swimming beach, fishing, boating (rentals). Hiking, biking, equestrian, nature trails. Bird watching. Interpretive center. Food concession. Open all year. $25 per night. 169 sites, no hookups. Drinking water. Restrooms; showers. Laundry facilities. Dump station.

Brendan T. Byrne State Forest

Mile Marker 1, Highway 72 E, Woodland Township, NJ 08088. Phone: (609) 726-1191. Located 16 miles SE of Vincentown via US 206, NJ 70, and NJ 72. GPS: 39.872106, -74.521582. Fishing, boating. Hiking, biking, equestrian, nature, walking trails. Bird watching. Scenic viewpoint. Interpretive center. Whitesbog Village Historic District. Cedar Swamp Natural Area. Open all year. $25 per night. 82 sites, no hookups. Drinking water. Restrooms; showers. Laundry facilities. Dump station.

Cheesequake State Park

300 Gordon Rd, Matawan, NJ 07747. Phone: (732) 566-2161. Located in Matawan off the Garden State Pkwy at Exit 120. GPS: 40.435073, -74.263735. Lake in park. Swimming beach, fishing, boating (no boat ramp). Hiking, biking, nature trails. Scenic viewpoint. Nature center. Food concession. There is an 11-foot height restriction for vehicles entering the camping area. Open Apr-Oct. $25 per night. 53 sites, no hookups. Drinking water. Restrooms; showers. Dump station.

Jenny Jump State Forest

Hope, NJ 07844. Phone: (908) 459-4366. Located 3 miles E of Hope via Johnsonburg Rd, Shiloh Rd, and State Park Rd. GPS: 40.912839, -74.922918. Lake in park. Fishing, boating. Hiking, nature trails. Scenic viewpoint. Astronomy observatory. Open Apr-Oct. $25 per night. 22 sites, no hookups. Drinking water. Restrooms; showers.

Parvin State Park

701 Almond Rd, Pittsgrove, NJ 08318. Phone: (856) 358-8616. Located 8 miles N of Bridgeton via NJ 77, NJ 56 and Parvins Mill Rd. GPS: 39.510665, -75.132585. Lakes in park. Swimming beach, fishing, boating (canoe rentals). Hiking, biking, nature, walking trails. Scenic viewpoint. Visitor center. Open Apr-Oct. $25 per night. 56 sites, no hookups. Drinking water. Restrooms; showers. Laundry facilities. Dump station.

Spruce Run Recreation Area

68 Van Sykel's Rd, Clinton, NJ 08809. Phone: (908) 638-8572. Located about 5 miles NW of I-78 Exit 17 near Clinton via NJ 31. GPS: 40.662741, -74.938843. Lake in park. Swimming beach, fishing, boating (rentals). Hiking, biking trails. Bird watching. Open Apr-Oct. $25-35 per night. 67 sites, 7 with water and electric hookups. Drinking water. Restrooms; showers. Dump station.

Stephens State Park

800 Willow Grove St, Hackettstown, NJ 07840. Phone: (908) 852-3790. Located 2 miles N of Hackettstown via Willow Grove St. GPS: 40.875177, -74.808692. Fishing (river), boating. Hiking, biking, equestrian trails. Rock climbing. Open Apr-Oct. $25

per night. 40 sites (small trailers), no hookups. Drinking water. Restrooms; showers.

Stokes State Forest

1 Coursen Rd, Branchville, NJ 07826. Phone: (973) 948-3820. Located about 4 miles N of Branchville via US 206. GPS: 41.185552, -74.795769. Lakes in park. Fishing, boating. Hiking, biking, equestrian trails. Wildlife viewing. Scenic viewpoint. Tillman Ravine Natural Area. Three camping areas open all year. $25 per night. 38 sites, no hookups. Drinking water. Restrooms; showers.

Swartswood State Park

1091 E Shore Rd, Swartswood, NJ 07877. Phone: (973) 383-5230. Located 7 miles SW of Branchville via Kemah Lake Rd and CR 521. GPS: 41.074149, -74.819642. Lakes in park. Swimming beach, fishing, boating (rentals). Hiking, biking, equestrian, nature trails. Bird watching. Scenic viewpoint. Food concession. Open all year. $25 per night. 65 sites, no hookups. Drinking water. Restrooms; showers. Dump station.

Voorhees State Park

251 County Road 513, Glen Gardner, NJ 08826. Phone: (908) 638-8572. Located about 2 miles N of High Bridge via Fairview Ave. GPS: 40.682201, -74.895413. Fishing. Hiking, biking, nature trails. Wildlife viewing. Scenic viewpoint. Astronomy observatory. Open Apr-Oct. $25 per night. 8 sites, no hookups. Drinking water. Restrooms; showers. Dump station.

Wharton State Forest

Wharton State Forest has two offices. Batsto Village is located on Route 542, eight miles E of Hammonton. Phone: (609) 561-0024. Atsion Recreation Area is on Route 206, eight miles N of Hammonton. Phone: (609) 268-0444. Numerous lakes and ponds in park. Swimming, fishing, boating. Hiking, biking, equestrian, nature trails. Wildlife viewing. Visitor center. Museum. Food concessions. Batsto Village, a former bog iron and glassmaking industrial center from 1766 to 1867. Village consists of thirty-three historic buildings and structures. Guided and self-guided tours. Historic Harrisville Village, a company town abandoned in 1891, self-guided tours. Atsion Mansion, built in 1826, the unfurnished home is offered as an architectural tour. Two camping areas.

Atsion Recreation Area. Atsion Road, Shamong NJ 08088. Phone: (609) 268-0444. Located 9 miles N of Hammonton via NJ 206. GPS: 39.745908, -74.743958. Open Apr-Oct. $25 per night. 50 sites, no hookups. Drinking water. 22-foot limit. Restrooms; showers. Dump station.

Godfrey Bridge Campground. Godfrey Bridge Rd, Chatsworth NJ 08019. Phone: (609) 561-0024. Located 20 miles E of Hammonton via CR 542 and CR 563. Single lane bridge, 5-ton limit. GPS: 39.689415, -74.549327. Open all year. $5 per night. 34 sites, no hookups. Drinking water. 21-foot limit. Vault toilets.

Worthington State Forest

Old Mine Rd, Columbia, NJ 07832. Phone: (908) 841-9575. Located about 3 miles N of I-80 Exit 1 near Columbia via River Rd and Old Mine Rd. GPS: 41.005164, -75.103332. Lake in park. Fishing, boating. Hiking, biking trails. Wildlife viewing. Scenic viewpoint. Visitor center. Open Apr-Dec. $25 per night. 54 sites, no hookups. Drinking water. Restrooms; showers.

New Mexico

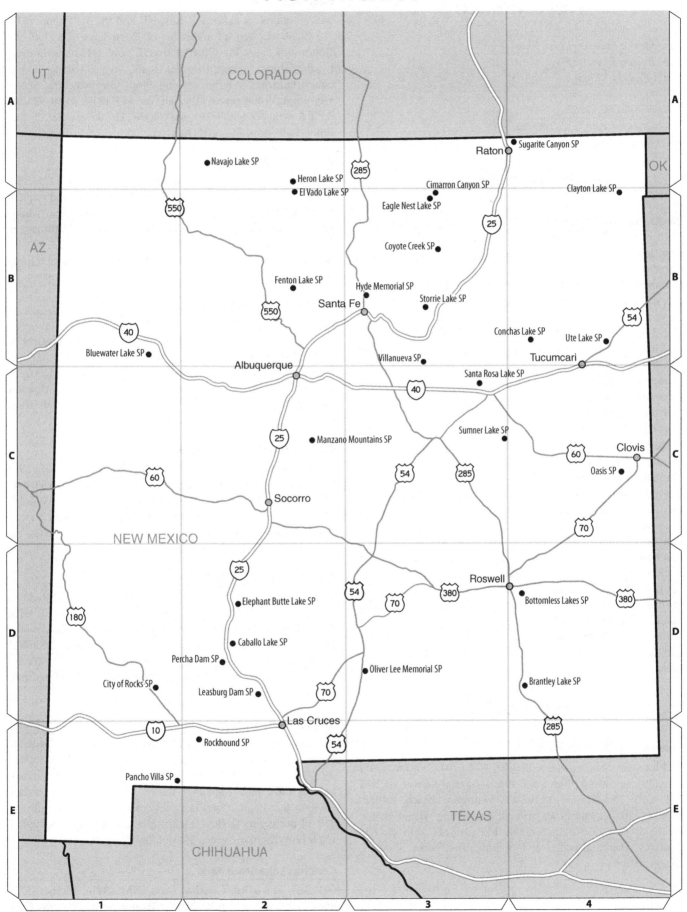

UT

COLORADO

OK

AZ

- Navajo Lake SP
- Heron Lake SP
- El Vado Lake SP
- **285**
- Raton
- Sugarite Canyon SP
- Cimarron Canyon SP
- Eagle Nest Lake SP
- Clayton Lake SP
- **550**
- Coyote Creek SP
- **25**
- Fenton Lake SP
- Hyde Memorial SP
- **550**
- Santa Fe
- Storrie Lake SP
- **40**
- Conchas Lake SP
- Ute Lake SP
- **54**
- Bluewater Lake SP
- Albuquerque
- Villanueva SP
- Tucumcari
- Santa Rosa Lake SP
- **40**
- NEW MEXICO
- **25**
- Manzano Mountains SP
- Sumner Lake SP
- **60**
- Clovis
- **60**
- **54**
- **285**
- Oasis SP
- Socorro
- **70**
- **25**
- **180**
- Roswell
- **54**
- **380**
- Bottomless Lakes SP
- **380**
- Elephant Butte Lake SP
- **70**
- Caballo Lake SP
- Percha Dam SP
- Oliver Lee Memorial SP
- Brantley Lake SP
- City of Rocks SP
- Leasburg Dam SP
- **70**
- **285**
- **10**
- Las Cruces
- Rockhound SP
- **54**
- Pancho Villa SP
- TEXAS
- CHIHUAHUA

1   2   3   4

New Mexico

New Mexico State Parks Division
1220 S Saint Francis Dr
Santa Fe, NM 87505

Phone: (888) 667-2757
Internet: www.emnrd.state.nm.us/SPD/
Reservations: Online or call park.

New Mexico Park Locator

New Mexico Parks

Bluewater Lake State Park

30 Bluewater State Park Rd, Prewitt, NM 87045. Phone: (505) 876-2391. Located 6 miles S of I-40 Exit 63 near Prewitt via NM 412. GPS: 35.302292, -108.107284. Swimming beach, fishing, boating. Hiking, equestrian trails. Bird watching. Visitor center. Open all year. $10-14 per night. 149 sites, 14 with electric hookups. Drinking water. 45-foot limit. Restrooms; showers. Dump station.

Bottomless Lakes State Park

545A Bottomless Lakes Rd, Roswell, NM 88201. Phone: (575) 988-3638. Located 17 miles SE of Roswell via US 380 and Bottomless Lakes Rd. GPS: 33.316377, -104.331320. Swimming beach, fishing, boating (rentals), scuba diving. Hiking, biking, equestrian trails. Wildlife viewing blinds. Bird watching. Scenic viewpoint. Visitor center. Open all year. $14-18 per night. 32 sites, 6 full hookup, 26 with water and electric. Drinking water. 60-foot limit. Restrooms; showers. Dump station.

Brantley Lake State Park

33 E Brantley Lake Rd, Carlsbad, NM 88221. Phone: (575) 457-2384. Located 17 miles NW of Carlsbad via US 285 and Capitan Reef Rd. GPS: 32.563197, -104.380111. Swimming beach, fishing, boating. Hiking, equestrian trails. Bird watching. Visitor center. Open all year. $14-18 per night. 51 sites, 3 full hookup, 48 with water and electric. 50-foot limit. Restrooms; showers. Dump station.

Caballo Lake State Park

Highway 187, Caballo, NM 87931. Phone: (575) 743-3942. Located 1 mile NE of I-25 Exit 59 near Truth or Consequences. GPS: 32.907553, -107.310181. Fishing, boating, skiing. Hiking, equestrian, nature trails. Bird watching. Four campgrounds open all year. $14-18 per night. 170 sites, 7 full hookup, 108 with water and electric, 55 no hookups. 50-foot limit. Restrooms; showers. Dump station.

Cimarron Canyon State Park

28869 Highway 64, Eagle Nest, NM 87718. Phone: (575) 377-6271. Located 3 miles E of Eagle Nest via US 64. GPS: 36.537688, -105.223289. Fishing (river). Hiking, equestrian trails. Wildlife viewing. Bird watching. On the Enchanted Circle Scenic Byway. Four campgrounds open all year. $10 per night. 94 sites, no hookups. 50-foot limit. Vault toilets.

City of Rocks State Park

327 Highway 61, Faywood, NM 88034. Phone: (505) 536-2800. Located 27 miles NW of Deming via US 80 and NM 61. GPS: 32.584460, -107.973080. Hiking, biking trails. Wildlife viewing. Bird watching. Scenic viewpoint. Visitor center. Desert botanical garden. Star observatory. Open all year. $10-14 per night. 50 sites, 9 with water and electric hookups. Drinking water. 50-foot limit. Restrooms; showers.

Clayton Lake State Park

141 Clayton Lake Rd, Clayton, NM 88415. Phone: (575) 374-8808. Located 12 miles NW of Clayton via NM 370 and NM 455. GPS: 36.573248, -103.301223. Fishing, boating. Hiking, equestrian, nature trails. Bird watching. Visitor center. Dinosaur tracks, pavilion. Star Point Observatory. Five campgrounds open all year. $10-14 per night. 42 sites, 9 with water and electric hookups, 7 water only. Drinking water. 50-foot limit. Restrooms; showers.

Conchas Lake State Park

501 Bell Ranch Rd, Conchas Dam, NM 88416. Phone: (575) 868-2270. Located 35 miles NW of Tucumcari via NM 104. GPS:

35.424962, -104.186332. Swimming beach, fishing, boating, skiing, scuba diving. Park store, cafe. Visitor center. Marina. Open all year. $10-14 per night. 74 sites, 33 with water and electric hookups, 33 water only, 8 no hookups. 50-foot limit. Restrooms; showers. Dump station.

Coyote Creek State Park

Hwy 434, Mile 17, Guadalupita, NM 87722. Phone: (575) 387-2328. Located 17 miles N of Mora via NM 434. GPS: 36.177883, -105.233885. Fishing, boating. Hiking trails. Bird watching. Visitor center. Open all year. $10-14 per night. 35 sites, 16 with water and electric hookups. Drinking water. 35-foot limit. Restrooms; showers. Dump station.

Eagle Nest Lake State Park

42 Marina Way, Eagle Nest, NM 87718. Phone: (575) 377-1594. Located 2 miles S of Eagle Nest via US 64. GPS: 36.534828, -105.264871. Fishing, boating. Hiking, biking, equestrian trails. Wildlife viewing. Scenic viewpoint. Visitor center. Marina. Open all year. $10 per night. 19 sites, no hookups. Drinking water. 56-foot limit. Vault toilets.

El Vado Lake State Park

State Road 112, Tierra Amarilla, NM 87575. Phone: (575) 588-7247. Located about 30 miles SW of Chama via US 64 and NM 112. GPS: 36.614451, -106.737965. Swimming beach, fishing, boating, skiing, scuba diving. Hiking, biking, equestrian trails. Bird watching. Open all year. $10-18 per night. 80 sites, 2 full hookup, 17 with water and electric, 61 no hookups. Drinking water. 50-foot limit. Restrooms; showers. Dump station.

Elephant Butte Lake State Park

101 Highway 195, Elephant Butte, NM 87935. Phone: (575) 744-5923. Located 4 miles E of I-35 Exit 79 near Truth or Consequences via NM 181 and Warm Springs Blvd. GPS: 33.181590, -107.207538. Swimming beach, fishing, boating (rentals), skiing. Hiking, biking, nature trails. Bird watching. Visitor center. Full service marinas. Restaurant. Open all year. $10-18 per night. 173 sites, 8 full hookup, 144 with water and electric, 21 no hookups. Drinking water. 40-foot limit. Restrooms; showers. Dump station.

Fenton Lake State Park

455 Fenton Lake Rd, Jemez Springs, NM 87025. Phone: (575) 829-3630. Located about 18 miles N of Jemez Springs via NM 4 and NM 126. GPS: 35.883149, -106.729925. Fishing, boating. Hiking, biking, equestrian trails. Bird watching. Open all year. $10-14 per night. 35 sites, 5 with water and electric hookups. Drinking water. 50-foot limit. Restrooms; no showers.

Heron Lake State Park

640 State Road 95, Los Ojos, NM 87551. Phone: (575) 588-7470. Located 7 miles SW of Los Ojos via NM 95. GPS: 36.696341, -106.653007. Swimming beach, fishing, boating (rentals). Hiking, biking trails. Bird watching. Scenic viewpoint. Visitor center. Marina. Ten campgrounds open all year. $10-14 per night. 250

sites, 54 with electric hookups. Drinking water. 50-foot limit. Restrooms; showers. Dump station.

Hyde Memorial State Park

740 Hyde Park Rd, Santa Fe, NM 87501. Phone: (505) 983-7175. Located 8 miles NE of Santa Fe via NM 475. GPS: 35.730436, -105.837282. Hiking trails. Wildlife viewing. Visitor center. Open all year. $10-14 per night. 50 sites, 7 with electric hookups. Drinking water. 50-foot limit. Vault toilets. Dump station.

Leasburg Dam State Park

12712 State Park Rd, Radium Springs, NM 88054. Phone: (575) 524-4068. Located 17 miles NW of Las Cruces via I-25 to Exit 19. GPS: 32.492787, -106.918052. Swimming beach, fishing (river), boating. Hiking, biking, nature trails. Wildlife viewing. Bird watching. Scenic viewpoint. Visitor center. Cactus/wildflower garden. Observatory. Open all year. $10-14 per night. 23 sites, 18 with water and electric hookups. Drinking water. 40-foot limit. Restrooms; showers. Dump station.

Manzano Mountains State Park

Mile Marker 3, NM Hwy 131, Mountainair, NM 87036. Phone: (505) 469-7608. Located 16 miles NW of Mountainair via NM 55 and NM 131. GPS: 36.603411, -106.360962. Hiking, nature trails. Wildlife viewing. Bird watching. Visitor center. Open Apr-Oct. $10-14 per night. 27 sites, 10 with electric hookups. Drinking water. 50-foot limit. Vault toilets. Dump station.

Navajo Lake State Park

36 Road 4110 #1, Navajo Dam, NM 87419. Phone: (505) 632-2278. Located 25 miles E of Bloomfield via US 64 and NM 511. GPS: 36.817377, -107.616503. Swimming beach, fishing, boating (rentals), skiing, scuba diving. Hiking, biking trails. Wildlife viewing. Visitor center. Two full service marinas. Restaurant. Seven campgrounds open all year. $10-18 per night. 244 sites, 8 full hookup, 56 with water and electric, 41 electric only, 139 no hookups. Drinking water. 50-foot limit. Restrooms; showers. Dump station.

Oasis State Park

1891 Oasis Rd, Portales, NM 88130. Phone: (575) 356-5331. Located 7.5 miles N of Portales via US 70 and NM 467. GPS: 34.259225, -103.351159. Small lake in park. Fishing. Hiking, biking, equestrian trails. Bird watching. Visitor center. Open all year. $10-18 per night. 26 sites, 2 full hookup, 8 with water and electric, 6 electric only, 10 no hookups. Drinking water. Up to 100-foot limit. Restrooms; showers. Dump station.

Oliver Lee Memorial State Park

409 Dog Canyon Rd, Alamogordo, NM 88310. Phone: (575) 437-8284. Located 16 miles SE of Alamogordo via US 54 and Dog Canyon Rd. GPS: 32.747975, -105.915181. Hiking, nature trails. Wildlife viewing. Bird watching. Visitor center. Historic ranch house. Open all year. $10-14 per night. 44 sites, 19 with water and electric hookups. Drinking water. 45-foot limit. Restrooms; showers. Dump station.

Pancho Villa State Park

400 W Highway 9, Columbus, NM 88029. Phone: (575) 531-2711. Located in Columbus along NM 9 just W of NM 11 intersection. GPS: 31.827637, -107.641892. Hiking, nature trails. Bird watching. Visitor center. Museum, historic structures. Botanical garden. Open all year. $10-14 per night. 79 sites, 75 with electric hookups. Drinking water. 50-foot limit. Restrooms; showers. Dump station.

Percha Dam State Park

Highway 187, Caballo, NM 87931. Phone: (575) 743-3942. Located S of Truth or Consequences about 2 miles S of I-25 Exit 59 via NM 187 and Percha Dam Canal Rd. GPS: 32.868987, -107.306025. Lake in park. Fishing, boating. Bird watching. Visitor center. Open all year. $10-18 per night. 50 sites, 1 full hookup, 29 with water and electric, 20 no hookups. Drinking water. 50-foot limit. Restrooms; showers.

Rockhound State Park

9880 Stirrup Rd SE, Deming, NM 88030. Phone: (575) 546-6182. Located 14 miles SE of Deming via NM 11 and NM 141. GPS: 32.185925, -107.612373. Hiking, biking, nature trails. Bird watching. Visitor center. Open all year. $10-14 per night. 29 sites, 23 with electric hookups. Drinking water. 40-foot limit. Restrooms; showers. Dump station.

Santa Rosa Lake State Park

Highway 91, Santa Rosa, NM 88435. Phone: (575) 472-3110. Located 9 miles N of Santa Rosa via NM 91. GPS: 35.030886, -104.695867. Swimming beach, fishing, boating, skiing, scuba diving. Hiking, equestrian, walking trails. Wildlife viewing blinds. Bird watching. Scenic viewpoint. Visitor center. Three campgrounds open all year. $10-14 per night. 78 sites, 26 with water and electric hookups. Drinking water. 50-foot limit. Restrooms; showers. Dump station.

Storrie Lake State Park

Highway 518, Mile Marker 3.5, Las Vegas, NM 87701. Phone: (505) 425-7278. Located about 5 miles N of Las Vegas via 7th St and NM 518. GPS: 35.657674, -105.231941. Swimming beach, fishing, boating, skiing. Bird watching. Visitor center. Six campgrounds open all year. $10-14 per night. 45 sites, 22 with water and electric hookups. Drinking water. 40-foot limit. Restrooms; showers. Dump station.

Sugarite Canyon State Park

211 Highway 526, Raton, NM 87740. Phone: (575) 445-5607. Located 5 miles east and north of I-25 Exit 452 near Raton via NM 72 and NM 526. GPS: 36.940207, -104.380152. Lakes in park. Fishing, boating. Hiking, biking, equestrian, nature trails. Wildlife viewing. Bird watching. Visitor center. Open all year. $10-18 per night. 40 sites, 2 full hookup, 8 with water and electric, 30 no hookups. Drinking water. 70-foot limit. Restrooms; showers. Dump station.

Sumner Lake State Park

32 Lakeview Ln, Sumner Lake, NM 88119. Phone: (575) 355-2541. Located 15 miles NW of Fort Sumner via US 84 and NM 203. GPS: 34.603935, -104.376592. Swimming beach, fishing, boating, skiing. Hiking, biking, equestrian, nature trails. Wildlife viewing. Scenic viewpoint. Visitor center. Open all year. $10-14 per night. 50 sites, 16 with water and electric hookups, 16 electric only, 18 no hookups. Drinking water. 70-foot limit. Restrooms; showers. Dump station.

Ute Lake State Park

1800 540 Loop, Logan, NM 88426. Phone: (575) 487-2284. Located 2 miles W of Logan via NM 540. GPS: 35.360405, -103.450696. Swimming beach, fishing, boating, skiing. Hiking, biking, equestrian trails. Bird watching. Visitor center. Marina. Two campgrounds open all year. $10-14 per night. 155 sites, 90 with water and electric hookups. Drinking water. 70-foot limit (some over 100'). Restrooms; showers. Dump station.

Villanueva State Park

135 Dodge Rd, Villanueva, NM 87583. Phone: (575) 421-2957. Located S of Las Vegas, off I-25 exit 323, off NM 3. GPS: 35.264118, -105.337840. Swimming, fishing, boating. Hiking, equestrian trails. Bird watching. Scenic viewpoint. Visitor center. Open all year. $10-14 per night. 33 sites, 12 with electric hookups. Drinking water. 65-foot limit. Restrooms; showers. Dump station.

New York

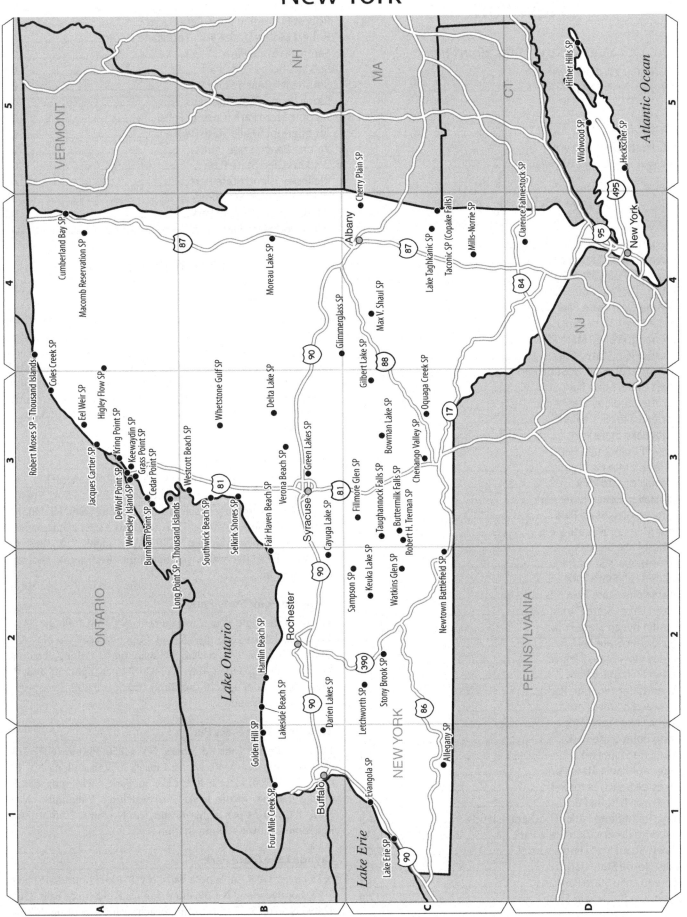

New York

New York State Office of Parks, Recreation &
Historic Preservation
Albany, NY 12238

Phone: (518) 474-0456
Internet: parks.ny.gov
Reservations: Online or call park.

New York Park Locator

New York Parks

Allegany State Park

2373 Allegany State Park Rd, Salamanca, NY 14779. Phone: (716) 354-9101. Located 7 miles S of Salamanca via Allegany State Park Rd. GPS: 42.10054, -78.74941. Lakes in park. Swimming beach, fishing, boating (rentals). Hiking, biking, equestrian trails. Park store. Visitor center. Restaurant. Museum. Two campgrounds open Apr-Oct. $18-30 per night. 424 sites, many with electric hookups. Drinking water. 48-foot limit. Restrooms; showers. Laundry facilities. Dump station.

Bowman Lake State Park

745 Bliven Sherman Rd, Oxford, NY 13830. Phone: (607) 334-2718. Located 8 miles NW of Oxford via NY 220. GPS: 42.516407, -75.677612. Swimming beach, fishing, boating (rentals). Hiking, biking trails. Bird watching. Disc golf. Park store. Nature center. Restaurant. Open May-Sep. $20-24 per night. 197 sites, no hookups. Drinking water. 50-foot limit. Restrooms; showers. Dump station.

Burnham Point State Park

340765 NYS Route 12E, Cape Vincent, NY 13618. Phone: (315) 654-2522. Located 4 miles NE of Cape Vincent via NY 12E. GPS: 44.161236, -76.263924. Lake in park. Fishing, boating. Wildlife viewing. Open May-Sep. $20-34 per night. 50 sites, 32 with electric hookups. 40-foot limit (many are 20'). Restrooms; showers. Dump station.

Buttermilk Falls State Park

112 E Buttermilk Falls Rd, Ithaca, NY 14850. Phone: (607) 273-5761 or (607) 273-3440. Located just S of Ithaca along NY 13. GPS: 42.417700, -76.523400. Lake in park. Swimming beach, fishing. Hiking, nature trails. Bird watching. Waterfalls. Open May-Oct. $20-24 per night. 46 sites, no hookups. 20-foot limit. Restrooms; showers. Dump station.

Cayuga Lake State Park

2678 Lower Lake Rd, Seneca Falls, NY 13148. Phone: (315) 568-5163. Located along NY 89 about 3 miles E of Seneca Falls. GPS: 42.89609, -76.75337. Swimming beach, fishing, boating. Biking.

Information center. Open Apr-Oct. $20-30 per night. 286 sites, 36 with electric hookups. Drinking water. 40-foot limit. Restrooms; showers. Dump station.

Cedar Point State Park

36661 Cedar Point State Park Dr, Clayton, NY 13624. Phone: (315) 654-2522. Located 6 miles SW of Clayton via NY 12E. GPS: 44.200558, -76.191666. Lake in park. Swimming beach, fishing, boating (rentals). Scenic viewpoint. Marina. Open May-Oct. $23-39 per night. 173 sites, 40 full hookup, 46 with electric, 87 no hookups. Drinking water. 40-foot limit. Restrooms; showers. Dump station.

Chenango Valley State Park

153 State Park Rd, Chenango Fork, NY 13746. Phone: (607) 648-5251. Located about 4 miles N of I-88 Exit 3 near Port Crane via NY 369. GPS: 42.214031, -75.828743. Lakes in park. Swimming beach, fishing, boating (rentals). Hiking, biking trails. Bird watching. Golf course, pro shop. Information center. Restaurant. Open May-Oct. $20-32 per night. 184 sites, 87 with electric hookups. Drinking water. 50-foot limit. Restrooms; showers. Dump station.

Cherry Plain State Park

10 State Park Rd, Petersburg, NY 12138. Phone: (518) 733-5400 or (518) 279-1155. Located 13 miles S of Petersburg via NY 22. GPS: 42.622093, -73.409424. Lake in park. Fishing, boating (rentals). Hiking, biking, nature trails. Open May-Sept. $17-24 per night. 10 sites, no hookups. 15-foot limit. Restrooms; showers.

Clarence Fahnestock State Park

1498 Route 301, Carmel, NY 10512. Phone: (845) 225-7207. Located 10 miles W of Carmel via NY 301. GPS: 41.466366, -73.824669. Lakes in park. Fishing, boating (rentals). Hiking, biking, equestrian trails. Bird watching. Scenic viewpoint. Nature center. Open Apr-Nov. $20-24 per night. 20 sites, no hookups. Drinking water. 30-foot limit. Restrooms; showers.

Coles Creek State Park

Route 37, Waddington, NY 13694. Phone: (315) 388-5636. Located 4 miles NE of Waddington via NY 37. GPS: 44.888611, -75.137665. Lake in park. Swimming beach, fishing, boating, skiing. Hiking, biking trails. Bird watching. Marina. Open May-Sep. $23-39 per night. 230 sites, 147 with electric hookups. Drinking water. 40-foot limit (many are 20'). Restrooms; showers. Dump station.

Cumberland Bay State Park

152 Cumberland Head Rd, Plattsburgh, NY 12901. Phone: (518) 563-5240. Located just E of Plattsburgh along NY 314. GPS: 44.724983, -73.422920. Lake in park. Swimming beach, fishing, boating, skiing. Biking. Park store. Open May-Oct. $20-34 per night. 133 sites, no hookups. 50-foot limit. Restrooms; showers. Dump station.

Darien Lakes State Park

10475 Harlow Rd, Darien Center, NY 14040. Phone: (585) 547-9242. Located 3 miles E of Alden via US 20. GPS: 42.903130, -78.432938. Swimming beach, fishing. Hiking, biking, equestrian trails. Disc golf. Open May-Oct. $23-35 per night. 154 sites, 141 with electric hookups. Drinking water. Restrooms; showers. Dump station.

Delta Lake State Park

8797 State Route 46, Rome, NY 13440. Phone: (315) 337-4670. Located 6 miles N of Rome via NY 46. GPS: 43.290138, -75.415115. Swimming beach, fishing, boating, skiing. Hiking, biking, nature trails. Bird watching. Restaurant. Open May-Oct. $20-38 per night. 101 sites with electric hookups. Drinking water. 40-foot limit. Restrooms; showers. Dump station.

DeWolf Point State Park

45920 County Route 191, Fineview, NY 13640. Phone: (315) 482-2012. Located on Wellesley Island off I-81 at Exit 51. GPS: 44.332329, -75.992378. Lake in park. Fishing, boating, skiing. Bird watching. Open May-Sep. $20-24 per night. 14 sites, no hookups. Drinking water. 20-foot limit. Restrooms; showers. Dump station.

Eel Weir State Park

RD #3, Ogdensburg, NY 13669. Phone: (315) 393-1138. Located 5 miles S of Ogdensburg via NY 812 and CR 4. GPS: 44.630367, -75.476891. Fishing (river), boating. Biking. Open May-Sep. $20-28 per night. 34 sites, no hookups. 40-foot limit. Restrooms; showers.

Evangola State Park

10191 Old Lake Shore Road, Irving, NY 14081. Phone: (716) 549-1802. Located 3 miles NE of Irving via NY 5. GPS: 42.601479, -79.082619. Lake in park. Swimming beach, fishing. Hiking, biking trails. Bird watching. Disc golf. Nature center. Concession stand. Open May-Oct. $20-32 per night. 78 sites, 49 with electric hookups. Drinking water. 40-foot limit. Restrooms; showers. Laundry facilities. Dump station.

Fair Haven Beach State Park

14985 State Park Road, Fair Haven, NY 13064. Phone: (315) 947-5205. Located just 1 mile NE of Fair Haven. GPS: 43.329971, -76.697014. Lake in park. Swimming beach, fishing, boating (rentals), skiing. Hiking, biking trails. Bird watching. Camp store. Marina. Three campgrounds open Apr-Oct. $23-33 per night. 184 sites, 46 with electric hookups. Drinking water. 35-foot limit. Restrooms; showers. Dump station.

Fillmore Glen State Park

1686 State Route 38, Moravia, NY 13118. Phone: (315) 497-0130. Located just S of Moravia on NY 38. GPS: 42.700130, -76.420166. Lake in park. Swimming beach, fishing. Hiking trails. Bird watching. Scenic viewpoint. Five waterfalls. Open May-Oct. $20-32 per night. 60 sites, 10 with electric hookups. 50-foot limit (many are 20'). Restrooms; showers. Dump station.

Four Mile Creek State Park

1055 Lake Road, Youngstown, NY 14174. Phone: (716) 745-3802. Located 4 miles E of Youngstown along NY 18. GPS: 43.271901, -78.996185. Lake in park. Fishing. Hiking, biking trails. Bird watching. Camp store. Open Apr-Oct. $23-39 per night. 275 sites, 139 with electric hookups. Drinking water. 50-foot limit. Restrooms; showers. Laundry facilities. Dump station.

Gilbert Lake State Park

18 CCC Road, Laurens, NY 13796. Phone: (607) 432-2114. Located 12 miles N of Oneonta via NY 205 and CR 12. GPS: 42.57272, -75.12817. Swimming beach, fishing, boating (rentals). Hiking, biking trails. Disc golf. Visitor center. Museum. Food concession. Open May-Sep. $20-32 per night. 135 sites, 32 with electric hookups. Drinking water. 50-foot limit. Restrooms; showers. Dump station.

Glimmerglass State Park

1527 County Highway 31, Cooperstown, NY 13326. Phone: (607) 547-8662. Located 7 miles N of Cooperstown via CR 31. GPS: 42.785576, -74.861572. Lake in park. Swimming beach, fishing, boating. Hiking, biking, nature trails. Wildlife viewing. Food concession. Open May-Oct. $20-30 per night. 50 sites with electric hookups. Drinking water. 40-foot limit. Restrooms; showers. Dump station.

Golden Hill State Park

9691 Lower Lake Rd, Barker, NY 14012. Phone: (716) 795-3885. Located 13 miles E of Olcott via NY 18. GPS: 43.366032, -78.473106. Lake in park. Fishing, boating, skiing. Hiking, biking, nature, walking trails. Bird watching. Scenic viewpoint. Disc golf. Interpretive center. Open May-Oct. $20-36 per night. 59 sites, 34 with electric hookups. Drinking water. 40-foot limit. Restrooms; showers. Laundry facilities. Dump station.

Grass Point State Park

42247 Grassy Point Rd, Alexandria Bay, NY 13607. Phone: (315) 686-4472. Located about 6 miles S of Alexandria Bay via NY 12. GPS: 44.278854, -75.995117. Lake in park. Swimming beach, fishing, boating (rentals). Hiking trails. Marina. Open May-Sep. $20-36 per night. 73 sites, 17 with electric hookups. Drinking water. 40-foot limit. Restrooms; showers. Dump station.

Green Lakes State Park

7900 Green Lakes Rd, Fayetteville, NY 13066. Phone: (315) 637-6111. Located 2 miles E of Fayetteville via NY 5. GPS: 43.039238, -75.966187. Two lakes in park. Swimming beach, fishing, boating (rentals required, no private boats). Hiking, biking trails. Bird watching. Golf course, clubhouse, restaurant. Disc golf. Interpretive center. Open May-Oct. $23-41 per night. 145 sites, 30 full hookup, 42 with electric, 73 no hookups. 60-foot limit (most are 30-40'). Restrooms; showers. Dump station.

Hamlin Beach State Park

1 Hamlin Beach Blvd W, Hamlin, NY 14464. Phone: (585) 964-2462. Located 6 miles NW of Hamlin via NY 19 and Lake Ontario State Pkwy. GPS: 43.359171, -77.950011. Lake in park. Swimming beach, fishing, boating. Hiking, biking, nature trails. Bird watching. Camp store. Open May-Oct. $29-35 per night. 264 sites with electric hookups. Drinking water. 40-foot limit. Restrooms; showers. Laundry facilities. Dump station.

Heckscher State Park

Heckscher State Pkwy, East Islip, NY 11730. Phone: (631) 581-2100. Located on the south shore of Long Island, just S of East Islip via Heckscher State Pkwy. GPS: 40.716801, -73.164268. Lake in park. Swimming beach, fishing, boating. Hiking, biking, walking trails. Wildlife viewing. Disc golf. Food concession. Open May-Sep. $20 per night. 67 sites, no hookups. 50-foot limit. Restrooms; showers. Dump station.

Higley Flow State Park

442 Cold Brook Dr, Colton, NY 13625. Phone: (315) 262-2880. Located about 7 miles S of Colton via NY 56. GPS: 44.492710, -74.916756. Lake in park. Swimming beach, fishing, boating. Hiking, nature trails. Wildlife viewing. Visitor center. Open May-Sep. $20-36 per night. 171 sites, 43 with electric hookups, 128 sewer only. Drinking water. 40-foot limit. Restrooms; showers. Dump station.

Hither Hills State Park

164 Old Montauk Hwy, Montauk, NY 11954. Phone: (631) 668-2554. Located about 4 miles W of Montauk via NY 27. GPS: 41.008937, -72.010631. On the ocean. Swimming beach, fishing. Hiking, biking, equestrian, nature trails. Bird watching. Camp store. Open Apr-Nov. $70 per night. 168 sites, no hookups. 40-foot limit. Restrooms; showers. Dump station.

Jacques Cartier State Park

Route 12, Morristown, NY 13664. Phone: (315) 375-6371. Located about 4 miles SW of Morristown via NY 12. GPS: 44.560173, -75.688438. Lake in park. Swimming beach, fishing, boating (rentals). Hiking, biking OHV trails. Food concession. Open May-Sep. $20-36 per night. 89 sites, 31 with electric hookups. 50-foot limit. Restrooms; showers. Dump station.

Keewaydin State Park

46165 Route 12, Alexandria Bay, NY 13607. Phone: (315) 482-3331. Located on Saint Lawrence River, 1 mile SW of Alexandria Bay via NY 12. GPS: 44.321007, -75.927994. Swimming pool, fishing (river), boating. Biking. Scenic viewpoint. Marina. Open May-Sep. $20-28 per night. 48 sites, no hookups. 40-foot limit. Restrooms; showers.

Keuka Lake State Park

3560 Pepper Rd, Bluff Point, NY 14478. Phone: (315) 536-3666. Located 24 miles N of Bath via NY 54 and NY 54A. GPS: 42.590580, -77.130287. Swimming beach, fishing, boating, skiing. Hiking, biking trails. Bird watching. Open May-Oct. $23-35 per night. 150 sites, 53 with electric hookups. Drinking water. 40-foot limit. Restrooms; showers. Dump station.

Kring Point State Park

25950 Kring Point Rd, Redwood, NY 13679. Phone: (315) 482-2444. On Saint Lawrence River, 8 miles NE of Alexandria Bay via NY 12. GPS: 44.380280, -75.852905. Lake in park. Swimming beach, fishing, boating. Bird watching. Open May-Oct. $23-39 per night. 100 sites, 28 with electric hookups. Drinking water. 40-foot limit. Restrooms; showers. Dump station.

Lake Erie State Park

5838 Route 5, Brocton, NY 14716. Phone: (716) 792-9214. Located on Lake Erie about 8 miles SW of Dunkirk via NY 5. GPS: 42.420944, -79.428612. Fishing, boating. Hiking, biking trails. Bird watching. Scenic viewpoint. Disc golf. Open May-Oct. $20-32 per night. 97 sites, 43 with electric hookups. Drinking water. 50-foot limit. Restrooms; showers. Laundry facilities. Dump station.

Lake Taghkanic State Park

1528 Route 82, Ancram, NY 12502. Phone: (518) 851-3631. Located 6 miles NW of Ancram via NY 82. GPS: 42.097488, -73.718307. Swimming beach, fishing, boating (rentals). Hiking, biking trails. Bird watching. Camp store. Nature center. Open May-Oct. $20-27 per night. 8 sites, no hookups. Drinking water. 20-foot limit. Restrooms; showers. Laundry facilities.

Lakeside Beach State Park

Route 18, Waterport, NY 14571. Phone: (585) 682-4888. Located about 10 miles N of Albion via NY 98 and NY 18. GPS: 43.364658, -78.234718. Lake in park. No swimming allowed. Fishing, boating. Hiking, biking trails. Bird watching. Disc golf. Camp store. Open May-Oct. $25-31 per night. 274 sites with electric hookups. Drinking water. 40-foot limit. Restrooms; showers. Laundry facilities. Dump station.

Letchworth State Park

1 Letchworth State Park Rd, Castile, NY 14427. Phone: (585) 493-3600. Located about 5 miles S of Castile via NY 19A. GPS: 42.570148, -78.051170. Swimming pool, fishing (river), boating/rafting. Hiking, biking, equestrian, nature trails. Bird watching. Scenic viewpoint. Visitor center. Nature center. Restaurant. Museum. Waterfalls. Open May-Oct. $29-35 per night. 270 sites with electric hookups. Drinking water. 50-foot limit. Restrooms; showers. Laundry facilities. Dump station.

Long Point State Park - Thousand Islands

7495 State Park Rd, Three Mile Bay, NY 13693. Phone: (315) 649-5258. Located about 28 miles W of Watertown via NY 12E and CR 57. GPS: 44.026028, -76.220802. Lake in park. Fishing, boating, skiing. Biking. Open May-Sep. $20-34 per night. 80 sites, 27 with electric hookups. 50-foot limit. Restrooms; showers. Laundry facilities. Dump station.

Macomb Reservation State Park

201 Campsite Rd, Schuyler Falls, NY 12985. Phone: (518) 643-9952. Located 7 miles NW of Peru via NY 22B and CR 33. GPS: 44.621754, -73.609131. Lake in park. Swimming beach, fishing, boating (non-motorized boats, rentals). Hiking, nature trails. Bird watching. Camp store. Open May-Sep. $20-30 per night. 123 sites, no hookups (15-amp power is available at some sites). 40-foot limit. Restrooms; showers. Dump station.

Max V. Shaul State Park

Route 30, Fultonham, NY 12071. Phone: (518) 827-4711. Located 6 miles SW of Middleburgh via NY 30. GPS: 42.546474, -74.410118. Fishing. Hiking, nature trails. Open May-Sep. $20-24 per night. 30 sites, no hookups. Drinking water. 34-foot limit. Restrooms; showers.

Mills-Norrie State Park

9 Old Post Road, Staatsburg, NY 12580. Phone: (845) 889-4646. Located on US 9, outside Staatsburg, on Hudson River. GPS: 41.840248, -73.930992. Lake in park. Fishing, boating. Hiking, biking, walking trails. Bird watching. Scenic viewpoint. Golf course. Interpretive center. Marina. Open May-Oct. $20-24 per night. 46 sites, no hookups. Drinking water. 30-foot limit (most are 20'). Restrooms; showers. Dump station.

Moreau Lake State Park

605 Old Saratoga Rd, Gansevoort, NY 12831. Phone: (518) 793-0511. Located on Moreau Lake, 10 miles N of Saratoga Springs off I-87, exit 17. GPS: 43.226288, -73.708176. Lake in park. Swimming beach, fishing, boating (rentals). Hiking, biking, nature trails. Bird watching. Visitor center. Nature center. Open May-Oct. $23-27 per night. 144 sites, no hookups. Drinking water. 40-foot limit (many are 30'). Restrooms; showers. Dump station.

Newtown Battlefield State Park

2346 County Road 60, Elmira, NY 14901. Phone: (607) 732-6067. Located just E of Elmira, off NY 17/I-86. GPS: 42.050869, -76.746971. Hiking trails. Wildlife viewing. Scenic viewpoint. Historic Revolutionary War battle site. Historic cabin, monument. Open May-Oct. $20-35 per night. 16 sites, 2 with electric hookups. Drinking water. 40-foot limit. Restrooms; showers. Dump station.

Oquaga Creek State Park

5995 County Road 20, Bainbridge, NY 13733. Phone: (607) 467-4160. Located E of Binghamton and S of Bennettsville off I-88 exit 8, on CR 20. GPS: 42.18903, -75.41825. Lake in park. Swimming beach, fishing, boating (rentals). Hiking, biking, nature trails. Bird watching. Disc golf. Food concession. Open May-Oct. $20-24 per night. 90 sites, no hookups. Drinking water. Restrooms; showers. Dump station.

Robert H. Treman State Park

105 Enfield Falls Rd, Ithaca, NY 14850. Phone: (607) 273-3440. Located on S end of Cayuga Lake, 5 miles SW of Ithaca on NY 327, near junction with NY 13. GPS: 42.402649, -76.548080. Lake in park. Swimming area (stream-fed pool), fishing. Hiking trails. Bird watching. 12 waterfalls. Open Apr-Nov. $23-33 per night. 70 sites, 11 with electric hookups. Drinking water. 50-foot limit. Restrooms; showers. Dump station.

Robert Moses State Park - Thousand Islands

32 Beach Marina Road, Massena, NY 13662. Phone: (315) 769-8663. Located about 8 miles N of Massena via NY 37 and NY 131. GPS: 44.998625, -74.851364. Lake in park. Swimming beach, fishing, boating (rentals). Hiking, biking trails. Bird watching. Scenic viewpoint. Visitor center. Nature center. Marina. Two campgrounds open May-Oct. $23-39 per night. 207 sites, 137

with electric hookups. Drinking water. 50-foot limit. Restrooms; showers. Dump station.

Sampson State Park

6096 Route 96A, Romulus, NY 14541. Phone: (315) 585-6392. Located 14 miles S of Geneva via NY 96A. GPS: 42.729141, -76.891724. Lake in park. Swimming beach, fishing, boating, skiing. Hiking, biking (rentals), walking trails. Wildlife viewing. Bird watching. Camp store. Marina. Restaurant. Museum. Open Apr-Nov. $20-36 per night. 309 sites, 243 with electric hookups. Drinking water. 40-foot limit. Restrooms; showers. Dump station.

Selkirk Shores State Park

7101 State Route 3, Pulaski, NY 13142. Phone: (315) 298-5737. Located 5 miles W of Pulaski via NY 13 and NY 3. GPS: 43.545937, -76.191216. Lake in park. Swimming beach, fishing, boating. Hiking, biking trails. Bird watching. Scenic viewpoint. Camp store. Open May-Oct. $26-32 per night. 132 sites with electric hookups. Drinking water. 40-foot limit. Restrooms; showers. Dump station.

Southwick Beach State Park

8119 Southwicks Place, Henderson, NY 13650. Phone: (315) 846-5338. Located 4 miles NW of Ellisburg via NY 193. GPS: 43.764709, -76.196342. Lake in park. Swimming beach, fishing, boating. Hiking, biking, nature trails. Wildlife viewing. Bird watching. Scenic viewpoint. Food concession. Open May-Oct. $23-35 per night. 100 sites, 41 with electric hookups. Drinking water. 40-foot limit. Restrooms; showers. Dump station.

Stony Brook State Park

10820 Route 36S, Dansville, NY 14437. Phone: (585) 335-8111. Located 2 miles S of Dansville via NY 36. GPS: 42.526417, -77.696533. Swimming (natural stream-fed pool). Hiking, nature trails. Scenic viewpoint. Park store. Food concession. Waterfalls. Open May-Oct. $20-34 per night. 88 sites, no hookups. Drinking water. 30-foot limit. Restrooms; showers. Dump station.

Taconic State Park (Copake Falls)

253 Route 344, Copake Falls, NY 12517. Phone: (518) 329-3993. Located about 13 miles N of Millerton via NY 22. GPS: 42.120987, -73.519562. Lake in park. Swimming beach, fishing, boating (rentals). Hiking, biking trails. Scenic viewpoint. Open May-Nov. $20-27 per night. 36 sites, no hookups. Drinking water. 20-foot limit. Restrooms; showers. Dump station.

Taughannock Falls State Park

2221 Taughannock Rd, Trumansburg, NY 14886. Phone: (607) 387-6739. Located 3 miles SE of Trumansburg via NY 96 and Taughannock Park Rd. GPS: 42.533184, -76.616402. Lake in park. Swimming beach, fishing, boating (rentals), skiing. Hiking trail. Bird watching. Scenic viewpoint. Visitor center. Marina. Waterfalls. Open Apr-Oct. $23-33 per night. 34 sites, 17 with electric hookups. Drinking water. 30-foot limit. Restrooms; showers. Dump station.

Verona Beach State Park

6541 Lakeshore Rd S, Verona Beach, NY 13162. Phone: (315) 762-4463. Located about 8 miles N of I-90 Exit 34 near Oneida via NY 13. GPS: 43.176266, -75.728050. Lake in park. Swimming beach, fishing, boating, skiing. Hiking, biking, equestrian, nature trails. Bird watching. Food concession. Open May-Sep. $23-35 per night. 47 sites, 12 with electric hookups. Drinking water. 50-foot limit. Restrooms; showers. Dump station.

Watkins Glen State Park

1009 N Franklin St, Watkins Glen, NY 14891. Phone: (607) 535-4511. Located just outside of Watkins Glen off NY 14. GPS: 42.37036, -76.87498. Lake in park. Swimming pool, fishing. Hiking, biking trails. Scenic viewpoint. Visitor center. Gift shops. Food concession. 19 waterfalls. Open May-Oct. $23-35 per night. 279 sites, 52 with electric hookups. Drinking water. 40-foot limit. Restrooms; showers. Dump station.

Wellesley Island State Park

44927 Cross Island Rd, Fineview, NY 13640. Phone: (315) 482-2722. Located on Wellesley Island about 4 miles west and north of I-81 Exit 51. GPS: 44.31726, -76.02143. Lake in park. Swimming beach, fishing, boating (rentals), skiing. Hiking, biking, walking trails. Bird watching. Golf course. Camp store. Visitor center. Nature center, gift shop. Full service marina. Open May-Oct. $23-41 per night. 432 sites, 53 full hookup, 90 with electric, 289 no hookups. Drinking water. 50-foot limit. Restrooms; showers. Laundry facilities. Dump station.

Westcott Beach State Park

Route 3, Henderson, NY 13650. Phone: (315) 646-2239. Located 3 miles S of Sackets Harbor via NY 3. GPS: 43.903517, -76.120779. Lake in park. Swimming beach, fishing, boating, skiing. Hiking, biking trails. Bird watching. Scenic viewpoint. Marina. Open May-Sep. $23-33 per night. 154 sites, 35 with electric hookups. Drinking water. 50-foot limit. Restrooms; showers. Dump station.

Whetstone Gulf State Park

6065 West Rd, Lowville, NY 13367. Phone: (315) 376-6630. Located about 7 miles S of Lowville via NY 26. GPS: 43.702629, -75.459938. Lake in park. Swimming beach, fishing, boating. Hiking, nature trails. Scenic viewpoint. Open May-Sep. $20-32 per night. 59 sites, 12 with electric hookups. 30-foot limit. Restrooms; showers. Dump station.

Wildwood State Park

790 Hulse Landing Rd, Wading River, NY 11792. Phone: (631) 929-4314. Located about 4 miles E of Wading River via NY 25A, Sound Ave, and Hulse Landing Rd. GPS: 40.96265, -72.80690. On the Long Island sound. Swimming beach, fishing. Hiking, biking, nature trails. Bird watching. Scenic viewpoint. Camp store. Beach gift shop. Food concession. Open Apr-Oct. $23-39 per night. 314 sites, 74 with full hookups. Drinking water. 50-foot limit (many in the 20'-30' range). Restrooms; showers. Dump station.

North Carolina

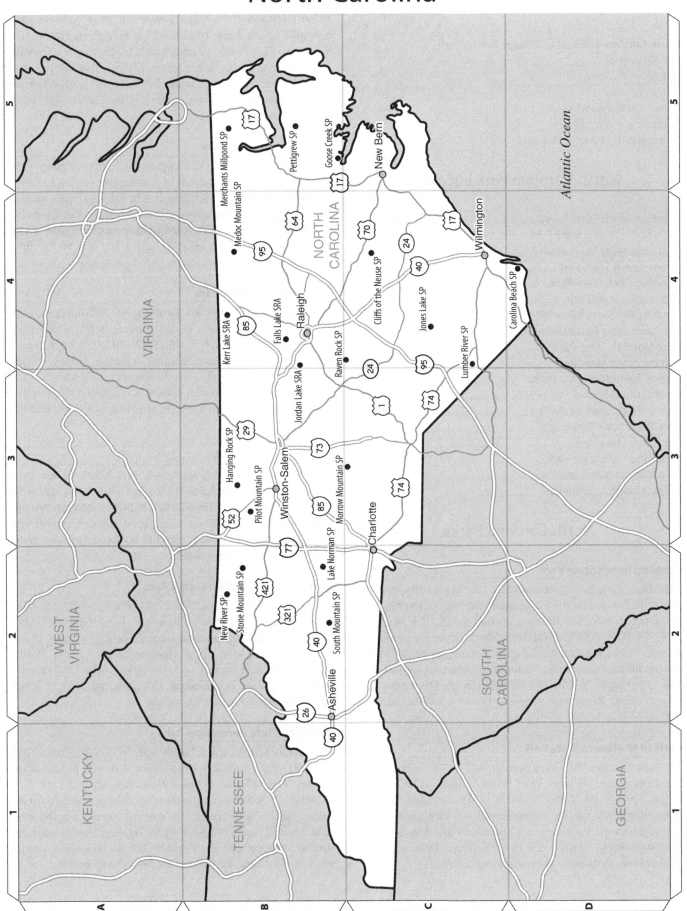

North Carolina

North Carolina Division of Parks & Recreation
121 W Jones St
Raleigh, NC 27699

Phone: (919) 707-9300
Internet: www.ncparks.gov
Reservations: Online or call park.

North Carolina Park Locator

North Carolina Parks

Carolina Beach State Park

1010 State Park Rd, Carolina Beach, NC 28428. Phone: (910) 458-8206. Located on the Intracoastal Waterway in southeastern NC about 10 miles S of Wilmington via US 421. GPS: 34.04673, 77.90708. Waters of Cape Fear River, Myrtle Grove Sound and the Atlantic Ocean. No swimming allowed. Fishing, boating (rentals). Hiking, biking, nature trails. Visitor center. Marina. Open all year. $19-33 per night. 79 sites, 10 with full hookups. Drinking water. 50-foot limit. Restrooms; showers. Laundry facilities. Dump station.

Cliffs of the Neuse State Park

240 Park Entrance Rd, Seven Springs, NC 28578. Phone: (919) 778-6234. Located 3 miles W of Seven Springs via NC 55 and Indian Springs Rd. GPS: 35.23623, -77.89133. Lake in park. Swimming beach, fishing, boating (rentals). Hiking, biking trails. Scenic viewpoint. Visitor center. Concession stand. Open all year. $19-30 per night. 32 sites, 12 with full hookups. Drinking water. 50-foot limit. Restrooms; showers. Dump station.

Falls Lake State Recreation Area

13304 Creedmoor Rd, Wake Forest, NC 27587. Phone: (919) 676-1027. Located about 12 miles N of Raleigh via NC 50. GPS: 36.01173, -78.68874. Swimming beach, fishing, boating (rentals). Hiking, biking trails. Visitor center. Marina. Two campgrounds open all year. $19-62 per night. 273 sites, 169 with water and electric hookups. Drinking water. 90-foot limit. Restrooms; showers. Dump station.

Goose Creek State Park

2190 Camp Leach Rd, Washington NC 27889. Phone: (252) 923-2191. Located 11 miles E of Washington via US 264. GPS: 35.47869, -76.90216. Swimming beach, fishing (river), boating. Hiking trails. Wildlife viewing. Visitor center. Environmental education center, extensive boardwalk across a freshwater marsh. Open all year. $30-36 per night. 22 full hookup sites. 90-foot limit. Restrooms; showers.

Hanging Rock State Park

1790 Hanging Rock Park Rd, Danbury, NC 27016. Phone: (336) 593-8480. Located 3 miles W of Danbury via NC 8/NC 89 and Hanging Rock Park Rd. GPS: 36.41159, -80.25397. Lake in park. Swimming beach, fishing, boating (rentals). Hiking, biking, equestrian, nature trails. Scenic viewpoint. Rock climbing. Visitor center. Museum. Concession stand. Open all year. $19-23 per night. 31 sites, no hookups. Drinking water. 50-foot limit. Restrooms; showers.

Jones Lake State Park

4117 Highway 242N, Elizabethtown, NC 28337. Phone: (910) 588-4550. Located 4 miles N of Elizabethtown via NC 242. GPS: 34.68325, -78.59466. Swimming beach, fishing, boating (rentals). Hiking trails. Visitor center. Concession stand. Open all year. $19-33 per night. 20 sites, 6 with full hookups. Drinking water. 50-foot limit. Restrooms; showers.

Jordan Lake State Recreation Area

280 State Park Rd, Apex, NC 27523. Phone: (919) 362-0586. Located about 12 miles W of Apex via US 64. GPS: 35.73329, -79.01656. Swimming beaches, fishing, boating (rentals). Hiking trails. Wildlife viewing. Scenic viewpoint. Visitor center. Marina. Five camping areas open all year. $19-50 per night. 1,011 sites, 665 with water and electric hookups. Drinking water. No RV length limit. Restrooms; showers. Dump station.

Kerr Lake State Recreation Area

6254 Satterwhite Point Rd, Henderson, NC 27537. Phone: (252) 438-7791. The recreation area's visitor center is located about 6 miles N of I-85 Exit 217 near Henderson via NC 1319. GPS: 36.44041, -78.36648. Swimming beaches, fishing, boating (rentals). Hiking trails. Visitor center. Two marinas. Seven camping areas; some open all year. $19-62 per night. 601 sites, 28 with water and electric hookups, 295 electric only, 278 no hookups. Drinking water. 80-foot limit. Restrooms; showers. Dump station.

Lake Norman State Park

759 State Park Road, Troutman, NC 28166. Phone: (704) 528-6350. Located about 7 miles W of I-77 Exit 42 near Troutman via US 21 and State Park Rd. GPS: 35.67380, -80.93209. Swimming beach, fishing, boating (rentals). Hiking, biking trails. Bird watching. Scenic viewpoint. Visitor center. Open all year. $23-33 per night. 44 sites, no hookups. Drinking water. 70-foot limit. Restrooms; showers. Dump station.

Lumber River State Park

26040 Raeford Rd, Wagram, NC 28396. Phone: (910) 628-4564. Located about 32 miles SW of Fayetteville via US 401. GPS: 34.89873, -79.35484. On a National Wild and Scenic River. Fishing, boating. Hiking, nature trails. Wildlife viewing. Scenic viewpoint. RV camping available in the Chalk Banks unit. Open all year. $12 per night. 14 sites, no hookups. Drinking water. 75-foot limit. Vault toilets.

Medoc Mountain State Park

1541 Medoc State Park Rd, Hollister, NC 27844. Phone: (252) 586-6588. Located 3 miles E of Hollister via Gibbs Ave and Medoc Mountain Rd. GPS: 36.25173, -77.89267. Fishing (creek), boating. Hiking, biking, equestrian trails. Wildlife viewing. Visitor center. Open all year. $19-28 per night. 34 sites, 12 with electric hookups. Drinking water. 80-foot limit. Restrooms; showers. Dump station. Equestrian area with 5 primitive sites.

Merchants Millpond State Park

176 Millpond Rd, Gatesville, NC 27938. Phone: (252) 357-1191. Located about 6 miles NE of Gatesville via NC 37 and US 158. GPS: 36.43744, -76.69961. Lake in park. Fishing, boating (canoe rentals). Hiking, biking trails. Wildlife viewing. Visitor center. Open all year. $19-23 per night. 20 sites, no hookups. Drinking water. 63-foot limit. Restrooms; showers.

Morrow Mountain State Park

49104 Morrow Mountain Rd, Albemarle, NC 28001. Phone: (704) 982-4402. Located 9 miles E of Albemarle via NC 740 and Morrow Mountain Rd. GPS: 35.37361, -80.07379. Lake in park. Swimming pool (lake swimming is not permitted), fishing, boating (rentals). Hiking, equestrian trails. Museum. Open all year. $19-28 per night. 105 sites, 22 with electric hookups. Drinking water. 50-foot limit. Restrooms; showers. Laundry sink at restrooms. Dump station.

New River State Park

358 New River State Park Road, Laurel Springs, NC 28644. Phone: (336) 982-2587. Located 10 miles NW of Laurel Springs via NC 113 and US 221. GPS: 36.46547, -81.34141. On a National Wild and Scenic River. Swimming beach, fishing, boating. Hiking, walking trails. Wildlife viewing. Scenic viewpoint. Visitor center. RV camping available at the US-221 access area. Open all year. $19-33 per night. 20 sites, 10 full hookup, 10 electric only. Drinking water. 60-foot limit. Restrooms; showers. Dump station.

Pettigrew State Park

2252 Lake Shore Rd, Creswell, NC 27928. Phone: (252) 797-4475. Located 6 miles S of Creswell via Spruill Bridge Rd and Thirty Foot Canal Rd. GPS: 35.79226, -76.40917. Lake in park. Swimming area, fishing, boating. Hiking, biking trails. Boardwalk Trail. Wildlife viewing. Open all year. $19-23 per night. 13 sites, no hookups. Drinking water. 75-foot limit. Restrooms; showers.

Pilot Mountain State Park

1792 Pilot Knob Park Rd, Pinnacle, NC 27043. Phone: (336) 444-5100. Located about 23 miles NW of Winston-Salem via US 52. GPS: 36.34203, -80.46364. Fishing (river), boating. Hiking, equestrian trails. Scenic viewpoint. Rock climbing. Visitor center. Open all year. $19-23 per night. 15 sites, no hookups. Drinking water. 30-foot limit. Restrooms; showers.

Raven Rock State Park

3009 Raven Rock Rd, Lillington, NC 27546. Phone: (910) 893-4888. Located in central NC, 9 miles NW of Lillington via US 421 and Raven Rock Rd (CR 1314). GPS: 35.457353, -78.912779. Fishing (river), boating. Hiking, biking, equestrian trails. Scenic viewpoint. Visitor center. Open all year. $23-33 per night. 24 sites, 9 with full hookups. Drinking water. No RV length limit. Restrooms; showers.

South Mountains State Park

3001 South Mountain Park Ave, Connelly Springs, NC 28612. Phone: (828) 433-4772. Located about 20 miles S of I-40 Exit 105 near Morganton via NC 18; follow signs. GPS: 35.59626, -81.60051. Lake in park. Fishing (river and lake), boating. Hiking, biking, equestrian trails. Visitor center. Waterfall. Open all year. $19-28 per night. 18 sites, 2 with electric hookups. Drinking water. 70-foot limit. Restrooms; showers.

Stone Mountain State Park

3042 Frank Pkwy, Roaring Gap, NC 28668. Phone: (336) 957-8185. Located 18 miles NW of Elkin via US 21. GPS: 36.37904, -81.02257. Fishing. Hiking, equestrian trails. Scenic viewpoint. Rock climbing. 600-foot granite dome that is a designated National Natural Landmark. Historic Hutchinson Homestead, a restored mid-19th-century farm. Open all year. $19-33 per night. 90 sites, 41 with water and electric hookups. Drinking water. 90-foot limit. Restrooms; showers. Dump station.

North Dakota

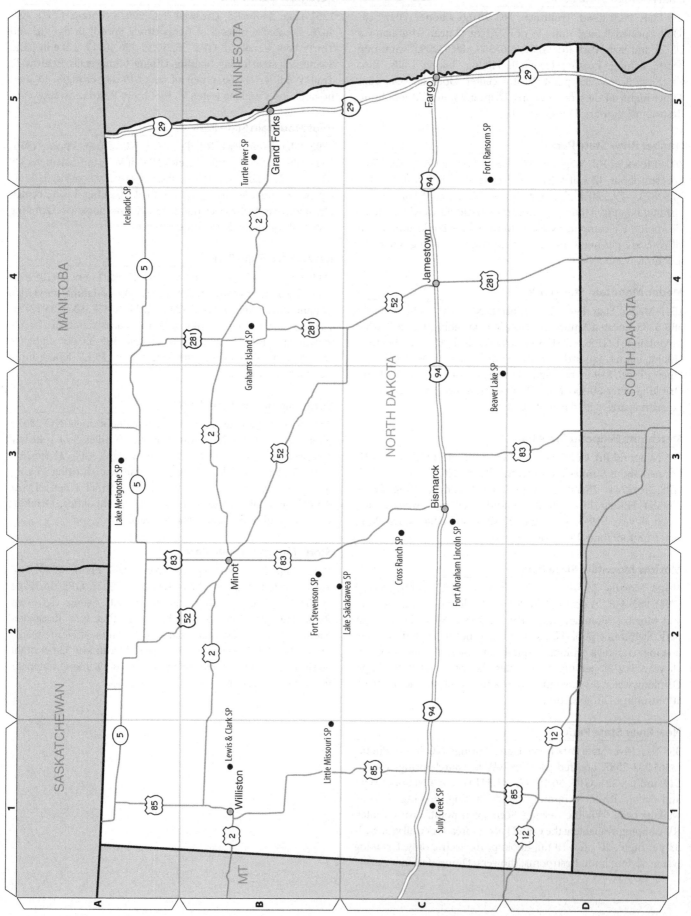

North Dakota

North Dakota Parks & Recreation Dept.
1600 E Century Ave, Ste. 3
Bismarck, ND 58506

Phone: (701) 328-5357
Internet: www.parkrec.nd.gov
Reservations: Online or call park.

North Dakota Park Locator

North Dakota Parks

Beaver Lake State Park

3850 70th St SE, Wishek, ND 58495. Phone: (701) 452-2752. Located 28 miles N of Wishek via ND 13 and ND 3. GPS: 46.39945, -99.61558. Swimming beach, fishing, boating. Hiking, biking, nature trails. Bird watching. Open all year. $25 per night. 25 sites with water and electric hookups. Restrooms; showers. Dump station.

Cross Ranch State Park

1403 River Rd, Center, ND 58530. Phone: (701) 794-3731. Located about 22 miles NE of Center via ND 25 and 28th Ave SW. GPS: 47.213827, -100.999762. On Missouri River. Fishing, boating (canoe/kayak rentals). Hiking, biking, nature trails. Visitor center. Open all year. $17-25 per night. 57 sites, 36 with water and electric hookups. 35-foot limit. Restrooms; showers. Dump station.

Fort Abraham Lincoln State Park

4480 Fort Lincoln Rd, Mandan, ND 58554. Phone: (701) 667-6340. Located 7 miles S of Mandan via Hwy 1806. GPS: 46.756125, -100.841839. Fishing (river). Hiking, biking, equestrian trails. Park store. Visitor center. Historic buildings, tours. Open all year. $17-25 per night. 107 sites, 82 with water and electric, 15 water only. Restrooms; showers. Dump station.

Fort Ransom State Park

5981 Walt Hjelle Pkwy, Fort Ransom, ND 58033. Phone: (701) 973-4331. Located 2 miles N of Fort Ransom via Walt Hjelle Pkwy. GPS: 46.547167, -97.932337. Fishing (river), boating (canoe/kayak rentals). Hiking, biking, equestrian, nature trails. Bird watching. Scenic viewpoint. Visitor center. Open all year. $17-25 per night. 26 sites, 14 with water and electric hookups. Restrooms; showers. Dump station. Equestrian area with 33 sites (24 with water and electric hookups).

Fort Stevenson State Park

1252A 41st Ave NW, Garrison, ND 58540. Phone: (701) 337-5576. Located 4 miles S of Garrison via CR 15. GPS: 47.59678, -101.42064. Lake in park. Swimming beach, fishing, boating (rentals). Hiking, biking (rentals) trails. Scenic viewpoint. Visitor center. Two marinas, store, grill. Museum. Open all year. $17-30 per night. 128 sites, 55 full hookup, 56 with water and electric, 17 no hookups. Restrooms; showers. Dump station.

Grahams Island State Park

152 S Duncan Rd, Devils Lake, ND 58301. Phone: (701) 766-4015. Located 15 miles SW of Devils Lake via ND 19. GPS: 48.043829, -99.056017. Lake in park. Swimming beach, fishing, boating. Hiking, biking trails. Park store. Visitor center. Open all year. $17-30 per night. 117 sites, 38 full hookup, 70 with water and electric, 9 no hookups. Restrooms; showers. Dump station.

Icelandic State Park

13571 Highway 5, Cavalier, ND 58220. Phone: (701) 265-4561. Located 7 miles W of Cavalier via ND 5. GPS: 48.780973, -97.756643. Lake in park. Swimming beach, fishing, boating (rentals). Hiking, biking trails. Bird watching. Park store. Museum. Nature preserve. Pioneer Heritage Center, restored historic buildings. Open all year. $17-25 per night. 150 sites, 140 with water and electric hookups. Restrooms; showers. Dump station.

Lake Metigoshe State Park

2 Lake Metigoshe State Park, Bottineau, ND 58318. Phone: (701) 263-4651. Located 14 miles NE of Bottineau via Town Line Rd and ND 43. GPS: 48.979932, -100.336342. Swimming beach, fishing, boating (canoe/kayak rentals). Hiking, biking trails. Bird watching. Outdoor Learning Center. Open all year. $17-25 per night. 124 sites, 85 with water and electric hookups. Restrooms; showers. Dump station.

Lake Sakakawea State Park

720 Park Ave, Pick City, ND 58545. Phone: (701) 487-3315. Located just N of Pick City off ND 200. GPS: 47.519352, -101.453747. Swimming beach, fishing, boating. Hiking, biking trails. Park store. Visitor center. Full service marina. Open all year. $17-25 per night. 191 sites, 149 with water and electric hookups. Restrooms; showers. Dump station.

Lewis & Clark State Park

4904 119th Rd NW, Epping, ND 58843. Phone: (701) 859-3071. Located 20 miles E of Williston via ND 1804. GPS: 48.124931, -103.234426. Lake in park. Swimming beach, fishing, boating (canoe/kayak rentals). Hiking, biking, nature trails. Wildlife viewing. Scenic viewpoint. Park store. Visitor center. Marina. Open all year. $17-30 per night. 96 sites, 41 full hookup, 47 with water and electric, 8 no hookups. Restrooms; showers. Dump station.

Little Missouri State Park

910 103rd Ave NW, Killdeer, ND 58640. Phone: (701) 764-5256. Located 20 miles N of Killdeer via ND 22. GPS: 47.545820, -102.736003. Hiking, equestrian trails. Designated horse park with 81 corrals and additional amenities to accommodate equestrian users. Open May-Oct. $12-15 per night. 31 sites, 28 with electric hookups. Restrooms; showers. Dump station.

Sully Creek State Park

1495 36th St, Medora, ND 58645. Phone: (701) 623-2024. Located 3 miles S of Medora via River Rd and 36th St. GPS: 46.889695, -103.537202. Fishing (river), boating. Hiking, biking, equestrian trails. Designated horse park with 66 corrals and additional amenities to accommodate equestrian users. Open May-Oct. $12 per night. 23 sites, 9 with water and electric hookups. Restrooms; showers. Dump station. Equestrian camp, 7 sites with wter and electric hookups.

Turtle River State Park

3084 Park Ave, Arvilla, ND 58214. Phone: (701) 795-3180. Located 19 miles W of I-29 Exit 141 in Grand Forks via US 2. GPS: 47.939399, -97.492487. Fishing (river). Hiking, biking trails. Scenic viewpoint. Visitor center. Open all year. $17-25 per night. 91 sites, 65 with water and electric hookups. Restrooms; showers. Dump station.

Ohio

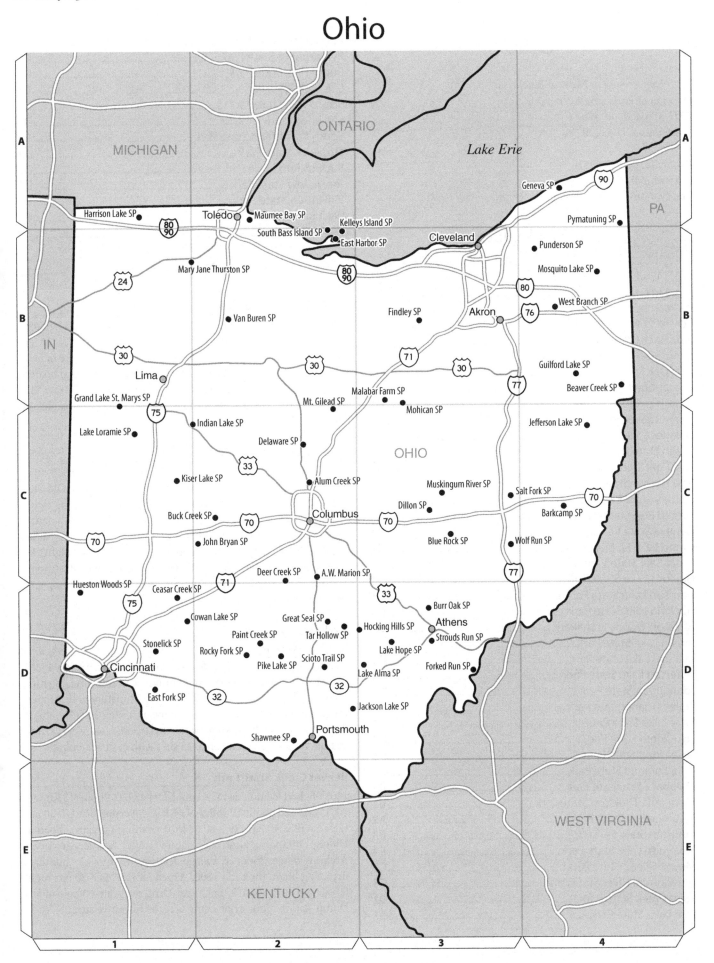

MICHIGAN

ONTARIO

Lake Erie

PA

Geneva SP

Harrison Lake SP

Toledo

Maumee Bay SP

Kelleys Island SP

South Bass Island SP

East Harbor SP

Cleveland

Pymatuning SP

Punderson SP

Mosquito Lake SP

Mary Jane Thurston SP

IN

Van Buren SP

Findley SP

Akron

West Branch SP

Guilford Lake SP

Lima

Grand Lake St. Marys SP

Mt. Gilead SP

Malabar Farm SP

Mohican SP

Beaver Creek SP

Jefferson Lake SP

Lake Loramie SP

Indian Lake SP

OHIO

Delaware SP

Kiser Lake SP

Alum Creek SP

Muskingum River SP

Salt Fork SP

Buck Creek SP

Columbus

Dillon SP

Barkcamp SP

John Bryan SP

Blue Rock SP

Wolf Run SP

Hueston Woods SP

Deer Creek SP

A.W. Marion SP

Ceasar Creek SP

Burr Oak SP

Cowan Lake SP

Great Seal SP

Hocking Hills SP

Athens

Paint Creek SP

Tar Hollow SP

Strouds Run SP

Stonelick SP

Rocky Fork SP

Scioto Trail SP

Lake Hope SP

Pike Lake SP

Lake Alma SP

Forked Run SP

Cincinnati

East Fork SP

Jackson Lake SP

Shawnee SP

Portsmouth

WEST VIRGINIA

KENTUCKY

Ohio

Ohio Department of Natural Resources
Division of Parks and Recreation
2045 Morse Road, Bldg C-4
Columbus, OH 43229

Phone: (614) 265-6561
Internet: parks.ohiodnr.gov
Reservations: Required, all parks. Online or call park.

Ohio Park Locator

Ohio Parks

A.W. Marion State Park

8498 Township Highway 77, Circleville OH 43113. Phone: (740) 474-9201. Located 6 miles NE of Circleville via US 22 and Ringgold Southern Rd. GPS: 39.634515, -82.873294. Lake in park. Swimming (from your boat in designated area), fishing, boating (rentals). Hiking, biking trails. Camp store. Open all year. $19-28 per night. 56 sites, 28 with electric hookups. Restrooms; no showers. Dump station.

Alum Creek State Park

2911 S Old State Rd, Delaware, OH 43015. Phone: (740) 548-4039. Located 7 miles SE of Delaware via US 36 and Lackey Old State Rd. GPS: 40.237056, -82.987013. Lake in park. Swimming beach, fishing, boating (rentals). Hiking, biking, equestrian, nature, walking trails. Disc golf. Miniature golf. Camp store. Nature center. Full service marina. Open all year. $29-45 per night. 310 sites, 24 full hookup, 286 with water and electric. Restrooms; showers. Laundry facilities. Dump station. Equestrian camp area, primitive sites.

Barkcamp State Park

65330 Barkcamp Rd, Belmont, OH 43718. Phone: (740) 484-4064. Located about 2 miles N of Belmont via OH 149. GPS: 40.046887, -81.031075. Lake in park. Swimming beach, fishing, boating. Hiking, biking, equestrian, nature trails. Miniature golf. Archery range. Open all year. $23-35 per night. 110 sites, 15 full hookup, 95 with electric. Drinking water. Restrooms; showers. Dump station. Equestrian camp area, 25 sites with electric hookups.

Beaver Creek State Park

12021 Echo Dell Rd, East Liverpool, OH 43920. Phone: (330) 385-3091. Located about 10 miles N of East Liverpool via US 30 and OH 7. GPS: 40.731429, -80.622670. Fishing (stream), boating. Hiking, biking, equestrian, nature trails. Scenic viewpoint. Archery range. Pioneer Village features 15 historic buildings depicting life in the early 1800s. Open all year. $17-26 per night. 50 sites, 6 with electric hookups. Drinking water. Vault toilets. Dump station. Equestrian camp area, 59 primitive sites.

Blue Rock State Park

7924 Cutler Lake Rd, Blue Rock, OH 43720. Phone: (740) 453-4377. Located about 3 miles NE of Blue Rock via Buttermilk Rd and Corns Rd. GPS: 39.819177, -81.852181. Small lake in park. Swimming beach, fishing, boating (rentals). Hiking, equestrian trails. Archery range. Camp store. Nature center. Open Mar-Dec. $17-24 per night. 53 sites, no hookups. Drinking water. Restrooms; showers. Dump station. Equestrian camp area, 12 primitive sites.

Buck Creek State Park

1901 Buck Creek Ln, Springfield, OH 45502. Phone: (937) 322-5284. Located about 6 miles NE of Springfield via US 40 and Bird Rd. GPS: 39.948808, -83.729732. Lake in park. Swimming beach, fishing, boating. Hiking, biking (rentals), equestrian trails. Bird watching. Disc golf. Camp store. Marina, store. Open all year. $23-32 per night. 108 sites, 86 with electric hookups. Drinking water. Restrooms; showers. Dump station.

Burr Oak State Park

10220 Burr Oak Lodge Rd, Glouster, OH 45732. Phone: (740) 767-3570. Located 6 miles NE of Glouster via OH 13 and Burr Oak Rd. GPS: 39.539588, -82.036235. Lake in park. Swimming beach, fishing, boating. Hiking, equestrian trails. Disc golf. Archery range. Nature center. Lodge, restaurant, lounge. Pioneer burial site. Open all year. $17-28 per night. 60 sites, 31 with electric hookups. Drinking water. Restrooms; showers. Laundry facilities. Dump station. Equestrian camp area, 10 primitive sites.

Caesar Creek State Park

8570 E State Route 73, Waynesville, OH 45068. Phone: (513) 897-3055. Located about 4 miles E of Waynesville via OH 73. GPS: 39.514645, -84.030083. Lake in park. Swimming beach, fishing, boating (kayak rentals). Hiking, biking, equestrian trails. Bird watching. Archery range. Camp store. Visitor center. Nature center. Full service marina. Open all year. $27-43 per night. 287 sites, 35 full hookup, 252 with electric. Drinking water. Restrooms; showers. Dump station. Equestrian camp area, 30 primitive sites.

Cowan Lake State Park

1750 Osborn Rd, Wilmington, OH 45177. Phone: (937) 382-1096. Located 5 miles S of Wilmington via US 68 and Dalton Rd. GPS: 39.388865, -83.883667. Swimming beach, fishing, boating (rentals). Hiking, biking (rentals) trails. Bird watching. Archery range. Camp store. Nature center. Marina. Open all year. $23-43 per night. 254 sites, 237 with electric hookups. Drinking water. Restrooms; showers. Laundry facilities. Dump station.

Deer Creek State Park

20635 State Park Road 20, Mount Sterling, OH 43143. Phone: (740) 869-3124. Located 5 miles S of Mount Sterling via OH 207 and Yankeetown Pike. GPS: 39.648593, -83.242160. Lake in park. Swimming beach, fishing, boating (rentals), skiing. Hiking, biking (rentals), equestrian trails. Golf course, pro shop. Disc golf. Miniature golf. Camp store. Nature center. Full service marina. Lodge, restaurant. Open all year. $27-32 per night. 232 sites with electric hookups. Drinking water. Restrooms; showers. Laundry facilities. Dump station.

Delaware State Park

5202 US Hwy 23 N, Delaware, OH 43015. Phone: (740) 548-4631. Located 6 miles N of Delaware via US 23. GPS: 40.396148, -83.063656. Lake in park. Swimming beach, fishing, boating (rentals). Hiking, biking trails. Bird watching. Disc golf. Camp store. Nature center. Full service marina. Open all year. $27-32 per night. 211 sites with electric hookups. Drinking water. Restrooms; showers. Laundry facilities. Dump station.

Dillon State Park

5265 Dillon Hills Dr, Nashport, OH 43830. Phone: (740) 453-4377. Located 9 miles N of I-70 Exit 153 near Zanesville via State St and OH 146. GPS: 40.010960, -82.104226. Lake in park. Swimming beach, fishing, boating (rentals), skiing. Hiking, biking, equestrian trails. Disc golf. Archery range. Camp store. Welcome center. Nature center. Marina. Open all year. $25-39 per night. 195 sites, 10 full hookup, 183 with electric, 2 no hookups. Drinking water. Restrooms; showers. Laundry facilities. Dump station. Equestrian camp area, 26 primitive sites.

East Fork State Park

3294 Elklick Rd, Bethel, OH 45106. Phone: (513) 734-2730. Located 10 miles N of Bethel via OH 133. GPS: 39.057205, -84.100463. Lake in park. Swimming beach, fishing, boating (rentals), skiing. Hiking, biking (rentals), equestrian trails. Miniature golf. Archery range. Visitor center (U.S. Army Corp of Engineers). Nature center. Open all year. $27-41 per night. 399 sites, 23 full hookup, 376 with electric. Drinking water. Restrooms; showers. Dump station. Equestrian camp area, 17 sites with electric hookups.

East Harbor State Park

1169 N Buck Rd, Lakeside-Marblehead, OH 43440. Phone: (419) 734-4424. Located 4 miles W of Lakeside-Marblehead via OH 163. GPS: 41.545080, -82.817565. Lake in park. Swimming beach, fishing, boating. Hiking, biking (rentals) trails. Bird watching. Disc golf. Archery range. Camp store. Welcome center. Nature center. Marina. Open all year. $25-45 per night. 573 sites, 51 full hookup, 354 with electric, 168 no hookups. Drinking water. Restrooms; showers. Laundry facilities. Dump station.

Findley State Park

25381 State Route 58, Wellington, OH 44090. Phone: (440) 647-4490. Located 3 miles S of Wellington via OH 58. GPS: 41.123090, -82.218445. Lake in park. Swimming beach, fishing, boating (canoe/kayak rentals). Hiking, biking trails. Wildlife viewing. Disc golf. Camp store. Nature center. Open all year. $23-41 per night. 257 sites, 15 full hookup, 91 with electric, 151 no hookups. Drinking water. Restrooms; showers. Laundry facilities. Dump station.

Forked Run State Park

63300 State Route 124, Reedsville, OH 45772. Phone: (740) 378-6206. Located on the Ohio River, 3 miles SW of Reedsville via OH 124. GPS: 39.085170, -81.770269. Lake in park. Swimming beach, fishing, boating (rentals). Hiking trails. Wildlife viewing. Disc golf. Camp store. Open all year. $19-28 per night. 143 sites, 79 with electric hookups. Drinking water. Vault toilets. Showers. Laundry facilities. Dump station.

Geneva State Park

4499 Padanarum Rd, Geneva, OH 44041. Phone: (440) 466-8400. Located 5 miles NW of Geneva via OH 534 and Lake Rd. GPS: 41.854442, -80.985749. Lake in park. Swimming beach, fishing, boating (rentals). Hiking, biking trails. Bird watching. Archery range. Camp store. Full service marina. Lodge, restaurant. Zipline and Challenge Course. Open all year. $23-41 per night. 93 sites, 19 full hookup, 74 with electric. Drinking water. Restrooms; showers. Laundry facilities. Dump station.

Grand Lake St. Marys State Park

834 Edgewater Dr, St. Marys, OH 45885. Phone: (419) 394-3611. Located about 3 miles W of Saint Marys via OH 703. GPS: 40.546737, -84.437936. Lake in park. Swimming pool and four beaches, fishing, boating. Hiking, biking (rentals) trails. Bird watching. Miniature golf. Camp store. Nature center. Restaurant. Open all year. $23-41 per night. 198 sites, 34 full hookup, 154 with electric, 10 no hookups. Drinking water. Restrooms; showers. Laundry facilities. Dump station.

Great Seal State Park

4908 Marietta Rd, Chillicothe, OH 45601. Phone: (740) 887-4818. Located about 7 miles N of Chillicothe via US 23. GPS: 39.402287, -82.941515. Hiking, biking, equestrian trails. Scenic viewpoint. Disc golf. Open all year. $17-22 per night. 15 sites, no hookups. Drinking water. Vault toilets.

Guilford Lake State Park

6835 E Lake Rd, Lisbon, OH 44432. Phone: (330) 222-1712. Located 8 miles NW of Lisbon via OH 172. GPS: 40.806296, -80.877516. Swimming beach, fishing, boating (rentals). Hiking trail. Bird watching. Open all year. $25-30 per night. 40 sites with electric hookups. Drinking water. Restrooms; showers. Dump station.

Harrison Lake State Park

26246 Harrison Lake Rd, Fayette, OH 43521. Phone: (419) 237-2593. Located 5 miles SW of Fayette via US 20 and CR 27. GPS: 41.643611, -84.366811. Swimming beach, fishing, boating (rentals). Hiking, biking (rentals) trails. Disc golf. Open all year. $21-30 per night. 179 sites, 143 with electric hookups. Drinking water. Restrooms; showers. Dump station.

Hocking Hills State Park

19852 State Route 664, Logan, OH 43138. Phone: (740) 385-6842. Located 12 miles SW of Logan via OH 664. GPS: 39.437449, -82.537889. Small lake in park. Swimming pool, fishing, boating (no ramp). Hiking, biking, equestrian, walking trails. Wildlife viewing. Disc golf. Archery range. Camp store. Visitor center. Lodge, restaurant. Waterfalls. Open all year. $25-45 per night. 169 sites, 47 full hookup, 109 with electric. Drinking water. Restrooms; showers. Laundry facilities. Dump station.

Hueston Woods State Park

6301 Park Office Rd, College Corner, OH 45003. Phone: (513) 523-6347. Located 4 miles NE of College Corner via Jones Rd and Butler Israel Rd. GPS: 39.585604, -84.770008. Lake in park. Swimming beach, fishing, boating (rentals). Hiking, biking, equestrian trails. Bird watching. Golf course, pro shop, driving range. Disc golf. Miniature golf. Archery range. Camp store. Nature center. Marina. Lodge, restaurant. Open all year. $21-39 per night. 365 sites, 20 full hookup, 208 with electric, 137 no hookups. Drinking water. Restrooms; showers. Laundry facilities. Dump station.

Indian Lake State Park

13156 State Route 235N, Lakeview, OH 43331. Phone: (937) 843-2717. Located about 3 miles NE of Lakeview via OH 235. GPS: 40.516240, -83.900470. Swimming pool and two beaches, fishing, boating (rentals). Hiking, biking, walking trails. Disc golf. Archery range. Camp store. Three marinas. Open all year. $27-41 per night. 443 sites, 43 full hookup, 400 with electric. Drinking water. Restrooms; showers. Laundry facilities. Dump station.

Jackson Lake State Park

921 Tommy Been Rd, Oak Hill, OH 45656. Phone: (740) 682-6197. Located 2 miles NW of Oak Hill via OH 279 and Tommy Been Rd. GPS: 38.903961, -82.596468. Swimming beach, fishing, boating. Hiking trails. Open Apr-Dec. $25-30 per night. 25 sites with electric hookups. Drinking water. Restrooms; no showers. Dump station.

Jefferson Lake State Park

501 Township Road 261A, Richmond, OH 43944. Phone: (740) 765-4459. Located 5 miles NW of Richmond via OH 43 and State Park Mooretown Rd. GPS: 40.466293, -80.807106. Swimming beach, fishing, boating (electric motors only). Hiking, biking, equestrian trails. Archery range. Open all year. $17-26 per night. 49 sites, 5 with electric hookups. Drinking water. Restrooms; no showers. Dump station.

John Bryan State Park

3790 State Route 370, Yellow Springs, OH 45387. Phone: (937) 322-5284. Located 2 miles SE of Yellow Springs via OH 343 and OH 370. GPS: 39.788902, -83.865085. Fishing (river), boating (paddle). Hiking, biking trails. Disc golf. Rock climbing. Camp store. Nature center. Limestone gorge, cut by the Little Miami State and National Scenic River, is a National Natural Landmark. Open all year. $19-28 per night. 61 sites, 9 with electric hookups. Drinking water. Restrooms; no showers. Dump station.

Kelleys Island State Park

920 Division St, Kelleys Island, OH 43438. Phone: (419) 734-4424. Located on Lake Erie. Access by ferry from Lakeside Marblehead. GPS: 41.614418, -82.706427. Lake in park. Swimming beach, fishing, boating (kayak rentals). Hiking, biking, walking trails. Wildlife viewing. Bird watching. Scenic viewpoint. Museum. Open Apr-Nov. $25-45 per night. 124 sites, 35 full hookup, 46 with electric, 43 no hookups. Drinking water. Restrooms; showers. Dump station.

Kiser Lake State Park

4889 N State Route 235, Conover, OH 45317. Phone: (937) 843-2717. Campground located 4 miles N of Saint Paris via Kiser Lake Rd. GPS: 40.181478, -83.949037. Swimming beach, fishing, boating (no motors, canoe/kayak rentals). Hiking, equestrian trails. Bird watching. Nature center. Marina. Open all year. $19-28 per night. 76 sites, 20 with electric hookups. Drinking water. Restrooms; no showers. Dump station.

Lake Alma State Park

422 Lake Alma Rd, Wellston, OH 45692. Phone: (740) 384-4474. Located 2 miles NE of Wellston via OH 349. GPS: 39.148305, -82.516160. Swimming beach, fishing, boating (no motors). Hiking, walking trails. Camp store. Nature center. Open all year. $19-35 per night. 76 sites, 6 full hookup, 60 with electric, 10 no hookups. Drinking water. Restrooms; showers. Dump station.

Lake Hope State Park

27331 State Route 278, McArthur, OH 45651. Phone: (740) 596-4938. Located 13 miles NE of McArthur via US 50, OH 677 and SR-278. GPS: 39.337062, -82.341544. Swimming beach, fishing, boating (rentals). Hiking, biking trails. Wildlife viewing. Archery range. Nature center. Restaurant. Park concession. Open all year. $19-28 per night. 189 sites, 46 with electric hookups. Drinking water. Restrooms; showers. Laundry facilities. Dump station.

Lake Loramie State Park

4401 Fort Loramie Swanders Rd, Minster, OH 45865. Phone: (419) 394-3611. Located 3 miles S of Minster via OH 362. GPS: 40.357595, -84.357179. Swimming beach, fishing, boating (rentals). Hiking, biking (rentals) trails. Disc golf. Miniature golf. Nature center. Museum. Open all year. $25-39 per night. 166 sites, 42 full hookup, 120 with electric, 4 no hookups. Drinking water. Restrooms; showers. Laundry facilities. Dump station.

Malabar Farm State Park

4050 Bromfield Rd, Lucas, OH 44843. Phone: (419) 892-2784. Located 5 miles S of Lucas via Moffett Rd and Pleasant Valley Rd. GPS: 40.643105, -82.401044. Fishing (ponds). Hiking, equestrian, nature trails. Scenic viewpoint. Visitor center, gift shop. Louis Bromfield home site, a working farm on the National Register of Historic Places. Tours available. Open all year. $17-22 per night. 15 sites, no hookups. Drinking water. Restrooms; no showers.

Mary Jane Thurston State Park

1466 State Route 65, McClure, OH 43534. Phone: (419) 832-7662. Located 6 miles NE of McClure via OH 65. GPS: 41.409720, -83.877659. Fishing (river), boating (rentals). Hiking trails. Archery range. Camp store. Marina. Open all year. $19-32 per night. 23 sites with electric hookups (4 with water hookup). Restrooms; no showers. Dump station.

Maumee Bay State Park

1400 State Park Rd, Oregon, OH 43616. Phone: (419) 836-7758. Located 7 miles NE of Oregon via Cedar Point Rd. GPS: 41.677970, -83.392330. Lake in park. Swimming beaches, fishing, boating (rentals). Hiking, biking (rentals), boardwalk trails. Wildlife viewing. Golf course, pro shop. Archery range. Camp store. Nature center. Marina. Lodge, restaurant. Open all year. $27-41 per night. 252 sites with electric hookups. Drinking water. Restrooms; showers. Laundry facilities. Dump station.

Mohican State Park

3116 State Route 3, Loudonville, OH 44842. Phone: (419) 994-5125. Located 2 miles SW of Loudonville via OH 3. GPS: 40.609963, -82.258884. Lake in park. Swimming pool, fishing, boating. Hiking, biking, equestrian trails. Camp store. Nature center. Lodge, restaurant. Open all year. $21-45 per night. 163 sites, 51 full hookup, 102 with electric, 10 no hookups. Drinking water. Restrooms; showers. Laundry facilities. Dump station.

Mosquito Lake State Park

1439 State Route 305, Cortland, OH 44410. Phone: (330) 637-2856. Located 5 miles W of Cortland via OH 305. GPS: 41.317016, -80.779177. One of the largest lakes in Ohio. Swimming beach, fishing, boating (rentals). Hiking, biking, equestrian trails. Wildlife viewing. Disc golf. Archery range. Camp store. Marina. Butterfly garden. Open all year. $21-39 per night. 232 sites, 40 full hookup, 176 with electric, 16 no hookups. Restrooms; showers. Laundry facilities. Dump station.

Mount Gilead State Park

4119 State Route 95, Mount Gilead, OH 43338. Phone: (419) 946-1961. Located 1 mile E of Mount Gilead via SR-95. GPS: 40.545929, -82.808908. Small lake in park. Fishing, boating (electric motors only). Hiking, equestrian trails. Bird watching. Disc golf. Camp store. Nature center. Open all year. $23-35 per night. 59 sites, 22 full hookup, 37 with electric. Restrooms; showers. Dump station.

Muskingum River State Park

1390 Ellis Dam Road, Zanesville OH 43701. Phone: (740) 767-3570. Located 9 miles N of Zanesville via Linden Ave and River Rd. GPS: 40.043961, -81.977875. Fishing, boating. Scenic viewpoint. On the National Register of Historic Places. It is the only remaining system of hand-operated locks in the nation. Open Apr-Oct. $17-22 per night. 19 sites, no hookups. Drinking water. Vault toilets.

Paint Creek State Park

280 Taylor Rd, Bainbridge, OH 45612. Phone: (937) 393-4284. Located 8 miles NW of Bainbridge via US 50 and Rapid Forge Rd. GPS: 39.270143, -83.381004. Lake in park. Swimming beach, fishing, boating. Hiking, biking, equestrian trails. Disc golf. Miniature golf. Rock climbing. Archery range. Camp store. Nature center. Marina. Open all year. $25-39 per night. 197 sites with electric hookups. Drinking water. Restrooms; showers. Laundry facilities. Dump station. Ten non-electric equestrian campsites.

Pike Lake State Park

1847 Pike Lake Rd, Bainbridge, OH 45612. Phone: (740) 493-2212. Located 7 miles SE of Bainbridge via county roads. GPS: 39.158502, -83.221182. Swimming beach, fishing, boating (canoe/kayak rentals, electric motors only). Hiking trails. Disc golf. Camp store. Nature center. Open all year. $21-26 per night. 75 sites with electric hookups. Drinking water. Restrooms; showers. Dump station.

Punderson State Park

11755 Kinsman Rd, Newbury, OH 44065. Phone: (440) 564-2279. Located 4 miles E of Newbury via OH 87. GPS: 41.456054, -81.205028. Lakes in park. Swimming beach, fishing, boating (kayak rentals, electric motors only). Hiking, biking (rentals) trails. Golf course, pro shop. Disc golf. Archery range. Camp store. Nature center. Marina. Lodge, restaurant. Open all year. $25-39 per night. 187 sites, 20 full hookup, 150 with electric, 17 no hookups. Drinking water. Restrooms; showers. Laundry facilities. Dump station.

Pymatuning State Park

6100 Pymatuning Lake Rd, Andover, OH 44003. Phone: (440) 293-6030. Located 6 miles SE of Andover via OH 7 and Slater Rd. GPS: 41.548447, -80.530034. Lake in park. Swimming beach, fishing, boating (rentals). Hiking trails. Archery range. Camp store. Nature center. Marina. Open all year. $21-39 per night. 370 sites, 18 full hookup, 331 with electric, 21 no hookups. Drinking water. Restrooms; showers. Laundry facilities. Dump station.

Rocky Fork State Park

9800 North Shore Dr, Hillsboro, OH 45133. Phone: (937) 393-4284. Located 5 miles E of Hillsboro via OH 124 and N Shore Dr. GPS: 39.187451, -83.530046. Lake in park. Swimming beaches, fishing, boating, skiing. Hiking trails. Bird watching. Disc golf. Miniature golf. Camp store. Nature center. Marina. Open all year. $21-39 per night. 171 sites, 45 full hookup, 99 with electric, 27 no hookups. Drinking water. Restrooms; showers. Laundry facilities. Dump station.

Salt Fork State Park

14755 Cadiz Rd, Lore City, OH 43755. Phone: (740) 439-3521. Located about 10 miles east and north of I-77 Exit 47 near Cambridge via US 22. GPS: 40.105007, -81.498152. Lake in park. Swimming beach, fishing, boating. Hiking, equestrian, nature trails. Golf course, pro shop, driving range. Miniature golf. Archery range. Camp store. Nature center. Two full service marinas. Lodge, restaurant. Historic Stone House Museum, tours. Open all year. $23-41 per night. 215 sites, 40 full hookup, 175 with electric. Drinking water. Restrooms; showers. Laundry facilities. Dump station.

Scioto Trail State Park

144 Lake Rd, Chillicothe, OH 45601. Phone: (740) 887-4818. Located 12 miles S of Chillicothe via US 23 and Stoney Creek Rd. GPS: 39.230296, -82.954515. Lake in park. Swimming beach, fishing, boating (canoe/kayak rentals, electric motors only). Hiking, equestrian trails. Camp store. Open all year. $23-28 per night. 55 sites with electric hookups. Drinking water. Vault toilets. Dump station.

Shawnee State Park

4404 State Route 125, Portsmouth, OH 45663. Phone: (740) 858-6652. Located 12 miles W of Portsmouth via US 52 and OH 125. GPS: 38.729910, -83.179761. Lakes in park. Swimming beaches, fishing, boating (rentals, electric motors only). Hiking, biking, equestrian trails. Wildlife viewing. Bird watching. Scenic viewpoint. Disc golf. Miniature golf. Archery range. Camp store. Nature center. Full service marina. Lodge, restaurant. Open all year. $19-28 per night. 107 sites, 94 with electric hookups. Drinking water. Restrooms; showers. Laundry facilities. Dump station.

South Bass Island State Park

1523 Catawba Ave, Put-In-Bay, OH 43456. Phone: (419) 285-2112. Located on South Bass Island in Lake Erie, N of Port Clinton; only accessible by ferry. GPS: 41.642914, -82.835582. Lake in park. Swimming beach, fishing, boating (rentals), skiing. Bird watching. Scenic viewpoint. Open Apr-Oct. $27-45 per night. 61 sites, 10 full hookup, 51 with electric. Drinking water. Restrooms; showers. Dump station.

Stonelick State Park

2895 Lake Dr, Pleasant Plain, OH 45162. Phone: (513) 734-4323. Located 11 miles E of I-275 Exit 57 near Cincinnati via OH 28 and Woodville Pike. GPS: 39.216852, -84.057422. Lake in park. Swimming beach, fishing, boating (canoe/kayak rentals, electric motors only). Hiking, biking (rentals) trails. Disc golf. Camp store. Open all year. $19-30 per night. 114 sites, 108 with electric hookups. Drinking water. Restrooms; showers. Laundry facilities. Dump station.

Strouds Run State Park

11661 State Park Rd, Athens, OH 45701. Phone: (740) 767-3570. Located 5 miles E of Athens via Strouds Run Dr. GPS: 39.355671, -82.039129. Lake in park. Swimming beach, fishing, boating (rentals). Hiking, biking, equestrian, nature trails. Scenic viewpoint. Open all year. $29 per night. 78 sites, no hookups. Vault toilets. Dump station.

Tar Hollow State Park

16396 Tar Hollow Rd, Laurelville, OH 43135. Phone: (740) 887-4818. Located 9 miles S of Laurelville via OH 327. GPS:

39.380138, -82.742628. Lake in park. Swimming beach, fishing, boating (rentals, electric motors only). Hiking, biking (rentals), equestrian trails. Miniature golf. General store, game room. Open all year. $21-30 per night. 82 sites, 70 with electric hookups. Drinking water. Restrooms; showers. Laundry facilities. Dump station.

Van Buren State Park

12259 Township Road 218, Van Buren, OH 45889. Phone: (419) 832-7662. Located 2 miles E of I-75 Exit 164 near Van Buren via OH 613 and Township Rd 218. GPS: 41.138087, -83.619265. Lake in park. Fishing, boating (electric motors only). Hiking, biking, equestrian trails. Disc golf. Open all year. $17-26 per night. 60 sites, 23 with electric hookups. Drinking water. Vault toilets. Dump station.

West Branch State Park

5708 Esworthy Rd, Ravenna, OH 44266. Phone: (330) 654-4989. Located 7 miles E of Ravenna via OH 5. GPS: 41.140673, -81.117547. Lake in park. Swimming beach, fishing, boating (rentals). Hiking, biking, equestrian trails. Disc golf. Camp store. Full service marina. Open all year. $23-41 per night. 198 sites, 42 full hookup, 155 with electric, 1 no hookups. Drinking water. Restrooms; showers. Laundry facilities. Dump station.

Wolf Run State Park

16170 Wolf Run Rd, Caldwell, OH 43724. Phone: (740) 732-5035. Located 1 mile E of I-77 Exit 28 via Wolf Run Rd. GPS: 39.791095, -81.540264. Lake in park. Swimming beach, fishing, boating. Hiking trails. Camp store. Nature center. Open all year. $19-28 per night. 139 sites, 72 with electric hookups. Drinking water. Restrooms; showers. Laundry facilities. Dump station.

Oklahoma

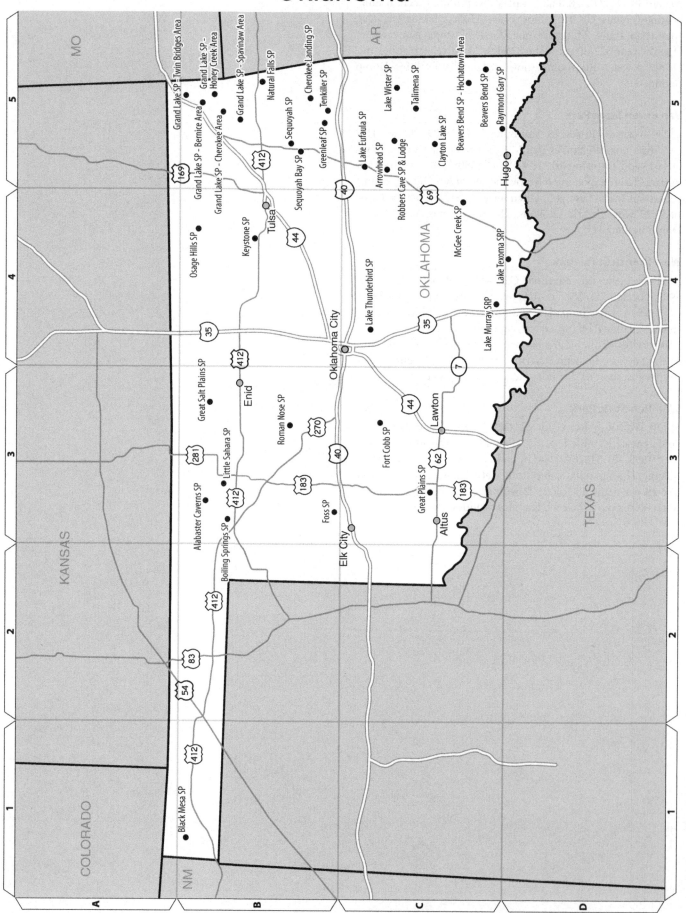

Oklahoma

Oklahoma Tourism Department
Travel Promotion Division
PO Box 52002
Oklahoma City, OK 73152

Phone: (800) 652-6552
Internet: www.travelok.com/state-parks
Reservations: Online or call park.

Oklahoma Park Locator

Oklahoma Parks

Alabaster Caverns State Park

217036 State Highway 50A, Freedom, OK 73842. Phone: (580) 621-3381. Located 6 miles S of Freedom via OK 50 and OK 50A. GPS: 36.697627, -99.148143. Hiking trails. Wildlife viewing. Cave tours, gift shop. Open all year. $25 per night. 11 sites with electric and water. Dump station. Restrooms; showers.

Arrowhead State Park

3995 Main Park Rd, Canadian, OK 74425. Phone: (918) 339-2204. Located 3 miles E of US 69 Exit 109 near the town of Canadian. GPS: 35.148184, -95.611951. Swimming beach, fishing, boating. Hiking, biking trails. Golf course. Marina. Restaurant. Four camping areas open all year. $23-33 per night. 91 sites, 20 full hookup, 71 with water and electric. Restrooms; showers. Dump station.

Beavers Bend State Park

4350 S Hwy 259A, Broken Bow, OK 74728. Phone: (580) 494-6300. Located 11 miles NE of Broken Bow via US 259 and OK 259A. GPS: 34.132414, -94.680812. Swimming beach, fishing, boating (rentals). Hiking, biking, equestrian trails. Golf course. Marina. Restaurant. Camp store. Open all year. $25-34 per night. 81 sites with water and electric. Restrooms; showers. Dump station.

Beavers Bend State Park - Hochatown Area

4350 S Hwy 259A, Broken Bow, OK 74728. Phone: (580) 494-6300. Located 11 miles N of Broken Bow via US 259 and Stevens Gap Rd. GPS: 34.168312, -94.735046. Swimming beach, fishing, boating (rentals), scuba diving. Hiking, biking, equestrian (rentals) trails. Nature center. Camp store. Restaurant. Marina. Golf course. River float trips. Open all year. $26-38 per night. 47 sites with water and electric. Restrooms; showers. Dump station.

Black Mesa State Park

County Road 325, Kenton, OK 73946. Phone: (580) 426-2222. Located 9 miles SE of Kenton via OK 325. GPS: 36.840489, -102.882362. Fishing, boating. Hiking trails. Wildlife viewing. Open all year. $25 per night. 25 sites with water and electric. Restrooms; showers. Dump station.

Boiling Springs State Park

207745 Boiling Springs Rd, Woodward, OK 73801. Phone: (580) 256-7664. Located 6 miles NE of Woodward via OK 34 and OK 34C. GPS: 36.453631, -99.304557. Swimming pool, fishing. Hiking, biking trails. Golf course (adjacent to park). Open all year. $25-34 per night. 40 sites with water and electric. Restrooms; showers. Dump station.

Cherokee Landing State Park

28610 Park 20, Park Hill, OK 74451. Phone: (918) 457-5716. Located about 10 miles SE of Park Hill via OK 82. GPS: 35.760210, -94.909624. Lake in park. Swimming beach, fishing, boating. Hiking, biking trails. Disc golf. Open all year. $25-30 per night. 60 sites with water and electric. Restrooms; showers. Dump station.

Clayton Lake State Park

170591 US Highway 271, Clayton, OK 74536. Phone: (918) 569-7981. Located 4 miles SE of Clayton via US 271. GPS: 34.540576, -95.306265. Swimming beach, fishing, boating (rentals). Hiking trails. Wildlife viewing. Open all year. $25-30 per night. 22 sites with water and electric. Restrooms; showers. Dump station.

Fort Cobb State Park

27022 Copperhead Rd, Fort Cobb, OK 73038. Phone: (405) 643-2249. Located 6 miles N of Fort Cobb via OK 9, OK 146 and CR

2550. GPS: 35.173954, -98.440252. Lake in park. Swimming, fishing, boating (rentals). Hiking, biking trails. Golf course. Marina, convenience store, restaurant. Ten camping areas open all year. $25-38 per night. 279 sites, 34 full hookup, 245 with electric. Restrooms; showers. Dump station.

Foss State Park

10252 Hwy 44, Foss, OK 73647. Phone: (580) 592-4433. Located about 6 miles N of I-40 exit 53 near Foss via OK 44. GPS: 35.529895, -99.187080. Lake in park. Swimming beach, fishing, boating (rentals). Hiking, biking, equestrian trails. Disc golf. Marina. Six camping areas open all year. $25-30 per night. 107 sites, 10 full hookup, 97 with water and electric. Restrooms; showers. Dump station.

Grand Lake State Park - Bernice Area

54101 E Hwy 85A, Bernice, OK 74331. Phone: (918) 786-9447. Located 1/2 mile E of Bernice via OK 85A. GPS: 36.626152, -94.904394. Swimming beach, fishing, boating. Hiking, biking trails. Nature center, wildlife feeding area and two watch towers. Open all year. $30 per night. 33 sites with water and electric. Restrooms; showers. Dump station.

Grand Lake State Park - Cherokee Area

13000 E 387 Rd, Langley, OK 74340 Phone: (918) 435-8066. Located below the dam just E of Langley. GPS: 36.465870, -95.032273. Swimming beach, fishing, boating. ATV area. Golf course. Wildlife viewing, birding. Three campgrounds open all year. $22-34 per night. 29 sites, 14 full hookup, 11 water and electric, 4 with electric only. Restrooms; showers. Dump station.

Grand Lake State Park - Honey Creek Area

901 State Park Rd, Grove, OK 74344. Phone: (918) 786-9447. Located 2 miles SW of Grove via US 59. GPS: 36.574855, -94.783348. Swimming pool, fishing, boating. Hiking, biking trails. Wildlife viewing. Open all year. $25-30 per night. 49 sites with water and electric. Restrooms; showers. Dump station.

Grand Lake State Park - Spavinaw Area

555 S Main St, Spavinaw, OK 74366. Phone: (918) 435-8066. Located below the dam just S of Spavinaw via OK 20. GPS: 36.387546, -95.054910. Swimming, fishing. Hiking trails are in the nearby Spavinaw Wildlife Management Area. Open Mar-Oct. $25-30 per night. 26 sites with water and electric. Restrooms; showers. Dump station.

Grand Lake State Park - Twin Bridges Area

14801 S Hwy 137, Fairland, OK 74343. Phone: (918) 542-6969. Located 6 miles NE of Fairland via US 60. GPS: 36.799512, -94.754527. Fishing, boating. Hiking, biking trails. Wildlife viewing. Six camping areas open all year. $25-30 per night. 64 sites with water and electric. Restrooms; showers. Dump station.

Great Plains State Park

22487 E 1566 Rd, Mountain Park, OK 73559. Phone: (580) 569-2032. Located 4 miles N of Mountain Park via US 183. GPS:

34.745695, -98.968651. Lake in park. Swimming beach, fishing, boating. Hiking, biking trails. Rock climbing. Camp store. Restaurant. The remnants of the 1904 Gold Bells Mill and Mine are located in the park. Three campgrounds open all year. $26-39 per night. 64 sites, 14 full hookup, 42 with water and electric. Restrooms; showers. Dump station.

Great Salt Plains State Park

23280 S Spillway Dr, Jet, OK 73749. Phone: (580) 626-4731. Located 8 miles N of Jet via OK 38. GPS: 36.743676, -98.128249. Swimming beach, fishing, boating. Hiking, biking, nature, equestrian trails. Bird watching. Selenite crystal dig area located SW of the lake in the Salt Plains National Wildlife Refuge. Open all year. $25-30 per night. 64 sites with water and electric. Restrooms; showers. Dump station. Equestrian area.

Greenleaf State Park

12022 Greenleaf Road, Braggs, OK 74423. Phone: (918) 487-5196. Located 22 miles SE of Muskogee via US 62 and OK 10. GPS: 35.624142, -95.170718. Lake in park. Swimming, fishing, boating (no motors, rentals). Hiking, biking trails. Miniature golf. Nature center, gift shop. Marina. Open all year. $25-29 per night. 98 sites, 22 full hookup, 76 with water and electric. Restrooms; showers. Dump station. Laundry facilities.

Keystone State Park

1926 S Hwy 151, Sand Springs, OK 74063. Phone: (918) 865-4991. Located 10 miles W of Sand Springs via US 412 and OK 151. GPS: 36.136815, -96.263581. Swimming beach, fishing, boating (rentals). Hiking, biking trails. Camp store. Marina, restaurant. Open all year. $25-29 per night. 114 sites, 41 full hookup, 73 with water and electric. Restrooms; showers. Dump station.

Lake Eufaula State Park

111563 Highway 150, Checotah, OK 74426. Phone: (918) 689-5311. Located 5 miles S of I-40 exit 259 near Checotah via OK 150. GPS: 35.400069, -95.605254. Swimming beach, fishing, boating. Hiking, biking, equestrian (rentals) trails. Marina. Disc golf. Archery range. Nature center. Camp store. Guided horseback rides. Golf course nearby. Open all year. $26-35 per night. 97 sites, 30 full hookup, 67 with water and electric. Restrooms; showers. Dump station.

Lake Murray State Resort Park

13528 Scenic Hwy 77, Ardmore, OK 73401. Phone: (580) 223-4044. Located 3 miles E of I-35 exit 24 near Ardmore via Lodge Rd. GPS: 34.071401, -97.101828. Swimming beach, fishing, boating (rentals). Hiking, biking, equestrian (rentals) trails. Golf course, miniature golf. Marina. ATV area. Camp store. Nine campgrounds open all year. $25-36 per night. 296 sites, 49 full hookup, 247 with water and electric. Restrooms; showers. Dump station. Laundry facilities.

Lake Texoma State Resort Park

11500 Park Office Rd, Kingston, OK 73439. Phone: (580) 564-2566. Located 14 miles W of Durant via US 70. GPS: 33.997639,

-96.639492. Swimming beach, fishing, boating (rentals). Hiking, biking trails. Marina, store. Three campgrounds open all year. $26-30 per night. 131 sites, 88 full hookup, 43 with water and electric. Restrooms; showers. Dump station.

Lake Thunderbird State Park

13101 Alameda Dr, Norman, OK 73026. Phone: (405) 360-3572. Located 11 miles E of Norman via Alameda St. GPS: 35.232488, -97.248010. Swimming beach, fishing, boating (rentals). Hiking, biking, nature, equestrian trails. Archery range. Nature center. Marina. Seven camping areas open all year. $26-35 per night. 197 sites, 178 with water and electric. Restrooms; showers. Dump station.

Lake Wister State Park

25679 US Hwy 270, Wister, OK 74966. Phone: (918) 655-7212. Located 2 miles S of Wister via US 270. GPS: 34.948007, -94.715190. Swimming beach, fishing, boating. Hiking, biking trails. Water spray park. Miniature golf. Four camping areas open all year. $25-34 per night. 97 sites, 26 full hookup, 71 with water and electric. Restrooms; showers. Dump station.

Little Sahara State Park

101 Main St, Waynoka, OK 73860. Phone: (580) 824-1471. Located about 4 miles S of Waynoka via US 281. GPS: 36.530197, -98.880041. Dune buggy and ATV riding across the sand dunes. Rentals available. Concessions are offered in the park seasonally. Open all year. $25-34 per night. 86 sites with water and electric. Restrooms; showers. Dump station.

McGee Creek State Park

5798 S McGee Creek Lake Rd, Atoka, OK 74525. Phone: (580) 889-5822. Located 21 miles E of Atoka via OK 3. GPS: 34.306059, -95.871917. Lake in park. Swimming beach, fishing, boating. Hiking, biking, equestrian trails. Open all year. $24-29 per night. 41 sites with water and electric. Restrooms; showers. Dump station.

Natural Falls State Park

19225 E 578 Road, Colcord, OK 74338. Phone: (918) 422-5802. Located 6 miles W of West Siloam Springs via US 59/US 412. GPS: 36.176009, -94.670370. Fishing. Hiking, biking, nature trails. Disc golf. Two observation areas for the 77-foot waterfall. Open all year. $25-34 per night. 44 sites, 7 full hookup, 37 with water and electric. Restrooms; showers. Dump station.

Osage Hills State Park

2131 Osage Hills State Park Rd, Pawhuska, OK 74056. Phone: (918) 336-4141. Located 13 miles W of Bartlesville via US 60. GPS: 36.745497, -96.179356. Swimming pool, fishing, boating (rentals). Hiking, biking trails. Open all year. $27 per night. 20 sites with water and electric. Restrooms; showers. Dump station.

Raymond Gary State Park

US Hwy 70, Fort Towson, OK 74735. Phone: (580) 873-2307. Located 2.5 miles S of Fort Towson via US 70 and OK 209. GPS: 33.993828, -95.256869. Lake in park. Swimming, fishing, boating.

Open all year. $22-27 per night. 19 RV sites, 10 full hookup, 9 with water and electric. Restrooms; showers. Dump station.

Robbers Cave State Park & Lodge

4628 NW 1027th, Wilburton, OK 74578. Phone: (918) 465-2562. Located 6 miles N of Wilburton via OK 2. GPS: 34.980010, -95.359408. Several lakes in park. Swimming pool and beach, fishing, boating (rentals). Hiking, biking (rentals), equestrian (rentals) trails. 250-acre ATV riding area. Rock climbing. Disc golf. Nature center. Camp store. Open all year. $26-35 per night. 114 sites, 22 full hookup, 92 with water and electric. Restrooms; showers. Dump station.

Roman Nose State Park

3236 S Highway 8A, Watonga, OK 73772. Phone: (580) 623-4218. Located 8 miles N of Watonga via OK 8 and OK 8A. GPS: 35.939625, -98.425513. Two lakes in park. Swimming, fishing, boating (rentals). Hiking, biking (rentals), equestrian (rentals) trails. Restaurant. Golf course. Camp store. Open all year. $25-34 per night. 46 sites, 12 full hookup, 34 with water and electric. Restrooms; showers. Dump station.

Sequoyah Bay State Park

6237 E 100th St N, Wagoner, OK 74467. Phone: (918) 772-2046. Located 10 miles SE of Wagoner via OK 16 and Gray Oaks Rd. GPS: 35.885721, -95.277819. Swimming beach, fishing, boating (rentals). Hiking, biking trails. Marina. Open all year. $25-27 per night. 71 sites with water and electric. Restrooms; showers. Dump station.

Sequoyah State Park

17131 Park 10, Hulbert, OK 74441. Phone: (918) 772-2046. Located 8 miles E of Wagoner via OK51. GPS: 35.929528, -95.250313. Swimming pool and beach, fishing, boating (rentals). Hiking, biking, equestrian (rentals) trails. Guided horseback trail rides. Nature center. Golf course, driving range. Marina. Restaurant. Open all year, some sites close in the winter. $30-34 per night. 124 sites, 44 full hookup, 80 with water and electric. Restrooms; showers. Dump station.

Talimena State Park

50884 Highway 271, Talihina, OK 74571. Phone: (918) 567-2052. Located 7 miles NE of Talihina via US 271. GPS: 34.784330, -94.951970. Hiking. Wildlife viewing. Entrance point for ATVs and dirt bikes into the national forest lands. Talimena National Scenic Drive. Open all year. $25 per night. 10 sites with water and electric. Restrooms; showers. Dump station.

Tenkiller State Park

448159 E 979 Road, Vian, OK 74962. Phone: (918) 489-5641. Located 12 miles NW of Vian via OK 82 and OK 100. GPS: 35.599494, -95.032256. Lake in park. Swimming pool and beach, fishing, boating (rentals). Tubing, scuba diving. Hiking, biking, nature trails. Disc golf. Nature center. Marina, cafe. Open all year. $22-42 per night. 86 sites, 11 full hookup, 45 with water and electric, 26 electric only. Restrooms; showers. Dump station.

Oregon

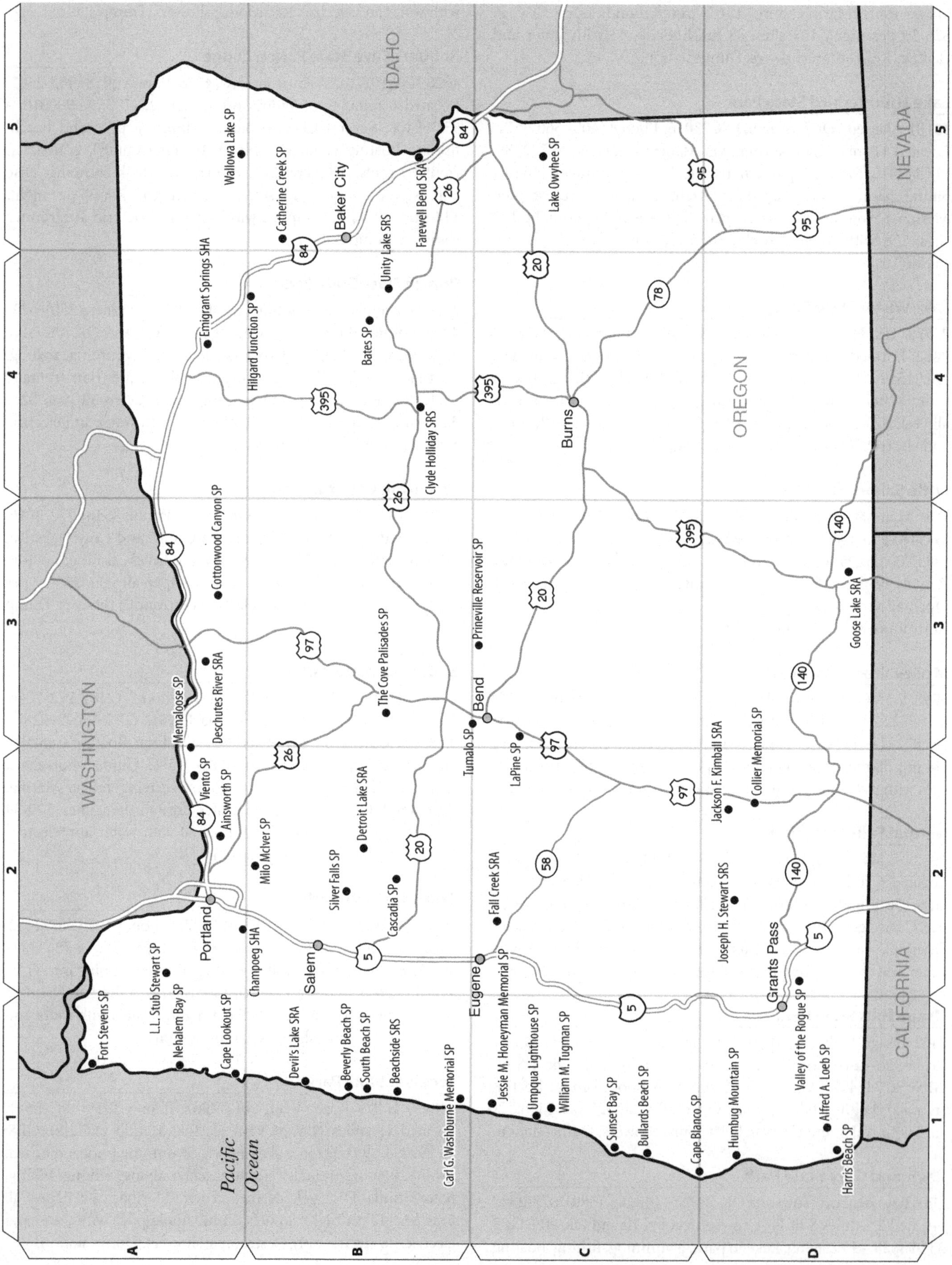

WASHINGTON
IDAHO
NEVADA
CALIFORNIA
OREGON
Pacific Ocean
Portland
Salem
Eugene
Grants Pass
Bend
Burns
Baker City
Wallowa Lake SP
Catherine Creek SP
Farewell Bend SRA
Lake Owyhee SP
Unity Lake SRS
Emigrant Springs SHA
Hilgard Junction SP
Bates SP
Clyde Holliday SRS
Cottonwood Canyon SP
Prineville Reservoir SP
Goose Lake SRA
Deschutes River SRA
Memaloose SP
The Cove Palisades SP
Tumalo SP
LaPine SP
Jackson F. Kimball SRA
Collier Memorial SP
Viento SP
Ainsworth SP
Detroit Lake SRA
Milo McIver SP
Silver Falls SP
Cascadia SP
Fall Creek SRA
Joseph H. Stewart SRS
Champoeg SHA
L.L. Stub Stewart SP
Fort Stevens SP
Nehalem Bay SP
Cape Lookout SP
Devil's Lake SRA
Beverly Beach SP
South Beach SP
Beachside SRS
Carl G. Washburne Memorial SP
Jessie M. Honeyman Memorial SP
Umpqua Lighthouse SP
William M. Tugman SP
Sunset Bay SP
Bullards Beach SP
Cape Blanco SP
Humbug Mountain SP
Valley of the Rogue SP
Alfred A. Loeb SP
Harris Beach SP
5
84
26
20
395
95
78
97
140
58
1
2
3
4
5
A
B
C
D

Oregon

Oregon Parks & Recreation Dept.
725 Summer St NE, Ste C
Salem, OR 97301

Phone: (503) 986-0707 or (800) 551-6949
Internet: www.oregonstateparks.org
Reservations: Online or (800) 452-5687

Oregon Park Locator

Oregon Parks

Ainsworth State Park

Historic Columbia River Highway, Cascade Locks, OR 97014. Phone: (503) 793-9885. Located 18 miles E of Troutdale just off I-84 Exit 35. GPS: 45.596544, -122.050954. Fishing. Hiking, biking trails. Open Mar-Oct. $26 per night. 40 full hookup sites. 60-foot limit. Restrooms; no showers. Dump station.

Alfred A Loeb State Park

1655 Highway 101, Brookings, OR 97415. Phone: (541) 469-2021. Located 8 miles NE of Brookins via US 101 and North Bank Chetco River Rd. GPS: 42.112981, -124.188453. Swimming, fishing, boating. Hiking, nature trails. Open all year. No reservations accepted. $26-34 per night. 48 sites with water and electric. 50-foot limit. Restrooms; showers.

Bates State Park

Old West Scenic Bikeway, Bates, OR 97817. Phone: (541) 448-2585. Located 30 miles east of John Day via US 26 and OR 7. GPS: 44.592492, -118.509905. Fishing. Hiking, biking trails. Scenic viewpoint. The campground sits between three nearby Wilderness Areas. Open May-Oct. No reservations accepted. $10 per night. 28 sites, no hookups. Water available. 50-foot limit. Vault toilets.

Beachside State Recreation Site

US Highway 101, Waldport, OR 97394. Phone: (541) 563-3220. Located 3.5 miles S of Waldport via US 101. GPS: 44.382886, -124.088422. Ocean beach access. Swimming, fishing. Hiking, biking trails. Wildlife viewing. Open Mar-Oct. $29-31 per night. 32 sites with water and electric. 30-foot limit. Restrooms; showers.

Beverly Beach State Park

198 NE 123rd St, Newport, OR 97365. Phone: (541) 265-9278. Located 6 miles N of Newport via US 101. GPS: 44.728597, -124.055391. Ocean beach access. Hiking, biking trails. Welcome center, gift shop. Open all year. $31-45 per night. 128 sites, 53 full hookup (27 with cable TV), 75 with water and electric. 65-foot limit. Restrooms; showers. Dump station.

Bullards Beach State Park

US Highway 101, Bandon, OR 97411. Phone: (541) 347-2209. Located about 3 miles N of Bandon town center via US 101. GPS: 43.151755, -124.395708. Ocean beach access. Fishing, boating. Hiking, biking, equestrian trails. Scenic viewpoint, wildlife viewing. Open all year. $28-33 per night. 185 sites, 103 full hookup, 82 with water and electric. 65-foot limit. Restrooms; showers. Dump station.

Cape Blanco State Park

US Hwy 101, Port Orford, OR 97465. Phone: (541) 332-6774. Located 8 miles N of Port Orford via US 101. GPS: 42.835901, -124.553860. Ocean beach access. Fishing. Hiking, biking, equestrian trails. Scenic viewpoint. Lighthouse tours. Open all year. $26-29 per night. 52 sites with water and electric. 65-foot limit. Restrooms; showers. Dump station. Equestrian area, 8 sites.

Cape Lookout State Park

13000 Whiskey Creek Rd W, Tillamook, OR 97141. Phone: (503) 842-4981. Located 12 miles SW of Tillamook via OR 131 and Whiskey Creek Rd. GPS: 45.362428, -123.968496. Ocean beach access. Fishing. Hiking, biking trails. Scenic viewpoint. Wildlife viewing. Open all year. $31-37 per night. 39 sites, 38 full hookup, 1 with water and electric. 60-foot limit. Restrooms; showers. Dump station.

Carl G. Washburne Memorial State Park

93111 US 101 N, Florence, OR 97439. Phone: (541) 547-3416. Located on central OR coast (not on the ocean), 12 miles N of Florence on US 101, near Heceta Head Lighthouse. GPS: 44.160312, -124.114687. Ocean beach access. Fishing. Hiking, biking trails. Scenic viewpoint. Wildlife viewing. Open all year. $31-33 per night. 55 sites, 45 full hookup, 10 with water and electric. 53-foot limit. Restrooms; showers. Dump station.

Cascadia State Park

48241 Cascadia Dr, Cascadia, OR 97329. Phone: (541) 967-3917 (Linn County Parks). Located in west-central OR at the confluence of Soda Creek and the South Santiam River, 14 miles E of Sweet Home on US 20. GPS: 44.397241, -122.481010. Swimming, fishing. Hiking trails. Open May-Sep. No reservations accepted. $10 per night. 22 sites, no hookups. Water available. 35-foot limit. Restrooms; no showers.

Catherine Creek State Park

Medical Springs Hwy, Union, OR 97883. Phone: (541) 983-2277. Located in northeastern OR, 8 miles SE of Union on OR 203. GPS: 45.152562, -117.743702. Fishing. Hiking trails. Open May-Oct. No reservations accepted. $10 per night. 20 sites, no hookups. Water available. 50-foot limit. Restrooms; no showers. Dump station.

Champoeg State Heritage Area

7679 Champoeg Rd NE, St. Paul, OR 97137. Phone: (503) 678-1251. Located in northwestern OR on Willamette River about 18 miles S of Portland and 5 miles W of I-5 exit 278. GPS: 45.249005, -122.893929. Fishing, boating (kayak). Hiking, biking trails. Disc golf. Wildlife viewing. Visitor center and historic buildings. On the National Register of Historic Places. Two camping areas. "A" loop open Apr-Oct, "B" loop open all year. $28-33 per night. 74 sites, 24 full hookup, 50 with water and electric. 55-foot limit. Restrooms; showers. Dump station.

Clyde Holliday State Recreation Site

US 26, Mount Vernon, OR 97865. Phone: (541) 932-4453. Located in central OR, 7 miles W of John Day on US 26, near US 395. GPS: 44.416710, -119.088046. Fishing. Nature trails. Wildlife viewing. Open Mar-Nov. No reservations accepted. $44-56 per night. 31 sites with water and electric. 60-foot limit. Restrooms; showers. Dump station.

Collier Memorial State Park

46000 US Hwy 97, Chiloquin, OR 97624. Phone: (541) 783-2471. Located in southern OR, 30 miles N of Klamath Falls on US 97. The Williamson River and Spring Creek converge in the park. GPS: 42.641805, -121.880580. Fishing, boating (non-motorized). Hiking, biking, equestrian trails. Wildlife viewing. Information center, gift shop. Logging Museum and historic cabin village. Open Apr-Oct. $28-29 per night. 44 sites with full hookups. 50-foot limit. Restrooms; showers. Dump station. Horse camp with 2 sites.

Cottonwood Canyon State Park

Mailing address: PO Box 32, Wasco, OR 97065. Phone: (541) 739-2322. Located on John Day River between Condon and Wasco, 15 miles SE of Wasco on OR 206. GPS: 45.480013, -120.464458. Fishing, boating (no motors). Hiking, biking, equestrian trails. Visitor center. Scenic viewpoint, wildlife viewing. Open all year. No reservations accepted. $10 per night. 21 sites, no hookups. Water available. 75-foot limit. Restrooms; no showers.

Deschutes River State Recreation Area

89600 Biggs-Rufus Hwy, Wasco, OR 97065. Phone: (541) 739-2322. Located on Deschutes & Columbia Rivers on OR 206, 15 miles E of The Dalles, off I-84 exit 97. GPS: 45.634379, -120.908397. Fishing, boating/rafting. Hiking, biking trails. Scenic viewpoint, wildlife viewing. Open all year. $10-24 per night. 59 sites, 34 with water and electric, 25 no hookups. 50-foot limit. Restrooms; showers.

Detroit Lake State Recreation Area

44125 N Santiam Hwy, Detroit, OR 97360. Phone: (503) 854-3766. Located in northwestern OR, 2 miles W of Detroit on OR 22. GPS: 44.731118, -122.173980. Swimming, fishing, boating. Hiking trail. Visitor center (gifts & basic camp supplies). Scenic viewpoint, wildlife viewing. Open May-Sep (some sites all year). $30-35 per night. 175 sites, 107 full hookup, 68 with water and electric. 60-foot limit. Restrooms; showers.

Devil's Lake State Recreation Area

1452 NE 6th Dr, Lincoln City, OR 97367. Phone: (541) 994-2002. Located in northwestern OR along the coast off US 101, outside Lincoln City, on Devil's Lake. GPS: 44.970704, -124.013128. Ocean beach access. Swimming, fishing, boating. Wildlife viewing, bird watching. Open all year (some sites will close in winter). $31-37 per night. 32 sites (all with cable TV), 28 full hookup, 4 with water and electric. 46-foot limit. Restrooms; showers. Dump station.

Emigrant Springs State Heritage Area

Meacham, OR 97859. Phone: (541) 983-2277. Located in northeastern OR between Pendleton and La Grand, 26 miles SE of Pendelton off US 30/I-84 exit 234. GPS: 45.541670, -118.461808. Hiking, equestrian trails. Park preserves a site where travelers on the Oregon Trail once replenished their water supplies. Open all year, limited facilities and camp sites in winter. $24-26 per night. 17 sites, 16 full hookup, 1 with water and electric. 66-foot limit. Restrooms; showers. Horse camp with 7 sites (closed in winter).

Fall Creek State Recreation Area

570 N Moss St, Lowell, OR 97452. Phone: (541) 973-1173. Located in western OR on Fall Creek Reservoir about 30 miles SE of Eugene-Springfield, 10 miles NE of Lowell via Big Fall Creek Rd. GPS: 43.972784, -122.664085. Swimming (dock and beach areas), fishing, boating. Cascara campground, on the upper end of the Fall Creek Arm of the lake is open May-Sep. No reservations accepted. $10 per night. 39 sites, no hookups. No water in campground. 45-foot limit. Vault toilets. Flush restrooms available in Winberry day-use area.

Farewell Bend State Recreation Area

23751 Old Hwy 30, Huntington, OR 97907. Phone: (541) 869-2365. Located on the Oregon/Idaho border on the banks of the Snake River's Brownlee Reservoir, 25 miles NW of Ontario, 1 mile N of I-84 exit 353. GPS: 44.303516, -117.227485. Fishing, boating. Hiking trails. Wildlife viewing. Historic markers and interpretive displays with information on the Oregon Trail. Open Mar-Nov. No reservations accepted Mar-Apr and Oct-Nov. $26 per night. 91 sites with water and electric. 50-foot limit. Restrooms; showers. Dump station.

Fort Stevens State Park

100 Peter Iredale Rd, Hammond, OR 97121. Phone: (503) 861-1671. Located in northwestern tip of OR off US 101, 10 miles W of Astoria at the mouth of the Columbia River. GPS: 46.184276, -123.957035. Swimming, fishing, boating (kayak tours). Hiking, biking (rentals) trails. Wildlife viewing blind. Scenic viewpoint. Military museum, visitor center. Historic shipwreck. Disc golf. Open all year. $32-38 per night. 476 sites, 174 full hookup, 302 with water and electric. 65-foot limit. Restrooms; showers. Dump station.

Goose Lake State Recreation Area

97003 State Line Rd, New Pine Creek, OR 97635. Phone: (541) 783-2471. Located on Goose Lake on the Oregon-California border, 1 mile W on State Line Rd from US 395 in New Pine Creek. GPS: 41.993311, -120.318418. Fishing, boating. Hiking trail. Wildlife viewing. Open Apr-Oct. No reservations accepted. $24 per night. 42 sites with water and electric. 55-foot limit. Restrooms; showers. Dump station.

Harris Beach State Park

1655 Hwy 101 N, Brookings, OR 97415. Phone: (541) 469-2021. Located in the SW corner of OR on Hwy 101 at the north end of Brookings city limits. GPS: 42.063958, -124.302839. Fishing, boating. Hiking, biking trails. Information center. Wildlife watching, scenic viewpoint. Campground 1/4 mile from the beach. Open all year (some sites close in winter). $30-35 per night. 90 sites, 65 full hookup, 25 with water and electric. 55-foot limit. Restrooms; showers. Dump station.

Hilgard Junction State Park

OR 244, LaGrande, OR 97850. Phone: (541) 983-2277. Located next to I-84 in northeastern OR, 8 miles W of LaGrande off I-84 exit 252, on Grande Ronde River. GPS: 45.342017, -118.233727. Swimming, fishing, boating. Wildlife viewing. Covered wagons on the Oregon Trail were maneuvered down the hill facing what is now this park. Interpretive center nearby. Open Apr-Oct. No reservations accepted. $10 per night. 18 sites, no hookups. Water available. 30-foot limit. Restrooms; no showers.

Humbug Mountain State Park

39745 US 101, Port Orford, OR 97465. Phone: (541) 332-6774. Located on southern OR coast, 6 miles S of Port Orford on US 101. GPS: 42.688258, -124.433984. Beach access. Swimming, scuba diving, surfing, fishing. Hiking, biking trails. Scenic viewpoint. Open all year. $26 per night. 39 sites with water and electric. 50-foot limit. Restrooms; showers. Dump station.

Jackson F. Kimball State Recreation Site

Chiloquin, OR 97624. Phone: (541) 783-2471. Located at the headwaters of the Wood River in southern OR, SE of Crater Lake National Park, 4 miles N of Fort Klamath via Dixon Rd off OR 62. GPS: 42.736323, -121.977057. Fishing, boating (hand boat launch). Hiking trail. Wildlife viewing. Open Apr-Oct. No reservations accepted. $10 per night. 12 sites, no hookups. No water. 45-foot limit. Vault toilets.

Jessie M. Honeyman Memorial State Park

84505 US 101 S, Florence, OR 97439. Phone: (541) 997-3641. Located on central OR coast, 3 miles S of Florence on US 101. Park is 2 miles from the ocean. GPS: 43.928727, -124.107380. Two lakes in park. Swimming beaches, fishing, boating/paddling (rentals), water skiing, and windsurfing. Hiking, biking (rentals) trails. Welcome center. Park is situated within a 47-mile stretch of dunes from Florence to Coos Bay. Large campground open all year. $29-36 per night. 168 sites, 47 full hookup, 121 with water and electric. 55-foot limit. Restrooms; showers. Dump station.

Joseph H. Stewart State Recreation Area

35251 OR 62, Trail, OR 97541. Phone: (541) 560-3334. Located in southwestern OR on Lost Lake Reservoir, 12 miles E of Trail (33 miles NE of Medford) on OR 62. GPS: 42.682486, -122.613734. Swimming beach, fishing, boating (rentals). Hiking, biking trails. Marina. Open all year. Park managed by Jackson County Parks; reservations: (541) 774 8183 or www.jacksoncountyparks.com. $24-30 per night. 151 sites with water and electric. 65-foot limit. Restrooms; showers. Dump station.

L.L. Stub Stewart State Park

30380 NW OR 47, Buxton, OR 97109. Phone: (503) 324-0606. Located 32 miles NW of Portland on OR 47, off US 26. GPS: 45.739043, -123.199414. Hiking, biking, equestrian trails. Disc golf. Welcome center. Open all year. $33-36 per night. 78 sites with full hookups. 63-foot limit. Restrooms; showers.

Lake Owyhee State Park

1298 Lake Owyhee Dam Rd, Adrian, OR 97901. Phone: (541) 339-2331. Remote location in eastern OR (west of Boise, ID), 27 miles SW of Owyhee. From OR 201 in Owyhee follow Owyhee Ave W for 5 miles, turn S onto Owyhee Dam Rd and follow 22 miles to park. Note: Parts of this road are steep and narrow with sharp turns. GPS: 43.614531, -117.250169. Fishing, boating. Wildlife viewing. Park store. Two campgrounds open Apr-Oct. $24 per night. 50 sites with water and electric. 60-foot limit. Restrooms; showers. Dump station.

LaPine State Park

15800 State Receration Rd, LaPine, OR 97739. Phone: (541) 536-2428. Located in central OR along the Deschutes River, 26 miles SW of Bend via State Recreation Rd off US 97. GPS: 43.763894, -121.528892. Swimming beach, fishing, boating, floating. Hiking, biking trails. Wildlife viewing, scenic viewpoint. Naturalist programs. Three camping loops, one open all year, two open May-Sep. $26-32 per night. 129 sites, 82 full hookup, 47 with water and electric. 75-foot limit. Restrooms; showers. Dump station.

Memaloose State Park

Park has no physical address which is located just E of Mosier, OR 97040. Mailing address: 7880 Hwy 84, The Dalles, OR 97058. Phone: (541) 478-3008. Located on the E end of the Columbia River Gorge, 11 miles W of The Dalles, directly off I-84 (westbound access only). Westbound on I-84 take exit 73, go through the rest area to reach park. Eastbound travelers use exit 76 to turn around, go westbound 3 miles on I-84 to exit 73. GPS: 45.695706, -121.340658. Hiking, biking trails. Scenic viewpoint. Open Mar-Oct. $24-31 per night. 44 full hookup sites. 53-foot limit. Restrooms; showers. Dump station.

Milo McIver State Park

24101 S Entrance Rd, Estacada, OR 97023. Phone: (503) 630-7150. Located in northwestern OR on the Clackamas River, 4 miles W of Estacada, off OR 211. GPS: 45.300967, -122.380840. Fishing, boating/rafting (rentals and guided tours). Hiking, biking, equestrian trails. Disc golf. Fish hatchery. Open Mar-Oct. Reservations required. $26 per night. 44 sites with water and electric. 74-foot limit. Restrooms; showers. Dump station.

Nehalem Bay State Park

34600 Garey St, Nehalem, OR 97131. Phone: (503) 368-5154. Located on OR coast W of Portland, 2 miles S of Manzanita junction, off US 101. GPS: 45.708677, -123.931488. Windsurfing, fishing, boating/kayaking. Crabbing, clamming. Hiking, biking, equestrian trails. Bay and ocean access. Kayak and horse tours. Open all year. $31-35 per night. 265 sites with water and electric.

55-foot limit. Restrooms; showers. Dump station. Equestrian area (17 primitive sites with corrals).

Prineville Reservoir State Park

19020 SE Parkland Dr, Prineville, OR 97754. Phone: (541) 447-4363. Located in central OR, 14 miles S of Prineville. From US 26 take OR 380 to Juniper Canyon Rd, follow to park entrance. GPS: 44.142869, -120.737611. Swimming, fishing, boating. Hiking trails. Scenic viewpoint. Wildlife viewing. Two campgrounds.

Main campground open all year. $31-33 per night. 44 sites, 22 full hookup, 22 with water and electric. 50-foot limit. Restrooms; showers.

Jasper Point campground is 3 miles E of main campground. Open May-Sep. No reservations accepted. $31-33 per night. 28 sites with water and electric. 35-foot limit. Restrooms; showers. Dump station.

Silver Falls State Park

20024 Silver Falls Hwy SE, Sublimity OR 97385. Phone: (503) 873-8681. Located 22 miles E of Salem via OR 22 (I-5, exit 253) and OR 214 (exit 9). Or 15 miles SE of Silverton on OR 214. GPS: 44.877445, -122.651519. Swimming, fishing. Hiking, biking, equestrian (rentals & guided tours) trails. Nature store, gifts. Lodge & cafe. The Trail of Ten Falls (hike exploring waterfalls, a National Recreation Trail). Open all year. Reservations required. $28-31 per night. 52 sites with water and electric. 60-foot limit. Restrooms; showers. Dump station. Equestrian area with 5 primitive sites and corrals (open May-Oct, $19).

South Beach State Park

5580 S Coast Hwy, Newport, OR 97366. Phone: (541) 867-4715. Located on central OR coast, 2 miles S of Newport on US 101. GPS: 44.599712, -124.058919. Fishing, boating, surfing, crabbing. Hiking, biking, equestrian trails. Hospitality Center, gifts, camp items. Disc golf. Open all year. Some sites close in the winter. $31-34 per night. 227 sites with water and electric. 50-foot limit. Restrooms; showers. Dump station.

Sunset Bay State Park

89814 Cape Arago Hwy, Coos Bay, OR 97420. Phone: (541) 888-4902. Located on southern OR coast, 12 miles SW of Coos Bay, on Cape Arago Hwy. GPS: 43.336818, -124.370260. Swimming, fishing, boating. Hiking trails. Scenic viewpoints, ocean vistas. Golf course next to park. Open all year. $28-33 per night. 63 sites, 29 full hookup, 34 with water and electric. 49-foot limit. Restrooms; showers. Dump station.

The Cove Palisades State Park

7300 Jordan Rd, Culver, OR 97734. Phone: (541) 546-3412. Located in central OR in Culver, 10 miles SW of Madras off US 97. GPS: 44.545783, -121.245092. Swimming beaches, fishing, boating (rentals). Hiking, nature trails. Marina with cafe and store. Scenic viewpoint, wildlife viewing. Two campgrounds generally open Mar Oct. $30-35 per night. 178 sites, 87 full hookup, 91 with water and electric. 50-foot limit. Restrooms; showers. Dump station.

Tumalo State Park

64120 OB Riley Rd, Bend, OR 97701. Phone: (541) 388-6055. Located in central OR on Deschutes River, 5 miles N of Bend off US 20. GPS: 44.128771, -121.331363. Swimming, fishing. Hiking, biking trails. Wildlife viewing. Open all year. $33-36 per night. 23 full hookup sites. 56-foot limit. Restrooms; showers. Dump station.

Umpqua Lighthouse State Park

460 Lighthouse Rd, Reedsport, OR 97467. Phone: (541) 271-4118. Located on south-central OR coast, 4 miles SW of Reedsport via US 101, near mouth of Winchester Bay. GPS: 43.662572, -124.193632. Lake in park. Swimming beach, fishing, boating (non-motorized). Hiking trails. OHV riding in nearby Oregon Dunes NRA. Lighthouse and museum 1/2 mile from park. Open all year. $28-31 per night. 17 sites, 10 full hookup, 7 with water and electric. 45-foot limit. Restrooms; showers.

Unity Lake State Recreation Site

18980 OR 245, Unity, OR 97884 (541) 932-4453. Located in eastern OR, 37 miles E of Prairie City off US 26 on OR 245 (4 miles N of Unity). GPS: 44.494674, -118.187545. Fishing, boating. Wildlife viewing. Hiking available in three wilderness areas near the park. Open Apr-Oct. No reservations accepted. $24 per night. 35 sites with water and electric. 40-foot limit. Restrooms; showers. Dump station.

Valley of the Rogue State Park

I-5 Exit 45B, Rogue River, OR 97525. Phone: (541) 582-3128. Located in southwestern OR along the Rogue River, 12 miles E of Grants Pass at I-5 exit 45B. GPS: 42.411081, -123.129887. Fishing, boating. Hiking, biking trails. Interpretive walking trail along the river. Open all year. (Some sites close in the winter.) $28-33 per night. 144 sites, 88 full hookup, 56 with water and electric. 85-foot limit. Restrooms; showers. Dump station.

Viento State Park

I-84 exit 56, Hood River, OR 97031. Phone: (541) 374-8811. Overlooks the Columbia River in northern OR, 8 miles W of Hood River at I-84 exit 56. Located on both sides of I-84. GPS: 45.696712, -121.668447. Swimming beach, fishing, boating. Hiking, biking trails. Bird watching. Windsurfing, paddle boarding. A one-mile trail to Starvation Creek waterfall. Open Mar-Oct. $24 per night. 56 sites with water and electric. 52-foot limit. Restrooms; showers.

Wallowa Lake State Park

72214 Marina Lane, Joseph, OR 97846. Phone: (541) 432-4185. Located in northeastern OR on the south end of Wallowa Lake, 6 miles S of Joseph off OR 351/82. GPS: 45.280904, -117.210195. Swimming beach, fishing, boating (rentals). Hiking trails. Wildlife viewing. Marina, supplies, gifts. Open all year. $32-35 per night.

121 sites with full hookups. 58-foot limit. Restrooms; showers. Dump station.

William M. Tugman State Park

72549 US 101, Lakeside, OR 97449. Phone: (541) 759-3604. Located on southern OR coast, 2 miles N of Lakeside, off US 101 on Eel Lake. GPS: 43.600274, -124.180052. Lake in park. Swimming, fishing, boating. Hiking trails. Wildlife viewing. Open all year. $26-29 per night. 93 sites with water and electric. 52-foot limit. Restrooms; showers. Dump station.

Pennsylvania

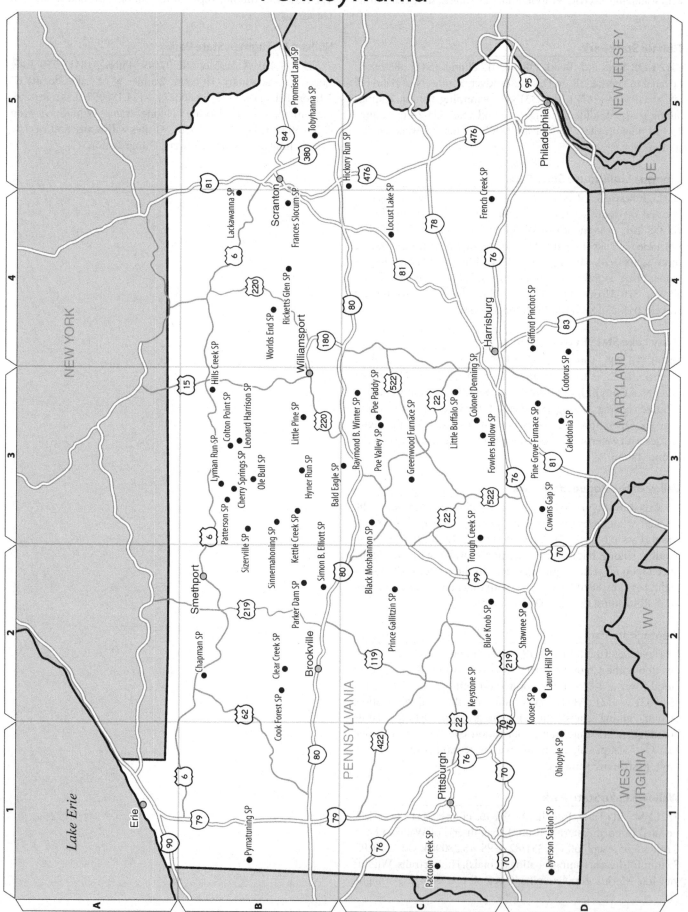

Pennsylvania

Bureau of State Parks
PO Box 8551
Harrisburg, PA 17105

Phone: (717) 787-6640
Internet: www.visitPAparks.com
Reservations: Online or (888) 727-2757

Pennsylvania Park Locator

Pennsylvania Parks

Bald Eagle State Park

149 Main Park Rd, Howard, PA 16841. Phone: (814) 625-2775. Located in north-central PA on PA 150 between Milesburg and Beech Creek on Foster Joseph Sayers Reservoir. GPS: 41.035707, -77.651473. Two campgrounds. Available to both areas: swimming beach, fishing, boating (rentals). Hiking, biking trails. Marina.

Russell P. Letterman campground on north side of lake. GPS: 41.035558, -77.647741. Open Apr-Dec. $20-48. 100 sites, 18 full hookup, 73 with electric, 9 no hookups. 50-foot limit. Restrooms; showers. Dump station.

Rustic campground on south side of lake. GPS: 41.018029, -77.641213. Open May-Oct. $20-24 per night. 36 RV sites, no hookups. 48-foot limit. Vault toilets, no showers. Dump station.

Black Moshannon State Park

4216 Beaver Rd, Philipsburg, PA 16866. Phone: (814) 342-5960. Located in central PA on PA 504, 9 miles E of Philipsburg on Black Moshannon Lake. GPS: 40.912111, -78.057166. Swimming beach, fishing, boating (rentals). Hiking, biking trails. Park store. Open Apr-Dec. $24-48 per night. 61 sites, 11 full hookup, 43 with electric, 7 no hookups. 73-foot limit. Restrooms; showers. Laundry facilities. Dump station.

Blue Knob State Park

124 Park Rd, Imler, PA 16655. Phone: (814) 276-3576. Located in southwestern PA, 6 miles NW of Imler via Mowrys Mill Rd and PA 869. Imler is 2 miles W of I-99 exit 10. GPS: 40.266658, -78.584111. Swimming (pool), fishing. Hiking, biking, equestrian trails. Open Apr-Oct. $24-35 per night. 48 sites with electric. 65-foot limit. Restrooms; showers. Dump station.

Caledonia State Park

101 Pine Grove Rd, Fayetteville, PA 17222. Phone: (717) 352-2161. Located in south-central PA on US 30 and PA 233, midway between Gettysburg (US 15) and Chambersburg (I-81). GPS: 39.908592, -77.477816. Swimming (pool), fishing. Hiking, biking trails. An 18-hole public golf course is adjacent to park. Open Apr-Oct (some sites thru Dec). $24-48 per night. 164 sites, 34 full hookup, 25 with electric, 105 no hookups. 60-foot limit. Restrooms; showers. Dump station.

Chapman State Park

4790 Chapman Dam Rd, Clarendon, PA 16313. Phone: (814) 723-0250. Located in northwestern PA next to Allegheny National Forest, 5 miles W of Clarendon, off US 6, via Railroad St and

Chapman Dam Rd. GPS: 41.757640, -79.170996. Lake Chapman in park. Swimming beach, fishing, boating. Hiking, biking trails. Concession stand. Open Apr-Dec. $24-35 per night. 67 sites, 55 with electric, 12 no hookups. 100-foot limit. Restrooms; showers. Dump station.

Cherry Springs State Park

4639 Cherry Springs Rd, Coudersport, PA 16915. Phone: (814) 435-1037. Located in north-central PA in Susquehannock State Forest, 15 miles SE of Coudersport via US 6 and PA 44. Remote park. GPS: 41.663293, -77.823421. One mile, self-guiding Working Forest Interpretive Trail. Overnight Astronomy Observation Field. Open Apr-Oct. $24-28 per night. 16 sites, no hookups. Restrooms; no showers. Dump station.

Clear Creek State Park

38 Clear Creek Park Rd, Sigel, PA 15860. Phone: (814) 752-2368. Located in northwestern PA, 4 miles NE of Sigel via PA 949. From I-80 near Corsica use exit 73 (PA 949) or exit 78 (PA 36) in Brookville. GPS: 41.322562, -79.076486. Swimming beach, fishing, boating. Hiking, biking trails. Disc golf. Open Apr-Dec. $24-35 per night. 52 sites, 41 with electric, 11 no hookups. 60-foot limit. Restrooms; showers. Dump station.

Codorus State Park

2600 Smith Station Rd, Hanover, PA 17331. Phone: (717) 637-2816. Located on Lake Marburg in southeastern PA, 3 miles E of Hanover via PA 216. GPS: 39.789786, -76.918657. Swimming (pool), fishing, boating (rentals). Hiking, biking, equestrian trails. Camp store. Bird watching. Marina. Disc golf. Open Apr-Oct. $24-35 per night. 176 sites, 113 with electric, 63 no hookups. 54-foot limit. Restrooms; showers. Dump station.

Colonel Denning State Park

1599 Doubling Gap Rd, Newville, PA 17241. Phone: (717) 776-5272. Located in south-central PA, north of I-76, 8 miles N of Newville via PA 233. GPS: 40.281017, -77.418623. Small lake in park. Swimming beach, fishing, boating (non-powered boats only). Two trails in the park, many miles of trails are in the adjoining Tuscarora State Forest. Open Apr-Dec. $24-35 per night. 44 sites, 31 with electric, 13 no hookups. 50-foot limit. Restrooms; showers. Dump station.

Colton Point State Park

927 Colton Rd, Wellsboro, PA 16901. Phone: (570) 724-3061. Located in north-central PA midway between Galeton and Wellsboro, 5 miles S of US 6 at Ansonia via Colton Rd. Colton Point and Leonard Harrison state parks are on opposite sides of the Pine Creek Gorge, called the Grand Canyon of Pennsylvania. GPS: 41.707116, -77.465887. Fishing (hike required). Hiking trails. Small camping area open May-Oct. No reservations accepted. $20-24 per night. 7 sites, no hookups. 38-foot limit. Vault toilets. No showers.

Cook Forest State Park

100 Rt 36, Cooksburg, PA 16217. Phone: (814) 744-8407. Located on the Clarion River in northwestern PA midway between Leeper

and Sigel via PA 36. GPS: 41.332827, -79.209406. Fishing, boating (rentals). Hiking, biking, equestrian trails. Open Apr-Oct. $24-51 per night. 210 sites, 26 full hookup, 68 with electric, 116 no hookups. 80-foot limit. Restrooms; showers. Laundry facilities. Dump station.

Cowans Gap State Park

6235 Aughwick Rd, Fort Loudon, PA 17224. Phone: (717) 485-3948. Located in south-central PA, N of US 30, off PA 75, 7 miles N of Fort Loudon. Buchanan State Forest surrounds the park. GPS: 39.995124, -77.924792. Swimming beach, fishing, boating (rentals). Hiking, biking trails. Food concession. Interpretive center. Two camping areas open Apr-Oct (some camp sites close in Dec). $24-35 per night. 179 sites, 126 with electric, 53 no hookups. 82-foot limit. Restrooms; showers. Dump station.

Fowlers Hollow State Park

5700 Fowler Hollow Rd, Blain, PA 17006. Phone: (717) 776-5272. Remote location in south-central PA. From PA 274 in Blain, turn S at the east end of town, drive 1/4 of a mile and turn right after the bridge onto Fowlers Hollow Road. Follow for 5.7 miles to park. The park can also be reached from PA 274 west of New Germantown via Upper Buck Ridge Rd. GPS: 40.275593, -77.576319. Fishing. Hiking, biking, equestrian trails. Open Apr-Dec. $24-35 per night. 12 sites with electric. 40-foot limit. Restrooms; no showers. Dump station.

Frances Slocum State Park

565 Mount Oilivet Rd, Wyoming, PA 18644. Phone: (570) 696-3525. Located in northeastern PA, 5 miles NW of Wyoming via W 8th St off US 11. GPS: 41.346721, -75.894214. Francis Slocum Lake in park. Swimming pool, fishing, boating (rentals). Hiking, biking trails. Open Apr-Oct. $24-35 per night. 86 sites, 54 with electric, 32 no hookups. 64-foot limit. Restrooms; showers. Dump station.

French Creek State Park

843 Park Rd, Elverson, PA 19520. Phone: (610) 582-9680. Located in southeastern PA off PA 345, midway between Pottstown and Morgantown. GPS: 40.198600, -75.793726. Two lakes in park. Swimming (pool), fishing, boating (rentals). Hiking, biking, equestrian trails. Bird watching. Food concession (at pool). Open Mar-Dec. $24-48 per night. 200 sites, 17 full hookup, 43 with electric, 140 no hookups. 45-foot limit. Restrooms; showers. Dump station.

Gifford Pinchot State Park

2200 Rosstown Rd, Lewisberry, PA 17339. Phone: (717) 432-5011. Located in southeastern PA, S of Harrisburg, 4 miles SW of Lewisberry on PA 177. GPS: 40.086929, -76.888230. Pinchot Lake in park. Swimming beach, fishing, boating (rentals). Hiking, biking, equestrian trails. Food concession. Disc golf. Open Apr-Oct. $24-48 per night. 289 sites, 23 full hookup, 123 with electric, 143 no hookups. 55-foot limit. Restrooms; showers. Dump station.

Greenwood Furnace State Park

15795 Greenwood Rd, Huntingdon, PA 16652. Phone: (814) 667-1800. Located in central PA on PA 305, 19 miles NE of Huntingdon via PA 26 and East Branch Rd. GPS: 40.650317, -77.753684. Lake in park. Swimming beach, fishing, boating (non-powered boats). Hiking, biking trails. Food concession. Open Apr-Nov. $24-35 per night. 45 sites, 42 with electric, 3 no hookups. 92-foot limit. Restrooms; showers. Dump station.

Hickory Run State Park

3 Family Camp Rd, White Haven, PA 18661. Phone: (272) 808-6192. Located S of I-80/I-476 junction in northeastern PA, 6 miles SE of White Haven on PA 534. GPS: 41.024905, -75.686598. Lake in park. Swimming beach, fishing. More than 40 miles of hiking trails (biking prohibited). Camp store. Visitor center. Disc golf. Food concession. Open Apr-Dec. $24-48 per night. 372 sites, 17 full hookup, 117 with electric, 238 no hookups. 93-foot limit. Restrooms; showers. Dump station.

Hills Creek State Park

111 Spillway Rd, Wellsboro, PA 16901. Phone: (570) 724-4246. Located in north-central PA between Wellsboro and Mansfield, N of US 6. Multiple access roads. GPS: 41.804501, -77.191177. Hills Creek Lake in park. Swimming beach, fishing, boating. Hiking trails. Nature center. Food concession. Open Apr-Oct. $24-48 per night. 82 sites, 16 full hookup, 22 with electric, 44 no hookups. 40-foot limit. Restrooms; showers. Laundry facilities. Dump station.

Hyner Run State Park

86 Hyner Park Rd, North Bend, PA 17760. Phone: (570) 923-6000. Located in north-central PA off PA 120, 6 miles NE of Renovo; 3 miles N of Hyner. GPS: 41.358374, -77.628169. Swimming (pool), fishing. Hiking trails. Open Apr-Dec. $24-35 per night. 30 sites, 21 with electric, 9 no hookups. 68-foot limit. Restrooms; showers. Dump station.

Kettle Creek State Park

97 Kettle Creek Park Ln, Renovo, PA 17764. Phone: (570) 923-6004. Located in north-central PA, on Kettle Creek Reservoir, on PA 4001, 7 miles NW of Westport (PA 120). GPS: 41.375294, -77.932715. Fishing, boating (electric motors only). Hiking, biking, equestrian trails. Nature center. Bird watching. Two camping areas open Apr-Oct (some sites open in December). $24-35 per night. 64 sites, 53 with electric, 11 no hookups. 92-foot limit. Restrooms; showers. Dump station.

Keystone State Park

1150 Keystone Park Rd, Derry, PA 15627. Phone: (724) 668-2939. Located in southwestern PA, about 45 miles E of Pittsburgh, off US 22 at New Alexandria. GPS: 40.375990, -79.380396. Lake in park. Swimming beach, fishing, boating (rentals). Hiking, biking trails. Food concession. Visitor center. Two campgrounds open Apr-Oct. $24-35 per night. 88 sites, 58 with electric, 30 no hookups. 55-foot limit. Restrooms; showers. Dump station.

Kooser State Park

943 Glades Pike, Somerset, PA 15501. Phone: (814) 445-8673. Located in southwestern PA, S of I-76, 9 miles NW of Somerset on PA 31. GPS: 40.059877, -79.228010. Small lake in park.

Fishing. Hiking trails. Open Apr-Dec. $24-48 per night. 29 sites, 5 full hookup, 23 with electric, 1 no hookups. 100-foot limit. Restrooms; showers. Laundry facilities. Dump station.

Lackawanna State Park

1839 Abington Rd, N Abington Township, PA 18414. Phone: (570) 945-3239. Located in northeastern PA, 10 miles N of Scranton on PA 407. GPS: 41.558856, -75.705504. Lake in park. Swimming, fishing, boating (rentals). Hiking, biking, equestrian trails. Food concession. Wildlife viewing blind. Open Apr-Oct. $24-31 per night. 68 sites, 56 with electric, 12 no hookups. 40-foot limit. Restrooms; showers. Dump station.

Laurel Hill State Park

1454 Laurel Hill Park Rd, Somerset, PA 15501. Phone: (814) 445-7725. Located in southwestern PA, S of I-76, 9 miles W of Somerset via Trent Rd off PA 31. GPS: 40.010393, -79.224782. Lake in park. Swimming beach, fishing, boating (rentals). Hiking, biking trails. Visitor center, gift shop. Open Apr-Oct. $24-48 per night. 258 sites, 14 full hookup, 153 with electric, 91 no hookups. 45-foot limit. Restrooms; showers. Laundry facilities. Dump station.

Leonard Harrison State Park

4797 PA 660, Wellsboro, PA 16901. Phone: (570) 724-3601. Located in north-central PA, 12 miles W of Wellsboro via PA 660. On east rim of the Pine Creek Gorge, also known as the Grand Canyon of Pennsylvania. Leonard Harrison and Colton Point state parks are on opposite sides of the gorge. GPS: 41.696451, -77.454632. Fishing (hike required). Hiking, biking trails. Visitor center, gift shop. Open Apr-Nov. $24-35 per night. 25 sites, 7 with electric, 18 no hookups. 75-foot limit. Restrooms; showers. Dump station.

Little Buffalo State Park

1579 State Park Rd, Newport, PA 17074. Phone: (717)567-9255. Located in south-central PA, 3 miles W of Newport via PA 34 and PA 4010 (Little Buffalo Rd). GPS: 40.459048, -77.169509. Lake in park. Swimming pool (prohibited in lake), fishing, boating (rentals). Hiking trails. Open Apr-Oct. $24-48 per night. 43 sites, 3 full hookup, 28 with electric, 12 no hookups. 45-foot limit. Restrooms; showers. Dump station.

Little Pine State Park

4205 Little Pine Creek Rd, Waterville, PA 17776. Phone: (570) 753-6000. Located in north-central PA about 25 miles NW of Williamsport, 4 miles N of Waterville via Little Pine Creek Rd off PA 44. GPS: 41.363501, -77.357042. Lake in park. Swimming beach, fishing, boating (rentals). Hiking trails. Open Apr-Dec. $24-35 per night. 91 sites, 72 with electric, 19 no hookups. 72-foot limit. Restrooms; showers. Dump station.

Locust Lake State Park

220 Locust Lake Rd, Barnesville, PA 18214. Phone: (570) 467-2404. Located in east-central PA, 3 miles S of Mahanoy City, 2 miles from PA 54 and I-81 interchange. GPS: 40.784989, -76.119247. Swimming beach, fishing, boating (rentals). Hiking, biking trails. Camp store. RV campground is on the S side of lake and is open

Apr-Oct. $24-35 per night. 203 sites, 79 with electric, 124 no hookups. 68-foot limit. Restrooms; showers. Dump station.

Lyman Run State Park

454 Lyman Run Rd, Galeton, PA 16922. Phone: (814) 435-5010. Located in north-central PA, 15 miles E of Coudersport; 7 miles W of Galeton via Rock Run Rd off US 6. GPS: 41.725121, -77.759936. Lake in park. Swimming beach, fishing, boating (electric motors only). Hiking, biking, ATV trails. Food concession. Open Apr-Nov. $31-35 per night. 30 sites with electric. 60-foot limit. Restrooms; showers. Dump station.

Ohiopyle State Park

124 Main St, Ohiopyle, PA 15470. Phone: (724) 329-8591. Park visitor center is in Ohiopyle on PA 381, in southwestern PA on Youghiogheny River. About 15 miles E of Uniontown. GPS: 39.867195, -79.494398. Fishing, boating (rentals), whitewater rafting section. Hiking, biking (rentals), equestrian trails. Rock climbing, bird watching. Visitor center. Open Apr-Dec. $24-35 per night. 184 sites, 61 with electric, 123 no hookups. 50-foot limit. Restrooms; showers. Dump station.

Ole Bull State Park

31 Valhalla Ln, Cross Fork, PA 17729. Phone: (814) 435-5000. Located in north-central PA on Kettle Creek, 7 miles NE of Cross Fork on PA 144. About 18 miles SW of Galeton (on US 6) via PA 144/44. GPS: 41.537058, -77.715319. Swimming beach, fishing. Hiking, biking, nature trails. Two camping areas. Area north of creek open Apr-Nov. Area south of creek open year-round (access not guaranteed during winter months). $24-35 per night. 79 sites, 56 with electric, 23 no hookups. 64-foot limit. Restrooms; showers. Dump station.

Parker Dam State Park

28 Fairview Rd, Penfield, PA 15849. Phone: (814) 765-0630. Located in west-central PA, 5 miles SE of Penfield via PA 153 and Mud Run Rd. Or 8 miles N of I-80 exit 111 (PA 153), and follow to Mud Run Rd. GPS: 41.193754, -78.511632. Swimming beach, fishing, boating (rentals). Hiking, biking trails. Camp store, food concession. Environmental education center. Civilian Conservation Corps Museum. Open Apr-Dec. $24-48 per night. 107 sites, 23 full hookup, 61 with electric, 23 no hookups. 93-foot limit. Restrooms; showers. Laundry facilities. Dump station.

Patterson State Park

2866 Cherry Springs Rd, Coudersport, PA 16915. Phone: (814) 435-5010. Located in north-central PA, 7 miles SE of Sweden Valley off US 6 on PA 44. GPS: 41.695561, -77.893319. Hiking, biking trails. Small remote park open Apr-Dec. No reservations accepted. $20-24 per night. 10 sites no hookups. Vault toilets.

Pine Grove Furnace State Park

1100 Pine Grove Rd, Gardners, PA 17324. Phone: (717) 486-7174. Located in south-central PA, SW of Carlisle on PA 233, 8 miles S of I-81 exit 37. GPS: 40.033130, -77.304565. Two lakes in park. Swimming beaches, fishing, boating (rentals). Hiking, biking trails. Camp store. Appalachian Trail Museum. Walking tour of historic buildings. Open Mar-Dec. $24-35 per night. 50 sites, 41 with electric, 9 no hookups. 60-foot limit. Restrooms; showers. Dump station.

Poe Paddy State Park

1087 Poe Paddy Dr, Woodward, PA 16882. Phone: (814) 349-2460. Located in central Pennsylvania at the confluence of Big Poe Creek and Penns Creek, 14 miles SE of Millheim (PA 45) and 4 miles E of Poe Valley State Park. GPS: 40.833798, -77.417697. Fishing. Hiking trails. Open Apr-Dec. $24-35 per night. 32 sites, 2 with electric, 30 no hookups. Drinking water. 90-foot limit. Vault toilets.

Poe Valley State Park

136 Poe Valley Park Circle, Coburn, PA 16832. Phone: (814) 349-2460. Located in central Pennsylvania, 10 miles S of Millheim (PA 45). Poe Paddy State Park is 4 miles E. GPS: 40.821100, -77.475653. Lake in park. Swimming beach, fishing, boating (rentals). Hiking trails. Food concession. Open Apr-Dec. $24-35 per night. 45 sites, 27 with electric, 18 no hookups. 40-foot limit. Restrooms; showers. Dump station.

Prince Gallitzin State Park

966 Marina Rd, Patton, PA 16668. Phone: (814) 674-1000. Located in west-central PA, 6 miles E of Patton via Glendale Lake Rd off PA 36. GPS: 40.651064, -78.555109. Lake in park. Swimming beach, fishing, boating (rentals). Hiking, biking trails. Camp store. Marina. Large camping area with 10 loops. Open Apr-Oct. $24-48 per night. 364 sites, 27 full hookup, 172 with electric, 165 no hookups. Restrooms; showers. Laundry facilities. Dump station.

Promised Land State Park

100 Lower Lake Rd, Greentown, PA 18426. Phone: (570) 676-3428. Located in northeastern PA on PA 390, S of I-84, 8 miles SE of Greentown (I-84 exit 20). Or from I-84 exit 26 (PA 390). GPS: 41.299621, -75.214150. Two lakes in park. Swimming beaches, fishing, boating (rentals). Hiking, biking, equestrian trails. Food concession. Museum. Four camping areas generally open Apr-Oct. $24-48 per night. 338 sites, 11 full hookup, 195 with electric, 132 no hookups. 87-foot limit. Restrooms; showers. Laundry facilities. Dump station. Equestrian area with 6 sites.

Pymatuning State Park

2660 Williamsfield Rd, Jamestown, PA 16134. Phone: (724) 932-3142. Located on Pymatuning Reservoir in northwestern PA, 2 miles NW of Jamestown to park office via US 322. GPS (park office): 41.499613, -80.468198. Swimming beaches, fishing, boating (rentals). Hiking trails. Wildlife viewing areas, fish hatchery and visitor center. Three marinas. Disc golf. Largest lake and state park in PA with two camping areas.

Jamestown Campground on southern end of reservoir, off US 322, near Ohio state line. GPS: 41.517655, -80.506628. Open Apr-Oct. $24-48 per night. 309 sites, 40 full hookup, 160 with electric, 109 no hookups. 65-foot limit. Restrooms; showers. Laundry facilities. Dump station. Camp store.

Linesville Campground on northern end of reservoir, off US 6, W of Linesville, PA. GPS:41.657840, -80.460961. Open Apr-Oct. $24-48 per night. 81 sites, 13 full hookup, 46 with electric, 22 no hookups. 65-foot limit. Restrooms; showers. Laundry facilities. Dump station.

Raccoon Creek State Park

3000 PA 18, Hookstown, PA 15050. Phone: (724) 899-2200. Located in southwestern PA, about 30 miles west of Pittsburgh on PA 18, off US 22 or US 30. GPS: 40.503511, -80.424977. Swimming beach, fishing, boating (rentals). Hiking, biking, equestrian trails. Concession stand. Open Apr-Oct. $24-35 per night. 145 sites, 64 with electric, 81 no hookups. 78-foot limit. Restrooms; showers. Dump station.

Raymond B. Winter State Park

17215 Buffalo Rd, Mifflinburg, PA 17844. Phone: (570) 966-1455. Located in central PA in Bald Eagle State Forest, 18 miles W of Lewisburg via PA 192 off US 15. GPS: 40.991249, -77.193875. Lake in park. Swimming beach, fishing. Hiking, biking trails. Environmental learning center, butterfly and bird gardens. Open Apr-Dec. $24-35 per night. 58 sites, 48 with electric, 10 no hookups. 50-foot limit. Restrooms; showers. Dump station.

Ricketts Glen State Park

695 PA 487, Benton, PA 17814. Phone: (570) 477-5675. Located in northeastern PA, 12 miles N of Benton via PA 487. About 28 miles N of Bloomsburg via PA 487 from I-80 exit 236 (236B for westbound travelers). Large RV access recommended from the N via PA 487 from US 220 in Dushore because of very steep road N of Red Rock. GPS: 41.335259, -76.301891. Lake in park. Swimming beach, fishing, boating (rentals). Hiking, equestrian trails. Scenic waterfalls. Glens Natural Area, a National Natural Landmark. Most sites open Apr-Oct, some open all year but access not guaranteed in winter months. $24-28 per night. 120 sites with no hookups. 50-foot limit. Restrooms; showers. Dump station.

Ryerson Station State Park

361 Bristoria Rd, Wind Ridge, PA 15380. Phone: (724) 428-4254. Located in the southwestern corner of PA, 3 miles S of Wind Ridge via PA 21 W to Bristoria Rd. Or take McNay Ridge Rd off PA 21 to Bristoria Rd. GPS: 39.886089, -80.445578. Swimming pool, fishing. Hiking trails. Campground is located at 217 McNay Ridge Rd. GPS: 39.890641, -80.439053. Open all year. $24-48 per night. 35 sites, 7 full hookup, 12 with electric, 16 no hookups. 50-foot limit. Restrooms; showers. Laundry facilities. Dump station.

Simon B. Elliott State Park

2112 Old PA 153, Penfield, PA 15849. Phone: (814) 765-0630. Located in the heart of Moshannon State Forest in west-central PA, 8 miles S of Penfield on PA 153. Or just off I-80 exit 111, NW of Clearfield. GPS: 41.113138, -78.526284. Fishing. Hiking trails. Open May-Oct. $24-28 per night. 25 sites, no hookups. 62-foot limit. Restrooms; no showers. Dump station.

Shawnee State Park

132 State Park Rd, Schellsburg, PA 15559. Phone: (814) 733-4218. Located in south-central PA, just south of Schellsburg, on PA 31 between US 30 and I-76. GPS: 40.026249, -78.635982. Lake in park. Swimming beach, fishing, boating (rentals). Hiking, biking trails. Open Apr-Dec. $24-48 per night. 207 sites, 15 full hookup, 93 with electric, 99 no hookups. 115-foot limit. Restrooms; showers. Dump station.

Sinnemahoning State Park

4843 Park Rd, Austin, PA 16720. Phone: (814) 647-8401. Located in north-central PA on Sinnemahoning Creek (George B. Stevenson Reservoir), on PA 872, 14 miles N of PA 120; 28 miles S of Coudersport (US 6). Park is long and narrow and includes lands on both sides of the water, reservoir is at the southern end of park. GPS: 41.473711, -78.056998. Fishing, boating (electric motors only). Hiking, biking trails. Wildlife watching, viewing blind. Park office/Wildlife center. Open Apr-Dec. $31-35 per night. 33 sites with electric. 85-foot limit. Restrooms; showers. Dump station.

Sizerville State Park

199 E Cowley Run Rd, Emporium, PA 15834. Phone: (814) 486-5605. Located in north-central PA surrounded by Elk State Forest, on PA 155, 7 miles N of Emporium (PA 120). GPS: 41.595972, -78.183379. Swimming pool, fishing. Hiking trails. Food concession. Open Apr-Dec. $24-35 per night. 23 sites, 18 with electric, 5 no hookups. 60-foot limit. Restrooms; showers. Dump station.

Tobyhanna State Park

114 Campground Rd, Tobyhanna, PA 18466. Phone: (570) 894-8336. Located in northeastern PA, southeast of Scranton, 2 miles NE of Tobyhanna on PA 423 (3 miles from I-380 exit 8). GPS: 41.207302, -75.396726. Lake in park. Swimming beach, fishing, boating (rentals). Hiking, biking trails. Open Apr-Oct. $24-35 per night. 131 sites, 26 with electric, 105 no hookups. 40-foot limit. Restrooms; showers. Dump station.

Trough Creek State Park

16362 Little Valley Rd, James Creek, PA 16657. Phone: (814) 658-3847. Located about 38 miles SE of Altoona, on PA 994, 6 miles E of Entriken (off PA 26). GPS: 40.311570, -78.130110. Fishing, boating. Hiking, biking trails. Open Apr-Dec. $31-35 per night. 24 sites with electric. 60-foot limit. Restrooms; no showers. Dump station.

Worlds End State Park

82 Cabin Bridge Rd, Forksville, PA 18616. Phone: (570) 924-3287. Located on Loyalsock Creek in north-central PA, 2 miles S of Forksville on PA 154. About 8 miles NW of Laporte off US 220. GPS: 41.472033, -76.581914. Swimming beach, fishing, whitewater boating. Hiking, biking trails. Scenic vista. Food concession. Visitor center. Open Apr-Dec. $24-35 per night. 62 sites, 32 with electric, 30 no hookups. 74-foot limit. Restrooms; showers. Dump station.

Rhode Island

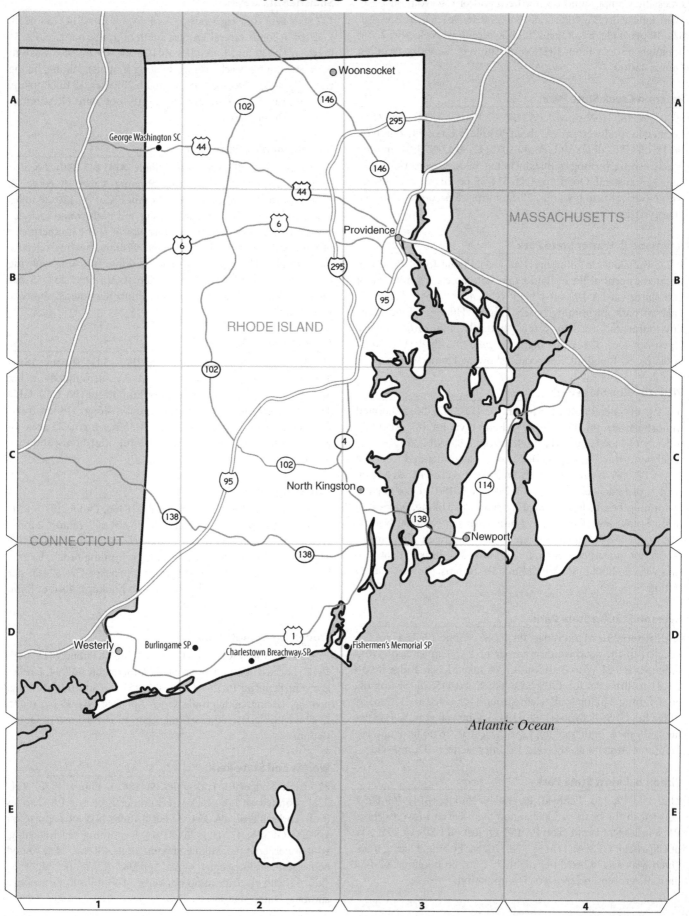

Rhode Island

Rhode Island State Parks
1100 Tower Hill Rd
North Kingstown RI 02852

Phone: (401) 667-6200
Internet: www.riparks.com
Reservations: 877-742-2675

Rhode Island Park Locator

Rhode Island Parks

Burlingame State Park

1 Burlingame State Park Rd, Charlestown, RI 02813. Phone: (401) 322-7337. Located 4 miles W of Charlestown via US 1. GPS: 41.362440, -71.700269. Fishing, swimming, boating. Open Apr-Oct. $36-45 per night. 692 sites, no hookups. Restrooms; showers. Dump station.

Charlestown Breachway State Park

Charlestown Beach Rd, Charlestown, RI 02813. Phone: (401) 364-7000. Located just S of Charlestown via Charlestown Beach Rd. GPS: 41.357175, -71.637168. Fishing, swimming, boating. Open Apr-Oct. Self contained RVs only. $36 per night. 75 sites, no hookups. Restrooms; showers.

Fishermen's Memorial State Park

1011 Point Judith Rd, Narragansett, RI 02882. Phone: (401) 789-8374. Located 4 miles S of US 1 near Narragansett via RI 108. GPS: 41.380074, -71.488424. Fishing. Open Apr-Oct. $45-55 per night. 147 sites, 40 full hookup, 107 with water and electric. Restrooms; showers. Dump station. Note: In season minimum stays may be required, check with park.

George Washington State Campground

2185 Putnam Pike, Chepachet, RI 02814. Phone: (401) 568-6700. Located 4.5 miles W of Chepachet via US 44. GPS: 41.919877, -71.754905. Swimming, fishing, boating. Hiking trails. Open Apr-Oct. $36 per night. 62 sites, no hookups. Restrooms; showers. Dump station.

South Carolina

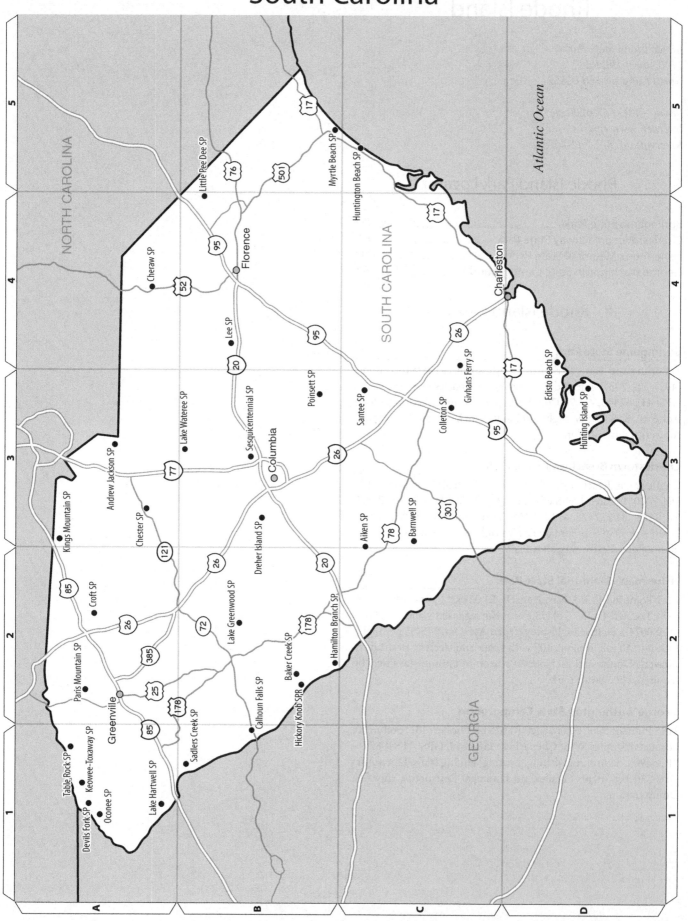

NORTH CAROLINA

SOUTH CAROLINA

GEORGIA

Atlantic Ocean

Little Pee Dee SP

Cheraw SP

Florence

Myrtle Beach SP

Huntington Beach SP

Charleston

Lee SP

Edisto Beach SP

Poinsett SP

Givhans Ferry SP

Hunting Island SP

Sesquicentennial SP

Santee SP

Colleton SP

Lake Wateree SP

Columbia

Andrew Jackson SP

Kings Mountain SP

Chester SP

Aiken SP

Barnwell SP

Dreher Island SP

Croft SP

Lake Greenwood SP

Paris Mountain SP

Baker Creek SP

Hamilton Branch SP

Greenville

Calhoun Falls SP

Hickory Knob SP

Sadlers Creek SP

Table Rock SP

Keowee-Toxaway SP

Devils Fork SP

Oconee SP

Lake Hartwell SP

South Carolina

South Carolina Dept. of Parks, Recreation & Tourism
1205 Pendelton St
Columbia, SC 29201

Phone: (803) 734-1700
Internet: www.southcarolinaparks.com
Reservations: Online or call park. Also (866) 345-7275

South Carolina Park Locator

South Carolina Parks

Aiken State Park

1145 State Park Rd, Windsor, SC 29856. Phone: (803) 649-2857. Located 5 miles N of Windsor via SC 53. About 14 miles E of Aiken. GPS: 33.550658, -81.489984. Swimming, fishing (river and 4 park lakes), boating (rentals). Hiking, biking trails. Park store, gift shop. Open all year. $18-21 per night. 25 sites with water and electric. 35-foot limit. Restrooms; showers. Dump station.

Andrew Jackson State Park

196 Andrew Jackson Park Rd, Lancaster, SC 29720. Phone: (803) 285-3344. Located 7 miles N of Lancaster via US 512. GPS: 34.837065, -80.806802. Fishing, boating (rentals). Hiking, biking trails. Park store, gift shop. Andrew Jackson Museum in park. Open all year. $28-32 per night. 25 sites with water and electric. 36-foot limit. Restrooms; showers. Dump station.

Baker Creek State Park

863 Baker Creek Rd, McCormick, SC 29835. Phone: (864) 443-2457. Located on Strom Thurmond Lake, 5 miles SW of McCormick, off US 378. GPS: 33.898468, -82.347003. Swimming, fishing, boating. Hiking, biking trails. Open Mar-Sep. $19-24 per night. 50 sites with water and electric. 40-foot limit. Restrooms; showers. Dump station.

Barnwell State Park

223 State Park Rd, Blackville, SC 29817. Phone: (803) 284-2212. Located along SC 3, 3 miles SW of Blackville (US 78 & SC 3). GPS: 33.329376, -81.302791. Swimming, fishing, boating (rentals). Small boats only, no boat ramp. Hiking, biking trails. Park store, gift shop. Open all year. $19-24 per night. 25 sites, 8 full hookup, 17 with water and electric. 36-foot limit. Restrooms; showers. Dump station.

Calhoun Falls State Park

46 Maintenance Shop Rd, Calhoun Falls, SC 29628. Phone: (864) 447- 8267. Located on Lake Russell, 2 miles NW of Calhoun Falls off SC 81. GPS: 34.105036, -82.604061. Swimming beach, fishing, boating. Hiking trail. Park store, gift shop. Marina. Two campgrounds open all year. $39-42 per night. 86 sites with water and electric. 40-foot limit. Restrooms; showers. Laundry facilities. Dump station.

Cheraw State Park

100 State Park Rd, Cheraw, SC 29520. Phone: (843) 537-9656. Located on Lake Juniper near junction of US 1 & US 52, about 5 miles S of Cheraw. GPS: 34.637332, -79.913425. Swimming beach, fishing, boating (rentals). Hiking, biking trails. Park store, gift shop. Golf course. Open all year. $19-24 per night. 17 sites with water and electric. 40-foot limit. Restrooms; showers. Dump station.

Chester State Park

759 State Park Dr, Chester, SC 29706. Phone: (803) 385-2680. Located 2 miles SW of Chester via SC 72. GPS: 34.682466, -81.244389. Swimming, fishing, boating (rentals). Hiking trail. Disc golf. Open all year. $22-28 per night. 25 sites with water and electric. 33-foot limit. Restrooms; showers. Dump station.

Colleton State Park

147 Wayside Ln, Walterboro, SC 29488. Phone: (843) 538-8206. Located on Edisto River, 11 miles N of Walterboro off US 15. Or

from I-95 exit 68 (SC 61) to US 15. GPS: 33.061075, -80.616153. Swimming (river), fishing, boating. Nature trail. Park store, gift shop. Open all year. $29 per night. 25 sites with water and electric. 40-foot limit. Restrooms; showers. Dump station.

Croft State Park

450 Croft State Park Rd, Spartanburg, SC 29302. Phone: (864) 585-1283. Located 7 miles SE of Spartanburg via US 176 or SC 56. GPS: 34.893651, -81.867786. Fishing, boating (rentals). Hiking, biking, equestrian trails. Bird watching. Park store, gift shop. Open all year. $30 per night. 50 sites with water and electric. 40-foot limit. Restrooms; showers. Dump station.

Devils Fork State Park

161 Holcombe Circle, Salem, SC 29676. Phone: (864) 944-2639. Located near SC/GA/NC state lines, 6 miles NE of Salem via Jocassee Lake Rd off SC 11. GPS: 34.952273, -82.946540. Swimming, scuba diving, fishing, boating (rentals). Nature trail. Park store, gift shop. Open all year. $42-46 per night. 59 sites with water and electric. 40-foot limit. Restrooms; showers. Laundry facilities. Dump station.

Dreher Island State Park

3677 State Park Rd, Prosperity, SC 29127. Phone: (803) 364-4152. Located on Lake Murray, 11 miles SE of Prosperity via S Main St/ Macedonia Church Rd. GPS: 34.096440, -81.415619. Swimming, scuba diving, fishing, boating. Hiking, biking trails. Park store, gift shop. Marina. Open all year. $34-42 per night. 97 sites with water and electric. 45-foot limit. Restrooms; showers. Dump station.

Edisto Beach State Park

8377 State Cabin Rd, Edisto Island, SC 29438. Phone: (843) 869-2156. Located in Edisto Beach on the Atlantic Ocean. Follow SC 174 off US 17 in Osborn. GPS: 32.512806, -80.300229. Swimming (ocean), fishing, boating. Hiking, biking, interpretive trails. Park store, gift shop. Open all year. $40-60 per night. 112 sites with water and electric. 40-foot limit. Restrooms; showers. Dump station.

Givhans Ferry State Park

746 Givhans Ferry Rd, Ridgeville, SC 29472. Phone: (843) 873-0692. Located on Edisto River, 8 miles SW of Ridgeville via S Main St or off SC 61 from the south. GPS: 33.027213, -80.385371. Swimming (river), fishing, boating. Hiking, biking trails. Park store, gift shop. Open all year. $32-37 per night. 25 sites, 6 full hookup, 19 with water and electric. 40-foot limit. Restrooms; showers. Dump station.

Hamilton Branch State Park

111 Campground Rd, Plum Branch, SC 29845. Phone: (864) 333-2223. Located on Strom Thurmond Lake near Georgia state line, 8 miles S of Plum Branch via SC 28/US 221. GPS: 33.754208, -82.203834. Swimming, fishing, boating. Hiking, biking (rentals) trails. Park store, gift shop. Open all year. $32-46 per night. 173 sites with water and electric. 40-foot limit. Restrooms; showers. Dump station.

Hickory Knob State Park Resort

1591 Resort Dr, McCormick, SC 29835. Phone: (864) 391-2450. Located on Strom Thurmond Lake, 7 miles W of McCormick via SC 7 off US 378. GPS: 33.882569, -82.414196. Swimming, fishing, boating (rentals). Hiking, biking trails. Archery range, skeet shooting. Park store, gift shop. Golf course. Restaurant. Open all year. $21 per night. 43 sites with water and electric. 30-foot limit. Restrooms; showers. Dump station.

Hunting Island State Park

2555 Sea Island Pkwy, Hunting Island, SC 29920. Phone: (843) 838-2011. Located on the Atlantic Ocean, 17 miles E of Beaufort at end of US 21. GPS: 32.373728, -80.446641. Swimming (ocean), fishing, boating. Hiking, biking, nature trails. Park store, gift shop. Bird watching. Hunting Island Lighthouse. Open all year. $60-65 per night. 102 sites with water and electric. 40-foot limit. Restrooms; showers. Dump station.

Huntington Beach State Park

16148 Ocean Hwy, Murrells Inlet, SC 29576. Phone: (843) 237-4440. Located about 18 miles SW of Myrtle Beach, off US 17, on the Atlantic Ocean. GPS: 33.512334, -79.071546. Swimming beach, fishing, boating. Boardwalk and nature trails. Bird watching. Nature center. Park store, gift shop. Open all year. $58-65 per night. 173 sites, 66 full hookup, 107 with water and electric. 40-foot limit. Restrooms; showers. Dump station.

Keowee-Toxaway State Park

108 Residence Dr, Sunset, SC 29685. Phone: (864) 868-2605. Located in the northwestern tip of SC, 12 miles NW of Pickens on SC 133 and SC 11. GPS: 34.931706, -82.884776. Swimming, fishing, boating. Hiking, nature trails. Bird watching. Visitor center, park store, gift shop. Open all year. $18-28 per night. 10 sites with water and electric. 40-foot limit. Restrooms; showers. Dump station.

Kings Mountain State Park

1277 Park Rd, Blacksburg, SC 29702. Phone: (803) 222-3209. Located near NC state line, about 10 miles NW of Clover via SC 55 and SC 161; adjacent to Kings Mountain National Military Park. GPS: 34.931706, -82.884776. Fishing, boating (rentals). Hiking, nature, equestrian trails. Park store, gift shop. Open all year. $27 per night. 115 sites with water and electric. 40-foot limit. Restrooms; showers. Dump station. Equestrian area (15 sites, central water).

Lake Greenwood State Park

302 State Park Rd, Ninety Six, SC 29666. Phone: (864) 543-3535. Located 6 miles E of Ninety Six (or 12 miles E of Greenwood) via SC 34 and Island Ford Rd. GPS: 34.195165, -81.948613. Swimming, fishing, boating. Nature trail. Civilian Conservation Corps museum. Open all year. $27-45 per night. 125 sites, 31 full hookup, 94 with water and electric. 40-foot limit. Restrooms; showers. Dump station.

Lake Hartwell State Park

19138-A SC 11S, Fair Play, SC 29643. Phone: (864) 972-3352. Located near SC/GA state lines, N of I-85 exit 1 via SC 11. GPS: 34.494877, -83.031514. Swimming, fishing, boating. Nature trail. Park store, gift shop. Open all year. $31-37 per night. 115 sites with water and electric. 40-foot limit. Restrooms; showers. Laundry facilities. Dump station.

Lake Wateree State Park

881 State Park Rd, Winnsboro, SC 29180. Phone: (803) 482-6401. Located 11 miles S of Great Falls via US 21 and Wateree Rd. GPS: 34.431109, -80.870231. Swimming, fishing, boating. Hiking, biking, nature trails. Park store, gift shop. Two campgrounds open all year. $32-43 per night. 100 sites (23 waterfront), 28 full hookup, 72 with water and electric. 40-foot limit. Restrooms; showers. Dump station.

Lee State Park

487 Loop Rd, Bishopville, SC 29010. Phone: (803) 428-5307. Located E of Bishopville via Lee State Park Rd off US 15 or off I-20 exit 123. GPS: 34.203042, -80.175869. Swimming, fishing, boating (4 miles to closest boat ramp). Hiking, biking, equestrian trails. Bird watching. Park store, gift shop. Education Center. Open all year. $20-31 per night. 25 sites, 6 full hookup, 19 with water and electric. 36-foot limit. Restrooms; showers. Dump station. Equestrian area with 23 sites, 5 full hookup, 18 with water and electric.

Little Pee Dee State Park

1298 State Park Rd, Dillon, SC 29536. Phone: (843) 774-8872. Located on Little Pee Dee River, 9 miles SE of Dillon off SC 57 or SC 9. GPS: 34.323531, -79.285184. Fishing, boating (rentals). Nature trail. Park store, gift shop. Open all year. $22-23 per night. 32 sites with water and electric. Restrooms; showers. Dump station.

Myrtle Beach State Park

4401 S Kings Hwy, Myrtle Beach, SC 29575. Phone: (843) 238-5325. Located on Bus. US 17 about 3 miles SW of Myrtle Beach, on the Atlantic Ocean. GPS: 33.649082, -78.938517. Swimming (ocean), fishing, boating. Hiking, biking, nature trails. Park store, gift shop. Nature Center, bird watching. Open all year. $49-62 per night. 278 sites, 138 full hookup, 140 with water and electric. 40-foot limit. Restrooms; showers. Laundry facilities. Dump station.

Oconee State Park

624 State Park Rd, Mountain Rest, SC 29664. Phone: (864) 638- 5353. Located in the northwestern tip of SC, 10 miles N of Walhalla on SC 107 off SC 28. GPS: 34.866973, -83.107868. Swimming, fishing, boating (rentals). Hiking, biking trails. Park store, gift shop. Mini golf. Open all year. $30-39 per night. 139 sites with water and electric. 40-foot limit. Restrooms; showers. Dump station.

Paris Mountain State Park

2401 State Park Rd, Greenville, SC 29609. Phone: (864) 244-5565. Located about 6 miles N of Greenville via CR 344 off SC 253 (from US 276). GPS: 34.926650, -82.365798. Swimming, fishing, boating (rentals, private boats not allowed). Hiking, biking, interpretive trails. Bird watching. Park store, gift shop. Open all year. $30 per night. 26 sites with water and electric. 40-foot limit. Restrooms; showers. Dump station.

Poinsett State Park

6660 Poinsett Park Rd, Wedgefield, SC 29168. Phone: (803) 494-8177. Located 7 miles S of Wedgefield off SC 261. About 18 miles SW of Sumter. GPS: 33.803107, -80.528828. Swimming, fishing, boating (rentals). Hiking, biking trails. Bird watching. Park store, gift shop. Open all year. $27 per night. 24 sites with water and electric. 40-foot limit. Restrooms; showers. Dump station.

Sadlers Creek State Park

940 Sadlers Creek Rd, Anderson, SC 29626. Phone: (864) 226-8950. Located on Lake Hartwell, 13 miles SW of Anderson via US 29 and SC 187. GPS: 34.421236, -82.818291. Swimming (lake), fishing, boating. Hiking, biking, nature trails. Open all year. $29-40 per night. 52 sites with water and electric. 40-foot limit. Restrooms; showers. Dump station.

Santee State Park

251 State Park Rd, Santee, SC 29142. Phone: (803) 854-2408. Located on Lake Marion, 4 miles N of Santee, off SC 6 near I-95 exit 98. GPS: 33.521143, -80.501682. Swimming, fishing, boating. Hiking, biking, nature trails. Bird watching. Park store, gift shop. Pontoon boat tours. Two campgrounds open all year. $24-32 per night. 146 sites with water and electric. 40-foot limit. Restrooms; showers. Dump station.

Sesquicentennial State Park

9564 Two Notch Rd, Columbia, SC 29223. Phone: (803) 788-2706. Located NE of Columbia off US 1 (I-77 exit 17). GPS: 34.101913, -80.911010. Splash Pad water attraction. Fishing, boating (rentals). Hiking, biking trails. Bird watching. Park store, gift shop. Open all year. $21-24 per night. 84 sites with water and electric. 35-foot limit. Restrooms; showers. Dump station.

Table Rock State Park

158 E Ellison Ln, Pickens, SC 29671. Phone: (864) 878-9813. Located 12 miles N of Pickens via US 178 and SC 11. GPS: 35.022777, -82.694314. Swimming, fishing, boating (rentals). Hiking trails. Park store, gift shop. Two camping areas open all year. $30-46 per night. 94 sites with water and electric. 40-foot limit. Restrooms; showers. Laundry facilities. Dump station.

South Dakota

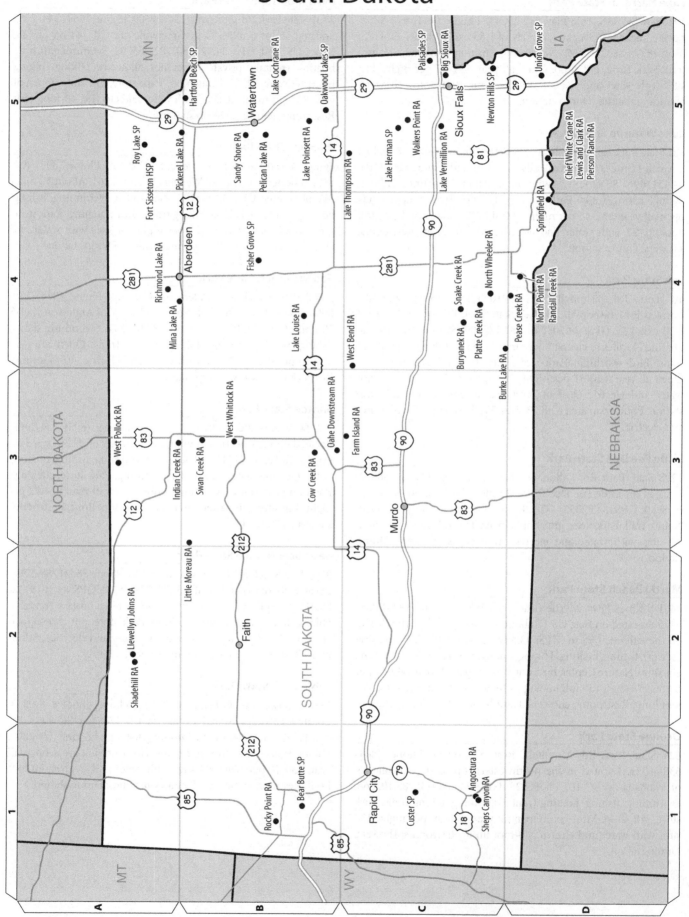

South Dakota

South Dakota Game, Fish and Parks
523 East Capitol Ave
Pierre, SD 57501

Phone: (605) 223-7660
Internet: gfp.sd.gov/parks/
Reservations: Online or (800) 710-2267

South Dakota Park Locator

South Dakota Parks

Angostura Recreation Area

13157 N Angostura Rd, Hot Springs, SD 57747. Phone: (605) 745-6996. Located on Angostura Reservoir, 10 miles SE of Hot Springs, off US 18/385. GPS: North entrance 43.346381, -103.421816, south entrance 43.292350, -103.381700. Swimming beach, fishing, boating (rentals). Hiking, biking (rentals) trails. Disc golf. Marina, store, restaurant. Visitor center. Four campgrounds open all year. $22-26 per night. 169 sites with electric. Restrooms; showers. Dump station.

Bear Butte State Park

20250 SD 79, Sturgis, SD 57785. Phone: (605) 347-5240. Located off SD 79, 6 miles NE of Sturgis. GPS: 44.461248, -103.435186. Fishing, boating. Hiking, equestrian trails. Visitor center. Open all year. No reservations accepted. $11 per night. 15 sites, no hookups. Drinking water available. Vault toilets.

Big Sioux Recreation Area

410 W Park St, Brandon, SD 57005. Phone: (605) 582-7243. Located E of Sioux Falls on Big Sioux River, 4 miles SW of Brandon off SD 11. GPS: 43.573013, -96.594479. Fishing, boating. Hiking, biking trails. Archery range. Disc golf. Open all year. $26 per night. 40 sites with 50 amp electric. Restrooms; showers. Dump station.

Burke Lake Recreation Area

29145 Burke Lake Rd, Burke, SD 57523. Phone: (605) 337-2587. Located off US 18, 2 miles E of Burke via SD 36. GPS: 43.183395, -99.260031. Fishing, boating. Hiking trail. Open all year. No reservations accepted. $11 per night. 15 sites, no hookups. Drinking water available. Vault toilets.

Buryanek Recreation Area

27450 Buryanek Rd, Burke, SD 57523. Phone: (605) 337-2587. Located on the Missouri River, 20 miles NW of Platte via Buryanek Rd off SD 44. GPS: 43.415486, -99.172706. Swimming beach, fishing, boating. Open all year. $19-23 per night. 44 sites with electric. Restrooms; showers. Dump station.

Chief White Crane Recreation Area

31323 Toe Rd, Yankton, SD 57078. Phone: (605) 668-2985. Located on Lake Yankton, 9 miles SW of Yankton via SD 52 and Toe Rd. GPS: 42.851243, -97.460297. Swimming, fishing, boating. Hiking, biking trails. Birdwatching. Open all year. $26 per night. 144 sites with 50 amp electric. Restrooms; showers. Dump station.

Cow Creek Recreation Area

28229 Cow Creek Rd, Fort Pierre, SD 57501. Phone: (605) 773-3117. Located on Lake Oahe Reservoir (on the Missouri River), 16 miles NW of Pierre off SD 1804. GPS: 44.554518, -100.474088. Swimming, fishing, boating. Hiking, biking trails. Open all year. $20 per night. 38 sites with electric. Dump station. Restrooms; showers.

Custer State Park

13329 US 16A, Custer, SD 57730. Phone: (605) 255-4515. Located in southwestern SD around Custer and Keystone. The east entrance (near park visitor center) is on US 16A near junction with SD 36. GPS: East entrance, park visitor center 43.760253, -103.369087. Swim beaches, fishing, boating. Hiking, biking, equestrian trails. Wildlife Station Visitor Center. Bison herd in park. Rock climbing. Scenic drives. Park visitor center. Restaurants. Park complex includes the following nine campgrounds.

a) Blue Bell Campground, located on SD 87 adjacent to the Blue Bell Lodge and Horse Stables. GPS: 43.716935, -103.482913. Open May-Oct. $30 per night. 28 sites with electric. Restrooms; showers.

b) Center Lake Campground, located off SD 87 on S Playhouse Rd, 3 miles N of US 16A. GPS: 43.808843, -103.425406. Open May-Sep. $19 per night. 57 sites, no hookups. Vault toilets. Showers.

c) French Creek Horse Camp - horse campers only. Located on Lame Johnny Rd. GPS: 43.714229, -103.456173. Open year-round (basic camping only, no electric Nov-Apr). $40 per night. 28 sites with electric. Restrooms; showers. Dump station.

d) Game Lodge Campground, located S of the visitor center, near the junction of US 16A and Wildlife Loop Rd. GPS: 43.760651, -103.371190. Open all year. $26-30 per night. 41 sites, 35 with electric. Restrooms; showers. Dump station.

e) Grace Coolidge Campground, located 2 miles W of the visitor center on US 16A. GPS: 43.776920, -103.400766. Open May-Oct. $30 per night. 20 sites with electric. Restrooms; showers.

f) Legion Lake Campground, located on US 16A across from Legion Lake and Legion Lake Lodge. GPS: 43.762127, -103.465075. Open May-Oct. $30 per night. 21 sites with electric. Restrooms; showers.

g) Stockade Lake North Campground, located on the western side of park off US 16A, 4 miles E of Custer. GPS: 43.773770, -103.520876. Open May-Sep. $26-30 per night. 38 sites, 31 with electric, 7 no hookups. Restrooms; showers.

h) Stockade Lake South Campground, located on the western side of park off US 16A, 4 miles E of Custer. GPS: 43.764493, -103.522626. Open May-Sep. $30 per night. 20 sites with electric. Restrooms; showers.

i) Sylvan Lake Campground, located ¼ mile S of Sylvan Lake on SD 87N (Needles Highway). Due to low, narrow tunnels large

RVs or vehicles towing campers should avoid SD 87N and approach the area using SD 89 north from US 16A in Custer. GPS: 43.840312, -103.556980. Open May-Sep. $30 per night. 25 sites with electric. 27-foot limit. Restrooms; showers.

Farm Island Recreation Area

1301 Farm Island Rd, Pierre, SD 57501. Phone: (605) 773-2885. Located 4 miles E of Pierre via SD 34. GPS: 44.349347, -100.279900. Swimming beach, fishing, boating (rentals). Hiking, biking (rentals) trails. Bird watching. Nature observation blind. Lewis and Clark family center. Two campgrounds open all year. $26 per night. 90 sites with electric. Restrooms; showers. Dump station.

Fisher Grove State Park

17290 Fishers Ln, Frankfort, SD 57440. Phone: (605) 626-3488. Located on James River off US 212, 7 miles E of Redfield. GPS: 44.882615, -98.356690. Fishing, boating. Hiking trail. Golf course adjacent to park. Open all year. $19-23 per night. 22 sites with electric. Restrooms; showers. Dump station.

Fort Sisseton Historic State Park

11907 434th Ave, Lake City, SD 57247. Phone: (605) 448-5474. Located in northeastern SD, 10 miles SW of Lake City on CR 5 off SD 10 (I-29 exit 232). GPS: 45.659356, -97.527944. Fishing, boating (rentals). Hiking trail. Restored 1864 army base in park. Visitor center, gift shop. Guided tours. Open all year. $26 per night. 10 sites with electric. Restrooms; showers.

Hartford Beach State Park

13672 Hartford Beach Rd, Corona, SD 57227. Phone: (605) 432-6374. Located on Big Stone Lake, 14 miles N of Milbank via SD 15. GPS: 45.402401, -96.673045. Swimming beach, fishing, boating (rentals). Hiking, biking trails. Park store. Disc golf. Two camping areas open all year. $26 per night. 117 sites with electric. Restrooms; showers. Dump station.

Indian Creek Recreation Area

12905 288th Ave, Mobridge, SD 57604. Phone: (605) 845-7112. Located on Lake Oahe off US 12, 2 miles SE of Mobridge in north-central SD. GPS: 45.522163, -100.386639. Fishing, boating (rentals). Hiking, biking trails. Marina, convenience store. Two camping areas open year-round. $20 per night. 123 sites with electric. Restrooms; showers. Dump station.

Lake Cochrane Recreation Area

3454 Edgewater Dr, Gary, SD 57237. Phone: (605) 882-5200. Located between two lakes in eastern SD, 10 miles E of Clear Lake, off SD 22 (I-29 exit 164). GPS: 44.714163, -96.478708. Swimming beach, fishing, boating. Open all year. $26 per night. 30 sites with electric. Restrooms; showers. Dump station.

Lake Herman State Park

23409 State Park Dr, Madison, SD 57042. Phone: (605) 256-5003. Located on Lake Herman, 2 miles W of Madison off SD 34. GPS: 43.992729, -97.160258. Swimming beach, fishing, boating (rentals). Hiking trails. Disc golf. Open all year. $22-26 per night. 72 sites, 69 with electric. Restrooms; showers. Dump station.

Lake Louise Recreation Area

35250 191st St, Miller, SD 57362. Phone: (605) 853-2533. Located 14 miles NW of Miller (junction US 14 & SD 45) via 191st St off SD 45. GPS: 44.620427, -99.140613. Swimming beach, fishing, boating. Hiking trail. Disc golf. Two camping areas open all year. $22-26 per night. 37 sites, 29 with electric. Restrooms. Dump station.

Lake Poinsett Recreation Area

45617 S Poinsett Dr, Arlington, SD 57212. Phone: (605) 983-5085. Located on Lake Poinsett, 14 miles N of Arlington, off US 81. GPS: 44.534279, -97.087215. Swimming beach, fishing, boating. Hiking, biking trail. Disc golf. Visitor center and museum. Two campgrounds open all year. $26 per night. 108 sites with electric. Restrooms; showers. Dump station.

Lake Thompson Recreation Area

21176 Flood Club Rd, Lake Preston, SD 57249. Phone: (605) 847-4893. Located on Lake Thompson off US 14, 6 miles SW of Lake Preston. GPS: 44.323828, -97.451070. Swimming beach, fishing, boating. Hiking, biking trail. Open all year. $26 per night. 97 sites with electric. Restrooms; showers. Dump station.

Lake Vermillion Recreation Area

26140 451st Ave, Canistota, SD 57012. Phone: (605) 296-3643. Located in southeastern SD, 6 miles E of Canisota via 261st St or 5 miles S of I-90 exit 374. GPS: 43.594891, -97.185161. Swimming beach, fishing, boating. Hiking, biking trail. Four camping areas open all year. $26 per night. 126 sites with electric. Restrooms; showers. Dump station.

Lewis and Clark Recreation Area

43349 SD 52, Yankton, SD 57078. Phone: (605) 668-2985. Located on Lewis & Clark Lake, about 6 miles W of Yankton (US 81 at NE/SD state line) off SD 52. GPS: 42.867260, -97.521108. Swimming beach, fishing, boating. Hiking, biking, equestrian trails. Visitor center. Marina. Archery range. Disc golf. Four camping areas open all year. $26 per night. 409 sites with electric. Restrooms; showers. Dump station. Equestrian camp, 8 sites with electric.

Little Moreau Recreation Area

19150 Summerville Rd, Shadehill, SD 57653. Phone: (605) 374-5114. Located on Little Moreau Lake, 6 miles south of Timber Lake off SD 20. GPS: 45.349027, -101.084478. Swimming beach, fishing, boating. Bird watching. Open all year. No reservations accepted. $11 per night. 5 sites, no hookups. Vault toilets.

Llewellyn Johns Recreation Area

19150 Summerville Rd, Shadehill, SD 57653. Phone: (605) 374-5114. Located on Flat Creek Lake, 12 miles south of Lemmon off SD 73. GPS: 45.775327, -102.177114. Swimming, fishing, boating. Bird watching. Open all year. $15 per night. 10 sites with electric. Vault toilets.

Mina Lake Recreation Area

402 Park Ave, Mina, SD 57451. Phone: (605) 626-3488. Located in northeastern SD, 12 miles W of Aberdeen off US 12. GPS: 45.446617, -98.740816. Swimming beach, fishing, boating (rentals). Hiking trail. Open all year. $26 per night. 37 sites with electric. Restrooms; showers. Dump station.

Newton Hills State Park

28767 482nd Ave, Canton, SD 57013. Phone: (605) 987-2263. Located on Lake Lakota, 6 miles S of Canton via CR 135 off US 18. GPS: 43.218855, -96.570210. Swimming beach, fishing, boating (rentals). Hiking, biking (rentals), equestrian trails. Welcome center. Open all year. $26 per night. 112 sites with electric. Restrooms; showers. Dump station.

North Point Recreation Area

38180 297th Ave, Lake Andes, SD 57356. Phone: (605) 487-7046. Located on Missouri River, off US 18, 1 mile NW of Pickstown. GPS: 43.084504, -98.534829. Swimming beach, fishing, boating. Hiking, biking trails. Archery range. Trapshooting/rifle range. Golf course. Marina. Open all year. $26 per night. 115 sites with electric. Restrooms; showers. Dump station.

North Wheeler Recreation Area

29084 N Wheeler Rd, Geddes, SD 57342 Phone: (605) 487-7046. Located on Lake Francis Case, 16 miles S of Platte via Main St off SD 44. GPS: 43.171689, -98.825525. Fishing, boating. Open all year. No reservations accepted. $15 per night. 25 sites with electric. Vault toilets.

Oahe Downstream Recreation Area

20439 Marina Loop Rd, Fort Pierre, SD 57532. Phone: (605) 223-7722. Located on Lake Sharpe on the south side of Oahe Dam, 6 miles N of Fort Pierre. Access via SD 1804 or SD 1806 off US 14. GPS: 44.437109, -100.400003. Swimming beach, fishing, boating. Hiking, biking trails. Disc golf. Archery range. Shooting range. OHV area. Marina. Visitor center. South Dakota prairie butterfly garden located near the main entrance. Three campgrounds open Apr-Nov. $23 per night. 205 sites with electric. Restrooms; showers. Dump station.

Oakwood Lakes State Park

20247 Oakwoood Dr, Bruce, SD 57220. Phone: (605) 627-5441. Located in eastern SD, 20 miles NW of Brookings. Park can be access off US 14, US 81 or I-29, exit 140. GPS: 44.449614, -96.982024. Swimming beach, fishing, boating (rentals). Hiking, biking, equestrian trails. Disc golf. Two campgrounds open all year. $26 per night. 136 sites with electric. Restrooms; showers. Dump station.

Palisades State Park

25491 485th Ave, Garretson, SD 57030. Phone: (605) 594-3824. Located on Split Rock Creek south of Garretson, about 10 miles N of I-90 exit 406 (SD 11 in Corson). GPS: 43.687127, -96.512030. Fishing, boating. Hiking trail. Rock climbing. Scenic overlooks. Open all year. $26 per night. 25 sites with electric. Restrooms;

showers. Dump station. Note: Dump station is located at the entrance to Devil's Gulch (5th St) in Garretson.

Pease Creek Recreation Area

37270 293rd St, Geddes, SD 57342. Phone: (605) 487-7046. Located on Missouri River's Lake Francis Case, 9 miles south of Geddess off SD 1804. GPS: 43.140186, -98.731929. Fishing, boating. Hiking, biking, equestrian trail. Open all year. $22-26 per night. 23 sites with electric. Restrooms; showers. Dump station. Equestrian area with 5 sites, no hookups.

Pelican Lake Recreation Area

17450 450th Ave, Watertown, SD 57201. Phone: (605) 882-5200. Located on Pelican Lake, 9 miles SW of Watertown in eastern SD, off US 212 or US 81. GPS: 44.852243, -97.208575. Swimming beach, fishing, boating (rentals). Hiking, biking, equestrian trails. Bird watching. Observation tower. Archery range. Open all year. $26 per night. 76 sites with electric. Restrooms; showers. Dump station. Equestrian area, 6 sites with electric hookups.

Pickerel Lake Recreation Area

12980 446th Ave, Grenville, SD 57239. Phone: (605) 486-4753. Located on Pickerel Lake in northeastern SD, 10 miles N of Waubay off US 12. GPS: East 45.485459, -97.248399 / West 45.502629, -97.283997. Swimming beach, fishing, boating (rentals). Hiking trails. Two campgrounds open all year. $26 per night. Campground on the east side of the lake has 30 sites with electric and the west side campground has 34 sites with electric. Restrooms; showers. Dump station.

Pierson Ranch Recreation Area

31144 Toe Rd, Yankton, SD 57078. Phone: (605) 668-2985. Located between Chief White Crane and Lewis and Clark Recreation Areas right off SD 52, 4 miles W of Yankton. GPS: 42.875507, -97.480697. Fishing, boating. Hiking, biking trail. Disc golf. Open all year. $26 per night. 67 sites with electric. Restrooms; showers. Dump station.

Platte Creek Recreation Area

35910 282nd St, Platte, SD 57369. Phone: (605) 337-2587. Located on Lake Francis Case on the Missouri River, 14 miles SW of Platte via 367th Ave S and 282nd St W to park entrance. GPS: 43.298444, -98.997307. Swimming beach, fishing, boating. Open all year. $20 per night. 36 sites with electric. Restrooms; showers. Dump station.

Randall Creek Recreation Area

136 Randall Creek Rd, Pickstown, SD 57367. Phone: (605) 487-7046. Located on the banks of the Missouri River, below Fort Randall Dam, 2 mile SW of Pickstown off US 281. GPS: 43.056221, -98.555468. Fishing, boating. Bird watching. Disc golf. Open Apr-Nov. $23 per night. 132 sites with electric. Restrooms; showers. Dump station.

Richmond Lake Recreation Area

37908 Youth Camp Rd, Aberdeen, SD 57401. Phone: (605) 626-3488. Located on Richmond Lake about 11 miles NW of Aberdeen off US 281 or US 12. The recreation area is on N side of lake, campground is on the S side. GPS: Recreation area 45.539900, -98.613313 / Campground 45.532610, -98.619212. Swimming beach, fishing, boating (rentals). Hiking, biking, equestrian trails. Disc golf. Open all year. $26 per night. 24 sites with electric. Restrooms; showers. Dump station.

Rocky Point Recreation Area

18513 Fisherman's Rd, Belle Fourche, SD 57717. Phone: (605) 641-0023. Located on Belle Fourche Reservoir, 8 miles E of Belle Fourche off US 212. GPS: 44.709307, -103.712612. Swimming beach, fishing, boating. Archery range. Dog park. Open all year. $26 per night. 57 sites with electric. Restrooms; showers. Dump station.

Roy Lake State Park

11545 Northside Dr, Lake City, SD 57247. Phone: (605) 448-5701. Located in northeastern SD on Roy Lake, 3 miles SW of Lake City off SD 10. GPS: 45.709642, -97.448789. Swimming beach, fishing, boating (rentals). Hiking trail. Convenience store. Disc golf. Two campgrounds open all year. $26 per night. 87 sites with electric. Restrooms; showers. Dump station.

Sandy Shore Recreation Area

1100 S Lake Dr, Watertown, SD 57201. Phone: (605) 882-5200. Located on Lake Kampeska, off US 212, 5 miles W of Watertown (I-29 exit 177). GPS: 44.893607, -97.241107. Swimming beach, fishing, boating (rentals). Open all year. $22-26 per night. 17 sites, 15 with electric. Restrooms; showers.

Shadehill Recreation Area

19150 Summerville Rd, Shadehill, SD 57638. Phone: (605) 374-5114. Located off SD 73, 15 miles S of Lemmon in northwestern SD on North Fork Grand River (Shadehill Reservoir). GPS: 45.766255, -102.232998. Swimming beach, fishing, boating. Hiking, biking, equestrian trail. Archery range. Open all year. $26 per night. 85 sites with electric. Restrooms; showers. Dump station.

Sheps Canyon Recreation Area

28150 S Boat Ramp Rd, Hot Springs, SD 57747. Phone: (605) 745-6996. Located on Angostura Reservoir, 12 miles south of Hot Springs VIA Sheps Canyon Rd off SD 71. GPS: 43.323456, -103.457637. Swimming, fishing, boating (rentals). Hiking, equestrian trail. Open all year. $22-26 per night. 22 sites with electric. Restrooms; showers. Equestrian area with 11 sites, no hookups. Dump station.

Snake Creek Recreation Area

35316 SD 44, Platte, SD 57369. Phone: (605) 337-2587. Located on Lake Francis Case (Missouri River) on SD 44, 14 miles W of Platte. GPS: 43.390691, -99.119553. Swimming beach, fishing, boating. Hiking trail. Scenic overlook. Marina. Concession, restaurant. Two campgrounds open all year. $26 per night. 127 sites with electric. Restrooms; showers. Dump station.

Springfield Recreation Area

1412 Boat Basin Dr, Springfield, SD 57062. Phone: (605) 668-2985. Located on the Missouri River just E of Springfield off SD 37. GPS: 42.860998, -97.882358. Fishing, boating. Hiking, biking trails. A trail connects the park to the town of Springfield. Golf course. Open all year. $23 per night. 20 sites with electric. Restrooms; showers. Dump station.

Swan Creek Recreation Area

c/o West Whitlock RA, 16157A W Whitlock Rd, Gettysburg, SD 57442. Phone: (605) 765-9410. Located on Lake Oahe (Missouri River) in north-central SD, 8 miles W of Akaska off US 83. GPS: 45.319105, -100.258278. Fishing, boating. Open all year. $20 per night. 26 sites with electric. Restrooms; showers. Dump station.

Union Grove State Park

30828 471st Ave, Beresford, SD 57004. Phone: (605) 987-2263. Located on Brule Creek in southeastern SD, 11 miles S of Beresford off I-29 exit 38 or exit 31 from the south. GPS: 42.920681, -96.785418. Fishing. Hiking, biking, equestrian trails. Bird watching. Open all year. $26 per night. 21 sites with electric. Restrooms; showers. Dump station. Equestrian area, 4 sites with electric.

Walkers Point Recreation Area

6431 Walkers Point Dr, Wentworth, SD 57075. Phone: (605) 256-5003. Located on Lake Madison, 7 miles SE of Madison, off SD 19 and CR 44. GPS: 43.956854, -97.029010. Swimming, fishing, boating, ski beach. Open all year. $26 per night. 42 sites with electric. Restrooms; showers. Dump station.

West Bend Recreation Area

22154 West Bend Rd, Harrold, SD 57536. Phone: (605) 773-2885. Located on Missouri River, off SD 34, 38 miles SE of Pierre. GPS: 44.170981, -99.721212. Swimming beach, fishing, boating, ski beach. Marina. Open all year. $19-23 per night. 122 sites, 112 with electric. Restrooms; showers. Dump station.

West Pollock Recreation Area

Mobridge, SD 57601. Phone: (605) 745-7112. Located on Lake Oahe (Missouri River), 3 miles SW of Pollock via SD 1804 and 104th St. GPS: 45.884557, -100.335807. Swimming, fishing, boating. Open all year. $20 per night. 29 sites with electric. Restrooms; showers. Dump station.

West Whitlock Recreation Area

16157 W Whitlock Rd, Gettysburg, SD 57442. Phone: (605) 765-9410. Located on Lake Oahe (Missouri River), 20 miles W of Gettysburg via SD 1804 off US 212. GPS: 45.048197, -100.266048. Swimming beach, fishing, boating (rentals). Bird watching. Hiking, biking trails. Open all year. $20 per night. 101 sites with electric. Restrooms; showers. Dump station.

Tennessee

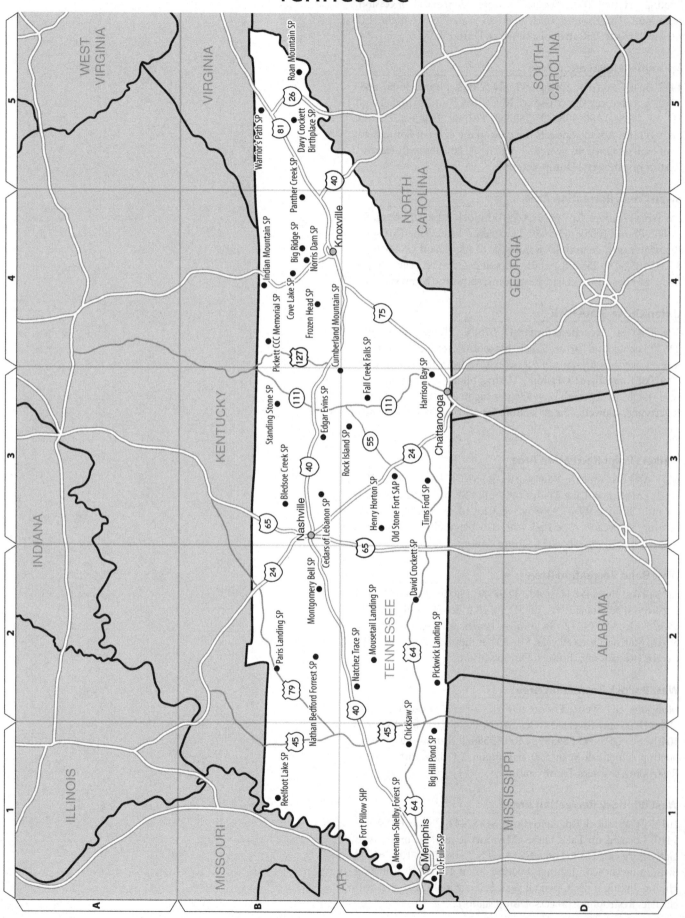

Tennessee

Tennessee State Parks
312 Rosa L Parks Ave
Nashville, TN 37243

Phone: (615) 532-0001
Internet: www.tnstateparks.com
Reservations: Online or call park.

Tennessee Park Locator

Tennessee Parks

Big Hill Pond State Park

1435 John Howell Rd, Pocahontas, TN 38061. Phone: (731) 645-7967. Located 6 miles E of Pocahontas via TN 57. GPS: 35.072578, -88.717019. Fishing, boating (rentals). Hiking, biking, equestrian trails. Visitor center. Observation tower. Open all year. $16-17 per night. 28 sites, no hookups. 20-foot limit. Restrooms; showers.

Big Ridge State Park

1015 Big Ridge Rd, Maynardville, TN 37807. Phone: (865) 992-5523 or (800) 471-5305. Located north of Knoxville, 10 miles W of Maynardville. From Maynardville and TN 61 take TN 144 to TN 170 (Hickory Valley Rd), then TN 61 N to park. GPS: 36.242311, -83.930427. Swimming beach, fishing, boating (rentals). Hiking, biking trails. Visitor center, gift shop. Norton Gristmill built circa 1825 and remnants of Sharp's Station Fort, built in the late 1700s. Open all year. $25-30 per night. 48 sites with water and electric. 35-foot limit. Restrooms; showers. Laundry facilities. Dump station.

Bledsoe Creek State Park

400 Zieglers Fort Rd, Gallatin, TN 37066. Phone: (615) 452-3706. Located on Old Hickory Lake, 5 miles E of Gallatin off TN 25. GPS: 36.378531, -86.360706. Fishing, boating (rentals). Hiking, nature trails. Visitor center, gift shop. Open all year. $26-38 per night. 58 sites with water and electric. 65-foot limit. Restrooms; showers. Laundry facilities. Dump station.

Cedars of Lebanon State Park

328 Cedar Forest Rd, Lebanon, TN 37090. Phone: (615) 443-2769. Located E of Nashville, 7 miles S of Lebanon via US 231. GPS: 36.091857, -86.330767. Swimming. Hiking, equestrian trails. Camp store. Visitor center. Disc golf. Open all year. $26-30 per night. 118 sites with water and electric. 80-foot limit (some 100-foot). Restrooms; showers. Laundry facilities. Dump station.

Chicksaw State Park

20 Cabin Ln, Henderson, TN 38340. Phone: (731) 989-5141. Located on Lake Placid, 8 miles W of Henderson on TN 100. GPS: 35.393106, -88.772310. Swimming beach, fishing, boating (rentals). Hiking, biking, equestrian (horse rentals) trails. Camp store. Visitor center. Golf course. Open all year. $28-34 per night. 53 sites, 26 full hookup, 27 with water and electric. 94-foot limit. Dump station. Restrooms; showers. Equestrian area, 32 sites with water and electric, accommodates RVs and horse trailers.

Cove Lake State Park

110 Cove Lake Ln, Caryville, TN 37714. Phone: (423) 566-9701. After hours camper check in: (423) 494-0806. Located on Cove Lake, 30 miles NW of Knoxville on US 25 W at I-75 exit 134 in Caryville. GPS: 36.309135, -84.210804. Swimming, fishing, boating. Hiking, biking trails. Bird watching. Camp store. Visitor center. BBQ Restaurant. Open all year. $26-30 per night. 98 sites with water and electric. 50-foot limit. Restrooms; showers. Dump station.

Cumberland Mountain State Park

24 Office Dr, Crossville, TN 38555. Phone: (931) 484-6138. Located on Byrd Lake on US 127 about 4.5 miles SE of Crossville. GPS: 35.898329, -84.995101. Swimming, fishing, boating (rentals). Hiking, biking trails. Camp store. Visitor center. Golf

course. Restaurant, gift shop. Open all year. $33-39 per night. 145 sites, 14 full hookup, 131 with water and electric. 45-foot limit. Restrooms; showers. Dump station.

David Crockett Birthplace State Park

1245 Davy Crockett Park Rd, Limestone, TN 37681. Phone: (423) 257-2167; Campground: (423) 257-4500. Located on Nolichucky River in northeastern TN, S of US 321, 3 miles SW of Limestone via Davy Crockett Rd. GPS: 36.209086, -82.658019. Swimming, fishing, boating. Hiking trails. Camp store. 18th-century farmstead with costumed living history interpreters, visitor center. Museum, gift shop. Open all year. $26-37 per night. 71 sites, 54 full hookup, 17 with water and electric. 68-foot limit. Restrooms; showers. Laundry facilities. Dump station.

David Crockett State Park

1400 W Gaines, Lawrenceburg, TN 38464. Phone: (931) 762-9408. Located on Shoal Creek, 1 mile W of Lawrenceburg via TN 242. GPS: 35.242884, -87.354293. Swimming, fishing, boating (rentals). Hiking, biking trails. Visitor center. Museum, gristmill. Restaurant. Two campgrounds. $26-37 per night. Campground #1 open Mar-Nov. 45 sites with water and electric. 52-foot limit. Campground #2 open year-round. 52 sites with water and electric. 57-foot limit. Both have a dump station and restrooms with showers.

Edgar Evins State Park

1630 Edgar Evins State Park Rd, Silver Point, TN 38582. Phone: (931) 646-3080 or (800) 250-8619. Located E of Nashville on Center Hill Lake, 7 miles W of Silver Point via TN 141. GPS: 36.102892, -85.819886. Swimming, fishing, boating (rentals). Hiking trails. Visitor center, observation tower. Marina, restaurant. Open all year. $26-38 per night. 60 sites with water and electric. 33-foot limit (some 40-foot). Restrooms; showers. Laundry facilities. Dump station.

Fall Creek Falls State Park

2009 Village Camp Rd, Spencer, TN 38585. Phone: (423) 881-5298 or (800) 250-8611. Located on Fall Creek Lake 16 miles SE of Spencer on TN 284 via TN 111 or TN 30. GPS: 35.654759, -85.356162. Swimming, fishing, boating. Hiking, biking trails. Nature center. Camp store. Golf course. Rock climbing. Open all year. $23-41 per night. 222 sites in five areas, 92 full hookup, 130 with water and electric. 65-foot limit. Restrooms; showers. Laundry facilities. Dump station.

Fort Pillow State Historic Park

3122 Park Rd, Henning, TN 38041. Phone: (731) 738-5581. Located north of Memphis in western TN, 17 miles W of Henning via TN 371 W and TN 87 W. GPS: 35.642539, -89.830275. Swimming, fishing, boating (rentals). Hiking trails. Camp store. Visitor center, museum. Open all year. $16-29 per night. 21 sites, 6 with water and electric, 15 electric only. 60-foot limit. Restrooms; showers. Dump station.

Frozen Head State Park

964 Flat Fork Rd, Wartburg, TN 37887. Phone: (423) 346-3318. Located in northeastern TN, 6 miles E of Wartburg via TN 62 and Flat Fork Rd. GPS: 36.125369, -84.504941. Swimming, fishing. Hiking, biking trails. Bird watching, observation deck. Visitor center, gift shop. Historic house, tours. Open all year. $16-20 per night. 20 sites, no hookups. 32-foot limit. Restrooms; showers.

Harrison Bay State Park

8411 Harrison Bay Rd, Harrison, TN 37341. Phone: (423) 344-6214. Located on Chickamauga Lake, northeast of Chattanooga, 5 miles N of Harrison via TN 58 and Harrison Bay Rd. GPS: 35.174075, -85.116736. Swimming, fishing, boating (rentals). Hiking, biking trails. Camp store. Marina. Restaurant. Golf course. Open all year. $22-37 per night. 128 sites with water and electric. 65-foot limit (limited). Restrooms; showers. Dump station.

Henry Horton State Park

4209 Nashville Hwy, Chapel Hill, TN 37034. Phone: (931) 364-2222 or (800) 250-8612. Located 40 miles S of Nashville on Duck River, 2 miles S of Chapel Hill on US 31-Alt. GPS: 35.591595, -86.695984. Swimming, tubing (guided river floats), fishing, boating (rentals). Hiking, biking trails. Camp store. Restaurant. Golf course. Disc golf. Trap and skeet range. Open all year. $33-38 per night. 54 sites with water and electric. 90-foot limit (limited). Restrooms; showers. Dump station.

Indian Mountain State Park

143 State Park Circle, Jellico, TN 37762. Phone: (423) 566-5870. Located just W of Jellico (I-75 exit 160) at KY state line; follow signs. GPS: 36.584562, -84.141576. Swimming, fishing, boating (rentals). Hiking trails. Bird watching. Camp store. Visitor center, gift shop. Open all year. $34-37 per night. 47 sites with full hookups. 55-foot limit. Restrooms; showers. Dump station.

Meeman-Shelby Forest State Park

910 Riddick Rd, Millington, TN 38053. Phone: (901) 876-5215. Located on the Mississippi River, 18 miles N of Memphis off US 51. GPS: 35.343649, -90.032358. Swimming, fishing, boating (rentals). Hiking, biking, equestrian trails. Visitor center, gift shop. Nature center. Bird watching. Disc golf. Open all year. $26-30 per night. 49 sites with water and electric. 40-foot limit. Restrooms; showers. Dump station.

Montgomery Bell State Park

1020 Jackson Hill Rd, Burns, TN 37029. Phone: (615) 797-9052. Located 30 miles W of Nashville, 6 miles E of Dickson via US 70 or TN 47. GPS: 36.100957, -87.284479. Swimming beach, fishing, boating (rentals). Hiking, biking trails. Camp store. Restaurant. Golf course. Bird watching. Open all year. $27-37 per night. 93 sites, 40 full hookup, 53 with water and electric. 60-foot limit. Restrooms; showers. Laundry facilities. Dump station.

Mousetail Landing State Park

3 Campground Rd, Linden, TN 37096. Phone: (731) 847-0841. Located in western TN on Tennessee River, 13 miles NW of

Linden on TN 438 off US 412. GPS: 35.655743, -88.006639. Swimming beach, fishing, boating. Hiking, biking trails. Visitor center, gift shop. Two camping areas open all year. $16-30 per night. 46 sites, 19 with water and electric. 90-foot limit (limited). Restrooms; showers. Laundry facilities. Dump station.

Natchez Trace State Park

24845 Natchez Trace Rd, Wildersville, TN 38388. Phone: (731) 968-3742. Located 35 miles east of Jackson on I-40 between Nashville and Memphis. Take Exit 116 from I-40 to the park's main entrance. GPS: 35.796400, -88.264324. Swimming beach, fishing, boating. Hiking, biking, equestrian trails. Camp store. Visitor center, museum, nature center. Restaurant. Equestrian center. Three camping areas.

Pin Oak Campground open all year. $34-40 per night. 77 sites with full hookups. 80-foot limit. Restrooms; showers. Laundry facilities.

Cub Creek Campground, seasonal. $16-35 per night. 23 sites with water and electric. Dump station. 25-foot limit. Restrooms; showers. An additional 46 primitive sites (no hookups) are available with 20-foot limit.

Bucksnort Wrangler Camp accommodates RVs and horse trailers. Open all year. $26-27 per night. 62 sites with water and electric. Restrooms; showers. Dump station.

Nathan Bedford Forrest State Park

1825 Pilot Knob Rd, Eva, TN 38333. Phone: (731) 593-6445. Located on Kentucky Lake in northwestern TN, 8 miles E of Camden via TN 191. GPS: 36.083255, -87.985625. Swimming beach, fishing, boating (rentals). Hiking trails. Camp store. Disc golf. Interpretive center & museum. Open all year. $24-26 per night. 37 sites with water and electric. 40-foot limit. Restrooms; showers. Dump station.

Norris Dam State Park

125 Village Green Circle, Rocky Top, TN 37769. Phone: (865) 425-4500. Located N of Knoxville on Norris Reservoir on US 441, 3 miles E of I-75 exit 128 in Rocky Top. GPS: 36.238441, -84.109446. Swimming, fishing, boating (rentals). Hiking, biking, equestrian trails. Camp store. Marina. Museun, old grist mill. Restaurant. Two camping areas open all year. $27-29 per night. 75 sites with water and electric. 50-foot limit. Restrooms; showers. Laundry facilities. Dump station.

Old Stone Fort State Archaeological Park

732 Stone Fort Dr, Manchester, TN 37355. Phone: (931) 461-7676. Located between Nashville and Chattanooga off US 41 in Manchester; from I-24 use exit 110 or 111. GPS: 35.486899, -86.101628. Fishing, boating. Hiking trails. Camp store. Visitor center, museum, gift shop. Open all year. $26-30 per night. 50 sites with water and electric. 50-foot limit. Restrooms; showers. Dump station.

Panther Creek State Park

2010 Panther Creek Park Rd, Morristown, TN 37814. Phone: (423) 587-7046. Located on Cherokee Reservoir in northeastern TN, 6 miles W of Morristown via TN 342 off US 11E. GPS: 36.206538, -83.406648. Swimming, fishing, boating (rentals). Hiking, biking, equestrian trails. Camp store. Visitor center, gift shop. Disc golf. Open all year. $28-37 per night. 50 sites, 8 full hookup, 42 with water and electric. 65-foot limit. Restrooms; showers. Laundry facilities. Dump station.

Paris Landing State Park

16055 TN 79 N, Buchanan, TN 38222. Phone: (731) 641-4465, reservations (800) 250-8614 or 731-642-4311. Located on the Tennessee River, 18 miles NE of Paris, on US 79. GPS: 36.439404, -88.083038. Swimming beach and pool, fishing, boating. Hiking trails. Camp store. Marina, store, restaurant. Golf course. Open all year. $26-30 per night. 39 sites with water and electric. 38-foot limit. Restrooms; showers. Laundry facilities. Dump station.

Pickett CCC Memorial State Park

4605 Pickett Park Hwy, Jamestown, TN 38556. Phone: (931) 879-5821. Located on TN 154, 12 miles NE of Jamestown (US 127), in Upper Cumberland Mountains. GPS: 36.550897, -84.796410. Swimming beach, fishing, boating. 58 miles of hiking trails in the park and surrounding forest. Dark Sky Park designation. Visitor center. Museum. Park on National Register of Historic Places. Open all year. $16-24 per night. 27 sites, 20 with water and electric, 7 water only. Restrooms; showers. Dump station.

Pickwick Landing State Park

116 State Park Ln, Counce, TN 38326. Phone: (731) 689-3129. Located 14 miles S of Savannah on the Tennessee River, two miles E of Counce via TN 57. GPS: 35.052618, -88.240987. Swimming beach, fishing, boating (rentals). Hiking trails. Visitor center. Golf course. Disc golf. Marina. Restaurant. Open all year. $22-25 per night. 48 sites with water and electric. 70-foot limit. Restrooms; showers. Laundry facilities. Dump station.

Reelfoot Lake State Park

2595 TN 21 E, Tiptonville, TN 38079. Phone: (731) 253-9652. Located in the northwestern corner of TN, 3 miles E of Tiptonville via TN 21. From the E follow TN 22 from Union City to park. GPS: 36.363095, -89.433085. Fishing, boating (rentals). Hiking trails. Visitor center, gift shop. Museum and nature center. Bald eagle and waterfowl tours. Two camping areas open all year. $26-33 per night. 100 sites with water and electric. 35-foot limit. Restrooms; showers. Laundry facilities. Dump station.

Roan Mountain State Park

1015 TN 143, Roan Mountain, TN 37687. Phone: (423) 547-3900 or (800) 250-8620 (reservations). Located in the northeastern tip of TN on Doe River, 2 miles S of Roan Mountain on TN 143. GPS: 36.176583, -82.079570. Swimming, fishing. Hiking, biking trails. Visitor center, museum, gristmill. Miller Farmstead (on National Register of Historic Places). Open all year. $27-40 per night. 86

sites with water and electric. 60-foot limit. Restrooms; showers. Laundry facilities. Dump station.

Rock Island State Park

82 Beach Rd, Rock Island, TN 38581. Phone: (931) 837-4770 or (800) 713-6065 (reservations). Located at confluence of Collins, Rocky and Caney Fork rivers on TN 287 between McMinnville and Sparta; off US 70S at Campaign. GPS: 35.809323, -85.642236. Swimming beach, fishing, boating. Hiking trails. Visitor center, gift shop. Open all year. $34-39 per night. 50 sites, 8 full hookup, 42 with water and electric. 46-foot limit. Restrooms; showers. Dump station.

Standing Stone State Park

1647 Standing Stone Park Hwy, Hilham, TN 38568. Phone: (931) 823-6347 or (800) 713-5157 (reservations). Located on TN 136, 6 miles N of Hilham off TN 85. Or 10 miles NW of Livingston off TN 52. Note: Any vehicle over 30 feet in total length must enter the park via TN 52 due to a bridge in the park that will not accommodate larger vehicles. GPS: 36.471308, -85.416062. Swimming, fishing, boating (rentals). Hiking trails. Visitor center, gift shop. Open all year. $26-29 per night. 36 sites with water and electric. 45-foot limit. Restrooms; showers. Dump station.

T.O. Fuller State Park

1500 W Mitchell Rd, Memphis, TN 38109. Phone: (901) 543-7581. Located within the southern city limits of Memphis via W Mitchell Rd off US 61S (I-55 exit 7). GPS: 35.059392, -90.114316. Swimming. Hiking trails. Bird watching. Visitor center. Interpretive nature and education center. Open all year. $26-28 per night. 45 sites with water and electric. 85-foot limit (limited). Restrooms; showers. Laundry facilities. Dump station.

Tims Ford State Park

570 Tims Ford Dr, Winchester, TN 37398. Phone: (931) 968-3536. Located on Tims Ford Reservoir in south-central TN, 11 miles W of Winchester via Mansford Rd off TN 50 or Awalt Rd off TN 130 S of Tullahoma, TN. GPS: 35.220711, -86.255649. Swimming, fishing, boating (rentals). Hiking, biking trails. Visitor center, gift shop. Golf course. Marinas. Restaurant. Two campgrounds open all year from $26-40 per night.

Tims Ford campground (main park area) 52 sites, 4 full hookup, 48 with water and electric. 40-foot limit. Restrooms; showers. Laundry facilities. Dump station.

Fairview campground (8 miles from main park) 82 sites, 31 full hookup, 51 with water and electric. 65-foot limit. Restrooms; showers. Dump station.

Warrior's Path State Park

490 Hemlock Rd, Kingsport, TN 37663. Phone: (423) 239-8531 or (423) 239-7141 (reservations). Located in the northeastern tip of TN, 2 miles SE of Kingsport on Patrick Henry Reservoir, accessible via TN 36; I-81 exit 59. GPS: 36.498531, -82.487071. Swimming, fishing, boating (rentals). Hiking, biking, equestrian trails. Camp store. Visitor center. Golf course. Disc golf. Marina

(snack bar). Riding Stables (guided trail rides and horse rentals). Open all year. $26-31 per night. 94 sites with water and electric. 40-foot limit. Restrooms; showers. Dump station. An additional 40 sites (no hookups) are available Memorial Day - Labor Day in the overflow campground.

Texas

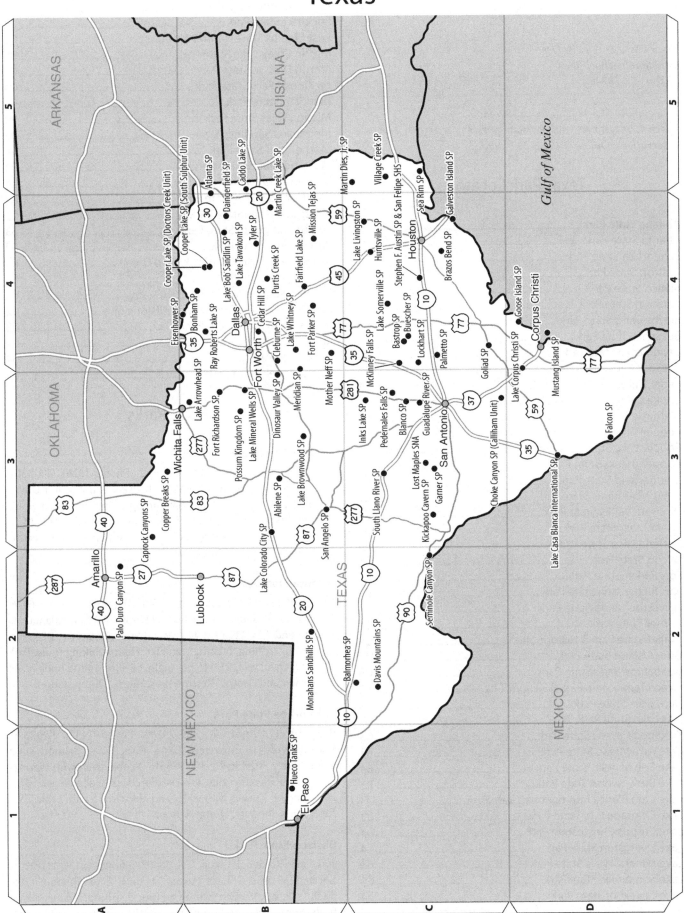

Texas

Texas Parks & Wildlife Dept.
4200 Smith School Road
Austin, TX 78744

Phone: (800) 792-1112 or (512) 389-4800
Internet: www.tpwd.texas.gov/state-parks/
Reservations: Online or (512) 389-8900

Texas Park Locator

Texas Parks

Abilene State Park

150 Park Rd 32, Tuscola, TX 79562. Phone: (325) 572-3204. Located SW of Abilene off FM 89, between US 277 and US 84. GPS: 32.240733, -99.879220. Swimming (pool), fishing, boating. Hiking, biking, nature trails. Park store. Open all year. $15-24 per night. 42 sites, 3 full hookup, 39 with water and electric. Restrooms; showers. Dump station.

Atlanta State Park

927 Park Rd 42, Atlanta, TX 75551. Phone: (903) 796-6476. Located on Wright Patman Lake, 11 miles NW of Atlanta, via FM 96 and FM 1154 off US 59. GPS: 33.229217, -94.246594. Swimming, fishing, boating (rentals). Hiking, biking trails. Park store. Open all year. $14-16 per night. 58 sites, 14 full hookup, 44 with water and electric. Restrooms; showers. Dump station.

Balmorhea State Park

9207 TX 17, Toyahvale, TX 79786. Phone: (432) 375-2370. Located S of I-10 in western TX, 4 miles SW of Balmorhea on TX 17. GPS: 30.945046, -103.786516. Scuba dive, swim (spring-fed pool). Park store, cafe. Observation deck. Open all year. $15-20 per night. 33 sites with water and electric (15 with cable TV). Restrooms; showers. Dump station.

Bastrop State Park

100 Park Rd 1A, Bastrop, TX 78602. Phone: (512) 321-2101. Located 30 miles SE of Austin, 1 mile E of Bastrop. GPS: 30.110438, -97.288438. Swimming (pool), fishing. Hiking, biking trails. Nature hikes and programs. Scenic drive between two state

parks. Park store. Open all year. $20-25 per night. 54 sites, 35 full hookup, 19 with water and electric. Restrooms; showers. Dump station.

Blanco State Park

101 Park Rd 23, Blanco, TX 78606. Phone: (830) 833-4333. Located on S side of Blanco on the Blanco River, 40 miles N of San Antonio on US 281. GPS: 30.090647, -98.424131. Swimming (river), fishing, boating (electric motors only). Nature trail, scenic overlook. Park store. Open all year. $20-25 per night. 29 sites, 17 full hookup, 12 with water and electric. Restrooms; showers. Dump station.

Bonham State Park

1363 State Park Rd 24, Bonham, TX 75418. Phone: (903) 583-5022. Located NE of Dallas and south of US 82, 1.5 miles SE of Bonham via TX 78 to FM 271. GPS: 33.547119, -96.144903. Swimming, fishing, boating. Hiking, biking trails. Open all year. $20-24 per night. 20 sites, 8 full hookup, 12 with water and electric. Restrooms; showers. Dump station.

Brazos Bend State Park

21901 FM 762, Needville, TX 77461. Phone: (979) 553-5101. Located on Brazos River, SW of Houston between TX 36 and TX 288, 13 miles W of Rosharon. GPS: 29.371473, -95.638603. Fishing. Hiking, biking, equestrian trails. Park store. Nature center, trail. Open all year. $20-25 per night. 73 sites with water and electric. Restrooms; showers. Laundry facility. Dump station.

Buescher State Park

100 Park Rd 1E, Smithville, TX 78957. Phone: (512) 237-2241. Located 2 miles N of Smithville via FM 153 off TX 71. GPS: 30.038387, -97.158320. Fishing, paddle boating (rentals). Hiking, biking trails. Park store. Scenic drive between two state parks. Open all year. $15-18 per night. 48 sites, 32 with water and electric, 16 water only. Restrooms; showers. Dump station.

Caddo Lake State Park

245 Park Rd 2, Karnack, TX 75661. Phone: (903) 679-3351. Located 13 miles NE of Marshall off TX 43. GPS: 32.678709, -94.175548. Fishing, paddle boating (rentals). Hiking trails. Interpretive center, trail. Park store. Open all year. $10-20 per night. 26 sites, 8 full hookup, 18 with water and electric. Additional 20 sites available for pop-ups and small trailers. Restrooms; showers. Dump station.

Caprock Canyons State Park

850 Caprock Canyon Rd, Quitaque, TX 79255. Phone: (806) 455-1492. Located in the Panhandle of TX, 4 miles N of Quitaque via Ranch Rd 1065 off TX 86. GPS: 34.409268, -101.053328. Swimming, fishing, boating. Hiking, biking, equestrian trails. Interpretive center, scenic overlook, historical marker. Park store. Scenic drive. Open all year. $14-22 per night. 44 sites, 35 with water and electric. Restrooms; showers. Dump station.

Cedar Hill State Park

1570 W FM 1382, Cedar Hill, TX 75104. Phone: (972) 291-3900. Located on Joe Pool Lake, 10 miles SW of Dallas between I-20 and US 67. GPS: 32.621120, -96.978621. Swimming, fishing, boating. Hiking, biking trails. Historical building. Open all year. $25-30 per night. 350 sites, 150 full hookup, 200 with water and electric. Restrooms; showers. Dump station.

Choke Canyon State Park (Calliham Unit)

358 Recreation Rd 8, Calliham, TX 78007. Phone: (361) 786-3868. Located on Choke Canyon Reservoir between San Antonio and Corpus Christi, 12 miles W of Three Rivers on TX 72. GPS: 28.464509, -98.355080. Swimming, fishing, boating. Hiking trails. Wildlife watching, birding. Scenic overlook. Open all year. $22 per night. 40 sites with water and electric. Restrooms; showers. Dump station.

Cleburne State Park

5800 Park Rd 21, Cleburne, TX 76033. Phone: (817) 645-4215. Located 10 miles SW of Cleburne via Park Rd 21 off US 67. GPS: 32.252445, -97.548882. Swimming, fishing, no-wake boating (rentals). Hiking, biking trails. Park store. Open all year. $20-30 per night. 58 sites, 27 full hookup, 31 with water and electric. Restrooms; showers. Dump station.

Cooper Lake State Park (Doctors Creek Unit)

1664 FM 1529 S, Cooper, TX 75432. Phone: (903) 395-3100. Located on NE side of Cooper Lake, 3 miles SE of Cooper off TX 154. GPS: 33.348995, -95.662333. Swimming, fishing, boating. Hiking, biking trails. Park store. Open all year. $20 per night. 39 sites with water and electric. Restrooms; showers. Dump station.

Cooper Lake State Park (South Sulphur Unit)

1690 FM 3505, Sulphur Springs, TX 75482. Phone: (903) 945-5256. Located on SE side of Cooper Lake, about 14 miles NW of Sulphur Springs via FM 71 off TX 19/154. GPS: 33.286546, -95.657105. Swimming, fishing, boating (rentals). Hiking, biking, equestrian trails. Park store. Open all year. $20 per night. 82 sites with water and electric. Restrooms; showers. 15 site equestrian area with electric hookup. Dump station.

Copper Breaks State Park

777 Park Rd 62, Quanah, TX 79252. Phone: (940) 839-4331. Located 12 miles S of Quanah, off TX 6. GPS: 34.112836, -99.732112. Swimming, fishing, no-wake boating. Hiking, biking, equestrian trails. Interpretive center, trail. Park store. International Dark Sky Park, star viewing area. Open all year. $12-20 per night. 49 sites, 24 with water and electric, 11 water only. Restrooms; showers. Dump station.

Daingerfield State Park

455 Park Rd 17, Daingerfield, TX 75638. Phone: (903) 645-2921. Located E of Dallas, 3 miles SE of Daingerfield on TX 11/49. GPS: 33.012452, -94.686730. Swimming, fishing, boating (rentals). Hiking trails. Park store. Interpretive center. Open all year. $20-25 per night. 40 sites with full hookups. Restrooms; showers.

Davis Mountains State Park

TX 118 N, Park Rd 3, Fort Davis, TX 79734. Phone: (432) 426-3337. Located 3 miles NW of Fort Davis on TX 118. GPS: 30.599832, -103.926794. Hiking, biking, equestrian trails. Park store. Interpretive center, scenic overlook. Open all year. $15-25 per night. 93 sites, 26 full hookup, 34 with water and electric. Restrooms; showers. Dump station.

Dinosaur Valley State Park

1629 Park Rd 59, Glen Rose, TX 76043. Phone: (254) 897-4588. Located 4 miles W of Glen Rose via FM 205 off US 67. GPS: 32.246691, -97.814201. Fishing, boating (rentals). Hiking, equestrian trails. Dinosaur tracks. Park store. Open all year. $25 per night. 8 sites with water and electric. Restrooms; showers. Dump station.

Eisenhower State Park

50 Park Rd 20, Denison, TX 75020. Phone: (903) 465-1956. Located off FM 1310 on Lake Texoma, NW of Denison. GPS: 33.810172, -96.599125. Swimming, fishing, boating (rentals). Hiking, biking, OHV trails. Park store. Marina. Open all year. $12-23 per night. 154 sites, 50 full hookup, 45 with water and electric, 47 water only. Restrooms; showers. Dump station.

Fairfield Lake State Park

123 State Park Rd 64, Fairfield, TX 75840. Phone: (903) 389-4514. Located on Fairfield Lake, 6 miles NE of Fairfield (I-45 exit 197) on FM 3285 via Main St/FM 488 and FM 1124. GPS: 31.765342, -96.074344. Swimming, fishing, boating (rentals). Hiking, biking, equestrian trails. Park store. Open all year. $15-20 per night. 126 sites, 93 with water and electric, 33 water only. Restrooms; showers. Dump station.

Falcon State Park

146 Park Rd 46, Falcon Heights, TX 78584. Phone: (956) 848-5327. Located in southern TX, near Mexico border, 2 miles NW of Falcon Heights via FM 2098. GPS: 26.579410, -99.136212. Swimming, fishing, boating. Hiking trail. Bird watching. Open all year. $10-18 per night. 98 sites, 31 full hookup, 31 with water and electric. Restrooms; showers. Dump station.

Fort Parker State Park

194 Park Rd 28, Mexia, TX 76667. Phone: (254) 562-5751. Located on Fort Parker Lake 7 miles S of Mexia on TX 14. GPS: 31.592709, -96.524050. Swimming, fishing, boating (rentals). Hiking, biking trails. Nature center. Open all year. $12-20 per night. 34 sites, 24 with water and electric. Restrooms; showers. Dump station.

Fort Richardson State Park

228 State Park Rd 61, Jacksboro, TX 76458. Phone: (940) 567-3506. Located NW of Fort Worth on Lost Creek Reservoir off US 281/380, about 1 mile S of Jacksboro. GPS: 33.207044, -98.155523. Swimming, fishing. Hiking, biking, equestrian trails. Park store. Interpretive center. Historic site, buildings. Open all year. $20-25 per night. 41 sites, 4 full hookup, 37 with water and electric. Restrooms; showers. Dump station.

Galveston Island State Park

14901 FM 3005, Galveston, TX 77554. Phone: (409) 737-1222. Located in Galveston near I-45 exit 1A on Seawall Blvd on Gulf of Mexico. GPS: 29.198803, -94.956456. Swimming, fishing, boating. Hiking, biking trails. Park store. Interpretive center. Observation tower. Open all year. $15-20 per night. 30 sites, 20 with water and electric, 10 water only. Restrooms; showers. Dump station.

Garner State Park

234 RR 1050, Concan, TX 78838. Phone: (830) 232-6132. Located in southern TX on the Frio River, 9 miles N of Concan, on US 83. GPS: 29.589403, -99.746633. Swim/float, fishing, boating (rentals). Hiking, biking trails. Scenic overlook. Miniature golf. Concessionaire; grill, snacks. Park store. Nature center. Open all year. $15-35 per night. 347 sites, 12 full hookup, 211 with water and electric, 124 water only (20-foot limit). Restrooms; showers. Dump station.

Goliad State Park & Historic Site

108 Park Rd 6, Goliad, TX 77963. Phone: (361) 645-3405. Located in southern TX, 1/4 mile S of Goliad on US 183 on San Antonio River. GPS: 28.656483, -97.385229. Swimming, fishing, boating (paddle). Hiking, biking, nature trails. Bird watching. Park store. Historic sites in park and nearby. Open all year. $20-25 per night. 34 sites, 20 full hookup, 14 with water and electric. Restrooms; showers. Dump station.

Goose Island State Park

202 S Palmetto St, Rockport, TX 78382. Phone: (361) 729-2858. Located next to the IC Waterway on St. Charles & Aransas bays, 10 miles NE of Rockport, off TX 35. GPS: 28.137969, -96.984298. Fishing, boating. Hiking trails. Bird watching. Park store. Open all year. $20-22 per night. 101 sites with water and electric. Restrooms; showers. Dump station.

Guadalupe River State Park

3350 Park Rd 31, Spring Branch, TX 78070. Phone: (830) 438-2656. Located on the Guadalupe River, 30 miles N of San Antonio on State Park Rd 31 off TX 46. GPS: 29.852112, -98.508212. Swim/tube, fishing, boating. Hiking, biking, equestrian trails. Bird watching. Park store. Interpretive center. Open all year. $20-24 per night. 85 sites with water and electric. Restrooms; showers. Dump station.

Hueco Tanks State Park & Historic Site

6900 Hueco Tanks Rd 1, El Paso, TX 79938. Phone: (915) 857-1135. Located 32 miles E of El Paso; US 62/180 east to Ranch Rd 2775. GPS: 31.926465, -106.042449. Hiking trails. Guided and self-guided tours. Rock climbing. Park store. Interpretive center. Open all year. $12-16 per night. 20 sites, 16 with water and electric, 6 water only. Restrooms; showers. Dump station.

Huntsville State Park

565 Park Rd 40 W, Huntsville, TX 77340. Phone: (936) 295-5644. Located 6 miles SW of Huntsville, off I-45 exit 109. GPS: 30.628390, -95.526001. Swimming, fishing, boating (rentals).

Hiking, biking trails. Park store. Nature center. Open all year. $15-25 per night. 160 sites, 23 full hookup, 77 with water and electric, 60 water only. Restrooms; showers. Dump station.

Inks Lake State Park

3630 Park Rd 4 W, Burnet, TX 78611. Phone: (512) 793-2223. Located 9 miles W of Burnet off TX 29. GPS: 30.756132, -98.373661. Swimming, scuba diving, fishing, boating (rentals). Hiking trails. Bird watching. Park store. Open all year. $16-23 per night. 174 sites, 125 with water and electric, 49 water only (26-foot limit). Restrooms; showers. Dump station.

Kickapoo Cavern State Park

20939 RR 674, Brackettville, TX 78832. Phone: (830) 563-2342. Located 21 miles N of Brackettville via Ranch Rd 674. GPS: 29.599118, -100.422949. Hiking, biking trails. Scenic overlook. Bird watching. Cave tours. Open all year. $12-20 per night. 15 sites, 5 full hookup. Restrooms; showers. Dump station.

Lake Arrowhead State Park

229 Park Rd 63, Wichita Falls, TX 76310. Phone: (940) 528-2211. Located 13 miles SE of Wichita Falls on FM 1954. Access FM 1954 from US 281 or US 287. GPS: 33.759593, -98.397123. Swimming, fishing, boating. Hiking, biking, equestrian trails. Disc golf. Park store. Open all year. $12-22 per night. 67 sites, 48 with water and electric. Restrooms; showers. Dump station.

Lake Bob Sandlin State Park

341 State Park Rd 2117, Pittsburg, TX 75686. Phone: (903) 572-5531. Located in northeast TX, 10 miles NW of Pittsburg via TX 11 and FM 21 N. GPS: 33.055240, -95.103180. Swimming, fishing, boating (rentals; kayaks). Hiking, biking trails. Bird watching. Park store. Historical cemetery. Open all year. $18 per night. 75 sites with water and electric. Restrooms; showers. Dump station.

Lake Brownwood State Park

200 State Hwy Park Rd 15, Brownwood, TX 76801. Phone: (325) 784-5223. Located in central TX, 19 miles N of Brownwood via TX 279 and Park Rd 15. GPS: 31.855349, -99.044106. Swimming, fishing, boating. Hiking, biking trails. Park store. Open all year. $15-25 per night. 66 sites, 20 full hookup, 46 with water and electric (11 sites have 27-foot limit). Restrooms; showers. Dump station.

Lake Casa Blanca International State Park

5102 Bob Bullock Loop, Laredo, TX 78044. Phone: (956) 725-3826. Located on Lake Casa Blanca, in northeast Laredo on US 59. GPS: 27.539342, -99.451365. Swimming, fishing, boating (rentals). Hiking, biking trails. Scenic overlook. Convenience store. Open all year. $18-21 per night. 66 sites, 11 full hookup, 55 with water and electric. Restrooms; showers. Dump station.

Lake Colorado City State Park

4582 FM 2836, Colorado City, TX 79512. Phone: (325) 728-3931. Located south of I-20 in central TX, 7 miles SW of Colorado City via TX 163. GPS: 32.316638, -100.935857. Swimming, fishing,

boating (rentals). Hiking trails. Open all year. $15-22 per night. 112 sites, 78 with water and electric, 34 water only. Restrooms; showers. Dump station.

Lake Corpus Christi State Park

23194 Park Rd 25, Mathis, TX 78368. Phone: (361) 547-2635. Located 4 miles southwest of Mathis off TX 359. GPS: 28.063322, -97.871048. Swimming, fishing, boating (rentals). Hiking, biking trails. Scenic overlook. Park store. Open all year. $10-25 per night. 108 sites, 26 full hookup, 23 with water and electric, 59 water only. Restrooms; showers. Dump station.

Lake Livingston State Park

300 Park Rd 65, Livingston, TX 77351. Phone: (936) 365-2201. Located 6 mile S of Livingston via FM 1988 off US 59. GPS: 30.656777, -95.000959. Swimming, fishing, boating (rentals). Hiking, biking trails. Park store. Interpretive center. Open all year. $18-28 per night. 127 sites, 75 full hookup, 52 with water and electric. Restrooms; showers. Dump station.

Lake Mineral Wells State Park

100 Park Rd 71, Mineral Wells, TX 76067. Phone: (940) 328-1171. Located 4 miles E of Mineral Wells off US 180. GPS: 32.812223, -98.043490. Swimming, fishing, boating (rentals). Hiking, biking, equestrian trails. Rock climbing. Wildlife viewing blind. Open all year. $14-26 per night. 108 sites, 77 with water and electric, 31 water only. Restrooms; showers. Dump station.

Lake Somerville State Park

Located in east-central Texas between Austin and Houston. Campgrounds are located in two park units. Birch Creek Unit is on the north side of the lake, while Nails Creek Unit is on the southwest side. Both units offer access to the lake for swimming, fishing and boating (rentals). Plus nearly 40-miles of hiking, biking and equestrian trails. Park store in each unit.

Birch Creek Unit: 14222 Park Rd 57, Somerville, TX 77879. Phone: (979) 535-7763. Located 15 miles W of Somerville via TX 36, FM 60, and Park Road 57. GPS: 30.309451, -96.635309. Open all year. $12-20 per night. 109 sites, 99 with water and electric. Restrooms; showers. Dump station.

Nails Creek Unit: 6280 FM 180, Ledbetter, TX 78946. Phone: (979) 289-2392. Located 15 miles NE of Ledbetter via FM 180 off US 290. GPS: 30.290380, -96.667817. Open all year. $12-20 per night. 50 sites, 20 with water and electric, 20 electric only. Restrooms; showers. Dump station.

Lake Tawakoni State Park

10822 FM 2475, Wills Point, TX 75169. Phone: (903) 560-7123. Located 10 miles N of Wills Point via FM 47 N and FM 2475 N. GPS: 32.841298, -95.994045. Swimming, fishing, boating. Hiking, biking trails. Lake Tawakoni Trading Post store. Open all year. $20-24 per night. 78 sites, 16 full hookup, 60 with water and electric, 2 electric only. Restrooms; showers. Dump station.

Lake Whitney State Park

433 FM 1244, Whitney, TX 76692. Phone: (254) 694-3793. Located S of Fort Worth, 3 miles W of Whitney on FM 1244. GPS: 31.931125, -97.356511. Swimming, fishing, boating. Hiking, biking trails. Park store. Open all year. $14-24 per night. 137 sites, 43 full hookup, 31 water and electric, 63 water only. Restrooms; showers. Dump station.

Lockhart State Park

2012 State Park Rd, Lockhart, TX 78644. Phone: (512) 398-3479. Located S of Lockhart, off FM 20, via US 183. GPS: 29.855448, -97.697482. Swimming (pool), fishing. Hiking, biking trails. Scenic overlook. Golf course (golf clubs rental). Park store/Pro shop. Open all year. $20-24 per night. 20 sites, 10 full hookup, 10 with water and electric. Restrooms; showers. Dump station.

Lost Maples State Natural Area

37221 FM 187, Vanderpool, TX 78885. Phone: (830) 966-3413. Located NW of San Antonio on the Sabinal River, 5 miles N of Vanderpool on FM 187. GPS: 29.806579, -99.570585. Fishing. Hiking, biking trails. Scenic overlook. Bird viewing blind. Interpretive center. Open all year. $20 per night. 28 sites with water and electric. Restrooms; showers. Dump station.

Martin Creek Lake State Park

9515 CR 2181 D, Tatum, TX 75691. Phone: (903) 836-4336. Located in eastern TX south of I-20, 5 miles SW of Tatum off TX 43. GPS: 32.278098, -94.566089. Swimming, fishing, boating. Hiking, biking trails. Open all year. $15-19 per night. 58 sites with water and electric. Restrooms; showers. Dump station.

Martin Dies, Jr. State Park

634 Park Rd 48 S, Jasper, TX 75951. Phone: (409) 384-5231. Located on B.A. Steinhagen Reservoir, 11 miles W of Jasper on US 190. GPS: 30.852769, -94.166903. Swimming, fishing, boating (rentals). Hiking, biking (rentals) trails. Park store. Open all year. $14-20 per night. 173 sites, 122 with water and electric. Restrooms; showers. Dump station.

McKinney Falls State Park

5808 McKinney Falls Pkwy, Austin, TX 78744. Phone: (512) 243-1643. Located in SE Austin, south of TX 71 and between US 183 and I-35. GPS: 30.180801, -97.721885. Swimming, fishing. Hiking, biking trails. Park store. Historic ruins. Open all year. $20-24 per night. 81 sites with water and electric. Restrooms; showers. Dump station.

Meridian State Park

173 Park Rd 7, Meridian, TX 76665. Phone: (254) 435-2536. Located S of Fort Worth, 3 miles SW of Meridian off TX 22. GPS: 31.892445, -97.695696. Swimming, fishing, boating (rentals). Hiking trails. Scenic overlook, bird blind. Park store. Open all year. $20-25 per night. 14 sites, 8 full hookup, 6 with water and electric. 20-foot limit. Restrooms; showers. Dump station.

Mission Tejas State Park

19343 TX 21 E, Grapeland, TX 75844. Phone: (936) 687-2394. Located midway between Dallas and Houston, 17 miles E of Grapeland via FM 227 and TX 21. GPS: 31.542192, -95.231981. Fishing. Wildlife viewing, bird blind. Hiking trails. Park store, visitor center. Open all year. $10-15 per night. 14 sites, 12 with water and electric. Restrooms; showers. Dump station.

Monahans Sandhills State Park

Park Rd 41, Monahans, TX 79756. Phone: (432) 557-3479. Located SW of Odessa, 5 miles E of Monahans; I-20 exit 86, follow signs to Park. GPS: 31.618541, -102.811575. Interpretive trail. Explore sand dunes on foot or horse back. Park store, visitor center. Open all year. $15 per night. 26 sites with water and electric. Restrooms; showers. Dump station. Additional 3 site equestrian area, water available (no tents).

Mother Neff State Park

1921 Park Rd 14, Moody, TX 76557. Phone: (254) 853-2389. Located midway between Fort Worth and Austin, 7 miles W of Moody via FM 107 off TX 317. GPS: 31.332748, -97.464763. Hiking trails. Park store. Interpretive/Visitor center. Natural scenic area, wildlife viewing area. Open all year. $12-25 per night. 35 sites, 20 full hookup. Restrooms; showers.

Mustang Island State Park

9394 TX 361, Corpus Christi, TX 78418. Phone: (361) 749-5246. Located on the Gulf of Mexico E of Corpus Christi; access via JFK Causeway to TX 361. GPS: 27.673720, -97.175016. Swimming, fishing, boating (paddling trail). Hiking, biking trails. Park store. Open all year. $10-20 per night. 48 sites with water and electric. Restrooms; showers. Dump station. 50 additional drive-up primitive sites (on Gulf, subject to high tides).

Palmetto State Park

78 Park Rd 11 S, Gonzales, TX 78629. Phone: (830) 672-3266. Located on San Marcos River, 10 miles NW of Gonzales off FM 1586 via US 183. GPS: 29.597567, -97.584540. Swim/tube, fishing, boating (rentals). Hiking, biking (rentals) trails. Scenic overlook. Park store. Open all year. $12-20 per night. 37 sites, 1 full hookup, 17 with water and electric. Restrooms; showers. Dump station.

Palo Duro Canyon State Park

11450 Park Rd 5, Canyon, TX 79015. Phone: (806) 488-2227. Located in northern Panhandle, 12 miles E of Canyon (I-27 exit 106) on TX 217. GPS: 34.985725, -101.702923. Palo Duro Canyon is second largest canyon in US. 30 miles of hiking, biking and equestrian trails. Visitor/Interpretive center, park store. Trading Post. Riding stable (canyon tours). Scenic overlook, historic marker. TEXAS Outdoor musical at amphitheater. Open all year. $26 per night. 97 sites with water and electric. Restrooms; showers. Dump station.

Pedernales Falls State Park

2585 Park Rd 6026, Johnson City, TX 78636. Phone: (830) 868-7304. Located 30 miles W of Austin on the Pedernales River, 9 miles E of Johnson City via FM 2766. GPS: 30.278085, -98.256541. Swim/tube, fishing, boating. Hiking, biking, equestrian trails. Park store. Scenic overlook, bird blind. Open all year. $20 per night. 69 sites with water and electric. Restrooms; showers. Dump station.

Possum Kingdom State Park

3901 State Park Rd, Caddo, TX 76429. Phone: (940) 549-1803. Located on Possum Kingdom Lake N of US 180, 14 miles NW of Caddo on State Park Rd 33. GPS: 32.854034, -98.574334. Swimming, fishing, boating (rentals). Scuba dive, snorkel. Hiking, biking trails. Marina, park store. Open all year. $12-25 per night. 114 sites (some close for the winter), 61 with water and electric. Restrooms; showers. Dump station.

Purtis Creek State Park

14225 FM 316 N, Eustace, TX 75124. Phone: (903) 425-2332. Located an hour SE of Dallas on Purtis Creek, 4 miles N of Eustace via FM 316. GPS: 32.353391, -95.993501. Swimming, fishing, boating. Hiking, biking trails. Park store. Open all year. $20 per night. 57 sites with water and electric. Restrooms; showers. Dump station.

Ray Roberts Lake State Park (Two Units)

Located an hour N of Dallas/Fort Worth area on Ray Roberts Lake. Campgrounds are located in two park units. Isle du Bois Unit is on the south side of the lake, while Johnson Branch Unit is on the north side. Both units offer access to the lake for swimming, fishing and boating. Plus miles of hiking, biking and equestrian trails. Full-service marinas near both units.

Isle du Bois Unit, 100 PW 4137, Pilot Point, TX 76258. Phone: (940) 686-2148. Located 5 miles SW of Pilot Point via FM 455 off US 377. GPS: 33.365641, -97.012132 Open all year. $15-26 per night. 129 sites, 102 with water and electric, 13 electric only. Restrooms; showers. Dump station.

Johnson Branch Unit, 100 PW 4153, Valley View, TX 76272. Phone: (940) 637-2294. Located 10 miles SE of Valley View via FM 3002 (Lone Oak Rd) off I-35, exit 483. GPS: 33.429876, -97.056585. Open all year. $25-26 per night. 104 sites, 93 with water and electric, 11 electric only. Restrooms; showers. Dump station.

San Angelo State Park

362 S FM 2288, San Angelo, TX 76901. Phone: (325) 949-4757. Located on O.C. Fisher Reservoir, just W of San Angelo on FM 2288, off US 67 or US 87 (two entrances). GPS: 31.463852, -100.507993. Swimming, fishing, boating. Hiking, biking, equestrian trails (50 miles). Scenic overlook. Wildlife observation area. Open all year. $20 per night. 71 sites with water and electric. 10 equestrian sites with electric. Restrooms; showers. Dump station.

Sea Rim State Park

19335 S Gulfway Dr, Sabine Pass, TX 77655. Phone: (409) 971-2559. Located on TX 87, on Gulf of Mexico, 20 miles S of Port Arthur. GPS: 29.676595, -94.044125. Swimming, fishing, boating

(kayak or canoe; rentals). Interpretive trail. Horseback riding. Open all year. $10-20 per night. 15 sites with water and electric. 75 primitive drive-up sites on the beach, non-reservable. Restrooms; rinse showers. Dump station.

Seminole Canyon State Park & Historic Site

PO Box 820, Comstock, TX 78837. Phone: (432) 292-4464. Located 9 miles W of Comstock (about 30 miles NW of Del Rio) on US 90. GPS: 29.705304, -101.318805. Hiking, biking trails. Guided interpretive trail, pictograph site, scenic overlook. Park store. Visitor center. Open all year. $10-20 per night. 46 sites, 23 with water and electric. Restrooms; showers. Dump station.

South Llano River State Park

1927 Park Rd 73, Junction, TX 76849. Phone: (325) 446-3994. Located on South Llano River, 7 miles SW of Junction (I-10 exit 456) on US 377. GPS: 30.445816, -99.804548. Swim/float, fishing, boating. Hiking, biking trails. Scenic overlook. Wildlife viewing, four bird blinds. Park store. International Dark Sky Park. Open all year. $20 per night. 58 sites with water and electric. Restrooms; showers. Dump station.

Stephen F. Austin State Park

Park Rd 38, San Felipe, TX 77473. Phone: (979) 885-3613. Located on Brazos River 50 miles W of Houston, in northern San Felipe. GPS: 29.811560, -96.108026. Hiking, biking trails. Scenic overlook, wildlife viewing. Park store. Interpretive center, statue/museum. Open all year. $28 per night. 38 full hookup sites. Restrooms; showers. Dump station.

Tyler State Park

789 Park Rd 16, Tyler, TX 75706. Phone: (903) 597-5338. Located 8 miles N of Tyler on FM 14 (State Park Hwy), off I-20 exit 562. GPS: 32.481703, -95.281700. Swimming, fishing, boating (rentals). Hiking, biking trails. Nature trails, bird blind. Park store. Open all year. $18-30 per night. 107 sites, 57 full hookup, 20 water and electric, 30 water only. Restrooms; showers. Dump station.

Village Creek State Park

8854 Park Rd 74, Lumberton, TX 77657. Phone: (409) 755-7322. Located on Village Creek in Lumberton, 10 miles N of Beaumont off US 96. GPS: 30.250594, -94.178905. Swimming, fishing, boating. Hiking, biking trails. Nature center. Park store. Open all year. $16 per night. 25 sites with water and electric. Restrooms; showers. Dump station.

Utah

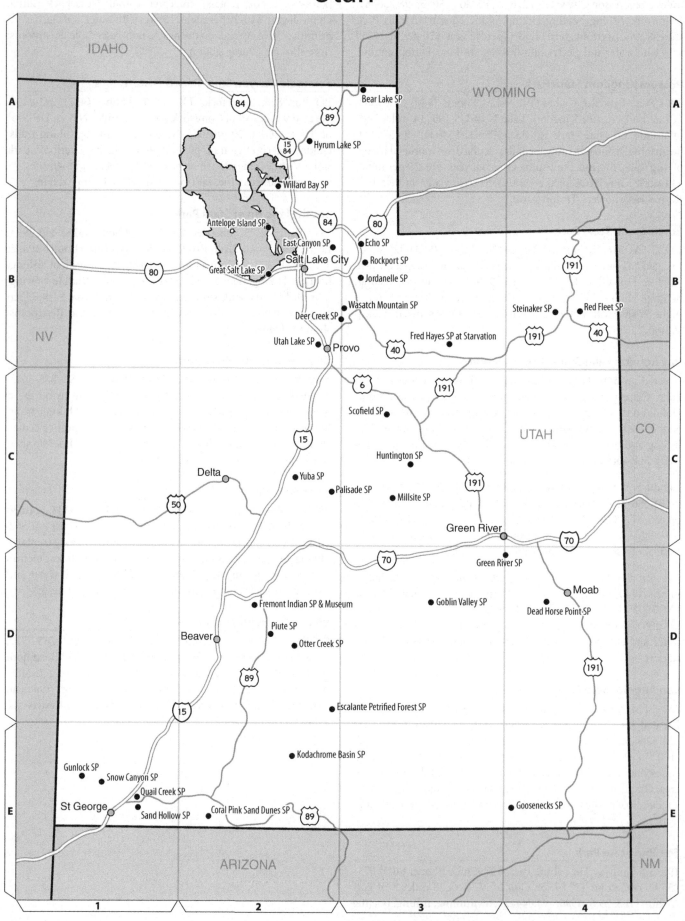

IDAHO

WYOMING

84

89

Bear Lake SP

15
84

Hyrum Lake SP

Willard Bay SP

84

80

Antelope Island SP

East Canyon SP

Echo SP

Salt Lake City

Rockport SP

191

80

Great Salt Lake SP

Jordanelle SP

NV

Wasatch Mountain SP

Steinaker SP

Red Fleet SP

Deer Creek SP

40

Utah Lake SP

Provo

Fred Hayes SP at Starvation

191

40

6

191

Scofield SP

UTAH

CO

15

Huntington SP

Delta

Yuba SP

191

Palisade SP

Millsite SP

50

Green River

70

70

Green River SP

Moab

Fremont Indian SP & Museum

Goblin Valley SP

Dead Horse Point SP

Piute SP

Beaver

Otter Creek SP

89

191

15

Escalante Petrified Forest SP

Kodachrome Basin SP

Gunlock SP

Snow Canyon SP

Quail Creek SP

St George

Goosenecks SP

Sand Hollow SP

Coral Pink Sand Dunes SP

89

ARIZONA

NM

Utah

Utah State Parks
1594 W North Temple, Suite 116
Salt Lake City, UT 84114

Information: (801) 538-7220
Internet: www.stateparks.utah.gov
Reservations: Online or (800) 322-3770

Utah Park Locator

Utah Parks

Antelope Island State Park

4528 W1700 S, Syracuse, UT 84075. Phone: (801) 773-2941. Located in the Great Salt Lake (via Causeway) 14 miles W of I-15 (exit 332) in Ogden via Antelope Dr. GPS: 41.060071, -112.237075. Swimming beach (restrooms with flush toilets and showers), fishing, boating (rentals). Hiking, biking, equestrian trails. Marina. Restaurant. Visitor center, gift shop. Two RV camping areas open all year. $20-40 per night. 46 sites, no hookups. Restrooms (vault toilets). Dump station.

Bear Lake State Park

940 N Bear Lake Blvd, Garden City, UT 84028. Phone: (435) 946-3343. Two locations on Bear Lake located at UT/ID state line. The State Marina is located on US 89, 2 miles N of Garden City. GPS: 41.963766, -111.399229. Rendezvous Beach, on the south shore, is near Laketown on UT 30. GPS: 41.845948, -111.350810. Swimming, fishing, boating (rentals). Hiking, biking trails. Food concession. Marina. Visitor center. Open all year. $18-35 per night. 130 sites, 101 full hookup, 29 with water and electric. Restrooms; showers. Dump station.

Coral Pink Sand Dunes State Park

PO Box 95, Kanab, UT 84741. Phone: (435) 648-2800. Located in southern UT, west of Kanab off US 89 via Hancock Rd. GPS: 37.037689, -112.731975. Hiking trails. OHV riding. Visitor center. Open all year. $35-50 per night. 22 sites, 10 with electric. Most are 40-foot or longer pull-through sites. Restrooms; showers. Dump station.

Dead Horse Point State Park

PO Box 609, Moab, UT 84532. Phone: (435) 259-2614. Located W of Moab on UT 313, 18 miles S off US 191. GPS: 38.520117, -109.731690. Hiking, biking trails. Visitor center, gift shop. Food concession. Two campgrounds open Feb-Nov. Reservations required. $40-50 per night. 41 sites with electric. 56-foot limit. Restrooms. Dump station.

Deer Creek State Park

PO Box 257, Midway, UT 84049. Phone: (435) 654-0171. Located 10 miles south of Midway along Highway 189, on Deer Creek Reservoir. GPS: 40.408549, -111.500521. Swimming, fishing, boating (rentals). Hiking, biking, equestrian trails. Marina, store, restaurant. Two campgrounds open May-Oct. $25-40 per night. 63 sites, 40 full hookup. 70-foot limit. Restrooms; showers. Dump station.

East Canyon State Park

5535 S UT 66, Morgan, UT 84050. Phone: (801) 829-6866. Located 10 miles S of Morgan on UT 65 & 66, NE of Salt Lake; off I-80 & I-84. GPS: 40.924978, -111.591060. Swimming, fishing, boating (rentals). Hiking, biking trails. Marina, store, grill. Open May-Sep. $25-40 per night. 45 sites, 13 full hookup, 15 water and electric. 40-foot limit. Restrooms; showers. Dump station.

Echo State Park

2115 N Echo Dam Rd, Coalville, UT 84017. Phone: (435) 336-4906. Located in northeastern Utah 3 miles N of Coalville (I-80, exit 162), along Echo Dam Rd on Echo Reservoir. GPS: 40.959877, -111.408467. Swimming, fishing, boating. Hiking, biking trails. Open all year. $40 per night. 18 sites with water and electric. Restrooms. Dump station.

Escalante Petrified Forest State Park

710 N Reservoir Rd, Escalante, UT 84726. Phone: (435) 826-4466. Located on Wide Hollow Reservoir 2 miles NW of Escalante, off UT 12 on Reservoir Rd. GPS: 37.786003, -111.630843. Swimming, fishing, boating (rentals). Hiking, biking trails. Visitor center. Open all year. $25-30 per night. 19 sites, 6 with water and electric. 40-foot limit. Restrooms; showers. Dump station.

Fred Hayes State Park at Starvation

PO Box 584, Duchesne, UT 84021. Phone: (435) 738-2326. Located on Starvation Reservoir, 4 miles NW of Duchesne on UT 311 off US 40. GPS: 40.188818, -110.451228. Swimming, fishing, boating. Hiking, biking, OHV trails. 3D archery course. Three campgrounds open May-Sep. $15-28 per night. 92 sites, 65 with water and electric. Restrooms; showers. Dump station. Additional primitive camping areas are available at serveral locations around the lake. These areas have no designated sites and facilities will vary.

Fremont Indian State Park & Museum

3820 W Clear Creek Canyon Rd, Sevier, UT 84766. Phone: (435) 527-4631. Located along I-70 (exit 17 or 23) in central UT, 10 miles SW of Joseph. GPS: 38.576712, -112.334721. Fishing. Hiking, biking trails. ATV trails nearby. Visitor center/museum. Two camping areas. $15-25 per night. 45-foot limit, both areas. Sam Stowe campground open year-round. 7 sites with full hookups. Restrooms; showers. Castle Rock campground closed in the winter. 31 sites, no hookups. Restrooms.

Goblin Valley State Park

PO Box 637, Green River, UT 84525. Phone: (435) 275-4584. Located south of I-70 between Hanksville and Green River on Goblin Valley Rd via Temple Mt Rd off UT 24. GPS: 38.578008, -110.707352. Hiking, biking, OHV trails. Disc golf. Open all year. $30-35 per night. 12 sites, no hookups. 40-foot limit. Restrooms; showers. Dump station.

Goosenecks State Park

c/o Edge of the Cedars State Park, 660 W 400 N, Blanding, UT 84511. Phone: (435) 678-2238. Located SW of Blanding, 25 miles W of Bluff on UT 316, 4 miles off UT 261. GPS: 37.175200, -109.926606. Hiking nearby, no trails in this small park. Open all year. No reservations accepted. $10 per night. 8 primitive sites. 30-foot limit. Vault toilets, no other facilities.

Great Salt Lake State Park

13312 W 1075 S, Magna, UT 84044. Phone: (801) 828-0787. Located 15 miles W of Salt Lake City on I-80, exit 104 (Saltair Dr). GPS: 40.732738, -112.204599. Swimming, fishing, boating. Marina. Visitor center, gift shop. Open all year. $35 per night. 5 sites with water and electric. 40-foot limit. Restrooms; showers. Dump station.

Green River State Park

PO Box 637, Green River, UT 84525. Phone: (435) 564-3633. Located on the Green River in the city of Green River off I-70 exit 160 or 164. GPS: 38.989715, -110.154513. Swimming, fishing, boating. OHV trails nearby. Golf course. Open all year. $35-45 per night. 37 sites, 4 full hookup, 33 with water and electric. 40-foot limit. Restrooms; showers. Dump station.

Gunlock State Park

Gunlock Rd, Gunlock, UT 84733. Phone: (435) 218-6544. Located on Gunlock Reservoir, 21 miles NW of St. George off Gunlock Rd via UT 18 or UT 8/Old US Hwy 91. GPS: 37.254672, -113.770375. Swimming, fishing, boating. Open all year. No reservations accepted. $20 per night. 5 sites, no hookups. No potable water. Restrooms; vault toilets.

Huntington State Park

PO Box 1343, Huntington, UT 84528. Phone: (435) 687-2491. Located on Huntington Reservoir, 2 miles NE of Huntington on UT 10. GPS: 39.347392, -110.942837. Swimming, fishing, boating. Open all year. $25-33 per night. 25 sites, 3 full hookup, 22 with water and electric. 45-foot limit. Restrooms; showers. Dump station.

Hyrum Lake State Park

405 W 300 S, Hyrum, UT 84319. Phone: (435) 245-6866. Located on Hyrum Reservoir in Hyrum, 8 miles S of Logan. GPS: 41.627985, -111.866538. Swimming, fishing, boating. Marina. OHV area nearby. Open May-Oct. $30-35 per night. 32 sites, 10 with electric. 40-foot limit. Restrooms; showers. Dump station.

Jordanelle State Park

SR 319, Heber City, UT 84032. Phone: (435) 649-9540. Located S of I-80 off US 189/40 on Jordanelle Reservoir, 9 miles N of Heber City. GPS: 40.621730, -111.428876. Swimming, fishing, boating (rentals). Hiking, biking, equestrian trails. Nature center, bird watching. Visitor center, marina, store. Open May-Oct. $45 per night. 100 sites, 14 full hookup, 86 with electric. 70-foot limit. Restrooms; showers. Laundry facilities. Dump station.

Kodachrome Basin State Park

Box 180069, Cannonville, UT 84718. Phone: (435) 679-8562. Located 9 miles SE of Cannonville via Kodachrome Rd and Cottonwood Canyon Rd. GPS: 37.501901, -111.993489. Hiking, biking, equestrian trails. Guided horseback rides available. Disc golf. Three campgrounds open Mar-Nov. $25-35 per night. 51 sites, 15 full hookup, 6 with electric. 45-foot limit. Restrooms; showers. Laundry facilities. Dump station.

Millsite State Park

Box 1343, Huntington, UT 84528. Phone: (435) 384-2552. Located on southern end of Millsite Reservoir, 5 miles W of Ferron via Ferron Canyon Rd off UT 10. GPS: 39.091205, -111.195954. Swimming, fishing, boating. Hiking, biking, OHV trails. 18-hole public golf course adjacent to park. Open all year. $20-25 per night. 27 sites, 12 with electric and water, 10 electric only. 45-foot limit. Restrooms; showers. Dump station.

Otter Creek State Park

PO Box 43, Antimony, UT 84712. Phone: (435) 624-3268. Located on southern end of Otter Creek Reservoir, 4 miles N from

Antimony on UT 22; about 12 miles E of US 89 at Kingston. GPS: 38.166022, -112.017194. Swimming, fishing, boating. Hiking, biking, OHV, equestrian trails. Bird watching. Open all year. $20-40 per night. 47 sites, 21 with electric. 45-foot limit. Restrooms; showers. Dump station.

Palisade State Park

2200 E Palisade Rd, Sterling, UT 84665. Phone: (435) 835-7275. Located on Palisade Lake, off US 89, 2 miles NE of Sterling. GPS: 39.202137, -111.665436. Swimming, fishing, electric or non-motorized boating (rentals). Hiking, biking trails. OHV trails nearby. Lakeside grill. Golf course. Open Apr-Oct. $25-35 per night. 59 sites, 23 with full hookups. 55-foot limit. Restrooms; showers. Dump station.

Piute State Park

PO Box 43, Antimony, UT 84712. Phone: (435) 624-3268. Located on the northern end of Piute Reservoir, 10 miles S of Marysvale via Piute State Park Rd off US 89. GPS: 38.320304, -112.198006. Swimming, fishing, boating. OHV riding. Open all year. No reservations accepted. $8 per night. 35 primitive sites, no hookups or water. Restrooms; pit toilets.

Quail Creek State Park

472 N 5300 W, Hurricane, UT 84737. Phone: (435) 879-2378. Located on Quail Creek Reservoir in the southwest corner of UT, 3 miles W of Hurricane off UT 9. Use exit 16 (UT 9) off I-15. GPS: 37.179129, -113.395936. Swimming, fishing, boating. Hiking, biking trails. Concessionaire with boat rentals. Open all year. $25-38 per night. 24 sites, 9 with water and electric. 40-foot limit. Restrooms; showers.

Red Fleet State Park

8750 N UT 191, Vernal, UT 84078. Phone: (435) 789-4432. Located on Red Fleet Reservoir in NE corner of UT, 10 miles N or Vernal, off US 191. GPS: 40.580581, -109.465014. Swimming, fishing, boating (rentals). Three-mile, round trip trail leads to dinosaur tracks. Open all year. $15-28 per night. 29 sites, 5 with full hookups. 30-foot limit. Restrooms. Dump station.

Rockport State Park

9040 N UT 302, Peoa, UT 84061. Phone: (435) 336-2241. Located on Rockport Reservoir along UT 32 about 45 miles E of Salt Lake City. Northern access near Wanship is via I-80, exit 155. GPS: 40.774393, -111.389756. Swimming, fishing, boating (rentals). Marina; store, grill. 3-D Archery Range. Five camping areas open all year. $15-35 per night. 93 sites, 23 with electric. 40-foot limit. Restrooms; showers. Dump station.

Sand Hollow State Park

3351 S Sand Hollow Rd, Hurricane, UT 84737. Phone: (435) 680-0715. Located in SW corner of UT on Sand Hollow Reservoir. From I-15 take exit 16 (UT 9/Hurricane) and travel E 5 miles, then 4 miles S off UT 9 on Sand Hollow Rd. GPS: 37.117650, -113.391552. Swimming, fishing, boating. Equestrian, hiking, biking, OHV trails. Two campgrounds open all year. $28-38 per night. 65 sites, 42 full hookup, 6 with water and electric. 60-foot limit. Restrooms; showers. Dump station.

Scofield State Park

PO Box 1343, Huntington, UT 84528. Phone: (435) 448-9449. Located on Scofield Reservoir NW of Helper, off US 6, on UT 96. GPS: 39.809915, -111.135049. Swimming, fishing, boating. Hiking, biking trails. Two camping areas open all year. $15-30 per night. 71 sites, 2 full hookup, 36 with electric. 35-foot limit. Restrooms; showers. Dump station.

Snow Canyon State Park

1002 N Snow Canyon Dr, Ivins, UT 84738. Phone: (435) 628-2255. Located 11 miles N of St. George, on UT 18 (exit 6 off I-15). GPS: 37.230794, -113.633926. Desert park, hot in summer. Hiking, biking, equestrian trails. Rock climbing. Open all year. $20-35 per night. 24 sites, 16 with water and electric. 40-foot limit. Restrooms; showers. Dump station.

Steinaker State Park

4335 N UT 191, Vernal, UT 84078. Phone: (435) 789-4432. Located on Steinaker Reservoir, 6 miles N of Vernal, off US 191. GPS: 40.533693, -109.522198. Swimming, fishing, boating. Hiking, OHV trails. 3-D Archery Range. Open all year. $15-30 per night. 27 sites, 8 full hookup, 8 with water and electric. 45-foot limit. Restrooms; showers. Dump station.

Utah Lake State Park

4400 W Center St, Provo, UT 84601. Phone: (801) 375-0731. Located on Utah's largest freshwater lake, 3 miles W of Provo, off I-15, exit 265 (W Center St). GPS: 40.236996, -111.732200. Swimming, fishing, boating (rentals). Hiking trail. Visitor center, marina. Frisbee golf. Open Apr-Oct. $35 per night. 30 sites with water and electric. 40-foot limit. Restrooms; showers. Dump station.

Wasatch Mountain State Park

1281 Warm Springs Rd, Midway, UT 84049. Phone: (435) 654-1791. Located about 40 miles SE of Salt Lake City, west and north of Midway on UT 222. GPS: 40.532909, -111.489830. Hiking, biking, OHV, equestrian trails. Four 18-hole golf courses. Two historic areas (Tate Barn and Huber Grove). Open May-Oct. $35-40 per night. 78 sites, 60 full hookup, 18 with water and electric. 50-foot limit. Restrooms; showers. Dump station.

Willard Bay State Park

900 W 650 N #A, Willard, UT 84340. Phone: (435) 734-9494. Located on Willard Bay Reservoir, north of Ogden on west side of I-15. There are two locations.

The northern camping area is about 15 miles N of Ogden off I-15 exit 357. GPS: 41.421681, -112.053515. Swimming, fishing, boating (rentals). Hiking trail. Marina. Open Apr-Oct. $30-40 per night. 71 sites, 36 with full hookups. 100-foot limit. Restrooms; showers. Dump station.

The southern camping area is about 9 miles N of Ogden via exit 351 off I-15. GPS: 41.348191, -112.064382. Swimming, fishing, boating (rentals). Marina. Open Apr-Oct. $35-40 per night. 16 sites with full hookups. 35-foot limit. Restrooms; showers. Dump station.

Yuba State Park

PO Box 159, Levan, UT 84639. Phone: (435) 758-2611. Located on Yuba Reservoir 25 miles S of Nephi, off I-15 exits 188 or 202. GPS: 39.379491, -112.028216. Swimming, fishing, boating (rentals). Hiking, biking, OHV trails. 3-D Archery Range. Zip lines. Open all year. $25-60 per night. 219 sites, 51 with electric. 90-foot limit. Restrooms; showers. Dump station.

Vermont

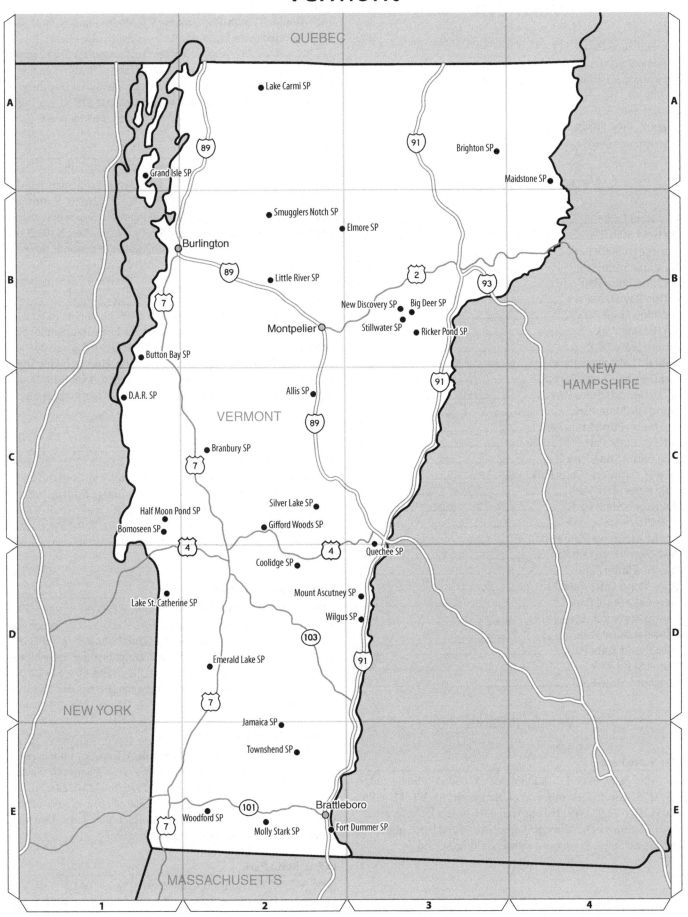

QUEBEC

Lake Carmi SP

Brighton SP

Grand Isle SP

Maidstone SP

Smugglers Notch SP

Elmore SP

Burlington

Little River SP

New Discovery SP

Big Deer SP

Stillwater SP

Ricker Pond SP

Montpelier

Button Bay SP

NEW HAMPSHIRE

D.A.R. SP

Allis SP

VERMONT

Branbury SP

Silver Lake SP

Half Moon Pond SP

Gifford Woods SP

Bomoseen SP

Quechee SP

Coolidge SP

Lake St. Catherine SP

Mount Ascutney SP

Wilgus SP

Emerald Lake SP

NEW YORK

Jamaica SP

Townshend SP

Brattleboro

Woodford SP

Molly Stark SP

Fort Dummer SP

MASSACHUSETTS

Vermont

Vermont State Parks
1 National Life Dr, Dewey 2
Montpelier, VT 05620

Phone: (888) 409-7579
Internet: www.vtstateparks.com
Reservations: Online or (888) 409-7579

Vermont Park Locator

Vermont Parks

Allis State Park

284 Allis State Park Rd, Randolph, VT 05060. Phone: (802) 276-3175. Located 10 miles N of Randolph via VT 12. GPS: 44.051257, -72.627349. Hiking trail (3/4 mile), lookout tower. Open Memorial Day through Labor Day. $19-21 per night. 18 sites, no hookups. Restrooms; showers. Dump station.

Big Deer State Park

1467 Boulder Beach Rd, Groton, VT 05046. Phone: (802) 584-3822. Located in the Groton State Fores, off Boulder Beach Rd, via US 302 and VT 232. About 10 miles N of Groton. GPS: 44.286686, -72.267575. Hiking and biking trails in state park and state forest. Close to the Groton Nature Center. Open Memorial Day through Labor Day. Check-in is at Stillwater State Park. $19-21 per night. 22 sites, no hookups. Drinking water. Restrooms; showers.

Bomoseen State Park

22 Cedar Mountain Rd, Castleton, VT 05743. Phone: (802) 265-4242. Located 5 miles N of Fair Haven via Scotch Hill Rd and W Castleton Rd. GPS: 43.656258, -73.228820. Swimming beach, fishing, boating (rentals). Hiking trails. Snack bar. Nature programs. Open Memorial Day through Labor Day. $19-23 per night. 55 sites, no hookups. Drinking water. Restrooms; showers. Dump station.

Branbury State Park

3570 Lake Dunmore Rd, Brandon, VT 05733. Phone: (802) 247-5925. Located on the eastern shore of Lake Dunmore, 9 miles N of Brandon on Rt 53 off US 7 or VT 73. GPS: 43.905608, -73.066047. Swimming beach, fishing, boating (rentals). Hiking, biking trails. Nature center. Food concession. Open May-Oct. $19-23 per night. 36 sites, no hookups. Drinking water. Restrooms; showers. Dump station.

Brighton State Park

102 State Park Rd, Island Pond, VT 05846. Phone: (802) 723-4360. Located on Spectacle Pond off VT 105, 2 miles SE of Island Pond, VT. GPS: 44.807170, -71.856402. Swimming, fishing, boating (rentals, no boat launch). Hiking, self-guided nature trail. Biking trails nearby. Nature museum. Open Jun-Oct. $19-23 per night. 54 sites, no hookups. Drinking water. Restrooms; showers. Dump station.

Button Bay State Park

5 Button Bay State Park Rd, Ferrisburgh, VT 05491. Phone: (802) 475-2377. Located on Lake Champlain, 7 miles W of Vergennes via Panton Rd, Basin Harbor Rd, and Button Bay Rd. GPS: 44.182924, -73.350223. Swimming, fishing, boating. Easy hiking trail through the park. Nature center. Open Jun-Oct. $19-23 per night. 53 sites, no hookups. Drinking water. Restrooms; showers. Dump station.

Coolidge State Park

855 Coolidge State Park Rd, Plymouth, VT 05056. Phone: (802) 672-3612. Located off VT 100A, 3 miles NE of Plymouth; 7 miles SW of Bridgewater off US 4. GPS: 43.552620, -72.707144. Hiking trails. More trails in nearby Coolidge State Forest. Nature center. Open Jun-Oct. $19-21 per night. 26 sites, no hookups. Drinking water. Restrooms; showers. Dump station.

D.A.R. State Park

6750 VT 17 W, Addison, VT 05491. Phone: (802) 759-2354. Located on Lake Champlain, 7 miles W of Addison via VT 17 (off

VT 22 A). GPS: 44.053357, -73.412195. Fishing. The parks steep bluff makes swimming and boating difficult. Open Memorial Day through Labor Day. $19-21 per night. 47 sites, no hookups. Drinking water. Restrooms; showers. Dump station.

Elmore State Park

856 VT 12, Lake Elmore, VT 05657. Phone: (802) 888-2982. Located on VT 12, 6 miles SE of Morrisville. GPS: 44.548039, -72.532776. Swimming beach, fishing, boating (rentals). Hiking, nature trail, lookout tower. Food concession. Open Jun-Oct. $19-23 per night. 44 sites, no hookups. Drinking water. Restrooms; showers. Dump station.

Emerald Lake State Park

65 Emerald Lake Ln, East Dorset, VT 05253. Phone: (802) 362-1655. Located in East Dorset on Emerald Lake on US 7 about 9 miles N of Manchester. GPS: 43.281552, -73.004696. Swimming beach, fishing, boating (no motors, rentals). Hiking trails. Food concession. Nature center. Open Jun-Oct. $19-23 per night. 66 sites, no hookups. Drinking water. Restrooms; showers. Dump station.

Fort Dummer State Park

517 Old Guilford Rd, Brattleboro, VT 05301. Phone: (802) 254-2610. Located along I-91, 1 mile south of Brattleboro via Old Guilford Rd. GPS: 42.824675, -72.566686. Swimming. Three hiking trails. Open Jun-Oct. $19-21 per night. 50 sites, no hookups. Drinking water. Restrooms; showers. Dump station.

Gifford Woods State Park

34 Gifford Woods, Killington, VT 05751. Phone: (802) 775-5354. Located near Killington, 1/2 mile N on VT 100 off US 4. GPS: 43.673539, -72.808782. Fishing, boating across from park. One mile hiking trail. More trails in nearby Coolidge State Forest. Open May-Oct. $19-23 per night. 21 sites, no hookups. Drinking water. Restrooms; showers. Dump station.

Grand Isle State Park

36 East Shore S, Grand Isle, VT 05458. Phone: (802) 372-4300. Located on South Hero Island in Lake Champlain, 3 miles S of Grand Isle via US 2. GPS: 43.673539, -72.808782. Swimming, fishing, boating (rentals). Nature trail, nature center. Observation tower. Most visited campground in the state park system. Open May-Oct. $19-23 per night. 115 sites, no hookups. Drinking water. Restrooms; showers. Dump station.

Half Moon Pond State Park

1621 Black Pond Rd, Hubbardton, VT 05743. Phone: (802) 273-2848. Located about 4 miles W of Hubbardton, off VT 30 via Hortonia Rd. GPS: 43.699211, -73.223166. Swimming beach, fishing, boating (no motors, rentals). Hiking trails. Nature center. Open Jun-Oct. Limited big rig sites. $19-23 per night. 52 sites, no hookups. Drinking water. Restrooms; showers. Dump station.

Jamaica State Park

48 Salmon Hole Ln, Jamaica, VT 05343. Phone: (802) 874-4600. Located on the West River, off VT 30 outside Jamaica. (8-ton weight limit on bridge leading to park.) GPS: 43.105550, -72.773304. Swimming, fishing, boating (no boat ramp). Hiking, biking trails. Nature center. Open May-Oct. $19-23 per night. 41 sites, no hookups. Drinking water. Restrooms; showers. Dump station.

Lake Carmi State Park

460 Marsh Farm Rd, Enosburg Falls, VT 05450. Phone: (802) 933-8383. Located 6 miles NW of Enosburg via VT 105 and VT 236. GPS: 44.953306, -72.862389. Swimming beaches, fishing, boating (rentals). Hiking trails. Nature center. Open May-Oct. $19-23 per night. 138 sites, no hookups. Drinking water. Restrooms; showers. Dump station.

Lake St. Catherine State Park

3034 VT 30, Poultney, VT 05764. Phone: (802) 287-9158. Located about 3 miles S of Poultney on VT 30. GPS: 43.480557, -73.201720. Swimming beachs, fishing, boating (rentals). Hiking trail. Nature center. Snack bar. Open Jun-Oct. $19-23 per night. 50 sites, no hookups. Drinking water. Restrooms; showers. Dump station.

Little River State Park

3444 Little River Rd, Waterbury, VT 05676. Phone: (802) 244-7103. Located in Mt. Mansfield State Forest on Little River, about 5 miles N of Waterbury (I-89 exit 10) via Little River Rd off US 2. GPS: 44.389754, -72.767482. Swimming beaches, fishing, boating (rentals). Hiking, biking trails. Nature center. Open May-Oct. $19-23 per night. 81 sites, no hookups. Drinking water. Restrooms; showers. Dump station.

Maidstone State Park

5956 Maidenstone Lake Rd, Guildhall, VT 05905. Phone: (802) 676-3930. Located on Maidstone Lake near NH state line, 10 miles S of Bloomfield via Maidenstone Lake Access Rd off VT 102. Most remote park in VT system. GPS: 44.653030, -71.638623. Swimming beaches, fishing, boating (no boat ramp, rentals). Hiking trails. Open Memorial Day through Labor Day. No big rigs. $19-23 per night. 34 sites, no hookups. Restrooms; showers. Dump station.

Molly Stark State Park

705 VT 9 E, Wilmington, VT 05363. Phone: (802) 464-5460. Located in southern VT, 3 miles E of Wilmington on VT 9. GPS: 42.854702, -72.814495. Hiking trail to Mt. Olga fire lookout tower. Open Jun-Oct. Big rig sites limited. $19-21 per night. 23 sites, no hookups. Drinking water. Restrooms; showers. Dump station.

Mount Ascutney State Park

1826 Back Mtn Rd, Windsor, VT 05089. Phone: (802) 674-2060. Located off US 5 on VT 44A (Back Mtn. Rd), 1 mile N of Windsor. GPS: 43.437778, -72.405821. Hiking trails (12 miles). Lookout tower. Open May-Oct. $19-21 per night. 38 sites, no hookups. Drinking water. Restrooms; showers. Dump station.

New Discovery State Park

4239 VT 232, Marshfield, VT 05658. Phone: (802) 426-3042. Located in Groton State Forest, 6 miles SE of Marshfield on VT 232 via US 2. GPS: 44.320527, -72.292196. Swimming (at Boulder Beach State Park), fishing. Hiking, biking trails in Groton State Forest. Nature center. Open Jun-Oct. $19-21 per night. 38 sites (plus 8 horse-camping sites), no hookups. Drinking water. Restrooms; showers. Dump station.

Quechee State Park

5800 Woodstock Rd, Hartford, VT 05047. Phone: (802) 295-2990. Located along US 4 (I-89 exit 1), 4 miles SW of Hartford. GPS: 43.638232, -72.410671. Fishing. Hiking trail to Quechee Gorge. Nature center. Open May-Oct. $19-23 per night. 45 sites, no hookups. Drinking water. Restrooms; showers. Dump station.

Ricker Pond State Park

18 Ricker Pond Campground Rd, Groton, VT 05046. Phone: (802) 584-3821. Located in Groton State Forest off VT 232, 5 miles NW of Groton (US 302). GPS: 44.245602, -72.253929. Swimming beach, fishing, boating (rentals). Hiking, biking trails in Groton State Forest. Nature center. Open Jun-Oct. $19-23 per night. 26 sites, no hookups. Drinking water. Restrooms; showers. Dump station.

Silver Lake State Park

20 State Park Beach Rd, Barnard, VT 05031. Phone: (802) 234-9451. Located just N of Barnard off VT 12. About 10 miles NW of Woodstock. GPS: 43.731392, -72.616555. Swimming beach, fishing, boating (rentals). Nature center. Food concession. Open Memorial Day through Labor Day. $19-23 per night. 39 sites, no hookups. Drinking water. Restrooms; showers. Dump station.

Smugglers Notch State Park

6443 Mountain Rd, Stowe, VT 05672. Phone: (802) 253-4014. Located about 9 miles NW of Stowe on VT 108. GPS 44.556601, -72.794279. Hiking trail, more multi-use trails nearby. Nature center. Open Jun-Oct. $19-23 per night. 6 sites, no hookups. 28-foot limit. Drinking water. Restrooms; showers. Dump station.

Stillwater State Park

44 Stillwater Rd, Groton, VT 05046. Phone: (802) 584-3822. Located in Groton State Forest, 9 miles N of Groton, via US 302 and VT 232. GPS: 44.279974, -72.274216. Swimming beach, fishing, boating (rentals). Hiking, biking trails in Groton State Forest. Nature center. Open Jun-Sep. $19-23 per night. 56 sites, no hookups. Dump station. Restrooms; showers. Drinking water.

Townshend State Park

2755 State Forest Rd, Townshend, VT 05353. Phone: (802) 365-7500. Located E of Townshend in Townshend State Forest, off VT 30 on the West River. GPS: 43.041190, -72.692435. Fishing. Hiking trails. Open Memorial Day through Labor Day. No big rigs. $19-21 per night. 22 sites, no hookups. Drinking water. Restrooms; showers. Dump station.

Wilgus State Park

3985 VT 5, Weathersfield, VT 05156. Phone: (802) 674-5422. Located on Connecticut River along US 5, 1 miles S of Ascutney (I-91 exit 8). GPS: 43.390071, -72.406983. Swimming, fishing, boating (rentals). One mile loop trail. Open May-Oct. $19-23 per night. 15 sites, no hookups. Drinking water. Restrooms; showers. Dump station.

Woodford State Park

142 State Park Rd, Bennington, VT 05201. Phone: (802) 447-7169. Located on Adams Reservoir on VT 9, 10 miles E of Bennington. GPS: 42.892062, -73.035679. Swimming beach, fishing, boating (rentals). Hiking trails. Nature center. Open Jun-Oct. $19-23 per night. 76 sites, no hookups. Drinking water. Restrooms; showers. Dump station.

Virginia

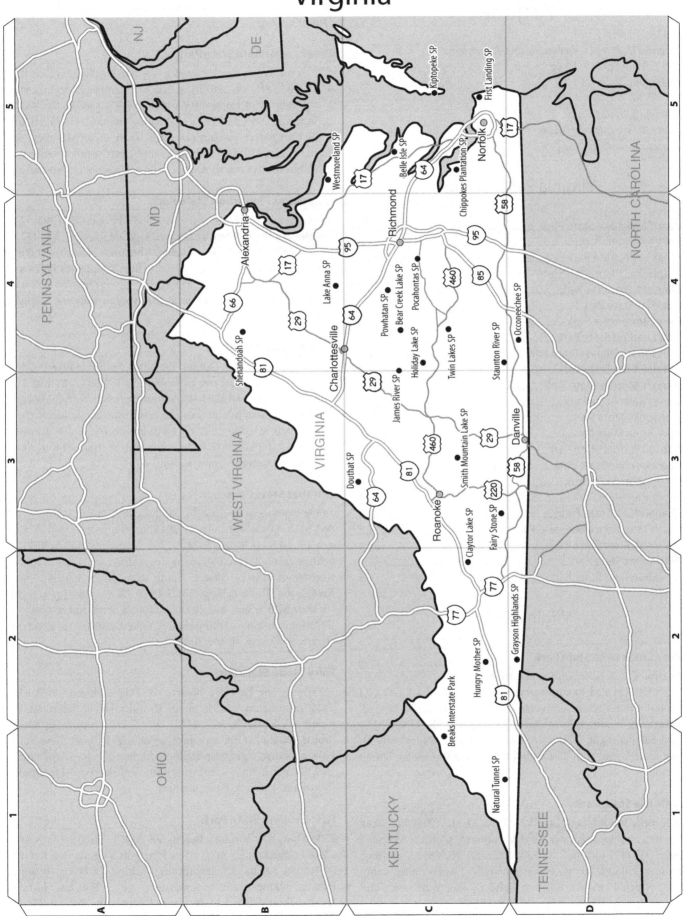

Virginia

Virginia Dept. of Conservation and Recreation
600 E Main St, 24th Floor
Richmond, VA 23219

Phone: (800) 933-7275
Internet: www.dcr.virginia.gov/state-parks/
Reservations: Online or (800) 933-7275

Virginia Park Locator

Virginia Parks

Bear Creek Lake State Park

22 Bear Creek Lake Rd, Cumberland, VA 23040. Phone: (804) 492-4410. Located in Cumberland State Forest off VA 622 (via US 60) 4 miles N of Cumberland. GPS: 37.533278, -78.274563. Swimming beach, fishing, boating. Hiking trails. Open Mar-Nov. $40 per night. 37 sites with water, electric. 28 sites with 20-foot limit, 9 with 35-foot limit. Restrooms; showers. Dump station.

Belle Isle State Park

1632 Belle Isle Rd, Lancaster, VA 22503. Phone: (804) 462-5030. Located on Rappahannock River in eastern VA, off VA 683, nine miles W of Lancaster. GPS: 37.782131, -76.585932. Fishing, boating. Hiking, biking, equestrian trails. Visitor center, camp store. Open Mar-Nov. $40 per night. 28 sites with water and electric. 45-foot limit. Restrooms; showers. Laundry facilities. Dump station.

Breaks Interstate State Park

627 Commission Circle, Breaks, VA 24607. Phone: (276) 865-4413 ext 3201, or 3202. Located on Kentucky/Virginia state line 8 miles N of Haysi off VA 80. GPS: 37.284851, -82.288569. Swimming; water park, fishing, boating (rentals). Hiking, biking trails. Camp store, restaurant, visitor center. Open Mar-Oct. $26-28 per night. 138 sites with water and electric; full hookup sites available. Restrooms; showers. Laundry facilities. Dump station.

Chippokes Plantation State Park

695 Chippokes Park Rd, Surry, VA 23883. Phone: (757) 294-3728. Located 5 miles E of Surry via VA 634, off VA 10. GPS: 37.142290, -76.727192. Swimming, fishing, boating. Hiking, biking, equestrian trails. Visitor center, gift shop. Chippokes Farm and Forestry Museum. Open Mar-Nov. $40-45 per night. 50 sites with water and electric. 50-foot limit. Restrooms; showers. Laundry facilities.

Claytor Lake State Park

6620 Ben H. Bolen Dr, Dublin, VA 24084. Phone: (540) 643-2500. Located 6 miles southeast of Dublin on VA 660, I-81 exit 101. GPS: 37.066652, -80.626454. Swimming beach, fishing, boating (rentals). Hiking, biking (rentals) trails. Marina. Snack bar, gift shop. Open Mar-Nov. $30 plus $10 for electric and water sites, per night. 103 sites, 39 with water and electric. 40-foot limit. Restrooms; showers. Dump station.

Douthat State Park

14239 Douthat State Park Rd, Millboro, VA 24460. Phone: (540) 862-8100. Located 8 miles N of Clifton Forge on VA 629, I-64 exit 27. GPS: 37.904821, -79.797266. Swimming beach, fishing, boating (rentals). Hiking, biking, equestrian trails. On National Register of Historic Places. Camp store, snack bar, gift shop. Restaurant. Three campgrounds open all year. $40 per night. 73 sites with water and electric. 50-foot limit (most 40-foot). Restrooms; showers. Dump station. Equestrian area, 14 sites with electric and water. 40-foot limit.

Fairy Stone State Park

967 Fairystone Lake Dr, Stuart, VA 24171. Phone: (276) 930-2424. Located on VA 346 about 15 miles NE of Stuart via VA 8 and VA 57. GPS: 36.792442, -80.117110. Swimming beach, fishing, boating (168-acre lake adjoining Philpott Reservoir). Hiking, biking, equestrian trails. Snack bar, gift shop. Open Mar-Nov. $40 per night. 51 sites with water and electric. 30-foot limit. Restrooms; showers. Dump station.

First Landing State Park

2500 Shore Dr, Virginia Beach, VA 23451. Phone: (757) 412-2300. Located on US 60 at Cape Henry in Virginia Beach. GPS: 36.918036, -76.053336. Swimming, fishing, crabbing, boating. Hiking, biking trails. Camp store, gifts. National Natural Landmark and listed in National Register of Historic Places.

The Chesapeake Bay Center houses historical and educational exhibits. Open Mar-Nov. $46 per night. 108 sites with water and electric. 50-foot limit. Restrooms; showers. Dump station.

Grayson Highlands State Park

829 Grayson Highland Ln, Mouth of Wilson, VA 24363. Phone: (276) 579-7092. Located 12 miles W of Mouth of Wilson via US 58. GPS: 36.612089, -81.491111. Fishing, boating. Hiking, biking, equestrian trails. Rock climbing. Visitor center. Open Mar-Nov. $30 plus $10 for water and electric, per night. 64 sites, 36 with water and electric. 40-foot limit. Restrooms; showers. Dump station. Equestrian campground, 23 sites with water and electric.

Holiday Lake State Park

2759 State Park Rd, Appomattox, VA 24522. Phone: (434) 248-6308. Located off VA 24 in the Appomattox-Buckingham State Forest, 13 miles E of Appomattox; access from VA 626 or 636. GPS: 37.402234, -78.643820. Swimming beach, fishing, boating (rentals). Hiking trails. Open Mar-Nov. $40 per night. 35 sites with water and electric. 40-foot limit. Restrooms; showers. Dump station.

Hungry Mother State Park

2854 Park Blvd, Marion, VA 24354. Phone: (276) 781-7400. Located on VA 16, 3 miles N of Marion (I-81 exit 45 or 47). GPS: 36.870942, -81.523932. Lake in park. Swimming beach, fishing, boating (rentals). Hiking, biking trails. Visitor center, gift shop, restaurant. Two campgrounds open all year. $40 plus $5 for full hookup sites, per night. 70 sites, 30 full hookup, 40 with water and electric. 35-foot limit. Restrooms; showers. Dump station.

James River State Park

104 Green Hill Dr, Gladstone, VA 24533. Phone: (434) 933-4355. Located on James River, 9 miles NE of Gladstone via US 60 and VA 605 (Riverside Dr). GPS: 37.623240, -78.796936. Fishing, boating/floating (rentals). Hiking, biking, equestrian trails. Visitor center, gift shop, camp store. Open Mar-Nov. $40 per night. 30 sites with water and electric. 40-foot limit. Restrooms; showers. Laundry facilities. Dump station. Equestrian area, 10 sites with water and electric.

Kiptopeke State Park

3540 Kiptopeke Dr, Cape Charles, VA 23310. Phone: (757) 331-2267. Located on eastern shore of Chesapeake Bay on VA 704 off US 13. Nine miles S of Cape Charles. From the south, park is 3 miles from the northern terminus of the Chesapeake Bay Bridge Tunnel. Tunnel has high toll fees. GPS: 37.173466, -75.975487. Two swimming beaches, fishing, crabbing, boating. Hiking, biking (rentals) trails. Major flyway for migratory birds. Camp store. Open Mar-Nov. $47 per night. 86 full hookup sites. 40-foot limit. Restrooms; showers. Dump station.

Lake Anna State Park

6800 Lawyers Rd, Spotsylvania, VA 22551. Phone: (540) 854-5503. Located 15 miles W of Spotsylvania, adjacent to VA 601 (Lawyers Rd) via VA 208. GPS: 38.143114, -77.813973. Swimming beach,

fishing, boating. Hiking, biking, equestrian trails. Snack bar. Visitor center, gift shop. Guided tours of the Goodwin Gold Mine. Open Mar-Nov. $35 plus $11 for water and electric, per night. 46 sites, 23 with water and electric. 60-foot limit. Restrooms; showers. Laundry facilities. Dump station.

Natural Tunnel State Park

1420 Natural Tunnel Pkwy, Duffield, VA 24244. Phone: (276) 940-2674. Located on VA 871 about 5 miles SE of Duffield via US 58. GPS: 36.703167, -82.746004. Swimming pool, limited creek fishing. Hiking, biking (rentals) trails. Visitor center, gift shop, snack bar, camp store. Cave tours and canoe trips. Daniel Boone Wilderness Trail Center. Two campgrounds open Mar-Nov. $40 per night. 34 sites with water and electric. 50-foot limit. Restrooms; showers. Laundry facilities. Dump station.

Occoneechee State Park

1192 Occoneechee Park Rd, Clarksvillle, VA 23927. Phone: (434) 374-2210. Located on Buggs Island Lake (John H. Kerr Reservoir), 2 miles E of Clarksville on US 58. GPS: 36.635511, -78.529213. Fishing, boating (rentals). Hiking, biking, equestrian trails. Marina, snack bar. Visitor center, museum. Open Mar-Nov. $30-35 plus $10 for water and electric, per night. 48 sites, 39 with water and electric. 35-foot limit. Restrooms; showers. Equestrian campground, 11 sites with electric. 65-foot limit.

Pocahontas State Park

10301 State Park Rd, Chesterfield, VA 23832. Phone: (804) 796-4255. Located on VA 655 about 5 miles W of Chesterfield. GPS: 37.369614, -77.576073. Aquatic recreation center, fishing, boating (rentals). Hiking, biking, equestrian trails (90-plus miles). Civilian Conservation Corps Museum. 2,000-seat amphitheater. Camp store. Open all year. $40 per night. 111 sites with water and electric. 40-foot limit. Restrooms; showers. Laundry facilities. Dump station.

Powhatan State Park

4616 Powhatan State Park Rd, Powhatan, VA 23139. Phone: (804) 598-7148. Located on the James River, 10 miles N of Powhatan via US 522 and VA 617. GPS: 37.660238, -77.922833. Fishing, boating (canoe or kayak launch only from inside the park). Hiking, biking, equestrian trails. Wildlife observation areas. Open Mar-Nov. $40 per night. 29 sites with water and electric. 60-foot limit. Restrooms; showers. Dump station.

Shenandoah State Park

350 Daughter of Stars Dr, Bentonville, VA 22610 Phone: (540) 622-6840. Located on the South Fork of the Shenandoah River, 8 miles SW of Front Royal, off US 340 in Bentonville. GPS 38.840560, -78.302344. Fishing, wading, floating, boating. Hiking, biking, equestrian trails. Visitor center. Open all year. $46 per night. 31 sites with water and electric. 60-foot limit. Restrooms; showers.

Smith Mountain Lake State Park

1235 State Park Rd, Huddleston, VA 24104. Phone: (540) 297-6066. Located on the second largest freshwater lake in the state,

8 miles SW of Huddleston on VA 626 (Smith Mountain Lake Pkwy). GPS: 37.099699, -79.586352. Swimming beach, fishing, boating (rentals). Hiking, biking trails. Visitor center, snack bar, gift shop. Open Mar-Nov. $40 per night. 24 sites with water and electric. 50-foot limit (19 have 30-foot limit). Restrooms; showers. Dump station.

Staunton River State Park

1170 Staunton Trail, Scottsburg, VA 24589. Phone: (434) 572-4623. Located 8 miles SE of Scottsburg, off US 360 via VA 344. GPS: 36.701658, -78.679127. Swimming pool, fishing, boating. Hiking, biking, equestrian trails. Visitor center, gift shop. Disc golf. Designated as an International Dark Sky Park. Open Mar-Nov. 14 sites with water and electric. Dump station. 45-foot limit (10 sites 30-foot limit). Additional 20 sites with water and electric for popup trailers, 20-foot limit. Restrooms; showers. Laundry facilities. Equestrian camp ($40 per night), 13 sites with water and electric. 50-foot limit. Restrooms; showers. Dump station. 20 covered horse stalls.

Twin Lakes State Park

788 Twin Lakes Rd, Green Bay, VA 23942. Phone: (434) 392-3435. Located between Green Bay and Burkeville off US 360. GPS: 37.162002, -78.287410. Swimming beach, fishing, boating. Hiking trails. Gift shop. Open Mar-Nov. $40 per night. 22 sites with water and electric. 36-foot limit. Additional 11 sites with water and electric for popup trailers, 20-foot limit. Restrooms; showers. Dump station.

Westmoreland State Park

145 Cliff Rd, Montross, VA 22520. Phone: (804) 493-8821. Located on Potomac River, 6 miles N of Montross via VA 3 and VA 347. GPS: 38.153037, -76.873370. Swimming pool, fishing, boating (rentals). Bird watching. Hiking, biking trails. Visitor center, snack bar, camp store. Listed on the National Register of Historic Places. Open Mar-Nov. $30 plus $10 for water and electric, per night. 116 sites, 42 with water and electric. 40-foot limit. Restrooms; showers. Laundry facilities. Dump station.

Washington

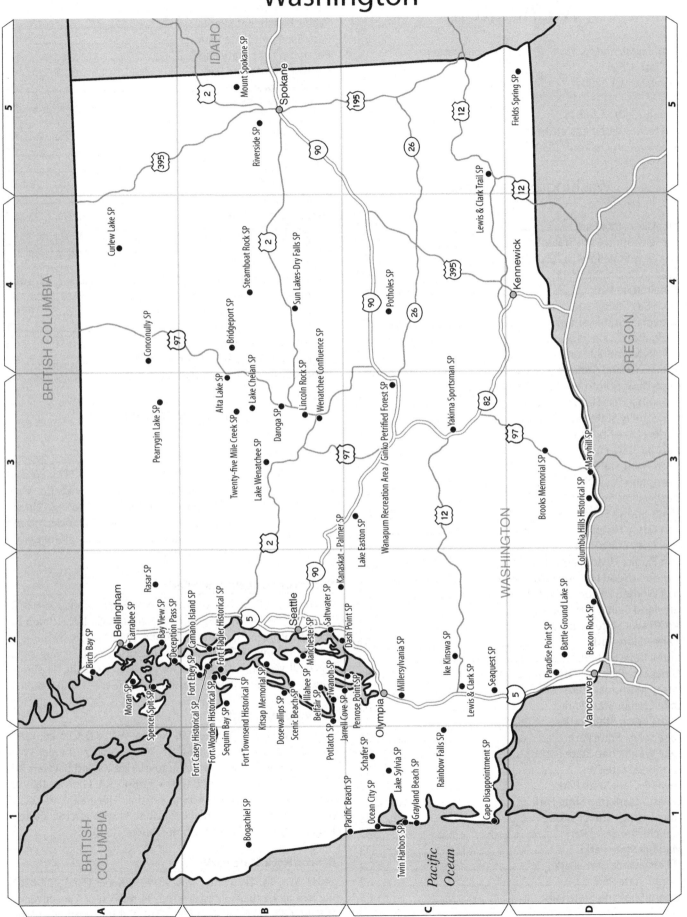

Washington

Washington State Parks & Recreation Commission
PO Box 42650
Olympia, WA 98504

Phone: (360) 902-8844
Internet: www.parks.state.wa.us
Reservations: Online or (888) 226-7688

Washington Park Locator

Washington Parks

Alta Lake State Park

1 B Otto Rd, Pateros, WA 98846. Phone: (509) 923-2473. Located 4 miles SW of Pateros via WA 153 and Alta Lake Rd. GPS: 48.031649, -119.934693. Swimming, fishing, boating. Hiking trails. Camp store. Open Apr-Oct. $27-37 plus $8 for electric and $5 for sewer, per night. 125 sites, 32 full hookup. 38-foot limit. Restrooms; showers. Dump station.

Battle Ground Lake State Park

18002 NE 249th St, Battle Ground, WA 98604. Phone: (360) 687-4621. Located 3 miles NE of Battle Ground via NE Heisson Rd and NE Palmer Rd. GPS: 45.802984, -122.486858. Swimming, fishing, boating. Hiking, biking, equestrian trails. Camp store. Open all year. $27-37 plus $8 for electric, per night. 41 sites, 6 with electric. 35-foot limit. Restrooms; showers. Dump station.

Bay View State Park

10901 Bay View-Edison Rd, Mt. Vernon, WA 98273. Phone: (360) 757-0227. Reservations: (888) 226-7688. Located 10 miles W of Burlington off WA 20. Use Farm to Market Rd and Bayview Rd. Then north into park via Bayview-Edison Rd. GPS: 48.487934, -122.480431. Swimming, fishing, boating. Open all year. $27-37 plus $8 for electric, per night. 76 sites, 30 with electric. 50-foot limit. Restrooms; showers. Dump station.

Beacon Rock State Park

34841 WA 14, Skamania, WA 98648. Phone: (509) 427-8265. Located along the Columbia River 34 miles E of Vancouver on WA 14. GPS: 45.630439, -122.018314. Fishing, boating. Hiking, biking, equestrian trails. Rock climbing. Open all year. $27-37 plus $13 for hookups, per night. 33 sites, 5 with full hookups. 40-foot limit. Restrooms; showers.

Belfair State Park

3151 NE WA 300, Belfair, WA 98528. Phone: (360) 275-0668. Located 3 miles SW of Belfair on WA 300. GPS: 47.430218, -122.878821. Swimming, fishing, walking trail. Open all year. $27-37 plus $13 for full hookups, per night. 133 sites, 41 with full hookups. 60-foot limit (limited availability). Restrooms; showers. Dump station.

Birch Bay State Park

5105 Helweg Rd, Blaine, WA 98230. Phone: (360) 371-2800. Located 8 miles S of Blaine via WA 548 and Bay Rd. Also accessible from I-5, exits 266 or 270. GPS: 48.903285, -122.759750. Swimming, fishing, boating. Crabbing, windsurfing, sailing and paddling. Natural game sanctuary. Open all year. $27-37 plus $8 for electric, per night. 167 sites, 20 with electric. 60-foot limit. Restrooms; showers. Dump station.

Bogachiel State Park

185983 US 101, Forks, WA 98331. Phone: (360) 374-6356. Located 6 miles S of Forks on US 101. GPS: 47.894851, -124.364348. Fishing. Bird watching, wildlife viewing. Open all year. $27-37 plus $8 for electric, per night. 32 sites, 6 with electric and water. 40-foot limit. Restrooms; showers. Dump station.

Bridgeport State Park

235A Half Sun Way, Bridgeport, WA 98813. Phone: (509) 686-7231. Located on the Columbia River 2 miles E of Bridgeport off WA 17 via Half Sun Way. GPS: 48.004311, -119.623809. Swimming, fishing, boating. Hiking trails. Golf course. Open all year. $35-45 per night. 20 sites with electric and water. 45-foot limit. Restrooms; showers. Dump station.

Brooks Memorial State Park

2465 US 97, Goldendale, WA 98620. Phone: (509) 773-4611. Located 12 miles N of Goldendale on US 97. GPS: 45.949770, -120.665487. Fishing. Hiking, biking, equestrian trails. Disc golf. Open Apr-Oct. $27-37 plus $13 for full hookup sites, per night. 45 sites, 23 full hookups. 60-foot limit. Restroom; showers. Dump station.

Camano Island State Park

2269 S Lowell Point Rd, Camano Island, WA 98282. Phone: (360) 387-3031. Located on Puget Sound, 14 miles SW of Stanwood (I-5 exit 212) via WA 532 and Camano Dr. GPS: 48.130322, -122.501921. Swimming, fishing, boating. Hiking, biking trails. Open all year. $27-37 per night. 77 sites, no hookups available. 40-foot limit. Restrooms; showers. Dump station.

Cape Disappointment State Park

244 Robert Gray Dr, Ilwaco, WA 98624. Phone: (360) 642-3078. Located on the Long Beach Peninsula near the mouth of the Columbia River, 2 miles S of Ilwaco via WA 100/Robert Gray Dr. GPS: 46.290171, -124.056379. Fishing, boating. Hiking trails. North Head Lighthouse, Lewis & Clark Interpretive Center. Camp store, cafe. Open all year. $27-37 plus $8 for electric and $5 for sewer, per night. 205 sites, 50 full hookups, 18 with water and electric. 45-foot limit. Restrooms; showers. Dump station.

Columbia Hills State Park

8514 Lewis & Clark Hwy, Lyle, WA 98617. Phone: (509) 773-3145. Located on the Columbia River, 10 miles SE of Lyle via WA 14. GPS: 45.643222, -121.108172. Swimming, fishing, boating. Hiking, biking trails. Rock climbing. Native American pictographs and petroglyphs. Dalles Mountain Ranch, historic homestead ranch. Open Apr-Oct. $27-37 plus $8 for electric, per night. 12 sites, 8 with electric. 60-foot limit. Restroom. Dump station.

Conconully State Park

119 Broadway St, Conconully, WA 98819. Phone: (509) 826-7408. Location on Conconully Reservoir, 18 miles NW of Omak via Kermel Rd and Conconully Rd. GPS: 48.556734, -119.751164. Swimming, fishing, boating. Hiking, biking trails. Open Apr-Oct. $27-37 plus $8 for electric, per night. 60 sites, 20 with electric. 75-foot limit. Restrooms; showers.

Curlew Lake State Park

62 State Park Rd, Republic, WA 99166. Phone: (509) 775-3592. Located 9 miles NE of Republic via WA 21. GPS: 48.721705, -118.657369. Swimming, fishing, boating. Hiking, biking trails. Open Apr-Oct. $27-37 plus $8 for electric and $5 for sewer, per night. 53 sites, 18 full hookup, 7 with electric and water. 40-foot limit. Restrooms; showers. Dump station.

Daroga State Park

1 S Daroga Park Rd, Orondo, WA 98843. Phone: (509) 784-0229. Located along the Columbia River, 18 miles N of Wenatchee via US 97. GPS: 47.705029, -120.195045. Swimming, fishing, boating. Hiking, biking trails. Open Apr-Sep. $35-45 per night. 28 sites with water and electric. 45-foot limit. Restrooms; showers. Dump station.

Dash Point State Park

5700 SW Dash Point Rd, Federal Way, WA 98023. Phone: (253) 661-4955. Located in western WA on Puget Sound, in Federal Way on WA 509. GPS: 47.317828, -122.407089. Swimming, fishing, boating (canoes and kayaks, no boat ramp). Hiking, biking trails. Open all year. $27-37 plus $8 for electric, per night. 141 sites, 27 with electric. 40-foot limit. Restrooms; showers. Dump station.

Deception Pass State Park

41229 WA 20, Oak Harbor, WA 98277. Phone: (360) 675-3767. Located in northwestern WA, 9 miles N of Oak Harbor on WA 20. GPS: 48.394331, -122.646034. Swimming, fishing, boating. Hiking, biking, equestrian trails. Civilian Conservation Corps Interpretive Center. Camp store. Three camping areas open all year. $27-37 plus $8 for electric, per night. 134 sites with electric. 60-foot limit. Restrooms; showers. Dump station.

Dosewallips State Park

306996 US 101, Brinnon, WA 98320. Phone: (360) 796-4415. Located in northwestern WA, 1 mile N of Brinnon on US 101. GPS: 47.687790, -122.899793. Swimming (river), fishing, boating (no boat launch). Hiking trails. Wildlife viewing platform. Open all year. $35-45 per night. 48 sites with electric. 40-foot limit. Restrooms; showers. Dump station.

Fields Spring State Park

992 Park Rd, Anatone, WA 99401. Phone: (509) 256-3332. Remote location in southeastern WA, 4 miles S of Anatone on WA 129. GPS: 46.088004, -117.167794. Hiking, biking trails. Wildlife viewing. Open all year. $27-37 per night. 20 sites, no hookups. 30-foot limit. Restrooms; showers. Dump station.

Fort Casey Historical State Park

1280 Engle Rd, Coupeville, WA 98239. Phone: (360) 678-4519. Located on Puget Sound, 4 miles S of Coupeville via Main St and S Engle Rd. GPS: 48.163873, -122.678257. Fishing, boating, scuba diving. Hiking trails. Lighthouse and gift shop. Camp store. Open all year. $27-37 plus $8 for electric, per night. 35 sites, 13 with electric and water. 40-foot limit. Restroom; showers.

Fort Ebey State Park

400 Hill Valley Dr, Coupeville, WA 98239. Phone: (360) 678-4636. Located 5 miles W of Coupeville off WA 20 via Libbey Rd and Hill Valley Dr. GPS: 48.224452, -122.757917. Fishing, surfing, paragliding. Hiking, biking trails. Camp store. Open Mar-Oct. $27-37 plus $8 for electric, per night. 50 sites, 11 with electric and water. 100-foot limit. Restrooms; showers.

Fort Flagler Historical State Park

10541 Flagler Rd, Nordland, WA 98358. Phone: (360) 385-1259. Located 9 miles NE of Port Hadlock via WA 116. GPS: 48.086109, -122.701611. Fishing, boating, scuba diving, surfing. Hiking, biking trails. Military museum, gift shop. Marina. Camp store. Open all year. $27-37 plus $13 for full hookups, per night. 114 sites, 55 full hookup. 50-foot limit. Restrooms. Dump station.

Fort Townsend Historical State Park

1370 Old Fort Townsend Rd, Port Townsend, WA 98368. Phone: (360) 385-3595. Located in northwestern WA, 4 miles S of Port Townsend off WA 20. GPS: 48.078054, -122.804264. Fishing, boating, sailing, scuba diving. Hiking, biking trails. Nature and Interpretive walks. Open Apr-Sep. $27-37 per night. 40 sites, no hookups. 40-foot limit. Restrooms; showers. Dump station.

Fort Worden Historical State Park

200 Battery Way, Port Townsend, WA 98368. Phone: (360) 344-4400. Located just N of Port Townsend on Puget Sound, off WA 20. GPS: 48.135707, -122.767050. Swimming, fishing, boating. Hiking, biking trails. Visitor center, gift shop. Marine Science Center, Coast Artillery Museum, Point Wilson Lighthouse. Two campgrounds open all year. $27-37 plus $8 for electric and $5 for sewer, per night. 80 sites, 50 full hookup, 30 with electric and water. 75-foot limit. Restrooms; showers. Dump station.

Grayland Beach State Park

925 Cranberry Beach Rd, Grayland, WA 98547. Phone: (360) 267-4301. Located on Washington coast, 1 mile S of Grayland on WA 105. GPS: 46.794215, -124.090004. Fishing, clamming, crabbing. Bird watching. Camp store. Open all year. $27-37 plus $8 for electric and $5 for sewer, per night. 97 sites, 55 full hookup, 38 with electric. 60-foot limit. Restrooms; showers. Dump station.

Ike Kinswa State Park

873 WA 122, Silver Creek, WA 98585. Phone: (360) 983-3402. Located on Mayfield Lake, 4 miles E of Silver Creek off US 12 via WA 122. GPS: 46.553336, -122.526329. Swimming, fishing, boating. Hiking, biking trails. Open all year. $27-37 plus $8 for electric, per night. 99 sites, 72 with electric. 60-foot limit. Restrooms; showers. Dump station.

Illahee State Park

3540 NE Sylvan Way, Bremerton, WA 98310. Phone: (360) 478-6460. Located on Port Orchard Bay, NE of Bremerton via Sylvan Way off WA 303. GPS: 47.595814, -122.597359. Swimming, fishing, boating. Clamming, crabbing, diving. Veteran's War Memorial. Open all year. $27-37 plus $13 for full hookup sites, per night. 25 sites, 2 with full hookups. 40-foot limit. Restrooms; showers. Dump station.

Jarrell Cove State Park

E 391 Wingert Rd, Shelton, WA 98584. Phone: (360) 426-9226. Located in the NW portion of Harstine Island in South Puget Sound, 16 miles E of Shelton off WA 3. GPS: 47.285734, -122.881198. Swimming, fishing, boating. Crabbing, diving. Hiking, biking trails. Open all year. $27-37 plus $8 for electric, per night. 21 sites, 2 with electric. 34-foot limit. Restrooms; showers.

Kanaskat - Palmer State Park

32101 Cumberland-Kanaskat Rd, Ravendale, WA 98051. Phone: (360) 886-0148. Located on the Green River, southeast of Seattle, 7 miles SE of Ravendale via local roads. GPS: 47.312245, -121.898826. Swimming, fishing. Rafting, kayaking (expert level). Hiking, biking trails. Bird watching. Camp store. Open all year. $35-45 per night. 19 sites with electric. 50-foot limit. Restrooms; showers. Dump station.

Kitsap Memorial State Park

202 NE Park St, Poulsbo, WA 98370. Phone: (360) 779-3205. Located NW of Seattle, 6 miles N of Poulsbo via WA 3. GPS: 47.816379, -122.644437. Swimming, fishing. Clamming, crabbing, diving. Hiking trail. Open all year. $27-37 plus $8 for electric and $5 for sewer, per night. 38 sites, 15 full hookup, 3 with electric. 40-foot limit. Restrooms; showers. Dump station.

Lake Chelan State Park

7544 S Lakeshore Rd, Chelan, WA 98816. Phone: (509) 687-3710. Located 9 miles W of Chelan, off Alt US 97 on WA 971. GPS: 47.873767, -120.200402. Swimming, fishing, boating. Hiking trails. Camp store. Open all year. $27-37 plus $8 for electric and $5 for sewer, per night. 138 sites, 17 full hookup, 18 with electric. 70-foot limit. Restrooms; showers. Dump station.

Lake Easton State Park

150 Lake Easton State Park Rd, Easton, WA 98925. Phone: (509) 656-2230. Located 1 mile N of Easton via Railroad St. Or Lake Easton Rd (exit 70) from I-90. GPS: 47.249505, -121.191606. Swimming, fishing, boating. Hiking, biking trails. Open May-Oct. $27-37 plus $13 for full hookup sites, per night. 135 sites, 45 with full hookups. 60-foot limit. Restrooms; showers. Dump station. Winter camping is available in the day-use area Dec-Mar ($12).

Lake Sylvia State Park

1812 N Lake Sylvia Rd, Montesano, WA 98563. Phone: (360) 249-3621. Located off US 12, 1 mile N of Montesano via Lake Sylvia Rd. GPS: 46.991782, -123.600997. Swimming, fishing, boating (electric motors only). Hiking, biking trails. Park is set in a former logging camp with displays of 20th-century logging gear. Open all year. $27-37 plus $8 for electric, per night. 35 sites, 4 with electric. 30-foot limit. Restrooms; showers. Dump station.

Lake Wenatchee State Park

21588 WA 207, Leavenworth, WA 98826. Phone: (509) 763-3101. Located in central WA, 18 miles N of Leavenworth, off US 2 on WA 207. GPS: 47.800320, -120.714235. Swimming, fishing, boating. Hiking, biking, equestrian (rentals and guided rides) trails. Camp store. Two developed campgrounds open Apr-Oct. $27-37 plus $8 for electric, per night. 197 sites (44 pull-thru), 42 with electric. 40-foot limit. Restrooms; showers. Dump station. Winter camping available in the south park day-use area, first-come, first-served basis.

Larrabee State Park

245 Chuckanut Dr, Bellingham, WA 98225. Phone: (360) 676-2093. Located in northwestern WA on Samish Bay, 6 miles S of Bellingham off WA 11, west of I-5. GPS: 48.652400, -122.490332. Swimming, fishing, boating. Clamming, crabbing, scuba diving. Hiking, biking trails. Open all year. $27-37 plus $13 for full hookups, per night. 77 sites, 26 full hookup. 60-foot limit. Restrooms; showers. Dump station.

Lewis & Clark State Park

4583 Jackson Hwy, Winlock, WA 98596. Phone: (360) 864-2643. Located in southwestern WA (east of I-5, south of US 12), 6 miles N of Toledo via WA 505 and Jackson Hwy. GPS: 46.522512, -122.813348. Hiking, biking trails. Environmental Learning Center, interpretive trail of the old growth forest. Open May-Sep. $27-37 plus $13 for full hookup sites, per night. 32 sites, 8 with full hookups. 60-foot limit. Restrooms; showers.

Lewis & Clark Trail State Park

36149 WA 12, Dayton, WA 99328. Phone: (509) 337-6457. Located in southeastern WA, 5 miles W of Dayton on US 12. GPS: 46.287460, -118.071976. Swimming, fishing, tubing. Short hiking trail. Interpretive display on Lewis and Clark and original area homesteaders. Open Apr-Oct. $27-37 per night. 24 sites, no hookups. 28-foot limit. Restrooms; showers.

Lincoln Rock State Park

13253 WA 2 E, East Wenatchee, WA 98802. Phone: (509) 884-8702. Located in central WA on the Columbia River (Lake Entiat), 7 miles N of East Wenatchee on US 2/97. GPS: 47.534301, -120.283459. Swimming beach, fishing, boating. Hiking, biking trails. Camp store. Open Mar-Oct. $35-45 plus $5 for full hookup sites, per night. 67 sites, 32 full hookup, 35 with electric and water. 65-foot limit. Restrooms; showers. Dump station.

Manchester State Park

7767 E Hilldale Rd, Port Orchard, WA 98366. Phone: (360) 871-4065. Located on Puget Sound on Olympic Peninsula, 5 miles NE of Port Orchard via Beach Dr E and E Hilldale Rd. GPS: 47.576472, -122.554353. Swimming beach, diving, fishing, boating. Two miles of hiking trails. Military history. Open all year. $27-37 plus $8 for electric, per night. 50 sites, 15 with electric. 60-foot limit. Restrooms; showers. Dump station.

Maryhill State Park

50 US 97, Goldendale, WA 98620. Phone: (509) 773-5007. Located on the Columbia River just W of Maryhill via Columbus Rd or Maryhill Hwy. Western end of park can be accessed via Maryhill Hwy off US 97. GPS: 45.684550, -120.820747. Swimming, fishing, boating. Park trail. Open all year. $27-37 plus $13 for full hookup sites, per night. 70 sites, 50 with full hookups. 60-foot limit. Restrooms; showers. Dump station.

Millersylvania State Park

12245 Tilley Rd S, Olympia, WA 98512. Phone: (360) 753-1519. Located 8 miles S of Olympia on WA 121 near I-5 exit 95 or 99. GPS: 46.915740, -122.907578. Two swimming beaches, fishing, boating. Hiking, biking trails. Lakeside Grill & Boats; food and boat rentals. Camp store. Open all year. $27-37 plus $8 for electric, per night. 139 sites, 45 with electric. 60-foot limit. Restrooms; showers. Dump station.

Moran State Park

3572 Olga Rd, Olga, WA 98279. Phone: (360) 376-2326. Located on Orcas Island, 2 miles N of Olga via Olga Rd. Access by Washington State ferry. GPS: 48.649442, -122.841197. Five freshwater lakes for swimming, fishing, and boating (electric motors only). Hiking, biking trails (49 miles). Equestrian area, trails (6 miles). Five camping areas open all year. $27-37 per night. 124 sites, no hookups. 45-foot limit. Restrooms; showers. Dump station.

Mount Spokane State Park

N 26107 Mount Spokane Park Dr, Mead, WA 99021. Phone: (509) 238-4258. Remote location in eastern WA (near Idaho border), 20 miles NE of Spokane on WA 206. GPS: 47.887689, -117.126669. Hiking, biking, equestrian trails (100 miles). The Mount Spokane Ski and Snowboard Park, located within the park, operates during the winter months. Open Jul-Sep. $27-37 per night. 8 sites with water. 30-foot limit. Restroom.

Ocean City State Park

148 WA 115, Hoquiam, WA 98550. Phone: (360) 289-3553. Located on Washington coast at intersection of WA 109 & 115, 1.5 miles N of Ocean Shores. GPS: 47.031482, -124.156769. Ocean beach, fishing, clamming. Hiking trails. Bird watching, wildlife viewing area. Open all year. $27-37 plus $13 for full hookup sites, per night. 178 sites, 39 full hookup. 50-foot limit. Restrooms; showers. Dump station.

Pacific Beach State Park

49 Second St, Pacific Beach, WA 98571. Phone: (360) 276-4297. Located on Washington coast, in Pacific Beach off WA 109. GPS: 47.206118, -124.202239. Ocean beach, fishing. Open all year. $27-37 plus $8 for electric, per night. 61 sites, 41 with electric. 60-foot limit. Restrooms; showers. Dump station.

Paradise Point State Park

33914 NW Paradise Park Rd, Ridgefield, WA 98642. Phone: (360) 263-2350. Located on Lewis River in southwestern WA, 4 miles N of Ridgefield via I-5 exit 16. GPS: 45.863719, -122.705521. Swimming (long sandy beach), fishing, boating. Hiking trail. Disc golf. Open all year. $27-37 plus $8 for electric, per night. 67 sites, 18 with electric. 40-foot limit. Restrooms; showers. Dump station.

Pearrygin Lake State Park

561 Bear Creek Rd, Winthrop, WA 98862. Phone: (509) 996-2370. Located 4 miles NE of Winthrop off WA 20 via Bluff St and E Chewuch Rd. GPS: 48.495710, -120.158400. Swimming, fishing, boating. Hiking, biking trails. Camp store, food service. Open Apr-Oct. $27-37 plus $8 for electric and $5 for sewer, per night. 169 sites, 50 full hookup, 27 with water and electric. 60-foot limit. Restrooms; showers. Dump station.

Penrose Point State Park

321 158th Ave SW, Lakebay, WA 98349. Phone: (253) 884-2514. Located on Puget Sound (Mayo Cove) on Olympic Peninsula, 1 mile E of Lakebay via Delano Rd. GPS: 47.253821, -122.748402. Swimming, fishing, boating. Crabbing, diving. Hiking, biking trails. Open all year. $27-37 per night. 82 sites, no hookups. 35-foot limit. Restrooms; showers. Dump station.

Potholes State Park

6762 WA 262 E, Othello, WA 99344. Phone: (509) 346-2759. Located in east-central WA on Potholes (O'Sullivan) Reservoir, 17 miles SW of Moses Lake (I-90 exit 179) on WA 262, via WA 17. GPS: 46.971008, -119.348569. Swimming, fishing, boating. Hiking, biking trails. Open all year. $27-37 plus $13 for full hookup sites, per night. 121 sites, 60 full hookup. 50-foot limit. Restrooms; showers. Dump station.

Potlatch State Park

21020 N US 101, Shelton, WA 98584. Phone: (360) 877-5361. Located on Hood Canal on Olympic Peninsula, 11 miles N of Shelton on US 101. GPS: 47.361143, -123.157736. Swimming, fishing, boating. Clamming, crabbing, diving. Short hiking trail.

Open all year. $27-37 plus $8 for electric, per night. 73 sites (some close in winter), 35 with water and electric. 60-foot limit. Restrooms; showers. Dump station.

Rainbow Falls State Park

633 Leudinghaus Rd, Chehalis, WA 98532. Phone: (360) 291-3767. Located on Chehalis River in southwestern WA, 16 miles W of Chehalis on WA 6. *Note*: WA 6 runs through the park on the south side of Chehalis River and the campground is on the north side. You will need to cross the river before or after entering the park to reach the campground. GPS: 46.634284, -123.234087. Swimming, fishing, boating. Hiking, biking, trails. Open all year. $27-37 plus $8 for electric, per night. 48 sites, 8 with electric. 60-foot limit. Restrooms; showers. Dump station.

Rasar State Park

38730 Cape Horn Rd, Concrete, WA 98237. Phone: (360) 826-3942. Located in northwestern WA on Skagit River, 8 miles W of Concrete off WA 20. GPS: 48.517698, -121.905309. Fishing. Hiking, biking trails. Wildlife viewing. Open all year. $27-37 plus $8 for electric, per night. 38 sites, 20 with water and electric. 40-foot limit. Restrooms; showers. Dump station.

Riverside State Park

9711 W Charles Rd, Nine Mile Falls, WA 99026. Phone: (509) 465-5064. Located in eastern WA on Spokane and Little Spokane rivers in NW Spokane, off Aubrey White Pkwy. GPS: 47.776843, -117.546872. Swimming, fishing, boating. Hiking, biking, equestrian trails. Rock climbing. ORV area. Two RV campgrounds open all year. $27-37 plus $8 for electric and $5 for sewer, per night. 53 sites, 4 full hookup, 33 with electric. 45-foot limit. Restrooms; showers. Equestrian area with 21 campsites. Dump station.

Saltwater State Park

25205 8th Place S, Des Moines, WA 98198. Phone: (253) 661-4956. Located in western WA south of Seattle on Puget Sound, 2 miles S of Des Moines via Marine View Dr off WA 509. GPS: 47.375000, -122.321299. Swimming beach, scuba diving, fishing, boating. Hiking, biking trails. Food station. Open May-Sep. $27-37 per night. 35 sites, no hookups. 50-foot limit. Restrooms; showers. Dump station.

Scenic Beach State Park

9565 Scenic Beach Rd NW, Seabeck, WA 98380. Phone: (360) 830-5079. Located on Hood Canal on the Olympic Peninsula, 9 miles W of Silverdale. From Seabeck follow Miami Beach Rd off Seabeck Holly Rd. GPS: 47.643498, -122.842261. Swimming, fishing, boating. Crabbing, scuba diving. Hiking trail. Open all year. $27-37 per night. 50 sites (some close in winter), no hookups. 32-foot limit. Restrooms; showers. Dump station.

Schafer State Park

1365 W Schafer Park Rd, Elma, WA 98541. Phone: (360) 249-3621. Located on Satsop River, 13 miles NW of Elma via US 12 and Satsop Rd. GPS: 47.096836, -123.466284. Swimming, fishing, inner-tube floating. Hiking trails. State and national historic site. Camp store. Open May-Sep. $27-37 plus $8 for electric and $5 for sewer, per night. 41 sites, 9 with electric. 40-foot limit. Restrooms; showers. Dump station.

Seaquest State Park

3030 Spirit Lake Hwy, Castle Rock, WA 98611. Phone: (360) 274-8633. Located in southwestern WA on Silver Lake, 6 miles E of Castle Rock on WA 504 (I-5 exit 49). GPS: 46.295778, -122.817636. Swimming, fishing, boating. Hiking, biking trails. Mount St. Helens Visitor Center. Open all year. $27-37 plus $8 for electric and $5 for sewer, per night. 85 sites (some close in winter), 15 full hookup, 18 with electric. 50-foot limit. Restrooms; showers. Dump station.

Sequim Bay State Park

269035 US 101, Sequim, WA 98382. Phone: (360) 683-4235. Located on northern Olympic Peninsula on Puget Sound, 5 miles SE of Sequim on US 101. GPS: 48.039784, -123.030820. Swimming, fishing, boating. Clamming, crabbing. Hiking, biking trails. Open all year. $27-37 plus $13 for full hookup sites, per night. 60 sites (some close in winter), 15 full hookup. 45-foot limit. Restrooms; showers. Dump station.

Spencer Spit State Park

521A Bakerview Rd, Lopez Island, WA 98261. Phone: (360) 468-2251. Located in northwestern WA on Lopez Island (Washington State ferry access only), S 4 miles from ferry landing. GPS: 48.532556, -122.864704. Swimming, fishing, boating. Clamming, crabbing, diving. Hiking trails. Open Mar-Oct. $27-37 per night. 37 sites, no hookups. Restrooms; no showers. Dump station.

Steamboat Rock State Park

51052 WA 155, Electric City, WA 99123. Phone: (509) 633-1304. Located on Banks Lake in east-central WA, 12 miles SW of Grand Coulee on WA 155. GPS: 47.852131, -119.132809. Swimming, fishing, boating. Hiking, biking, horse trails. Camp store, food service. Open all year. $27-37 plus $13 for full hookup sites, per night. 162 sites (some close in winter), 136 full hookup. 50-foot limit. Restrooms; showers. Dump station.

Sun Lakes-Dry Falls State Park

34875 Park Lake Rd NE, Coulee City, WA 99115. Phone: (509) 632-5583. Located in east-central WA, 6 miles W of Coulee City on WA 17. GPS: 47.596844, -119.398863. Swimming, fishing, boating. Hiking, biking trails. Golf course & miniature golf. Museum. National Natural Landmark. Visitor center, gift shop. Park store. Open all year. $27-37 plus $13 for full hookup sites, per night. 191 sites (some close in winter), 41 full hookup. 65-foot limit. Restrooms; showers. Laundry facilities. Dump station.

Twanoh State Park

12190 E WA 106, Union, WA 98592. Phone: (360) 275-2222. Located on Hood Canal in South Puget Sound, 7 miles E of Union on WA 106. GPS: 47.377939, -122.973079. Crabbing, swimming, fishing, boating. Hiking trails. Food service. Open all year. $27-37

plus $13 for full hookup sites, per night. 47 sites, 22 full hookup. 35-foot limit. Restrooms; shower.

Twenty-five Mile Creek State Park

20530 S Lakeshore Rd, Chelan, WA 98816. Phone: (509) 687-3610. Remote location in central WA on Lake Chelan, 19 miles NW of Chelan via US 97 Alt, WA 971, and South Lakeshore Rd. GPS: 47.992118, -120.259353. Swimming, fishing, boating, scuba diving. Hiking, biking trails. Marina. Park store. Open Apr-Oct. $27-37 plus $8 for electric and $5 for sewer, per night. 36 sites, 7 full hookup, 4 with electric. 30-foot limit. Restrooms; showers. Dump station.

Twin Harbors State Park

3120 WA 105, Westport, WA 98595. Phone: (360) 268-9717. Located just S of Grays Harbor on central WA coast, 4 miles S of Westport on WA 105. GPS: 46.856136, -124.108205. Surf fishing, clamming, diving. Beach trails. Welcome Center. Open all year. From Sep 15 thru Apr 1, camping is on a first-come, first-serve basis. $27-37 plus $13 for full hookup sites, per night. 157 sites, 42 full hookup. 35-foot limit. Restrooms; showers. Dump station.

Wanapum Recreation Area /Ginko Petrified Forest SP

4511 Huntzinger Rd, Vantage, WA 98950. Phone: (509) 856-2700. Located on Wanapum Lake along the Columbia River in south-central WA surrounding Vantage (I-90 exit 136). Ginkgo Petrified Forest State Park is a National Natural Landmark comprised of three primary locations.

1) Wanapum Recreation Area. The only area with camping. Open Mar-Oct. 50 full hookup sites. 60-foot limit. Restrooms. Swim beach, fishing, boat ramp. $40-50 per night. GPS: 46.938791, -119.990104.

2) Ginkgo Petrified Forest Interpretive Center. Open all year. Day-use picnic areas, exterior displays and an interpretive facility.

3) The Trailside Museum and Trees of Stone Interpretive Trail. Museum features an interpretive exhibit. The trail guides you through an ancient fossil bed.

Wenatchee Confluence State Park

333 Olds Station Rd, Wenatchee, WA 98801. Phone: (509) 664-6373. Located in central WA in Wenatchee at confluence of Wenatchee and Columbia rivers. Access via US 2 or WA 285. GPS: 47.462339, -120.328804. Swimming, fishing, boating. Hiking, biking trails. Horan Natural Area. Open all year. $27-37 plus $13 for full hookup sites, per night. 60 sites, 52 full hookup. 65-foot limit. Restrooms; showers. Dump station.

Yakima Sportsman State Park

904 University Pkwy, Yakima, WA 98901. Phone: (509) 575-2774. Located in south-central WA, near Yakima off I-82 exit 33 or 34. GPS: 46.591873, -120.453067. Fishing. Hiking, biking, equestrian trails. Wetland area, bird watching. Open all year. $27-37 plus $13 for full hookup sites, per night. 70 sites, 37 full hookup. 60-foot limit. Restrooms; showers. Dump station.

West Virginia

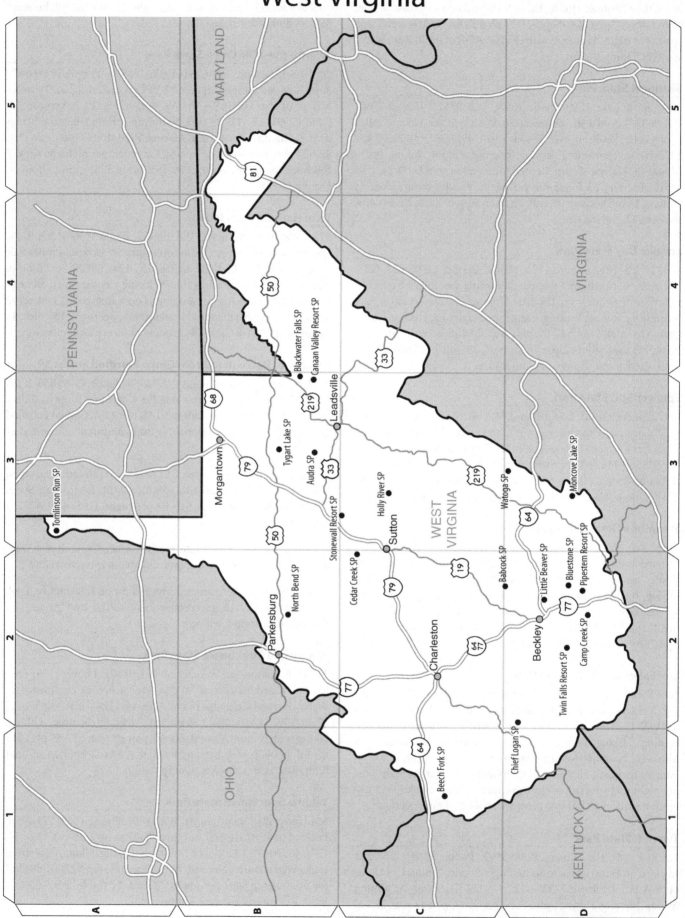

West Virginia

West Virginia State Parks & Forests
324 4th Ave
Charleston, WV 25305

Information: (833) 987-2757
Internet: www.wvstateparks.com
Reservations: Online or call park.

West Virginia Park Locator

West Virginia Parks

Audra State Park

8397 Audra Park Rd, Buckhannon, WV 26201. Phone: (304) 457-1162. Located 9 miles NW of Belington via Audra Park Rd. GPS: 39.042229, -80.068829. Swimming, fishing, boating. Hiking, biking trails. Camp store. Open spring through fall. $25-30 per night. 65 sites, 39 with electric. Restrooms; showers. Laundry facilities. Dump station.

Babcock State Park

486 Babcock Rd, Clifftop, WV 25831. Phone: (304) 438-3004. Located about 28 miles NE of Beckley on WV 41, 4 miles SW of US 60. GPS: 37.979888, -80.945816. Swimming, fishing, boating. Hiking, biking trails. Glade Creek Grist Mill. Open spring through fall. $25-30 per night. 52 sites, 28 with electric. Restroom; showers Laundry facilities. Dump station.

Beech Fork State Park

5601 Long Branch Rd, Barboursville, WV 25504. Phone: (304) 528-5794. Located 12 miles S of Huntington via WV 10 (I-64 exit 11) and CR 43. GPS: 38.308127, -82.345816. Swimming, fishing, boating. Hiking, biking trails. Four campgrounds, one is open all year. $30-40 per night. 275 sites (99 lakefront) all with electric, some with water and sewer. Camp store. Restrooms; showers Laundry facilities. Dump station.

Blackwater Falls State Park

1584 Blackwater Lodge Rd, Davis, WV 26260. Phone: (304) 259-5216. Located 3 miles SW of Davis via Blackwater Falls Rd and Blackwater Lodge Rd. GPS: 39.107659, -79.495471. Swimming, fishing, boating. Numerous hiking trails. Lodge; restaurant. Open all year. $27-32 per night. 65 sites, 30 with electric. Restrooms; showers. Laundry facilities. Dump station.

Bluestone State Park

HC 78 Box 3, Hinton, WV 25951. Phone: (304) 466-2805. Located 7 miles SW of Hinton via WV 20 and Bluestone Park Rd. GPS: 37.616677, -80.933048. Fishing, boating. Hiking trails. Two RV campgrounds open spring through fall. $30-35 per night. 76 sites, 22 with electric. Restrooms; showers. Dump station.

Camp Creek State Park and Forest

2390 Camp Creek Rd, Camp Creek, WV 25820. Phone: (304) 425-9481. Located about 15 miles N of Princeton off I-77 exit 20. GPS: 37.504388, -81.133349. Fishing. Hiking, equestrian trails. One RV campground open year-round. $30-35 per night. 26 sites with electric, some with water and sewer. Restrooms; showers. Laundry facilities. Equestrian camp.

Canaan Valley Resort State Park

230 Main Lodge Rd, Davis, WV 26260. Phone: (304) 866-4121. Located 12 miles S of Davis via WV 72 and Main Park Rd. GPS: 39.024252, -79.465338. Swimming, fishing. Hiking, biking trails. Golf and ski resort. Lodge, restaurants. Camp store. Open all year. $40-50 per night. 34 sites with full-hookups. Restrooms; showers. Laundry facilities. Dump station.

Cedar Creek State Park

2947 Cedar Creek Rd, Glenville, WV 26351. Phone: (304) 462-8517. Located 8 miles S of Glenville via US 119, US 33 and CR 17. GPS: 38.882729, -80.853744. Swimming pool, fishing. Hiking, biking trails. Miniature golf. Open spring through fall. $30-35 per night. 66 sites with electric and water. Restrooms; showers. Laundry facilities. Dump station.

Chief Logan State Park

1000 Conference Center Dr, Logan, WV 25601. Phone: (304) 855-6100. Located 4 miles N of Logan via WV 10 and Little Buffalo Creek Rd. GPS: 37.897046, -81.999169. Swimming, fishing. Hiking, biking trails. Museum, lodge, restaurant. Open spring through summer. $30-35 per night. 26 sites with electric and water, some with sewer hookups. Restrooms; showers. Dump station.

Holly River State Park

680 State Park Rd, Hacker Valley, WV 26222. Phone: (304) 493-6353. Remote location in central WV, 32 miles S of Buckhannon

on WV 20. GPS: 38.670414, -80.370515. Swimming, fishing. Hiking, biking, equestrian trails. Restaurant. Open spring through fall. $25-30 per night. 88 sites with electric. Restrooms; showers. Laundry facilities. Dump station.

Little Beaver State Park

1402 Grandview Rd, Beaver, WV 25813. Phone: (304) 763-2494. Located 8 miles E of Beckley via Grandview Rd off I-64, exit 129A. GPS: 37.756066, -81.080319. Fishing, boating. Hiking, biking trails. Camp store. Open spring through fall. $30-35 per night. 46 sites, 30 with water and electric, 16 water only. Restrooms; showers. Laundry facilities. Dump station.

Moncove Lake State Park

695 Moncove Lake Access Rd, Gap Mills, WV 24941. Phone: (304) 772-3450. Located 17 miles SW of White Sulphur Springs via Tuckahoe Rd and CR 8. GPS: 37.621219, -80.353382. Swimming, fishing, boating. Hiking trails. Bird watching, 160 species in area. Gift shop. Open spring through fall. $20-30 per night. 48 sites, 34 with electric. Restrooms; showers. Dump station.

North Bend State Park

202 North Bend State Park Rd, Cairo, WV 26337. Phone: (304) 643-2931. Located 5 miles NE of Cairo via Low Gap Rd. GPS: 39.221995, -81.111519. Swimming, fishing, boating. Hiking, biking trails. Lodge, nature center, gift shop. Miniature golf. Two campgrounds open spring through fall. $25-30 per night. 75 sites, 26 with water and electric, 26 electric only. Restrooms; showers. Laundry facilities. Dump station.

Pipestem Resort State Park

3405 Pipestem Dr, Pipestem, WV 25979. Phone: (304) 466-1800. Located 15 miles NE of Princeton via WV 20 to Pipestem Rd. GPS: 37.531458, -80.993649. Swimming, fishing, boating, rafting. Hiking, biking, equestrian trails. Rock climbing. Golf course. Two lodges, zipline tours, aerial tramway, splash park & adventure lake. Camp store. Open all year. $35-40 per night. 82 sites, 31 full hookup, 19 with electric. Restrooms; showers. Laundry facilities.

Stonewall Resort State Park

940 Resort Dr, Roanoke, WV 26447. Phone: (304) 269-7400. Located 9 miles S of Weston off US 19. GPS: 38.937443, -80.499538. Swimming, fishing, boating. Hiking, biking trails. Marina, boat tours. Golf course. Lodge, restaurants, gift shop. Open all year. $60 per night. 40 full hookup sites. Restrooms; showers.

Tomlinson Run State Park

84 Osage Rd, New Manchester, WV 26056. Phone: (304) 564-3651. Located 5 miles NE of New Cumberland off WV 8/Veterans Blvd. GPS: 40.540608, -80.574845. Swimming, fishing, boating. Hiking trails. miniature golf, disc golf. Camp store, snack bar, gift shop. Open spring through fall. $25-30 per night. 55 sites, 39 with electric. Restrooms;showers. Laundry facilities. Dump station.

Twin Falls Resort State Park

Rte 97, Mullens, WV 25882. Phone: (304) 294-4000. Located 20 miles SW of Beckley via WV 97 and Black Fork Rd. GPS: 37.634638, -81.438942. Swimming pool. Hiking, biking trails. Lodge, restaurant. Golf course. Working Pioneer Farm. Open all year. $25-30 per night. 50 sites, 25 with electric. Restrooms; showers. Laundry facilities. Dump station.

Tygart Lake State Park

1240 Paul E. Malone Rd, Grafton, WV 26354. Phone: (304) 265-6144. Located 3 miles S of Grafton via Barrett St and Woodyard Rd. GPS: 39.304988, -80.022627. Swimming beach, fishing, boating. Hiking trails. Lodge, restaurant. Marina. Nature center. Open spring through fall. $25-30 per night. 36 sites, 10 with electric and water. Restrooms. Dump station.

Watoga State Park

4800 Watoga Park Rd, Marlinton, WV 24954. Phone: (304) 799-4087. Located 16 miles S of Marlinton via US 219 and CR 27. GPS: 38.117765, -80.128510. Swimming, fishing, boating. Hiking, biking, equestrian trails. Museum, gift shop. Observation tower. Two campgrounds open spring through fall. $25-35 per night. 88 sites, 50 with electric. Restrooms; showers. Laundry facilities. Dump station.

Wisconsin

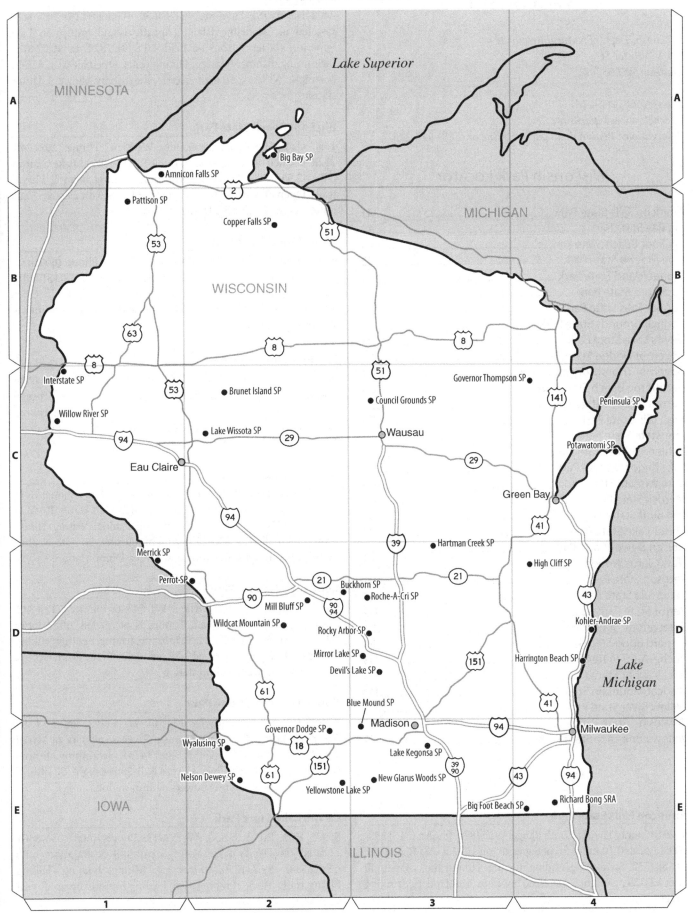

Wisconsin

Wisconsin Dept. of Natural Resources
101 S Webster St
Madison, WI 53707

Phone: (608) 266-2181
Internet: www.wiparks.net
Reservations: Required, all parks. Online or (888) 947-2757

Wisconsin Park Locator

Wisconsin Parks

Amnicon Falls State Park

4279 S County Hwy U, South Range, WI 54874. Phone: (715) 398-3000. Located 10 miles SE of Superior, off US 2. GPS: 46.608465, -91.887332. Swimming/wading, fishing. Hiking trails. Open all year. $21-23 per night. 36 sites; no hookups. Vault toilets, drinking water.

Big Bay State Park

2402 Hagen Rd, LaPointe, WI 54850. Phone: (715) 747-6425. Located on Madeline Island (Apostle Island group) in Lake Superior, via ferry from Bayfield. GPS: 46.787874, -90.674074. Swimming, fishing, boating. Hiking trails. Open all year. $25-27 per night. 53 sites, 21 with electric. Restrooms; showers. Dump station.

Big Foot Beach State Park

1550 S Lake Shore Dr, Lake Geneva, WI 53147. Phone: (262) 248-2528. Located on Lake Geneva, 1 mile S of the city of Lake Geneva. GPS: 42.566299, -88.434709. Swimming, fishing, boating. Hiking trails. Open all year. $20-25 per night. 34 sites with electric. Vault toilets, shower building. Dump station.

Blue Mound State Park

4350 Mounds Park Rd, Blue Mounds, WI 53517. Phone: (608) 437-5711. Located about 25 miles W of Madison via US 18/151. GPS: 43.024531, -89.837339. Swimming. Hiking, biking trails. Open all year. $20-23 per night. 77 sites; 30 with electric. Restrooms; showers. Dump station.

Brunet Island State Park

23125 255th St, Cornell, WI 54732. Phone: (715) 239-6888. Located on Chippewa & Fisher rivers, 1 mile NW of Cornell. GPS: 45.180126, -91.162373. Swimming, fishing; boating. Hiking, biking trails. Two campgrounds open all year. $23-25 per night. 69 sites, 24 with electric. Restrooms; showers.

Buckhorn State Park

W8450 Buckhorn Park Ave, Necedah, WI 54646. Phone: (608) 565-2789. Located 10 miles SE of Necedah via County Road G. GPS: 43.948340, -90.004315. Swimming, fishing; boating. Hiking trails. Open all year. $20-25 per night. 69 sites, 20 with electric. Some pull-throughs. Restrooms; showers. Dump station.

Copper Falls State Park

36764 Copper Falls Rd, Mellen, WI 54546. Phone: (715) 274-5123. Located on Bad River, 2 miles N of Mellen, off WI 169. GPS: 46.351556, -90.643424. Swimming, fishing, boating. Hiking, biking trails. Open all year. $25-27 per night. 20 sites with electric. Restrooms; showers. Dump station.

Council Grounds State Park

N1895 Council Grounds Dr, Merrill, WI 54452. Phone: (715) 536-8773. Located on the Wisconsin River, 4 miles W of Merrill via WI 107. GPS: 45.183035, -89.734231. Swimming, fishing; boating. Hiking trails. Open all year. $20-25 per night. 52 sites, 19 with electric. Restrooms; showers. Dump station.

Devil's Lake State Park

S5975 Park Rd, Baraboo, WI 53913. Phone: (608) 356-8301. Located on Devil's Lake about 3 miles S of Baraboo. GPS: 43.428534, -89.731770. Swimming, fishing, boating. Hiking, biking trails. Rock climbing. Three campgrounds open all year.

$25-27 per night. 423 sites, 146 with electric. Restrooms; showers. Dump station.

Governor Dodge State Park

4175 State Hwy 23 N, Dodgeville, WI 53533. Phone: (608) 935-2315. Located about 3 miles N of US 18 in Dodgeville via WI 23. GPS: 43.017202, -90.140514. Swimming, fishing, boating. Hiking, biking, equestrian trails. Two campgrounds open all year. $25 per night. 261 sites, 80 with electric. Restrooms; showers. Dump station.

Governor Thompson State Park

N10008 Paust Ln, Crivitz, WI 54114. Phone: (715) 757-3979. Located 15 miles NW of Crivitz via county roads. GPS: 45.322360, -88.219881. Swimming, fishing, boating. Hiking trails. Open all year. $21-23 per night. 100 sites, 16 with electric. Restrooms; showers. Dump station.

Harrington Beach State Park

531 CR D, Belgium, WI 53004. Phone: (262) 285-3015. Located about 1 mile E of Belgium, off I-43 exit 107. GPS: 43.497435, -87.810905. Swimming, fishing, boating. Hiking, biking, equestrian trails. Open May-Oct. $23-25 per night. 64 sites, 31 with electric. Dump station. Restrooms; showers. Laundry facilities.

Hartman Creek State Park

N2480 Hartman Creek Rd, Waupaca, WI 54981. Phone: (715) 258-2372. Located about 7 miles W of Waupaca via Hartman Creek Rd, off WI 54. GPS: 44.330369, -89.213826. Swimming, fishing, boating. Hiking, biking, equestrian trails. Open May-Nov. $23-25 per night. 103 sites, 25 with electric. Restrooms; showers. Dump station.

High Cliff State Park

N7630 State Park Rd, Sherwood, WI 54169. Phone: (920) 989-1106. Located on the NE corner of Lake Winnebago, 2 miles W of Sherwood off WI 114/55. GPS: 44.166896, -88.291160. Swimming, fishing, boating. Hiking, biking, equestrian trails. Marina. Open all year. $25 per night. 112 sites, 32 with electric. Restrooms; showers. Dump station.

Interstate State Park

1275 WI 35, St. Croix Falls, WI 54024. Phone: (715) 483-3747. Located on Lake O'the Dalles in western WI, off WI 35, 1/2 mile S of US 8. GPS: 45.395416, -92.640409. Swimming, fishing, boating. Hiking trails. Rock climbing. Open all year. $20-25 per night. 82 sites, 27 with electric. Restrooms; showers. Dump station.

Kohler-Andrae State Park

1020 Beach Park Ln, Sheboygan, WI 53081. Phone: (920) 451-4080. Located on Lake Michigan about 6 miles S of Sheboygan via CR V, exit 120 from I-43. GPS: 43.672663, -87.718238. Swimming, fishing, boating. Hiking, biking, equestrian trails. Open all year. $25 per night. 137 sites, 52 with electric. Restrooms; showers. Laundry facilities. Dump station.

Lake Kegonsa State Park

2405 Door Creek Rd, Stoughton, WI 53589. Phone: (608) 873-9695. Located about 5 miles N of Stoughton via Williams Dr. GPS: 42.975327, -89.225218. Swimming, fishing, boating. Hiking trails. Open May-Oct. $20-27 per night. 96 sites, 29 with electric. Restrooms; showers. Dump station.

Lake Wissota State Park

18127 CR O, Chippewa Falls, WI 54729. Phone: (715) 382-4574. Located about 5 miles NE of Chippewa Falls via WI 178 and county roads S and O. GPS: 44.980856, -91.304856. Swimming, fishing, boating. Hiking, biking, equestrian trails. Nature Center. Open all year. $20-25 per night. 116 sites, 58 with electric. Restrooms; showers. Dump station.

Merrick State Park

S2965 WI 35, Fountain City, WI 54629. Phone: (608) 687-4936. Located on Mississippi River, 6 miles S of Cochrane, or 3 miles N of Fountain City, along WI 35. GPS: 44.160347, -91.761182. Fishing, boating (rentals). Self-guided canoe trail. Hiking trails. Open all year. $20-21 per night. 60 sites, 22 with electric. Restrooms; showers. Dump station.

Mill Bluff State Park

15819 Funnel Rd, Camp Douglas, WI 54618. Phone: (608) 427-6692 or 337-4775 (off season). Located on both sides of Interstate 90/94. Take the Oakdale exit #48 or Camp Douglas exit #55 to US 12/16 and follow signs to park. Part of the Ice Age National Scientific Reserve. GPS: 43.950614, -90.319388. Swimming. Hiking, biking trails. Open May-Sep. $20-21 per night. 21 sites, 6 with electric. Water available. Vault toilets.

Mirror Lake State Park

E10320 Fern Dell Rd, Baraboo, WI 53913. Phone: (608) 254-2333. Located 8 miles N of Baraboo via US 12 and Farm Dell Rd. GPS: 43.561369, -89.808130. Swimming, fishing, boating. Hiking, biking trails. Visitor center. Three campgrounds open all year. $25-27 per night. 156 sites, 61 with electric. Restrooms; showers. Dump station.

Nelson Dewey State Park

12190 CR VV, Cassville, WI 53806. Phone: (608) 725-5374. Located 2 miles NW of Cassville via CR VV. GPS: 42.731235, -91.016951. Five short hiking trails. Open May thru Columbus Day weekend. $20-21 per night. 41 sites, 18 with electric. Restrooms; showers. Dump station.

New Glarus Woods State Park

W5508 CR NN, New Glarus, WI 53574. Phone: (608) 527-2335. Located 2 miles S of New Glarus via WI 69 to CR NN. GPS: 42.787001, -89.630020. Hiking, biking trails. Open all year. $20-23 per night. 18 sites, 1 with electric. Drinking water. Vault toilets.

Pattison State Park

6294 S WI 35, Superior, WI 54880. Phone: (715) 399-3111. Located on WI 35 about 15 miles S of Superior. Park features the highest waterfalls in Wisconsin and the fourth highest waterfall east of the Rocky Mountains. GPS: 46.537148, -92.120080. Lake in park. Swimming beach, fishing. Hiking trails. Nature center. Open all year. $25-27 per night. 59 sites, 18 with electric. Restrooms; showers. Dump station.

Peninsula State Park

9462 Shore Rd, Fish Creek, WI 54212. Phone: (920) 868-3258. Located on Lake Michigan, between Fish Creek and Ephraim along WI 42. GPS: 45.127991, -87.236572. Swimming beach, fishing, boating. Hiking, biking trails. Golf Course. Lighthouse; tours. Camp store. Five campgrounds open all year. $25-27 per night. 468 sites, 163 with electric. Restrooms; showers. Dump station.

Perrot State Park

W26247 Sullivan Rd, Trempealeau, WI 54661. Phone: (608) 534-6409. Located on the Mississippi River, 1 mile NW of Trempealeau via Sullivan Rd. GPS: 44.012096, -91.466218. Fishing, boating. Hiking, biking trails. Open all year. $20-25 per night. 102 sites, 45 with electric. Restrooms; showers. Dump station.

Potawatomi State Park

3740 CR PD, Sturgeon Bay, WI 54235. Phone: (920) 746-2890. Located about 5 miles NW of Sturgeon Bay via WI 42, Stagg Rd and Park Dr. GPS: 44.851964, -87.426382. Fishing, boating. Hiking, biking trails. Open all year. $23-25 per night. 123 sites, 40 with electric. Restrooms; showers. Dump station.

Richard Bong State Recreation Area

26313 Burlington Rd, Kansasville, WI 53139. Phone: (262) 878-5600. Located 8 miles SE of Burlington on WI 142. GPS: 42.633842, -88.127134. Swimming, fishing, boating. Biking, hiking, ATV trails. Visitor center. Two campgrounds open all year. $20-23 per night. 217 sites, 54 with electric. Restrooms; showers. Dump station.

Roche-A-Cri State Park

1767 WI 13, Friendship, WI 53934. Phone: (608) 339-6881 or 565-2789 off season. Located about 2 miles N of Frienship on WI 13, on the west side of the highway. GPS: 44.001201, -89.813046. Fishing. Hiking trails. Native American petroglyphs and pictographs. Open late spring to early fall. $20-21 per night. 33 sites, 4 with electric. Drinking water. Vault toilets. Dump station.

Rocky Arbor State Park

N101 US 12/16, Wisconsin Dells, WI 53965. Phone: (608) 254-8001 or 254-2333 off season. Located about 2 miles N of Wisconsin Dells via US 12. GPS: 43.641029, -89.802174. Nature trail. Open Memorial Day weekend through Labor Day weekend. $20-25 per night. 89 sites, 19 with electric. Drinking water. Restrooms; showers. Dump station.

Wildcat Mountain State Park

E13660 WI 33, Ontario, WI 54651. Phone: (608) 337-4775. Located on the Kickapoo River, just S of Ontario via WI 33. GPS: 43.697776, -90.574127. Fishing, canoeing, kayaking. Hiking, equestrian trails. Open all year. $20-25 per night. 15 sites, 9 with electric. Restrooms; showers. Dump station.

Willow River State Park

1034 CR A, Hudson, WI 54016. Phone: (715) 386-5931. Located about 11 miles SW of New Richmond via CR A. Or from I-94 exit 4 follow US 12 N to CR A. GPS: 45.012403, -92.678199. Swimming beach, fishing, boating (rentals). Hiking trails. Nature center. Open all year. $25 per night. 1,600 sites, 64 with electric. Restrooms; showers. Dump station.

Wyalusing State Park

13081 State Park Ln, Bagley, WI 53801. Phone: (608) 996-2261. Located on the Mississippi River, 7 miles N of Bagley via county roads. GPS: 42.977861, -91.113939. Fishing, boating (rentals), 6-mile canoe trail. Hiking, biking trails. Native American burial mounds. Open all year. $23 per night. 109 sites, 38 with electric. Restrooms; showers. Dump station.

Yellowstone Lake State Park

8495 Lake Rd, Blandchardville, WI 53516. Phone: (608) 523-4427. Located about 9 miles SW of Blandchardville via CR F. GPS: 42.771081, -89.985558. Swimming beach, fishing, boating (rentals). Hiking, biking trails. Concession stand. Open Apr-Nov. $20-25 per night. 128 sites, 38 with electric. Restrooms; showers. Dump station.

Wyoming

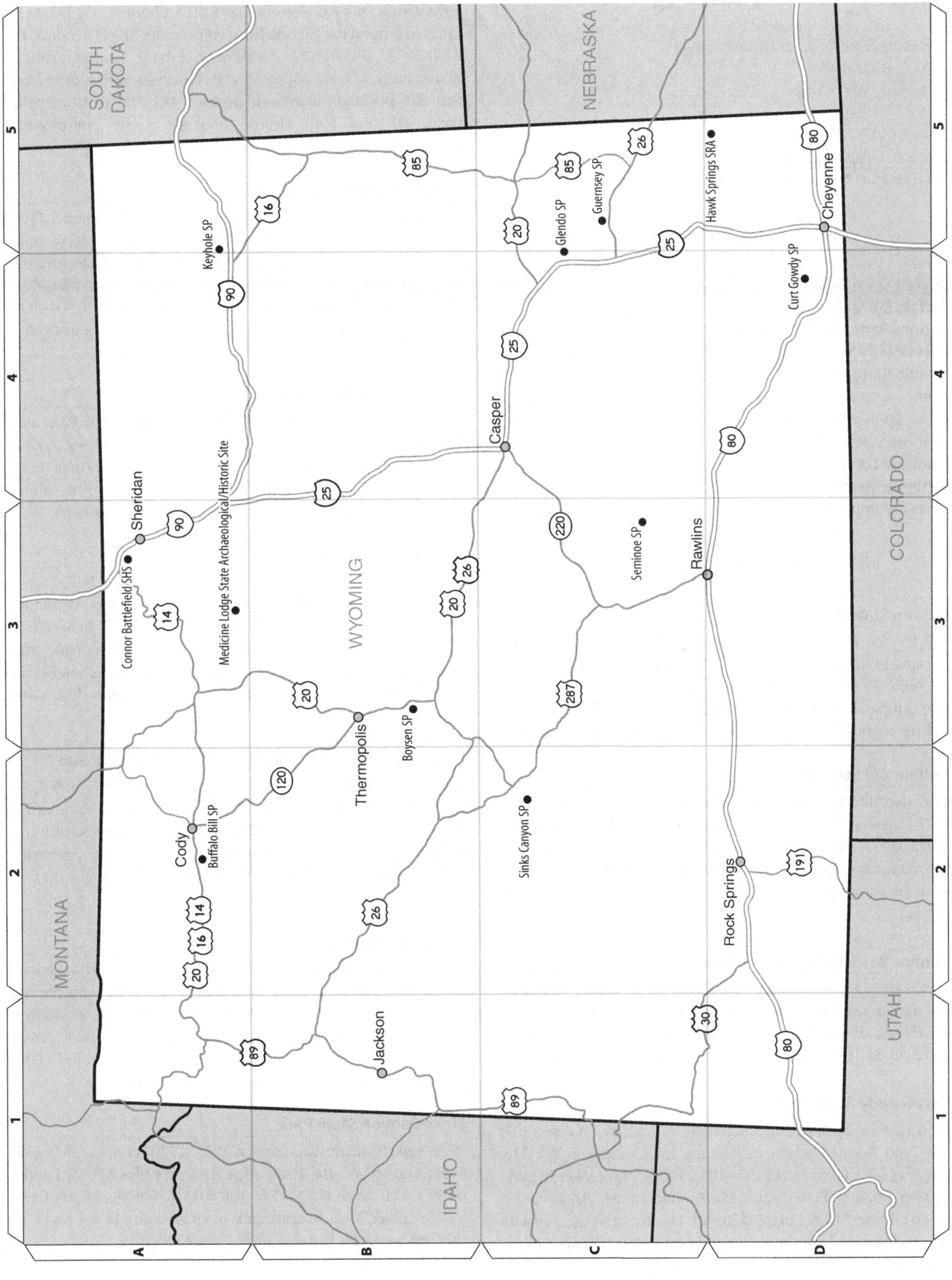
SOUTH DAKOTA
NEBRASKA
MONTANA
IDAHO
UTAH
COLORADO
WYOMING
Cheyenne
Casper
Sheridan
Rawlins
Thermopolis
Cody
Rock Springs
Jackson
Keyhole SP
Glendo SP
Guernsey SP
Hawk Springs SRA
Curt Gowdy SP
Seminoe SP
Boysen SP
Sinks Canyon SP
Buffalo Bill SP
Connor Battlefield SHS
Medicine Lodge State Archaeological/Historic Site
A
B
C
D
1
2
3
4
5

Wyoming

Wyoming State Parks & Historic Sites
2301 Central Ave
Cheyenne, WY 82002

Phone: (307) 777-6323
Internet: wyoparks.wyo.gov
Reservations: Online or (877) 996-7275

Wyoming Park Locator

Wyoming Parks

Boysen State Park

120 Boysen Dr, Shoshoni, WY 82649. Phone: (307) 876-2796. Located 13 miles N of Shoshoni on US 20; also accessible from US 26. GPS: 43.402610, -108.167228. Swimming, fishing, boating. Five campgrounds open all year. May-Sep $16 per night. Oct-Apr $11 per night. 192 sites, no hookups. Restrooms. Dump station.

Buffalo Bill State Park

4192 Northfork Hwy, Cody, WY 82414. Phone: (307) 587-9227. Located 9 miles W of Cody on US 14. GPS: 44.501579, -109.233397. Fishing, boating. Two campgrounds open May-Sep. $16 per night ($26 with electric). 97 sites, 37 with electric; some pull-through. Water available. Restrooms; showers. Dump station.

Connor Battlefield State Historic Site

55 US Hwy 14, Ranchester, WY 82839. Phone: (307) 684-7629. Located on the Tongue River in Ranchester, just off US 14. GPS: 44.905539, -107.162913. Fishing. Open May-Sep. No reservations accepted. $16 per night. 20 sites, no hookups. Restrooms.

Curt Gowdy State Park

1264 Granite Springs Rd, Cheyenne, WY 82009. Phone: (307) 632-7946. Located between Cheyenne and Laramie on WY 210, just N of I-80. GPS: 41.180205, -105.239089. Three lakes in park. Fishing, boating. Equestrian trails. Archery range. Visitor center. Open all year. $16 per night ($26 with electric). 164 sites, 49 with electric; some pull-through. Restrooms; showers. Dump station.

Glendo State Park

397 Glendo Park Rd, Glendo, WY 82213. Phone: (307) 735-4433. Located around the Glendo Reservoir, 6 miles SE of Glendo. GPS: 42.485053, -105.011055. Swimming, fishing, boating. Hiking, biking trails. Marina. Open all year. Reservations required May-Sep. $16 per night ($26 with electric). 482 sites in 19 camping areas, 60 sites with electric hookups; some pull-through. Restrooms. Dump station.

Guernsey State Park/Museum

2187 Lakeside Shore Dr, Guernsey, WY 82214. Phone: (307) 836-2334. Located on North Platte River off US 26, 2 miles NW of Guernsey. GPS: 42.291017, -104.765761. Swimming, fishing, boating. Hiking, biking trails. Museum (open May-Sep). Campgrounds located around the Guernsey Reservoir. Open all year. $16 per night ($26 with electric). 199 sites, 33 with electric, some with water. Restrooms; showers. Dump station.

Hawk Springs State Recreation Area

c/o Guernsey State Park, 2187 Lakeside Shore Dr, Guernsey, WY 82214. Phone: (307) 836-2334. Located on Hawk Springs Reservoir in southeastern WY, 9 miles SE of Hawk Springs via US 85 and Road 22. GPS: 41.712129, -104.197217. Swimming, fishing, boating. Open all year. $16 per night. 24 sites; no hookups.

Keyhole State Park

22 Marina Rd, Moorcroft, WY 82721. Phone: (307) 756-3596. Located on Keyhole Reservoir in the NE corner of Wyoming, 6 miles N of I-90 exit 165 9Pine Ridge Rd). GPS: 44.356235, -104.750170. Swimming beach, fishing, boating. Hiking, equestrian trails. Marina. Five campgrounds open all year. $16 per night ($26 with electric). 231 sites, 32 with electric and water. Restrooms; showers. Dump station.

Medicine Lodge State Archaeological/Historical Site

4800 CR 52, Hyattville, WY 82428. Phone: (307) 469-2234. Located 6 miles NE of Hyattville, off WY 31 on W slope of Big Horn Mountains. GPS: 44.296465, -107.541299. Swimming, fishing. Hiking, biking, equestrian trails. Visitor center, museum, petroglyphs. Open all year. $16 per night ($26 with electric). 28 sites, 4 with electric. Restroom.

Seminoe State Park

County Rd 351, Sinclair, WY 82334. Phone: (307) 320-3013. Located on the NW side of Seminoe Reservoir, 32 miles NE of Sinclair via Seminoe Rd (CR 351). GPS: 42.136588, -106.906536. Swimming, fishing, boating. Hiking, biking, equestrian trails. Visitor center. Three camping areas open all year. $16 per night ($26 with electric). 82 sites, 13 with electric. Restrooms. Dump station.

Sinks Canyon State Park

3079 Sinks Canyon Rd, Lander, WY 82520. Phone: (307) 332-6333. Located on the Popo Agie River, 6 miles SW of Lander on WY 131. GPS: 42.752959, -108.804316. Hiking, biking trails. Visitor center. Two campgrounds open all year. $16 per night. 27 sites, no hookups. Water available. Vault toilets.

Made in United States
Orlando, FL
24 December 2024

56496817R00124